THE REBEL PUBLISHING HOUSE

Editing by Ma Prem Taranga, B.A.,
Ma Shivam Suvarna, B.Sc.
Typing by Swami Atirup, Ma Prem Veeresha
Design by Swami Shivananda, M.A.
(Graphic Design)
Back cover Painting by
Ma Anand Meera Kasué Hashimoto, B.F.A.
(Musashino Art University, Tokyo)
Production by Ma Prem Arya,
Swami Prem Visarjan
Printing by Mohndruck, Gütersloh,
West Germany

Published by The Rebel Publishing House GmbH,
Cologne, West Germany
Copyright © Neo-Sannyas International
First Edition

Distributed in Europe by
The Rebel Publishing House GmbH, Cologne,
West Germany

ISBN 3-89338-028-0

In loving gratitude to Bhagwan
Rajneesh Foundation Australia

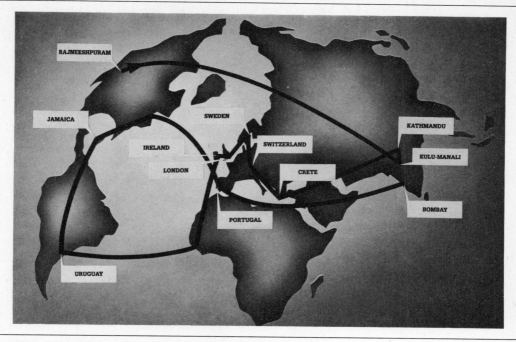

The 46,000 mile World Tour of Bhagwan Shree Rajneesh

Bhagwan Shree Rajneesh is this century's most talked about and controversial figure. He suffered twelve days of various tortures in American jails in complete innocence. After his release he began to be regarded as this century's "most dangerous" man! As a result he went wandering through twenty-one countries in search of "a few yards of earth."

There was no country ready to receive him.

History tells us there are always people born into this world who put their lives at risk. Socrates was poisoned, Jesus was raised on a cross, Sarmad and Mansoor's heads were chopped, Kabir was sent to be trampled under an elephant, Mira was given poison.

But these are the very people that set the course of the "chariots of civilization." If these people were not, we could not be where we are today.

The newest link in this chain of dangerous people is Bhagwan Shree Rajneesh. He has to suffer everything that this caliber of enlightened person has suffered before.

Drinking poison and sharing nectar – this is the invariable fate of every great revolutionary seer. Human society can not put up with one who wants to move ahead of his time.

The well-known Hindi poet Gopaldas Neeraj

Talks given to the
Rajneesh Mystery School in Uruguay
from April 12 - May 4, 1986

BEYOND PSYCHOLOGY

Talks in Uruguay

Bhagwan Shree Rajneesh

Contents

Introduction

These discourses, the first which Bhagwan spoke after His arrest in Crete, Greece, are among the "hidden jewels" of sannyas. They were delivered to a very small group of intimate disciples and, as such, are unique, unequaled, historic – and almost unknown.

They were delivered in Punta del Este, the chic gambling and recreational mecca of South America, after Bhagwan had been refused even two-week visas in those European countries which pride themselves most for their love of freedom, liberty, free speech, and their so-called democracies.

Bhagwan, by risking everything, had shown us that such claims were simply not true. Switzerland and Sweden had refused Him literally at the point of a gun. He was arrested and detained in England, and forced to "disappear" in the Irish countryside for weeks, while arrangements could be made for another destination country. Finally, those of us with Him got the point. He was showing us that the entire so-called "free" world is not free. That freedom of speech was just a catch term for the latest in our millennia-long, unbroken chain of liar politicians and their enslaved "constituencies."

Bhagwan, having no other choice, agreed to fly from Ireland to Uruguay via Africa. It was stranger than it sounds…the plane we were flying in was not legally cleared to fly the incredible distance from Senegal, Africa to Recife, Brazil, in South America. Under international law the flight was "illegal" because if either of the two huge jet engines have a system failure the plane cannot reach its destination – or go back – it simply crashes into the sea.

This regulation had never been waived in the history of international air control rules. But for Bhagwan? No problem; no one cared. The waiver was immediately granted. It was dangerous, but the pilots agreed and Bhagwan agreed. Because Canada had refused, under United States pressure, to allow Bhagwan to land on their soil even to fuel the plane He was riding in, we were forced to drop down into Africa and cross the Atlantic at one of its widest points.

When He finally reached Uruguay I often wondered if He would ever speak again. After treatment like that, why would He? And yet, He did. Suddenly, after we spent several weeks in Uruguay working out the details for a possible residency, Bhagwan said He was ready to talk again.

Television and audio equipment was flown in from Europe, a room in the elegant home where Bhagwan was staying was prepared, lighting equipment was tested, and videotapes were air-shipped from America.

Each day Bhagwan sat peacefully by the side of the swimming pool, wearing large gold Cazal sunglasses, unmoving, except for His almost imperceptible breathing and His occasional slow glance at the brilliant green parrots which perched near Him in the eucalyptus trees. The Atlantic Ocean thundered against the sand bunkers of Punta del Este's legendary beach just a few hundred feet away.

When He first spoke I wept. Barely more than a dozen people heard those first words.

It was just so much to hear Him again, so soft and loving, so forgiving of the treatment He had received and…there *was* something else. A different quality than ever before…an intimacy, a focus. I couldn't quite grasp it until I realized that Bhagwan had never spoken to so few about so much since perhaps His earliest days, just after it became known that He was enlightened.

These talks are to His beloveds, His intimates, His "family," as He used the word. And because of it, perhaps, the feel of these discourses *is* different. And He introduced and emphasized new dimensions to His work, aspects of His very transmission of wisdom and light.

He spoke in detail of the seven layers of man's consciousness, and how the disciple must meet them, explore them, expose them. He introduced His vision of hypnotic techniques for entering and opening the vast unconscious mind and its volcanic energies. He told us how to do it and when to do it.

He described hidden techniques for self-discovery, spoke of His true relationship with His disciples…and defined what it means to be a "friend" of the Master.

There is nothing like it. It is a striking vertical leap in His guidance, directed to the meditator, the sincere and earnest seeker, the authentic disciple. The three volumes in this series – of which this book is the first one – point the way to the future of mankind, the possibilities and the promise, seen through the eyes of the Living Master, Bhagwan.

Swami Dhyan Yogi, M.D.
Poona, February 1988

Chapter 1
April 12, 1986, Evening

Truth is the Greatest Offender

Beloved Bhagwan,

In the Poona years, I remember You so often using the phrase, "Be in the marketplace, but not of it." I thought this meant that when I was away from You, I would need to constantly remind myself that I was no longer part of the marketplace mentality — I was a sannyasin.

Recently, dropped into the so-called normal reality of bargain-hunting and flat-finding, of supermarkets and skinheads, I realized Your people aren't part of the marketplace; that now there is no need to remind ourselves — we are very obviously and irrevocably a race apart.

Only weeks ago, my question was about helping Your vision to be realized. Now, after my recent experience of the world, and seeing its treatment of You, I don't even have the energy to talk to people about You. Does this mean they are too far gone — or am I?

The way the world has treated me is absolutely natural, you should not feel offended by it. If they had been respectful, understanding, and loving towards me, *that* would have been a shock. Their treatment is absolutely expected.

You have not gone far away, they have gone far away and they have been going on and on for millions of years. The distance between the real man and the man that exists in the world has become almost unbridgeable. They are so far away from their own reality, they have forgotten the way back home.

They have forgotten what was the purpose of their being here.

There is an ancient parable… A very wise king wanted his son — the only son, who was going to be his successor — to be a wise man before he succeeded him and became the king of a vast kingdom. The old man chose a way which was very strange: he sent the son away from the kingdom, told him that he was abandoned, that he should forget completely that he was a prince – "He is no longer a prince and I am not going to make him my successor."

All his beautiful clothes, ornaments – everything was taken away. He was given the clothes of a beggar and sent away in the middle of the night in a chariot to be thrown out of the kingdom. And there were strict orders that he should not be allowed back in the kingdom from anywhere.

Years passed; the prince really became a beggar. He really forgot that he was a prince. In fact there had been no effort on his part to forget – he *was* a beggar. He was begging for clothes, for food, for shelter, and he had slowly accepted the condition he was in.

After many years, one day he was sitting outside a hotel, begging. It was hot summer and he wanted enough money to purchase a pair of shoes – secondhand of course – because the earth was almost like fire, and to walk without shoes was becoming impossible. He had wounds on his feet, and he was crying out for just a few coins. At that very moment a golden chariot stopped before the hotel, and a man descended. The man said, "Your father has called you back. He is very old and dying, and he wants you to be his successor."

In a single split second the beggar disappeared. The man was totally different; you could see it in his face, his eyes…the clothes were of the beggar still, but the man was totally different. A crowd gathered – the same crowd before whom he had been spreading his hands for a few coins – and they all started showing great friendship. But he was not even paying attention to them. He went up to the chariot, sat in the chariot and told the man who had come to get him, "First take me to a beautiful place where I can have a good bath, find clothes worthy of me, shoes, ornaments

…because I can go before the king only as a prince."

He came home, and he came as a prince. He said to his father, "Just one thing I want to ask: Why did I have to be a beggar for so many years? I had really forgotten… If you had not called me back, I would have died as a beggar, never remembering that once I was a prince."

The father said, "This is what my father did to me. It was not done to harm you, but to give you the experience of the extremes of life – the beggar and the king. And between these two, everybody exists.

"That day I told you to forget that you were a prince; now I want you to remember that being a prince or being a beggar are just identities given by others. It is not your reality, it is not you – neither the king, nor the beggar. And the moment you realize that you are not what the world thinks of you, you are not what you appear to be, but you are something so deeply hidden in yourself that except for you, nobody else can see you, then a man becomes wise. Knowing it, wisdom follows.

"I was angry with my father and I know you must have been angry with me. But forgive me, I had to do it to make it clear to you: don't get identified with being a king, don't get identified with being a beggar, because in a split second these identities can be changed. And that which can be changed is not you. You are something eternal, something unchangeable."

People have gone far away from their reality, and to remind them of their reality hurts them. Their treatment of me is nothing but an expression of their wounded heart. They don't want to see those wounds; they don't want to be reminded of anything else which they have tried so hard to forget, to forgive.

Somehow they have managed a certain identity in the world…and here comes a man

TRUTH IS THE GREATEST OFFENDER

who shatters it completely. It is natural they should be angry with me. It is natural they will stone me. It is natural they will do everything that they have always done with people like me.

That does not mean that you have to lose hope, that you have to become pessimistic, that you have to stop even talking about me. That way you are not helping them, and that way you are not helping yourself either.

Their behavior should not be taken into account at all. They are absolutely asleep. We are trying something which goes against their sleep, and naturally they feel disturbed and react. This is absolutely acceptable. But how long can they react? It is a question of a great challenge.

Losing hope means you have lost the game. I am not going to lose the game.

To my very last breath I will go on doing the same, whatever their reaction. It is only by bringing their reaction to the surface that there is a possibility of change. It will take time, because millions of years have taken them away from themselves. You should have patience with them. They need your compassion, they need your patience.

They will come home; they *want* to come home, but it goes against their ego to recognize that they are not at home already. It goes against their ego to recognize that they are false, that they are phony.

But their reaction – their throwing stones at me, or throwing knives at me, or putting me in jails, or crucifying me – is going to change them. This is the only way that they will start thinking about what they are doing and why they feel offended.

You feel offended only when something truthful about you is told, something which you have been hiding. You are never offended by lies.

Truth is the greatest offender.

Their very disturbance, their fear that I will destroy their morality, I will destroy their religion, I will destroy their tradition, shows one thing: they don't have religion, they don't have morality, they don't have any tradition. They are managing to believe that they have, but it is only a belief which can be easily destroyed; otherwise what happened in Greece?

I was just a tourist for four weeks in a country thousands of years old. The Greek Orthodox church is the oldest church in the world – the Vatican is not that old. Jesus and his sayings were first translated into Greek; that's why he became "Christ," and his followers became "Christians." These are Greek words.

Now, this country – which for two thousand years has been perpetually propagating Christianity, teaching every child a conditioning – is afraid of a tourist who is going to be there for only four weeks. The archbishop was disturbed so much that he threatened that my house would be burned, that I would be stoned if I was not removed immediately from the country, because my presence would destroy the morality of the country, it would destroy the religion of the country, the family, the church, the tradition – just in four weeks!

If I can manage to do that in four weeks, then whatever I am destroying *deserves* to be destroyed. It simply means that it is phony. People are not really in it – they are just pretending. Only pretensions can be destroyed in four weeks; realities cannot be destroyed. But the archbishop of the oldest church of Christianity is so much afraid, and he goes on saying things which are absolute lies. But that's what I have been telling you again and again – that all your religions are based on lies, and hence they are afraid.

The archbishop was sending telegrams to the president of the country, to the prime minister, to other ministers, and he was saying that I had been sent specially from hell to destroy the Christian Orthodox church in Greece. Can you believe a sane man saying something like that? And he holds the highest post, so even the president is afraid, the prime minister is afraid, and they have to do something criminal because that man can provoke the masses against them.

But I enjoyed the whole thing for the simple reason that it shows that truth has really a strength and power of its own. Truth has an authority which lies cannot have. You may have been conditioning people with those lies for centuries, but just a ray of light, just a small truth, can destroy that whole structure.

So there is no need to be hopeless. Talk to people – and if they are offended, rejoice. It means whatever you have said has disturbed their conditioning, and they are trying to protect it.

You cannot disturb an unconditioned man. You can say anything about him, but you cannot disturb him.

Now my sannyasins are in the world, and I have told them to mix with the world so that they can spread the truth more easily. You are fortunate – just our people, a small minority in the world of five billion people, is enough to create a wildfire. But don't be in a hurry and don't be impatient. And there is no need ever to be in a state of losing hope. Truth is intrinsically indefatigable, intrinsically impossible to defeat.

It may take time, but there is no scarcity of time. And there is no need that the revolution should happen before our eyes.

It is contentment enough that you were part of a movement that changed the world, that you played your role in favor of truth, that you will be part of the victory that is going to happen ultimately.

Beloved Bhagwan,
Why is money such a loaded issue? It seems as though when we have money, either we feel guilty about it, and thus compelled to spend it, or insecure, and therefore want to hold onto it.
Obviously it affects a multitude of areas that revolve around the pivot of power and freedom. The curious thing is that even to discuss the subject of money is somehow as much a taboo as discussing sex or death at the dinner table. Please comment.

Money is a loaded subject for the simple reason that we have not been able to work out a sane system in which money can be a servant to the whole humanity, and not the master of a few greedy people.

Money is a loaded subject because man's psychology is full of greed; otherwise money is a simple means of exchanging things, a perfect means. There is nothing wrong in it, but the way we have worked it out, everything seems to be wrong in it.

If you don't have money, you are condemned; your whole life is a curse, and your whole life you are trying to have money by any means.

If you have money it does not change the basic thing: you want more, and there is no end to wanting more. And when finally you have too much money – although it is not enough, it is never enough, but it is more than anybody else has – then you start feeling guilty, because the means that you have used to accumulate the money are ugly, inhuman, violent. You have been exploting, you have been sucking the blood of people, you have been a parasite. So now you have got the money but it reminds you of all the crimes that you have committed in gaining it.

That creates two kinds of people: one who starts donating to charitable institutions to get rid of guilt. They are doing "good work," they are doing "God's work." They are opening hospitals, and schools. All they are doing is trying somehow not to go mad because of the feeling of guilt. All your hospitals, and all your schools and colleges, and all your charitable institutions are outcomes of guilty people.

For example, the Nobel prize was founded by a man who earned money in the first world war by creating all kinds of destructive bombs, machines. The first world war was fought using the means supplied by Mr. Nobel. And he earned such a huge amount of money... Both the parties were getting war material from the same source; he was the only person who was creating war materials on a vast scale. So whoever was killed, was killed by him. It doesn't matter whether he belonged to this side or to that side; whoever was killed was killed by his bombs.

So in old age, when he had all the money in the world a man can have, he established the Nobel prize. It is given as a peace award – by a man who earned the money by war! Whoever is working for peace receives a Nobel prize. It is given for great scientific inventions, great artistic, creative inventions. And with the Nobel prize comes big money – right now it is near about two hundred and fifty thousand dollars. The best award, and two hundred and fifty thousand dollars with it; and it goes on increasing because money goes on becoming less and less valuable. And such a fortune that man must have created that all these Nobel prizes that are distributed every year are given

only out of the interest. The basic money remains intact, will remain intact forever. Every year so much interest accumulates that you can give twenty Nobel prizes.

All charitable work is really an effort to wash your guilt – literally. When Pontius Pilate ordered the crucifixion of Jesus, the first thing he did was to wash his hands. Strange! The order for crucifixion does not make your hands dirty, why should you wash your hands? It is something significant: he is feeling guilty. It took two thousand years for man to understand this, because for two thousand years nobody even mentioned or bothered to comment on why Pontius Pilate washed his hands. It was Sigmund Freud who found out that people who are feeling guilty start washing their hands. It is symbolic...as if their hands are full of blood.

So if you have money, it creates guilt. One way is to wash your hands by helping charitable institutions, and this is exploited by the religions. They are exploiting your guilt, but they go on buttressing your ego, saying you are doing great spiritual work. It is nothing to do with spirituality; it is just that they are trying to console the criminals.

The first way is what religions have been doing. The other is that the man feels so guilty that either he goes mad or commits suicide. His own existence becomes just anguish. Each breath becomes heavy. And the strange thing is that he has worked his whole life to attain all this money, because the society provokes the desire, the ambition, to be rich, to be powerful. And money does bring power; it can purchase everything, except those few things which cannot be purchased by it. But nobody bothers about those things.

Meditation cannot be purchased, love cannot be purchased, friendship cannot be purchased, gratitude cannot be purchased –

but nobody is concerned with these things. Everything else, the whole world of things, can be purchased. So every child starts climbing the ladder of ambitions, and he knows if he has money then everything is possible. So the society breeds the idea of ambition, of being powerful, of being rich.

It is an absolutely wrong society. It creates psychologically sick, insane people. And when they have reached the goal that the society and the educational system have given to them, they find themselves at a dead end. The road ends there; there is nothing beyond. So either they become a phony religious person or they just jump into madness, into suicide, and destroy themselves.

Money can be a beautiful thing if it is not in the hands of the individuals, if it is part of the communes, part of the societies, and the society takes care of everybody. Everybody creates, everybody contributes, but everybody is not paid by money; they are paid by respect, paid by love, paid by gratitude, and are given all that is necessary for life.

Money should not be in the hands of individuals; otherwise it will create this problem of being burdened with guilt. And money can make people's lives very rich. If the commune owns the money, the commune can give you all the facilities that you need, all the education, all creative dimensions of life. The society will be enriched and nobody will feel guilty. And because the society has done so much for you, you would like to pay it back by your services.

If you are a doctor you will do the best you can do; if you are a surgeon you will do the best you can do, because it is the society that has helped you to become the best surgeon, given you all the education, given you every facility, taken care of you from your very childhood. That's what I mean when I say that children should belong to the communes, and the commune should take care of everything.

And all that is created by people will not be hoarded by individuals; it will be a commune resourcefulness. It will be yours. It will be for you, but it will not be in your hands. It will not make you ambitious; it will make you more creative, more generous, more grateful, so the society goes on becoming better and more beautiful. Then money is not a problem.

Communes can use money for exchange, because every commune cannot have all the things it needs. It can purchase from another commune; then money can be used as a means of exchange – but from commune to commune, not from individual to individual, so that every commune is capable of bringing in things which are not available there. So money's basic function remains, but its ownership changes from the individual to the collective. To me this is basic communism: the money's function changes from the individual to the collective.

But the religions will not want that. Politicians will not want it, because their whole game will be destroyed. Their whole game depends on ambition, power, greed, lust.

It seems very strange to say that the religions exist almost on irreligious things, or it will be better to say, on anti-religious things. They use those things, but on the surface you don't see that. You see charity, but you don't see from where charity comes, and why. In the first place, why should there be a need for charity? Why should there be orphans, why should there be beggars? Why in the first place should we allow beggars to happen and orphans to happen? And in the second place, why are there people who are very willing to do charity work, to give money, to give their whole lives to charity and serving the poor?

On the surface everything seems to be right because we have lived in this kind of structure for so long; otherwise it is absolutely absurd. No child is an orphan if the commune owns the children, and if the commune owns everything, then nobody is a beggar; we all share whatsoever we have. But then religions will not have their sources of exploitation. They will not have the poor to console, they will not have the rich to help get rid of their guilt. These are the reasons why they are so much against me.

My work is almost like that of a gravedigger who goes on digging up beautiful marble graves and bringing out skeletons. Nobody wants to see them. People are afraid of skeletons.

One of my friends was a student in a medical college, and I used to stay with him once in a while, while traveling. If I had to stay the whole night, rather than staying at the station I would stay in the hostel with this student. One day it happened that somehow, late in the night, the discussion went on about so many things, and came around to ghosts. And I was simply joking; I said, "They are a reality. It is strange that you have not come across them."

Almost fifteen students were there in the room, and they said, "No, we don't believe in them. We have dissected so many bodies; we have never found any soul, and there is no ghost, nothing."

So I prepared my friend… In their surgical ward they had many skeletons, and they also had another ward where autopsies are done, when beggars die or somebody is killed or commits suicide – it was a big city, it was the capital of a state. The wards were joined together. On this side of the hall were the skeletons, and the other side of the hall many dead bodies used to wait. And who cares about the beggars and this and that? – whenever there was time the professors would do the autopsies and decide.

I told my friend, "You do one thing: tomorrow night, you lie down on a stretcher where the dead bodies are lying, and I will bring in your friends. You have to do nothing. In the middle of the conversation, when I am there with your friends, you just have to sit up. From the lying position you simply sit up."

It was a simple thing, there was no problem. He said, "I will do it."

But a problem arose…it became very complicated. We went into the surgical hall, and my friend was lying down. As we entered he got up, and all the fifteen people started trembling. They could not believe their eyes that a dead body…! But the problem became real because a real dead body got up! So my friend who was pretending jumped up and he said, "There *are* really ghosts! Just look at that body!"

There had been some misunderstanding: that man was in a coma. Some servants had brought him in the night so they put him in with the dead bodies. Then he came back to consciousness, so he stood up. When he saw these people he thought it must be morning and now it is time to get up and ask what is going on. Even I could not manage at first to work out what had happened, because I had sent only one. This second man…! We closed the doors and started to leave. The man was shouting, "Wait, I am alive! Why I am being put here?"

We closed the doors. We said, "It is not our business," and we left. It was difficult to convince my friend who had been lying there that it was not a ghost, that the other man was just a mistake. He said, "But never a next time! It was good that he stood up only when you all had come. If he had stood up when I was lying there alone I would have died! I could not have survived."

If you go on digging at the roots – which are ugly, which nobody wants to see…. That's why words like 'sex' or 'death' or 'money' have become taboos. There is nothing in them that you cannot discuss at the dining table, but the reason is that we have repressed them deep down and we don't want anybody to dig them out. We are afraid.

We are afraid of death because we know we are going to die, and we don't want to die. We want to keep our eyes closed. We want to live in a state as if "everybody else is going to die, but not me." That is the normal psychology of everybody: "*I* am not going to die."

To bring up death is taboo. People become afraid because it reminds them of their own death. They are so much concerned with trivia, and death is coming. But they want that trivia to keep them engaged. It functions as a curtain: they are not going to die, at least not now. Later on…"whenever it happens, we will see."

Sex they are afraid of because so many jealousies are involved. Their own life experiences have been bitter. They have loved and failed, and they really don't want to bring the subject up – it hurts.

And so is the case with money, because money immediately brings in the hierarchy of the society. So if there are twelve persons sitting around the table, immediately you can put them in a hierarchy; the similarity, the equality, for the moment is lost. Then somebody is richer than you, somebody is poorer than you, and suddenly you see yourselves not as friends but as enemies, because you are all fighting for the same money, you are grabbing at the same money. You are not friends, you are all competitors, enemies.

So at least at the dining table when you are eating you want no hierarchy, not the struggle of the ordinary life. You want for a moment to forget all those things. You want to talk only of good things – but these are all façades.

Why not create a life which is really good? Why not create a life where money does not create a hierarchy, but simply gives more and more opportunity to everybody? Why not create a life where sex does not make bitter experiences, jealousies, failures; where sex becomes just fun – nothing more than any other game, just a biological game.

A simple understanding… I can't conceive why…if I love some woman and she enjoys some man, it is perfectly okay. It does not disturb my love. In fact I love her more because she is being loved by more people; I have chosen really a beautiful woman. It will be really ugly to find a woman whom only *I* love, and she cannot find anybody else in the whole world to love her. That will be really hell.

And what is wrong if she is happy sometimes with somebody else? An understanding heart will be happy that she is happy. You love a person and you want him to be happy. If she is happy with you, good; if she is happy with somebody else it is as good. There is no problem in it.

Once we stop the old nonsense that has been poured into our minds continuously – of monogamy, of one-to-one relationship, of fidelity – which is all nonsense… When there are so many beautiful people in the world, why shouldn't they be intermixing? You play tennis; that does not mean your whole life you have to play tennis with the same partner, fidelity…! Life should be richer.

So it is only that a little understanding is needed and love will not be a problem, sex will not be taboo. Nor will death be a taboo once your life has no problems, no anxieties; once you have accepted your life in its totality, death is not the end of life, it is part of it.

In accepting life in its totality, you have accepted death too; it is just a rest. The whole day you have been working – and in the night do you want to rest, or not?

There are a few insane people who don't want to sleep. I have come across one person who was brought to me because he did not want to sleep. The whole night he made every effort to keep himself awake. The problem was that he was afraid that if he sleeps, then what is the guarantee that he will wake up? Now, who can give the guarantee? That is really a great problem – who can give him a guarantee?

He wants a guarantee that "I will wake up. What is the guarantee that I will not go on sleeping? – because I have seen many people just go to sleep and…finished! People say that they are dead, and they take them to the burning place and burn those people. I don't want to be burned. So why take the risk? This sleep is risky!" Now sleep can become a problem.

Death is a little longer sleep, a little deeper. The daily sleep rejuvenates you, makes you again capable of functioning better, efficiently. All tiredness is gone, you are again young. Death does the same on a deeper level. It changes the body, because now the body cannot be rejuvenated only by ordinary sleep; it has become too old. It needs a more drastic change, it needs a new body. Your life energy wants a new form. Death is simply a sleep so that you can easily move into a new form.

Once you accept life in its totality, life includes death. Then death is not against it but is just a servant, just as sleep is. Your life is eternal, it is going to be there forever and forever. But the body is not eternal; it has to be changed. It becomes old, and then it is better to have a new body, a new form, rather than dragging the old.

To me, a man of understanding will not have any problems. He will have only a clarity to see – and the problems evaporate. And tremendous silence is left behind, a silence of great beauty and great benediction.

Beloved Bhagwan,
I hear You saying that we are all leaves on the same tree, and that enlightenment is only possible when we really come together. On the other hand, I hear You saying that only the single individual can fulfill his being in deep aloneness.
I feel both of these are right, but still I have no real understanding of it.
Please comment.

Both are right, but they appear to be contradictory; hence the confusion. On the one hand I am saying that when you are one with existence, you come to realization – and to be one with existence means you disappear, you are no more. And on the other hand I am telling you to be yourself, to be authentically your original face; only then can you experience realization.

I can see your dilemma. You feel that they are both right – that is significant to remember – that you *feel* that they are both right, but your mind is not convinced, your thinking is not convinced. Your thinking creates questions: How can they both be right?

Mind functions in an either/or way: either this can be right or its opposite can be right. Both together cannot be right – as far as mind, its logic, its rationality, is concerned.

If mind is either/or, then the heart is both/and. The heart has no logic, but a sensitivity, a perceptivity. It can see that not only can both be together; in fact, they are not two. It is just one phenomenon, seen from two different aspects. And there is much more than the two – that's why I say "both/and."

And the heart is always right. If there is a question of choosing between the mind and the heart…because mind is a creation of the society. It has been educated. It has been given to you by the society, not by existence.

Your Mind
is the Judas

The heart is unpolluted.
It is pure existence:
Hence it has a sensitivity.
Look from the viewpoint of the heart, and the contradiction starts melting like ice.

I say to you, be one with the universe; you have to disappear and let the existence be. You just have to be absent so that the existence can be present in its totality. But the person who has to disappear is not your reality, it is only your personality. It is just an idea in you. In reality you are already one with existence; you cannot exist in any other way.

You *are* existence.

But the personality creates a deception, and makes you feel separate. You can assume yourself to be separate – existence gives you total freedom, even against itself. You can think of yourself as a separate entity, an ego. And that is the barrier that is holding you back from melting into the vastness that surrounds you every moment.

It has no closed doors, all its doors are open. Sometimes you *do* feel a certain door open – but only for a fragment of a moment; your personality cannot afford more. Those moments you call moments of beauty, moments of ecstasy.

Looking at a sunset, just for a second you forget your separateness. You *are* the sunset. That is the moment when you feel the beauty of it. But the moment you say that it is a beautiful sunset, you are no longer feeling it; you have come back to your separate, enclosed entity of the ego. Now the mind is speaking.

And this is one of the mysteries, that the mind can speak – and knows nothing; and the heart knows everything – and cannot speak.

Perhaps to know too much makes it difficult to speak. The mind knows so little, it is possible for it to speak. Language is enough for it, but is not enough for the heart.

But sometimes, under the impact of a certain moment – a starry night, a sunrise, a beautiful flower – and just for a moment you forget that you are separate. And even forgetting it releases tremendous beauty and ecstasy.

When I say you have to disappear for the realization of the ultimate, I do not mean *you;* I mean the you that you are not. I mean the you that you think you are.

And the second statement, that only in feeling one with existence, totally dissolved in it, do you realize yourself, you realize truth… there is no contradiction for the heart, because this "you" that you realize when you are one with existence is not the old you. That was your personality, and this is your individuality. That was given by the society, and this is nature, reality, a gift of existence. You can forget it, but you cannot destroy it.

The other you, the false you – you can create it, but you cannot make it real. It will remain a shadow, a painted face. It will never become your original face.

When I was a professor in the university, in the professors' campus there used to be a small street. Very few bungalows were there and those were the best bungalows – for the deans and the vice-chancellor and the heads of the departments. So very silent, empty, no traffic…and the street was not long. It went just half a mile and then there was an end, a dead end, and a deep valley.

Whenever there was rain… I loved to walk in the rain. The last house had made it a point…because they saw it happening again and again, that whenever it rains I am certain to appear on the street. And that was the last house; then the valley was there.

They thought I must be mad – without umbrella, soaking with water, with a beard, long hair, and walking so slowly and at ease…

as if there is no problem of the rain. And then I used to stand by the side of a big bodhi tree, just at the very end of the street.

The bodhi tree has many beauties. One of the beauties is that its leaves are such that when it is raining you can stand underneath it and save yourself from the rains: the leaves prevent the water from reaching to you. And it has very thick foliage, so the water goes on gathering on the leaves. And the leaves are like cups, so they hold much.

So if you are suddenly caught in the rain, and don't want to spoil your clothes, the bodhi tree protects you longer than any other tree. But the other beauty is – which was more important for me – that when the rain has stopped, then under the bodhi tree, rain starts! – because how long can it contain all that water? Sooner or later it becomes weightier, and leaves start… So when the whole world is silent, under the bodhi tree it is raining.

So I used to go to the end of the street and rest under the bodhi tree. That was another madness to the people of the house. Only in the beginning few minutes of rain can the bodhi tree protect you; after, that is dangerous, the most dangerous. The rain has stopped, but it will not stop under the bodhi tree for at least one hour.

The children of the house, the wife, daughters, sons – they all would gather in the verandah and look at me. And it became an absolute thing to them, that both things happen together – rain, and my coming to their house.

The house was given to one of the most important physicists, the head of the physics department. And he was very much interested in me, because once in a while I was making statements which were bringing physics and mysticism closer than ever. Perhaps the same statement can be made by the physicist as is being made by the mystics.

He was a very humble man. He had been teaching all over the world in different universities. Whenever I was giving a lecture in the students' union – because almost every week, once or twice… He was an absolute audience – he would come, certainly. Many other professors used to come, but he was the most regular. And we became friends.

He was very old. He had worked with Albert Einstein, and after Albert Einstein's death he came to America in his place – because he was his closest colleague, and nobody could have taken that place except him.

We became such great friends that he said, "Sometime I would like you to come to my house; I would like to introduce you to my wife and my children." I had no idea that those were the people who knew me already, and I knew them already.

When I reached their house they all started giggling, and he was very angry. He said, "I have brought a friend. Accepted that he is very young and I am very old, and the friendship looks strange, but our conceptions about reality are very close, and you should not behave like this – you have never behaved like this."

But the wife said, "You don't know this man."

And I said to him, "She is right: we have been well-acquainted for almost two years."

He said, "What! You are acquainted with my wife and children?"

I said, "Not actually, but a sort of acquaintance is there." And then I told him, "I come here on this street when it is raining; I love rains, and these people love to see me – a madman. And don't think they are unmannerly – that you are introducing me and they are laughing and giggling…even your wife cannot contain herself."

This physicist met some sannyasin in America, and sent me a message: "The last person I want to see is you, and I am coming back to India as soon as possible just to see you. And the reason is that I feel you are perfectly right that the way of the heart in seeing things is far closer to reality than the way of the mind."

But before he could come to India, he died. I feel that I must have been in his thoughts when he died.

We are one as far as our reality is concerned.

We look separate as far as our fabricated egos are concerned.

So when I say dissolve your "you," I mean your own creation, or the creation of the society in you. And just feel the silence of the moment when you are not; then you will feel so much in tune with clouds and the ocean and the mountains.

The day you drop it completely is the greatest day in your life, because this brings you the whole universe. You lose nothing – you lose only a false idea – and you attain everything: the whole universe, the infinite universe with all its beauties, with all its treasures.

But before you can drop the false "I" you have to find your real "I"; otherwise dropping the false "I," you will feel you are becoming empty.

That's why I say become an individual, be yourself.

That simply means that, feeling your reality you will be – without any trouble – capable of dropping the false. In fact the false will drop itself. As the real comes in, the false goes out. And the real is from one standpoint, individual – individual against personality.

The personality was just hodgepodge; something was put by your mother, something was put by your father, something by your neighbors, friends, wife, teachers, priests, leaders… It was a patchwork, it was not indivisible.

It was almost falling apart – any moment, a small accident and it will fall apart – it had no soul connecting all its parts. It had no wholeness, it was only parts.

Against 'personality' I use the word 'individuality' in the meaning of indivisibility. Individual means indivisible: you cannot divide it, there are no parts – it cannot fall apart. It is solid rock, it is one piece, seen in comparison with personality. But that is only one aspect.

Seen from the universal, you are no longer individual either. Even that much demarcation disappears. You are the whole. The winds, the trees, the moon are not separated anywhere; neither are you. You are breathing every moment. Existence is not separate from you, even when you think you are separate.

And when you know that you are not separate, it is a tremendous realization. Then all fear of losing your face, all fear of losing your personality – which is always slipping – disappears. You have come to the origins. You have come to the eternal, to the universal.

This is what I call enlightenment.

You have become full of light and clarity.

Now you live the whole mystery of existence.

Seeing a roseflower, you become it. You don't see it from outside; you feel it from its innermost being. Its petals are yours, its perfume is yours. You are not an observer – you *are* it.

Krishnamurti used to say again and again – his whole life he was saying it; I don't think the people who were listening were really listening to him. This is his most repeated observation: that the observed becomes the observer, or the observer becomes the observed.

You don't see a sunset setting far away; you are *in* it, you are part of all those beautiful colors. And to live existence in such deep empathy is the richest experience man is capable of.

Trust your feeling; never trust your mind.

Your mind is the Judas.

Beloved Bhagwan,
The more I move into the meditation, the more I feel responsible for myself and for the situation in the whole world. How is that possible?

It is the same thing – just the same question. The more you become yourself, the more you will feel responsible for the world because the more you are becoming part of the world – you are not separate from it. Your being authentically yourself means a tremendous responsibility – but it is not a burden. It is a rejoicing that you can do something for existence.

Existence has done so much for you, there is no way to pay it back. But we can do something. It will be very small compared to what existence has done for us, but it will show our gratitude. It is not a question of whether it is big or small; the question is that it is our prayer, our gratitude, and our totality is involved in it.

Yes, it will happen: the more you become yourself, the more you will start feeling responsibilities which you had never felt before.

I am reminded…. In the life of Mahavira, the most important Jaina philosopher…. He is going from one village to another village with his close disciple, Goshalak. And this is the question they are discussing: Mahavira is insisting, "Your responsibility towards existence shows how much you have attained to your authentic reality. We cannot see your authentic reality but we can see your responsibility."

As they are walking, they come across a small plant. And Goshalak is a logician – he pulls the plant and throws it away. It was a small plant with small roots.

Mahavira said, "This is irresponsibility. But you cannot do anything against existence. You can try, but it is going to backfire."

Goshalak said, "What can existence do to me? I have pulled this plant; now existence cannot bring it to life again."

Mahavira laughed. They went into the town, they were going to beg for their food. After taking food, they were coming back, and they were surprised: the plant was rooted again. While they were in the town it had started raining, and the roots of the plant, finding the support of the rain, went back into the soil. They were small roots, it was windy, and the wind helped the plant to stand up again.

By the time they had come back, the plant was back to its normal position. Mahavira said, "Look at the plant. I told you you cannot do anything against existence. You can try, but that will turn against you, because that will go on separating you from existence. It will not bring you closer.

"Just see that plant. Nobody could have imagined that this will happen, that the rain and the wind together will manage that small plant back, rooted into the earth. It is going to live its life.

"It seems to us a small plant but it is part of a vast universe, a vast existence, of the greatest power there is."

And Mahavira said to Goshalak, "From this point our paths separate. I cannot allow a man to live with me who is against existence and feels no responsibility."

Mahavira's whole philosophy of non-violence can be better expressed as the philosophy of reverence for existence. Non-violence is simply a part of it.

It will go on happening: the more you find yourself, the more you will find yourself responsible for many things you have never cared about. Let that be a criterion: the more you find yourself responsible for people, things, existence, the more you can be at ease that you are on the right track.

One of my professors, Dr. Ras Biharidas – he was a very old man – has lived his life alone, because he was so contented, and so joyous in himself that he never needed anybody else.

He was the head of the department, so he had a big bungalow – he was living alone in it. And as we became acquainted with each other, he became very loving towards me, like a father.

He said, "There is no need for you to live in the hostel – you can come and live with me. I have lived all alone in my life…" He used to play the sitar – perhaps better than anybody else I have heard, and I have heard all the best sitarists. But he never played it to entertain people; he just played out of his joy.

And his timing was such that nobody would have ever thought…three o'clock in the morning every day he will play his sitar. For seventy years he had been playing. The difficulty arose the first day, because I used to read up to three, and then I would go to bed – and that was the time for him to wake up.

And this was a disturbance for both of us, because I loved to read things that I liked, not silently but loudly. When you are just reading with your eyes there is only a partial connection. But when you read poetry loudly you are involved in it; for the moment, you become the poet. You forget it is somebody else's poetry; it starts becoming part of your blood and bones and marrow.

Naturally it was difficult for him to sleep. And when I would go to sleep at three it was difficult for me to sleep. Just by my side, in the next room, he was playing his electric instruments – the guitar, sitar, and other instruments. In two days we both were tired.

He said to me, "You live in this house – I am leaving!"

I said, "You need not leave – and where will you go? I have at least a place in the hostel. I will leave."

But he said, "I cannot say to you to leave. I love you, I love your presence here. But our habits are dangerous to each other. I have never interfered with anybody; there has never been anybody with me to interfere with. And I know you – you will not interfere with me. But this will kill both of us! You will not say, 'Change your time.' I cannot say that you should leave the house; that's why I said that I am leaving – you live in the house."

I persuaded him, "I cannot live in the house. Once you leave, the university cannot allow me to live in this house – this house is meant for you. I have to go to my hostel." With tears in his eyes he came to lead me to the hostel.

I remembered him at this point because I have never seen anybody else in my life who was so responsive, so sensitive. Even if by mistake he had hit the chair, he will apologize – to the chair. I told him, "Dr. Biharidas, this is going too far!"

He said, "That's how I feel. I have hit the

poor chair. She cannot speak; otherwise she would have been angry. And she is part of this whole cosmos, and she has served me, and I have not been friendly towards her; I have hit her. I have to apologize."

People in the university thought that he was mad – a man who asks forgiveness from a chair in this world cannot be thought to be sane. I have watched him closely; he was one of the sanest persons. But his responsibility was tremendous.

He could not say to me…it was his house. He could have said to me, "You can read silently" or, "You can read at some other time" or, "You can read while I am playing my instrument." But that he would not do. It would have been easy – that's what everybody else is doing in the world. But his sensitivity and deep respect for the other person…even his reverence for things was impeccable.

People have looked at his behavior and have thought, "He is not in the right state of mind." But nobody bothered to think that the right state of mind makes people responsible, so responsible that they start looking – to others – mad.

For example, Mahavira slept his whole life only on one side. He would not change his side in the night. Asked why, he said – because he was living naked, having nothing, lying down on the bare floor…. If he changes his side, some ant, some small insects may be crushed by his turning, and he will not do such a thing. His responsibility towards very small things simply shows his integrity with existence.

His way of begging will explain to you what I mean. Nowhere else in the world has anybody done such a thing – so much trust for existence! In the morning, after his meditations, he would visualize in what condition he was going to accept today's food. And sometimes it happened that thirty days would pass and he would not be able to receive food because what he has visualized, a particular condition, was not fulfilled. Strange things….

For example, he thinks that he will accept food if a woman at the house where he stands begging comes out of the house with her baby still sucking milk from her breast. Then only will he accept food from that woman; otherwise that day is gone. Then next day he will try again.

His people persistently said to him, "This is strange! There have been great ascetics …you can fast as much as you want, that is another thing."

He said, "This is not a question of fasting. I am leaving it to existence, and I am making a condition so that I can know if existence wants me to eat today or not. It is between me and existence. If the condition is not fulfilled that simply means existence wants me to fast. It is not *my* fast, it is simply that existence does not want me to eat today, and the wisdom of the whole is bigger."

And sometimes such strange conditions were fulfilled that nobody could have imagined that it would be possible. For example, one of the conditions was fulfilled…. After thirteen days remaining hungry, fasting, he continued: unless that condition was fulfilled he would not change the condition. He would change it only when it is fulfilled; then he would add the second condition.

The condition was that a princess – no ordinary woman, but a great princess – chains on her legs, handcuffed…if she offers food to him, he will accept. Now, this is asking something absurd. In the first place, if she is a princess, why should she be handcuffed, with chains on her feet? And if she is handcuffed and with chains on her feet, she will be in jail! She may be a princess but she will not be able to offer food.

But it happened that one of the kings got very angry with his daughter – her name was Chandana – and out of anger he ordered that she should be handcuffed and chained for twenty-four hours. She was not put in jail, but she was free in the home.

And when Mahavira came... And that was the argument that created the whole problem: she wanted to offer food to Mahavira. She loved the man, she loved his way of thinking, and her father was absolutely against it. That's why she was handcuffed and chained – she would not be able to go out of the house in that way because this would be so embarrassing.

When Mahavira came, he came with thousands of his followers.

But she went out with the food, and those thousands of followers could not believe their eyes, because that very day, after thirteen days, they had insisted, "Mahavira, we would like to know: what is the condition? We are not going to tell anybody; we just want to see whether there is any meaning in your conditions. Is existence compassionate enough, is existence caring enough? Does it bother about you? Just for once, we want to know: what is your condition?"

He said, "This is my condition..."

They said, "My God, this may never be fulfilled!"

Mahavira said, "That simply means existence does not need me. I have no complaint; perhaps my work is completed, and I am unnecessarily being a burden." But the condition was fulfilled.

Such trust in existence, such unwavering trust, comes when you start taking responsibilities. As you feel more responsible towards small things around you, existence goes on responding in a thousand-fold way. You are not a loser.

Beloved Bhagwan,
Can a chain-smoker become meditative? I have smoked for twenty-five years, and I feel that in smoking I stop going deeply into meditation. Still, I can't stop smoking. Can You tell me something about it?

A meditator cannot smoke, for the simple reason that he never feels nervous, in anxiety, in tension.

Smoking helps – on a momentary basis – to forget about your anxieties, your tensions, your nervousness. Other things can do the same – chewing gum can do the same, but smoking does it the best.

In your deep unconscious, smoking is related with sucking milk from your mother's breast. And as civilization has grown, no woman wants the child to be brought up by breast-feeding – naturally; he will destroy the breast. The breast will lose its roundness, its beauty.

The child has different needs. The child does not need a round breast, because with a round breast the child will die. If the breast is really round, while he is sucking the milk he cannot breathe; his nose will be stopped by the breast. He will get suffocated.

The child's needs are different from a painter's need, from a poet's need, from that of a man of aesthetic sensibility. The child needs a long breast so his nose is free and he can do both – he can breathe and also feed himself. So every child will try to make the breast according to his needs. And no woman wants the breast to be destroyed. It is part of her beauty, her body, her shape.

So as civilization has grown, children are taken away from the breast of the mother sooner and sooner. And the longing to drink from the breast goes on in their minds. And whenever people are in some nervous state, in tension, in anxiety, the cigarette helps. It helps them to become a child again, relaxed in their mother's lap.

The cigarette is very symbolic. It is just like the nipple of the mother, and the smoke that goes through it is warm just like the milk is warm. So it has a certain symmetry, and you become engaged in it, and for the moment you are reduced to a child who has no anxieties, no problems, no responsibilities.

You say that for thirty years you have been smoking, a chain-smoker; you want to stop it but you cannot stop it. You cannot – because you have to change the causes that have produced it.

I have been successful with many of my sannyasins. First they laughed when I suggested to them…they could not believe that such a simple solution could help them. I said to them, "Don't try to stop smoking, but rather bring a milk bottle that is used for small children. And in the night when nobody can see you, under your blanket enjoy the milk, the warm milk. It is not going to do any harm at least."

They said, "But how is it going to help?"

I said, "You forget about it – how and why – you just do it. It will give you good food before you go to sleep, and there is no harm. And my feeling is that the next day you will not feel so much need for cigarettes. So you count."

And they were surprised…slowly, slowly the cigarettes were disappearing, because their basic need which had remained hanging in the middle was fulfilled: they are no more children, they are maturing, and the cigarette disappears.

You cannot stop it. You have to do something which is not harmful, which is healthier, as a substitute for the time being so that you grow up and the cigarettes stop themselves.

Small children know this – I have learned the secret from them. If a child is crying or weeping and is hungry, and the mother is far away, then he will put his thumb in his mouth and start sucking it. And he will forget all about hunger and crying and weeping, and will fall asleep. He has found a substitute – although that substitute is not going to give him food, at least it gives a sense that something similar is happening. It relaxes him.

I have tried with a few of my sannyasins, even sucking the thumb. If you are too afraid to bring a bottle and fill it with milk, and if your wife comes to know about it, or your children see you doing it, then the best way is: you go to sleep with the thumb in the mouth. Suck it and enjoy it.

They have always laughed but they have always come back and said, "It helps, and the number of cigarettes next day is less and it goes on becoming less." Perhaps it will take a few weeks, then the cigarettes will disappear. And once they have disappeared without your stopping them…. Your stopping is repression, and anything repressed will try to come up again with greater force, with vengeance.

Never stop anything.

Find the basic cause of it and try to work out some substitute which is not harmful. So the basic cause disappears – the cigarette is only a symptom. So the first thing is, stop stopping it. The second thing is, get a good bottle, and don't be embarrassed. If you are embarrassed then use your own thumb. Your own thumb will not be that great, but it will help.

And I have never seen anybody failing who has used what I am saying. One day suddenly he cannot believe that he was unnecessarily destroying his health rather than having pure and clean air, smoking dirty smoke and destroying his lungs.

And this is going to become a problem

more and more because as the women's liberation movement grows children will not be breast-fed. I am not saying that they *should* be breast-fed; but they should be given some substitute breast so that their unconscious does not carry some wound that will create problems for them – chewing gum and cigarettes and cigars.... These are all symptoms. In different countries they are different.

In India they go on chewing *pan* leaves, or there are many people who use snuff. These are all the same. The snuff looks far away, but it is not that far away. The people who are nervous, tense, in anxiety, will take a dose of snuff. It gives a good sneeze, clears their mind, shakes their whole being, and it feels good.

But those anxieties will come back. The snuff cannot destroy them. You have to destroy the very base of your being nervous. Why should you be nervous?

Many journalists have told me, "With you one of the greatest difficulties is that we feel nervous." And they have said, "This is strange because we interview politicians – they feel nervous, we make them nervous. You make *us* nervous, and immediately the desire to smoke arises. Then you prevent us smoking: 'You cannot smoke here.' You are allergic.

"You have a great strategy! – we cannot smoke, and you are making us nervous and tense, and this allergy you have which prevents us from smoking...so you have no way out for us."

But why should they feel nervous before me? Those politicians are powerful people – if they feel nervous before them, it can be understood. But the reality is those powerful people are just hollow inside, and that power is borrowed from others, and they are afraid for their respectability. Each word they have

to speak, they have to think twice. They are nervous that these journalists may create a situation in which their influence over people is destroyed. Their image that they have created has to become better and better. That is their fear. Because of that fear, the journalist – any journalist, who has no power – can make them nervous.

To me there is no problem. I have no desire for respectability. I am notorious enough – they cannot make me more notorious. I have done everything that could have made me nervous; I have managed already. What can they do to me? – I don't have any power to lose, and I can say anything that I want because I am not worried about being contradictory, inconsistent. On the contrary, I enjoy being contradictory, inconsistent.

They start feeling nervous, and the nervousness immediately brings the idea to do something, to get engaged, so nobody feels that you are nervous. Just watch: when you start feeling that you need a cigarette, just watch why you need it. There is something that is making you nervous, and you don't want to be caught.

I am reminded... One day in a New York church, as the bishop entered he saw a strange man, a perfect hippy-type. But he made the bishop nervous, because that man looked into his eyes, and said, "Do you know who I am? I am Lord Jesus Christ."

The bishop phoned Rome: "What am I supposed to do?" he asked the pope. "A hippy-looking man, but he also looks like Jesus Christ. And I am alone here, early in the morning and he has come here. I have never been told what we have to do when Jesus Christ comes, so I want instruction. Clearly, so I don't commit any mistake."

The pope was himself nervous. He said, "Do only one thing: look busy! What else can be done? Meanwhile give a phone call to the police station. And look busy so that man cannot see your nervousness."

Cigarettes help you to look busy; your nervousness is covered by it. So don't try to stop it; otherwise you will feel nervous and then you will fall back to the old pattern. The desire is there because something is left incomplete in you.

Complete it – and there are simple methods to complete it. Just a baby's milk bottle will do. It will give you good food, it will make you healthier and it will take away all your desire for looking busy!

Chapter 3
April 13, 1986, Evening

Just Counting Other People's Cows

Beloved Bhagwan,
The pope and his bishops — are they really fully aware of how they are cheating their people? I can't imagine that they are just a big heap of criminals, without any respect for truth.

The religious leaders are as much asleep as the people they are leading. The only difference between the leaders and the led is theoretical. The leaders have a great store of theological knowledge, all borrowed; nothing in it is of their own experience, but it gives them great authority over the people who don't have even borrowed knowledge. And these leaders are consistently emphasizing the fact: "You are sinners, you are ignorant. We are the saints, we are the knowers."

The poor masses cannot make a distinction between authentic knowing and borrowed knowledge. Even these leaders — popes, bishops, *shankaracharyas,* ayatollahs — even they are not alert of the distinction. They know only one kind of knowledge, and that is borrowed knowledge. They have no awareness of a different dimension of knowing, so whatever they are doing is done in deep sleep. They are not cheating people consciously.

You *cannot* cheat anybody consciously.

Consciousness will prevent you from doing anything as ugly as cheating, deceiving, pretending, being a hypocrite, condemning people as sinners and fulfilling your own egos as great saints. No, it is not done consciously.

I never suspect for a single moment their good intentions. Whatever these people are doing, they are doing with good intentions; but the question is *not* of good intentions, the question is: what is the result?

You may murder me with good intentions, but your good intentions cannot justify my murder.

I have come into contact with almost all kinds of religious scholars, and on one point they are the same, whether Hindu, Mohammedan, Christian, Jew. That point is that they are perfectly at ease, feeling very good, in whatever they are doing – they are doing God's work, and they are spreading wisdom. They don't even know the *meaning* of wisdom. They have never tasted anything like that; they have heard about it, they have read about it, they have crammed hundreds of scriptures.

I am reminded of an historical event... When Alexander the Great invaded India, his master was no one other than Aristotle, the father of logic in the western hemisphere. And he had asked him, "When you come back, bring the four *Vedas* of the Hindus. The rumors have been, for hundreds of years, that those four books contain all the knowledge that is in the world; if you know those four *Vedas,* you know all. So bring those four *Vedas* for me."

Alexander said, "That is very simple." But in those days the *Vedas* were not printed. Hindus resisted printing them for hundreds of years after the printing press was invented. They never wanted their sources of wisdom to be printed and sold in the market.

Knowledge cannot be sold, and you cannot purchase wisdom. And purchasing the four *Vedas* from a bookstall, you will be deceiving yourself. Those words are dead.

Alexander enquired because he was thinking he could get them easily, but it was difficult. Only a few prominent brahmin families had copies of the *Vedas,* and that was their whole treasure. But finally he found one old brahmin...people said, "He has one of the most authentic copies of the *Vedas*. And he is old; you can get them from him."

Alexander went to the old man. The old man said, "There is no problem, but traditionally we can give the *Vedas* only when the sun is rising. You have come at the wrong time – the sun is setting. Come tomorrow morning, just before sunrise, just as the sun is rising, and I will hand over all the four *Vedas* to you."

Alexander said, "I was not thinking that it is going to be so simple. You don't ask anything in return?"

He said, "No, this is enough, that you will be taking the *Vedas* into the wide world. Come early in the morning." But that old man was *really* clever....

The whole night he and his four sons remained awake sitting around a fire. He told the sons, "Read one page of the book that I have given to you." He distributed the four *Vedas* to the four sons, according to their age. The eldest got the *Rigveda,* the oldest scripture. "You read aloud one page so that I can hear that you are reading it rightly, and then remember it and drop it into the fire. By the morning all four *Vedas* have to be burned, and by the morning all you four have to become my four *Vedas*. I am going to present you to Alexander the Great."

In ancient India, memory was particularly trained. Still, all universities, and colleges' educational systems depend on cultivating memory. They deceive you and themselves, thinking that this is intelligence. Memory is not intelligence, because memory can be part of a computer – which has no consciousness, which has no intelligence. Your mind is also a natural bio-computer. Memory is simply remembering but not understanding; understanding is totally different. Memory needs a very mechanical mind, and understanding needs a very non-mechanical mind. In fact the ways are diametrically opposite.

In the morning when Alexander appeared he was stunned. All the four *Vedas* were burned, and the old man said, "Now you can take my four sons. They have perfect memory. They will·repeat the *Vedas* exactly. I could not give you the *Vedas* – that is never done – but I can give my sons to you. My whole life I have trained them in memorizing. You just have to repeat something one time and it remains in their memory, as if written on a stone."

Alexander was defeated by the old man. He could not take those four sons because they didn't know the *meaning* of what they were saying; they could not explain anything. The language was different, and they could not translate it – they didn't know Greek. What purpose would be served by taking these people?

But *all* your religious scholars and leaders are nothing but memories, trained memories. They don't know what they are saying, but they say it correctly. Their language is right, their grammar is right, their pronunciation is right, their accent is right, but all these are futile because they don't know the meaning, they have never lived it. That meaning comes through living, through experiencing. But they will remain in a deception, and they will spread the same deception to other people.

So I say again: the popes, the bishops, the *shankaracharyas* – they are not doing intentionally any crime. They are fast asleep; they cannot do anything intentionally! They are living an unconscious life. Their words are beautiful – they have collected them from beautiful sources – but the words have not grown within their being. The words are not part of their life. They are as ignorant as the people they are teaching.

Socrates used to say that there is a knowledge which is ignorant, and there is an ignorance which is knowledge.

Borrowed knowledge is ignorance.

Experienced truth makes you not knowledgeable, but humble. The more you know it, the less you claim to know it. The day you know it perfectly, you can only say, "I am utter ignorance. I am just a child, collecting seashells on the beach. I know nothing."

"I do not know," can only be said by a man who knows perfectly.

The people who say, "We know," are utterly ignorant people – but their memories are full. And those memories are dead, because they have not given birth to any experience of their own.

Gautam Buddha used to say, "I used to know a man – he was my servant. Sitting by the door, he would count the cows that were going early in the morning to the pasture, to the river." He would count them – it had become almost an automatic thing with him. His duty was to sit in front of the door of Gautam Buddha, in case he needs anything; otherwise he was sitting there the whole day. And by the time the cows returned… It is one of the most beautiful times. In Indian villages, which are still not modernized, the time when the sun is setting has got a special name, *goadhooli. Goa* means cow, and *dhooli* means dust: the cows are coming, raising dust. The sun is setting, the birds are returning to their trees – it is a very peaceful moment.

So at the time of *goadhooli* he would count again the cows that were returning home. And he would become very much worried if some cow was missing, if the count was not exactly as it should have been. Later, when Gautam Buddha became a great master, he used the story of that man and his habit to explain something immensely meaningful.

He said, "I used to ask that poor fellow, 'Do you have a cow?' And he would say, 'I am so poor, I don't have a cow.' And I would say to him, 'Then why do you unnecessarily go on counting thousands of cows in the morning, then in the evening again – thousands of cows? And if one cow is missing – or perhaps you have miscounted – then you are worried, you cannot sleep. And it is not your cow, it is not your concern!'"

Buddha used to say to his disciples, "All knowledge that is not yours is not your concern. You are counting other people's cows, unnecessarily wasting your time. It is better to have one cow of your own – that will be nourishment."

But all your scholars are just counting other people's cows. And they are doing immense harm without knowing it, because they are helping people to become knowers without knowing. This is the greatest harm that can be done to man, to give him a sense that he knows – and he knows nothing. You have destroyed his whole life. You have destroyed the opportunity in which he may have known, experienced, lived. You have taken all his opportunities, all his possibilities of growth.

I am against all these scholars, not because their intentions are bad but because the outcome of their very good intentions is disastrous. They have destroyed millions of people on the earth; they never allowed them to grow, they gave them a false notion that they know already. This is pure poison.

George Gurdjieff used to tell a story… there was a magician who had many sheep. And it was a trouble to get them home from the forest every night – wild animals were there, and he was losing many of his sheep. Finally the idea came to him, "Why do I not use my expertise, my magic?"

He hypnotized all his sheep and told them different things. To one sheep he said, "You are a lion. You need not be afraid; you are the king amongst the animals." To another he said, "You are a tiger," to another, "You are a man." And he told to everybody, to all the sheep: "You are not going to be butchered because you are not sheep, so you need not be afraid to come back home. You should come early, before nightfall."

And from that day no sheep went missing. In fact, from that day no sheep was behaving like a sheep: somebody was roaring like a lion, somebody was behaving like a man, and nobody was afraid of being butchered, killed – the very question was irrelevant. And the magician was butchering them every day for his food. They may have been roaring like lions – that did not matter; they were sheep after all.

But he managed very beautifully. Giving one sheep the notion of being a lion, there was no need now to be bothered that he would try to escape, seeing that other sheep are being killed. Still sheep were being killed, but this sheep will know, "I am a lion, I am not a sheep. Sheep are bound to be killed!" When *he* is killed, others will be thinking, "He was just a sheep, we are men. And he was not only a sheep, but a foolish sheep who used to think that he is a lion, and never listened to us. We argued many times, 'You are a sheep. We are men, we know better. You stop roaring, that is not going to help.'" But the magician was in absolute control.

The story Gurdjieff was telling was about your religious leaders. They have managed to tell you things which you are not. They have managed to convince you that you know things which you know not. And this is the greatest crime that can be committed. But you cannot call them criminals, because they are not doing it to harm you. They are trying to serve you, they are trying to help you.

Just because all the religions have been doing the same thing, the whole world is under a certain hypnosis. And why have I created so many enemies? – for the simple reason that I am telling you that your knowledge is not knowledge, that it is a cover-up. You are *utterly* ignorant. You know nothing, and you believe that you know. It hurts!

I am taking away your knowledge, I am taking away your virtue, I am taking away your morality. I am taking away everything that you used to think is a great treasure, everything that has been cherished by you, nourished by you, protected by you, because you thought that you have got the real secrets of life, that you know the real mysteries of life. And to take away these things from people is naturally going to create enemies.

It is a strange world. The enemies are popes, are archbishops, are *shankaracharyas,* are ayatollahs – they are the respected people of the world, and the friend looks like the greatest enemy. The enemies appear to be friends, and the friends appear to be enemies. Humanity has misbehaved with its friends and given all its respect to its enemies. And that is the reason why the whole world is in misery: you have listened to the enemies and you have destroyed your friends.

And the same story continues.

I have talked to so many wise people, and found that all their wisdom is just memory. Not even a small bit is their own; all has come from others. And this is something fundamental to realize, that truth can only be your own experience. There is no other way to get it. Lies you can get in abundance. There are supermarkets all over the world, Christian, Jewish, Hindu, Mohammedan, Buddhist – all kinds of lies, all colors, all shapes and sizes, whichever you prefer. They are available and suitable to you. You are not to fit with them, they fit with you. It is very easy. They are made for you, they are tailored for you.

Truth is a totally different matter.
You will have to fit with it.
Truth knows no compromise.
You will have to change according to it. You will have to go through a transformation.

So I am creating enemies, not without any reason. The reason is clear. I am creating a few friends also, but those few friends have to go through a deep fire test. They have to drop their false personalities, their egos, their knowledge – *everything* they have. They have to be ready to be utterly naked and empty. Only then are they at the right point of the journey, the journey towards truth.

Naked, empty, and alone....

But it is such a joy, and each moment is such a glory, such a paradise that once you have tasted a single moment on the way towards truth, you will never look back on all that you had to leave. It is a great unburdening, a freedom.

Now you can open your wings unto the sky. The whole sky now is yours.

Beloved Bhagwan,
You were saying that the new will be victorious. Will it really be the new, or will it be the old polished up here and there? There are publications now in Germany that use You. Some mention You in the list of literature as the source, but others use You and don't mention You – or they even condemn You. I am really afraid of those people. What is their intention? Can You please take away that fear?

There is no need to be afraid of those people. That is happening in every language all over the world. People are taking my statements and not mentioning my name.

There is no harm in it, because my name is not important; what is important is the statement. Even if these people are stealing, there is no harm. That statement may start something in somebody which these people cannot fulfill. That statement may trigger a process in somebody who will *have* to come to the original source.

They are not mentioning my name for two reasons. One reason is, they would like to appear original. Secondly, they are afraid that if they mention my name they will be condemned – then their book is not going to be praised, respected.

But don't be afraid of these people, whatever their reason. Anything taken from me is fire, and it does not matter in what way the fire reaches to somebody's heart. These people who are doing such things cannot be great writers, poets, creative thinkers; otherwise they would not do such an act of stealing. These people are third rate.

So if they have stolen something from me it is going to stand out in their whole book as separate, unrelated, out of context. Anybody who has a little intelligence will see that this part has not come from the same man who has written the book, because the book has a third class flavor; there is no originality, there is no understanding of the deeper problems of life, and there is no courage to say the truth as it is. So anything that they have stolen to decorate their books, to make their books valuable, unknowingly that very part is going to destroy their whole book. They have stolen fire and put it into their book.

In India, one radio station was reading my statements every day, for ten minutes in the morning, without mentioning my name – but passages from books, stories. Hundreds of letters came to me saying, "These people are stealing from your books."

I said, "Don't be worried. My name is not significant, my message is. They are cowards, or perhaps they love me but they are government servants."

In India radio is owned by the government, television is owned by the government. If they use my name, they may lose their jobs. And certainly during that series, which was continuing for six months, even ministers, cabinet ministers and the prime minister, were quoting from those statements, thinking that they have nothing to do with me. But the people who were listening knew that those statements were not coming from Indira Gandhi – they could not be, they had no relevance with the person – they were stolen. And they started searching for the place from where the statements had been stolen.

Finally I met the person, the director of that radio station. He was a lover of me, and he said, "I have been condemned. Hundreds of letters are coming to me, saying, 'You are stealing. You are not mentioning Bhagwan's name.' But if I mention your name then the series will be stopped that very day. I will continue as long as they don't discover..."

And the moment it was discovered, immediately the series was stopped and the man was removed. He told me, "It happened because of that series. People started writing letters to the prime minister saying, 'This man is stealing passages from Bhagwan.'"

The prime minister herself had been stealing. Her lectures have been sent to me, and word for word, long passages have been stolen from me. But I have always taken the standpoint: let the truth reach to people by any means, by anyone.

I have been thinking that if the great powerful governments of the world are so afraid that they will not allow me entry into their country – just as a tourist for three or four weeks – if they are so impotent with all their power that they will not even allow me an overnight stay at the airport, which is *legally* my right…

In England my jet plane was standing at the airport, and the pilots had to rest. According to the law, after a certain period they cannot fly, so only in the morning would they be able to fly. I had every right to stay in the lounge at the airport, but they refused – as if with me there are different laws!

One of my friends who was traveling with me just happened to see the file of the man who was preventing me, because he went to the bathroom, leaving the file on the table. And my friend just looked and was surprised, because there were government instructions…. I had just arrived, but the file was ready, saying that if I try to stay even overnight I should not be allowed to stay in the first class lounge, but I should be put in jail; I am a dangerous person.

In the airport lounge, from where I cannot get into the country…there is no way to get into the country from the lounge. Every instruction was there about how they had to treat me. In England we had to stay for one night in jail, without any crime – just because the pilots could not fly overtime. And the government was ready beforehand. It was not a spontaneous decision, it was well planned.

Now there are countries who have decided in their parliaments that I should not be allowed into their country. And they have a certain European parliament… Just the other day I was informed that now they are considering in the European parliament – which is just a combined body of all the parliaments of Europe – a decision that I should not be allowed even to land my plane at any airport in Europe.

Today they will be doing this in Europe – America has done it already. Tomorrow they will be doing it in Asia, in Australia, in Africa. It is possible, very possible, that if they are so much afraid of me, they will start banning my books. And it may become necessary that my books go without my name, or with any name – like Holy Ghost!

The name does not matter.

But the message has to reach.

It is unprecedented. The whole world against a single man – a man who has no power, no nuclear weapons, who cannot do any harm to anybody. The whole world is at war with a single person. It simply shows that I am hitting at their very roots.

You need not be worried. If somebody has taken some passage, that passage will prove more important than his whole book. And I would like more and more writers, poets, film makers to steal as much as they can, because truth is not my property, I am not its owner. Let it reach in any way, in anybody's name, in any form, but let it reach.

Beloved Bhagwan,
These words "taking responsibility for yourself," confuse me. I am an individualist and enjoy being on my own. If I do what feels good to support myself, is it not a way of feeding my ego? Where is the limit between taking responsibility for oneself and feeding the ego by fulfilling its tendencies?

There is no limit for taking responsibility for yourself. And the question has arisen…and not only this question, many questions arise because you only think about them; they are not your existential experiences. If you take responsibility for yourself you cannot be an egoist, because to be an egoist simply means you are fast asleep and you cannot take any responsibility.

Responsibility comes with awareness, alertness.

You are asking an intellectual question like, "When we bring light into the room, what are we are going to do with the darkness? Where have we to throw it?" Intellectually it is perfectly right. There *is* darkness in the room and you say, "Bringing light into the room, the question arises, 'Where then has the darkness to be pushed? Where has it to be thrown? In what way?'" But it is not existential. Just try to bring light in and there will be no question about darkness. There will be no darkness!

Responsibility is awareness, alertness, consciousness.

Ego is just unconsciousness.

They cannot coexist.

As you grow more conscious you grow more towards light, and anything belonging to the world of darkness starts disappearing. Ego is nothing but darkness.

So remember one thing: try to ask questions which are existential. Intellectual questions may look logical, but are really absurd. You *try* responsibility, and by being responsible you will have to be conscious and alert.

Remaining responsible, you will create the light that automatically dispels the darkness of the ego.

Chapter 4
April 14, 1986, Morning

**Dancingly,
Disappear**

Beloved Bhagwan,
Often, when I am deeply relaxed, a strong feeling to die comes up in me. In these moments I feel myself as part of the whole cosmos, and I want to disappear into it. On one hand, it is such a beautiful feeling, and I am so grateful for it. On the other hand I mistrust it: maybe I have not said "yes" to myself, to my being, if the desire to die is so strong. Is it a suicidal desire?

It is not a suicidal desire.

One basic thing about suicide is that it arises only in people who are clinging very much to life. And when they fail in their clinging, the mind moves to the opposite pole. The function of the mind is of either/or: either it wants the whole, or none of it. The lust for life cannot be fulfilled totally, because life as such is a temporal thing; it is bound to end at a point, just as it began one day at a point. You cannot have a line with only the beginning; somewhere or other there is bound to be an end.

So the people who commit suicide are not against life; it only appears so. They want life in its totality, they want to grab it whole, and when they fail – and they are bound to fail – then out of frustration, out of failure, they start thinking of death. Then suicide is the only alternative. They will not be satisfied with whatsoever life gives them; they want more and more and more.

Life is short, and the series of the desire for more and more is infinite, so the failure is certain. Somewhere or other there is bound to come a moment when they will feel they have been cheated by life. Nobody is cheating them – they have cheated themselves. They have been asking too much, and they have only been asking, they have not been giving anything, not even gratefulness. In anger, in rage, in revenge the pendulum of the mind moves to the other end – still they do not know with whom they are taking the revenge. They are killing themselves: it does not destroy life, it does not destroy existence.

So this experience is not of a suicidal nature. It is something similar to suicide, but on a very different level and from a very different dimension. When you are relaxed, when there is no tension in you, when there is no desire, when the mind is as silent as a lake without any ripples, a deep feeling arises in you to disappear in this moment, because life has not given you anything better than this. There have been moments of happiness, of pleasure, but this is something far beyond happiness and pleasure; it is pure blissfulness.

To turn back from it is really hard. One wants to go deeper, and one can see going deeper means disappearing. Most of him has already disappeared in relaxation, in silence, in desirelessness. Most of his personality has already gone, just a small thread of the ego is still hanging around. And he would like to take a jump out of this circle of the ego, because if relaxing even within the ego brings so much benediction, one cannot imagine what will be the result if everything is dissolved, so that one can say, "I am not and existence is."

This is not a suicidal instinct. This is what basically is meant by spiritual liberation: it is liberation from the ego, from desire, even from the lust for life. It is total liberation, it is absolute freedom.

But in this situation the question is bound to arise in everyone. The question is arising not out of your intelligence; the question is arising out of your cowardice. You really want some excuse not to dissolve, not to evaporate into the infinite. Immediately the mind gives you the idea that this is what suicide is –

"Don't commit suicide. Suicide is a sin, suicide is a crime. Come back!" And you start coming back. And coming back means you become again tense, again full of anxieties, again full of desires. Again the whole tragic drama of your life…

It is your fear of total dissolution. But you don't want to accept it as a fear, so you give it a condemnatory name – suicide. It has nothing to do with suicide; it is really going deeper into life.

Life has two dimensions. One is horizontal – in which you are all living, in which you are always asking for more and more and more. The quantity is not the question; no quantity is going to satisfy you. The horizontal line is the quantitative line. You can go on and on. It is like the horizon – as you go on, the horizon goes on receding back. The distance between you and the goal of your more and more, the goal of your desire, remains always exactly the same. It was the same when you were a child, it was the same when you were young, it is the same when you are old. It will remain the same to your last breath.

The horizontal line is exactly an illusion. The horizon does not exist, it only appears – there, perhaps just a few miles away, the sky is meeting the earth. It meets nowhere. And out of the horizon comes the horizontal line – unending, because the goal is illusory; you cannot come to make it a reality. And your patience is limited, your span of life is limited. One day you realize that it seems all futile, meaningless: "I am unnecessarily dragging myself, torturing myself, reaching nowhere." Then the opposite of it arises in you – destroy yourself. It is not worthwhile to live, because life promises, but never delivers the goods.

But life has another line – a vertical line. The vertical line moves in a totally different dimension. In such an experience, for a moment you have turned your face towards the vertical.

You are not asking – that's why you are being given.

You are not desiring – that's why so much is made available to you.

You don't have any goal – that's why you are so close to it.

Because there is no desire, no goal, no asking, no begging, you don't have any tension; you are utterly relaxed.

In this relaxed state is the meeting with existence.

The fear comes at the moment when you come to dissolve your last part, because then it will be irrevocable; you will not be able to come back.

I have told many times a beautiful poem of Rabindranath Tagore. The poet has been searching for God for millions of lives. He has seen him sometimes, far away, near a star, and he started moving that way, but by the time he reached that star, God has moved to some other place. But he went on searching and searching – he was determined to find God's home – and the surprise of surprises was, one day he actually reached a house where on the door was written: "God's Home."

You can understand his ecstasy, you can understand his joy. He runs up the steps, and just as he is going to knock on the door, suddenly his hand freezes. An idea arises in him: "If by chance this is really the home of God, then I am finished, my seeking is finished. I have become identified with my seeking, with my search. I don't know anything else. If the door opens and I face God, I am finished – the search is over. Then what? Then there is an eternity of boredom – no excitement, no discovery, no new challenge, because there cannot be any challenge

greater than God."

He starts trembling with fear, takes his shoes off his feet, and descends back down the beautiful marble steps. He took the shoes off so that no noise was made, for his fear was that even a noise on the steps…God may open the door, although he has not knocked. And then he runs as fast as he has never run before. He used to think that he had been running after God as fast as he can, but today, suddenly, he finds energy which was never available to him before. He runs as he has never run, not looking back.

The poem ends, "I am still searching for God. I know his home, so I avoid it and search everywhere else. The excitement is great, the challenge is great, and in my search, *I* continue, I continue to exist. God is a danger – *I* will be annihilated. But now I am not afraid even of God, because I know His home. So, leaving His home aside, I go on searching for him all around the universe. And deep down I know my search is not for God; my search is to nourish my ego."

I place Rabindranath Tagore as one of the greatest religious men of our century, although he is not ordinarily related with religion. But only a religious man of tremendous experience can write this poem. It is not just ordinary poetry; it contains such a great truth. And that's what your question is raising. Relaxed, you come to a moment where you feel you are going to disappear, and then you think, "Perhaps this is a suicidal instinct," and you come back to your old miserable world. But that miserable world has one thing: it protects your ego, it allows you to be.

This is the strange situation: blissfulness does not allow *you;* you have to disappear. That's why you don't see many blissful people in the world. Misery nourishes your ego – that's why you see so many miserable people in the world. The basic central point is the ego.

So you have not come to a point of suicide. You have come to a point of nirvana, of cessation, of disappearance, of blowing out the candle. This is the ultimate experience. If you can gather courage, just one step more… Existence is only one step away from you.

Don't listen to this garbage of your mind saying that this is suicide. You are neither drinking poison, nor are you hanging yourself from a tree, and you are not shooting yourself with a gun – what suicide? You are simply becoming thinner and thinner and thinner. And the moment comes when you are so thin and so spread all over existence that you cannot say you are, but you can say that existence is.

This we have called enlightenment, not suicide.

This we have called realization of the ultimate truth. But you have to pay the price. And the price is nothing but dropping the ego. So when such a moment comes, don't hesitate. Dancingly, disappear…with a great laughter, disappear; with songs on your lips, disappear.

I am not a theoretician, this is not my philosophy. I have come to the same borderline many times and turned back. I have also found the home of God many times and could not knock. Jesus has a few sayings. One of the sayings is, "Knock, and the door shall be opened unto you." If this sentence has any meaning, it is this meaning that I am giving you now.

So when this moment comes, rejoice and melt. It is human nature – and understandable – that many times you will come back. But those many times don't count. One time, gather all courage and take a jump.

You will be, but in such a new way that you cannot connect it with the old. It will be a discontinuity. The old was so tiny, so small, so mean, and the new is so vast. From a small dewdrop you have become the ocean. But even the dewdrop slipping from a lotus leaf trembles for a moment, tries to hang on a little more, because he can see the ocean… once he has fallen from the lotus leaf he is gone. Yes, in a way he will not be; as a dewdrop he will be gone. But it is not a loss. He will be oceanic.

And all other oceans are limited.

The ocean of existence is unlimited.

Beloved Bhagwan,
When I close my eyes I often hear the sound of a tiny bell ringing within.
Can You please tell us about hearing, meditation, sound and silence?

It is possible that hearing inside you a tiny bell when you enter into meditation may be related to your past life, particularly as a Tibetan, because for centuries in Tibet this has been the conditioning of the mind – that when you enter meditation, you hear tiny bells. And if a conditioning has been continued too long, it is carried into new lives.

But hearing the tiny bell is not meditation; it is just a conditioning. When you start entering into total silence where no bells are ringing, then meditation begins. The tiny bell rings in the mind, and meditation is a state of no-mind. Tiny or not tiny, no bell can ring there; it is utter silence.

But many religions, particularly in the East… and the most prominent is the Tibetan religion which has used tiny bells. It is a significant technique but dangerous, as all techniques are: you can get attached to the technique. If you listen to a tiny bell for hours it will have a hypnotizing effect on your mind. Thinking will stop, only the bell will go on ringing. Even when in reality the bell has stopped, it will go on ringing in the mind. The idea behind the technique was that slowly, slowly the sound of the bell will fade away into silence. If it happens, good. But the greater possibility is that you will become attached to the bell. And it gives great peace, it will give you a feeling of great well-being, because the mind will not be thinking; it cannot do two things.

It is not only the bell – anything can be used. Lord Tennyson, the great poet, was embarrassed to recognize in his autobiography that from his very childhood, he does not know how – perhaps sleeping in a separate room as a small child – he was afraid of the darkness. Just to make him feel that he is not alone, he started repeating his own name, "Tennyson, Tennyson…" Repeating his own name he forgot all about the darkness and the ghosts, and all kinds of creatures that humanity has invented for poor children to be tortured with. He would repeat a few times, "Tennyson, Tennyson, Tennyson…" and he would become silent and would fall into a deep sleep.

Later on, as he grew up, it became his usual practice. Without it he could not fall asleep – it became a necessary ritual. But it started giving him new insights: it not only brought sleep, but repeating, "Tennyson, Tennyson," his own name, he became silent, peaceful; he became somehow more than the body, somehow immaterial. And then, as he came to know about meditation…he had already developed a technique through his whole life. He tried it for meditation, and it worked. Just as it was leading him into deep sleep, it started leading him into deep relaxation, a great peacefulness.

So it is not a question of what mantra, what chanting, what name of which God, or just the sound of a bell…it doesn't matter. All that matters basically is that you become concentrated on one thing, that the mind is so full of one thing that all other thoughts stop. And any one thing for a long time is going to give you a certain kind of hypnotic state.

Just a few days ago, Anando brought me a press clipping. The man was authentic in writing it…he was puzzled, he could not understand what is happening. He had been listening to me – he had come as a journalist to report – he had never heard such long discourses, and on subjects which were not his area! So he reports on me: "What is striking," he reports, "is Bhagwan speaks very slowly, with gaps – sometimes with closed eyes, and sometimes he looks very intensely at you. He speaks so long that one feels bored, but the strange thing is that after this boredom one feels a deep serenity, a silence – which is strange, because usually out of boredom one feels frustration, one feels angry."

But he has observed well his own mind…one feels a certain serenity, silence, peacefulness, and finally it seems that a kind of hypnosis has happened: "Perhaps this is Bhagwan's method – to speak slowly, to speak with gaps, so that you start feeling bored. But out of that boredom comes a serenity."

It is strange for him – it is strange for Western psychology too – that if boredom is used rightly it is going to create serenity, peacefulness and a state of hypnosis. And hypnosis is healthy. It is not meditation, but it still somehow reflects meditation. It is like the moon reflected in the water; it is not the moon, but this is still a reflection of the moon.

So all the religions – in the East particularly, but in the West also – have used very similar techniques. Now a Buddhist monk in

Tibet, in the silence of the Himalayas, goes on ringing a small bell for hours…no other sound – the whole universe around him is silent – the only sound is the bell. Naturally his mind starts getting bored, starts feeling disinterested. There is no excitement, it is just repetition, but that is the point: if the bell can be stopped – and the bell has to be stopped – the mind will go on listening to it for a little time longer.

The monk has become so accustomed to listening to it that he will go on listening to it. And as the sound of the bell recedes, becomes thinner, becomes distant, more distant, the mind is left in a certain silence. This silence either can give you hypnosis… Hypnosis is another name for deliberately created sleep: it is deeper than your ordinary sleep, healthier than your ordinary sleep; it rejuvenates you within minutes, which your ordinary sleep can do only in eight hours. That is one line that it can move on, but that is not meditation.

The other line is…listening to the bell inside you getting more and more distant, you become more and more alert so that you can listen to it, even though the sound is going away from you.

Now you have to be more conscious to listen to it. First you were unconscious and you were listening to it; now it is getting distant so you have to be very alert, very conscious. And a moment comes when the sound disappears…you have to be perfectly conscious. You have taken a different route.

This state of consciousness is meditation.

I am not against hypnosis; what I am against is…hypnosis should *not* be understood as meditation. Hypnosis is of the mind, and good for the mind, good for the body. Meditation is neither of the body nor of the mind, but belongs to the third within you – your being. It is good for the being, it is nourishment for the being.

So it is possible that if sitting in meditation, you suddenly start hearing bells, you may have practiced this in your past lives. I don't talk about past lives for the simple reason that for you it will be just a belief. But the question was such that I had to bring the past life in, because it had nothing to do with this life. You had not practiced meditation on the sound of bells, so from where can it come into your mind? It can come only from the past conditioning, and a very deep conditioning.

Nothing is wrong in it. Enjoy it, but remember not to go towards sleep. Go towards more consciousness. Sleep is unconsciousness, so they are diametrically opposite directions. And there comes a point from where you can move either way. When the sound of bells is receding, disappearing, that is the moment. Either you can fall asleep… which is good but this is not meditation, and it is not going to give you any spiritual experience. If you remain alert, aware, the sound disappears; only silence remains.

Consciousness and silence together is what meditation is all about.

Beloved Bhagwan,
I once drew a picture of a flower blossoming. The flower was simple and lovely; it had a faint light coming out of the just- opening bud, and the leaves were strong and healthy. But the roots were underdeveloped and weak, as if they didn't belong to this flower at all. This picture was to symbolize me, and I have a deep attachment to it. But I am constantly worried by the roots, as they contradict the promise of the blossom.

There are many questions connected with this picture, but I would be very happy if You would answer me somehow.

This is not only your situation. This is the situation of almost all human beings: their roots are weak, and without strong roots the promise of a healthy blossoming of thousands of flowers is impossible. Why are the roots weak? They are kept weak.

In Japan they have trees four hundred, five hundred years old, and six inches high. It is considered to be an art. To me it is simple murder. Generations of gardeners have been keeping those trees in this situation.

Now, a tree which is five hundred years old…you can see its branches are old, although small; it is a very tiny old man, but it shows on the leaves, on the trunk, on the branches. And the strategy that has been used is this: they plant a tree in a mud pot which has no bottom, then they go on cutting the roots – because the pot has no bottom. When the roots come out and try to reach the earth, they will cut them. They will not do anything to the tree; they will simply go on cutting the roots. Now for five hundred years a family has been continually cutting the roots. The tree may live for thousands of years, but the tree never blossoms, it never comes to fruition.

The same has been done to man all over the world. His roots have been cut from the very beginning, about everything.

Every child has to be obedient. You are cutting his roots. You are not giving him a chance to think whether to say yes to you, or to say no. You are not allowing him to think, you are not allowing him to make a decision on his own. You are not giving him responsibility – you are taking responsibility away, behind the beautiful word 'obedience'. You are taking his freedom away, you are taking his individuality away, by a simple strategy – insisting that he is a child, he does not know anything. The parents have to decide, and the child has to be absolutely obedient.

The obedient child is the respected child. But so much is implied in it that you are destroying him completely. He will grow old, but he will not grow up. He will grow old, but there will be no blossoming and there will be no fruition. He will live, but his life will not be a dance, will not be a song, will not be a rejoicing. You have destroyed the basic possibility for all that makes a man individual, authentic, sincere, gives him a certain integrity.

In my childhood…there were many children in my family. I had ten brothers and sisters myself, then there were one uncle's children, and another uncle's children…and I saw this happening: whoever was obedient was respected. I had to decide one thing for my whole life – not only for being in my family or for my childhood – that if I in any way desire respect, respectability, then I cannot blossom as an individual. From my very childhood I dropped the idea of respectability.

I told my father, "I have to make a certain statement to you."

He was always worried whenever I would go to him, because he knew that there would be some trouble. He said, "This is not the way a child speaks to his father – 'I am going to make a statement to you.'"

I said, "It is a statement through you to the whole world. Right now the whole world is not available to me; to me you represent the whole world. It is not just an issue between son and father; it is an issue between an individual and the collectivity, the mass. The statement is that I have renounced the idea of respectability, so in the name of respectability never ask anything from me; otherwise I will do just the opposite.

"I cannot be obedient. That does not mean I will always be disobedient, it simply means it will be my choice to obey or not to obey. You can request, but the decision is going to be mine. If I feel my intelligence supports it, I will do it; but it is not obedience to you, it is obedience to my own intelligence. If I feel it is not right, I am going to refuse it. I am sorry, but you have to understand one thing clearly: unless I am able to say no, my yes is meaningless."

And that's what obedience does: it cripples you – you cannot say no, you have to say yes. But when a man has become incapable of saying no, his yes is just meaningless; he is functioning like a machine. You have turned a man into a robot. So I said to him, "This is my statement. Whether you agree or not, that is up to you; but I have decided, and whatever the consequences, I am going to follow it."

It is such a world… In this world to remain free, to think on your own, to decide with your own consciousness, to act out of your own conscience has been made almost impossible. Everywhere – in the church, in the temple, in the mosque, in the school, in the university, in the family – everywhere you are expected to be obedient.

Just recently I was arrested in Crete. They did not show me my arrest warrant. I told them, "This is absolutely criminal."

They said, "We have got it, but it is in Greek."

And I said, "Do you have another warrant to search the house?" They had none – they had never thought about it. I said, "You were allowed by your warrant to arrest me outside the house; you were not allowed to enter the house. You not only entered the house, but Anando, my secretary, was trying to tell you, 'Just wait! Bhagwan is asleep and I will go and awaken Him. It will take only five minutes.' You could not even wait five minutes.

"You threw Anando from the porch, four feet high, onto the ground – which was gravel and stone – and dragged her away and arrested her with no warrant. And the only crime she had done was to tell you, 'Just wait. We are bringing Bhagwan down, then you can show your papers to Him.'"

When I was awakened by John, they had already started throwing rocks at the windows, at the doors, trying to break into the house from all sides. I heard noises as if bombs were being thrown. They had dynamite bombs, and were threatening to dynamite the house.

On the way to the police station they stopped in an empty, silent space and gave me a paper, describing all that had happened, that I should sign it. I said, "I would be happy to sign it, but it is not a true description. You have not mentioned anything about breaking the windows, the doors of the house, threatening that you will destroy the house with dynamite. You have not mentioned anything about Anando, that you threw her on the ground, dragged her along the stones without any arrest warrant for her. I will not sign it! You want to cover it up. If I sign it, that means I cannot go to the court because you can present this paper that I have signed already. You make it exactly factual, saying all that has happened; then I will be willing to sign it."

They understood that I am not a person who can be threatened, and they took the paper away. And they never again asked me to sign it, because they were not in a position to write all those things that they had done; that would have been their condemnation. They wanted immediately to send me to India by boat, and I refused.

I said, "Sailing by boat on the sea does not suit me. I will be seasick, and who will be responsible for it? So you have to give me a written document saying that you will be responsible for my sea-sickness and the damages." They forgot all about that boat!

I said, "My jet plane is waiting in Athens. You have to take me on a plane from here to Athens, or you have to allow my plane to come here. I am not interested in living in such a country even for two weeks" – because my visa was valid only for two weeks more – "where government authorities behave in such a primitive, ugly, inhuman way."

I told the police officer, "Wherever the pope goes, he kisses the ground after landing. I should start spitting on the ground, because that's what you deserve." The comment that he made to me reminded me of all this. He said, "It seems that from your very childhood, nobody has disciplined you in obedience."

I said, "That's right, that's an absolutely right observation. I am not against obedience, I am not disobedient, but I want to decide my life in my own way. I don't want to be interfered with by with anybody else, and I don't want to interfere in anybody else's life either."

Man can only be truly human when this becomes an accepted rule. But up to now the accepted rule has been to destroy the person in such a way that his whole life he remains servile, submissive to every kind of authority, to cut his roots so that he doesn't have enough juice to fight for freedom, to fight for individuality, to fight for anything. Then he will have only a small amount of life, which will enable him to survive till death relieves him from this slavery that we have accepted as life. Children are slaves of their parents; wives are slaves, husbands are slaves, old people become slaves of the younger people who have all the power. If you look around, everybody is living in slavery, hiding the wounds behind beautiful words.

So that drawing of yours, of a flower with beautiful petals and a light aura, but with very weak roots…you felt that it describes you: it describes all human beings.

The roots can be strong only if we stop what we have been doing up to now, and do just the opposite of it. Every child should be given a chance to think. We should help him to sharpen his intelligence. We should help him by giving him situations and opportunities where he has to decide on his own. We should make it a point that nobody is forced to be obedient, and everybody is taught the beauty and the grandeur of freedom. Then the roots will be strong.

But even your God has been cutting the roots of his own children because they were not obedient. Their disobedience became the greatest sin, such a great sin that hundreds of generations have passed, but the sin continues; you have not committed it, but you come in the line of hundreds of generations. Somebody in the beginning disobeyed God, and God is so furious that not only Adam and Eve should be punished, but all their future generations, forever.

These are the religions which have made human beings live without any blossomings and without any fragrance; otherwise each individual has the capacity to be a Socrates, to be a Pythagoras, to be a Heraclitus, to be a Gautam Buddha, to be a Chuang Tzu. Each individual has potential, but the potential is not getting enough nourishment. It remains potential…and the man dies, but the potential never becomes actuality.

My whole effort and approach is to give each individual opportunities to develop his potential, whatsoever it is. Nobody should try to divert his life – nobody has the right to do it. And then we can have a world which is truly a garden of human beings. Right now we are living in hell.

Chapter 5
April 14, 1986, Evening

You Have to Go Nowhere

Beloved Bhagwan,
I feel divided in two parts — half going towards the unknown, and half towards all that is familiar from my past. When I get close to letting go of what I believe is mine, I panic — even though I yearn to go to the place You talk about.
Please give me courage to take the next step.

The real question is not of courage; the real question is that you don't understand that the known is the dead, and the unknown is the living.

Clinging to the known is clinging to a corpse. It does not need courage to drop the clinging; in fact it needs courage to go on clinging to a corpse. You just have to see… That which is familiar to you, which you have lived – what has it given? Where have you reached? Are you not still empty? Is there not immense discontent, a deep frustration and meaninglessness? Somehow you go on managing, hiding the truth and creating lies to remain engaged, involved.

This is the question: to see with clarity that everything that you know is of the past, it is already gone. It is part of a graveyard. Do you want to be in a grave, or do you want to be alive? And this is not only the question today; it will be the same question tomorrow, and the day after tomorrow. It will be the same question at your last breath.

Whatever you know, accumulate – information, knowledge, experience – the moment you have explored them you are finished with them. Now carrying those empty words, that dead load, is crushing your life, burdening your life, preventing you from entering into a living, rejoicing being – which is awaiting you each moment.

The man of understanding dies every

moment to the past and is reborn again to the future. His present is always a transformation, a rebirth, a resurrection. It is not a question of courage at all, that is the first thing to be understood. It is a question of clarity, of being clear about what is what.

And secondly, whenever there is really a question of courage, nobody can give it to you. It is not something that can be presented as a gift. It is something that you are born with, you just have not allowed it to grow, you have not allowed it to assert itself, because the whole society is against it.

The society does not want lions, it wants a crowd of sheep. Then it is easy to enslave people, exploit people, do whatever you want to do with them.

They don't have a soul; they are almost robots. You order, and they will obey. They are not free individuals.

No society wants you to be courageous. Every society wants you to be a coward, but nobody says it so sincerely; they have found beautiful words instead. They will not say, "Be cowardly," because that will look offensive to the person and he will start thinking, "Why should I be cowardly?" – and a coward is not something respectable.

No, they say, "Be cautious. Think twice before you leap. Remember your tradition, your religion is thousands of years old; it has wisdom. You are a newcomer, you cannot afford to disbelieve in it. There is no comparison. You have just come in, and your religion has been there for ten thousand years, accumulating more and more experience, knowledge. It is a Himalayan phenomenon.

"You are a small pebble. You cannot fight with tradition – that is fighting against yourself, it is self-destructive. You can only submit to tradition; that is wise, intelligent." To be with the crowd you are protected, you are secure, you are assured that you will not go astray. In so many ways you will be told a simple thing: Just be a coward; it pays to be cowardly. It is dangerous to be courageous, because it is going to bring you in conflict with all the vested interests – and you are a small human being.

You cannot fight with the whole world.

My grandfather used to say to me, "Whatever you say is right. I am old, but I can understand that you are saying something true. But I will suggest – don't say it to anybody. You will be in trouble. You cannot be against the whole world. You may have the truth, but truth does not count; what counts is the crowd. Somebody may be simply lying" – and all religions have been doing that, lying about God, lying about heaven, lying about hell, lying about a thousand and one things – "but the crowd is with them. Their lies are supported by the immense humanity and its long tradition. You are nobody."

I was very friendly with my grandfather. He used to take me to the saints who were visiting the town. He enjoyed very much my arguments with the so-called saints, creating a situation absolutely embarrassing for the saint because he was unable to answer me. But coming back he would tell me, "Remember, it is good as a game but don't make it your life; otherwise you will be alone against the whole world. And you cannot win against the whole world."

The last thing he said was the same. Before he died, he called me close and told me, "Remember, don't fight against the world. You cannot win."

I said, "Now you are dying. You have been with the world – what have you gained? What is your victory? I cannot promise you what you are asking. I want it to be absolutely clear to you that whatever the cost...I may lose in the fight, but it will be *my* fight, and I will be immensely satisfied because I was in favor of truth. It does not matter whether I win or lose – that is irrelevant, the defeat or the victory. What is important is that whatever you feel is right, you stand for it."

This courage is in everybody. It is not a quality to be practiced; it is something that is part of your life, your very breathing. It is just that the society has created so many barriers against your natural growth that you have started thinking from where to get courage? from where to get intelligence? from where to get truth?

You have to go nowhere. You contain in the seed form everything that you want to be. Realizing this and seeing the other side… The people who live with the crowd – what is their gain? They lose everything. In fact they don't live at all; they only die. From their birth they start dying, and go on dying till the last breath. Their whole life is a long series of deaths. Just look at the whole crowd of people. You can be with them, but the same is going to be your fate.

It is so simple if you see it: the only way to live life is to live on your own. It is an individual phenomenon, it is an independence, it is freedom.

It is a constant unburdening of all that is dead, so that life can go on growing and is not crushed under the weight of the dead.

Beloved Bhagwan,
You are my inspiration.
I have heard You say You never had a master; but was there any source of inspiration for You when You began Your journey?

Life itself is enough.

Seeing people all around – walking corpses – is inspiration enough not to move with them, not to go their way, but to find a small footpath of your own if you want to be alive.

I have never had a master, and I am fortunate that I never had a master. I have been, in my past lives, with a few living masters. They were beautiful people, lovable, but one thing has been clear all along to me – that nobody can be a source of inspiration for me, because that word 'inspiration' is dangerous.

First it is inspiration, then it becomes following, then it becomes imitation – and you end up being a carbon copy. There is no need to be inspired by anybody. Not only is there no need, it is dangerous too. Just watching, I have seen…each individual is unique. He cannot follow anybody else.

He can try – millions have been trying for thousands of years. Millions are Christians, millions are Hindus, millions are Buddhists. What are they doing? Inspiration from Gautam Buddha has made millions of people Buddhists, and now they are trying to follow in his footsteps. And they are not reaching anywhere; they cannot.

You are not a Gautam Buddha, and his footprints won't fit you, neither will his shoes fit you; you will have to find the exact size of shoes that fit you. He is beautiful, but that does not mean that you have to become like him. And that's the meaning of the word 'inspiration'. It means you are so much influenced that the man becomes your ideal, that you would like to be like him. That has misled the whole humanity.

Inspiration has been a curse, not a blessing.

I would like you to learn from every source, to enjoy every unique being that you come across. But never follow anybody and never try to become exactly like somebody else; that is not allowed by existence. You can be only yourself.

And it is a strange phenomenon: the people who have become an inspiration for millions of other people were themselves never inspired by anybody – but nobody takes note of this fact. Gautam Buddha was never inspired by anybody, and that's what made him a great source of inspiration. Socrates was not inspired by anybody, but that's what makes him so unique.

All these people whom you think of as sources of inspiration have never been inspired by anybody else. That is something very fundamental to be understood. Yes, they learned; they tried to understand all kinds of people. They loved unique individuals, but nobody was to be followed. They still tried to be themselves.

So please don't be inspired by me; otherwise you will never become a source of inspiration. You will be just a carbon copy, you won't have your authentic, original face. You will be a hypocrite: you will say one thing – you will do another. You will show your face in different situations with different masks, and slowly, slowly you will forget which one is your real face; so many masks…

I have heard about a man… One hundred years had passed since Abraham Lincoln was shot dead, so for one year a great celebration was arranged in his honor all over America. One man looked like Abraham Lincoln; just a few touches here and there and he was almost a photographic copy of Abraham Lincoln.

He was trained to speak the way Abraham Lincoln used to speak, with his gestures, his emphasis, his accent, everything, small details – even the way he walked – for twenty-four hours a day…and he was to perform this drama of the life of Abraham Lincoln all over the country, moving from one place to another place the whole year.

He was shot dead so many times, every night in every show, sometimes even twice a day. That year was a long year – he died so many times – and his part in the drama became almost his second nature. So when the celebrations were finished, people were surprised: he walked out of the hall the same way Abraham Lincoln used to walk – he used to limp a little. He was limping.

His wife said, "Come to your senses!" – because he spoke in the same way, in an accent one hundred years old. His wife said, "Don't stretch the joke too much. Just become your real self and come home."

He said, "I *am* my real self, I am Abraham Lincoln." For one year continuously he had lived as Abraham Lincoln, he died thousands of deaths as Abraham Lincoln; he had completely forgotten that he was ever anybody else.

He was brought to a doctor. The doctor talked to him, but he was still in his dramatic role. The doctor said, "Just forget that drama."

The man said, "What drama?"

The doctor turned to his wife and said to her, "This man won't listen unless he is shot dead!"

The family was getting mad. He lost his job; nobody was ready to treat him because he was not sick. He was simply glued with a mask. One year is a long time, and every day, twenty-four hours a day, he was Abraham Lincoln. And to be Abraham Lincoln for one year and then suddenly become an ordinary human being – who would like it? He had seen the glorious days, the golden days, and he was clinging tightly to them.

That man lived for a few years as Abraham

Lincoln; he used to sign "Abraham Lincoln" exactly the same as Abraham Lincoln used to sign. Would you say this man has attained something or lost something? He has lost himself, and what he has gained is just a dramatic act. He has become absolutely phony.

And this is the situation of almost everybody in the world – not so dramatic, not so outstanding, but everybody is playing a certain role that has been taught to him, for which he has been brought up.

A child is born – he is not Christian, he is not a Jew, he is not Mohammedan – and then we start putting a mask on him. His innocent face disappears. And he will die believing that he is a Christian. So don't laugh at that poor man who died believing that he was Abraham Lincoln, because everybody else is doing the same. People are dying as Hindus – they were not born as Hindus.

It was a continual trouble for me whenever there was census. The officers would come to me to fill out the form, and when it came to religion, I would say, "I don't have any religion."

They would be shocked, but they would say, "You must have been born into some religion. Your parents must have been Hindus, Mohammedans, Jainas."

I said, "That does not make any difference. My father can be a doctor or an engineer – that will not make me a doctor or an engineer. He may be a Hindu or a Mohammedan – that is his business. He cannot biologically transfer his religion to me. If he cannot transfer his medical knowledge to me, how can he transfer his spiritual knowledge to me? It is a deception, and I don't want to be part of any deception."

People are being trained as actors; in this whole big world you will find everybody acting. Everybody is brought up to act… beautiful names – etiquette, manners – but hidden behind is a subtle psychology to make you forget your originality and imbibe some actor which the vested interests want you to be.

Never be inspired by anybody.

Remain open.

When you see a beautiful sunset, you enjoy the beauty of it; when you see a Buddha, enjoy the beauty of the man, enjoy the authenticity of the man, enjoy the silence, enjoy the truth the man has realized, but don't become a follower. All followers are lost.

Remain yourself – because this man Gautam Buddha has found because he has remained himself. And all these beautiful names – Lao Tzu, Chuang Tzu, Lieh Tzu, Bodhidharma, Nagarjuna, Pythagoras, Socrates, Heraclitus, Epicurus – all these beautiful names which have been a great inspiration to many people were themselves never inspired by anybody. That's how they protected their originality; that's how they remained themselves.

I have been with masters, and I have loved them. But to me the very desire to be like them is ugly. One man is enough; a second like him will not enrich existence, it will only burden it.

To me, uniqueness of individuals is the greatest truth.

Love people when you find them in some dimension true and authentic, blossoming. But remember, they are blossoming because of their authenticity and originality; so be mindful not to fall in the trap of following them. Be yourself.

The famous maxim from Socrates is: "Know thyself." But it should be completed – it is incomplete. Before "Know thyself" another maxim is needed, "Be thyself"; otherwise you may know only some actor that you are pretending to be. Knowing thyself comes second; first is being thyself.

The real great masters have been only friends, a helping hand, fingers pointing to the moon; they have never created a slavery. But the moment they died they left such a great impact around them that cunning people – theologians, priests, scholars – started preaching to people, "Follow Gautam Buddha."

Now the man is dead and he cannot deny anything…and these people started exploiting the great impact that Buddha had left. Now the whole of Asia, millions of people for twenty-five centuries have followed in the steps of Gautam Buddha, but not a single Gautam Buddha has been created. It is enough proof: two thousand years and not a single Jesus again; three thousand years, not a single Moses again.

Existence never repeats.

History repeats itself because history belongs to the unconscious mob.

Existence never repeats itself. It is very creative and very inventive. And it is good; otherwise, although Gautam Buddha is a beautiful man, if there are thousands of Gautam Buddhas around – if wherever you go you meet Gautam Buddha, in every restaurant! – you will be really bored and tired. It will destroy the whole beauty of the man. It is good that existence never repeats. It only creates one of a kind, so it remains always rare.

You are also one of a kind. You just have to blossom, to open your petals and release your fragrance.

Beloved Bhagwan,

I have heard it said that some sannyasin therapists now imagine that they are on the same plane as You are, doing the same kind of work – if perhaps on a somewhat smaller scale. They no longer even mention Your name, and appear to have discarded the mala and red clothes entirely.

Have they achieved – or what is really going on with Your therapists?

What is going on is hilarious.

These people think they have become individuals, they have attained freedom. But they don't even see a simple thing. I said to them, "You can drop your malas, and you can drop your clothes, and you can be free" – and they immediately followed! They proved that they are followers – *chronic* followers! If I had not said that, they would have been wearing the mala and red clothes still. Their freedom is not their attainment, but just my joke!

Naturally when I said, "I am your friend," they started thinking that they are *my* friends. These are two totally different things! When I say I am your friend, that does not mean that you are my friend. For the second to be real, you will have to travel long.

I say out of my compassion that I am your friend, and you say out of your ego that you are my friend. Naturally, when you are my friend, then you are doing the same work as I am doing. It is just out of humbleness that they are saying, "Perhaps you are doing it on a bigger scale and we are doing it on a smaller scale." But deep down they may be thinking that they are doing it on a bigger scale – or a more personal and intimate scale.

They have been with me for years, but they have been less with me than with their patients. The people who have missed me most are the therapists.

Once I declared some people enlightened – and they became enlightened! And when I said it was just a joke, they became unenlightened again. I had told them, "You are now free." So they are free! Tomorrow I can call them back and put them in red clothes and in the mala: "This much freedom is enough; more than that is dangerous. Just come back and be your old self!"

If you are really understanding me, you will see the point: I give you chances to show your ego to yourself, to show your reality to yourself. And that's what is happening, and it is really hilarious. I saw one therapist who has even shaved his beard and mustache. Perhaps he thinks by shaving the beard and mustache, he has shaved himself spiritually too. And all that he looks like is like a well-shaved ape – just stupid.

It is unfortunate but it is true that the therapists have missed me most, for the simple reason that in the commune they were working on people's psychology and they started getting a subtle ego that they are helping my work. They forgot completely that they have not even started working on themselves.

They had a certain knowledge of therapy; they were useful for people and they helped to bring people close to me. Their patients became more intimate to me, more open to me, became more understanding of my work than the therapists. Because they were therapists and they were answering questions from people, running groups, they would not ask questions to me about themselves.

They had come for themselves, but they got lost because they had brought a load of knowledge. It was useful for others, and I told them that they should help people. But all their knowledge was not able to indicate a simple small thing to them, that "we have come here to realize ourselves. We can do the therapy, but that is not what we have come here for."

They went on doing therapy, and when the commune dispersed, they went back to their countries thinking that now they are doing exactly the work I am doing – and they don't know even the ABC of my work. They were the most blind and the most deaf, because they were the most knowledgeable people.

They have missed the first opportunity. Now in the second opportunity, all those therapists who are just behaving like buffoons will be called back and put to some other work – not therapy. They have to be completely removed from their knowledge; otherwise it is very simple for them to think like this.

They are afraid to mention my name because that may create the feeling in people that they are still not free of me. Their fear shows that they are not free of me. If they were really free of me, there would have been gratitude. They would have taken my name to different parts of the world with great respect and love if they were really free.

But they know they are not free; hence the fear. If somebody discovers that they have been my sannyasins, then what will happen to the sudden mastery that they have attained? A few of them have become "enlightened," a few of them have become "liberated" – and they are simply proving one thing, that they are utter fools. And the sooner they realize it, the better!

Beloved Bhagwan,
It seems to me that perhaps all the master needs to do is to hand out to each of his disciples a length of rope. Over the course of time, we either use that rope to skip with or to hang ourselves with. Please comment.

That's true – it needs no comment!

Chapter 6
April 15, 1986, Morning

A Lot –
And Nothing

Beloved Bhagwan,
Can You tell us what happened to You since we last met on that beautiful morning in Crete, some weeks ago?

A lot – and nothing.
A lot on the periphery, and nothing to my being – nothing to me.

The first thing that I became aware of was that man has not been evolving, that perhaps the concept of evolution is wrong, because for thousands of years he has been behaving in the same pattern.

That beautiful morning on the island of Crete, the people and their mistreatment of me and my friends who were with me, reminded me of Socrates. These were the same people, and strangely the crime alleged against Socrates was the same: corrupting the young minds, destroying their morality. Their allegation against me was exactly the same.

It seems twenty-five centuries have simply passed by and man is stuck, not evolving. Their behavior was brutal, inhuman. They could have told me to leave the country – it is their country – there was no need for brutality, smashing the windows and the doors of the house with rocks. To me, coming from the top floor, it sounded as if bombs were being exploded. They had dynamite with them, and they were threatening that they would dynamite the whole house. It seems as if to send me out of the country was just an excuse to give expression to this brutality; otherwise it was a simple matter to tell me that I am not welcome.

The man who had given me the tourist visa for four weeks was the chief of police; and the man who canceled it after fifteen days was the deputy chief of police. That seems to be absolutely improper – that the chief should give the permission and the deputy should cancel it.

At the airport in Athens there were at least forty police officers, just for a single unarmed man, and that deputy chief was also present. There was a huge crowd of press people from newspapers, radio, television, and dozens of cameras – they all wanted an interview with me. And I said, "There is not much to say, other than it seems man is not going to be civilized, ever."

The press people were in front of me and those forty police dogs – all big officers – were surrounding me, and the deputy chief was standing by my side. When I said, "With this kind of police, this kind of government, you are destroying the very future of humanity, particularly of your own country. These people were responsible for killing Socrates...."

When I said this, pointing towards the deputy chief, he wanted to interfere.

For the first time in thirty-five years, I pretended to be angry. I could not succeed because inside I was giggling! But I told that man, "Shut up, and stand by the side where you belong. And don't come close to me."

And I shouted so loudly, "Shut up!" that he really became silent and went back and stood in the crowd. Later on I saw the reports: they thought I was ferocious, very angry – I was nothing! But that is the only language those people will understand. And when you are talking to somebody, you have to use the language he understands.

But I enjoyed that. Anger can be acted – you can remain absolutely silent within and you can be ferocious outside. And there is no contradiction, because that ferociousness is only acting.

On the plane I remembered George Gurdjieff, who was trained in many Sufi schools in different kinds of methods. In a certain school one method was used, and that was acting – when you are not feeling angry, *act* angry; when you are feeling very happy, act miserable. The method has a tremendous implication.

It means that when you are miserable you will be capable of acting happy; when you are angry you will be able to act peaceful. Not only that, it implies that you are neither misery nor happiness. These are faces you can make: you are different, your being is not involved in it. Strange methods have been used for meditation, to discover your being, to detach it from your emotions, sentiments, actions. And Gurdjieff became so proficient in it, and the school was training him for this particular method....

Gurdjieff became so capable that if he was sitting between two persons, to one person he would appear immensely peaceful and silent – half of his face, one side profile. And to the other he will appear to be murderous, danger- ous, criminal – the other profile, the other side. And when both persons would talk about Gurdjieff, how could they agree? They were bound to disagree: according to one they have met a very silent, peaceful person, and according to the other – a very murderous, dangerous, criminal type.

When asked, Gurdjieff would say, "They are both right. I can manage not only to divide my being and my action, I can manage to divide even my face into two parts."

I was presented a statue of Buddha from Japan – a very beautiful statue, but very strange. In one hand he is holding a naked sword, and in the other hand he is holding a small lamp. In the East they use mud lamps, which are just small cups of mud filled with oil. They are almost like candles with a flame, so the flame was there. The flame was shining on one part of his face; it was lighted, silent, peaceful. And the sword was reflected on the other side of his face – a warrior, a fighter, a born rebel, a revolutionary.

At the airport in Athens, I saw those forty police officers…they must have been the topmost people – except the chief, because he could not gather courage to come. I would have asked him, "On what grounds has the visa issued by you been cancelled by your assistant?" – only he was not there.

But the others…I saw a strange thing: they were behaving in very inhuman ways, but they were all cowards. When I shouted, "Shut up!" that deputy chief simply slipped back like a small child, afraid that the television would catch my words and me, and him with all the honors of the police on his coat, with a pistol hanging by his side. But inside there was a child, a cowardly child.

It was an experience – because democracy was born in Athens.

Democracy is a Greek idea, and yet the man who created the idea of democratic values was poisoned by Athenians – that's what history goes on saying. But that day I became suspicious of history.

Socrates was not poisoned by the people of Athens, but by the bureaucracy of Athens. And one should make a distinction, because I was mistreated on the island of Crete by the police. But the people of the village where I was staying, Saint Nicholas, were not with the bureaucracy. And when one journalist asked me, "What is your message to the people of Saint Nicholas?" I said, "Just tell them to come to the airport, to show the police that they are with me and not with them."

Three thousand people were at the airport in the middle of the night, filling the whole terrace of the airport. They had been standing there for hours. The whole village was empty; those who were left behind had to walk because they could not get any taxi, any bus – everything had moved to the airport. But people walked miles to reach the airport to demonstrate a simple fact: they are not with the brutality and the fascist behavior of the government; they are with me.

People have always been blamed for the bureaucracy and its brutality. I don't think Socrates would have been killed by the people of Athens. He was such a loving person, and with no egoistic idea of being holier than you.

In the morning he would go to fetch some vegetable, and he would not return even by the night – because everywhere on the streets, in the vegetable shop, in the market, he was discussing with everybody things which are beyond the ordinary man. He was the teacher of the whole of Athens.

A single man made Athens one of the most intelligent cities that has ever existed in the world – single-handedly, just moving, meeting anybody. To say hello to him meant you were entering into a dialogue – in spite of yourself. You may have been in a hurry – Socrates was not in a hurry.

These people could not have killed him. The bureaucracy became afraid. The Crete experience made me look again at history. The books are lying – the people have not killed the man. They could not have even imagined it. But the government…and why should the government kill the man? – because the man was making the masses so intelligent, so independent, so freedom-loving, so individualistic, that the government would soon find itself in troubled waters. It would not be able to control these people, it would not be able to enslave these people.

It is better to kill Socrates than let him go on sharpening people's minds to such an extent that the bureaucrats look like fools! Before it happens, it is better to kill him. But the history books go on saying that the people of Athens killed Socrates. Now, I saw the people of Saint Nicholas come running to the airport to demonstrate that they are not with the police. And even when I had left their country, a deputation from Saint Nicholas, on their own decision, went to see the president of the country to protest about what had happened in their village.

I had been there only two weeks, and I had never gone out of the house; but they could see my people – at least five hundred sannyasins from all over Europe had gathered. They were well accustomed to tourists, because it is a tourist place, but they had never seen such loving people. And just because of my sannyasins, although they could not understand me – the language was a great barrier – still, a few of the village people started coming just to sit with me in the morning, in the evening. And that's what was hurting the religious hierarchy.

The archbishop was getting mad because nobody comes to his congregation; and I had been there for fifteen days and I had created a big congregation. In his congregation, between six to twelve old women – who were almost dead – they used to come to listen to him.

He was getting afraid, sending telegrams to the president, to the prime minister, to other ministers, to the police chief, giving interviews which were full of lies – because he knew nothing about me. And his fear became infectious: the government also became afraid.

One of my sannyasins, Amrito – who had invited me to Greece – was a close friend of the president, of the prime minister. She was well connected with all the high-position people, because twenty years before she had been chosen as the beauty queen, "Miss Greece," and she had become famous. And since then she had been modeling, so all the film directors, businessmen…all kinds of people were related to her. She was never asked to make an appointment; she simply went to their houses – the president or the prime minister.

But that day she went to the president and for six hours she remained there, and she was not allowed into the house. Why was the president afraid of a woman whom he knows, who has been coming to him and they have been friends…? The fear was because…what will he say? What had been done to me and my people by his government, he had no answer for.

And you will be surprised: the answer came in a very strange way. I left Athens because they wouldn't allow me even to stay for the night in a hotel under their supervision, or at the airport.

As I left, they immediately started searching for Amrito. She must have found out from some source: "Now you will be the target – why did you invite Bhagwan here, knowing him?" And she had to escape out of the country. And still the police went….

Amrito is a very simple and loving person. She is not rich; she has only a small juice bar. And still the police went to the juice bar and tried to find out strange things with which the police had no concern – that it was not clean.

Of course it was not clean, because for three days she had been out of the country. And it was not clean because for fifteen days she was on the island of Crete with me, so only the servant was running it. But that is not a crime – at least not for the police. Perhaps the municipal authorities who look for cleanliness in restaurants, hotels may have come – but they were not there; the police were finding faults.

But I have told her to go back and give a fight, because she has not done anything wrong. Everything wrong is on the part of the government. Because they could not do any harm to me, afraid of its international consequences, they found a scapegoat: they can harass her, they can torture a woman who is divorced, has a little child, an old mother, and she is the only earning person. And what earning can come out of a juice bar?

These people always throw their crimes on the masses – and the masses are dumb. And history is really bunk: there are more lies in history books than anywhere else. The incident was small, but the implications were great.

I had not stepped out of the house, I was not talking in Greek. The people of the country could not understand me. The people who were listening to me were all from outside of Greece. To say that I am corrupting the minds of youth, destroying the morality of the country, its tradition, its church, the family…but the people who were listening to me were not Greek! In what way could I have had any effect on their morality, on their religion?

But it seems bureaucracy does not think; it simply lives out of fear. And the fear is that somebody could raise questions about the very roots of their society. But it is foolish because wherever I am, I am going to do the same, and my word is going to reach everywhere in the world.

What can I do if their roots are rotten? What can I do if their morality is not morality but only a pretension? What can I do if their marriage is hypocrisy and not love? What can I do if the family has been outlived, and needs to be replaced by something better? It has done its work. It has done a few good things which can be done by a different way. It has

done a few very dangerous, poisonous things which can be avoided.

The family as it has existed down the ages cannot be allowed to exist. If it exists, then man has to die. To save man we have to change the social structure around him, to bring a new man – because the old has been an utter failure.

For ten thousand years at least, we have moved on the same lines – reaching nowhere.

It is time to understand that we have taken a wrong route. It is stale; it leads to death. It does not allow people joy, rejoicing; it does not allow people to sing and to dance.

It makes people serious, heavy – for themselves and for others.

In the family are the seeds of all wars, of all religions, of all nations. That's why they call the family, the "unit of our civilization."

There is no civilization – and the unit is rotten. It creates only a pathological man, who needs all kinds of psychotherapies and still remains pathological.

We have not been able to create a sane humanity.

So on the periphery I thought what happened in Greece perhaps may happen in other countries, because it is the same structure – and it happened.

From Greece we moved to Geneva, just for an overnight rest, and the moment they came to know my name they said, "No way! We cannot allow him into our country."

I was not even allowed to get out of the plane.

We moved to Sweden, thinking that people go on saying that Sweden is far more progressive than any country in Europe or in the world, that Sweden has been giving refuge to many terrorists, revolutionaries, expelled politicians, that it is very generous.

We reached Sweden. We wanted to stay

overnight because the pilots were running out of time. They could not go on anymore; otherwise it would become illegal. And we were happy because the man at the airport…we had asked only for an overnight stay, but he gave seven-day visas to everybody. Either he was drunk or just sleepy – it was midnight, past midnight.

The person who had gone for the visas came back very happy that we had been given seven-day visas. But immediately the police came and cancelled the visas, and told us to move immediately: "This man we cannot allow in our country."

They can allow terrorists, they can allow murderers, they can allow Mafia people, and they can give them refuge – but they cannot allow me. And I was not asking for refuge or permanent residence, just an overnight stay.

We turned to London, because it was simply a question of our basic right. And we made it twice legal – we purchased first-class tickets for the next day. Our own jet was there but still we purchased them in case they started saying, "You don't have tickets for tomorrow, so we won't allow you to stay in the first-class lounge."

We purchased tickets for everybody, just so that we could stay in the lounge, and we told them, "We have our own jet – and we also have tickets." But they came upon a bylaw of the airport that the government or anybody cannot interfere with: "It is at our discretion – and this man we won't allow in the lounge."

In the lounge, I thought: How can I destroy their morality, their religion? In the first place I will be sleeping, and by the morning we will be gone.

But no, these so-called civilized countries are as primitive and barbarous as you can conceive. They said, "All that we can do is, we can put you in jail for the night."

And just by chance one of our friends looked into their file. They had all the instructions from the government already about how they were to treat me: I should not be allowed in any way to enter into the country, even for an overnight stay in a hotel or in the lounge; the only way was that I should be kept in jail.

In the morning we moved to Ireland. Perhaps the man did not take note of my name amongst the passengers. We had asked just to stay for two, three days – "at the most seven, if you can give us." We wanted time because some other decision was being made, and they were delaying it, and our movement was dependent on that decision.

The man was really generous…must have taken too much beer: he gave everybody twenty-one days. We moved to the hotel and immediately the police arrived at the hotel to cancel it, saying, "That man is mad – he does not know anything."

They cancelled the visas, but they were in a difficult situation – what to do with us?

We were already in the land, we were in the hotel; we had passed a few hours in the hotel. They had given us twenty-one days on the passports. Now he had cancelled them, and we were not ready to go. We had to wait still a few days.

You can see how bureaucracy covers its own errors.

They said, "You can stay here, but nobody should come to know about it – no press, nobody should come to know that Bhagwan is here, because then we will be in trouble. And of course we cannot do anything because that will stir up problems immediately.

"If you don't want to go – and we have given you twenty-one days' permission…. On what grounds are we cancelling? You have not done anything – you have only slept the night here – unless sleeping is a crime. So we are in a difficulty. The only way is, you remain silent and absolutely hidden."

Now, it was absolutely illegal to stay without a visa; and the police were suggesting to us to remain silent so that nobody knows it – and leave silently. And they were keeping the press away; they were giving them false clues so they were looking in some different places.

But the strange thing is that these people are in direct communication with the government.

The question was raised in the parliament, "What happened? Their jet is standing at the airport. They have entered the country – where have they disappeared to?" And the minister simply lied, saying, "They had come, and they have left." We were in the country, and the parliament was told that we have left the country....

This whole journey has been an exposure of the bureaucracies.

And just now I have received the information that all the countries of Europe, jointly, are deciding that I cannot land my plane at any airport.

How will that affect their morality – refueling the plane? But they simply want to cut me away from humanity. That's why I had to leave India. Their conditions were clear: they wanted me to remain in India – naturally *they* cannot deny me; it is my birthland. "You can remain," they said, "but no foreign disciple can be allowed to reach you, and no news media can be allowed to reach you."

That was a way to cut me off from the world, from my people, and even from news media, so nobody knows whether I am alive or dead. It was a strategy to make me almost dead – although I am alive – to cut me away from everybody.

I refused their conditions. I have never lived under any conditions, and particularly such ugly conditions. I left the country and went to Nepal – because that is the only country where I can go without a visa; otherwise the Indian government had informed all the embassies that no visa should be issued to me so that I cannot leave India. They have a treaty with Nepal; no visa is needed.

But Nepal is a small and very poor country – the poorest – and under tremendous pressure from India.... India can take it over any moment. It has no army worth the name.

When it became from reliable sources absolutely certain that they would compel the Nepalese government either to arrest me or to send me back to India, I had to leave Nepal.

It makes no difference to my being.

But it makes a lot of difference to my attitude about the society in which we are living. It is absolutely ugly, barbarous, uncultured, uncivilized.

That's why I said, "A lot – and nothing."

Beloved Bhagwan,
I found the story You told us about Mahavira when he went begging very odd. That he should stipulate how existence should present his daily food seemed to me like a trip, and not the attitude of someone totally available to, and accepting of, life's ways. Probably I have misunderstood the whole point.

You have said we need not be in a hurry in our search; but around You I always feel such a great sense of how precious time is, so I want to use it to the maximum. And to me at the moment that means asking all and any questions I once might have held back, from fear of appearing stupid. I really do want to stand before You, "naked, empty, and alone."

The story of Mahavira has always been misunderstood – it is not only you who have misunderstood it – because we understand things according to our minds. If you were in place of Mahavira then perhaps it would be stipulating existence, but for Mahavira it is not so; it is not stipulating existence.

As far as Mahavira is concerned, he simply wants a signal from existence – whether he should continue, or he is no longer needed. He never complains. At times he has remained fasting for three months continuously, but not a single word of complaint.

If he was stipulating then there would be frustration, there would be complaint. If he was trying to manipulate existence then there would be a certain sense of failure. For three months he had not been able even to get food – but there was no complaint. He was one of the most peaceful, loving, silent beings.

Why did he make this decision? – simply not to be a burden on existence. Let existence decide. He is not stipulating existence; he is allowing existence to take total charge of his life, even of his breathing, of his food. *Everything* he is leaving in the hands of existence.

But how will he know? There is no linguistic communication between you and existence; there can be only a symbolic communication – and that was nothing but a symbolic communication. He wanted a symbol.

One thing has to be remembered, that these people like Mahavira, Parsunatha, Buddha, are very unique beings. They have their own ways, and their ways fit perfectly with their personality.

Now *I* will never do that kind of thing. I am a totally different person – but I will not misunderstand Mahavira either. I accept his uniqueness, and I respect the way he lived his life – always undemanding. This was not a demand – that existence should fulfill this condition – it was simply an agreement: "Because language is not possible, I will choose a certain symbol, and then it is up to existence." He is leaving himself in the hands of existence so totally that he does not want to breathe even a single breath on his own.

But I am a totally different person, almost the very opposite of Mahavira. I will never ask such a thing from existence. My whole way is of let-go – and why bother? Once and for all, leave it to existence, and when existence does not need you, you will be absorbed into the universe. There is no need every day to ask again and again – that is a kind of nagging. I have done it once, and that's all. I will not do it twice, because to do it twice means that the first time you were not total; otherwise who is doing it again?

Let-go can be done only once.

When I was a child we used to have many puzzles, and particularly we used to ask a teacher – who was a little dumb – simple things, and he would get into such a nervous state.

For example we used to ask him, "One man tried to commit suicide four times. Can you tell us when he succeeded? – the first time, the second time.... Which time did he succeed?"

And he would start thinking about it. He would say, "How should I know?" If a man succeeds then the last time is really the first time!

In my understanding, let-go is only once. If you need it again, that means the first time…whom were you deceiving? And what is the guarantee that the second time is not going to be just like the first?

Let-go is an understanding.

It is not something that you have to *do*.

It is not something that you have to say to existence; it is simply an understanding: "I will not swim against the current, because that is simply stupid." You are going to be tired soon, you can never be victorious against the current. Understanding that, you accept the current's way as your way.

That is let-go.

Now, wherever the river leads you…you don't have to check every day; you simply go with the river. Some day – any day – you may reach the ocean, you may disappear.

So I will not suggest to anybody to do what Mahavira used to do. But Mahavira has his own unique being.

His real name was not Mahavira; *Mahavira* means "a great warrior." His real name was Vardhmana, but nobody remembers his real name for the simple reason that his whole approach is that of a warrior, a fighter. Even with existence he is in a constant fight. He is saying, "I can live only if I am welcome. I don't want to live even a single moment more if I am not welcome."

Deep down he was fighting, but his fighting had a beauty of its own. He was total in it – that was its beauty. It was not a partial war, it was total. And the secret is, whatever is total transforms you; your let-go, if it is total, will transform you; your fight, if total, will transform you.

What transforms is neither let-go nor war, but your totality.

Even today there are monks doing the same, who follow Mahavira. There are not many because as soon as Mahavira died there was a division. There were people who were not ready for such a fight. And that division has many monks. They have compromised on many points on which Mahavira would not compromise.

For example, they wear clothes; Mahavira remained naked. These people stay in homes; Mahavira never stayed under a roof. It may have been raining, it may have been cold, it may have been hot – he was always under a tree. So the people who wanted to compromise could not compromise when he was alive. He was a tremendously powerful man. But the day he died, his followers divided.

So the orthodox ones, who still follow Mahavira… There are only twenty-two of them – there *were* when I was in India; a few may have died, because they were all old people. And once one monk dies, it is very difficult to replace him.

The other party, the compromisers, have almost five thousand monks – and they go on growing. And they go on compromising.

First they started using clothes; then they started using people's houses to stay in. Now they have started using even airplanes. Mahavira walked all his life, never using any vehicle. I have seen these compromisers hiding toothpaste; Mahavira never washed his teeth.

I know about these monks, that whenever they have a chance they take a shower; Mahavira never took a shower himself unless the sky was raining and he was standing under a tree. I have seen in one monk's place, where he was staying…he was very friendly to me, and he was not worried that I would expose him.

He said, "What you will take? – Fanta or Coca Cola?"

I said, "What are you saying?"

He said, "Just don't tell anybody!" – and he opened a closet and he was hiding Coca Cola, Fanta. Compromise has no limit. But what is harmful in it? – it is absolutely nonviolent junk; you can drink it.

But those who have followed Mahavira,

their number has been getting less and less; one dies and is not replaced. Even they, in an underground way, have compromised. It is difficult to be exactly like Mahavira – that's what I say, following is impossible.

These people also make, after their meditation in the morning, a certain condition that should be fulfilled. But those conditions are limited – six or eight – and everybody knows, so if they are staying in a city, then they will go to all the Jaina houses and all the Jaina houses will be fulfilling different conditions. And they have made very simple conditions.

For example, if on the door of a house two bananas are hanging, then the food will be accepted. And this is known, so every Jaina is hanging two bananas, and they come and they accept the food – the condition is fulfilled. Just such small conditions which are known, and which must be made known by the monks.

They cannot eat food from anybody other than a Jaina family, so you will be surprised to see that they have renounced their family, one family, but when they are moving… And they are constantly moving. They cannot stay more than three days in one place, because this is Mahavira's understanding – and I feel that he is right – that after three days some kind of attachment starts growing.

For example, for the first day you will not find the place suitable to you. You may not sleep well, you may have a certain tension in you. But after the third day, things start settling; and after the twenty-first day you become well-accustomed to the place, as if you had been born in it.

A certain amount of time is needed for adjustment, so Mahavira does not allow more than three days. And in India, Jainas are very few, so there are many, many places where there are no Jainas – so what will the Jaina monk do? So twenty families follow him with their buses and their cars and tents, and wherever there is no Jaina family they make a small campus of tents and bananas are hanging…and all eight conditions that are known are fulfilled. And every family has prepared food – and the man must have made one condition out of eight – so he will get food.

Now, formally he is following, but this was not what Mahavira was doing. That was a totally different thing. It was not let-go; he was not a man for let-go, he was a warrior.

Truth has to be conquered, according to him, and to conquer it you have to fight totally. And the story I told you is part of his fight. His whole life is the path of fight.

I will tell you one story more.

He remained for twelve years silent, till he became enlightened. Those twelve years are filled with great incidents. One day he is meditating…and his meditation is also not that of a relaxed way. The meditation ordinarily done in the East is in the lotus posture, and the lotus posture physiologically is the most relaxed once you have learnt it, because your spine is straight and the gravitation is the least, and that makes your body hang on the straight spine like a loose cloth.

Mahavira meditates standing. In his every attitude he is a warrior. There are people who meditate with closed eyes – this is more relaxed. There are people who meditate with open eyes, just the natural way – blinking. That too is not a fight. Mahavira meditates with eyes half closed and half open, and no blinking.

In those twelve years one day he is standing and meditating by the side of the river, and a man comes and says to Mahavira, "You are standing here, just watch my cows. I am leaving – I have to go urgently to my home; my mother is sick and somebody has come to inform me that she is dying. So I will be back soon, but just…you are standing here for the whole day: just have a look so my cows don't get lost in the jungle."

And Mahavira, because he cannot speak, is silent. And the man is in such a hurry – his mother is dying – he does not bother that this man is not speaking. He simply takes his silence as a yes.

When he comes back after one or two hours, Mahavira is still standing there but all the cows are gone. Now he gets furious. He says, "You seem to be a cunning man. So you were standing here the whole day just for my cows. Where are my cows?"

And because he does not speak, the man becomes more and more furious: "So you are trying to be dumb! I will make you speak!"

And he takes two pieces of wood and forces those two pieces into Mahavira's two ears and hits them hard with a rock, so that he becomes deaf for his whole life. But still he will not speak, he will not blink.

The man thought, "He seems to be mad. Anybody would have spoken…" And he goes and looks in the forest. In the evening the cows come back, and when the man comes back, he finds they are all sitting around Mahavira where he had left them before.

He said, "You are really a man! I destroyed your ears and you did not speak! I have been going all over the forest, and the cows are sitting here! Where have you been hiding them?" And he beats him – he is naked. And Mahavira remains standing. The man is thinking that he is really mad – neither beating has any effect…you cannot do *anything* to him, he will not react. That is total silence – that whatever happens, he will remain centered without any reaction. It is not only a question of speaking.

The story is beautiful. Up to this point it is factual, but it takes a mythological ending. In India there are many gods. India does not believe in one god – one god seems to be like believing in a dictator; it is undemocratic – India believes in many gods, actually thirty-three million. That was the population of India when they invented gods: one god for everyone. That seems to be right and fair.

Indra, one of the gods, feels terribly hurt and disturbed by what has happened to Mahavira – a silent man who has done nothing. The cows moved themselves, came back again, and he is utterly innocent.

Indra came – and gods can speak without words – so he spoke to Mahavira, "I can give you two gods as bodyguards, because it is unthinkable, unbelievable! This should not happen." And to gods you may not speak but they can read your thought.

Indra reads Mahavira's thought: "Just leave me alone. I don't want anybody's help; I want to fight it alone. I don't want to be indebted to anybody – forgive me. Whatever happens, I am going to fight this whole war alone until I am victorious."

Now, his victory will sound strange to anybody who has been listening to the idea of let-go, surrender to existence. But this is a good place to remind you: Be compassionate about others, their uniqueness. It does not mean that you have to follow their path; it simply means a deep understanding that people are unique; and if people are unique then their ways are going to be unique. And sometimes very opposite ways lead to the same goal.

It is very easy to misunderstand, but I would like you to understand different ways, different people, different uniquenesses. All that will help to broaden your heart, your compassion, your comprehension. And whatever path you are following, it will be helpful to it.

A LOT – AND NOTHING

This is broadness – that it can contain contradictions.

Chapter 7
April 15, 1986, Evening

Empty from Birth to Death

Beloved Bhagwan,
I remember while You were in the police station in Crete, those two young smiling Greek women, dressed in black like typical Cretan women, coming to the window, holding Your hand and saying in very broken English, "Bhagwan, we love You. We are Cretan, we want You to stay here."

It seems that as the governments become increasingly strident in their attacks on You — in spite of the increasingly obvious love the common man has for You — one of the most important parts of Your work will be to show how the bureaucracy, far from representing the common man, is in fact in complete opposition to him.

I certainly remember those two young women holding my hand and trying to convey to me that "We, the people of this island, want you to stay here. We love you."

The question you have raised has occurred to me many times in my life, again and again. The bureaucracy is *not* for the people, it is against them. It uses them, it exploits them, it manipulates them; it makes them believe that it is serving their purposes. But the reality is just the opposite.

They define democracy as the government of the people, for the people, by the people. It is none of these things. It is neither by the people, nor of the people, nor for the people.

The people who have been holding power down the centuries have always been able to persuade people that whatever is being done, is done for their sake. And the people have believed it because they have been trained to believe; it is a conspiracy between religion and state to exploit humanity.

The religion goes on preaching belief and destroys the intelligence of people to question, makes them retarded. And the state goes on exploiting them in every possible way – still managing to keep the people's support, because the people have been trained to believe, not to question. Any kind of government – it may be monarchy, it may be aristocracy, it may be democracy, it may be any kind of government... Just the names change but deep down the reality remains the same.

In Japan before the second world war, Hirohito, the emperor of Japan, was believed to be the direct descendant of the God Sun, and whatever he was saying was not human, it was divine; his order had just to be followed. For centuries Japanese people have believed in him as a Sun God, And they have died in hundreds of wars, willingly, *joyously,* because they are dying for God himself. What more blissful and beautiful a death could one aspire to?

Japan is a small country but no other country has been able to conquer it – even countries like China, vast countries. China is the greatest country as far as numbers are concerned, as far as land is concerned, but a small tiny Japan was able to defeat the Chinese because the people had this fanatic belief that God is behind them, so victory is theirs. And more or less the same has been the situation all over the world.

That day when those two Cretan women, holding my hand with great love, said to me, "We are not against you. We love you and we want you to stay here," they represented the real consciousness of the people. And then I saw at the airport, three thousand people – it must have been the whole population of Saint Nicholas – came to show their support, and to show that they are not with the brutality and nazi actions of the police against me, that they are for me.

Yes, it has to be one of my works to awaken people to the real situation: you are being exploited in different names. The exploiters even call themselves public servants, to tell you that they serve you. For thousands of years they have been "serving" – and the people are in immense misery, ignorance. They don't have anything to their life; they are born, they somehow live, and they die. Nothing happens to them which could be called ecstatic, which could be called an experience.

Empty from birth to death, nothing flowers, nothing blossoms...and they have all the potential of being a song of joy. But these bureaucracies, religious and political, would not allow it. They are so afraid of joyous people.

It was a strange feeling for me in the beginning. I had never thought that people should be so afraid of joyous people. Slowly slowly, I became aware that joy has many implications:

A joyous person is not retarded.

A joyous person is intelligent.

A joyous person knows the art of life; otherwise he cannot be joyous. And a joyous person is dangerous to all those vested interests which go against humanity.

Those interests want humanity to live in hell forever. They have managed in every possible way to keep you in misery. They destroy everything that you can rejoice in, and they give you ample opportunity to be miserable. A miserable person is not a danger to this rotten society.

Yes, it has to be one of my basic works to make people aware that the powerful ones – either religious or political – are not your friends. They are your enemies. And unless the common humanity goes through a rebellion against all types of bureaucracies, man will remain stuck, not evolving, not reaching to the heights which are his birthright.

Beloved Bhagwan,

Has anyone really understood Your message of love? Recently it has been painfully clear to me that I haven't, and I wonder if we aren't all, with some slight variations on the theme, still singing the same old song.

Why is it so difficult to live something that is so simple and natural?

Just because it is so simple and so natural, that's why it is so difficult.

You are not simple and you are not natural.

And it *is* simple *and* natural.

My message of love is absolutely simple; nothing can be more simple than that. But your mind is very complex, very tricky. It makes simple things complicated – that's its work. And for centuries it has been trained for only one thing: to make things so complicated that your life becomes impossible.

Your mind has become expert in destroying you, because your life consists of simple things. The whole existence is simple, but man's mind has been cultivated, conditioned, educated, programmed in such a way that the simplest thing becomes crooked. The moment it reaches to your mind it is no longer simple. The mind starts interpreting it, finding things in it which are not there, ignoring things which are there.

And you think that you have heard whatever I have been telling you? It is not so. I have been telling you one thing, and you have been hearing something else because your hearing is not direct. There is a mediator – your mind. It functions in many ways as a censor, it does not allow many things to enter inside you.

You will be surprised to know how much it prevents – ninety-eight percent. It allows in only two percent of what is being said to you, and that too not in its purity. First it pollutes it by its own interpretations, by its own past experiences, conditionings, and by the time the mind comes to have the sense that it has understood, what was said and what was heard are poles apart.

Gautam Buddha used to tell a story…it is strange that all great masters have depended on stories. There is some reason for it: the mind relaxes when it is a question of a story; when it is just a joke the mind relaxes. There is no need to be tense and serious, just a story is being told, you can relax.

But when something like love or freedom or silence is being explained, you are tense. That's why the masters have to use simple stories. Perhaps by the end of the story they can manage it so a small message enters in from the back door while you are still relaxed.

Gautam Buddha used to say – it was his custom after his evening talk – he used to say to his disciples, "Now go and do the last thing before you go to sleep." That last thing was the meditation.

One day it happened that a prostitute was listening and a thief was also in the audience. When Buddha said, "Now it is time for you to go and do the last thing before you go to sleep," all the sannyasins went to meditate. The thief simply became awakened – "What am I doing here?" This was the time to do his business.

The prostitute looked around and felt that Buddha was really very perceptive, because when Buddha had said that, he was looking at her. She bowed down in gratitude because she was reminded, "Go to do your business before you go to sleep."

A simple statement, but three types of people heard three meanings. In fact there must have been more meanings, because to somebody meditation must have been a joy, to somebody else meditation must have been something one has to do; and then the meaning differs. To all those meditators the message was the same, but what was heard by them could not have been the same.

All my life I have never taught anything complex to anybody. Life is already too complex, and I don't want to burden you more. But I have been more misunderstood than perhaps anybody else in this whole century, for the simple reason that I am saying simple things which nobody says. I am talking about the obvious which everybody has forgotten, which has been taken for granted. Nobody talks about it.

You can look at the great theological treatises of the Christians, at great works of religion by Hindus, Mohammedans, Jews – very scholarly, very difficult to understand. The more difficult they are, the more they are respected. When people cannot understand something they think it is something great, mysterious, something far above their comprehension. And naturally it becomes respectable.

The Hindus use a language for their religious treatises, Sanskrit, which has never been a living language. It has never been spoken by the people in the marketplace; it has been a language of the experts. But they have resisted continuously that Hindu scriptures should be translated.

I was always wondering, why this resistance? In fact they should be happy that their scriptures are being translated and their message is being spread to all corners of the earth. But when I studied their scriptures, I understood the reason.

The reason was that those scriptures have nothing. Just the language is so difficult, and people don't understand it, so they go on paying respect to it. Once it is translated into the language of the people, it loses all glory, all spirituality. It becomes so ordinary because it

is no longer difficult.

And the same is true about others – for example the Jews. The rabbis will still prefer Hebrew. Now it is not a living language, why go on insisting on it? But it gives the mind the impression of something mysterious, impenetrable, holy, far beyond, so that all that you can do is to bow down. Once it is translated, it has nothing. And specially, it has nothing that you need.

None of these scriptures teach about love, its implications, its different dimensions. None of these scriptures teach about freedom. None of these scriptures teach about *you,* your life, and how it can be transformed into a celebration. They talk about God! I have never come across a single man who has any problem with God – it is so irrelevant. Is God anybody's problem? Is the Holy Ghost anybody's problem? – things which are absolutely irrelevant to human existence.

The mind has been filled with all kinds of unnecessary luggage. No space is left in the mind for the realities that you have to live. So even your greatest theologian is as foolish about love as you are, has no understanding of freedom, has never enquired into the distinction between personality and individuality.

I had one professor who was teaching religion. After listening for a few days I stood up and told him, "I think you are talking about irrelevant things. I don't see a single student here for whom God is a problem, and I don't see either that God is a problem to you" – because I used to live just in front of his house, and his wife was the problem.

I told him, "Your wife is the real problem; *that* you can discuss. God is absolutely abstract. I have never seen you thinking about God in your house. And all that you are teaching about God has nothing of your experience in it, it has not been your quest.

You are filling the minds of these innocent people with ideas which are of no use. Talk about love!"

He was very angry. He said, "You have to come with me to the principal."

I said, "I can come even to God. You cannot threaten me."

On the way towards the principal's office he said, "You don't feel afraid?"

I said, "Why should I feel afraid? You should feel afraid! I know all the students; their problem is love, and your problem is love. And I am going to tell the principal, 'If you don't believe me, just call this professor's wife, and you will know what I mean by problem.'"

He said, "You are making it too complex."

I said, "I am making it absolutely simple, factual. I can bring all the students to the office; they all have problems of love. Somebody is chasing a woman, and is not getting her – that's his problem. Somebody has got her – and that is *his* problem."

He said, "It is better you should come back; there is no need."

I said, "I never go back from anywhere. If you are not coming, I am going alone."

He said, "When I am saying there is no need…"

I said, "It may not be a need for you; it is a need for me. I have to decide it finally, because to me love is a religious phenomenon, while God is not. God is only a hypothesis. It means nothing because there is nothing corresponding to it.

"And love is a religious phenomenon. Unless it is understood in its totality, a man is bound to become miserable by something which could have made his life divine. The same thing which could have been his heaven is going to become hell because he has no

understanding. And it is certainly an art. Who cares about God? So you start talking sense. We have come here to understand religion, not nonsense."

"But," he said, "in the whole syllabus there is no mention of love, freedom, individuality, silence…we have to complete the syllabus."

Universities complete their syllabuses without bothering about the real life of man, his real problems.

Because I am talking about simple things, many people simply feel that this is not what religion has to be. They have got an idea of religion, of complicated abstract hypotheses, you can go on thinking about them but it makes no difference to your life – you remain the same.

You may be a Hindu, or a Mohammedan, or a Christian, it does not matter; your real problems are the same. Your unreal problems are different, but those unreal problems are nothing but a burden to the mind.

It is possible to understand me if you can just put aside your mind and its complicated mechanism. It is not needed because my work is heart to heart.

I am speaking from my heart.

I am not a theoretician, I am not speaking from my mind. I am pouring my heart to you, but if you are going to listen from the mind you are going to miss it.

If you are also ready to open a new door into your being, if you are ready to hear from the heart, then whatever I am saying is so simple that there is no need to believe in it because there is no way to disbelieve it. It is so simple that there is no way to doubt it.

I am against belief for the simple reason that for all my teaching, no belief is needed. I am all for doubt because for my simple teaching, you cannot doubt. All the religions of the world insist on belief, because what they are teaching can be doubted. And they are all against doubt because doubt can destroy their whole edifice.

I am simple and real. I am not metaphysical; hence there is no need to believe in me. If you have heard me, a trust is bound to arise which is not belief, which is closer to love; even if you try to doubt, you cannot. And when you cannot doubt something, then there is real trust, indubitable trust. It transforms simply by being within you.

In the whole history of man, only Mahavira has made a distinction to be remembered – which is significant in this reference. He says that there are two ways to reach to the truth. One is the way of the *shravaka*. *Shravaka* means one who can hear, one who is able to hear from the heart. Then he need not do anything. Just hearing is enough, and he will be transformed. The other is the way of the monk, who will have to try hard to reach to the truth.

My effort has been not to create monks. That's why I have chosen to speak – because just hearing me, you can be reborn. Nothing else is needed on your part, except a willingness to open the doors of your heart. Just let me in and you will not be the same again.

I have seen thousands of my people changing without their knowing; they have changed so drastically, but the change has happened almost underground. Their mind has not been even allowed to take part in it – just from heart to heart.

These people had not needed any therapy. These people here have not needed any meditation. If they have heard, the way I am telling you, then this is their meditation, and this is their therapy, and this is their revolution.

Beloved Bhagwan,
I have heard you extol "commune-ism" as the highest form of economic system, the equal sharing of abundance and richness in a loving family of man. However, I have heard you say that the poor should be brought up to the level of the rich rather than the rich being dragged down into poverty, as has happened in all existing communistic societies. But how can the rich share wealth now, and live in "commune-ism" without being dragged down into economic mediocrity?

The first thing is that the rich people of the world should start living in communes. Let those communes be of the rich! – so they will not be dragged down from their standard of life, their comforts, their luxuries. Let there be around the world hundreds of communes of rich people – rich communes.

And to me, wealth is a certain kind of creativity. If five thousand rich people who have all created wealth individually are together, they can create wealth a millionfold. Their standard will not go lower; their standard can even go higher. Or they can start sharing. They can start inviting people who are not rich but who are creative in some other way, who will enhance the life of their commune although they may be poor.

Five thousand rich people together with their genius for creating wealth are capable of creating so much wealth that they can invite thousands of other people who may not be rich in the sense of being wealthy, but who may be rich as painters, as poets, as dancers, as singers.

What are you going to do only with wealth? You cannot play music on money; you cannot dance just because you have so much cash in the bank. And these rich communes can start becoming bigger, absorbing more and more creative people. These rich communes will need every kind of thing.

Talking about the rich commune, I am reminded of the Jaina community. There was a time, in India, in the history of Jainism…because Jainism is a small community and it is a community of rich people. In India you cannot find a single Jaina beggar, a single Jaina orphan. In the ancient days it was a fundamental rule that if a Jaina was poor, then all other Jainas would simply contribute just little bits.

For example, if he needs a house, the whole commune simply provides it. Somebody provides the wood, somebody provides the bricks, somebody provides the tiles and the whole community provides some money for the man to start off with. You have changed a poor man into a rich man. Nobody has been forced to do it, it is just out of generosity. And that man will do the same when a new arrival happens to come to the commune.

You are asking me right now what the rich people should do. They should drop their private ownership and make a rich commune wherever they can manage – and they can manage everywhere, anywhere. They can make beautiful places all around the world, and slowly, slowly more people can be absorbed.

For example, you will need plumbers, however rich you may be; you will need mechanical people; you will need technicians; you will need shoemakers. Invite these people – and they come to you not as servants, but as members of the commune. They will be enriching the commune doing whatever they can do the best. And it is the commune's duty to raise those people to the same standard of life.

Slowly slowly we can transform the whole world – without any bloodshed and without any dictatorship.

A communism that comes out of love, out of intelligence, out of generosity, will be real. A communism that comes through force is going to be unreal. And there is not a single man in the world, howsoever poor, who has nothing to contribute.

I am reminded of Abraham Lincoln…I love this anecdote so much! It was his first address in the Senate as president. He was a poor man's son, his father was a shoemaker – in India he would have been an untouchable. Even in America people were very annoyed, irritated, angry that a shoemaker's son had become the president; the aristocrats, the rich, the super-rich naturally were angry. There was great tension on the first day when he addressed them.

As he stood up, one aristocrat also stood up and said, "Mr President, before you start speaking, I would like you to remember that your father used to make shoes for my family. Right now I am using the shoes made by your father, so don't forget that. Just becoming president does not mean anything. Don't forget that you are a shoemaker's son."

There was absolute silence, pin-drop silence. Everybody felt that Abraham Lincoln would feel embarrassed, but instead of feeling embarrassed, he made the whole Senate feel embarrassed.

He said, "It is good, I am immensely thankful to you that you reminded me about my father" – and tears came to his eyes. And he said, "How can I forget him? I know that he was a perfect shoemaker and I can never be *that* perfect a president. I cannot defeat the old man.

"You are still wearing shoes he has made – many of you must be wearing them. If they do not fit you, if they are pinching, if you are feeling uncomfortable, don't be worried. Although my father is dead, he made me learn the art enough to mend your shoes. I cannot replace him; he was a perfect master. I am just an amateur, but I can mend your shoes and I will always remember to try at least to become as good a president as he was a shoemaker. I cannot hope to be better than him – that is impossible, because I know him."

The poorest man in the world has also got something to contribute.

Create rich communes and suddenly you will find that you need many people, not just the rich. They may be able to create wealth, but wealth is not all.

Life is much more than wealth. It needs so many things that naturally you will have to invite many people. Around the world all the rich communes will need people; and slowly, slowly your commune will become bigger and bigger.

The richer will not become poorer, but the poorer will become richer, and respectable, and equal – in no way inferior to anybody else – because they are also functioning in the same way as anybody else. And whatever *they* are doing is needed as much as anybody else's expertise is needed.

I conceive of this just like a flower opening up, becoming bigger – all the petals opening up. A commune, full-blown, complete, lacking nothing, will not be only of rich people. Many poor people will have been transformed into richness. And they will be contributing – they will not be a burden, and they will not be beggars. They will have their pride. You cannot exist without them.

We can transform the whole earth into a rich society, but it should start the way I am telling you: not by the dictatorship of the proletariat, but by communes of the rich.

Beloved Bhagwan,
I really felt affected when You talked about Rajen the other night, because I feel friend- ship for him, and I feel he loves You as he did before. I feel that in dropping the mala and the red clothes, he is simply trying to experience something new.

I must admit, though, that having worked with him for years, in the most recent group experience with him just a few days ago the quality of his work felt different: I missed the feeling of Your presence through him. Please comment.

Your question itself is the answer. If he loves me, then in his groups my presence would have become even more tangible. If my presence in his groups has disappeared, then what he calls love is just an empty word. This is a simple thing.

Neither dropping the mala nor the red clothes is important, because I have allowed it myself. But in his groups he is saying, "I used to serve Bhagwan through surrender. I am still serving him, through making you free of Bhagwan."

The whole world is free of me. Nobody needs to work to make people free of me. The whole world is already free of me.

But why is my presence being missed? He has lost contact with my heart; his heart is no longer beating with my heart. And it is not only with Rajen. It is so with many other therapists. Only a few have proved the fire test, like Prasad. He has not just remained the same, but has become more deeply involved with me on a new basis, a new flowering of love. In his groups my presence has become deeper. And his work has changed; his therapy has become different, more effective.

But all these people are unconscious. Their love is not what I mean by love. Perhaps at the most, their love means that they don't hate me. Even that much will be great, because most of them may even be angry with me for the simple reason that they had become accustomed to being just a follower. The whole responsibility was on me. Now I have given back the responsibility to them; they can be angry – they are bound to be angry. They may go on saying like old parrots, "I love you," but their actions don't prove it.

Ananda Teertha and a few others with him have opened a meditation academy in Italy. Devageet was there. In finding the place, in arranging the place he worked hard, but finally he was very disappointed because they did not want my name to be associated with the academy.

Devageet said, "I have been working day and night just so that we can create an academy for Bhagwan, and you are not ready even to mention His name in the brochure!" They all had their pictures in the brochure, and they were not willing to have my picture in the brochure.

Devageet had to leave in disgust. They all were saying, "We love Bhagwan," but no mention of me in the brochure, no mention of me in their groups. And all their groups are filled by sannyasins, and those sannyasins are coming because of me. Devageet made it clear that this is pure exploitation. "These people are coming to your groups because of Bhagwan, not because of you. And you are no longer working for Bhagwan."

Devageet came to see me in Crete, and I told him, "Don't be disturbed. This is how unconscious humanity is. Let them do what they are doing. If it is good for people, people will go on coming to them; if it is not good, they will disappear."

"But," he said, "it hurts that you made these people great therapists. You made their name famous around the world."

I said, "You don't understand the unconscious mind's logic: now they are taking revenge. They cannot forgive me because I have made them; they feel a certain inferiority, and they would like to proclaim their superiority. So let them do it – don't be worried. This is how this world goes on."

It makes no difference to me whether my name is associated with their academy, because there are thousands of other therapists in the world who have nothing to do with me, so these few also can be part of that. Or they may realize sooner or later that what they are doing is ugly, unloving, and to a man who has made you world-famous; otherwise nobody knew about you, nobody would have ever heard about you.

But this is the problem: it is very difficult to forgive a person who has helped you in any way. You cannot pay it back to me; there is no way of repaying, and you feel indebted. A certain inferiority that you are not self-made creates anger, revenge. But all this will subside.

Just look at your question. You say that you have been with Rajen, and you feel, "He loves You just as he loved You before." And still you observe that in his work I am no longer there; I am absent.

Can't you see the contradiction? If he loves me, I should be more present and he should be more absent. If he loves me totally, then only I will be present and he will not be present at all; otherwise the word 'love' is just a word as everybody else is using it.

But these people will come to understand soon. It will take a little time because while they were with me, and they were working with the people in therapy groups, it was as if they were constantly nourished by my love.

Soon they will find that nourishment is no

longer there because their hearts are closed, and they will start feeling tired, exhausted, because all those people who come for therapy are going to take their energies. Soon they will find that they have lost their roots, that now they cannot blossom. But it will take a little time. You can cut the roots – still the flowers will remain for a few days, but not for long.

So let them come to the understanding by themselves, that here they used to work so much with so many people – thousands of people they worked with – but they never felt as if their energies were sucked. But they were not aware why they were not feeling like that – because their roots were within me.

But in the name of freedom, they have withdrawn their roots. They will start dying. It will be sad if they don't understand it.

Chapter 8
April 16, 1986, Morning

The Head
is Compulsory,
But Not the Cap

Beloved Bhagwan,
You talked the other morning of the child being forced to be obedient. That child is still sitting here: I hate being told what to do. But in a way that should be the other person's problem; however, I insist on making it my problem by reacting with anger, resentment, and the need to justify myself. It is clear that those who do the telling also hate being told what to do. It seems as if we are all caught in the same intricate web, playing different roles at different times. As an adult how can I convert reaction into response and responsibility?

The first thing to be understood very clearly is what I mean by disobedience. It is not the disobedience you will find in the dictionaries. My idea of disobedience is not to hate being told what to do or, in reaction, to do just the opposite.

Obedience needs no intelligence.

All machines are obedient; nobody has ever heard of a disobedient machine. Obedience is simple, too. It takes from you the burden of any responsibility. There is no need to react, you have simply to do what is being said. The responsibility rests with the source from where the order comes. In a certain way you are very free: you cannot be condemned for your act.

After the second world war, in the Nuremberg trials, so many of Adolf Hitler's top men simply said that they were not responsible, and they don't feel guilty. They were simply being obedient – whatever was told they did it, and they did it with as much efficiency as they were capable of.

In fact to make them responsible and condemn them, punish them, send them to the gallows, according to me was not fair. It was not justice, it was revenge. If Adolf Hitler had won the war, then Churchill's people, Roosevelt's people, Stalin's people or they themselves would have been in the same situation, and they would have said exactly the same – that they are not responsible.

If Stalin had been on the stand in the court, he would have said that it was the order of the high command of the communist party. It was not his responsibility because it was not his decision; he had not done anything on his own. So if you want to punish, punish the source of the order. But you are punishing a person who simply fulfilled what all the religions teach, and all the leaders of the world teach – obedience.

Obedience has a simplicity; disobedience needs a little higher order of intelligence. Any idiot can be obedient, in fact only idiots can be obedient. The person of intelligence is bound to ask why – "Why am I supposed to do it?" And, "Unless I know the reasons and the consequences of it, I am not going to be involved in it." Then he is becoming responsible.

Responsibility is not a game. It is one of the most authentic ways of living – dangerous too – but it does not mean disobedience for disobedience's sake. That will be again idiotic.

There is a story about a Sufi mystic, Mulla Nasruddin. From the very beginning it was thought that he was upside down. His parents were in trouble. If they would say, "Go to the right," he would go to the left. Finally his old father thought that rather than bothering with him, it is better, if they want him to go to the left, to order him to go to the right – and he is bound to go to the left.

One day they were crossing the river. On their donkey they had a big bag of sugar, and the bag was leaning more towards the right so there was a danger that it may slip into the river; it had to remain balanced on the donkey. But to tell Nasruddin, "Move the bag towards the left," will mean losing the sugar – he will move it towards the right.

So he said to Nasruddin, "My son, your bag is slipping; move it towards the right." And Nasruddin moved it towards the right.

The father said, "This is strange, for the first time you have been obedient!"

Nasruddin said, "For the first time you have been cunning. I knew you wanted this to be moved towards the left; I could see with my eyes where it needs to be moved. Even in such a subtle way you cannot make me obedient."

But just to go against obedience is not moving your intelligence higher. You remain on the same plane, obedient or disobedient, but there is no change of intelligence.

To me disobedience is a great revolution.

It does not mean saying an absolute no in every situation. It simply means deciding whether to do it or not, whether it is beneficial to do it or not. It is taking the responsibility on yourself. It is not a question of hating the person or hating to be told, because in that hating you cannot act obediently, disobediently; you act very unconsciously. You cannot act intelligently.

When you are told to do something, you are given an opportunity to respond. Perhaps what is being told is right; then do it, and be grateful to the person who told you at the right moment to do it. Perhaps it is not right – then make it clear. Bring your reasons, why it is not right; then help the person – what he is thinking is going in a wrong way. But *hate* has no place.

If it is right, do it lovingly.

If it is not right, then even more love is needed, because you will have to tell the person, explain to the person that it is not right.

The way of disobedience is not stagnant,

just going against every order and feeling anger and hate and revenge towards the person. The way of disobedience is a way of great intelligence.

So it is not ultimately obedience or disobedience. Reduced to the basic fact, it is simply a question of intelligence – behave intelligently. Sometimes you will have to obey, and sometimes you will have to say, "I am sorry, I cannot do it." But there is no question of hate, there is no question of revenge, anger. If hate, anger or revenge arises, that simply means you know that what is being told *is* right, but it goes against your ego to obey it; it hurts your ego. That hurt feeling comes up as hate, as anger.

But the question is not your ego; the question is the act that you have to do – and you have to bring your total intelligence to figure it out. If it is right, then be obedient; if it is wrong, be disobedient. But there is no conflict, there is no hurt feeling.

If you are obeying it, it is easier; you need not explain to anybody. But if you are not obeying it, then you owe an explanation. And perhaps your explanation is not right. Then you have to move back, you have to do it.

A man should live intelligently – that's all. Then whatever he does is his responsibility.

It happens that even great intellectuals are not living intelligently. Martin Heidegger, one of the greatest intellectuals of this age, was a follower of Adolf Hitler. And after Adolf Hitler's defeat and the exposure of his basic animality, brutality, murderousness, violence, even Martin Heidegger shrank back and said, "I was simply following the leader of the nation."

But a philosopher has no business to follow the leader of the nation. In fact a philosopher's basic duty is to guide the leaders of the nation, not to be guided by them, because he is out of active politics, his vision is more clear. He is standing aloof, he can see things which people who are involved in action cannot see.

But it is easy to throw responsibility…

If Adolf Hitler had been victorious, I am certain Martin Heidegger would have said, "He is victorious because he followed my philosophy." And certainly he was a great intellectual compared to Adolf Hitler. Adolf Hitler was just a retarded person. But power…

We have been brought up to follow the powerful – the father, the mother, the teacher, the priest, the God. Essentially we have been told that whoever has the power is right: "Might is right." And you have to follow it. It is simple because it needs no intelligence. It is simple because you can never be told that it was your responsibility, that whatever happened was your responsibility.

In all the armies around the world only one thing is taught through years of training, and that is obedience. In Germany, in the second world war, there were good people, but they were heads of concentration camps. They were good fathers, good husbands, good friends. Nobody could have conceived – watching them in their families, with their friends, in the club – that these people are burning thousands of Jews every day.

And they were not feeling guilty at all, because it is only an order from above. And that is their whole training, that you have to follow the order. It has become part of their blood and their bones and their marrow. When the order comes, obedience is the only way.

This is how man has lived up to now, and that's why I say obedience is one of the greatest crimes, because all other crimes are born out of it. It deprives you of intelligence, it deprives you of decisiveness, it deprives you of responsibility. It destroys you as an individual. It converts you into a robot.

Hence I am all for disobedience. But disobedience is not just against obedience. Disobedience is above obedience and the so-called disobedience described in the dictionaries. Disobedience is simply the assertion of your intelligence: "I take the responsibility, and I will do everything that feels right to my heart, to my being. And I will not do anything that goes against my intelligence."

My whole life, from my childhood to the university, I was condemned continuously for being disobedient. And I insisted, "I am *not* disobedient. I am simply trying to figure out, with my own intelligence, what is right, what should be done, and I take the whole responsibility for it. If something goes wrong, it was my fault. I don't want to condemn somebody else because he has told me to do it."

But it was difficult for my parents, for my teachers, professors. In my school it was compulsory to wear caps, and I entered the high school without a cap. Immediately the teacher said, "Are you aware or not that the cap is compulsory?"

I said, "A thing like a cap cannot be compulsory. How can it be compulsory to put something on your head or not? The head is compulsory, but not the cap. And I have come with the head; perhaps you have come only with the cap."

He said, "You look a strange type. It is just written in the school code that without a cap, no student can enter the school."

I said, "Then that code has to be changed. It is written by human beings, not by God; and human beings commit mistakes."

The teacher could not believe it. He said, "What is the matter with you? Why can't you just wear a cap?"

I said, "The trouble is not with the cap; I want to find out *why* it is compulsory, its reason, its results. If you are unable...you can take me to the principal and we can discuss it." And he had to take me to the principal.

In India, Bengalis are the most intelligent people; they don't use caps. And Punjabis are the most unintelligent, simple people, and they use turbans. So I said to the principal, "Looking at the situation – Bengalis don't use any caps and they are the most intelligent people in the country, and Punjabis use not only a cap but a very tight turban, and they are the most unintelligent people. It has something to do with your intelligence. I would rather not take the risk."

The principal listened to me and he said, "The boy *is* stubborn, but what he is saying makes sense. I had never thought about it – this is true. And we can make this code non-compulsory. Anybody who wants to wear a cap can wear one; anybody who does not want to use, there is no need – because it has nothing to do with learning, teaching."

The teacher could not believe it. On the way back he told me, "What did you do?"

I said, "I have done nothing, I simply explained the situation. I am not angry, I am perfectly willing to use a cap. If you feel it helps intelligence, why only one? I can use two caps, three caps, caps upon caps, if it helps intelligence...! I am not angry. But you have to prove it."

The teacher said to me – I still remember his words – "You will be in trouble your whole life. You will not fit in anywhere."

I said, "That's perfectly okay, but I don't want to be an idiot and fit in everywhere. It is good to be an 'unfit' but intelligent. And I have come to the school to learn intelligence, so I can be an unfit intelligently! Please never try again to change me from an individual into a cog in the wheel." And from the next day the caps disappeared; only he had come with a cap.

And looking at the class and the school… because the new rule has come into force that caps are not compulsory, all other teachers, even the principal, had come without caps. He looked so idiotic. I said to him, "There is still time. You can take it off and put it in your pocket." And he did it!

He said, "That's right. If everybody is against the cap…I was simply being obedient to the law."

I said, "The law is made by us. We can change it, without any anger. Can we not discuss each and everything intelligently?"

So remember, when I say disobedience I don't mean replace obedience by disobedience. That will not make you better. I use the word disobedience only to make it clear to you that it is up to you, that you have to be the decisive factor of all your actions in life. And that gives tremendous strength, because whatever you do, you do with a certain rational support to it.

I entered the university, and the first question the vice-chancellor asked me was, "Why have you been growing your beard and mustache?" And it was in a way natural because no other student was doing that.

I said to him, "I have come here to see you for a scholarship, but I can risk the scholarship. I cannot risk a chance for an argument."

He said, "What do you mean?"

I said, "I mean *I* should ask *you* why you have shaved your beard, your mustache. *I* have done nothing; they are growing by themselves. You have done something; you have not allowed them to grow – you are shaving twice a day. You owe me an explanation. What is the reason why you are doing it?"

He said, "I have never thought about it…

because everybody else was doing it, I started doing it."

I said, "That is not a very intelligent answer. You can think over it. I will come every day and knock on the door, so whenever you have found the answer you can give me the answer, and from that day I will start shaving."

Three days only I had to go to his office to knock. On the fourth day he said to me, "Excuse me, you have taken away my sleep. The whole day I am thinking about my beard and mustache, and the whole day I am looking at the door, thinking that you must be coming to knock. And sometimes I hear that there has been a knock, and I open the door and there is nobody, so I am hallucinating! You have made me so afraid! You simply take your scholarship and do whatever you want; it is your beard and your mustache. And just please forgive me that I asked you."

I said, "It is not so easy. You have to stop shaving; otherwise I will continue coming every day, knocking on the door, waiting for the answer."

He said, "My God! I am giving you the scholarship, which really should not be given to you because you don't belong to this university – you are coming from another university, and according to our rules, the first preference will be for a graduate of this university. I am not bothering about the rule; I am giving you the scholarship because I simply want you to stop knocking on my door."

I said, "You can keep your scholarship and you can give it to anybody you want, but you will have to stop shaving."

He said, "Don't be so hard on an old man – because what will people say? Don't make me a laughingstock!"

I said, "You *will* become a laughingstock if you don't listen to me, because then I am going to tell everybody the whole story of what has been happening in these four days."

And you will not believe it: he gave me the scholarship, and he started growing the beard! The whole university was surprised, because he was very fussy about his clothes, and about shaving – he had been in Oxford, a professor of history, head of the department of history there.

Everybody started asking him, "What has happened?"

He said, "Nothing has happened. I just came to realize that I was doing something wrong, because I cannot give any reason. This young man has made me aware that you should live your life rationally. I have been an imitator, I have been very obedient to the surroundings. Nobody has told me – I have been obedient on my own. But because I don't have any reason, I will let my beard grow. And this young man seems to be right, that if women start growing beards, mustaches…"

And it is not very difficult. There are hormones which can be injected and they will start growing beards. Do you think it will be a beautiful world, where men are shaving beards, and women are growing beards? A woman with a beard will freak out anybody! And the same happens with the man; just the women are very patient, very tolerant. They even tolerate people without beards. No man can tolerate his wife with a beard, I tell you; it is absolutely certain. Either he will throw her out, or he will hang himself! But millions of women are tolerating beardless men.

Nature never does anything without any reason. I have tried to look at men without beards. It seems something is missing in the man. Just look at Milarepa! When I first saw him here I was so shocked. He was looking so beautiful with a beard and now he is looking simply idiotic! He has lost all his grandeur.

Just live intelligently.

If something is told to you, decide whether it is right or wrong, then you can avoid all guilt feelings. Otherwise, if you don't do it, then you feel guilty; if you do it, again you feel guilty. If you do it you feel that you are being obedient, subservient, that you are not being assertive, that you are not being yourself. And if you don't do it, then you start feeling guilty again – because perhaps it was the right thing to do, and you are not doing it.

There is no need for all this clumsiness. Just be simple. If something is told to you, respond intelligently. And whatsoever your intelligence decides, do it this way or that – but you are responsible. Then there is no question of guilt.

If you are not going to do it, explain to the person why you are not going to do it. And explain without any anger, because anger simply shows that you are weak, that you don't really have an intelligent answer. Anger is always a sign of weakness. Just plainly and simply explain the whole thing; perhaps the other person may find that you are right and may be thankful to you. Or perhaps the other person may have better reasons than you; then you will be thankful to the other person because he has raised your consciousness.

Use every opportunity in life for raising your intelligence, your consciousness.

Ordinarily what we are doing is using every opportunity to create a hell for ourselves. Only *you* suffer, and because of your suffering, you make others suffer. And when so many people are living together, and if they all create suffering for each other, it goes on multiplying. That's how the whole world has become a hell.

It can be instantly changed.

Just the basic thing has to be understood, that without intelligence there is no heaven.

You have been called "the genius of the absurd." Your way in this world seems so relentlessly wild and crazy that many people – perhaps all people – are filled with wonder, or confusion; and sometimes, even anger. But the European Parliament, gathering votes to ban You from Europe forever seems also absurd and crazy. I wonder who is more absurd: You or them? What can we discover about truth in Your absurdity?

They are not absurd; they are functioning very logically. They can see the potential danger that I can bring to the younger generation, and which can destroy their centuries of vested interests.

They are not absurd. It may look absurd – the whole world against one single man – but it is very logical. They can see that what I am saying is true, and they have no way to defend their morality, their marriage, their family, their social structure. Naturally, they would not like me to come in contact with their youth, because their youth is going to be powerful tomorrow; and if their youth becomes aflame with my ideas, tomorrow the old world will have completely collapsed.

To save the old and to prevent the new, they are taking every measure – and it is very logical.

I am certainly absurd.

You have to understand the meaning of absurd. In life everything that is significant is absurd. When you fall in love with someone it is absurd, it is not logical. You cannot give us a logical answer why you have fallen in love with a particular person – man or woman. It is something beyond you that has *gripped* you. It is not your doing. Even if you wanted to prevent it, you could not have succeeded; in fact you were absolutely helpless.

Your joy in a world full of misery is absurd. It has no relatedness to the miserable humanity. You are completely alone. Everything that is valuable – you love music, you are enchanted with beauty, you are seeking truth, you want to know yourself – all these are absurd activities.

Meditating is absurd; it would be better and more logical to earn money.

Just before I left Nepal, a group of sannyasins from Delhi had come to prevent me from going out of Nepal or out of India – a kind of deputation. They were ready to purchase a big palace and make every arrangement for a commune. But I told them, "Right now you are being emotional. You will be in difficulty. The palace costs one million dollars. Perhaps you can collect that much donation, saying that if the palace is not purchased, I am going to leave. But the palace is not the only thing; then there will be at least fifty people living there, and you will not be able to support them.

"It is not a question of one day, so be logical. Your asking me to remain in India is out of love, but it is absurd. You will create trouble for me and trouble for yourselves. So you go back, think over it. I will wait here ten days more. You can come after seven days with the decision."

They never came. They must have understood the implications – they will not be able to manage it. But their insistence was out of love, not out of reason.

I am absurd because whatever I am teaching to you goes against everything that you have been taught. And you have been taught things for so long that you have forgotten completely that they are questionable.

For example, every culture in the world has believed, has conditioned its younger generations, with an idea that love is permanent, that if you love a person you love that person forever. This idea has prevailed for centuries all over the world. It looks logical that if you love a person, the very phenomenon of love will make it permanent.

And why has everybody accepted it? – because you also desire that it should be permanent. Everybody wants his love to be permanent.

So the traditional idea and your desire synchronize, and it becomes a truth…so much so that if your love changes, then not only others but you yourself start thinking that it was not love – that's why it changed. You don't change the basic idea of permanent love; you start thinking, "Perhaps what I thought was love was not love, because it has changed – and love does not change."

I am bound to be absurd, because I want to say to you that in life everything changes – in spite of your desire for no change. It does not matter that sitting by the side of the river you desire that the river should not go on flowing, that the seasons should not change, that the flowers should not die, that youth should never turn into old age, that life should never end up in a graveyard.

Your desires apart…existence does not listen to your desires, and does not follow your desires, however beautiful and however pious. Existence goes on in its own way.

Everything changes – and love is not an exception.

Now, perhaps I am the first person who wants to make it understood by everyone that love changes: it begins, it comes of age, it becomes old, it dies. And I think it is good the way it is. It gives you many more chances of loving other people, to make life richer – because each person has something special to contribute to you. The more you love, the more rich you are, the more loving you become.

And if the false idea of permanence is dropped, jealousy will drop automatically; then jealousy is meaningless. Just as you fall in love and you cannot do anything about it, one day you fall out of love and you cannot do anything about it. A breeze came into your life and passed. It was good and beautiful and fragrant and cool, and you would have liked it to remain always there. You tried hard to close all the windows and all the doors, to keep the breeze fragrant, fresh. But by closing the windows and the doors, you killed the breeze, its freshness, its fragrance; it became stale.

Every marriage is stale.

I am absurd, because I don't want to enforce logic – which is man-made – on existence. In trying to impose logic on existence you simply create misery for yourself, because you are going to fail; your failure is absolute. Millions of people are simply pretending that they go on loving each other. Once they had loved, but now it is only a memory, and becoming fainter and fainter every day. But because of the idea of permanency they are afraid to say the truth.

And it is not anger, it is not hate; it is nothing against the other. It is simply the way of life – love changes. It is seasonal, and it is good to have summer and to have winter, and to have rain…to have the fall and the spring.

Your whole life can be lived either as logic or as existence. Existence will be absurd. One moment it is one thing; another moment, it is something else. And you are left with the choice either to go on pretending that it is still the same, or to be honest and sincere and to say that it was a beautiful moment but it has passed. The oasis is passed and now we are in a desert, and we know that we are in a desert;

we cannot enjoy, we cannot rejoice. But still we are bound to each other with the idea of permanent love. That permanent love is a logical idea.

Real love is a real roseflower: it is going to change. From morning to evening it is going to take different shapes, different shades, and by the evening it will be gone. And I don't think that there is anything wrong.

Love is just one example. Your whole life is full of such things. For example, every child is taught respect for the parents, respect for the teachers, respect for the elders. Respect is a beautiful experience, but when you have to be respectful just as a mannerism, it is ugly.

I was told again and again in my childhood, "You have to be respectful."

I used to tell my father, "Before you tell me to be respectful towards somebody, you should at least be certain whether he is worthy of respect; otherwise you are making me phony. I know that a man is not worthy of respect; but he is elder, and I am supposed to be respectful. I am ready to be respectful, but there must be something corresponding to it. For what am I going to be respectful?"

But for centuries upon centuries, the same idea in different dimensions…be respectful towards your parents. But why? Just because they have given birth to you? Was it not a joy to them? If it was a joy to them, they have already got their reward. Now if they want respect from you, then they should be worthy of respect.

And my father would say, "You are always talking absurdities. We have to live in a society, and the society runs through a certain discipline. Certain manners have to be followed; otherwise you will be crushed by the society. So don't be absurd," he was continuously saying to me.

And I said, "I would not like to be crushed by the society, but I cannot behave logically, seeing that existence is moving in a different direction. What you are saying is logical. You are saying, 'This is the way things have always been done; and this is the way things should be done.'"

And there *is* a logic in it – that if you are respectful towards others, others will be respectful towards you; if you help the society, the society will help you. But if you go on criticizing the society, if you go on finding faults everywhere, you will fall alone, and you cannot win against the vast majority.

Logic is the way of winning in the society.

Be logical, and it will be easier for you to climb the ladders.

I said, "I would like to remain true to existence – and existence is absurd. It has no logic, it has no meaning. It has immense beauty, it has tremendous possibilities for ecstasy, but you cannot make a logical system out of it."

So remember it: the European parliament, the American government – and others will soon be following – are all behaving very logically.

But I am not a logician.

I am an existentialist.

I believe in this meaningless, beautiful chaos of existence, and I am ready to go with it wherever it leads.

I don't have a goal, because existence has no goal. It simply is, flowering, blossoming, dancing – but don't ask why. Just an overflow of energy, for no reason at all.

I am with existence.

And that's what I call being a sannyasin:

To be with existence.

The only thing you will have to renounce will be your logical mind. So start living in an existential but illogical way.

The world may call you absurd, mad…

So what?

Chapter 9
April 16, 1986, Evening

I Want to Provoke Your Jealousy

Beloved Bhagwan,

Because of Your genius in combining and then going beyond the material and the spiritual, and because You seem to have an abundance of both worlds, I think that many non-sannyasins and sannyasins feel jealous of You. People resent and don't want to feed abundance. If they feed anything, they feed poverty. If You were sitting in a cave, naked, cold, and meditating, it would be one thing, but You are not. Sannyasins who never dreamed of having a Rolls Royce seem to yearn for one more than for the state of meditation even after spending years with You. You seem to be sparking greed for the material, rather than a yearning for the beyond — or at least that's the message that's being received by some. Could You comment.

It is part of my whole device to change the very structure of human consciousness.

The past has revered poverty, asceticism, masochistic attitudes. A man was respected if he was renouncing all that is pleasant, all that is comfortable. He was respected for torturing himself; the greater the torture, the greater the respect. The whole human past is masochistic, and all the religions have contributed to this insanity.

My effort is to change such a vast past and its influence. So it has been only a device. I have not been creating desires for materialistic things in people; they are there without anybody's creating them. Yes, they have been repressed so deeply that people have even forgotten that they had them. I am not creating them; I simply want to remove the cover-up, the repression, and to make the person realize that he wants a Rolls Royce more than enlightenment.

This realization will be a basic step towards enlightenment, because it will make him aware of his own reality, his greed.

There was no need for ninety-three Rolls Royces. I could not use ninety-three Rolls Royces simultaneously – the same model, the same car. But I wanted to make it clear to you that you would be ready to drop all your desires for truth, for love, for spiritual growth to have a Rolls Royce. I was knowingly creating a situation in which you would feel jealous.

The function of a master is very strange. He has to help you come to an understanding of your inner structure of consciousness: it is full of jealousy.

All the traditions and the whole past have done just the opposite. The so-called saint, in all the traditions, lives in such a way that you will never feel jealous of him. Note that point.

You will feel sympathetic towards him, respectful towards him; but respectfulness is not your reality, sympathy is not your nature. The saint is torturing himself, that is not *his* nature either. He is being unnatural to gain respect, to fulfill his ego. He is not interested in spiritual growth; he is interested in respectability, in being worshipped like a god. And he is ready to do *anything* for it.

He is living in an illusion, and he is creating a great illusion in people who come to him. He helps them to feel that they are religious, that they are spiritual, because they respect a saint, they worship a saint. They are not yet ready to do such ascetic disciplines for themselves, but they hope some day...this is their ideal. They are completely forgetting that they are jealous human beings. And the saint is helping them to forget their jealousy; he is helping them to repress it.

My work is bound to be totally different. I want to provoke your jealousy, because that is the only way to get rid of it. First you have to know that you have it; then you can drop it, because it is misery and hell. But you can repress it so deeply that the question of dropping it does not arise.

I have lived in abundance because to me there is no division between the material and the spiritual.

The teaching to live in poverty is dangerous: you will be materially poor, and you will be spiritually poor too, because there *is* no division. I teach you to live richly, in abundance, materially *and* spiritually – both. It is not a question of whether you should live materially in abundance, or spiritually. The basic question is whether you should live in abundance, in richness – which is natural and existential. It is your very basic urge to blossom in abundance, to know all the colors, to know all the songs, to know all the beauties of life.

But certainly I am bound to come in conflict with the old, because the whole human past has been praising poverty and making it equal to spirituality, which is absolute nonsense.

Spirituality is the greatest richness that can happen to a man, and it contains all other richnesses. It is not against any other richness; it is simply against *all* kinds of poverty. So what I have been trying is something so radical that it is bound to create antagonism all around the world from every corner. People have lived with certain values for so long that although those values have given them only misery, they don't see the connection. Those values have not made them fulfilled, contented – but they don't see the connection.

I want my people to become symbolic...to make the whole world aware that their misery is caused by their wrong values, that they are poor because they have respected poverty – and their behavior is so insane. On the one hand they will respect poverty, and on the other hand they will say, "Serve the poor."

Strange! If poverty is so spiritual then the most spiritual thing will be to make every rich man poor, to help the rich man to be poor, so he can become spiritual. Why help the poor? Do you want to destroy their spirituality?

But a deep unconsciousness, a great blindness exists, and I am fighting against a mountainous unconsciousness, darkness. Naturally they will be very much annoyed. They would have loved me, they would have worshipped me. And it was so easy for me to do what they wanted, but then I would have been continuing the old misery, the old disease, the old stupidity. I decided to be unrespectable, but not to help any nonsensical value system.

It is a very simple thing to see why ascetics – self-destructive people engaged in a kind of slow suicide – have been respected; it is because it is unnatural, because *you* cannot do it. They are doing something which you cannot do. If somebody is standing on their head on the road, there will be a crowd immediately, but you are walking on your legs – no crowd will be there!

What is that man doing that attracts the crowd? He is doing something that the crowd cannot do. He is proving mind over body, he is proving spirit over nature. Torturing his body he is proving that he is not the body, it does not affect him. By fasting, not sleeping, or standing for days he is proving that what you cannot do he can do; he is superior to you. You also *can* do what he is doing, you just have to be a little stupid, you just have to be a little suicidal, destructive. All that you need is a certain pleasure in pain and you can become a great spiritual saint.

I have looked at the whole history and found not one single man revolting against this suicidal attitude towards life, this anti-life attitude. Perhaps they were afraid that nobody was going to listen to them, afraid that they would lose their respectability.

I decided in the very beginning days of my life that there is one thing I have to be aware of, and that is not to be bothered about respectability. Then things are very simple. Then I can do what is natural and what is healthy. And then I can manage a bridge between matter and spirit, between this world and that world.

And to me, to live in abundance is the only spiritual thing in the world.

Just look at existence and its abundance. What is the need of so many flowers in the world? Just roses would have been enough, but existence is abundant: millions and millions of flowers, millions of birds, millions of animals – everything in abundance. Nature is not ascetic; it is everywhere dancing – in the ocean, in the trees. It is everywhere singing – in the wind passing through the pine trees, in the birds…

What is the need of millions of solar systems, each solar system having millions of stars? There seems to be no need, except that abundance is the very nature of existence, that richness is the very core, that existence does not believe in poverty. Look at nature, look at existence, and you will see that what man has done is against it.

My effort is to bring man back to his natural self.

I will be condemned, I will be criticized. Every religion, every tradition, every morality, every ethical code is going to condemn me. That does not surprise me! I expect it, because what I am saying and doing is changing the very course of human consciousness.

I don't think that by torturing yourself you can meditate more easily; on the contrary, if your body is pleasantly at ease you can meditate more easily. I don't think that when you are fasting you can meditate. You can only think of food and nothing else; you will dream of food and nothing else. But if you are well fed, well nourished, you don't think of food – there is no need. The body is completely satisfied, it does not create any disturbance.

To live pleasurably, to live joyously is not against meditation. It is really the basic need of meditation. I know many kinds of ascetics but I have never seen any intelligence in them, I have never seen any creativity in them. I have never seen in their eyes a light of the beyond, or in their gestures some message that cannot be said through words. They don't have anything. They are simply starving – and starving because it fulfills the ego, because the more they starve, the more they torture themselves, more and more people come to worship them.

Now this is to me just an insane chapter in the history of man; it has to be closed. It is time that we start a new chapter – natural, existential, life-affirmative – and create a bridge between the body and the soul…not a wall but a bridge.

There is no need for any conflict and war. Fighting with yourself, you are not going to get anything; you will be simply destroying yourself slowly. All your so-called saints are mostly mentally sick, and they have made the whole of humanity sick.

Your question is significant. I have been asked again and again, "Spiritual people are respected everywhere, why are you opposed everywhere?"

I said, "Only one thing is certain: either they are not spiritual, or I am not spiritual. We both cannot be spiritual, that is certain. And as far as I am concerned, I say that they are sick, not spiritual, and they are worshipped by a sick society."

It is a vicious circle: the society creates the sick saint, the sick saint creates the sick society – and it goes on and on. I have no part in this sickness, the so-called spirituality. I am just a contented, fulfilled human being. What more do you want? And what more can spirituality be?

We want people to be fulfilled and contented, and this journey towards contentment, fulfillment, enlightenment should start with the body. You cannot begin from anywhere else. You can begin only from the beginning. You cannot ignore the roots and just go on praising the flowers. Your flowers will die, and you will have to replace them with plastic flowers if the roots are not taken care of. Is there any conflict between the roots and the blossoms? It is the same juice – and you have to begin with the roots, because flowers will come only in the end.

But with humanity we have been almost mad. We have never bothered about the roots, and we have talked only about flowers. We talk about people being nonviolent, being compassionate, being loving – so much that you can love your enemy, so much that you can even love your neighbor. We talk about flowers, but nobody is interested in the roots.

The question is: "Why are we not loving beings?"

It is not a question of being loving to this person, to that person, to the friend, to the enemy. The question is whether you are loving or not. Do you love your own body? Have you ever *cared* to touch your own body with a loving caress? Do you love yourself? No, all your religions teach you to hate yourself: you are a wrong person and you have to put yourself right; you are a sinner and you have to become a saint. How can you love yourself? – you cannot even accept yourself. And these are the roots!

I will teach you to love yourself. And if you

can love yourself, if you can rejoice in being yourself, naturally your love will go on spreading. It will become an aura around you; you will love your friends, and in a certain way you will love your enemies too – because just the way the friend defines you, your enemy also defines you.

I am reminded of a recent incident. In India, before freedom came to that country, there was great struggle between Hindus and Mohammedans because Hindus wanted the country to remain one, undivided. It was favorable to them because they were the majority religion. If India was undivided, then Mohammedans had no possibility of ever being in power; they were the second majority religion.

The Mohammedans wanted a separate country and they had their reasons: "We have a different language, we have a different religion, we are a different race, we cannot live together." But the basic reason was not language, not culture, not race, because they had lived together for two thousand years, so there was no problem about that. The real thing was, if they had a separate country of their own they would have power.

The leader for an undivided India was Mahatma Gandhi, and the leader for the division of India and for a new land, Pakistan, for Mohammedans was Mohammed Ali Jinnah. They were archenemies their whole life.

In 1948 Gandhi was shot dead. Now Mohammed Ali Jinnah was governor-general of Pakistan. He was sitting on the lawn as the news reached him that Gandhi had been shot. The person who had brought this news thought that he would be happy to hear it – that his lifelong enemy is dead. But he was surprised: Jinnah became sad, and he went into the house and told his secretary that he should not be disturbed. "If Gandhi is dead, much of me is dead too, because we defined each other."

A great insight – the enemy also defines you, in the same way as the friend defines you. Jinnah lived only one year longer, and he was never again seen so happy as he used to be; this last year was just sadness. Without Gandhi a gap, a great gap... A lifelong enmity is a relationship, a deep relationship. So the man of understanding will love the enemy too – not for any spiritual reason, but for the simple reason that he is defining him, he is part of his existence. Without him there will be a gap which nobody else can fill.

The question is not "love your enemies" the way Jesus says it. That is simply egoistic: love your enemies because you are a superior spiritual being, and he is just an ordinary human being; so love him, show him the true path of spirituality. But it is just fulfilling your own ego.

I will also say, "Love him," but not for the same reasons. I will say, "Love him," because he defines you; he is part of you, just as you are part of him – not only the friend, but the enemy too. It does not make you "holier than thou." It is a simple understanding of how psychology functions.

Love yourself. But you can love yourself only if you drop the idea of being a sinner. You can drop the idea of being a sinner if you drop the idea that there is a god.

If there is a God, you are a sinner; you cannot be anything else. If there is a God, then you are a sinner. You have been expelled from the kingdom of God, and you will be accepted back only if you become obedient – so obedient that you lose your individuality to a hypothetical god whom you have never ever seen and whom you will never see.

Your religions don't allow you to love yourself, but then they talk all this bullshit of loving your enemies and loving your neighbors. But you can see the point. If you cannot love yourself, you cannot love anybody else in the world. That loving energy has to come from your heart, and there, there is sitting a sinner, condemned, waiting to be thrown into hellfire.

I have heard... In the middle ages when people, particularly women, were more naive, more simple, there were Christian preachers who would go on threatening them with hellfire, describing in minute details how they will be tortured. And it used to happen that many women would faint in the churches listening to the sermons, because the hellfire and the minute details would drive them nuts. Now these women, can they accept themselves as they are? – No!

All the religions stand upon one single word, and that is how you *should* be. That word is 'should' – that word is not 'is'. The 'is' is condemned, and the 'should' is praised; and the 'should' is opposed to your 'is'.

You cannot love yourself, your wife cannot love herself – and you both are supposed to love each other. I don't understand how it is possible. You can pretend, but basically you will hate, because the wife knows you are dragging her farther into hell, you know that she is dragging you farther into hell – how can you love? Jesus is clever. He talks about loving your enemies but he does not say anything about loving your wives. Strange, that should have been the first thing to be reminded of – "Love your husbands." But no, these things are not mentioned.

The religions have been talking about flowers; I am working with the roots. And I am against plastic flowers. Real flowers have many differences; plastic flowers are permanent – plastic love will be permanent. The real flower is not permanent, it is changing moment to moment. Today it is there dancing in the wind and in the sun and in the rain. Tomorrow you will not be able to find it – it has disappeared just as mysteriously as it had appeared. Real love is like a real flower.

But all religions teach you plastic love. And then they destroy the very possibility of ever coming to know a real flower. The real flower will have fragrance; the plastic flower has nothing to contribute to your life. It only looks like a flower, it is not a flower. The plastic flower is easy. You do not need to water it, you do not need to take care of the roots. Real flowers need some creativity on your part. *Every* real value needs creativity.

And just look at your saints: *none* of them are creative. All their qualities are just hilarious – somebody can lie down in a grave for seven days, and then you dig him up and he is still alive; and he becomes a great saint. But I don't see that there is any contribution, any creativity in it. He may lie for seven hundred years in a grave; that does not matter. How can he become a saint by lying in a grave for seven days, by learning a certain technique of holding the breath in?

Paul Brunton, a great seeker going from one country to another country all over the East, came across many people who were worshipped as saints in the beginning of this century. In Ajmer in India he came across a Mohammedan saint who used to put both his eyes down, hanging out of their sockets – that was his only quality. And he was worshipped far and wide, because he was doing really the impossible!

He came across a Hindu yogi who was able to drink any kind of poison. He had exhibited his great achievement at many universities – in Oxford, in Cambridge, in Varanasi, in Calcutta. But in Calcutta an accident happened. He was capable of keeping the poison in his body, without getting it into his bloodstream, only for half an hour: more than that he was incapable of. He had learned his whole life how to do it, but in Calcutta the traffic defeated him.

In India, you know, the traffic is great; all the centuries are moving on the road – a bullock cart, a horse-driven vehicle, a donkey, a camel-driven cart, cars, buses, trams. Particularly in Calcutta you will find all the centuries together on the street. From the very beginning when man first invented a vehicle, to the latest car – everything is available. You just stand by the side of the road and watch.

So he was stuck somewhere in a traffic jam and could not reach the place where he was going to vomit; that was the whole art. For half an hour he could keep it; and then he would vomit – not to let it go into his bloodstream. But he was late; it reached to his bloodstream and he died. But he was a world famous saint. What is his contribution?

I cannot conceive why these people should be called saints. Perhaps they should be called certain kinds of experts; they have a certain expertise, but it has nothing to do with spirituality. In the name of spirituality you have been worshipping utter nonsense. And behind this nonsense is the real man – suffering, uncared for, unlooked at. Nobody bothers about him and his problems; nobody answers his real need.

My whole effort is to make a fresh beginning. It is bound to create condemnation of me from all over the world. But it doesn't matter – who cares!

I care only for those who are ready to change the very course of human consciousness. I will offend others, I will annoy others, I will irritate others, I will create jealousy in others. These are part of my devices. I am

really exposing them. If they have any intelligence they will understand it.

Ninety-three Rolls Royces…but I have not looked back at them, at what happened. They were not mine, and I am as happy without them as I was with them. I never went to see those Rolls Royces in the garage. The director of my garage, Avesh, is here. I went on saying to him, "One day I am coming," but that day never came. I have never seen those cars together. It was he who would bring a car for a one-hour drive, it was his choice. And I have not looked back.

Those cars fulfilled their purpose. They created jealousy in the whole of America, in all the super-rich people. If they were intelligent enough, then rather than being my enemies they would have come to me to find a way to get rid of their jealousy, because it is their problem. Jealousy is a fire that burns you, and burns you badly. You are in the hands of somebody else.

I was just a tourist there, and I made the whole of America disturbed. They had enough money; they could have purchased more Rolls Royces if they wanted. But they had no guts for that either. They were condemning me, saying that I am a materialist. And you will be surprised; one bishop who was continuously condemning me as a materialist, wrote me a letter, privately, saying, "It would be very compassionate of you if you could donate a Rolls Royce to my church. It won't make any difference to you – ninety-three or ninety-two – but it will make much difference to us." And every Sunday he was condemning me. His condemnation was not about my materialism; his condemnation was to hide his jealousy.

The politicians, the rich, could have managed it for themselves – why were they worried? But the worry was that a tourist, who has not even a valid visa, has defeated all the super-rich; it hurts! If they were intelligent enough, they could have understood that there must be a purpose behind these Rolls Royces. It cannot be just the one-hour ride. For that, one Rolls Royce would have been enough.

Everything that I have done in my life has a purpose. It is a device to bring out something in you of which you are not aware.

If you are intelligent you would like to get rid of it because it is a poison which is killing you. A jealous mind is incapable of love; a jealous mind is incapable of rejoicing…and not only incapable of rejoicing, he is incapable of seeing anybody else rejoice. This kind of people fill the whole earth. And your so-called saints have not been a help to them. Your so-called saints have exploited them.

It is hilarious! Your saints are exploiting you by being poor, torturing themselves; they are helping you not to feel jealous, not to feel hurt. They are protecting your ego. And it is not one-sided. That's why I say it is hilarious. The game is strange: they are helping you to remain in your misery, in your insanity, and you are helping them to remain in their suicidal, torturous life – a mutual conspiracy of the whole of humanity to remain in hell.

The commune in America was also a device. It did its work. It made people aware that to be joyous, to be loving is possible on this earth; you do not have to wait for heaven. And I can't see, I can't understand…a person who has never been dancing and singing here, when he enters heaven and a harp is provided for him – what is he going to do with the harp? He will be at a loss! He will ask, "What is it, and what am I supposed to do with it?"

Only my people will be immediately able to do something, whichever instrument is provided. It is not only a question of rejoic-ing…all other things too. If here for your whole life you learn only torture, what are you going to do in heaven? That self-torture has become a second nature to you.

I am reminded of a story… There was a very beautiful man, Eknath, who was going on a pilgrimage with his disciples. One well-known thief approached him, and asked the master, "Although I am a sinner – you know me, everybody knows I am a thief – a great desire has arisen in me to go on a pilgrimage with you, if you allow me in your company. Thirty people are going; it won't make much difference, one person more…"

Eknath said, "There is no harm, but one condition: while you are with me, and it is going to take nine months" – because they were going to be traveling by foot all around the country, covering all the holy places, singing and dancing – "you will not steal anything from the group or from somebody else where we are staying in a village. You will have to stop your art for nine months. If you promise me you are allowed."

The man said, "I promise absolutely that I will not steal anything for the coming nine months." But just within two, three days there was trouble. A strange kind of thing started happening, and that was that your money bag was found in somebody else's luggage, somebody else's coat was found in somebody else's bag! Strange…things were missing from here, but they were found there.

Finally Eknath one night had to remain awake to see what was going on, because it was very disturbing. Every morning you would have to find out where your things were; they were always found, but it was an unnecessary nuisance. Eknath had a suspicion that that man may be the cause of it – and he was. In the middle of the night he started changing things around, and Eknath caught him redhanded. He said, "You had promised me that you would not steal."

He said, "I am completely following my promise; I am not stealing. But I never promised you that I would not change things from one bag to another – that is not stealing. I am not putting anybody's things into my bag. But just to practice…otherwise in nine months I may forget my whole art. And moreover, I cannot sleep unless I do something. It is a lifelong habit."

Eknath said, "I understand your problem, but you must understand my problem too: every morning everybody is disturbed and upset – money has gone, somebody's shirt is missing, somebody's blanket is missing. And unnecessarily every morning, for one hour, we have to sort it out."

But he said, "This much you will have to tolerate. This I have never promised. And I am not doing too much – just one hour in the night then I can sleep at ease."

A man who has tortured himself for his whole life – do you think he will be able to rejoice in heaven? He will have forgotten how to smile, he will have forgotten what joy means. No, I say to you the whole human past has been ugly, insane; it has created a kind of spirituality which is another name for schizophrenia. I have to fight against it, whatsoever the cost.

Somebody has to raise his hand and say to the people, "You have been misled. Your misery is a proof; no other proof is needed."

Beloved Bhagwan,
Recently I read an old saying: A man who loves one woman will surely lose his mind; but a man who loves two women loses his soul. Is there any truth to understand in this?

I am sure this question must be from Milarepa!
It is true: if you love one woman you will lose your mind; if you love two you will lose your soul. But if you go on loving more and more, you have nothing else to lose – with the second you are finished!

When Milarepa came I asked Vivek, "Has he brought his guitar? And what else does he do?"

She said, "He does nothing else – just plays on his guitar and chases women."

I said, "Enquire if he has got his guitar. Then he should start playing guitar; otherwise chasing women the whole time will not be good for his health. So once in a while, just to get some rest, he can play guitar."

But he has not brought his guitar. I think you should provide him with a guitar, because he has lost everything. Now he has nothing to be worried about losing; he can go on chasing…

That's why the saying stops at two women, because for the third you have nothing to lose. And it is good to go beyond the second, because then you really become humble – you have nothing.

To me that is spirituality.

The Ostrich Argument

Beloved Bhagwan,
A little while ago the British government refused Your admission to England, even for an overnight stay, on the basis that Your exclusion from the country was "conducive to the public good."

Just a few weeks later, the head of that same government authorized the use of military bases by American bombers for the recent attack on Libya. The prime minister justified the decision to assist America's bombing of Middle Eastern cities saying that it was her duty to "prevent the evils of terrorism." The notions of good and evil expressed by the British government are simply mind-boggling.

Please comment.

One has to understand that everything is relative, not ultimate; hence what appears to be good to one person may look evil to another. And there is no contradiction: both may be right.

What is good depends on your preconceived ideas; so does evil.

The British government thinks my entry even for an overnight stay in England, is not conducive to the public good. The same government is ready to allow American bombers, missiles, to use their bases, to destroy a small country like Libya, and to the government this seems to be conducive to public good.

There is no inconsistency. In their eyes their society, their culture, their religion, their country has to be saved at any cost, because they think they stand for good – although the British government has tortured humanity more than any other government in the world. For three hundred years it has been the greatest terrorist possible; it killed millions of people around the world, to create the greatest empire of history. This government is absolutely in tune with the American imperialistic ideology.

Out of necessity it has been compelled to give freedom to the countries of its empire, but not willingly and joyously. Those countries had to fight for almost one century, without any arms. They were butchered, without any consideration of human values.

I am reminded... In India there happened an incident which can be considered one of the most inhuman in history. In Amritsar, the holy place of the Sikhs, they have a beautiful public garden, a vast area that can contain at least one million people for any gathering, meeting, discourse. And it has been used for that purpose. It has a very high wall so that no traffic noise comes in and it has only one door, so small that only one person can come out or go in; two persons together cannot pass through the door.

They were having a silent meeting of almost one million people – children, women, old men. The prayer was, "The British government should change its heart and should leave our country." Now, it is not terrorism; they were simply praying for a change of heart. But Colonel Dyer, who was in charge of the area, went there with his troops, fixed machine guns on the people, and started firing – because it is revolution against the empire, this prayer that the government should change its heart!

There was only one door, and from that door they were shooting bullets at random, with no discrimination – children, women, old men. And nobody could escape from there because of the high wall. Dyer killed the whole crowd; not a single human being came alive out of that door. Now, it was *their* country; the British had been terrorists, had been ruling their country, exploiting their country.

India has been rich, known for thousands of years as "a golden bird" – that's how Pythagoras describes it, that's how Alexander the Great describes it. So many invaders...but still India seemed to be inexhaustibly rich. People would come, invade the country, take away their treasures, take over their beautiful women...

This had been going on for thousands of years; the Britishers were the last. For three hundred years they squeezed every richness, the last drop of it, from Indian soil. And people were not even allowed to pray for a change of heart – this became an act against the empire. And there was no need for any magistrate, for any judge; there was no need for any trial. Just...a colonel simply kills all those people!

The British government has been one of the ugliest phenomena that we know of. It created the biggest empire – it was said that in the British empire the sun never set. And it was true, because the empire was all around the earth. The sun may have set in one part, but it was rising in another part; there was not any gap. The sun was always rising somewhere in the British empire.

These imperialists have a deep sympathy, friendship, with America. Naturally, it is for the public good to allow American troops, to allow America a base to destroy a small country.

And why destroy Libya? Because the man who is leading Libya now is one of the most outspoken politicians in the whole world. Just a few days ago, Kaddafi said that Ronald Reagan is "Adolf Hitler Number Two." And I, commenting on it, say that Kaddafi is wrong. And he will agree with me when he understands the reason why I am saying he is wrong: Adolf Hitler himself is now Number Two. Ronald Reagan is Adolf Hitler Number One, because what power did Adolf Hitler have? Reagan has a million times more power. Adolf Hitler could not have destroyed the world; Reagan can do that.

To allow Reagan a base in England seems, to the British government, to be for the public good. Both are imperialists, both are agreed on exploiting people, both are agreed that nothing like communism should happen in the world, both are agreed that Christianity should be imposed on people who are not Christian: naturally Ronald Reagan is a friend, although he is going to do something inhuman which may trigger the third world war.

And I understand Kaddafi. He is not a man to sit back. And he is not sitting back. He has a small country but he is not just a politician, he is a warrior. He would rather the country die than to allow the country to be enslaved. And I praise him for being a pioneer. He has responded well. Now he is bombing American bases all over Europe. He has bombed in Spain; in other countries he is going to bomb – in Greece…wherever in Europe American bases exist, he is going to bomb them. And he will have the sympathy of all the downtrodden countries. He will rise as a world leader.

Ronald Reagan may have the power, but he will not have any sympathy.

This imperialist government of Britain feels afraid of me. Just my overnight stay at the airport – I was not asking to enter their country – and against their own laws they refused me. They said it was not good for their public; my overnight stay would have destroyed their morality, their religion, all their cherished values!

There is something to understand clearly: I am against imperialism. I am against exploiting man, other human beings. I am against torturing people just so that you can

have power. Perhaps they were afraid that overnight my sannyasins from all over England may gather…just one night may be enough to give them a fresh insight, a new life to go against all traditional values.

And it *is* a conspiracy. Not only Britain is responsible for it. All those who are living and thriving on traditional values are really afraid – of a man who has no power except that he can show people that their misery is caused by their own wrong ideas, and that those wrong ideas are being emphasized by their government, by their church.

There is a conspiracy.

All the European governments are agreeing on the point that I cannot land at their airports. They do not understand that this is defeatism, that they have already accepted defeat. They are showing that they have no arguments to save their religion, their morality, their politics, it is all rotten.

And they are afraid that their youth will be on my side, not on their side. I can give an open challenge to *any* country: Let me speak to your young people, and you speak to the same young people, and let it be decided by those young people who are going to own the future. These governments know perfectly well they cannot defend anything that they believe.

These efforts to prevent me are good signs; they are good news. It means they have accepted their defeat; otherwise, what was the fear? – they could have allowed me to talk to people. And they have their archbishops and popes and priests who could have demolished my arguments; that would have been a cultured way, a human way.

I am alone – they have millions of priests. But they don't have a single argument for anything that they think is the basis of their society.

THE OSTRICH ARGUMENT

Yes, it is not conducive to their rotten society. It may ring the death bell. But they cannot prevent me. It is not me who is going to destroy the rottenness; it is the time itself which is not in favor of them. If not me, then somebody else will have to do it.

It is impossible to protect those societies, those governments, those churches. They have lost all roots. And they are aware of it, that just a push and they will fall down. They cannot even resist – even that much power is not left. You can make a corpse stand, but if you push it, it cannot retaliate; it is bound to fall down.

All these countries are corpses.

And they don't want their youth to come in contact with anybody who can show them that the old is dead and you have to find a new way of life.

This is not a question of one country; it is a question of the whole human past. Just a deep attachment, a deep conditioning…

There is a beautiful story in India. Shiva is one of the Hindu trinity of gods. It is not called a trinity, it is called *trimurti* – three faces of one God. Shiva is one. He fell in love with a beautiful woman, Parvarti, and he loved her so much that when she died he would not accept that she was dead.

Nobody could dare to tell him that she was dead and now it was time to take her to the crematorium. Instead, he carried the corpse of Parvarti on his shoulder all over India, in search of some physician, some healer, who could bring her back to life. You cannot carry a corpse… It took twelve years for him to move around the country – it was a big country. Wherever he heard that there was some physician, he would go there.

In those twelve years the parts of the woman he was carrying started falling off – the hand fell, the leg fell, the head fell. But he was not worried about that; he was not even looking at her, because he was *afraid* to look.

Note that point:

He was afraid to look at her, because deep down he also knew that she was dead. But his mind did not want to believe it; he wanted to believe she was alive. Now she was not even whole. The head had fallen somewhere, the legs had fallen somewhere else, the hands had fallen somewhere else.

India is a country of stories, signifying tremendous meanings. Now there are twelve pilgrimage temples which are made at points where one part of Parvarti fell, to give the story a feeling of reality. Twelve temples exist all over the country representing…because some part of Parvarti had fallen there, they have become sacred.

But Shiva remained completely blind, knowingly blind. And this is the situation of the world. The societies are rotten, the religions are dead; the politicians are only promising, knowing perfectly well they cannot fulfill any promise.

The future is dark, but nobody wants to see it – the past is dead, and if you go on clinging to the past the future is going to become darker and darker.

I will be avoided by every country.

I will be persecuted by every power, for the simple reason that I want them to see the reality. They are keeping their eyes closed.

In logic it is called the "ostrich argument." The ostrich has a tendency: whenever he comes against an enemy and knows that death is certain, he simply puts his head into the sand. He lives in the desert, eyes closed, head in the sand. He is perfectly happy because he cannot see any enemy anywhere.

But this does not eliminate the enemy; in fact it makes the enemy more powerful. Now this ostrich is not going to do anything to escape, to fight, to negotiate, to do something. Now there is no question: he is simply available as food. And ostriches are eaten by their predators without any fight, because the ostrich is living with the idea that, "I don't see any enemy here."

This "ostrich argument" is widespread today around the world. Nobody wants to see the reality – that you are sinking, that all your values are false, that all your civilization is hypocrisy, that all your smiles are just exercises of lips, and there is no heart in it; that you have forgotten to live, to love, to laugh, that you don't know what life *means* at all.

And you go on clinging because there is nothing else, there is no alternative – and I am being prevented because I can give you the alternative.

I can show you that this is not the only way a society can exist, this is not the only way that a marriage can exist, this is not the only way that children can be brought up, this is not the only way that governments should function. There are alternative ways.

But even to hear of the alternative, they are afraid. The message should not reach to the young – because the young are bound to be affected by the news that there is an alternative, that you need not remain in this misery, continuously fighting, killing human beings unnecessarily.

Now Libya is destroying American bases. America cannot remain silent: it will start destroying Libya – not only its military bases but its civilians. It is a small country, but Libya knows that if America starts to destroy the civilians, the whole East – particularly the Middle East – will be on its side. And behind the scenes will be the Soviet Union.

So if America has guts, it is not going to start a fight between America and Libya – which is very unbalanced: Libya has nothing

with which to fight against one of the greatest nuclear powers. But Libya has the assurance of the Soviet Union: "Don't be worried, Libya is just a facade, just a front." And once these two powers start fighting, they cannot resist using nuclear weapons; it is impossible.

But the government of England is not afraid of this. The government of England should have prevented America: "This is not a right beginning; this is not conducive to the public good. This will lead more and more into war. Don't take the first step; otherwise the last step will not be far away." But they would prefer to have a third world war rather than change the human mind.

Why? – because to change the human mind means that for millions of years you have been behaving stupidly, that all your great ancestors have been simply fools and nothing else. They knew nothing about human consciousness; they were unconscious, they were blind. And blind people have been leading other blind people towards the goal of light. It seems it is difficult to accept that our whole past has been wrong. It is better to destroy the whole future but remain stubborn that our past has been right: Let man die, but save your ego.

That will give you a clue to why I am a danger, just for an overnight stay, and American nuclear missiles are not dangerous. They think alike; their mathematics is the same.

To them I am a dangerous person because I have no pride in the past. I am a dangerous person because I do not consider that for thousands of years man has lived intelligently; otherwise why so much misery, why so much anxiety, why so much anguish? The fruit shows the quality of the tree. And the fruit that we have shows that the whole human past went somewhere wrong, and just out of ego went on pushing in a wrong direction.

I am ready and willing to change my ideas if somebody can show me that they are wrong, that they will not lead to the good of the people. But nobody is ready to do that; they simply accept it. No argument is needed, no discussion is needed.

The government of Spain was wondering for one month continuously whether to allow me into Spain or not. They have nuclear bases for the American army; they are members of NATO, and the man who is the prime minister became prime minister by promising the people of Spain that he would pull Spain out of NATO, and that he would order the American bases to be removed from Spain. And the people of Spain don't want…because they have seen Franco, who ruled for forty years with absolute dictatorship; he destroyed all freedom of thinking and killed anybody who said anything against him. After forty years of this experience, this nightmare, they don't want to get into another nightmare again.

They voted in this man on a single point – that he was promising that he would pull out of NATO and force the Americans to leave Spain. Two years have passed and the people have been asking, "What happened? You are not pulling out of NATO, and neither are the American bases moving out of Spain."

In these two years, the man…when he had come to power he was not a politician, but these two years have turned him into a politician. He said, "My experience of two years in power makes me change my idea: we are going to remain in NATO, and American bases are going to remain in Spain."

It was such a betrayal that the people demanded a vote on the point, a referendum. But the prime minister, the whole bureaucracy, the whole government, is now *for*

American military bases and membership in NATO. Still, they do not have a big majority. The young people of Spain have still voted against them: forty-five percent of the people have voted against NATO. But the government with all their powers…certainly they managed to get just a little bit bigger number of votes in favor.

If this man had any sense of dignity he would have resigned, because he was chosen for a simple program. *He* was not chosen – the program was chosen, and because he has dropped the program he should resign immediately. But these politicians seem to be so shameless, with no dignity, with no honor, with no self-respect.

He wanted me to stay in Spain, but the problem was the American pressure. For one month he went on postponing. He informed me that I should not leak the news that Spain had invited me, because the royal family of Spain, the prime minister, the president, the cabinet – they would all be at the airport to receive me. I was going to be their invited guest, so *they* would proclaim the date and time, and they would inform me.

But slowly, slowly he saw that if forty-five percent of the people can vote against him, then to bring a man like me into the country is dangerous because these young people are bound to be influenced by me.

The parliament decided that I should be welcomed, the cabinet decided that I should be welcomed, but finally the prime minister informed me that it would not be possible; politically it would be difficult.

I know the difficulty; the difficulty came after the referendum. And I have been telling John every day that if any decision has to be taken, it should be taken before the referendum. After the referendum I don't see any hope, because once the prime minister sees how many people can vote against him, he will not be courageous enough to invite a person who can influence his people.

This is the fear, and the fear is now almost all over the world, in every country – strange fears. In this small, beautiful country, I was told that we should not mention that we have one million sannyasins around the world and three million sympathizers, because that may become a fear – this country has only three million people, and they would not like such a powerful man in the country, who has four million people around the world who love him.

The country should be proud to have someone…and I am not a political person, I am not going to have any political contest with anybody; but still, fear is fear. All these powerful people are deep down very inferior and very fearful.

They go on thinking…the only thing in their minds is power, what can enhance their power and what can destroy their power. And they put conditions….

The president of Greece was willing for me to have a commune in Greece, and in fact he *wanted* it. His reasons were different – that it would bring thousands of tourists and that it would boost the economy. In fact *he* was the cause that I was allowed a four-week visa for Greece.

But then the condition came in – that if I wanted to stay there and make a commune, I should remember a few things: "The Greek Orthodox church is respected by our constitution; you cannot criticize it. The family is our foundation; you cannot criticize it. Our code of morality; you cannot criticize it. We believe in virginity; you cannot criticize it."

They certainly believe in virginity, but it is difficult to find a single virgin in the whole of Greece. That's okay – but you should not

criticize it. You can see the political mind: the reality can be tolerated but it should not be exposed.

I cannot accept anybody's conditions.

Whatever happens to me, whatever the consequences…but to accept conditions, and that too for a little piece of land…

How much land does a man require? I might like to live without a country – a wanderer in the *true* sense. There have been wanderers but they had a home base. I will be really a wanderer without any home base – being rejected from one country to another country. But their rejection of me is simply an acceptance of their defeat, their impotency. Sooner or later they will have to pay for it, pay highly for it, because in every country there are intelligent people. How long can these intelligent people tolerate this? Sooner or later it will become a revolution. Without my entering those lands, I will find my friends there.

I cannot lose hope, because I cannot see that intelligence is dead. It is repressed, but it is alive. It has become an undercurrent, but my rejection is going to provoke it to come to the surface. Soon there will be protests in every country which is denying me entry.

In Italy they have been postponing for almost three months, just for a three-week tourist visa. And the president and the prime minister and the minister of foreign affairs, all are saying, "We are going to give it to him – just tomorrow…." And sannyasins are going every day; they are sitting there in their offices, saying, "Whenever you want we are ready. But when will your tomorrow come?" And after three months they got so frustrated, because the pope is holding it back. They cannot say no to the sannyasins because they have no reason to say no.

And they know my impact in Italy. Just a

few days ago, a television interview of one and a half hours was seen by thirty- four million people – unprecedented. The director informed me, "We could not believe that so many people would be interested in you. You have never come to this country." No other program in his whole life had attracted so many people. And not only the show – the show was finished in one and a half hours – but people are discussing each and every point in the marketplace, in the university – everywhere. Somebody is for, somebody is against, but everybody is intensely involved.

So the government could not say no because that might create trouble. And the pope is insisting that I should not be allowed into Italy. So they go on postponing. Finally the sannyasins got so frustrated that they started making a protest, and one of the most famous Italian film directors, Fellini, has signed their petition first. They have thirty-six other world-known people who have signed the protest, and they are collecting more names – and I have never been there.

But one thing is certain, whether you agree with me or not: I cannot be prevented from presenting my views, my perspective, to the people. And what is happening there will happen in Germany, will happen in Greece, will happen in England, will happen in Spain, is going to happen everywhere. Sannyasins have to create a worldwide chain of protests, signed by all the important creative artists, novelists, musicians, sculptors, dancers, actors, directors – people of all dimensions who have made an impact on the world.

Collect their names for the protest first, in every country, and then send a final protest to the U.N., with all the protests of all the countries together – because now it is not a question of one country; if the European parliament decides that I cannot even land my plane at their airports, you cannot now take me just as an individual.

I have become representative of a worldwide intelligence of creative, talented people.

That is my country.

And my sannyasins have to go to the U.N., because this is simply ugly.

But as I said in the beginning, it is something relative.

To me it is ugly. And to all those who can understand, it will be ugly. But to those who believe in the ostrich logic, it is good, it is "for the public good."

We will show the world what is good for the public and what is bad for the public!

Beloved Bhagwan,
I was one of those who was taken for a ride when the list of enlightened people was announced, because I thought, "If Bhagwan says I'm enlightened, why not try it out?"
I enjoyed it: I threw a party for a hundred or so friends, and for the next six months – until I became endarkened again – tried to use what I saw as a really potential situation.
The main thing I saw was that I really am okay. Am I kidding myself about that experience?

No, if you can understand it you cannot be kidding.
First let me explain a few other things.

After I declared a few people enlightened – Santosh was also one of them. He wrote me a letter saying, "Your declaration of my enlightenment gives me no excitement, but my being accepted as a member of the committee of the enlightened ones makes me feel very great."

I sent him the message, "Why does your being enlightened not make you feel excited? The reason is that you think that you are already enlightened – and that is not true. That's why your becoming a member of the committee of the enlightened ones makes you feel great – at last your enlightenment has been recognized. It is not a declaration for you but a recognition that you have been enlightened long before.

"But if enlightenment is not an excitement, then how can it be a great thing to be a member of the party, or the committee, of enlightened people? If enlightenment itself makes no sense to you, then being the member of the committee cannot make any sense, except this: that it fulfills your ego.

"You were enlightened, and nobody was taking note of it. Finally I have recognized it, and now you are part of the committee of enlightened people, so it is sealed. But you are wrong – because it was all a joke! The committee was a joke, the declaration was a joke. And it was a device."

Somendra immediately sent a telegram to Teertha, saying, "I have got it – what about you?" He was continuously in competition – that was his problem, that he should be higher than Teertha. And this was a good chance.

He has dropped sannyas, he has not been in any contact with us, but my declaration of his enlightenment – that he accepts. Sannyas he has dropped – he is no longer part of my family – but enlightenment…immediately a telegram: "I have got it – what about you?"

It was a device to see how people would react. Your response to it was perfectly beautiful.

Your response was, "If Bhagwan says I am enlightened, I must be."

It simply shows trust, love. It has nothing to do with ego. And your throwing a party and rejoicing the moment with your friends was perfectly right.

And when I said it was a joke, you were not angry. You simply took it again the same way: "If Bhagwan says I am not enlightened, and it was a joke, perhaps I am not enlightened and it was really a joke." And the six months that you lived as enlightened, the joy and the peace and the serenity that you felt was not of enlightenment – it was of trust and love.

It was a good experience for you.

But different experiences happen to different people.

There were only two Indians in the group who were declared enlightened, and they understand traditionally what enlightenment means. One was Vinod Bharti.

He became very nervous, was crying, came to Vivek to give me the message, "Bhagwan, I am not enlightened. And you have created a trouble for me: I cannot say you are wrong, and I know perfectly well myself that I am not enlightened. So what am I supposed to do? I am just torn apart. You just tell me the truth!"

He knows about enlightenment. He knows that for centuries in India enlightenment has been the ultimate peak of spiritual search. In the West the very idea has never existed. So he cannot conceive of himself as Gautam Buddha, and he cannot deny me because he loves me and trusts me. So I can see his trouble. So I sent him the message, "Don't be worried, it was just a joke. You are not enlightened, relax!"

Until he heard that he was not enlightened, he could not sleep for two days. Then he relaxed – he is not enlightened; there is no problem.

The other man was Swami Anand Maitreya, who was the only one who understood the joke immediately, because as he left the room he said, "Bhagwan is really a rascal! Saying to me that I am enlightened proves it!"

But he is also an Indian and particularly he comes from Bihar where most of the enlightened people happened in India – Gautam Buddha, Mahavira, Parsunatha, Naminatha, Adinatha... a long series of enlightened people. All the twenty-four enlightened masters of the Jainas...Gautam Buddha – they all happened in Bihar. Bihar has the deepest understanding and experience of enlightenment. So naturally he said, "Bhagwan is a rascal." But it was also his love.

He was not disturbed, because once you know that it is a joke, there is no question of any difficulty about it.

A few people simply remained silent: they neither reacted this way or that. That too is good. They were not affected by it; they simply remained themselves, as they were. "If Bhagwan says it is enlightenment, it may be; if he says it is not, it may not be." But it did not make any difference to them; they remained aloof and detached.

And it was a good experience to see how people react to a single idea, with their different minds. Those who were not included in the committee were angry. I received a few letters saying, "If these people have become enlightened, then why have I not become enlightened?" As if it were something..."You have given it to these people. Why have you not given it to me?"

Somebody wrote, "I have been with you longer than these people, and I am not enlightened yet. Have you forgotten me or what?" But it was good to know how people react.

Your reaction was perfectly beautiful on both ends. "If Bhagwan says it is enlightenment, it must be" – that is a simple trust. "And if he says it is not...." Then you don't feel any contradiction or inconsistency, you simply accept it: "If he says it is not, then it must not be." You have transcended the world of consistencies, inconsistencies.

Love knows no contradiction.

It knows no comparison.

Each moment it is available.

It is
Pure Light...
Pure Delight

**Beloved Bhagwan,
What is a natural death?**

It is a significant question, but there are many possible implications in it. The simplest and the most obvious is that a man dies without any cause; he simply becomes old, older, and the change from old age to death is not through any disease. Death is simply the ultimate old age – everything in your body, in your brain, has stopped functioning. This will be the ordinary and obvious meaning of a natural death.

But to me natural death has a far deeper meaning: one has to live a natural life to attain a natural death. Natural death is the culmination of a life lived naturally, without any inhibition, without any repression – just the way the animals live, the birds live, the trees live, without any split...a life of let-go, allowing nature to flow through you without any obstructions from your side, as if you are absent and life is moving on its own.

Rather than you living life, life lives you, you are secondary; then the culmination will be a natural death. According to my definition, only an awakened man can die a natural death; otherwise all deaths are unnatural, because all lives are unnatural.

How can you arrive at a natural death, living an unnatural life? Death will reflect the ultimate culmination, the crescendo of your whole life. In a condensed form, it is all that you have lived. So only very few people in the world have died naturally, because only very few people have lived naturally. Our conditionings don't allow us to be natural.

Our conditionings, from the very beginning, teach us that we have to be something more than nature, that just to be natural is to be animal; we have to be supernatural. And it seems very logical. All the religions have been teaching this – that to be man means going above nature – and they have convinced centuries of humanity to go above nature.

Nobody has succeeded in going above nature. All that they have succeeded in, is destroying their natural, spontaneous beauty, their innocence.

Man need not transcend nature.

I say unto you, man has to fulfill nature – which no animal can do.

That is the difference.

The religions were cunning, cheating and deceiving people. They made the distinction that animals are natural and you have to be supernatural. No animal can do fasting; you cannot convince any animal that fasting is something divine. The animal only knows that it is hungry, and there is no difference between fasting and being hungry. You cannot convince any animal to go against nature.

This gave an opportunity to the so-called religious people, because man has the capacity at least to fight against nature. He will never be victorious, but he can fight. And in fighting he will not be destroying nature; he will be destroying only himself.

That's how man has destroyed himself – all his joy, all his love, all his grandeur – and has become not something higher than animals, but something lower, in every possible way. Perhaps you have never thought about it: no animal in the wild is homosexual. The very idea, and the whole world of animals will burst into laughter. It is simply stupid! But in a zoo, where females are not available, animals turn into homosexuals out of sheer necessity.

But man has turned the whole world into a zoo: millions and millions of people are homosexuals, lesbians, sodomists, and what-not – all kinds of perversions. And who is responsible? The people who were teaching you to go beyond nature, to attain super-natural divineness.

This is only one example. In every other way they have done the same. For example, in India Mahavira was so much attached to the idea of nonviolence that even cultivation – gardening – was prohibited to his followers, because if you cultivate you will have to cut plants…and plants have life, and that will be violence.

His followers were mostly coming from the warrior race, the *kshatriyas;* he himself was a warrior king. Now they could not fight because fighting was violence; they could not be cultivators because cultivation was violence. They could not be teachers because that was the monopoly of the brahmins, and a brahmin is born; you cannot enter into the brahmin fold, howsoever wise you are. You may be wiser than all those brahmins, but you cannot become a teacher of the people – that is the birthright of a brahmin. So they could not be accepted by the brahmins. They would not like to become the sudras, the untouch-ables, making shoes, cleaning streets and toilets.

Now the only way possible for them was to become businessmen; all other possibilities were closed. So all the Jainas in India became businessmen, and a strange phenomenon happened: all their violence…because just not being a fighter or a hunter or a cultivator makes no difference; you are the same person. All their violence became exploita-tion: they cannot cut off your head, but they can suck your blood. And they became the richest people in the country, for the simple reason that all their violence became concen-trated only on one thing, and that was money.

This was not evolution. These people were not better people. Mahavira's teaching of nonviolence has not helped them to become better – they have become worse! They are the greediest, the most materialist, the most money-minded; their whole world is money, because every other avenue is closed. They talk about money, they think about money, they dream about money. And they can do anything to accumulate money.

Whenever you enforce something, the result is not going to bring a betterment. They have not become compassionate; to be nonviolent means to be loving and to be compassionate. They have become just the opposite. They are not compassionate, they are not kind, they are not loving.

In many other spheres, different religions have tried to make man something above nature. The result has been without any exception, failure. You are born as a natural being. You cannot go above yourself. It is just like trying to lift yourself off the ground by pulling your legs. You may hop a little, but sooner or later you are going to fall to the ground, and you may have a few fractures. You cannot fly.

And that's what has been done. People have been trying to raise themselves above nature, which means above themselves. They are not separate from nature, but the idea suited their egos: you are not animals so you have to be above nature; you cannot behave like animals. People have even tried to make animals not behave like animals; they have tried to make them go a little above nature.

In the Victorian age in England, dogs were clothed when people used to take them for a walk. The dogs had coats to prevent them being natural, to prevent them being naked and nude – which is suitable to animals. These kind of people are trying to raise their dogs a little higher than animals.

You will be surprised to know that in the Victorian age in England, even the legs of chairs were covered – for the simple reason that they were called legs, and legs should be covered. Bertrand Russell, who lived almost one century – a long life – remembers in his childhood that seeing the feet of a woman was enough to get sexually excited. The dresses were made in such a way that they covered the feet; you could not see the feet.

It was believed, even just one hundred years ago, that the women of the royal family don't have two legs. Royalty has to be somehow different than ordinary, common humanity, and nobody had seen – and there was no possibility to see – whether their legs were separate from each other.

But the ego…neither did those royal people make it clear: "This is nonsense, we are as human as you are." The ego prevented them. If the people are putting them on a higher pedestal, then why bother? – just remain royal. That was one of the reasons why royal families would not allow anybody, a commoner, to be married into the royal family, because he may expose the whole thing: "These people are just as human as everybody else; there is nothing royal about them." But for centuries they maintained the idea.

I would also like you to be different from the animals, but not in the sense that you can go above nature – no. You can go deeper into nature, you can be more natural than animals. They are not free, they are in a deep coma; they cannot do anything other than what their ancestors have been doing for millennia.

You can be more natural than any animal. You can go to the abysmal depths of nature, and you can go to the very heights of nature, but you will not be going beyond in any way. You will be becoming more natural, more multidimensionally natural.

To me the religious man is not one who is above nature, but is the man who is totally natural, fully natural, who has explored nature in all its dimensions, who has not left anything unexplored.

Animals are prisoners; they have a certain limited area of being.

Man has the capacity, the intelligence, the freedom to explore.

And if you have explored nature totally, you have come home.

Nature is your home.

And then death is a joy, is a celebration. Then you die without any complaint; you die with deep gratitude, because life gave you so much, and death is simply the ultimate height of all that you have lived.

It is just like before the flame of a candle goes out it burns brightest...the natural man, before he dies, lives brightest for a moment; he is all light, all truth.

To me this is natural death.

But it has to be earned; it is not given to you. The opportunity is given to you, but you have to explore, you have to earn, you have to deserve.

Even to see the death of an authentic man, just to be near him while he is dying, you will be filled suddenly with a strange joy. Your tears will not be of sadness, sorrow; they will be of gratitude and blissfulness – because when a man dies naturally, living his life fully, he spreads his being into the whole of nature. Those who are present and close to him are bathed...a sudden freshness, a breeze, a new fragrance and a new feeling that death is not something bad, that death is not something to be afraid of, that death is something to be earned, to be deserved.

I teach you the art of life.

But it can be called also the art of death.

They are both the same.

Beloved Bhagwan,
How can one get out of the trap the mind creates of never being quite blissful in the moment, and be patient, letting the grass grow by itself?
I'm always wanting to move faster, to push the river, and missing the beauty of it taking me in its own time.
Would You please comment?

It is one of the eternal questions.

The East has come up with something very close to the truth. There are religions born in India and religions born outside India; the religions born outside all believe in one life – that is, seventy years. Naturally, one is in a hurry; one has to be in a hurry – such a small life and so much to do, so much to experience, so much to explore. That's why the Western mind is speedy, wanting to do everything faster and faster, quickly, because his conception of life is too small. You cannot blame him.

The religions born in India have an eternal expanse – life after life. There is no hurry, there is no haste. But man is so stupid that you solve one question, and out of the solution a thousand other questions will arise. The idea of many lives was really to help you to relax: there is no hurry; the eternity is yours, so don't run, just walk the way you go for a morning walk – at ease, relaxed.

That was the idea of the people who gave the conception of reincarnation, but people are such that rather than becoming relaxed, they became lazy. They said, "There is no hurry, so why bother even to walk? Running is out of the question but even to go for a morning walk, what is the need? Eternity is yours – you can go any time for your morning walk."

The East became poor because of this, because no technology evolved. Technology is just to make things quickly, to produce things faster than man can do with his own hands. The people remained poor, went on becoming poorer. The idea was good, but the consequences proved not to be good.

The West has just the opposite idea – of a small life. It created great tension and anxiety, but it created technology, scientific developments, richness, comfort, luxuries; it created everything. But the man inside was lost, because he was always running. He was never where he was; he was always going for something else. And that goal where you can stop never comes. So in the West people have means of speed, and they are going fast. But don't ask them, "Where are you going?" Don't waste their time in asking such stupid questions! All that matters is that they are going fast; it does not matter where they are going and *why* they are going.

Both ideas have failed. Eastern religions have not been of help; Western religions have not been of help. They both tried to give you an idea, but they never gave you an insight into your own being.

That's where I differ.

For example, your question is that you understand, "Relax and let the grass grow by itself," but still you go on pushing.

No, you don't understand. The first thing for you to understand is that you don't understand the meaning of the grass growing by itself. If you understand that, the pushing, the forcing, will disappear. When I say it will disappear, I am not saying it will stop. It will differ with different people.

If you understand what it means that the grass grows by itself…such a vast universe is going so silently, so peacefully; millions of solar systems, millions of stars moving day in, day out, from eternity to eternity… If you understand that existence is happening, it is

not *doing,* then if pushing is your nature you will accept it.

It is not a question of stopping it, because that will be again doing. You simply understand that things are happening, that this is how you are: that you push, that you force. Then there is a great acceptance of it, and in that acceptance, the tension disappears.

For a few others the pushing may disappear – if it is not part of their nature, if they are imitating somebody else, if they are competing with somebody else and because everybody else is pushing, *they* are pushing. It may stop, understanding that things are happening, and you need not unnecessarily bother about them; you can enjoy silently the way things are happening. You can contribute without any anxiety anything that comes naturally to you; but not beyond that.

So *each* individual will have different things happening out of the same understanding. If pushing is your nature, then there is nothing wrong in it. Enjoy it, push as much as you can – but with a song and with a dance, and without being worried that you are pushing. This is you. This is your grass, and it grows this way. There are grasses and grasses.

Just one thing has to be remembered, that anything that you are doing is joyfully done, rejoicingly done – that's enough. Different people will be doing different things, and the world needs that different people should do different things. It is the richness of the world that all are not alike, and should not be alike. But on one point they should meet; and that is the cosmic center of being relaxed.

In Japan they have developed strange things for meditative purposes…Japan has done a tremendous service to humanity. Meditation was developed in India, but it remained a very limited phenomenon – just sitting in a lotus posture witnessing your thoughts, becoming silent. It did the work, but Japan tried different dimensions, strange dimensions: swordsmanship, but with meditation. Two swordsmen bent upon killing each other have to remain centered in themselves without tension, without fear, without anger, without revenge, just playful. To the observer it is a question of life and death, but to those two meditators it is playfulness.

And a strange thing has been observed again and again: if both the meditators are of the same depth in meditation, nobody wins, nobody is killed. Even before one person raises the sword to hit the other person at a certain point – even before he has done that – just that *idea* of his has reached to the other and his sword is ready to protect him. It is impossible to declare who is the winner.

Ordinarily it is difficult to think of swordsmanship and meditation, aikido and meditation, jujitsu and meditation, wrestling and meditation. But in Japan they have tried every dimension possible, and they have found that it doesn't matter what you are doing; what matters is, are you centered?

If you are centered then you can do anything and it will not create any tension; your relaxation will remain the same.

So don't be worried about pushing. Just try to understand that we are so small compared to this immense universe; what we do or don't do makes no difference to existence. We are not to be serious about it. I was not here and existence continued; I will not be here, and existence will continue. I should not take myself seriously.

That is a fundamental understanding of a meditator – that he does not take himself seriously. Then relaxation comes automatically. And with relaxation, whatsoever is natural to you continues, and whatsoever is not natural to you falls on its own accord.

Beloved Bhagwan,
The question for the meditator used to be, "How to be in the world and not of it?"
Since the Ranch and having moved back into the world, many of us feel alien, different, not of it.
The question now seems to be, "How to be in it?"

No, still the question is to be in the world and not to be of it. To be in it does not change the first position.

The first position allows you to be in the world but not worldly. It is perfectly good that you feel alien – there is nothing wrong in it. You should feel so, that this world in which you have to be is not the world where you can synchronize with people, with their ideas, with their behavior.

This world is not the right world – I mean the human world. And you want to be in it, part of it? Then you have to be a Christian in a Christian society. Then you have to go to the church, then you have to believe in *The Holy Bible.* Do you want to be in this way in the world? Then all that you have done before has been a sheer wastage of time.

Being in the world only means that you will be doing a job, that you will be earning your bread, that you will be living with people who are not of the same mind as you, that you will be living amongst foreigners; and naturally, you will feel alien. But that is something to be happy about.

I have not sent you into the world to get lost. I have sent you into the world to remain yourself in spite of the world.

And that was the meaning of the original statement: To be in the world but not of it. It remains unchanged.

It is so fundamental that it will remain unchanged.

Beloved Bhagwan,

One of the things I enjoy most in this life is hearing You describe the state of enlightenment. For those of us who love to listen, can You once again say something about the unsayable?

It is true that there is nothing more beautiful, more blissful than enlightenment – even the talk of it, even the faraway echo, even the shadow of it. The moon reflected in the water is not the real moon, but still it has tremendous beauty; and if the waters of your mind are silent, then the moon reflected in those waters is exactly the same.

It is not your experience, but it is the experience of someone you love, it is the experience of someone you trust. And just because you love and you trust, you start sharing the experience in a subtle way.

It is certainly difficult to say anything about it, although my whole life I have been saying things about it – and only about it. Even if, though, I am talking about other things, I am only talking to lead you towards an understanding of enlightenment.

It is your state of silence, it is your state of universal-hood.

It is you without the ego and its problems.

It is you without any questions and without any answer either – simply silent.

And there is no joy which can transcend this silence.

It is pure light, it is pure delight.

I can understand your question. Just to hear about it again and again is necessary, a need, so you don't forget why you are here.

Chapter 12
April 18, 1986, Morning

**Obedience
Needs No Art**

Beloved Bhagwan,
When I hear You speaking of Your vision, I can't help but feel that those few daring people around You will live to experience the new man. But it feels more like a hundred years away before man at large will come to see and live the genius of Your ways. Is this true?

It is true.
Even if it happens in a hundred years time it will be soon.

But the question is significant in a totally different way. It is not the realization of the vision, the coming of the new man, a new humanity...that will come in its own time. The more important thing is to be able to visualize it.

Everything great that has happened in the world has been an idea first. Sometimes it took hundreds of years for it to become a reality, but the joy of having a vision, an insight into the future, is immense.

The people who are with me should rejoice that they can see a possibility of the old, rotten world disappearing and a new, fresh human being taking its place.

Just the vision will change *you* at least, will shift your being from the past to the future. In a certain way you will start living the new man, who has not yet come. You will start living the new man in small ways, and each moment of that living will be a blessing. And as you become acquainted, within yourself, with the explosion of the new and the destruction of the old, you are changing, you are going through a revolution.

I am interested in *you*. Who cares about what is going to happen after a hundred years? Something must be going to happen, but it is not our business.

And when I talk about the new man I am

really talking about *you,* for you to become aware of the possibility, because that very awareness will change you. I am not interested in the future; I am simply interested in the immediate present.

The future will go on for eternity, but if your mind can be cleaned of the past rubbish, and if you can see the faraway rising sun...

I am not interested in the sun, I am interested in your vision, in your capacity to see, in your understanding, in your hope that it is possible. That very hope will become a seed in you.

The new man will come whenever it has to come. But the new vision can come right now.

And with the new vision, you participate in a subtle way with the man who has not come yet, with the humanity which is still in the womb. You start having a synchronicity, a certain relationship. Your roots from the past start dropping, and you start growing your roots into the future.

But my interest, I repeat, is basically in you. Neither am I interested in the past, nor in the future. I talk about the past so you can get rid of it; I talk about the future so you can remain open to it. But *you* are the point of my emphasis.

Beloved Bhagwan,
Nothing thrills me more than when You speak about nirvana. How mysterious it is that I can long for something so much that I don't know and You can't say. The word itself is still unpolluted and so wondrous.
On the other hand, I noticed the other week that we now have "enlightened" insurance policies!
Would You please thrill my heart once more?

This must be Kaveesha, because the question can come only from California. In California you can have enlightened insurance policies. In California everything is possible! But there is no insurance, no guarantee for enlightenment. You have to earn it, you have to deserve it. Nobody can give it to you; it is not a commodity.

And I can see why the word nirvana thrills you into ecstasies. It is certainly one of the words which is unpolluted. There is a reason why it remained unpolluted. The first reason that it remained unpolluted was its meaning. Unless you have come to a deep understanding of yourself and existence, the word nirvana will create fear in you. It is a negative word. Literally it means "blowing out the candle."

Gautam Buddha used the word for the ultimate state of consciousness. He could have chosen some positive word, and in India there were many positive words for it: *moksha,* freedom, liberation; *kaivalya,* aloneness, absolute aloneness; *brahmanubava,* the experience of the ultimate. But he chose a strange word, which has never been used in spiritual contexts: "blowing out the candle." How can you relate it with a spiritual experience?

Buddha says your so-called self is nothing but a flame, and it is being kept burning through your desires. When all desires disappear the candle has disappeared. Now the flame cannot exist anymore. The flame also disappears – disappears into the vast universe, leaving no trace behind it; you cannot find it again. It is there but it has gone forever from any identity, from any limitation.

Hence Buddha chose the word nirvana rather than realization, because realization still can give you some egoistic superiority – that you are a realized person, that you are a liberated being, that you are enlightened, that you are illuminated, that you have found it. But *you* remain. And Buddha is saying *you* are lost – who is going to find it? You disperse, you were only a combination. Now each element goes to its original source. The identity of the individual is no more. Yes, you will exist as the universe…

So Buddha avoided any positive word, knowing the human tendency, because each positive word can give you a feeling of ego. No negative word can do that; that's why it remains unpolluted. You cannot pollute something which is not. And people were very much afraid to use the word – with a deep inner trembling – nirvana.

Thousands of times Buddha was asked, "Your word nirvana does not create in us an excitement, does not create in us a desire to achieve it. The ultimate truth, self-realization, the realization of God – all those create a desire, a great desire. Your word creates no desire."

And Buddha said again and again, "That is the beauty of the word. All those words which create desire in you are not going to help you, because desire itself is the root cause of your misery. Longing for something is your tension. Nirvana makes you absolutely free from tension: there is nothing to desire. On the contrary, you have to prepare yourself to accept a dissolution. In dissolution you cannot claim the ego, hence the word remains unpolluted."

No other word has remained unpolluted. Its negativity is the reason – and only a great master can contribute to humanity something which, even if you want, you cannot pollute. Twenty-five centuries…but there is no way. Nirvana is going to dissolve you; you cannot do anything to nirvana.

It is certainly the purest word. Even its sound, whether you understand the meaning or not, is soothing, gives a deep serenity and silence, which no other word – god-realization, the absolute, the ultimate…no other word gives that feeling of silence.

The moment you hear the word nirvana it seems as if time has stopped, as if there is nowhere to go.

In this very moment you can melt, dissolve, disappear, without leaving any trace behind.

Beloved Bhagwan,
The anecdote You told about Mulla Nasruddin and the sack of sugar pinpointed the reason for my occasional resistance to being told what to do. When Nasruddin's father saw what was happening to the sugar, he need only have made his son aware of it, without providing a solution. Having had the situation pointed out to him, the Mulla, if he had any intelligence – and it seems he had his fair share – could have immediately seen what was needed to be done and acted accordingly. But his father did not allow him the chance to think it out for himself.
To encourage people to use their intelligence and initiative seems to be a creative way of putting one's authority into action.
I would be grateful for your comment.

The story is simply a way of saying very complex and complicated things. As far as the story is concerned, you are right; the father could have explained. There was no need for any order, and no need for obedience or disobedience. But it is a story.

In actual life there are things – particularly for example God, or the soul, or paradise, the temple, worship, the prayer to an unknown God…there is no way to explain. The father cannot explain God – he himself does not know. He has been told, he accepted it, and he has believed it. Now it is time for him to tell the son – how can he explain? And that's where I come into the story.

Your whole society and the mind of your society is based on things which can be only believed but cannot be explained; hence the necessity of obedience; hence the angry reaction of your elders if you disobey.

It was a problem for me also in my childhood. My whole family was going to the temple and I was resistant. I was willing – if they could explain what this whole thing was all about. They had no explanation except, "It has been done always, and it is good to follow your elders, to follow your old generations, to follow the ancient heritage…it is good." This is not an explanation.

I told them, "I am not asking whether it is good or bad; I am asking what it is. I don't see any God, I see only a stone statue. And you know perfectly well that it is a stone statue – you know better than me, because you have purchased it from the market. So God is being sold in the market? You have installed it with your own hands in the temple; at what point did it become God? – because in the shop of the sculptor it is not worshipped. People are haggling for its price; nobody is praying to it! Nobody thinks that these are gods, because there are so many statues. And you can choose according to *your* liking.

"You haggled for the price, you purchased the statue, and I have been an observer all the time, waiting to see at what moment the stone statue becomes God, at what moment it is not a commodity to be purchased and sold, but a divinity to be worshipped."

They had no explanation. There *is* no explanation, because in fact it never becomes God; it is still a statue. It is just no longer in the shop, it is in the temple.

And what is the temple? – another house.

I was asking them, "I want to participate with you in your prayers, in your worship; I don't want to remain an outsider. But I cannot do it against myself. First I have to be satisfied, and you don't give any answer that is satisfying. And what are you saying in your prayers?

"'Give us this,' 'Give us that' – and do you see the whole hilarious scene? You have purchased a stone statue, installed it in a house, and now you are begging from the statue, which is purchased by you, 'Give us this,' 'Give us that…prosperity to our family, health to our family.' You are behaving very strangely, in a weird way, and I cannot participate in it.

"I don't want to disobey for disobedience's sake. And this is not disobedience; I am ready to follow your order, but you are not prepared to give it to me. You never asked your own parents. They lived in ignorance, you are living in ignorance, and you want me also to live in ignorance."

They thought that I would cool down by and by. They used to take me to the temple. They would all bow down, and I would stand by the side. And my father would say to me, "Just for our sake…it doesn't look good. It looks odd that you stand by the side when everybody is bowing down with so much religiousness."

I said, "I don't see any religiousness; I simply see a certain kind of exercise. And if these people are so much interested in exercise, they can go to a gymnasium, which will *really* give them health.

"Here they are asking, 'Give us health,' and 'Give us wealth.' Go to the gymnasium and there you will get health, and you will have real exercises. This is not much! And you are right that it looks odd – not my standing here, but you all doing all kinds of stupid rituals. *You* are odd. I may be in the minority, but I am not odd.

"And you say for your sake I should participate. Why are you not participating with me for my sake? You all should stand in a line in the corner – that will show that you really want to participate."

Finally he told me, "It is better you don't come to the temple, because other people come and they see you, and you are always doing something nasty."

I said, "What?"…because I was always sitting with my back towards God, which is not allowed – that is "nasty."

I said, "If God is omnipotent, he can change his position. Why should I be bothered about it? But he goes on sitting in the same position. If he does not want to see my back, he can move; he can start looking at the other side. I am more alive than your God, that's why you tell *me* to change my position; you don't tell your God. You know that he is dead."

And they said, "Don't say such things!"

I said, "What can I do? He does not breathe, he does not speak, and I don't think he hears, because a man who is not breathing, who is not seeing, who cannot move, cannot hear – all these things happen in an organic unity, and the organism has to be alive. So to whom are you praying?"

And slowly, slowly I persuaded my family to get rid of the temple. It was made by my family, but then they gave it to the community; they stopped going there. I told them, "Unless you explain it to me, your going shows that you are not behaving intelligently."

So the question is not the story. The story is a simplification of the complicated life situations where explanations have never been given. For thousands of years man has lived without explanations, has lived in obedience, has not questioned, has not doubted, has not been skeptical; has been afraid to, because these are all sins – obedience is virtue.

To me obedience is not virtue: intelligence is virtue. If you follow something because it appeals to your intelligence, it becomes virtuous. And if you don't follow something because your intelligence is against it, it has not to be condemned as sin.

The mind of man, for centuries, has been conditioned to obey.

I want a society where we will drop all those things which cannot be explained. Then only, obedience can be dropped.

I have not removed God without any reason; it is all a connected whole. If God is not removed, obedience remains in religion. Then religion never becomes a scientific approach towards your own interiority.

So *anything* that cannot be explained should not be ordered. Those things should be taken out of the human mind. But then, what remains of your religion? God disappears, hell and heaven disappear.

Mahavira believed in three hells, because people are committing sins of different categories. Naturally, to put all of them in one hell and punish them in the same way is illogical. He was a man of logic; he was very mathematical. You will be surprised to know that twenty-five centuries ago he said everything about the theory of relativity that Einstein discovered in this century. Of course not in such minute detail, because he had no way to experiment; it was just his vision….

So he has three hells. Christianity has only one, Mohammedanism has only one, Judaism has only one – why does Mahavira insist on three? Because he can see that it is unjustified: somebody has committed a small sin, has simply stolen a little money from somebody else, and somebody has killed many people, murdered, raped. Now putting them together with the same punishment is illogical. So he has three categories.

In the first will be the light sinners: the people who have been smoking, and drinking tea and coffee, and eating ice cream, etc. They are not doing very great sins, so just the first hell will be for them, just to give them a little torture. Not to give them their ice cream will be enough; to put them in hellfire seems too much!

In the second will be the heavier sinners. And in the third will be the most heavy ones, the greatest sinners.

But it is not so easy to categorize into three. Buddha has seven hells, because he sees that with three you still cannot be fair, because there are so many kinds of people and so many kinds of sins that a little more scope is needed to be fair. He has seven hells. But nobody has any explanation; nobody can prove their existence. It is just hypothetical.

There was a man, Sanjay Belattiputta who was also a great teacher, contemporary to Buddha and Mahavira. He has seven hundred hells because, he says, "These people don't understand the complexity." And I think he is right.

As far as complexity is concerned, even seven hundred hells may not be enough. You may have to find a hell for everyone, for every single sinner, because two sinners cannot be put together: it will be unfair to this person, or to that person. There is no criterion, no weighing machine so that you can decide how much sin you have done, how many kilos.

But it is all hypothetical. And whom to listen to? – all the three persons are great teachers, great masters. But what they are saying, although it seems to be reasonable, is still hypothetical. Somebody may come and

may talk about seven thousand, and you cannot refute them and you cannot prove what they say.

Once you ask for an explanation for everything, your religions will start withering away. Your political ideologies will be found to be based on nonsense.

For example, communism is based on the equality of man – and there are not two men who are equal, or have ever been equal. It is psychological nonsense to talk of the equality of man.

Each individual is unique; there is no question of comparison.

All that your mind is filled with – if you take it item by item and try to find out evidence, proof, explanation, you will be surprised: you are carrying an unnecessary load.

Yes, there are things which cannot be explained but still they are true. But they are not to be ordered either; they have to be learned in a deep, loving atmosphere.

If you trust a master, if you love a master, if you can feel his authenticity, sincerity, his humanness, then perhaps he can talk about things which *are* but can only be experienced, which cannot be explained. But such a man will not order you to believe in him.

For example, I cannot tell you to believe in reincarnation, although I know it is a truth. But because I cannot prove it, I cannot ask you to believe in it. I can only ask you to explore, to go deeper into your meditation, to go deeper into your own being, so that you can reach to when you were born; and still a little deeper, so that you can feel that you are in your mother's womb.

You have been in your mother's womb, and the memory of it is carried by you. Go further back, and you can see the moment in which you were conceived, the moment when your father and mother provided the opportunity for your soul to enter into a body. Go back a little more, and you can see yourself dying – your past life's end. You can move backwards into a few lives, but that will be your experience; still you cannot explain to anybody else, and you cannot insist that they should believe your experience. You may be hallucinating, it may be an illusion, it may be a dream. It is not – because dreams have different definitions.

You cannot repeat a dream. Have you thought about it? You see a dream, and tomorrow you want to repeat it – can you repeat it?

It is beyond you. It may come sometime, but you cannot repeat it.

But by going into your past life, you can repeat; it is within your hands, it is not a dream.

A hallucination needs unconsciousness, a drugged state. In meditation you are not unconscious, you are conscious – more conscious than ever; hence your experience of past lives cannot be a hallucination. But these are your inner experiences, and they remain individual.

There are things which cannot be explained; they are there, but they need not be ordered. They have also been ordered – to be a Hindu you have to believe in reincarnation. But the person who believes in reincarnation knows nothing about it. And every belief dulls your intelligence.

So it is right that Mulla Nasruddin's father could have explained to his son rather than ordering him, but he is ordering because otherwise the story would have lost all meaning. The story is a Sufi story; it has a certain purpose. If the father had explained, and Mulla Nasruddin had followed the explanation, what story would there be?

The story is there to indicate something about human beliefs, which can only be ordered, which can only be obeyed, which cannot be explained. And if the younger generation wants to get rid of them, the only way is to disobey *everything* that does not convince them.

Disobedience is an art.

It is not against anybody, and it is not something hard. You can be very polite, you can be really nice, and yet disobedient. It looks difficult because we have become accustomed to the association that the disobedient person is a hard person, that he is not gentle, that he is not nice. That is a wrong association.

I have disobeyed my whole life – my parents, my teachers, my elders – but I have never let them feel that I am in any way disrespectful to them, or that I am being nasty to them.

Disobedience is a greater art than obedience. Obedience needs no art.

One of my professors, Professor S.S. Roy, was in deep love with me – so much so that at times he would say, "Okay, so you come here, near the board, and you explain to the class if you feel my explanation is not enough, or is not adequate." And he would go and sit in my place, and I would stand in his place and teach the class.

I asked him again and again, "Do you feel that I am disrespectful to you?"

He said, "Never. Don't be worried about it." He was very much concerned that I go to the examination hall, because he knew perfectly well that I was not interested in examinations or in getting degrees or anything. I was in the university to sharpen my intelligence, not to get a certificate. So he would come to my room, take me in his car to the examination hall, see with his own eyes that I had entered into the hall – and then he would leave.

I told him the first day, "I have not prepared at all about this subject. And I am going to be absolutely original, because any answer that I am going to give will not be found in any book!"

He said, "My God, why did you not tell me? – because I have set this paper. Don't be worried, there is still time."

He took out his notebook and gave me five questions, and told me, sitting in the car, answers to each, in short. He said, "I am giving you just the essential answers, then you can elaborate."

When he was finished, I told him, "Don't feel hurt – I will not use a single sentence of what you have told me, because it is unfair. You have set the paper; you should not let me know. You have created more difficulty for me. Now I will have to avoid everything that you have said."

He said, "You are strange!"

I said, "I am not strange, I am simply saying that you have done wrong; now please don't force me to do wrong." And it was a difficult paper because he had given me the questions, he had given me the answers, and I had to avoid his answers. But it was a great exercise to find my own answers – absolutely clean, unpolluted. And he was also the examiner of that paper, so as my paper reached to him and he saw it, he could not believe his eyes: I had really avoided *every-thing* that he had said; I had not even used one word.

He called me, and said, "I am sorry that I gave you such trouble. I can see how difficult it must have been for you to avoid all the right answers, and yet remain right. But you did well, and I am giving you ninety-nine percent marks. I wanted to give you one hundred percent, but that would look a little too much, so I have cut one mark. But to you I can say that that was my desire – to give you one hundred percent marks, for the simple reason that you have been able to avoid all the real answers and yet you have managed to answer my questions relevantly. And these answers you have given cannot be found in any textbook; it must have been a strain on you."

I said, "No, it has not been. It has been just a play, just an exercise."

"Still," he asked, "why did you not listen to me? That would have been the easiest thing."

I said, "You know that I cannot do anything which is unfair; no other student knew it. Now these ninety-nine percent are my own earning. If I had repeated your answers I would have always felt guilty that I was part of some unfair process. But don't feel hurt; I have not rejected your answers for any other reason."

You can be disobedient with great artfulness; in fact you will have to learn much artfulness to be disobedient. So to anything that has no explanation, and is being forced on you, it is good to say no.

But there will come a moment in your life when you are close to a mystic – then don't ask for explanations, because he is not ordering you to believe anything or disbelieve anything. He is simply opening his heart to you. He is not asking for any response from you, so the question of obedience and disobedience does not arise.

Don't ask explanations from him.

Ask how to experience what he is saying.

So there is a world of explanations, which is mundane.

And there is a world of experience, which is really the very truth, the very essence of life, the very foundation of existence.

Beloved Bhagwan,
Are we really looking for the answer to our numerous questions?

It occurs to me there must be, for each of us present here, one question that characterizes us, and which, if we could just pinpoint it, would act like a beacon. Then that question would be enough in itself and without the need for an answer.

In fact there is *no* question which will be an answer to you. The reality is unquestionably here. All your questions are not really in search of answers – but they can put you in great trouble.

If the man you are asking the question to is a scholar, a pedagogue, then he can give you an answer which will create thousands of questions. You had come only with one question; he has given one answer. Now that answer creates thousands of questions – and that's how it has been going on in philosophy, in theology. Each question leads to an answer, and that answer leads to many questions. And this goes on growing.

In fact, if the man you are asking knows, then he is not answering your question; he is destroying it. He is trying that you get rid of it. He is not putting an answer in its place, because then that will torture you.

This is the real work of a master, a mystic, that sooner or later the people who are with him start feeling questionless.

To be questionless is the answer.

There is no answer…it is not that when you are questionless all your questions have been demolished. It is not that you come upon a hidden answer.

No, there is nothing hidden.

All the rubbish has been removed. You feel just a clean and clear consciousness. This is the answer… Not the answer to any question, but the state of no question is the answer that we are seeking and searching. Every question is a burden, every question is a wound, every question is a tension. And to be questionless, to be completely free of all questions…

There is a story in the life of Mevlana Jalaluddin Rumi. He was working with his disciples in the desert, in a small monastery. A few travelers passing by, just out of curiosity stopped and went in. They saw that in the courtyard the students were sitting, the disciples were sitting, and Mevlana – Mevlana means the beloved master – Mevlana Rumi was answering them.

They got fed up, because strange questions and strange answers…they went on their way. After years of traveling, they came back, and stopped again to see what was happening. Only Mevlana Rumi was sitting there, and there were no disciples. They were really shocked – what had happened? They went to Mevlana and they said, "What happened?"

Mevlana laughed. He said, "This is my whole work. I crushed all their questions, and now they have no questions so I have told them, 'Go and do the same to others: crush their questions. And if you find somebody you cannot manage, send him here!'"

When all questions are removed, you are again a child, utterly innocent. Then your mind is bound to be silent, and there is no possibility of it getting disturbed. And a great serenity…

This is the answer. There are no words in it, and it is not relevant to any question in particular; it is only a state of silence.

Chapter 13
April 18, 1986, Evening

Beloved Bhagwan,

Modern Christians are making desperate attempts to save their religion from its primitive, superstitious past — and from the fundamentalists!

For example, a modernist in the Church of England believes, it is said, in a God who works through evolutionary processes only, does not doubt the existence of Jesus Christ, but would not lose his faith if it were to be proved that Jesus never existed, and claims to believe in the supernatural, but not in the miraculous. His Jesus did not perform miracles and was not born of a virgin. The tomb was not empty. Ethics are more important to the modernist than doctrine.

Down the same path is traveling our old friend, the Bishop of Durham, who got into trouble for his comments last year about the virgin birth and resurrection. He was recently quoted as saying, "Either God does not exist or else he must establish his own existence."

Is the resurrection of Christianity any more likely than that of a Jesus Christ himself?

Christianity Is An Empty Box

The resurrection of Jesus Christ may be possible, but not the resurrection of Christianity.

In fact Jesus never died on the cross. It takes at least forty-eight hours for a person to die on the Jewish cross; and there have been known cases where people have existed almost six days on the cross without dying. Because Jesus was taken down from the cross after only six hours, there is no possibility of his dying on the cross. It was a conspiracy between a rich sympathizer of Jesus and Pontius Pilate to crucify Jesus as late as possible on Friday – because on Saturday, Jews stop everything; their Sabbath does not allow any act. By the evening of Friday everything stops.

The arrangement was that Jesus would be crucified late in the afternoon, so before sunset he would be brought down. He might have been unconscious because so much blood had flowed out of the body, but he was not dead. Then he would be kept in a cave, and before the Sabbath ended and the Jews hung him again, his body would be stolen by his followers. The tomb was found empty, and Jesus was removed from Judea as quickly as possible. As he again became healthy and healed, he moved to India and he lived a long life – one hundred and twelve years – in Kashmir.

It is a coincidence, but a beautiful coincidence, that Moses died in Kashmir and Jesus also died in Kashmir. I have been to the graves of both. The graves are ample proof, because those are the only two graves that are not pointing towards Mecca. Mohammedans make their graves with the head pointing towards Mecca, so in the whole world all the graves of Mohammedans point towards Mecca, and Kashmir is Mohammedan.

These two graves don't point towards Mecca, and the writing on the graves is in Hebrew, which is impossible on a Mohammedan grave – Hebrew is not their language. The name of Jesus is written exactly as it was pronounced by the Jews, "Joshua." "Jesus" is a Christian conversion of the Jewish name. The grave is certainly of Jesus.

A family has been taking care of both the graves – they are very close together in one place, Pahalgam – and only one family has been taking care of them down the centuries. They are Jews – they are still Jews – and I had to take their help to read to me what is written on the graves.

Moses had come to Kashmir to find a tribe of Jews who were lost on the way from Egypt to Jerusalem. When he reached Jerusalem his deep concern was the whole tribe that had got lost somewhere in the desert. When his people were established in Jerusalem, he went in search of the lost tribe, and he found the lost tribe established in Kashmir. Kashmiris are basically Jewish – later on Mohammedans forcibly converted them – and Moses lived with them and died there.

Jesus also went to Kashmir, because then it was known that Moses had found the lost tribe there. The doors of Judea were closed – he would be hanged again – and the only place where he would find the people who speak the same language, the people who have a same kind of mind, where he would not be a foreigner, was Kashmir. So it was natural for him to go to Kashmir.

But he had learned his lesson. He had dropped the idea of being the only begotten son of God; otherwise these Jews would crucify him too. He dropped the idea of being a messiah. He lived with his few intimate friends and followers in Pahalgam.

Pahalgam is named after Jesus, because he used to call himself "the shepherd" – Pahalgam means "the town of the shepherd." So it was a small colony of Jesus and his friends, surrounding the grave of their forefather and the founder of Judaic tradition. Jesus remained a Jew to the very end; he never heard about Christianity.

But the followers who were left in Judea managed to create the story of resurrection. And there was no way to prove it this way or that. Neither could they produce Jesus – if he was resurrected then where was he? Nor could the other party prove what had happened. They had put such a big rock on the mouth of the cave that it was impossible for Jesus to have removed it, and there was a Roman soldier on duty twenty-four hours, so there was no possibility of anybody else removing the rock and taking the body.

But because Pontius Pilate was from the very beginning against crucifying Jesus.... He could see the man was absolutely innocent. He has some crazy ideas, but they are not criminal. And what harm does it do to somebody? If someone thinks he is the only begotten son of God, let him enjoy it. Why disturb him, and why get disturbed? If somebody thinks he is the messiah and he has brought the message of God...if you want to listen, listen; if you don't want to listen, don't listen. But there is no need to crucify the man.

But Jesus learned his lesson – learned the hard way. In Kashmir he lived very silently with his group, praying, living peacefully, no longer trying to change the world. And Kashmir was so far away from Judea that in Judea the story of resurrection, amongst the followers of Jesus, became significant.

So I say a kind of resurrection certainly happened – it was a conspiracy more than a resurrection. But certainly Jesus did not die on the cross, he did not die in the cave where he was put; he lived long enough.

But Christianity cannot even *conspire* to revive itself, to resurrect itself. There is a great movement among Christian theologians, and they are making desperate efforts. Their very efforts show that they are going to fail. In fact their efforts are ridiculous.

There is one theologian who says, "There is no God, and we have to accept godless Christianity." He knows that it is impossible to prove God to the coming generation; to the young and the fresh mind it is impossible to prove God. And the days of belief are over. It is a scientific age: you must prove, give the evidence; nobody is going to accept something just by your saying it. So he is ready to sacrifice God to save Christianity. What will Christianity be without God?

There is another theologian who is ready to believe that perhaps Jesus is only a myth, he never existed. It is as difficult to prove Jesus' existence as the existence of God, because no contemporary literature even mentions his name. There is no proof other than those four gospels of his own disciples – they cannot be called proof. This theologian is willing to drop Jesus to save Christianity, but what will Christianity be without God, without Jesus? But they are so desperate to save Christianity that they don't see the implications of what they are doing.

Another theologian says there have been no miracles; all miracles are just inventions of the followers. Up to now, for two thousand years, Christianity has depended on the miracles. Those were its basic foundations to prove it a superior religion to any other religion – because Gautam Buddha does not walk on water, Mahavira cannot revive a dead man, Krishna cannot heal the sick just by touching them, Mohammed cannot make wine out of water.

These miracles have been, for two thousand years, the superiority of Christianity over all religions; otherwise what has Christianity got? But he is ready to drop the miracles because now they are continuously hammered. Nobody is ready to believe in them – they go against the very way things are. And nature does not change its rules, its laws, for anybody; it does not take anybody as an exception. So the new theologian feels embarrassed. He knows himself that it is impossible to prove the miracles.

I asked the archbishop in Bombay, "You represent Jesus, the pope represents Jesus. You should do at least some little miracles as evidence that you are really representatives; otherwise what have you got to prove that you *are* the representative? Walk on water, and the whole world will become Christian. And you say faith in Jesus can do miracles – then try it! You must have faith."

But no theologian, nor any pope, is ready to walk on water. They all know that nature does not change its laws for anybody.

So it is a bold step, but very dangerous. If you take away all the miracles of Jesus then a very poor man, just a carpenter's son, is left behind, with nothing to be compared with Gautam Buddha or Mahavira or Zarathustra. Really you take away all his glory which depends on miracles. But you cannot prove miracles, and because you cannot prove miracles you create suspicion about Jesus. So it is better to drop miracles; at least the suspicion about Jesus will be dropped. But you don't understand the implication: without miracles Jesus means nothing.

Without miracles Buddha remains the same, because he never did any miracles. People loved him not for his miracles. People loved him for his clarity of perception, of seeing into the very root of things, of giving insights to people to transform life. Walking on water is simply stupid. Even if you can do it, then too it is not a miracle, it is simply stupidity, because you will remain the same. You will not come out of the water a transformed human being.

Just to give you an idea of how Gautam Buddha and Jesus will behave in a similar situation…. Lazarus is dead. His sisters are great devotees – Lazarus was a great friend of Jesus. They send a message to him, "Come, Lazarus is dead!" And they keep his body inside a cave. Jesus comes and he calls Lazarus, standing outside the cave, "Lazarus, come out!"

Lazarus says, "Have you come? Great, I am coming!" And he comes out. It seems to be dramatic, it seems to be all planned. It seems the man was not dead. He was a friend, his two sisters were devotees – it was as if he was simply sitting there, waiting.

But it is not a miracle. And even if it is a miracle, even if Lazarus comes back to life, he is not transformed. We don't hear anything else again of Lazarus. A man who has died, a man who has gone through the process of death to the beyond, who comes back, cannot be the same. Lazarus would have become a great master, but he remained the same person – no change at all.

In a similar situation Gautam Buddha behaves differently, and I think that is the way any wise man will behave. A woman, Krishagautami, had only one son. Her husband had died, her other children had died; she had seen death in its brutal ugliness. Only one son remained, and she was living only for him; otherwise there was nothing for her to live for. She wanted to kill herself; she had lost everything – all those people she had loved and lived for. But her neighbors suggested, "One son is alive – without you he will also be dead. Take care of him. We understand your sorrow…"

But one day that boy also died, and Krishagautami went completely mad. It was a coincidence that Buddha was staying in the same city of Shravasti. Somebody suggested to Krishagautami, "A great mystic is here. Why don't you take your son to him? He can do anything; he is a man of tremendous power. Seeing your situation, and knowing his compassion, something is possible. Perhaps your son may come back to life."

Krishagautami went with the dead body. She put the body at the feet of Gautam Buddha and said, "I have lost everything – all my children, my husband. I was living only for this son; now he is also dead. I have heard much about your compassion. Now is the time to show it. Let my son get up again, resurrect him."

Buddha said, "On one condition: you go into the town…to resurrect your child I need a few mustard seeds, but they should be from a family where nobody has ever died."

Krishagautami was not in a state of mind to realize that this was impossible, that the condition could not be fulfilled. She went from one house to another and people said, "We can give you as many mustard seeds as you want. We can fill our bullock carts with mustard seeds and bring them to Gautam Buddha if your son can be revived. But our mustard seeds won't help, because not only one but thousands must have died in our family. For generations after generations, people have been dying. These mustard seeds are not going to fulfill the condition."

She went on, and the same was the answer everywhere. She went to the king of Shravasti and told him, "Can't you do just a small thing for me? A few mustard seeds and my son can be back, alive."

The king said, "You can have as many mustard seeds as you want."

But the woman said, "There is a condition, and the condition is that in your family no one should have died. And your family is royal – certainly you will fulfill my condition."

The king said, with tears in his eyes, "Royal or not royal, death makes no difference. My father has died, my son has died, and an unaccountable number of people must have died in my family before I was born. You have to forgive me; I can give you anything you want, but that condition cannot be fulfilled."

The whole day going round the city, the woman became alert of a fact…death is inevitable, today or tomorrow.

After seeing the king she came back to Buddha, touched his feet and said, "Please forgive me. I was asking you to do something against nature, and you were wise enough not to say no to me. Instead you gave me an opportunity to understand that my asking was wrong. Please initiate me. I don't have anything to live for, but I would like to know what it is that lives and what it is that dies." Buddha initiated her, and she became one of the great meditators among his followers.

Now, which one do you think is a miracle, Lazarus or Krishagautami? Which one do you think is doing the miracle? – Jesus or Gautam Buddha?

Gautam Buddha is not doing a miracle at all, but if you understand it rightly, he *is* doing the miracle, because he is changing the woman from a mad state into a meditative state. Even if Lazarus becomes alive he remains Lazarus, and one day he will die again, so what is the point?

But Christianity has depended on these miracles in proving its superiority over other religions; in fact those religions are far superior, because they don't depend on such stupid, childish ideas. So there are theologians who are ready to drop all miracles. But if you drop all miracles then Jesus is left naked; you have taken all his clothes, he has nothing to give to the world.

One theologian takes God away, another theologian makes Jesus himself a myth, another theologian takes miracles away, and the fourth theologian takes religion itself away – he wants a religionless Christianity, but Christianity has to remain! I don't understand: when you have taken all the contents, why cling to the box? Now even religion has to be taken away because half of humanity is already religionless.

The communists don't believe in religion, and the communists are not only in the

CHRISTIANITY IS AN EMPTY BOX

communist countries, which is half of humanity; communists are in other countries also. In fact, three-fourths of humanity has already dropped religion. The remaining ones are only formally religious. They are not much disturbed by the idea of taking religion out. But then what remains?

It seems you are clinging just to the label, to the name "Christianity." It is a desperate effort, and stupid too. Why not accept that Christianity is dead? God is dead, miracles are dead, religion is dead, Jesus is no longer born out of a virgin Mary – so what are you saving?

I have been looking into all these theologians who are prominent people in the Christian world. They have taken all the contents; only an empty box… But why carry on this empty box? For what reason? Just an old habit, an old attachment.

And then there is another effort…because you cannot carry an empty box for long; you will also feel that you are doing something foolish. And others will start feeling, when they look into your box, that you have a great Christianity! – Jesus is missing, God is missing, miracles are not there, the virgin Mary is not there. All that was Christianity is not there; then why are you carrying this empty box? So there is another effort going on, side by side, to fill the box with something.

So Christian theologians are studying other religions, so as to have something similar. It is going to be imitation, unauthentic, because it is not *their* experience. They call it "comparative religion"; in all Christian colleges they study comparative religion.

I asked the professors and the principals of those colleges, "Why should you be worried about other religions? – you have Christianity." But the problem is that they have to fill the box with something, so from other religions they are collecting ideas.

They are studying psychoanalysis. Now every Christian preacher has compulsorily to study psychoanalysis. Now, what does psychoanalysis have to do with religion? But the problem is, what religion used to do was to console people in their misery. Now they don't have that religion at all, so they have to find some contemporary way to console people. And psychoanalysis is a very thriving business all around the world; the most highly-paid professionals are psychoanalysts. So Christians think, "They must be doing something for people. Let us learn their art and use it to save Christianity." But they don't understand that Freud was against religion, the whole of psychoanalysis is against religion. They *cannot* use it.

They are studying Karl Marx because the man has converted three-fourths of humanity; he must have something – the idea of equality of human beings. Although he is against religion and against God, he has certain values; those values can be taken.

They are collecting all kinds of things in the box where Christianity used to be. It is so eclectic that it does not make one organic whole. If you look into the box you will get into a madness, because the things they are taking belong to different systems. Within those systems they have a living quality; out of those systems they are dead. Somebody's eyes, somebody's hand, somebody's legs, somebody's heart….

And do you think in your box there will come a man, because you have arranged everything that is needed for a man? – hands, head, eyes, heart. Everything is there, but it is just nonsense. Those eyes were able to see in an organic unity in a body; now they cannot see. There is no organic unity, and you cannot bring an organic unity.

Christianity *is* dead.

Their desperate effort to save it simply *confirms* that it is dead. But it needs guts to accept it.

You will be surprised to know that when Joseph Stalin died it was not declared to the world. It took a few days for the communist high command...because they had believed that this man is immortal. Stalin, man of steel, he cannot die! But men of steel, whatever your conception may be, have to follow nature: he died. For a few days they delayed informing the world. In fact they could not believe it, but finally they had to accept that Stalin was dead.

The same happened with Mao Tse-tung. His death was not immediately reported to the world because he had become a god.

I know about Sri Aurobindo, because he himself was teaching his whole life that his special work was to give methods to people to attain physical immortality. All old teachers have taught you *spiritual* immortality; that's not a big problem, because the spiritual element in you is already immortal.

He used to say, "I am doing the *real* thing. The physical body, which is not immortal, I am going to make it immortal." And one day he died.

One of my friends was there in Pondicherry, in his ashram. He told me, "For seven days we were hiding the fact that Aurobindo had died. We could not believe it ourselves, because if he himself is not immortal, then what about us who have gathered here just to become physically immortal? And the man who was going to make us physically immortal is dead! Now we cannot even say him, 'You deceived us. What happened?' To declare it to the world looks so embarrassing.'"

The chief disciple, "the Mother" of the Sri Aurobindo ashram, finally found a solution to it. She said, "He is not dead, he has gone into deep samadhi, the deepest that anyone has ever gone. He will wake up again – he is simply asleep."

So they made a marble grave for him, with all the comforts, because he was just sleeping and one day he was going to wake up; this was his last experiment in physical immortality. Then years passed, but he did not knock from the grave.

People started suspecting, but the mother was over ninety, and she was still preaching physical immortality.

Then one day *she* died. And it was very difficult for the believers, because the believers had some investment; their investment was their own immortality. If both the leaders were dead, then there was no hope for them. And they had not yet told them the real secret; they had been telling them that they were working on it.

Sri Aurobindo used to give an audience only once a year to his disciples. The rest of the year he was working constantly – that was the idea in the ashram for physical immortality. Now both are lying in their graves, and there are still idiots living in the ashram, believing that they will awake one day.

Idiots are also miracles – they still believe. My friend who has been there, and still is there, is a doctor of philosophy, but he still believes. He has been coming to see me, but there is no way to convince him. I tried every possible way, but he said, "Patanjali himself says in the *Yoga Sutras* that *samadhi* and *susupti* – samadhi and deep sleep – are exactly alike. They have gone into deep sleep to find out the secret of physical immortality."

I said, "But how long will it take? By that time you will all be dead! Even if they come... You just go and open the grave, and you will know that it is no longer sleep. There are only skeletons, stinking of death, not the fragrance of immortality."

But the believer is such that he goes on believing, because his belief is basically for a reason: he is afraid that perhaps they are dead, and then what about him? And that stops him – the idea that they are dead. Do you see the point? He cannot accept that Sri Aurobindo and the mother are dead because that means *he* will have to die – and he does not want to die. That's why he has come and lived there for years, waiting for the secret to be revealed. He will wait: "They are asleep and working."

Desperate efforts…and they happen only when something is really gone and you don't have it. Then you get into a frenzy of creating some way that you can continue to believe in it. For example, *The Bible* believes that God created the world four thousand and four years before Jesus Christ, which is only six thousand years before now. Now, that is disproved so abundantly that it is absolutely wrong.

In India we have found cities which were lying hidden underneath the earth, seven thousand years old – and not ordinary cities. I have been to Harrapur, Mohanjodro – both are in Pakistan now – and it is something to see. Seven thousand is a very orthodox idea; there are scholars who say they must be more than fifteen thousand years old. But even if they are only seven thousand years old, there must have been a long past to those cities, because that kind of city cannot be created instantly.

They have bigger roads than New York. Now, a city seven thousand years old, having a wider road than New York…it means they must have had vehicles, traffic, otherwise why create such a road? They had beautiful bathrooms, they had a system of running water. Even if they were seven thousand years old, they must have been developed for thousands of years to come to such technology, to such plumbing, that they can have running water in their bathrooms, in their houses. They had swimming pools…

In China we have found human bodies, frozen in ice, ninety thousand years old. Now, when all these facts came to the Christian theologians, there was great turmoil: What to do? – because God created the world six thousand years ago.

I am giving you this example of how a desperate believer functions.

One theologian came up with the idea, which became accepted by the whole Christianity, that God created the world exactly as it is said in *The Bible,* six thousand years ago, with cities under the earth, with bathrooms, with plumbing, with wide roads, with ninety-thousand-year-old bodies…just to test your faith! "God can do anything. If he can create the world, do you think he cannot create something that looks ninety thousand years old to all scientific investigation? But the world *was* created six thousand years ago."

A desperate effort to cling to superstitions! But there comes a point where all your superstitions are proved to be superstitions. Then this situation arises that you start saying, "They are all superstitions, and we can drop them and still we can save Christianity."

You cannot. Those superstitions have been the very backbone of your Christianity. Without those superstitions your Christianity will lose all its life. And it will be *more* absurd to believe in a Christianity devoid of all superstitions, miracles, God – even of religion.

Now they are saying it is only ethics, not doctrine. But ethics need not be Christian – ethics has nothing to do with Christianity. Ethics is a science in itself. I have been a teacher of ethics, and I had never thought that ethics can be Christian. Ethics asks what is truth? what is good? what is bad? It has nothing to do with religion; it has something to do with your actions. And it is the same for everybody. Whether you are in Tibet or China or in America, it does not make any difference, the ethical standard will be the same. Ethics is a science complete in itself.

Now, finding nothing in their doctrines, they are falling back on ethics, saying that the essential thing is not doctrine – because all their doctrines have been proved wrong. Up to now it was doctrine; now because all doctrines are proved wrong, or at least questionable, and they have not been able substantially to support their doctrines and their truth…

This is the last effort of a dying religion. You drop those doctrines – they are dangerous, they are killing you – so you jump upon something else that can give you a resurrection. But ethics is purely a science in itself. It thinks about values – which have nothing to do with being Hindu, Mohammedan or Christian. Ethics is not going to save Christianity; it is not going to give a resurrection.

There is no possibility for Christianity, and it will be good that they accept it and drop the dead body. It is a great load, and by carrying it unnecessarily, you are missing your life. And living with a dead religion you are bound to become dead. Your churches are graveyards. There is no song of life, there is no dance of existence.

It is better to simply get out of the old habit. These are just old habits. I don't know why Christian priests', nuns', bishops' old clothes are called habits – I don't know. But one thing I know: just drop the habit! – whatever it means. Just be natural and human.

It is not only a question of Christianity.

Your question was concerned with Christianity; otherwise the same is the situation with other religions.

Man has come of age, and he does not need those old, superstitious religions; he needs a more scientific approach to explore his being. And that will be possible only if he gets rid of the old habits. And they are very dirty, because for thousands of years the same habits have been used by so many people. They are stinking! Get out of those habits as quickly as possible.

Beloved Bhagwan,
This morning, as You spoke of the "questionless answer," I watched my questions dissolving into silence, which I shared for a moment with You. But one question survived, and that is: If we don't ask You questions, how are we going to play with You?

That's really a question!
It will be difficult, so whether you have the questions or not, still you can go on asking just the same. Your question need not be yours, but it must be somebody else's, somewhere. And my answer may help somebody somewhere, sometime. So let us continue the game.

I cannot say anything on my own. Unless there is a question, I am silent. Because of the question it is possible for me to respond. So it does not matter whether the question is yours; what matters is that the question is bound to be somebody's somewhere.

And I am not only answering you. I am answering, through you, the whole of humanity…not only the contemporary humanity, but also the humanity that will be coming when I will not be here to answer.

So find out all the possible angles and questions, so that anybody, even in the future when I am not here, who has a question can find an answer in my words.

To us it is a play. To somebody it may become really a question of life and death.

Beloved Bhagwan,
Questions seem to be the offspring of the capacity to doubt; and doubt, the spark of an alive and active intelligence.
Without questions – and thus, without doubt – how can intelligence continue to flourish?
And yet within You is the ultimate in silence and the ultimate in intelligence.

It is true in the beginning. Doubt helps your intelligence, sharpens it. Questioning makes you aware of many possibilities of which you may not have been aware before.

But this is only the beginning of the journey. At the end, when all your questions have disappeared...and the real master never gives you the answer. Let me repeat it: the real master never gives you the answer, so you cannot doubt it. He brings you to a point where all your questions disappear. His answers are murderous, killing your questions, destroying them mercilessly, to bring you to a point where there is no question in your consciousness.

The master does not give you any answer that you can doubt. This non-questioning consciousness *is* the answer. And it is your experience; you cannot doubt it, it is there.

From *this* point, silence and intelligence are just two aspects of the same thing. From this point, not knowing, innocence, and knowing are two aspects of the same thing.

This is the mysterious world which is available to you if you can pass the jungle of questions and doubts and reach into the clear, where there are no questions and doubts, and no answers either.

Just you are – in utter silence, with immense clarity, with tremendous sharpness.

That's why I am against belief, because it will never allow you to reach to this stage. It will stop you in the very beginning of the journey. It will not help to make you more intelligent; it will make you more unintelligent. It will make you more fanatic, superstitious, but it will not allow you to come into the clarity which can be called the very goal of what transpires between master and disciple: the moment of total silence, the moment where everything is crystal clear.

But it has to be earned. Belief is cheap. This will bring you something totally different, what I call trust in existence. In the dictionaries, trust and belief and faith are all synonymous – but not in reality.

Belief is opposite to trust. You believe because you have doubt; the belief is an antidote to doubt, it is a need to cover up the doubt. Trust is when you don't have any doubt, so trust is not a belief. Belief is always in *something* – in some doctrine, in some principle, in some philosophy.

Trust is in the totality of the cosmos. It has nothing to do with books – *Holy Bibles, Gitas, Korans* – no. Then there is only one scripture which is spread all around you – in the trees, in the rivers, in the ocean, in the stars. And you don't have to read it; you have to be just silent, and it starts showering on you all its wisdom, which is eternal.

I am against belief because I want you to come to the point of trust.

Chapter 14
April 19, 1986, Morning

Beloved Bhagwan,
Recently I heard You say that transcendence of life's misery and confusion can occur by either a let-go of life or by fight – as long as either is done with totality. Mahavira's way was fight, and Yours is let-go. Could You say more about let-go and its relationship to intelligence and responsibility? I don't have this understanding, and my life seems to be an odd mixture of let-go and fight. Let-go seems more natural, and fight seems more responsible.

It is not only your question, it is everybody's question – a mixture of let-go and fight. But your let-go is not my let-go; your let-go is simply a defeatist attitude. Basically you want to fight, but there are situations where you *cannot* fight, or perhaps you have come to the very end of your energy for fighting. Then, to cover up your defeat, you start thinking of let-go. Your let-go is not true, it is phony.

Real let-go is not against fight.

Real let-go is absence of fighting.

And you cannot mix real let-go with fighting attitudes, for the simple reason that the presence of let-go means the absence of a fighting attitude. How can you mix something which is present with something which is absent? Just as you cannot mix light and darkness, however great an artist you may be – you cannot mix light and darkness for the simple reason that darkness is only an absence of light. You cannot bring them together; only one can be present.

So the first thing to remember is that the basic attitude of every human being is to fight. So don't think of it particularly as your problem. It will help you immensely to understand that it is a human problem. Then you can stand aloof and watch it, observe it, understand it.

Let it Soak Within Your Heart

Fighting is a basic attitude because it feeds the ego. The more you fight, the more your ego becomes stronger. If you become victorious the ego has great joy. You are giving life to ego by your victories. But on the other hand, as the ego becomes stronger, your being is receding farther and farther away from you.

As your ego becomes stronger you are losing yourself. You may be fighting and being victorious, not knowing at all that it is not a gain but a loss. Each child is taught to fight in different ways. Competition is a fight, to come first in your class is a fight, to win a trophy in a game is a fight. These are preparations for your life. Then fight in the elections, fight for money, fight for prestige. This whole society is based on fighting, competition, struggle, putting each individual against the whole.

So it is almost everybody's situation. And then you listen to me about let-go.

Let-go means no competition, no struggle, no fight…just relaxing with existence, wherever it leads. Not trying to control your future, not trying to control consequences, but allowing them to happen…not even thinking about them. Let-go is in the present; consequences are tomorrow. And let-go is such a delightful experience, a total relaxation, a deep synchronicity with existence.

I am reminded of a parable. I call it a parable because it is so good it cannot be true. In the East, the name of Majnu is very famous. It is a Sufi story – perhaps nobody of that name existed, but it is irrelevant whether he existed or not. He has become the symbolic lover.

Majnu was a poor young man, with tremendous love and a great heart, and he fell in love with the richest man's daughter. The marriage was not possible; even meetings were not possible. He could only see once in a while, from far away, his beloved, Laila. But the rumor about his love started spreading, and the rich man, the father of Laila, was afraid that it would contaminate the family's name and he would not be able to find the right man for his daughter. So he left the village to go to a faraway country, where nobody will know anything about Majnu.

The day they were going, a great caravan…because he had so much money and so many things to take, hundreds of camels carrying things. Majnu was standing by the road, by the side of a tree, hiding himself in the foliage of the tree – because the father was so mad he even could shoot him, although he had not done anything. He had not even spoken to Laila.

He was standing there just to see her for the last time. It was enough for him that she was happy and healthy – and he would wait. If his love has any power, she will come back. There was tremendous trust in him. He had seen the love, the same flame that was burning in his heart, in the eyes of Laila too. Laila was also searching and looking all around from the camel she was riding. She knew Majnu must be waiting somewhere on the way, and then she saw him hiding under a tree in its thick foliage. For a moment, without a single word or gesture, they were one; and then the caravan passed.

But for Majnu time stopped then and there. He remained standing by the side of the tree waiting and waiting. It is said years passed. Laila came, but came a little late. She enquired; people said, "We have never heard about him. Since you left he has not come to the town again."

She rushed to the tree where she had left him. He was still there, but a strange thing had happened – he had become one with the tree. That's why I say it is a parable: it is too good to be true. He relaxed so utterly because there was nothing else to do but to wait. He relaxed with the tree, and slowly, slowly they started merging with each other. The tree became his nourishment; they were no longer separate, they became one. Branches grew out of his body. He was no longer hiding under the foliage; the foliage was on his body – beautiful leaves and beautiful, fragrant flowers.

Laila could not recognize him. But the whole tree was saying only one thing, "Laila...Laila!" She was getting mad, and asking, "Where are you hiding?" And the tree said, "I am not hiding. Waiting so long, doing nothing, and just being relaxed, I have become one with the tree. You came a little late.

"What was going to happen between us has happened between me and the tree. We were going to become one – that was not acceptable to destiny perhaps. But I was ready to relax in the moment, without thinking of any consequences. And I am happy that you are alive, still young, and more beautiful. But I am gone, far away. I am immensely happy...alone, relaxed, in a let-go."

To me, let-go means you are not fighting for anything in life, but giving everything to life to take care of. You say "let-go seems to be natural." It only 'seems'...because your whole conditioning is against it. You have been brought up for millions of years to fight. Fighting, either you can be defeated – which will create a wound, which will create revenge – or you can be victorious; which will again create another kind of wound. That is the ego. In either case you are a loser. Defeated you lose, victorious you lose. In either case you are going farther away from yourself.

Let-go has not been taught to people because it will go against the whole structure of the society – which is based on competition and fighting, where everybody is your enemy. Even your friend is your enemy, even your wife is your enemy, even your children are your enemies, because everybody is trying to snatch as much from you as possible.

And the same thing you are trying to do. The world of misery is created because everybody is snatching things from everybody else. It is not a peaceful, silent, loving existence; we are still barbarous and animalistic.

Let-go is totally a different approach. Its first step is dropping the ego, remembering that you are not separate from existence: with whom are you fighting? You are not separate from people: with whom are you fighting? With yourself...and that's the root cause of misery. With whomsoever you are fighting, you are fighting with yourself – because there is nobody else.

Let-go is a deep understanding of the phenomenon that we are part of one existence. We cannot afford to have separate egos; we are one with all. And the all is vast, immense. Your understanding will help you to go with the whole, wherever it is going. You don't have a goal separate from the whole, and the whole has no goal. It is not going anywhere. It is being simply here.

The understanding of let-go helps you to be simply here, without any goals, without any idea of achievement, without any conflict, struggle, fight, knowing that it is fighting with yourself – which is simply foolish.

Let-go is a deep understanding.

It is not an act that you have to do.

Every act is part of the world of fight. That which you have to *do* is going to be a fight. Let-go is simply understanding.

And then a silent relaxation, flowing with the river, unconcerned where it is going, unworried that you can get lost...no anxiety, no anguish, because you are not separate from the totality, so whatever is going to happen is going to be good.

With this understanding you will find there is no mixing: understanding cannot mix with ignorance; insight into existence cannot mix with blindness; consciousness cannot mix with unconsciousness.

And let-go cannot mix with different kinds of struggles – that is an impossibility.

Just let it sink within your heart, and you will find a new dimension opening up, in which each moment is a joy, in which each moment is an eternity unto itself.

Beloved Bhagwan,
I have heard You say, in connection with Martin Heidegger, that the work of a philosopher is to guide the leaders of the nations, not to follow them. Your work at this time seems to be moving in that direction. Your work is more global, involving whole nations and their people, and even transcending nations. Diogenes stood naked – and largely unknown – holding a lamp in broad daylight, and repeated the statement, "I am looking for a man." Is Your work really different from Diogenes' or does it only appear so? Are You also looking for a man?

Diogenes is one of the most loved human beings, as far as I am concerned. As far as the world is concerned, he is one of those who are destined to be condemned for their behavior, for their ideas. And Diogenes particularly, because he is so unique.

His ways would have been understood in the far East, in Japan; he would have become a great Zen master. In Greece he was simply condemned. He was not in the right place. First, he was naked – for a certain reason: naked we have come into the world, and all the animals are naked, why should man hide his wild body behind clothes?

And the strange insight was that it is not weather, cold or heat, that has prompted man to use clothes – because if all the animals can exist without clothes, there is no reason. And your face is naked, but it becomes immune. That's how the whole animal world lives. Small birds are more powerful than you: they are immune to cold and to heat. They don't need any clothes. Why did man need clothes? Not to protect his body but to hide it, because he is the only animal who has not been natural, and his body has become ugly. Now, Diogenes has a strange insight.

I agree with him, that clothes help you immensely to hide your body. Man has lost his natural beauty, agility, and that's why he had to discover clothes. It is very strange: if your naked body is brought before you, or just a photograph of your naked body is brought before you, you will not be able to recognize that it is your body. People are recognizable only by their faces; the whole body is ignored. And through clothes you can create the illusion of beauty. You can hide the ugly parts and you can expose the beautiful parts; you can emphasize the beautiful parts.

Diogenes was disgusted with the whole idea. This is exhibitionism, not what Sigmund Freud thinks is exhibitionism. I agree with Diogenes and not with Sigmund Freud.

Sigmund Freud calls a man exhibitionist if he tries to show his naked body to somebody. Diogenes calls all people who have been forced by your so-called civilization to wear clothes, exhibitionists. This is a beginning of deception, hypocrisy. And my feeling is that one day man will return to being naked, because only then he will regain his health again – for the simple reason that then he will have to be healthy, otherwise he will feel embarrassed. Then he will have to exercise, then he will have to go to some gymnasium and maintain his body and his beauty, because now it is not only his face that is his identity; now his whole body is his identity. And he will not be ashamed of it; it is his body and nature has given it to him. He will be proud of it.

Diogenes was as beautiful a man as Mahavira – both lived naked – so proportionate, so beautiful. In India Mahavira's nakedness became spiritual; in Greece Diogenes became a madman. He used to carry a lamp with him, and whomsoever he met – even in the full daylight – he would raise his lamp and look at the man. And people would ask, "What are you doing? It is full daylight, the sun is shining; why are you carrying a lamp? And why do you go on looking in people's faces?"

He used to say, "I am looking for a real, authentic man."

My search is, in a way, similar: I am also looking for a real, authentic man. But the real, authentic man cannot be searched for with a lamp.

Diogenes' lamp is only symbolic. It simply says that he is putting his whole lighted being as a beam on the person, as an X-ray, to see whether there is anything left or everything is hypocrisy. The day he died he had his lamp by his side, still in his hand. One man, just to joke, asked Diogenes, "Now you are dying. Before you die, please answer one question. Your whole life you have been searching for the authentic, real man, with your lamp. Have you found him or not?"

Diogenes was really a beautiful man. He laughed and said, "I have not found him, but I am grateful to the whole of humanity that nobody stole my lamp, because I found all kinds of thieves all around. An authentic man I have not been able to come across, but even this is enough, that they have left my lamp with me; otherwise when I looked at these people they were criminals, murderers, thieves, and I was worried about my lamp – that's the only thing I possess. So one thing I can say before I die – one good thing about humanity – is that my lamp was not stolen."

At the moment of death also he could laugh and joke. In Greece he was not understood at all. He belongs to the category of people like Bodhidharma, Chuang Tzu, Hotei. That was his category, but he was with the wrong people. Aristotle had defined man – Diogenes was a contemporary of Aristotle – as "a two-legged animal without feathers." That shows the depth of logic, and the insight of Aristotle. When Diogenes heard it, he caught hold of an animal with two legs, took away all the feathers, and sent it as a present to Aristotle, saying, "This is your man: a two-legged animal without feathers."

Aristotle was very angry: "It is not a joke, and this Diogenes is never serious!" But I say to you, he was serious. He was saying to Aristotle, "This is not the way to define man – two-legged, without feathers. You are degrading man to animals, just a little different variety – without feathers. That's the only difference: there are many animals with two legs."

He was not just joking – he was serious. And he was serious in his search for the authentic man. It is not a question of defining it; it is a question of finding it. You can define it only after you have found it.

The man that exists is not authentic.

Yes, my work is similar in a way: I am also searching for the authentic man, destroying all that is not authentic in you, at the risk of being condemned all over the world. But I am not carrying a lamp in my hand because I know that was only a gesture.

I am really working with each individual who has come in contact with me to help him to drop all unnecessary conditionings and to have a communion with nature.

To be natural you will be authentic.

To be natural you will be human.

And to be natural you will be a being full of rejoicings.

It is your unnaturalness that is creating the whole misery, and just as money brings more money, misery brings more misery. Whatever you have attracts its own kind. If you have a little joy, you will attract much joy; if you have a little silence, then even from the faraway stars you will be attracting silence, then even in a crowd, in the marketplace you will be attracting silence.

It depends what you have within you; that becomes the gravitation, and it attracts its own kind. Just a little experience and then there is no need to push you; you will go in that direction on your own.

My whole effort is to give you just a glimpse, just to open a window so you can see the sky with all its colors and sunset.

And I know you will come out of the hole to see the whole sky, to see the birds returning home, to see the trees going to sleep, preparing their beds. But right now you have only misery, and that misery goes on attracting more misery.

My work is somehow to create a small gap in your miserable existence…just a little window.

Beloved Bhagwan,
Does a natural death also transcend nature?

Nothing transcends nature. Everything goes on becoming more and more natural – deeper and deeper nature, higher and higher nature – but nothing transcends nature, because there is nothing else but nature.

You have to drop the old categories – that there is nature and then there is supernature. What has been called supernature is nothing but the highest peak of being natural. Why create categories, when nature alone is capable of containing all?

The lowest and the highest point of life are both natural. The murderer and the enlightened man, both are natural. The murderer is at the lowest point, the enlightened man is at the highest point. But as man they are part of the same nature, and being natural, they are similar. And this opens a new possibility: the murderer can become enlightened. We are not preventing him, we are not putting him in a separate category. He can become enlightened, because he is part of nature. Perhaps he was upside down, he just has to change his posture.

But nature is profound. It contains everything – the good, the bad, the evil, the divine – and I want them all to be part of nature, so transformation is not impossible. Old religions have created categories, and created such gaps that it is impossible…

For example, Christianity believes in eternal hell – which is absolutely absurd. You cannot commit so many sins in a small life of seventy years. One third of it is lost in sleep; much of it is lost in childhood, in sickness, in earning the bread, in quarreling with your husbands, with your wives, with your neighbors. You don't have much time to commit sin. And even if you continuously commit sin, from your very birth to the last breath, without any coffee break – just sinning and sinning – then too eternal hell is not justified. Then at least seventy years in hell will do. But eternal hell, unending, forever and forever… Christianity does not leave any possibility for the sinner to change. It cuts all his future.

My approach is simple: the worst and the best are both part of the same nature. One may be at the lowest, one may be at the highest, but they belong to the same nature, and hence have the possibility of transformation. The lowest person can start climbing to the highest peak – and it has happened many times.

There is a Hindu story in India… The oldest book on the life of Rama is written by Balmik. Balmik was a robber, thief, murderer – everything that you can conceive of he had done. That was his only profession. Uneducated but a tremendously powerful man, just on the highway he would be waiting for people, and anybody who was caught had to give everything; otherwise he was finished. Balmik's family was living in luxury – he was bringing so much every day.

One day it happened that one beautiful saint, Nardar, who was always carrying his *ektara* – a simple musical instrument, with only one string, that had become his symbol – singing and playing on his ektara he was passing, and Balmik caught hold of him. But he was still singing and playing on his ektara.

Balmik said, "Are you mad or something? Can't you see me, can't you see my sword? Give me everything that you have!"

Nardar said, "You have caught a beggar; I have only this ektara. And that too I am not going to give easily, because what will you do with this? But if you want it, I can give it to you. If you want my life I can give that too. But before I give you anything, I want to ask one question to you."

Balmik said, "Question? What question?"

Nardar said, "You go home, ask your wife: you have been killing people, robbing people – is she ready to share the responsibility of it? Ask your father, your mother, your son, your daughter. Are they willing to share the responsibility of what you are doing?"

Balmik had never thought about such a thing; he was an uneducated man. He said, "I have never thought about it. They must share the responsibility. I am doing it for them."

Nardar said, "I will be here. Don't be worried, you can just tie me to the tree so I cannot escape." He was tied to the tree and Balmik rushed to his home and asked his wife. His wife said, "I have nothing to do with your responsibilities. It is your responsibility to feed your wife; how you do it I have no concern for." And the same was the response of everybody.

Even the mother said, "It is your responsibility to take care of your old father and mother. Now how you are doing it – that you have to work out. We have not told you to kill people and rob people; you are doing it on your own. We are simply not responsible for any of your acts."

Not a single man in his house was ready to share responsibility. He was shocked! He went back, untied Nardar, touched his feet and said, "I have been my whole life a wrong person. Is there any possibility for me to get rid of all that I have done?"

Nardar said, "There is no problem. You stop doing it, because the people you are doing it for are not even ready to take responsibility for it! And I will teach you my song. My song is very simple; I simply repeat the name of Rama. It is so simple, no education is needed. You sit under the tree and repeat, 'Rama, Rama…' as long as you can, and you will be transformed – because intrinsically your innermost core always remains pure. It is only the layers on it which can be dropped."

After a few months Nardar came back and he was surprised: Balmik was sitting there under the tree. Nardar had been his whole life repeating the name of Rama, the Hindu god, but nothing like this had happened to him. Balmik was surrounded by an aura of light. Just going close to him you felt a tremendous silence, a great rejoicing.

He said, "My God, I have been repeating the name of God my whole life. And this man is a murderer, a robber, he has done every sin possible, and he is my student – I have taught him to repeat the name of Rama – and he seems to be transformed, transmuted!"

Nardar had to wait. He did not dare to touch him or to disturb him; his presence was so sacred. When Balmik opened his eyes, he touched the feet of Nardar. Nardar said, "You need not touch my feet – I have to touch *your* feet. What has happened? Within a few months you are a new man! Have you found something more than I have given to you? because I have been using that mantra, 'Rama, Rama…' my whole life. And now I feel like a fool; within a few months… You must have got something else!"

He said, "My God, is it Ram? I forgot." Because repeating it continuously…if you repeat, "Rama, Rama Rama…." And he was uneducated, a robber, murderer; he had never done any such thing. "Rama" repeated continuously without any gaps…he forgot, and started repeating, "Mara, Mara…" Instead of "Rama," two "Ramas" became joined and he forgot what it was, so he started, "Mara, Mara…" *Mara* means dead.

Balmik says, "This is another miracle! You have been repeating, 'Mara' which means 'dead'; it is not the name of God. But your sincerity, your innocence, your totality has changed it. You are far away from me.

Never touch my feet again!"

The lowest can change to the highest.

There is no barrier, there is no wall.

And nature is all that is there.

So even a natural death does not transcend nature; it simply fulfills nature in its totality.

**Bhagwan,
We've run out of questions.**

You don't have any more? Anando, some question about poor Avesh? No? Okay!

I Have Kept My Wondering Eyes Alive

Beloved Bhagwan,

Soon I will be spending a few days with my two teenage daughters. They want a full-time mother and are angry that I have chosen to be with You instead of them. I am torn, because although I have been told that my greatest gift to them is getting free, it is only an idea. On the other hand, my desire for approval for being a good mother is very strong and I feel guilty being with You while they continue to suffer alone.

Would You please talk about how to break free of society's conditioning about motherhood?

Everything depends on a very simple understanding. The whole idea that children are your possession is wrong. They are born through you but they do not belong to you. You have a past; they have only future. They are not going to live according to you. To live according to you will be almost equivalent to not living at all. They have to live according to themselves – in freedom, in responsibility, in danger, in challenge. That's how one becomes strong.

Parents down the ages have carried the idea that children belong to them, and that they have to be just carbon copies of them. A carbon copy is not a beautiful thing, and existence does not believe in carbon copies; it rejoices in originality.

Once you understand that your children do not belong to you – that they belong to existence, you have been just a passage – you have to be grateful to existence that it has chosen you to be a passage for a few beautiful children. But you are not to interfere in their growth, in their potential. You are not to impose yourself upon them. They are not going to live in the same times, they are not going to face the same problems; they will be part of another world. Don't prepare them for this world, this society, this time, because then you will be creating troubles for them. They will find themselves unfit, unqualified.

You have to help them to grow beyond you; you have to help them not to imitate you. That is really the duty of the parents – to help the children not to fall into imitation. Children are imitative, and naturally, who are they going to imitate? The parents are the closest people. And up to now parents have enjoyed it very much that their children are just like them. The father feels proud because his son is just like him; he should be ashamed that his son is just like him. Then one life is wasted; then his son is not needed – he was enough. Because of this wrong conception of pride in children imitating you, we have created a society of imitators.

One of the most famous Christian books was written by Kempis: *Imitation of Christ*. It is almost second to *The Holy Bible*. One great Christian theologian and a world-famous author of many, many treatises, Stanley Jones, used to stay with me whenever he used to come to my city. He was continuously going around the world, and he always kept the book, *Imitation of Christ*. Once I told him, "If you really understand, then this book should be burned."

To teach anybody to imitate Christ is to destroy that person. One Christ is enough, more than enough. Many, many Christs carrying their crosses on their shoulders would make a very hilarious scene...and everybody proclaiming himself to be the only begotten son of God!

The word 'imitation' has never been condemned, but it should be condemned. The religious founders have been wanting people to imitate them, the parents have been wanting their children to imitate them; the teachers, the professors, the priests – everybody is wanting children to imitate them. The children become a mass phenomenon; carbon copies of many people...much ado about nothing!

I remember, I must have been seven years old and a friend of my father's who had not seen me, who had not come for seven years...he had gone for a long pilgrimage around the Ganges. Hindus do that – go around the whole Ganges, both sides. That is thousands of miles, deep in the Himalayas, dangerous valleys, mountains. After seven years he came and he wanted to see me. And he said to my father, "His eyes look like yours," and to my grandfather, "His nose looks like yours," and to my uncle, "His face looks like yours."

I said, "Wait! Does anything look like me? Am I here or not? You are being utterly disrespectful to me." He was shocked. He could not conceive that it would be a disrespect, because this is commonly done, every day, in every home: the child's eyes look like the mother's, his face looks like the father's. And they all feel proud; and nobody bothers about the child, whether anything looks like him or not.

But I made it clear to him, "Just take your words back, because I can say to you that my eyes don't look like my father's. You have another look. And my face does not look like my uncle's – how can it look...? I have my own eyes and I have my own face, and I am going into the world with my face and with my eyes."

He asked to be forgiven. Later on he told my father, "Your son seems to be dangerous. I have never seen anybody so assertive – and at this age!"

My father said, "At first we used to feel very embarrassed by the things he did or said, but now we have started feeling proud, because he seems to be right. You are not the first man who has compared my eyes with his – many others have done that. And he has taken me to the mirror and told me, 'Look, they are not the same.' And I have to say to you that they are not the same; he is right."

The whole of humanity has lived in such a wrong way, and for so long, that we have completely forgotten that there can be some other way, that there can be an alternative.

You are here with me. In fact, you should make your children understand that this is a great opportunity for you, to be yourself: "If I was with you there is every possibility that, knowingly or unknowingly, I may treat you habitually – just the old things, behaving the way my parents have behaved with me – and that would be ugly."

And tell them not to feel angry at me; rather, bring them to me sometimes. Once in a while, when they have holidays, let them come to me. They will understand me more clearly than you, because they are fresher, younger, closer to nature, yet unspoiled. They are not going to be angry at me.

Once they start understanding me, they will be proud of you – not feeling that they have been abandoned by you, but feeling that they have been given freedom, which is the greatest gift possible in the world. And your children will start feeling proud of you, because you are one of the rarest mothers who can give them freedom, and bring them to a man who can help them see how to be free and how to be responsible...how to be oneself.

In this world of imitators, how to be original and authentic? – because only those few individuals who are themselves feel fulfilled. Others simply live miserably, hoping that tomorrow things will be better; but that tomorrow never comes.

Once your children start understanding something of what I am doing here and why *you* are here, they will be proud of you. And their being proud of you will immediately erase the feeling of guilt in you.

You are feeling guilty that you have left children alone – that perhaps this is not right. According to the old mind, it is not right. According to the old mind everything has to be taught: they are not to be allowed to be themselves; they have to be molded into a certain ideal. This very process of molding is going to kill them. And there are corpses all around the world – moving, doing things – but I say that they are corpses because they are not themselves. If they had been given freedom, if they had been given a chance to grow naturally, to be themselves, they would never have been the person they are. And only then would they have been able to find a certain contentment and satisfaction.

You need not feel guilty. Those who are destroying their children, *they* should feel guilty. Giving children freedom.... And once in a while you will be going, once in a while you will be with your children and that is a pure gift, to be with them once in a while, because then you can be loving. You have gathered so much love; for so many days you have been far away. There has been so much longing. You will shower upon them your whole love. They will see only your loving being.

Twenty-four hours being with them, every day, year in year out – you cannot remain loving. You are bound to be angry, you are bound to be jealous; you are bound to be *everything* that you should not be before your children, and they will learn those things from you.

My whole idea is that parents should meet their children only occasionally, so they can pour out their whole heart, and the children know their mothers and their fathers only as pure love. They don't know that both these persons fight continuously, that they nag, they throw things at each other.

I used to live in a place where everybody was surprised. It was a big apartment house with thin, modern walls. You could hear everything that was going on, on the other side. You need not go to the movies or any other entertainment, it was available free, and just without any effort – just lying on your bed and all around things were happening.

The most amazing part was that from every apartment was always coming screams, shouting, fighting, beating, things being thrown, plates being broken. Just from one house there was always heard great laughter. The whole neighborhood was surprised; they seemed to be the ideal couple – never anything except great laughter was heard from that apartment.

One day, going for a morning walk, I met the man and I asked him, "You are the ideal couple – not only in this building, but perhaps in the whole world. Nothing else is ever heard except laughter. Can you tell me the secret?"

He said, "Don't ask me. It is better not to ask, not to say anything about it, because I feel like crying."

I said, "I am praising you and you feel like crying?"

He said, "You don't understand at all. The reality is, she throws things at me. When she hits me, she laughs; when she misses, I laugh. But don't tell it to anybody. This arrangement is going well." But the same man, after five years, went to the court – he wanted a divorce.

The whole neighborhood was surprised. I had never told anybody, because it was such a private thing. Everybody was just amazed, "What happened that they have gone to the court? And, we hear, for divorce!" I was going to the university. I thought that first I should visit them – the court was just on the way – so I stopped at the court and went into the court.

The judge was asking, "How long have you been married?"

They said, "For six years."

"So why do you want now to divorce? What has happened?"

He said, "What has happened? She throws things at me."

The judge said, "Recently she has started throwing things at you?"

He said, "No, she has been throwing things from the very first night."

The judge said, "You amaze me. If she has been throwing things from the very first night, then for six years what have you been doing? Why did you not come earlier for a divorce?"

He said, "You don't understand. Now she has become so practiced that she never misses. It is always she who is laughing. For months I have not laughed; now I cannot tolerate it. At first it used to be almost fifty-fifty: one time she will laugh, one time I will laugh. It was okay, we were equal. Now it is intolerable – only she laughs, and I am just standing there like an idiot, with never a chance to laugh."

It is better that the children don't see your ugly faces. If the child never comes to know about these ugly faces, his life will be totally different. It will be a life of love, without jealousies, without nagging, without throwing things, because he had no chance to learn these things.

You need not feel guilty; those parents should feel guilty who never leave their children alone. Once in a while go and be with them, and then you can be as totally with them as possible. And once in a while bring them here.

You have to share me with your children.

If you love me, you would like your children also to love me. Don't leave them in anger at me; that is not right.

And their love towards me will help you immensely not to feel guilty. It will help the children also to feel that it is good that you are here. They would also like to be here someday – when their educations are complete, when they are grown up and they are ready to move into life. They would like to learn more about the complexities of existence, the intricacies of life, its delights, and the art of how to achieve it.

Beloved Bhagwan,
I realized this morning when You were talking that I am a fighter, but I don't know anything except fighting, that unfortunately I am a proud fighter – and even worse, that I love fighting. I love to stand in the face of the strongest storm and laugh. It is great joy. I don't like to lie in the sun and melt. And yet behind my mind, my heart longs to melt. It yearns, but it never seems to have even a fighting chance. How can I salvage my being?

There is no problem in it.
If you feel you are a fighter, if you enjoy fighting, not only that, if you are proud of being a fighter – then relax. Fight totally! Then don't fight your fighting nature. That will be let-go for you.

It is perfectly beautiful to stand before the strongest storm and laugh. Don't feel guilty. Just try to understand one thing: when I say let-go, I don't mean you have to change anything. I simply mean, whatever you feel you are, just allow it its totality.

Be a fighter with your whole being, and in this totality you will find the melting of the heart. That will be the reward of your being total. You do not need to do anything for it; rewards come on their own. Just be total in anything that you feel you love, that you feel proud of – just be total in it. Don't create a split. Don't be half and half; don't be partial.

If you are total, one day – standing against the strongest storm, laughing – you will suddenly feel your heart melting in the sun. That will come to you as a reward.

Man unnecessarily creates problems. I want you to understand that there are no problems in life except those you create. Just try to see: whatsoever feels good for you is good. Then go the whole way. Even if the whole world is against it, it doesn't matter. And whether you have gone total and whole will be decided by the reward.

If you start feeling at one point a sudden melting then you know that you have not cheated yourself, that you have been sincere, true. That now is really the point where you can be proud.

Beloved Bhagwan,
What do You feel the next phase of Your work will be, once you have found a stable residence? And what do You see your sannyasins doing?

That's really a problem – an unanswerable one too, because I never think of tomorrow, and I don't know what is going to happen tomorrow. I leave it up to tomorrow! I don't burden myself too much. Today is enough unto itself.

Tomorrow I will be there, the problems will be there, the challenges will be there; and I will be available to those challenges, to those problems.

My whole life I have lived this way – without any predecision, without any commitment for the future, without any promise to myself or to anybody else for the next moment. And that has given me the most precious gift of life. I have become attuned with existence; knowing not where I am going, I am going joyously.

One thing I know: existence has no goal, and as part of existence I cannot have any goal. The moment you have a goal, you cut yourself away from existence. Then a small dewdrop is trying to fight against the ocean. Unnecessary is the trouble, meaningless is the struggle.

I never think of the yesterdays.

And I never think of the tomorrows.

That leaves me just a small moment, the present moment – unburdened, uncluttered, clean, free.

So I don't know the answer to your question. All that has happened in my life…if you try to recapitulate it, you will find certainly a tremendously systematic program – as if I had planned everything from the very beginning in minute detail. But this is an absolutely wrong idea.

As far as I am concerned, I have never planned anything; I have simply lived, wondering what is going to happen next. I have kept my wondering eyes alive, just like a small child.

Hasya has to plan, Jayesh has to plan, John has to plan – so they are all suffering from fever, tired.

Just look at Jayesh!

But I am simply wondering what is going to happen.

Beloved Bhagwan,
You are giving Your life to help people find inner freedom, and the whole world is trying to take away Your freedom – that is, freedom of speech, of movement, and so on. How is it possible that You do not give up? What is compassion? Does compassion possess You like love, or can You choose whether or not to be compassionate?

The question has many questions in it.

Firstly, I am not making any effort to give to people freedom from the bondage of their rotten past. It is not my effort, it is simply my joy. I enjoy doing it; hence there is no tension about it, whether I succeed or not. I am not serious – it is just playfulness. I am free, I have enjoyed it, and out of that joy arises an overflow of energy, spreading on its own accord.

I am just a watcher, not a doer.

Secondly, the world cannot take my freedom. It can try, but its failure is absolutely certain – for the simple reason that to me freedom is more valuable than my life. I would rather risk my life than choose to lose my freedom; hence nobody can take it. They can kill me, but they cannot kill my spirit, they cannot kill my freedom. They are doing everything in their hands – they seem to be desperate. And I am joyfully trying to find new ways to reach people. At the most they can take my life, but they *cannot* take my freedom.

They can take your freedom only when you value your life more than freedom; then your freedom can be taken very easily. Just a threat to your life and your freedom can be taken. But they cannot take my freedom because to me life has no value, and freedom has all value.

To me, freedom is life.

They can destroy my body but they cannot destroy my consciousness.

So there is no question of their taking my freedom. They may be powerful – they are powerful. All the governments of the world are together against a single individual, and still they cannot take his freedom. And I can say it with absolute certainty that they cannot take my freedom, because I am ready to offer my life at any moment.

Thirdly, you ask, is your compassion as possessive of you as love? No, compassion is not possessive. In love you fall; hence the phrase "falling in love." Have you ever heard of somebody "falling in compassion"? That kind of phrase does not exist in any language. You *rise* in compassion.

Compassion does not possess you; neither do you possess compassion.

That is something subtle to be understood. It is easy to understand whether it possesses you or not, but my answer is: compassion does not possess me, neither do I possess it.

Compassion has become my nature. There is no duality of the possessor and the possessed. So it is a very different situation from love.

It is not in my hands to stop being compassionate, because I am not separate from it. In either case, whether you possess something or something possesses you, the duality remains.

But in compassion the duality disappears.

You are it, there is nobody else; so you can simply be it.

There is no other way of being.

Beloved Bhagwan,
To have such an incredible opportunity to ask You a question, and to be so fearful of doing so, shows me how little trust I have. Can I still be Your sannyasin?

The question is not of being *my* sannyasin, the question is of being *a* sannyasin.

To be my sannyasin certainly needs a certain commitment, a certain surrender. And I do not want you to be surrendered to me, or to be committed to me. I want you to be surrendered to nature, committed to existence. You need not be *my* sannyasin, you have just to be *a* sannyasin – and that's the only way of being my sannyasin.

It is not a direct phenomenon – that directly you commit yourself and surrender to existence. But the deeper you surrender to existence, life, nature, the more loving, the more understanding, the more insightful you become; and that insight will bring you closer to me. You will find in me, indirectly, the state of total surrender, total trust.

Don't be worried that you don't have that total trust now. Even if you have a little bit of trust, that is enough to begin with. Just open the bank account; you need not have millions to open the bank account with. With the smallest trust you can start the journey, and as the journey grows deeper, the trust grows deeper. Soon you will find yourself surrounded with only trust.

That moment you will feel you are my sannyasin.

Those who have come directly to me can betray. Those who have come indirectly to me cannot betray, because even before coming to me they had already tasted something of the beyond, and to betray is impossible. But there have been many sannyasins who have come directly to me. They started their commitment, their trust, towards me as a beginning. That is not a right beginning, because that means there is a certain belief. They don't know me, they can't know me – and still they have believed.

There is danger because the doubt is there;

the doubt can any day take over their belief. But the authentic sannyasins, the real ones, have come to me in a very indirect way. It is very difficult for you to find out who has come in what way, because it is something inner that you cannot see. But the people who have come slowly, trying to understand me, step by step, moving towards being natural, authentic, sincere...suddenly one day they find they are related to me. Strange – they had never tried for it, they had not made any effort. It is a discovery.

So sannyas to me has to be a discovery.

Then you cannot lose it; it is your own discovery.

Don't be worried that your trust is partial – that's enough, that much will do. You want to learn swimming...you need not jump into the deep water immediately; otherwise there is a danger you will get scared for your whole life. You will never come close to water again.

There is a Sufi story that Mulla Nasruddin wanted to learn swimming. But as he went close to the river with the teacher who was going to teach him, he slipped and fell into the river – and it was a deep river. He was saved by the teacher, but he went a few times under the water; and as he was taken out, he took his shoes and ran away.

The teacher said, "Where are you going? You have come to learn swimming."

He said, "Now, first I will learn swimming and then I will come near the water; otherwise I am not going to come near the water – it is too dangerous. First I will learn swimming." But where is he going to learn swimming? You cannot learn swimming in your bedroom.

There is no other way...but unfortunately he entered the river from the wrong end. The teacher would have taken him to where the water was shallow, and slowly would have encouraged him to go towards deeper waters.

As he would have become more proficient, the teacher would have encouraged him to go farther and farther.

Just a little trust is enough.

In the beginning you cannot hope to have total trust. That's how we start making impossible demands upon ourselves, and then we cannot fulfill them. Guilt arises, a condemnation of oneself arises, a rejection: "I am not worthy...." But all these things are unnecessary.

And *this* has happened all over the world. Everybody is feeling unworthy because he aspired in the very beginning to find the end. Naturally it was impossible – he could not reach it – and that stopped him even starting the journey again.

I used to live with one of my professors, in the same house. I was living alone and he felt that, looking at the condition of my cottage... he said, "It will be better you come and start living with me" – because I had my bed just near the door, so that I could simply jump into bed, jump out of it...I never used to enter the house, because who is going to clean it?

When he saw this situation he said, "I have never seen such a way of living." Just in front of me was my bathroom; that much space was all that I used to move in – from the bed to the bathroom. All my books were around the bed so I could pick up any book that I needed, and whenever the bed became too dirty I simply used to put the light off – then everything looks the same!

He said, "This is not good. My wife will take care of you; you come with me. And we don't have any children." He was an old man – he was just like my father. He said, "I won't let you live here. I had never thought that you are living in this way. You have invented an absolutely new way of life – that you put the light off if you see that it is too dirty."

So I went to live in his house. He was an atheist; he did not believe in God. And he was interested in me because he thought I was also an atheist – because he had heard me speaking in the university and at other places, declaring that there is no God. So he thought we were both atheists.

But on the way I made it plain to him, "You may be under a wrong impression. I am not an atheist."

He said, "What! And you declare everywhere that there is no God."

I said, "Yes, I declare there is no God. That's why I cannot be a theist; a God is needed to be a theist – to believe in it. But a God is needed *also* to be an atheist – *not* to believe in it. And there is no God, so I don't fall into any category."

He said, "My God! So you don't fall into any category?" I said, "No."

I lived with him for a few months, and the more I tried to understand him, the more I came to the conclusion – a very strange conclusion, which proved right about many other atheists I had to meet during my life – that this man had been a great theist in his past life, and because he failed to find God he reversed his position to the other extreme. Otherwise it is unexplainable that atheists should waste so much time in denying God. When there is no God, why bother about it? And they write books and pamphlets, and they make associations. They have their own philosophy, and they are more argumentative than theists. Almost all the time, the whole time, whoever they meet, sooner or later the conversation turns to atheism, that there is no God.

This insistence, this wastage on something negative simply means they are taking revenge with themselves. They have been theists.

I came to the conclusion because I started hypnotizing this old man. I told him, "This is my logical conclusion, but I want to know exactly where you were in your past life – in what belief, in what religion." He was excited to know about it, so he was willing.

Unless someone is willing you cannot hypnotize him. The art of hypnosis needs a very intelligent man and a very willing man. You cannot hypnotize an idiot – that is an impossibility. You can hypnotize only very few people who are very intelligent, sharply intelligent, and yet ready to go on an inner journey, willingly. You cannot force…they have simply to go with you.

Living with him, slowly, slowly I persuaded him. And he became a good medium for hypnosis. His wife was the judge – I used to tell her to sit there and to see the situation, because this man would not remember when he woke up, and he would deny what I said. She had to be my witness. That man was a very great theist, lived his whole life worshipping God, renounced his family, did all kinds of ascetic disciplines. And he failed, as he was bound to, because there is no God to achieve. That failure turned the whole pendulum of his consciousness to the other extreme and now he was revengeful – unknowingly, unconsciously. And when I woke him up and told him, he would deny it: "No, I have never been a theist and I don't believe in a past life."

I said, "I have a witness – your wife – that you can regress, under hypnosis, back into your past life." And I did it dozens of times, and it was always the same result: without any exception he was a great theist. He had turned against himself because he had wasted one life.

I said to him, "Now you are wasting another life. That's why I say I don't belong to

139   I HAVE KEPT MY WONDERING EYES ALIVE

any category. I don't want to waste my life for God – this way or that."

To me, man has in him the highest potential of existence and consciousness. If he explores it he will reach to a state of godliness – not of God, but only of godliness.

But don't be worried that you are starting with a small amount of trust; that much is enough. To begin with, *anything* is enough, Just the desire to go on a pilgrimage is enough. And don't be bothered that you have to be my sannyasin; just be a sannyasin. Just be a seeker of truth. And perhaps somewhere on the way I will be meeting you.

I will tell you one Sufi story: A man is going in search of truth. As he comes out of his city, he finds an old man sitting under a tree. The young man does not know where to go in search of truth. He has heard that one has to go somewhere in search of truth, one has to go on a pilgrimage – but where? Roads go to all sides. Which road is *the* road?

Seeing the old man sitting under the tree, he thought: perhaps this man is old enough; he must know which road leads to truth. And he asked the man. He said, "Yes I know the road. Follow the right and go on until you come to a certain tree" – he described the tree in detail, its leaves, its fruit – "and you will find under it a very old man…just to give you an example, something like me but thirty years older. This is the man who is going to be your guide."

The man was very happy. He thanked the old man and rushed towards the way he had shown him. For thirty years he was wandering and wandering, and the tree never came and the old man never came. He was getting tired, and he himself was getting old, and he said, "What nonsense!"

Finally he decided, "It is better to go back home…enough is enough! Thirty years I have wasted in searching truth, and I have not even met the old man who is going to be my guide. And God knows, when the guide meets me, what kind of guidance it will be and how long it will take. It seems to be too complicated; it is better to go home. I was running a good business. I destroyed the business and unnecessarily got into trouble hearing this word 'truth' again and again."

He came back. Again he passed the tree – and he was shocked! This was the tree the old man had described. And he looked under the tree and the old man was there – the same old man, thirty years older and exactly the same as the description in every way. He said, "My God! Then why did you waste my thirty years?"

He said, "I wasted your thirty years – or you wasted my thirty years? At that time you were not ripe enough to be guided, because I gave all the guidance and you didn't even look at the tree – and I was describing it in minute detail. I was describing your guide in minute detail, and you did not look at me, to see that I am describing myself. You were in such a hurry; you were too young. But nothing is wasted. I was waiting, knowing that one day you will come back, one day you will recognize this tree, one day you will recognize this old man, that I am your guide!"

The young man said, "This seems to be a strange business."

The story is immensely significant. You have a little trust. Don't be worried, go to the right… This time not under a tree, this time on a beautiful chair, you will find an old man – someone looking similar to me.

But that will be the right time for you to become *my* sannyasin. Right now just be a sannyasin; don't be greedy!

Emptiness Has its Own Fullness

Beloved Bhagwan,

For years I have contemplated what seems to me to be the basic message for well-being: love yourself. When I was a therapist, all day hearing, "I hate myself; I feel sorry for myself; I am proud of myself; I want to destroy myself; I feel good about myself," I started wondering — Who is this self?

I love when You say there is no self. That seems so freeing. Could You please say more?

The whole therapeutic movement has gone wrong on that point: Love thyself.

Socrates used to say, "Know thyself." And there have been masters, particularly Sufis, who say, "Be thyself." But there is only one person in the whole history of man, Gautam Buddha, who said, "There is no self. You are an emptiness, utter silence, a non-being."

His message was much opposed by all the traditions, because they all depended in some way or other on the idea of the self. There may have been differences on other points, but on one point they were all totally in agreement — and that was the existence of the self. Even people like George Gurdjieff, who used to talk about a very novel idea – that you are not born with a self, you have to earn it: "Deserve thyself" – finally, he also ends up with the self.

Gautam Buddha does not make any distinction between the self and the ego – and there is none. It is just sophistry, linguistic gymnastics, to make such distinctions; then you can discard the ego and save the self. But the self is simply another name of the ego. You are only changing names, and no transformation of being is happening.

Buddha's message is tremendously significant: you are an emptiness; there is no point in you which can say "I."

Looked at from my vision, when I say to

you, "Melt, dissolve into existence," I am simply saying the same thing in more positive terms.

Buddha's way of saying it was so negative that many people were stopped, because the question arose, naturally, that if there is no self, why bother? what is there to achieve? Just to know that you are not?

A whole life of discipline, great effort for meditation, and the result is to know that you are not? The result does not seem to be worth it! At least without the meditation, without the discipline you have some sense of *being*. It may be wrong, but at least you are not feeling hollow and empty. Knowing that you are not, how will you live? Out of nothingness there is no possibility of any love, of any compassion – no possibility of *anything*. Out of nothing comes only nothing.

So the opponents of Buddha described his method as a subtle way of spiritual suicide – far more dangerous than ordinary suicide, because with ordinary suicide you *will* survive, you will take a new form, a new birth. But with Buddha you will be committing total suicide, annihilation. There will be no longer anything left of you, and you will be never heard from again, never found again.

You never were in the first place.

Buddhism died in India, and one of the basic reasons was Buddha's way of putting his philosophy. I can understand why he was so insistent on negatives, because all other philosophies were so positivistic, and all their positivism was turning into stronger and stronger egos. He moved to the other extreme, seeing that positivism is going to give you egoistic ideas – and that is a hindrance between you and existence.

To stop this idea he became totally negative.

You cannot complain about it, because the positivistic ideologies were in a strange situation: you have to drop the ego to find yourself, you have to drop the ego to find God, you have to drop the ego to become God, you have to drop the ego to find ultimate liberation – liberation of whom? Liberation of your self.

So there was achievement, and achievement is always of the ego.

There is a goal, and the goal is always of the ego.

Seeing all this, Buddha said, "There is no self. There is nothing to be achieved, and there is no goal to be found. You have never existed, you do not exist, you will not exist. You can only imagine, you can only *dream* that you are."

Chuang Tzu's story is famous. I never get tired of Chuang Tzu because his small, absurd stories have so many aspects to explore, each time I can bring it in with a new light, with a new meaning, with a new perspective.

One morning he wakes up, calls all his disciples and says, "I am in great trouble, and you have to help me."

The disciples said, "We have come to be helped by *you,* and you want our help?" Chuang Tzu said, "It was okay, but this night everything got disturbed: I dreamt that I had become a butterfly."

They all laughed. They said, "All nonsense! Dreaming does not create any mess."

Chuang Tzu said, "It has created, because now I am thinking that perhaps I am a butterfly, thinking, dreaming that I am Chuang Tzu. Now, who am I? And I have to be certain, in order to live, whether I am Chuang Tzu or I am a butterfly."

He looks absurd, but he is really bringing the absurdity of logic to the surface. If a butterfly cannot dream of being a Chuang

Tzu, then how can Chuang Tzu dream of being a butterfly? And if Chuang Tzu can dream of being a butterfly, then there is no logical objection to a butterfly falling asleep under the morning sun on a beautiful flower, and dreaming of herself being Chuang Tzu.

None of his disciples could help him. For centuries Taoists have been using that as a koan, because it is insoluble – but to Buddha it is not so.

Chuang Tzu and Gautam Buddha were contemporaries, but far away; one was in China, one in India. They were divided by the great Himalayas, so no communication; otherwise Buddha would have solved Chuang Tzu's problem, because he says, "Both are dreams. It does not matter whether Chuang Tzu dreams of being a butterfly, or the butterfly dreams of being a Chuang Tzu – *both* are dreams. You simply don't exist."

Many came to Buddha and turned away, because nobody can make nothingness be his life's achievement – for what? So much discipline and so much great trouble in getting into meditation just to find out that you are not...strange kind of man this Gautam Buddha. We are good as we are, what is the need of digging so deep that you find there is nothing? Even if we are dreaming, at least there is something.

My own approach is just the same, but from a very different angle. I say to you that you don't have a self, because you are part of the universe; you are not nothing. Only the universe can have a self, only the universe can have a center, only the whole can have a soul. My hand cannot have a soul, my fingers cannot have a soul; only the organic unity can have a soul. And we are only parts. We are, but we are only parts; hence we cannot claim that we have a self.

So Buddha is right – there is no self – but he is not helping people, poor people, because they cannot figure out all the implications of the statement.

I say to you: You *don't* have a self because you are part of a great self, the whole. You cannot have any separate, private, self of your own. This takes away the negativity, and this does not give you the positive desire for becoming more and more egoistic. It avoids both the extremes and finds a new approach: The universe is, I am not. And whatever happens and appears to be in me, as me, is simply universal.

To call it "I" is to make it too small. That is what makes it untrue; it does not correspond to reality. To call it "self" makes it unreal, because the self is possible only if you are totally independent – and you are not. Even for a single breath you are not independent. Even for a single moment you are not independent of the sun, of the moon, of the stars. The whole is contributing all the time. That's why you are.

To recognize it is not a loss, it is a gain; and yet it is not an egoistic gain. If you can see the subtlety of it...it is a tremendous achievement to understand that you are part of the whole, that the whole belongs to you, that you belong to the whole. And yet with such a great achievement, there is no shadow of the self.

It is one of the most beautiful understandings, that we are not separate – not separate from the mountains, not separate from the trees, not separate from the ocean, not separate from anybody. We are all connected, interwoven into oneness. The gain is immense, but there is no sense of I, of me, of my, of mine. As far as these things are concerned, there is utter silence and emptiness. But this emptiness is not just empty.

We can empty this room – we can take all the furniture, everything in the room out – and anybody coming in will say, "The room is empty." That is one way of looking at it – but not the right way.

The right way is that now the room is full of emptiness. Before, the emptiness was hindered, cut into parts, because so much furniture, and so many things were not allowing it to be one: now it is one.

Emptiness too *is*. It is existential; it does not mean that it is not. Somebody empty of jealousy will become full of love, somebody empty of stupidness will become full of intelligence. Each emptiness has its own fullness. And if you miss seeing the fullness that comes with emptiness, absolutely and certainly, then you are blind.

There is no self.

And that's a great relief.

You don't have to love it, you don't have to hate it, you don't have to accept it, you don't have to reject it; you don't have to do anything: it simply is not there. You can relax, and in this relaxation is the melting into the universe.

Then nothingness becomes wholeness.

Buddha was very miserly; he would never say that nothingness is wholeness. He knew it; it is impossible that a man who knows nothingness to such depths will not know the other side of the coin – wholeness. But he was very miserly – and for a reason, because the moment you utter "wholeness," immediately the ego feels at ease.

The ego says, "So there is no fear. You have to attain to wholeness. Nothing was a danger; wholeness gives hope." That's why he was so persistently denying something which is ultimately real. He was leading people towards it, but denying it because the moment you assert it those people start going astray.

But I would like tell you the whole thing.

One day Buddha is passing through a forest. It is fall, and the whole forest is full of dry and dead leaves, and the wind is taking those dry and dead leaves from here and there and making beautiful music; and just to walk on those leaves is a joy.

Ananda asked Buddha, "Can I ask you…there is nobody around, and I rarely get a chance to be alone with you. Although I am twenty-four hours a day with you, somebody is always there, and of course he has preference to ask, to talk, because it is an opportunity for him; I am always with you. But today there is nobody. Can I ask you one thing: Have you said everything that you know? Or have you been keeping a few things back and not revealing them to people?"

Buddha stooped down and filled one of his fists with dead leaves. Ananda said, "What are you doing?"

He said, "I am trying to answer your question. What do you see in my hand?"

And Anand said, "I see a few leaves."

Buddha said, "What do you see all over the forest?"

He said, "Millions and millions of dead leaves."

Buddha said, "What I have said is just this much, and what I have not said is equal to the leaves that are in the whole forest. But my whole desire is to take you to the forest, to leave you to listen to the music of the whole, to walk and run on dry leaves, just like children. I don't want to give you a few leaves in my fist. No, I want to give you the whole.

"And this is my understanding: you may trust me or not, but I trust you. You may change, you may even become an enemy to me, but my trust will remain the same in you. Because my trust is not something conditional upon you, it does not depend on you. My trust is my joy, and I want to give the whole."

Nothingness is half of the truth –

immensely relieving, but it leaves something like a wound, something unfulfilled. You will be relieved, relaxed, but you will be still looking for something, because emptiness *cannot* become the end.

The other side, wholeness, has to be made available to you. Then your emptiness is full – full of wholeness.

Then your nothingness is all.

It is not just nothing, but all.

These are the moments when contradictory terms are transcended, and whenever you transcend any contradictory terms you become enlightened. Whatever the contradiction may be, all contradictions transcended bring enlightenment to you. And this is one of the fundamental contradictions: emptiness and wholeness.

The transcendence needs nothing but just a silent understanding.

Beloved Bhagwan,
Since being with You, I have noticed that when a person becomes closely related to You they sometimes get a fixed idea about who You are. It seems like they forget who You really are and even why they have come to You.

This situation puzzles me, even scares me a little.

Would You please comment?

The mind has a natural tendency to quickly get fixed ideas. It is very much afraid of change, because change means rearrangement. Each time you change something, you have to rearrange your whole inner being.

Mind wants to live with fixed ideas, so when a person comes to me – and it has been happening for thirty-five years continuously –

he starts loving me. He comes closer, becomes intimate, and then gets a fixed idea. And that's where he misses, because now his fixed idea is going to create trouble.

I am not an idea and I am not fixed. I am changing. I am in absolute agreement with Heraclitus that you cannot step twice in the same river. Translated, it means you cannot meet the same person again. I not only agree with him, I go a little further: I say you cannot step in the same river even once. Again translated to the human world, it means you cannot meet the same person even once, because even while you are meeting him he is changing, you are changing, the whole world is changing.

But once you get a fixed idea you cling to it, and I am constantly going to change. Tomorrow you will find yourself in a conflict.

So many have come, so many have gone, and this has been one of the basic reasons: they became so much fascinated with their own idea of me that *I* became secondary. Their idea of me became primary – and that too, old, dated. I am with them, fresh and young, but I became secondary. And if there was any conflict between their idea and my reality, they went with their idea – even to the point of becoming enemies to me, telling people that I am no longer the same, I am no longer the person I used to be; they have worshipped a great saint, but I am no longer the same person. They will keep their memory of me deep in their heart, but it is simply a photograph. Photographs don't change.

Once it happened…one of my friends was collecting photographs of me from my childhood – from wherever he could get them. He had made a big album, and he was showing me. He had done a great deal of work; he had gone to many places, to many people. Wherever he heard that somebody had a picture of me he went there, either to get the

EMPTINESS HAS ITS OWN FULLNESS

original or a copy of it. But while he was showing them to me he felt I was not interested. He stopped and said to me, "You don't seem to be interested."

I said, "I don't seem to be interested because none of these photographs represent me; they only represent that which is dead. The photograph can only represent that which is dead. A photograph is always of the dead; you cannot find a photograph which is of the living."

In Picasso's home there used to be a portrait, a self-portrait of Picasso. He never sold it, at any price, that was the only picture he insisted on not selling. And the more he insisted on not selling, the more and more people were coming, with bigger and bigger offers for the picture. It became a challenge for art collectors.

One beautiful woman had come with the same idea, to purchase the picture. Whatever the price she was ready to pay; she was rich enough. She said to Picasso, "I am willing to pay you as much as you want for your portrait."

Picasso said, "People are mad. For a dead thing they go on harassing me. You can have it without any price, but remember, it is not me."

The woman looked puzzled. She said, "It is not you? What do you mean?"

He said, "If it were me it would have kissed you by now! It does not speak, it does not love, it does not sing, it does not dance. Such a beautiful woman is standing before it and the idiot is not even kissing. You just can take it. It is dead. Remove it from here – it is not me!"

People get fixed ideas – and very soon. Ordinarily it goes perfectly well, because you meet only dead people who are not changing, who go on saying the same thing their whole life just like a parrot. They are consistent people; they have all your respect.

I seem to you self-contradictory, inconsistent, for the simple reason that I have decided not to die before I die. I am going to live to the very last breath, so you cannot be certain about me till my last breath. After that you can make any image of me and be satisfied with it. But remember, it will not be me.

To be with me needs courage, and the greatest courage is being capable of seeing the change and moving with it. It may be difficult; it is easy to have one idea once and then be finished.

A Sufi story... Mulla Nasruddin is appointed as the prime minister of a king because he was known to be very wise; somewhat weird was his wisdom, but still, wisdom is wisdom. The first day when they went to have their dinner together, a certain vegetable called *bindhi* was made by the cook, stuffed with Eastern spices. It is a delicacy.

The king appreciated the cook, and after that Mulla said, in appreciation of the bindhi, "This is the most precious vegetable in the world. It gives you long life, it keeps you healthy, it gives you resistance against diseases," and so on and so forth.

The king said, "I never knew that you know so much about vegetables."

The cook heard about it, so he thought, "If bindhi is such a thing that our king can live long and healthy and young..." Next day again bindhi was made, and again Mulla praised it, going even higher than the first day. The third day bindhi was made and Mulla went still higher. The fourth day bindhi was made and Mulla was going higher and higher. The fifth day Mulla even said that bindhi is a divine food – God eats only bindhi.

But the king was bored. He threw the plate of bindhi and told Mulla Nasruddin,

"You are an idiot. Bindhi…and God eats bindhi every day? You will drive me mad!"

Mulla said, "Lord, you are getting unnecessarily hot. I am your servant; you said bindhi was good, I simply followed you, and when I do something I do it perfectly. I am not a servant to bindhi, I am your servant. The truth is that bindhi is the worst thing in the world – even devils don't eat it. You did well that you threw it."

He threw his plate farther away than the king. He said, "You should always remember that I am your servant, and you are always right. And I am a consistent man; I will remain *consistently* your servant, whatever happens."

There are people – almost the whole world – who live in a certain consistency. It is easier. But when you come close to a man like me, you are going to be in difficulty; either you will have to drop your idea of consistency or you will have to drop me. And people are so infatuated with their own ideas that they can drop me, but they cannot drop their ideas.

My first book was published in 1960. I was staying in someone's home, and the housewife of the home told me, "My father is a monk, a Jaina monk; he is old, ninety years old. He has been told by the Jaina order that he need not go begging, he is too old, so he remains outside the town in a hut, and we take his food there. But he wants to come to see you – he insists. We've told him, 'We can bring the person you want to see…'"

In fact I used to go on that road every morning. She said, "It is very easy for you to go to meet the old man, but he insists, 'No, that will not be respectful.' He reads your books; he has stopped reading all other books. And he says, 'If it was in my power I would declare this man as our twenty-fifth *tirthankara.*'"

They have twenty-four tirthankaras in one cycle of existence; in Jainism there are cycles of existence. It is a very mathematical philosophy. Everything moves in the world in cycles – existence also has a cycle: it begins, it ends, it begins again, it ends again…it is a long, long way. In fact, India has the biggest terms for counting; no other language has such big terms for counting. And it has to use its biggest terms to count how long it takes one cycle to complete.

In one cycle there are twenty-four tirthankaras, just as in one day there are twenty-four hours. For each hour in the cycle of existence there is one master. This old Jaina monk had said something almost sacrilegious: that if it was in his power he would declare me the twenty-fifth tirthankara. He was so infatuated with the book that he said that he had never understood things which the book had made him understand, and he was happy that he had found it before his death.

He came to see me; it must have been nearabout six in the evening when he came. The daughter of the woman I was staying with came and told me, "You should take your bath because your supper is ready."

I said, "Wait, this old man has come from so far." And the old man had already said – just within the few minutes he had been there – "You are the twenty-fifth tirthankara. Perhaps if it is not possible according to existence, then you will be the first tirthankara in the new cycle. Your book has given me so much; all the books that I have read in my whole life – all the scriptures – have proved useless."

He had touched my feet. I told him, "It is not good. You are ninety years old, and a Jaina monk is not supposed to touch anybody's feet."

He said, "I don't care. I consider you as my master." But when he heard the girl asking me to get ready, he was shocked –

EMPTINESS HAS ITS OWN FULLNESS

because the sun had set, and Jainas don't eat after the sun has set. Immediately everything changed.

He said, "Do you eat after the sunset?"

I said, "Ordinarily, no. But you have come from so far, an old man, and I wanted to be with you. It doesn't matter if it is a little late. I can take my supper a little late."

He said, "Then forgive me. Whatever I have said to you, I want to take it back. You are not even a Jaina, how can you become a Jaina tirthankara? First you should learn how to discipline your life."

He started teaching me. Just a moment before I was the master, and I was going to be the first tirthankara of the new cycle; now I was not even a disciple! And there was absolute condemnation in his mind. The book that he had brought with him – my book – he simply left there. He didn't take it with him.

I asked him, "What happened? That book... I may have fallen from your mind, but that book does not eat supper. You can take the book."

He said, "I cannot even touch it. You have written it and you don't know even simple things, that after sunset one cannot eat. If one eats after sunset, one can never know what reality is."

It was really hilarious to see the whole thing; the whole family gathered to see. The husband of the woman was a rare man. He said to me, "Except me, everybody in my family is going to betray you. Only I will remain in the end with you, because I am not a religious person; they all are against me. I don't go to the temple, I don't read their scriptures, I don't follow the discipline of a Jaina – not eating in the night, not eating before sunrise, and other things. I will be the last one to still be with you, because whatever you do will not hurt me; I don't make any image, I simply see it.

"Each time you come to my home you are different, and all these people get into difficulty. They are puzzled – last time you said something and this time you have been saying something which goes against it. Only to me it does not seem puzzling simply because last time was last time! The water in the Ganges has gone down so much. This time is this time, and to me you are each time beautiful."

And he was right. By and by all the people in his family started getting stuck with some image of me. Only he remained to the very last. He is dead now. Just before dying he said, "Convey to Bhagwan, 'Only you are in my mind right now, when I am leaving my body.'" He was a man who really had guts to go along with me through all the seasons of the year, all the changes of life.

If you really want to be with me you have to stop making images. What is the need to make an image? The need is to cling.

Remain without an image so that your eyes are not cluttered with old images and you are available to me directly, each moment.

This direct immediacy is the true relationship between me and you.

Anything less than that is worthless.

Beloved Bhagwan,
The other day I heard You saying, "Just listening to me can be enough to be transformed." I felt so grateful to You and relaxed for a moment. But a part of me was doubtfully asking, "Is it really that easy? Can I really relax and let existence take over?" My chattering mind wants to do something. How can I be more patient and really trust?

Just for a moment you had the glimpse. Now make yourself available more and more...that glimpse comes again and again, becomes deepened. And don't be bothered by your chattering mind.

Use that chattering mind to make new questions.

Chapter 17
April 20, 1986, Evening

The World is Where the World Is

Beloved Bhagwan,

In the land of money, power, designer drugs like "ecstasy" and enlightened insurance, many of Your sannyasins are now working, with a job, and earning their livelihood. Laughter, a sense of humor, and a deep love and gratitude towards You, keep us all connected with each other somehow. With Your people in the world now and physically so far away, has Your work with us taken on a new significance?

It has certainly taken on a new significance, a new turn.

I always wanted my people to be in the world, occasionally coming to me, being with me, refreshing themselves, then going back again to the world – because the world has to be changed. We are not the ones who renounce the world.

All the religions have been teaching, "Renounce the world."

I teach you, transform the world.

Renouncing it is sheer cowardice, and by renouncing it, nothing significant happens – the world goes on living, producing new generations in the old pattern. And the persons who have renounced the world – they also don't go through a transformation, for a simple reason that they lose all opportunities where they can test whether they are growing or not. You can sit in the Himalayas for a half a century and you will feel silent, but that silence is not yours; it belongs to the Himalayas. Everything is silent, eternally silent, and there is nobody to disturb you.

Just to get out of the situations where you get disturbed does not mean that you are attaining peacefulness; it simply means you are running away from situations where you are certain that your peace will be disturbed. Renouncing the world has never been my idea; it was always to change it. Millions of people are suffering, and suffering for stupid reasons. It is absolutely inhuman to turn your back on it and move to the mountains or to the deserts to live peacefully there. That peace is very cheap, very superficial; it has almost no meaning. Just come back to the world and it will be disturbed, it will be shattered into pieces.

And that will be immensely significant to awaken you, that what you have been thinking of as peace, silence, has been just a dream which is shattered by the reality, just as a mirror is shattered when hit by a rock…and it is shattered forever. That mirror you cannot put together again, and all those years that you were enjoying the idea that you have attained peace have gone down the drain.

So my idea has always been: come to me to rejoice, come to me for a holiday. Come to me for pure joy. Be filled with the fragrance, be filled with my presence, then take it back into the world. There is the real test: whether it remains with you or not. If you want to keep it, spread it, share it, and it will grow within you. But whenever you feel somewhere stuck, not growing, I am available – come back to me, be with me. When you feel the clarity again, go back to the world.

If you start living with me you will be a loser on two counts. One: you will by and by start taking me for granted – which is a great loss, because I will be available to you. It is dangerous, because the more I am available to you, the less you will become available to me.

I have lived for almost twenty years in Jabalpur in India; it has one of the most beautiful spots in the world. For two to three miles continuously a beautiful river, Narmada, flows between two mountains of marble…just three miles of pure white marble on both sides, high mountains. And the river is deep.

On a full-moon night, when the moon comes in the middle and you can see those rocks also reflected into the waters, it creates almost a magical world. I don't think there is anything in the world which can be compared to that magic. It is simply unimaginable.

I insisted again and again to my professor, Doctor S.K. Saxena…I had loved him very much because he was the only teacher I came across who never treated me as a student. We argued, we fought on small points, and if he was wrong he was always ready to accept it, and he was grateful.

He had a Ph.D. from America – he lived his whole life in America, and taught as a professor of Indian philosophy there. Just at the end, he wanted to go back to his own country. He had been searching for someone who could translate his doctoral thesis into Hindi, but he never came across a man who could. And his thesis was really of great significance; just a literal translation would not have done. It needed someone with a deep understanding. The subject matter of the thesis was, "The evolution of consciousness in the East." It was one of the most difficult subjects, very elusive, but he had managed, worked hard, and had come to certain very significant conclusions.

He asked me – I was only a student – to translate it. I said, "You should ask some professor, at least someone qualified."

He said, "I have seen many professors, many qualified people; they can translate only literally. And I trust you. Arguing with you I have come to the conclusion that this is the man who can translate it."

It took me two months continuously – my whole holiday one summer. It was hard work. And it was harder because there were faults, there were mistakes, and I could not tolerate them. So I pointed out to him, "These are mistakes; out of your seven conclusions, three are wrong, and if it was in my hands I would take your doctorate back. The people who have given you a doctorate know nothing about consciousness."

He said, "I was afraid of this!"

But I said to him, "I have translated it; just in the footnotes I have made my comments where you have gone wrong, why you have gone wrong. Perhaps anybody would have gone wrong. Just as a scholar it was bound to happen, this mistake. I am not a scholar."

I gave the thesis to him and I said, "You look at it, and you tell me how you feel."

He hugged me and told me, "You have done such a tremendous job that I feel ashamed. It looks like my book is a translation and your book is the original! And I am not going to publish it because that would destroy my whole reputation. You have also made comments which I agree with – you are right and my examiners were wrong. I was wrong, my examiners were wrong."

So he kept the translated thesis with him and never allowed anyone to see it, never allowed anyone to publish it.

I said, "You wasted my two months unnecessarily!" I said, "Just to compensate, now you have to come with me to Jabalpur." It was one hundred miles from the university where he was professor, to the marble rocks. "I would not let you die without seeing it."

But he said, "Howsoever beautiful it is, I have seen the whole world" – he had been a world traveler – "I have seen everything that is worth seeing. What can be there?"

I said, "I cannot describe…you just come with me." And I took him there. He was asking again and again, when we were moving in the boat, "Do you call this the most beautiful place?"

I said, "You just wait. We have not entered into it yet." And then suddenly the boat entered into the world of marble, the mountains of marble. And in the full-moon night they were just so pure, so virgin-pure, and their reflections… The old man had tears in his eyes. He said, "If you had not insisted, I would have missed something in my life. Just take the boat close to the mountains, because I would like to touch then. It looks so illusory! Without touching I cannot believe that what I am seeing is real."

I told the boatman to come close to the mountains. He touched the mountains, and he said, "Now I can leave – they are real! But for three miles continuously…!"

This man wrote beautifully, spoke beautifully, but still was miserable. And I said, "Neither your writings mean anything, nor your speeches mean anything. To me what is significant is whether you have been able to drop all the causes of misery. You are so miserable that you drink, just to forget. You are so miserable that you smoke, just to forget. You gamble, just to forget."

Now, this world is not to be renounced. There are beautiful people, there are immensely capable people; they just have never come across a person who could have triggered a process of mutation in their life. So my idea has always been: come to me whenever you start feeling, "Perhaps I am living in an illusion." Then come and just touch me. Let yourself be showered by my presence, my love, so that you can regain confidence, courage, and you can go back to the world.

But the world is where the work is.

This is a mystery school.

We prepare people to send them to change the world.

That was from the very beginning my idea of a commune, but because I was silent and in isolation, things went not according to my idea. The commune, rather than becoming a refreshing place, a place for holiday, became just another world of work, of hierarchy, of bureaucracy. All those things that we wanted to change evolved in the commune itself.

So my new phase of work will be that there will be a mystery school. It will live like a commune, but the people will be changing. People will be coming whenever they can manage, whenever they need. There will be a certain number of people who will be permanent, to take care of all the visitors. But the commune will be a continuous pilgrimage place – where you learn something, where you drink something, and go back to the world.

We are not the renouncers – we are the revolutionaries.

We want to change the whole world.

And in changing the world, you will change yourself. You cannot change anything else unless you go through the change simultaneously.

So on one count it was a loss that if you were staying with me continuously…you are human, and it is a human mistake that one starts taking things for granted. I am available.

I told you about this beautiful spot because in Jabalpur there are thousands of people who have not seen it. It is only thirteen miles away, and I have asked those people – professors, doctors, engineers – "Just go and see!"

And they say, "We can see it anytime. It is there; it is not going to go away."

In the second world war it happened that suddenly, when Adolf Hitler declared that he was going to bomb the Tower of London, thousands of people rushed to see it. They had been living in London their whole life; they were born there. They were passing the Tower every day on the way to their job – going to the office, coming back home, it was there. People were coming from faraway places to see it, but *they* were taking it for granted: it is there, so what is the hurry?

It is absolutely certain that thousands of people have been born in London and died in London without seeing the tower. I know about Jabalpur; thousands of people must have died… It is always there, but *you* are not always there.

As far as the relationship with me is concerned, neither you are forever nor am I forever. But you can take it for granted, and by and by a fog surrounds your mind. Rather than my presence there is a fog – which separates you, not connects you.

This was the most disastrous thing that was happening in the commune. People were with me, but they had created a fog around themselves. Seen from the outside, physically they were close, but spiritually they had gone far away.

Secondly, when five thousand or ten thousand people start living in a commune, their whole orientation, why they have come there, changes without their knowledge. They had come there to meditate, to be with me, to be as much as possible open and available to my experience…to enjoy, to relax, to sing, to dance, to be ecstatic. They had all come for that.

But when ten thousand people have to live together, you have to make houses, you have to make roads, you have to prepare food, you have to prepare clothes; a thousand and one things are needed, they go on taking all your time. Slowly, slowly you completely forget the real reason you had come. You go on getting into other things, and the original intention is completely forgotten.

This time I am working in a totally different way, so these two things can be avoided.

For me, I always want to be just a holiday.

For me, I always want to mean nothing but

ecstasy, music, dance. It is good to be only for a few days with me and then go into the world. Take the music, take the ecstasy with you, spread it, and whenever you feel thirsty, come back again.

So it will be a world school of mysticism where people will be coming and going, taking the message to all the nooks and corners of the world. And I don't want you to be in any way associated with anything…road-making, making houses, and creating a dam – all that is just damned foolery!

I simply want you to remember me as a flower, a fragrance, a flame, a light; associate me with these things. That is going to be the purpose of the new mystery school. I would like to call it the mystery school rather than a commune, because that name has become associated with the commune we had.

I am not in any way thinking that the disappearance of that commune has been a loss. Not at all – because the way it was functioning, it was a non-ending rut. You would have needed new roads, because new houses were to be built, then new roads would have had to be connected. You would have needed more restaurants, bigger restaurants; you would have needed more clothes…and finally, you were going to have to produce. You would have had to make factories and other productive directions – because how long can five thousand people live only on donations? Friends can support for a time being, but not forever.

So soon you would have completely forgotten that you are separate from the world. In fact you would have been in more difficulty, because in the other world somebody else takes care of the roads, somebody else takes care of the post office, and somebody else takes care of other things. You have just to work five hours, six hours. In the commune you were working for twelve hours, sometimes fourteen hours; even then the work was unending.

So the resources that were helping the commune were going to be soon exhausted; the commune was going to collapse. I was telling the people who were in power in the commune, "The commune will collapse, because how long can you live on other people's support? And if you become productive – you open factories and you start making things – then why bother? All these things are being done everywhere else."

This time, from the very beginning, only a small nucleus of people who are absolutely necessary to run the mystery school will be living with me. Everybody else will be a guest for a few days, a few weeks, a few months…as much as he can manage. But his being here with me will be all relaxation, meditation, so he can be rejuvenated. And then he can go back. The whole world is there to work on.

This way we will avoid the most basic thing – that he does not take me for granted. And the second thing – that he does not forget his basic intention in coming to me.

Beloved Bhagwan,
Once, when I was sitting with a dying patient – it was Anna Freud, Sigmund Freud's youngest daughter – I was in conversation with her companion, and it happened I was speaking of You. When, an hour or so later, my patient died, I recalled I had mentioned Your name, and in retrospect it felt as if because of that, rosewater had been sprinkled into the atmosphere. Is it just being fanciful to feel that simply the mention of Your name, or even a brief glimpse of Your face on our lockets, can in some way have an effect on people?

It all depends on you – not on my name, not on my face on your locket, but on your heart.

If you are talking about me with deep love, with trust, with reverence, your heart creates a certain milieu. If you are talking not just from the mind but from the very innermost core of your being, it can happen: you can feel as if rosewater has been sprinkled…a great cleanliness, a great freshness, a fragrance. But they are not contained in my name or in my photograph; those are just instrumental. The reality that is created is by your heart.

There are people who are against me, who are saying my name continually, and they will never feel that rosewater has been sprinkled.

The archbishop in Greece has some source of information! As I was arrested, and the whole population of Saint Nicholas was at the airport to show their support to me, alone, with his half a dozen old, almost dead women, he was ringing the bell of victory – that God had won over the devil, that I was sent specially from hell to destroy God's land, his church, his morality. It depends! To him it may be that my name may give him such electric shocks that he will think that this man must be evil.

Just a few days before, when I was here in the ministry of interior, there were many people – a great crowd. Nobody recognized me because they were all people either from this country or from Argentina or Brazil where I have never been. But as I was being taken in, one woman immediately pulled back her three children and whispered to them, "Don't touch him!" She must have been either English or American, afraid that if you touch him, and if he is really the devil or comes from hell, it is going to be disastrous.

So it all depends on you.

But it was good that you were mentioning me when Anna Freud, Sigmund Freud's youngest daughter, was dying, and she heard about me with deep love and reverence from you. And she was not an orthodox woman. She was really representative of Sigmund Freud – the same quality of mind, the same sharpness, the same fearless intelligence to cut through all nonsense, superstitions. She was one of the most significant women of this century – and sensitive, alert.

I hope that what you felt, she also may have felt a little bit. At the moment of death, nothing could have been a greater gift to her – and she deserved it.

> **Beloved Bhagwan,**
> **An old Tibetan is quoted as saying:**
> "Like a lion, I have no fear.
> Like an elephant, I have no anxiety.
> Like a madman, I have no hope.
> I tell you the honest truth."
> **Bhagwan, what is so wondrous and precious about the honest truth?**

In fact, to use these two words together shows a deep misunderstanding.

"Honest truth" implies that there can be dishonest truth.

Truth is enough.

Honesty is a very ordinary quality that comes as a shadow of truth, with many other qualities. There is something immensely important about truth. But remember, never use the words *honest truth*. That means you have a suspicion: deep down you yourself are not convinced of the truthfulness of truth. To substitute, to compensate, you add honesty to it.

Nothing can be added to truth.

Truth is always pure, nude, alone.

And there is great beauty, because truth is the very essence of life, existence, nature. Except for man, nobody lies. A rosebush cannot lie. It has to produce roses; it cannot produce marigolds – it cannot deceive. It is not possible for it to be other than it is. Except for man, the whole existence lives in truth.

Truth is the religion of the whole of existence – except man.

And the moment a man also decides to become part of existence, truth becomes his religion. It is the glorious moment.

When I say that except for man everything is living truth – the ocean, the clouds, the stars, the stones, the flowers – that everything is nothing but truthfulness, nothing but just itself, with no mask, and only man is capable of deceiving others, of deceiving himself – it has to be remembered that this is a great opportunity. It has not to be condemned, it has to be praised, because even if a rosebush or a lotus *wants* to lie, it cannot. Its truth is not freedom; its truth is a bondage. It cannot go beyond the boundaries.

Man has the prerogative, the privilege of being untrue. That means man has the freedom to choose. If he chooses to be truthful, he is not choosing bondage, he is choosing truth and freedom. Freedom is his privilege. In the whole of existence, nobody else has freedom.

But there are dangers when you have opportunities. When you have freedom, you can go wrong. No rose can go wrong, no rock can go wrong. You can go wrong; hence a deep awareness of each act, of each thought, of each feeling, has to penetrate you.

To me that is what is the meaning of a seeker of truth.

Only man needs to seek it; everybody has already got it, but the glory of freedom is not there. You have to seek it, and find it. And in that very seeking and finding you are glorious, you are the very crown of existence.

But truth is enough.

Don't burden it with honesty or anything else.

**Beloved Bhagwan,
How can I thank You?**

There is no need: just be what you can be. Allow yourself to blossom. Enjoy in glory – and that will be thankfulness enough.

Anybody who blossoms close to me has already shown his gratitude. Saying it would be profane. Saying it would destroy the beauty of the unsaid, the silent.

If you have really come to a point when you want to say thank you to me, then don't say it; I will understand it. By saying it, you will be bringing down something from a very high level.

You will be surprised to know that in India, one of the oldest civilizations in the world, perhaps the oldest, you rarely hear anybody thanking somebody else. No child will thank his parents; no parents will thank their child. In the West that is part of your formal training: on each occasion say, "Thank you."

I was thinking about the difference, why it has not developed in this old civilization. And I understand…what I said, that is the reason. If you are really thankful, then saying it is useless, because you cannot put your heart into it. And if you are not thankful, then why unnecessarily destroy a beautiful word?

And to make it a formality means that you are making it an unconscious part of your behavior. So just as somebody presents you with a cup of coffee and you say thank you, if somebody brings enlightenment to your consciousness, are you going to use the same words? It is absolutely impossible to use those same words; they have become so formal. You say them without even thinking about it. You simply say them like a robot.

It is a good question, to ask me how to say thank you to me, because there must be a great feeling of gratitude, but all words seem to be meaningless. Thankfulness, gratefulness – they all seem to be too small. What has happened to you is so vast.

My suggestion is: you need not give me any thank you. I will take it myself.

It will be so apparent through your eyes and through your face, but there will be no need to say it. I will simply understand it from there.

Chapter 18
April 21, 1986, Morning

Terrorism is in Your Unconsciousness

Beloved Bhagwan,
I've heard that in Europe the threat of terrorism is striking fear in everyone. Airplanes are delayed by extraordinary security measures, many of the seats are empty, and some airports are closing. People are even thinking twice about going out in the evening. And all this is more prevalent since the recent bombing of Libya. Is the rise of terrorism over the last decade in some way symbolic of what is happening to society in general?

Everything is deeply related with everything else that happens.

The event of terrorism is certainly related with what is happening in the society. The society is falling apart. Its old order, discipline, morality, religion, everything has been found to be wrongly based. It has lost its power over people's conscience.

Terrorism simply symbolizes that to destroy human beings does not matter, that there is nothing in human beings which is indestructible, that it is all matter – and you cannot kill matter, you can only change its form. Once man is taken to be only a combination of matter, and no place is given for a spiritual being inside him, then to kill becomes just play.

The nations are irrelevant because of nuclear weapons. If the whole world can be destroyed together within minutes the alternative can only be that the whole world should be together. Now it cannot remain divided; its division is dangerous, because division can become war any moment. The division cannot be tolerated. Only one war is enough to destroy everything, and there is not much time left for man to understand that we should create a world where the very possibility of war does not exist.

Terrorism has many undercurrents. One is that because of nuclear weapons, the nations are pouring their energy into that field, thinking that the old weapons are out of date. They *are* out of date, but individuals can start using them. And you cannot use nuclear weapons against individuals – that would be simply stupid. One individual terrorist throws a bomb – it does not justify that a nuclear missile should be sent.

What I want to emphasize is that the nuclear weapon has given individual people a certain freedom to use old weapons, a freedom which was not possible in the old days because the governments were also using the same weapons.

Now the governments are concentrated on destroying the old weapons, throwing them in the ocean, selling them to countries which are poor and cannot afford nuclear weapons. And all those terrorists are coming from these poor countries, with the same weapons that have been sold to their countries. And they have a strange protection: you cannot use nuclear weapons against them, you cannot throw atom bombs at them.

They can throw bombs at you and you are suddenly impotent. You have a vast amount of atomic bombs, nuclear bombs in your hands – but sometimes where a needle is useful, a sword may not be of any use. You may have the sword; that does not mean that you are necessarily in a superior position to the man who has a needle, because there are purposes in which only the needle will work – the sword will not be of any use.

Those small weapons from the old times were piling up, and the big powers had to dispose of them – either drown them in the ocean.... That meant so much money, so much manpower, so much energy had gone to waste; economically it was disastrous. But just to go on piling them up was also economically impossible. How many weapons can you gather? There is a limit. And when you get a new way of killing people more efficiently, then the old simply has to be got rid of.

It was thought that it would be better to sell them to poor countries. Poor countries cannot create nuclear weapons – it costs too much. And these weapons were coming cheap – as help; they accepted it, but these weapons cannot be used in a war. In a war these weapons are already useless. But nobody has seen the possibility that these weapons can be used individually, and a new phenomenon – terrorism – can come out of it.

Now, a terrorist has a strange power, even over the greatest powers. He can throw bombs at the White House without any fear, because what you have is too big and you cannot throw it at him. And these are the weapons sold by you! But the phenomenon was not conceived of, because human psychology is not understood.

My understanding is that the way he has lived, man needs every ten to twelve years, a war. He accumulates so much anger, so much rage, so much violence, that nothing short of a war will give him release. So, war after war, there is a gap of only ten to fifteen years. That gap is a kind of relaxation. But again you start accumulating, because the same psychology is working – the same jealousy, the same violence.

And man is basically a hunter; he is not by nature vegetarian. First he became a hunter, and for thousands of years he was just a meat-eater, and cannibalism was prevalent everywhere. To eat human beings caught from the opposing tribe you were fighting with was perfectly ethical. All that is carried in the unconscious of humanity.

Religions have imposed things on man

very superficially; his unconscious is not in agreement. Every man is living in a disagreement with himself. So whenever he can find a chance – for a beautiful cause; freedom, democracy, socialism – *any* beautiful word can become an umbrella to hide his ugly unconscious, which simply wants to destroy and enjoys destruction.

Now the world war has become almost impossible; otherwise there would have been no terrorism. Enough time has passed since the second world war; the third world war should have happened nearabout 1960. It has not happened. This has been the routine for the whole of history, and man is programmed for it.

It has been observed by psychologists that in wartime people are more happy than in peacetime. In wartime their life has a thrill; in peacetime they look bored. In wartime, early in the morning they are searching for the newspaper, listening to the radio. Things may be happening far away, but they are excited. Something in them feels an affinity.

A war that should have happened somewhere between 1955 and 1960 has not happened, and man is burdened with the desire to kill, with the desire to destroy. It is just that he wants good names for it.

Terrorism is going to become bigger and bigger, because the third world war is almost impossible. And the stupid politicians have no other alternative. Terrorism simply means that what was being done on a social scale now has to be done individually. It will grow. It can only be prevented if we change the very base of human understanding – which is a Himalayan task; more so because these same people whom you want to change will fight you. They won't allow you to change them easily.

In fact they love bloodshed; they don't have the courage to say so. In one of the existentialist's novels, there is a beautiful incident which can almost be said to be true. A man is presented before the court because he has killed a stranger who was sitting on the beach. He had never seen the stranger. He did not kill him for money. He does not yet know how that man looked, because he killed him from the back, just with a big knife.

They had never met – there was no question of enmity. They were not even familiar; they had not even seen each other's faces.

The magistrate could not figure it out, and he asked the murderer, "Why did you do it?"

He said, "When I stabbed that man with a knife, and a fountain of blood came out of his back, that was one of the most beautiful moments I have ever known. I know that the price will be my death, but I am ready to pay for it; it was worth it. My whole life I have lived in boredom – no excitement, no adventure. Finally I had to decide to *do* something. And this act has made me world famous; my picture is in every newspaper. And I am perfectly happy that I did it."

There was no need for any evidence. The man was not denying – on the contrary, he was glorifying it. But the court has its own routine way – witnesses still have to be produced; just his word cannot be accepted. He may have be lying, he may not have killed the man. Nobody saw him – there was not a single eyewitness – so circumstantial evidences had to be presented by the police.

One of them was that possibly this man has killed according to his past life and his background. When he was young, his mother died. And when he heard that his mother had died, he said, "Shit! That woman will not leave me even while dying! It is Sunday, and I have booked tickets for the theater with my girlfriend. But I knew she would do something to destroy my whole day – and she has destroyed it."

His mother has died and he is saying that she has destroyed his Sunday! He was going to the theater with his girlfriend, and now he has to go to the funeral. And the people who heard his reaction were shocked. They said, "This is not right, what are you saying?"

He said, "What? What is right and what is wrong? Couldn't she die on any other day? There are seven days in the week – from Monday to Saturday, she could have died any day. But you don't know my mother – I know her. She is a bitch! She did it on purpose."

The second evidence was that he attended the funeral, and in the evening he was found dancing with his girlfriend in a disco. And somebody asked, "What! What are you doing? Your mother has just died."

He said, "So what? Do you mean now I can never dance again? My mother is never going to be alive, she will remain dead; so what does it matter whether I dance after six hours, eight hours, eight months, eight years? What does it matter? – she is *dead*. And I have to dance and I have to live and I have to love, in *spite* of her death. If everybody stopped living with the death of their mother, with the death of their father, then there would be no dance in the world, no song in the world."

His logic is very right. He is saying, "Where do you draw the demarcation line? After how many hours can I dance? – twelve hours, fourteen hours, six weeks? Where will you draw the line? on what grounds? What is the criterion? So it doesn't matter. One thing is certain: whenever I dance I will be dancing after the death of my mother, so I decided to dance today. Why wait for tomorrow?"

Such circumstantial evidences are presented to the court – that this man is strange, he can do such an act. But if you look closely at this poor man, you will not feel angry at him; you will feel very compassionate. Now, it is not his fault that his mother has died; and anyway, he has to dance some day, so it makes no difference. You cannot blame this man for saying ugly things: "She deliberately died on Sunday to spoil my joy," because his whole experience of life must have been that she was again and again spoiling any possibility of joy. This was the last conclusion: "Even in death she will not leave me."

And you cannot condemn the man for killing a stranger…because he is not a thief; he did not take anything from him. He is not an enemy; he did not even see who was the man he was killing. He was simply bored with life and he wanted to do something that made him feel significant, important. He is happy that all the newspapers have his photo. If they had published his photo before, he would not have killed; but they waited – until he kills they will not publish his photo. And he wanted to be a celebrity…just ordinary human desires.

And he was ready to pay with his life to become, at least for one day, known to the whole world, recognized by everybody.

Until we change the basic grounds of humanity, terrorism is going to become more and more a normal, everyday affair. It will happen in the airplanes, it will happen in the buses. It will start happening in the cars. It will start happening to strangers. Somebody will suddenly come and shoot you – not that you have done anything to him, but just, the hunter is back.

The hunter was satisfied in the war. Now the war has stopped and perhaps there is no possibility for it.

The hunter is back; now we cannot fight collectively. Each individual has to do something to release his own steam.

Things are interconnected. The first thing that has to be changed is that man should be made more rejoicing – which all the religions have killed. The real criminals are not caught. These are the victims, the terrorists and other criminals.

It is all the religions who are the real criminals, because they have destroyed all possibilities of rejoicing. They have destroyed the possibility of enjoying small things of life; they have condemned everything that nature provides you to make you happy, to make you feel excited, feel pleasant.

They have taken *everything* away; and if they have not been able to take a few things away because they are so ingrained in your biology – like sex – they have at least been able to poison them.

Friedrich Nietzsche, according to me, is one of the greatest seers of the Western world; his eyes really go penetrating to the very root of a problem. But because others could not see it – their eyes were not so penetrating, nor was their intelligence so sharp – the man lived alone, abandoned, isolated, unloved, unrespected.

He says in one of his statements that man has been taught by religions to condemn sex, to renounce sex. Religion has not been able to manage it; and man has tried hard but has failed, because it is so deeply rooted in his biology – it constitutes his whole body. He is born out of sex – how can he get rid of it except by committing suicide?

So man has tried, and religions have helped him to get rid of it – thousands of disciplines and strategies have been used. The total result is that sex is there, but poisoned. That word 'poisoned' is a tremendous insight. Religions have not been able to take it away, but they have been certainly successful in poisoning it.

And the same is the situation about other things: religions are condemning your living in comfort. Now, a man who is living in comfort and luxury cannot become a terrorist. Religions have condemned riches, praised poverty; now, a man who is rich cannot be a terrorist. Only the "blessed ones" who are poor can be terrorists – because they have nothing to lose, and they are boiling up against the whole of society because others have things they don't have.

Religions have been trying to console them. But then came communism – a materialist religion – which provoked people and said to them, "Your old religions are all opium to the people, and it is not because of your evil actions in this life or in past lives that you are suffering poverty. It is because of the evil exploitation of the bourgeois, the super-rich that you are suffering."

The last sentence in Karl Marx's *Communist Manifesto* is: Proletariats of the whole world unite; you have nothing to lose and you have the whole world to gain.

"You are already poor, hungry, naked – so what can you lose? Your death will not make you more miserable than your life is making you. So why not take a chance and destroy those people who have taken everything away from you. And take those things back, distribute them."

What religions have somehow been consoling people with – although it was wrong and it was cunning and it was a lie, but it kept people in a state of being half asleep – communism suddenly made them aware of. That means this world is now never going to be peaceful if we don't withdraw all the rotten ideas that have been implanted in man.

The first are the religions – their values should be removed so that man can smile again, can laugh again, can rejoice again, can be natural again. Second, what communism is saying has to be put clearly before the people – that it is psychologically wrong. You are falling from one trap into another. No two men are equal; hence the idea of equality is nonsense. And if you decide to be equal then you have to accept a dictatorship of the proletariat. That means you have to lose your freedom.

First the church took away your freedom, the God took away your freedom. Now communism replaces your church, and *it* will take away your freedom.

And without freedom you cannot rejoice.

You live in fear, not in joy.

If we can clean the basement of the human mind's unconscious…and that's what my work is. It can be cleaned away.

The terrorism is not in the bombs, in your hands; the terrorism is in your unconscious.

Otherwise, this state of affairs is going to grow more bitter. And it seems all kinds of blind people have bombs in their hands and are throwing them at random.

The third world war would have released people for ten or fifteen years. But the third world war cannot happen because if it happens it won't relieve people, it will only destroy people.

So individual violence will increase – it is increasing. And all your governments and all your religions will go on perpetuating the old strategies without understanding the new situation.

The new situation is that every human being needs to go through therapies, needs to understand his unconscious intentions, needs to go through meditations so that he can calm down, become cool – and look towards the world with a new perspective, of silence.

Beloved Bhagwan,
Whenever in life I've had a bout of feeling miserable, a point always comes when I just laugh at myself, feel freedom return, and see that all I had done was to stop loving myself.

This insight in itself is perhaps not particularly profound but at the moment of its realization, I am always amazed to see how easily, for what, and for how long I am willing to forsake my own self-love. Is this at the roots of most people's suffering, or is it just *my* trip?

It is not just your trip. It is at the root of most people's suffering – but not with the meaning you are giving to it.

It is not because you have stopped loving yourself that you fall in misery.

It is that you have created a self which does not exist at all, so sometimes this unreal self suffers misery in loving others, because out of unreality, love is not possible. And it is not on one side: two unrealities trying to love each other…sooner or later this arrangement is going to fail. When this arrangement fails, you fall upon yourself – there is nowhere else to go. So you think, "I had forgotten to love myself."

In a way it is a small relief: at least instead of two unrealities now you have only one. But what will you do by loving yourself? And how long can you manage to remain loving yourself? It is unreal; it won't allow you to see it for a long time because that is dangerous: if you see it for a long time, this so-called self will disappear, and that will be a real freedom from misery.

Love will remain, unaddressed, to someone else or to yourself.

Love will remain unaddressed, because there is nobody to address, and when love is there unaddressed, there is great bliss.

But this unreal self won't allow you much time. Soon you will be falling in love with someone else again, because the unreal self needs the support of other unrealities. So people fall in love and fall out of love and fall in love and fall out of love – and strange is the phenomenon, that dozens of times they do it and still they don't see the point. They are miserable when they are in love with someone else; they are miserable when they are alone and not in love, a bit relieved – for the moment.

In India, when a person dies, people carry him on a stretcher-like construction on their shoulders. But they go on changing it on the way, on their shoulders – from this shoulder they will put it on the right, and after a few minutes they will again change and put it on the left. It feels a relief when you put it from the left shoulder onto the right. Nothing is being changed – the weight is there, and on you, but this left shoulder feels a kind of relief. It is momentary, because soon the right shoulder will start hurting so you will have to change it again.

And this is what your life is. You go on changing the other, thinking that perhaps this woman, this man, will bring you the paradise you have always been longing for. But everybody brings hell – without fail! And nobody is to be condemned for it, because they are doing exactly the same as you are doing: they are carrying an unreal self out of which nothing can grow. It cannot blossom. It is empty – decorated, but inside empty and hollow.

So when you see somebody from far away he or she is appealing. As you come closer the appeal becomes less. When you meet, it is not a meeting but a clash. And suddenly you see the other person is empty, and you have been deceived, cheated, because the other person has nothing which had been promised.

The same is the situation of the other person about you. All promises fail, and you become a burden to each other, a misery to each other, a sadness to each other, destructive to each other. You separate. For a little while there is relief, but your inner unreality cannot leave you in this state for long; soon you will be searching for another woman, another man, and you will get into the same trap. Only the faces are different; the inner reality is the same – empty.

If you really want to get rid of misery and suffering then you will have to understand – you don't have a self. Then it will be not just a small relief but a tremendous relief. And if you don't have a self, the need for the other disappears. It was the need of the unreal self to go on being nourished by the other. You don't need the other.

And listen carefully: when you don't need the other, you can love.

And that love will not bring misery.

Going beyond needs, demands, desires, love becomes a very soft sharing, a great understanding.

When you understand yourself, that very day you have understood the whole of humanity. Then nobody can make you miserable. You know that they are suffering from an unreal self, and they are throwing their misery on anybody who is close by.

Your love will make you capable of helping the person you love to get rid of the self.

I know only of one present....

Love can present you only with one thing: That you are not, that your self is just imaginary. This realization between two persons suddenly makes them one, because two nothings cannot be two. Two somethings will be two, but two nothings cannot be two: Two nothings start melting and merging. They are bound to become one.

For example, if we are sitting here.... If everybody is an ego then there are so many people; they can be counted. But there are moments I can see – perhaps many times you see them too – when there is utter silence. Then you cannot count how many people are here. There is only one consciousness, one silence, one nothingness, one selflessness. And only in that state can two persons live in eternal joy, can any group live in tremendous beauty; the whole of humanity can live in great benediction.

But try to see the self, and you will not find it. Not finding it is of great importance.

I have told many times the story of Bodhidharma and his meeting with the Chinese emperor Wu – a very strange meeting, very fruitful. Emperor Wu perhaps was at that time the greatest emperor in the world; he ruled all over China, Mongolia, Korea, the whole of Asia, except India.

He became convinced of the truth of Gautam Buddha's teachings, but the people who had brought the message of Buddha were scholars. None of them were mystics. And then the news came that Bodhidharma was coming, and there was a great thrill all over the land. Because Emperor Wu had become influenced by Gautam Buddha, that had made his whole empire influenced by the same teaching.

And now a *real* mystic, a buddha, was coming. It was such a great joy!

Emperor Wù had never before come to the boundaries where India and China meet to receive anyone. With great respect he welcomed Bodhidharma, and he asked , "I have been asking all the monks and the scholars who have been coming, but nobody has been of any help – I have tried everything. But how to get rid of this self? And Buddha says, 'Unless you become a no-self, your misery cannot end.'"

He was sincere. Bodhidharma looked into his eyes, and he said, "I will be staying by the side of the river near the mountain in the temple. Tomorrow morning, at four o'clock exactly, you come and I will finish this self forever. But remember, you are not to bring any arms with you, any guards with you; you have to come alone."

Wu was a little worried – the man was strange! "How can he just destroy my self so quickly? It takes – it has been told by the scholars – lives and lives of meditation; then the self disappears. This man is weird! And he is wanting me to come in the darkness, early in the morning at four o'clock, alone, even without a sword, no guards, no other companion. This man seems to be strange – he could do anything.

"And what does he mean that he will kill the self forever? He can kill me, but how will he kill the self?"

The whole night he could not sleep. He changed his mind again and again – to go or not to go? But there was something in the man's eyes, and there was something in his voice, and there was some aura of authority when he said, "Just come at four o'clock sharp, and I will finish this self forever! You need not be worried about it."

What he said looked absurd, but the way he said it, and the way he looked were so authoritative: he knows what he is saying. Finally Wu had to decide to go. He decided to risk, "At the most he can kill me – what else? And I have tried everything. I cannot attain this no-self, and without attaining this no-self there is no end to misery."

He knocked on the temple door, and Bodhidharma said, "I knew you would come;

165

I knew also that the whole night you would be changing your mind. But that does not matter – you have come. Now sit down in the lotus posture, close your eyes, and I am going to sit in front of you.

"The *moment* you find, inside, your self, catch hold of it so I can kill it. Just catch hold of it tightly and tell me that you have caught it, and I will kill it and it will be finished. It is a question of minutes."

Wu was a little afraid. Bodhidharma looked like a madman; he is painted like a madman – he was not like that, but the paintings are symbolic. That's the impression he must have left on people. It was not his real face, but that must be the face that people were remembering.

He was sitting with his big staff in front of Wu, and he said to him, "Don't miss a second. Just the moment you catch hold of it – search inside every nook and corner – open your eyes and then tell me that you have caught it, and I will finish it."

Then there was silence. One hour passed, two hours passed and the sun was rising, and Wu was a different man. In those two hours he looked inside himself, in every nook and corner. He *had* to look – that man was sitting there; he could have hit him on his head with his staff.

You could expect anything; whatever.... He was not a man of etiquette, manner; he was not part of Wu's court, so he had to look intently, intensively. And as he looked, he became relaxed, because it was nowhere. And in looking for it, all thoughts disappeared. The search was so intense that his whole energy was involved in it; there was nothing left to think and desire, and this and that.

As the sun was rising Bodhidharma saw Wu's face; he was not the same man – such silence, such depth. He had disappeared.

Bodhidharma shook him and told him, "Open your eyes – it is not there. I don't have to kill it. I am a nonviolent man, I don't kill anything! But this self does not exist. Because you never look at it, it goes on existing. It is in your not looking for it, in your unawareness, that it exists. Now it is gone."

Two hours had passed, and Wu was immensely glad. He had never tasted such sweetness, such freshness, such newness, such beauty. And he was not.

Bodhidharma had fulfilled his promise. Emperor Wu bowed down, touched his feet and said, "Please forgive me thinking that you are mad, thinking that you don't know manners, thinking that you you are weird, thinking that you you can be dangerous. I have never seen a more compassionate man than you…I am totally fulfilled. Now there is no question in me."

Emperor Wu said that when he died, on his grave, the memorial, Bodhidharma's statement should be engraved in gold, for the people in centuries to come to know… "There was a man who looked mad, but who was capable of doing miracles. Without doing anything he helped me to be a non-self. And since then everything has changed. Everything is the same but I am not the same, and life has become just a pure song of silence."

Beloved Bhagwan,

Sometimes, when dark sides of my mind come up, it really scares me. It is very difficult for me to accept that it is just the polar opposite of the bright ones. I feel dirty and guilty and not worthy of sitting with You in Your immaculate presence.

I want to face all facets of my mind and accept them because I hear You often say that acceptance is the condition to transcend the mind.

Can You please talk about acceptance?

The basic thing to be understood is that you are not the mind – neither the bright one nor the dark one. If you get identified with the beautiful part, then it is impossible to disidentify yourself from the ugly part; they are two sides of the same coin. You can have it whole, or you can throw it away whole, but you cannot divide it.

And the whole anxiety of man is that he wants to choose that which looks beautiful, bright; he wants to choose all the silver linings, leaving the dark cloud behind. But he does not know that silver linings cannot exist without the dark cloud. The dark cloud is the background, absolutely necessary for silver linings to show.

Choosing is anxiety.

Choosing is creating trouble for yourself.

Being choiceless means: the mind is there and it has a dark side and it has a bright side – so what? What has it to do with you? Why should you be worried about it?

The moment you are not choosing, all worry disappears. A great acceptance arises, that this is how the mind has to be, this is the nature of the mind – and it is not your problem, because you are not the mind. If you were the mind, there would have been no problem at all. Then who would choose and

Step Aside, Let the Mind Pass

who would think of transcending? And who would try to accept and understand acceptance?

You are separate, totally separate.

You are only a witness and nothing else.

But you are being an observer who gets identified with anything that he finds pleasant – and forgets that the unpleasant is coming just behind it as a shadow. You are not troubled by the pleasant side – you rejoice in it. The trouble comes when the polar opposite asserts – then you are torn apart.

But you started the whole trouble. Falling from being just a witness, you became identified. The biblical story of the fall is just a fiction. But this is the real fall – the fall from being a witness into getting identified with something and losing your witnessing.

Just try once in a while: Let the mind be whatever it is. Remember, you are not it. And you are going to have a great surprise. As you are less identified, the mind starts becoming less powerful, because its power comes from your identification; it sucks your blood. But when you start standing aloof and away, the mind starts shrinking.

The day you are completely unidentified with the mind, even for a single moment, there is the revelation: mind simply dies; it is no longer there. Where it was so full, where it was so continuous – day in, day out, waking, sleeping, it was there – suddenly it is not there. You look all around and it is emptiness, it is nothingness.

And with the mind disappears the self. Then there is only a certain quality of awareness, with no "I" in it. At the most you can call it something similar to "am-ness," but not "I-ness." To be even more exact, it is "is-ness" because even in am-ness some shadow of the "I" is still there. The moment you know its is-ness, it has become universal.

With the disappearance of the mind disappears the self. And so many things disappear which were so important to you, so troublesome to you. You were trying to solve them and they were becoming more and more complicated; everything was a problem, an anxiety, and there seemed to be no way out.

I remind you of the story, "The Goose is Out." It is concerned with the mind and your is-ness.

The master tells the disciple to meditate on a koan: A small goose is put into a bottle, fed and nourished. The goose goes on becoming bigger and bigger and bigger, and fills the whole bottle. Now it is too big; it cannot come out of the bottle's mouth – the mouth is too small. And the koan is that you have to bring the goose out without destroying the bottle, without killing the goose.

Now it is mind-boggling.

What can you do? The goose is too big; you cannot take it out unless you break the bottle, but that is not allowed. Or you can bring it out by killing it; then you don't care whether it comes out alive or dead. That is not allowed either.

Day in, day out, the disciple meditates, finds no way, thinks this way and that way – but in fact there is no way. Tired, utterly exhausted, a sudden revelation…suddenly he understands that the master cannot be interested in the bottle and the goose; they must represent something else. The bottle is the mind, you are the goose…and with witnessing, it is possible. Without being *in* the mind, you can become identified with it so much that you start feeling you *are* in it!

He runs to the master to say that the goose is out. And the master says, "You have understood it. Now keep it out. It has never been in."

If you go on struggling with the goose and

the bottle, there is no way for you to solve it. It is the realization that, "It must represent something else; otherwise the master cannot give it to me. And what can it be?" – because the whole function between the master and the disciple, the whole business is about the mind and awareness.

Awareness is the goose which is not in the bottle of the mind. But you are believing that it *is* in it and asking everyone how to get it out. And there are idiots who will help you, with techniques, to get out of it. I call them idiots because they have not understood the thing at all.

The goose *is* out, has never been in, so the question of bringing it out does not arise.

Mind is just a procession of thoughts passing in front of you on the screen of the brain. You are an observer. But you start getting identified with beautiful things – those are bribes. And once you get caught in the beautiful things you are also caught in the ugly things, because mind cannot exist without duality.

Awareness cannot exist *with* duality, and mind cannot exist *without* duality.

Awareness is non-dual, and mind is dual.

So just watch. I don't teach you any solutions. I teach you *the* solution:

Just get back a little and watch.

Create a distance between you and your mind.

Whether it is good, beautiful, delicious, something that you would like to enjoy closely, or it is ugly – remain as far away as possible. Look at it just the way you look at a film. But people get identified even with films.

I have seen, when I was young... I have not seen any movie for a long time. But I have seen people weeping, tears coming down – and nothing is happening! It is good that in a movie house it is dark; it saves them from feel-ing embarrassed. I used to ask my father, "Did you see? The fellow by your side was crying!"

He said, "The whole hall was crying. The scene was such..."

"But," I said, "there is only a screen and nothing else. Nobody is killed, there is no tragedy happening – just a projection of a film, just pictures moving on the screen. And people laugh, and people weep, and for three hours they are almost lost. They become part of the movie, they become identified with some character..."

My father said to me, "If you are raising questions about people's reactions then you cannot enjoy the film."

I said, "I can enjoy the film, but I don't want to cry; I don't see any enjoyment in it. I can see it as a film, but I don't want to become a part of it. These people are all becoming a part of it."

My grandfather had an old barber who was an opium addict. For something which was possible to do in five minutes he would take two hours, and he would talk continuously. But they were old friends from their childhood. I can still see my grandfather sitting in the chair of the old barber... And he was a lovely talker. These opium addicts have a certain quality, a beauty of talking, telling stories about themselves, what is happening day-to-day; it is true.

My grandfather would simply be saying, "Yes, right, that's great..."

I said to him one day, "About everything you go on saying, 'Yes, right, it is great.' Sometimes he is talking nonsense, simply irrelevant."

He said, "What do you want? That man is an opium addict..."

In India razor blades are not used; things almost like six-inch long knives are used as razor blades. "Now what do you want me to say? – with that man who has a knife, a sharp knife in his hand, just on my throat. To say no to him…he will kill me! And he knows it. He sometimes tells me, 'You never say no. You always say yes, you always say great.' And I have told him, 'You should understand that you are always under the influence of opium. It is impossible to talk with you, to discuss with you or to disagree with you. You have a knife on my throat, and you want me to say no to something?'"

I said, "Then why don't you change from this man? There are so many other barbers, and this man takes two hours for a five-minute job. Sometimes he takes half your beard and then he says, 'I am coming back, you sit.' And he is gone for an hour, because he gets involved in a discussion with somebody and forgets completely that a customer is sitting in his chair. Then he comes and says, 'My God, so you are still sitting here?'"

And my grandfather would say, "What can I do? I cannot go home with half the beard shaved. You just complete it. Where have you been?"

The barber would say, "I got in such a good argument with somebody that I completely forgot about you. It is good that that man had to go; otherwise you would have been sitting here the whole day. And sometimes I don't even close the shop at night. I simply go home, just forget to close, and once in a while a customer is still sitting in the chair and I am sleeping. Somebody has to say to him, 'Now you can go; that man will not be seen again before tomorrow morning. He is fast asleep in his home. He has forgotten to close his shop and he has forgotten about you.'"

And if you were angry… Sometimes new people got into his shop, and became angry.

He would say, "Calm down. At the most you need not pay me. I have cut only half of the beard; you can just go. I don't want to argue. You need not pay me; I don't ask even for half payment."

But nobody can leave his chair with half the beard shaved – or half the head shaved! You ask him just to shave the beard and he starts shaving your head, and by the time you notice, he has already done the job. So he asks you, "Now what do you want? – because almost one-fourth of the work is done. If you want to keep it this way I can leave it; otherwise I can finish it. But I will not charge for it because if you say that you never wanted it to be cut, then it is my fault and I should take the punishment. I will not charge you."

This man was dangerous! But my grandfather used to say, "He is dangerous but he is lovely and I have become so much identified with him that I cannot conceive that if he dies before me I will be able to go to another barber's shop. I cannot conceive…for my whole life he has been my barber. The identity has become so deep that I may stop shaving my beard, but I cannot change my barber."

But fortunately my grandfather died before the opium-addict barber.

You get identified with anything. People get identified with persons and then they create misery for themselves. They get identified with things, then they get miserable if that thing is missing.

Identification is the root cause of your misery.

And every identification is identification with the mind.

Just step aside, let the mind pass.

And soon you will be able to see that there is no problem at all – the goose is out. You don't have to break the bottle, you don't have to kill the goose either.

Beloved Bhagwan,
How best to deal with fear? It affects me variously...from a vague uneasiness or knotted stomach to a dizzying panic, as if the world is ending.
Where does it come from?
Where does it go?

It is the same question that I was just answering. All your fears are by-products of your identification.

You love a woman and with the love, in the same parcel comes fear: she may leave you – she has already left somebody and come with you. There is a precedent; perhaps she will do the same to you. There is fear, you feel knots in the stomach. You are too much attached.

You cannot get a simple fact: you have come alone in the world; you have been here yesterday also, without this woman, perfectly well, without any knots in the stomach. And tomorrow if this woman goes...what is the need of the knots? You know how to be without her, and you will be able to be without her.

The fear that things may change tomorrow... Somebody may die, you may go bankrupt, your job may be taken away. There are a thousand and one things which may change. You are burdened with fears and fears, and none of them are valid – because yesterday also you were full of all these fears, unnecessarily. Things may have changed, but you are still alive. And man has an immense capacity to adjust himself in any situation.

They say that only man and cockroaches have this immense capacity of adjustment. That's why wherever you find man you will find cockroaches, and wherever you find cockroaches you will find man. They go together, they have a similarity. Even in faraway places like the North Pole or the South Pole... When man traveled to those places he suddenly found that he had brought cockroaches with him, and they were perfectly healthy and living and reproducing.

If you just look around the earth you can see – man lives in thousands of different climates, geographical situations, political situations, sociological situations, religious situations, but he manages to live. And he has lived for centuries...things go on changing, he goes on adjusting himself.

There is nothing to fear. Even if the world ends, so what? You will be ending with it. Do you think you will be standing on an island and the whole world will end, leaving you alone? Don't be worried. At least you will have a few cockroaches with you!

What is the problem if the world ends? It has been asked to me many times. But what is the problem? – if it ends, it ends. It does not create any problem because we will not be here; we will be ending with it, and there will be no one to worry about. It will be really the greatest freedom from fear.

The world ending means every problem ending, every disturbance ending, every knot in your stomach ending. I don't see the problem. But I know that everybody is full of fear.

But the question is the same: the fear is part of the mind. The mind is a coward, and *has* to be a coward because it doesn't have any substance – it is empty and hollow, and it is afraid of everything. And basically it is afraid that one day you may become aware. That will be *really* the end of the world!

Not the end of the world but your becoming aware, your coming to a state of meditation where mind has to disappear – that is its basic fear. Because of that fear it keeps people away from meditation, makes them enemies of people like me who are trying to spread something of meditation, some way of awareness and witnessing. They become antagonistic to me – not without any reason; their fear is well-founded.

They may not be aware of it, but their mind is really afraid to come close to anything that can create more awareness. That will be the beginning of the end of the mind. That will be the death of the mind.

But for you there is no fear. The death of the mind will be your rebirth, your beginning to *really* live. You should be happy, you should rejoice in the death of the mind, because nothing can be a greater freedom. Nothing else can give you wings to fly into the sky; nothing else can make the whole sky yours.

Mind is a prison.

Awareness is getting out of the prison – or realizing it has never been in the prison; it was just thinking that it was in the prison. All fears disappear.

I am also living in the same world, but I have never felt for a single moment any fear because nothing can be taken away from me. I can be killed – but I will be seeing it happening, so what is being killed is not me, is not my awareness.

The greatest discovery in life, the most precious treasure, is of awareness. Without it you are bound to be in darkness, full of fears. And you will go on creating new fears – there is no end to it. You will live in fear, you will die in fear, and you will never be able to taste something of freedom. And it was all the time your potential; any moment you could have claimed it, but you never claimed it.

It is your responsibility.

Beloved Bhagwan,
When You came to say farewell to Dadaji on the podium in Buddha Hall, suddenly the area where You and Dadaji's body were became like a film. You both seemed to be without substance. The other half of the podium where Mataji sat, and the rest of Buddha Hall where we were all sitting, seemed normal. Just the part where You were seemed different. What happened?

Death, if it happens with enlightenment, is a tremendous experience. On the one hand the man dies; on the other hand he achieves the totality of life.

When I touched my father's seventh chakra, just on the top of the head, those who were perceptive, silent, meditative, may have experienced something strange happening. According to the centuries-old science of inner reality, a man's life energy is released from the center, the chakra, at which he was living.

Most people die from the lowest chakra, the sex center. There are seven chakras in the body from where life can go out of the body. The last is on top of the head, and unless you are enlightened life cannot go out from that chakra.

When I touched my father's seventh chakra, it was still warm. Life had left it, but it was as if the physical part of the chakra was still throbbing with the tremendous happening.

It is a rare happening. And in that moment it may have appeared to many that the small section on the podium where I was with my father's body was in a different world. It was, in a sense, because it was on a different level. Just by his feet was my mother…and ten thousand sannyasins in Buddha Hall – that was the normal world.

But something abnormal had happened. The chakra was still warm, the body was as if it was still rejoicing in the phenomenon. If you had eyes to see, then this distinction was bound to be seen.

It is good that it came to your vision, the difference. It is a difference of levels. The lowest is where most people are living, and the effort here is, in this mystery school, to bring everybody to the highest.

Slowly, slowly, moving from one center into another, you will also feel within your body a few things. For example, if you are existing at the sex center, you will find a subtle division – *below* the lower center and *above* the lower center. You can feel it, that in the body below it and the body above it there seems to be a division, because the lower body has no centers, no chakras. It is the same for anybody. Wherever he is, the body below the sex center remains the same; it is our roots in the earth.

But if your center changes, comes to a higher level – for example if your heart becomes your very life – you will see again that below your heart the whole body is separate, and above the heart the whole body is separate. Wherever your energy is there will be a separation line.

When you reach to the seventh chakra, then the whole body is below it and there is no division. The seventh chakra is only *in a sense* in the body; otherwise it is above the body, as if a line touching your head is pulsing. Your whole body will become one, and for the first time you will see there are no divisions – and this you can watch.

With each chakra coming into function, your actions will change, your responses will change, your dreams will change, your aspirations will change, your whole personality will go through a change. As you move higher, newer dimensions start happening which were not available to you before.

For example, the heart center is almost in the middle; three centers are above it and three centers are below it. The man of the heart will be the most balanced man. In his actions, in his feelings, in everything he does he will find a subtle balance, an equilibrium. He will never be hectic; there will be a grace.

In other words, he has found the center of his life, exactly the middle path. You will not see any extremes in him, and because all extremes have disappeared from his life he will have a balanced view of everything. He will not be rightist, he will not be leftist; he will always be fair and just.

If the world was run according to me, then I would choose as magistrates and judges only people who are at their heart center, because only they can be just and fair. It is not a question of intellectual qualifications or seniority; it is a question of your inner balance.

The Sufi story is…. Mulla Nasruddin is chosen an honorary magistrate. The first case appears. He hears one side and declares to the court, "Within five minutes I will be back with the judgment."

The court clerk could not believe it – he has not heard the other side! The clerk whispered in his ear, "What are you doing? Don't you see a simple thing? You have heard only one party, one side. The other side is waiting, and without hearing them you cannot give any judgment."

Mulla Nasruddin said, "Don't try to confuse me. Just now I am absolutely clear. If I hear the other side too, then there is bound to be confusion."

These Sufi stories are not just ordinary stories, they are extraordinary. It is saying that every judge is listening only to one side because he already has a prejudiced mind; he is not capable of listening to both sides. For that a totally different kind of man is needed – which no educationalist concerning law and jurisprudence has even thought about.

No one thinks – you ask the judge to be fair, but his mind is prejudiced. He cannot even hear both stories, both sides, with the same clarity – impossible. He only pretends. In all the courts of the world there are pretensions.

And now that I have been in the courts I can see, and say with absolute authority that they don't listen to both sides. They can't! I am not complaining: I am simply stating a fact. Their education is wrong.

As you go above the heart center, new things that may not have ever been a part of your life start happening. The second chakra above the heart is the throat. If that chakra has your life energy, then whatever you say has a deep authority in it. Without any effort to convert anybody, it converts, because it convinces.

The chakra above that is the most famous and well-known – the one on the forehead between the two eyes. That kind of energy moving through the *agnya* chakra, the sixth, has a deep hypnotic influence. It is managed …the person is not doing anything; it simply happens, his eyes become so full of some unknown magnetism.

The man with the seventh chakra open has the capacity, the intrinsic flowering, so that his presence becomes infectious. Below the seventh, the presence is not infectious; with the seventh chakra opening, it is as if the consciousness has blossomed and there is a fragrance, an aura.

Whoever is available to this presence, to this aura, will feel the freshness of a breeze, the freshness after a shower. And many rotten things – rubbish that you have been entangled in, fighting – will simply disappear from your life. Just a touch from this kind of man will be a transformation.

But that evening something was transpiring, and what you noted was an energy phenomenon; many others must have noted the same.

I answer such questions in order for you to become aware of your own situation and start moving upwards.

Beloved Bhagwan,
Do You ever surprise Yourself? – and if You do, who is surprising whom?

There is no one to surprise or to be surprised.
I am as absent as I will be when I will be dead, with only one difference…that right now my absence has a body, and then, my absence will not have a body.

It is
All Happening
Silently

Beloved Bhagwan,

For me, being here with You is as if I have arrived at the end of a long journey, no desire to be anywhere else. My heart should jump high and I should bliss out, but looking at myself, carrying this great gift of being with You, there seems to be only a great sense of calm. Happiness and sadness are always simultaneously in me and it is as if they cancel each other out. It seems as if my life flame burns constantly but low, and this worries me.

This question of whether I am living intensely enough or not is with me always and pulls my energy down even more. Please destroy it.

It is good that you feel calm and quiet, rather than ecstatic, excited, because every ecstasy, every excitement is bound to come down; it cannot remain high forever. It burns your energy and burns it intensely. But you don't have an inexhaustible source; as an individual, in the body, all you have is limited.

To be with me, silently and calmly, peacefully is the right way; you can afford it. Even with the limited sources of individual beings, a calm state of mind can remain forever.

I have seen both types of people coming to me. Those who come and become too much excited are soon exhausted, and when they are exhausted they are angry at me; when they are exhausted they turn into enemies rather than into friends. Obviously to them I am the cause for their breakdown, and they cannot forgive me. Deep down in their mind they carry an idea that ecstasy was given to them and now it has been taken away.

I don't give you anything and I don't take anything away. Whatever happens in you simply happens in you; I am not more than a catalytic agent. So the best that can happen to you is a deep calmness. It is more reliable

because it is going to last your whole life –
maybe even beyond life.

And you are getting mixed up in your
question between this happening in my
presence, with me, and your intensive living.
Intensive living I teach to people just so that
they can transcend their desires, their turmoil,
quickly. If they live very miserly, as many live,
then in this life there is no hope for them to
experience transcendence.

Don't mix that with your state, because
your calmness is the beginning of transcendence. That's why you are feeling that your
happiness and sadness are happening
together. It cannot happen – either you can be
happy, or you can be sad. You cannot be sadly
happy, neither can you be happily sad. That
would be a very strange situation!

What is happening is that your calmness is
giving you this impression, because in your
calmness you are feeling something that
belongs to happiness and something that
belongs to sadness. Sadness is not all wrong;
happiness is not all right.

The essential part of happiness is a feeling
of well-being; that you are feeling in your
calmness, so you think you are happy. And
the essential part of sadness is silence; that you
are feeling in your calmness. These both can
exist together, in fact they can only exist
together.

A silent feeling of well-being…whatever is
happening is perfectly right. Don't ask me to
destroy it, ask me to enhance it. Don't make it
a problem! It is not. It is a tremendous gift that
the master never gives and the disciple always
receives.

There are things the master never says and
the disciple always hears. It is one of those
mysterious phenomena that are not handed
over by the master to you – but you receive it,
it arises within you.

It is just like the sunrise when millions of
birds start singing. They are not even aware of
the sunrise, but something in their heart is
triggered by the presence of the sun; the sun is
not aware of so many birds. Millions of
flowers suddenly open their petals. The sun is
not going to each single flower saying, "Wake
up! It is time, and I have come." Neither are
the flowers aware why they are opening their
petals, why they are releasing their perfume.
It all is happening silently. The presence of the
sun is needed, but that presence does not do
anything. Just its being there is enough.

Gurdjieff used to say that the situation of
the human mind is like that of a small school
class. The master is out, and all children are
shouting and screaming and jumping and
every kind of thing is going on, books are
being thrown at each other…. And then
suddenly the master appears and there is absolute silence. All screaming, all jumping, all
throwing books stops. They are all leaning on
their books – although they are not reading,
but pretending that they are reading.

One thing is certain, that the very presence
of the master makes a difference. He does not
do anything, he does not say anything. If he
needs to say anything, if he needs to do
anything, he is not a master; he is not
respected, he is not loved. The children don't
feel that he is worthy enough that they should
be behaving differently in his presence than
they behave in his absence.

In ancient Eastern scriptures it is again and
again discussed, because it has been one of the
eternal questions: should the disciple respect
the master, or not? All the organized religions
have decided that he should respect.

I have been talking to different religious
leaders and I have said to them, "That is just
wrong. The disciple should not respect. The
master should be respectable." That is a

totally different thing. The master should have the weight; he should be lovable, he should be respectable. Don't put the responsibility on the disciple, who is after all a disciple, a learner. It is easy for him to err.

One of my vice-chancellors said, in his convocation address, that the respect for the teacher is disappearing from the world of students, and this is dangerous. Ordinarily nobody stands up in a convocation address, because that is not a place to discuss. But I stood up and I said, "Before you say anything more, let me correct you. You are right in your observation that respect is disappearing from the student community, but you are wrong in your conclusion. The responsibility is not of the students but of the teachers. Can you say with authority that the teachers are worthy of respect? And if you cannot say it with authority that the teachers are worthy of respect, then why make a student responsible for this whole situation? If the teacher is worthy of respect, the question of respect from the students does not arise at all."

I said to him, "This I am saying to you with my own experience." For five years at that time I had been a teacher in the university and I had not come across a single student who was not respectful. "And if you come across students who are disrespectful to you, you should go home and think over it. Something must be wrong in you. Somewhere you have lost the worth."

There was immense silence in the whole auditorium. The professors were shocked, the students were shocked, the chancellor was suddenly frozen like a statue, and the vice-chancellor could not think what to say. I said, "You can see this silence – I have not told anybody to be silent, but most of them are my students or have been my students and they know what I mean."

And the vice-chancellor had to take his words back. He said, "I can understand it. The responsibility should always be on the stronger person, not on the weaker person. The student is weak, a learner, has no power; the teacher has all the powers, all the learning, all the authority…and if he cannot manage respect, then he is responsible. You are right."

But he used the word "manage". I didn't say anything, but that was a wrong word. To manage means you are thinking about it, you are using certain tactics, strategies for it. A real master simply comes amongst his disciples and there is silence, and there is calm.

And the same happens within you. You need not be worried about intensive living. If you can live this calmness, if this calmness can become your very life, where happiness and sadness contribute their essential beauty, then there is no need to think of people who talk of ecstasy. Their ecstasy will be gone in two days; your calmness will go with you beyond the grave.

Beloved Bhagwan,
Only in moments of love do I feel my body dancing with joyful sweetness, and only in moments of love do musicians create music which touches my heart. To feel the music moving my body and the dance moving the fingers of the musicians is for me the most beautiful experience.
Can You please say something about it?

It is a beautiful moment and a beautiful experience – but there is much more in life. There is much more than music, because music is after all sound, and there is silence too. Music is beautiful but you should not forget silence. Dance is beautiful, but there is something beyond it: an absolute unmoving state of consciousness...no dance.

There are beauties and beauties...and there are categories. Music and dance are very physical. As far as they go they are beautiful, but one should not get stuck with them, one should not be stopped by them. They should open the door for the higher realm. For example, if you are really a lover of music, soon music will be forgotten and you will be entering into silence. If you are really in deep attachment with dance, soon the dance has to disappear, so that you can be in an unmoving state of being.

In China there is an ancient story. A man declared himself to be the greatest archer, and he went to the king and said, "I am ready to accept anybody's challenge. I have practiced archery for thirty years, and I know that there is nobody in the whole empire who can be a competitor to me. It should be declared...a time should be given and within this time, if there is somebody who wants to compete with me, I am ready; otherwise you have to declare me the champion of the whole empire, the master archer."

The king knew that he was the greatest archer he had seen and what he was saying was not boasting, it was really true. There was nobody in the whole empire even close to him; he had gone into the art so deeply. But an old man who was the constant companion of the king...he was a servant, but he was very respected by the king because the king's father had died early and this servant had been almost a father to him; he had protected him, he had disciplined him, he had trained him to be a king, and he managed to put him on the throne, to make him the emperor. He was sitting by his side on the ground, and he laughed.

The king said, "Why are you laughing? What he is saying is true. I know this man, I know his archery. Even with closed eyes he never misses his target; with closed eyes he can kill a flying bird. There is nobody who is in any way comparable to him."

The old man said, "You are too young. I know a man before whom this man is just an amateur. He is very ancient, very old – older than me. He lives deep in the mountains. Before you declare this man the champion, he has to meet that old man. Just meeting him will be enough – competition is out of the question."

This was a great challenge...just meeting him will be enough, competition is out of the question. You cannot compete with that man. He is a master. And he showed him the way to the place where he could be found, the cave where he lived. The archer went miles into the mountains, finally found the cave and laughed, because there was the old man sitting, not even with a bow in the cave anywhere, no arrows – what kind of master archer is he? And he was so old, maybe ninety, ninety-five or more. He could not hit the target, his hands would tremble; he was so old! But the man said, "I have been sent by the king to meet you."

The old man said, "I have received the message of the king, but before I meet you I will give a little test. I don't meet each and everybody! At least you must be capable of being an archer; you will have to do for me a little test." To be a master archer is out of question...he wanted to check whether he had any capacity for archery, any talent, any genius.

The old man came out of his cave, took the young man with him and he said, "The moment I saw you coming with your bow and with your arrows, I knew that you were an amateur, because the real master does not need these things. Have you not heard the ancient saying: when a master reaches to his ultimate genius, if he is an archer he throws away his bow and his arrows; if he is a musician he throws away his musical instruments; if he is a painter he throws away his brushes, his canvases."

He said, "I have heard it but I have never understood it."

The old man said, "Now you have come to the place where you will understand it. Come with me." There was a rock protruding into the valley, and the valley was thousands of feet deep. If you fell from the rock there was no possibility of your being alive; in fact you could not even be found as a whole body, you would be scattered. It was a dangerous valley.

The old man went onto the protruding rock; the young man was standing there trembling – he was not going onto the rock. The old man was going and the young man was trembling. The old man said, "Stop that trembling. That is not the sign of a master archer." And the old man went to the very end of the rock, standing with half of his feet off the edge of the rock. He was standing there and he said to the young man, "Now you come and stand by my side."

The young man took one step, two steps – and then fell flat, trembling, everything whirling. He said, "You have to forgive me. I cannot come where you are standing. Just a little mistake, a little breeze of wind, a little forgetfulness and you are gone forever! I have come here to meet you, not to commit suicide. I cannot believe how you are standing there."

The old man said, "That's what archery brings to a man – an untrembling heart, a non-moving mind. Now I do not need the bow and the arrows. I know that you have looked around in my cave and I have seen your subtle

smile, 'How can this man be an archer?' Now I will show you my archery."

He looked up and there were nine birds flying – and as he looked up all the nine birds fell down on the earth. He said, "If you are absolutely immobile inside, even your eyes are enough; arrows are not needed. So go back, practice archery. Championship is far away. While I am alive, never think again of championship – although I am not a competitor. Even if you were declared champion I would not have bothered to object – who cares? Your championships, your titles are children's games.

"But the old man in the palace knows me. Now as long as I am living you cannot be a champion; you can be a champion if you really go deeper into archery, practice. And only I can make you a champion, not the king. What does he know about archery? So tell him, 'You don't have any authority.' I will come in the right time if I am alive. Or I will send somebody, or I will make some arrangement, even if I am dead."

Ten years passed and the old man was dying. He called his son from the village down in the plains and told him – he was also very old – "Go to this certain archer and just report to me the situation."

He went there. The archer was very loving, very happy that the old man still remembered him and had sent his son. The son saw the big bow hanging on the wall. He asked, "What is it?"

And the archer said, "I used to know what it is… Now I don't know. I will have to ask; somebody must know."

But the son said, "I have heard you are an archer."

He said, "I used to be in my youth, and in youth everybody is foolish. I used to be, but your father brought me to my senses."

This was reported to the old man, that he had forgotten the name of the bow. The old man said, "That means he has proved his mettle. I will have to go down before I die to declare him the champion, the master archer."

Now he was also capable – just looking at a bird was enough to kill it. Just those two rays going from the eyes were enough, because his inner being was so solidly immobile that those two rays became like arrows. He said, "Now I understand the meaning of the old saying: The musician breaks his musical instruments when he really becomes a master. Then what is the use of those instruments? because they are still part of the world of sound and the real music is silence."

Even when you are listening to music, what really touches your heart is not the sound but the gap between two sounds. How to bring that gap to your heart is the whole art of music. But if a man can bring that gap just by his presence, and you fall into deep silence, you will know the real music. Then you will know that what you used to think of as music was only a preliminary training. And the same is true about dancing, the same is true about every creative art. What it appears to be is not the reality; it is just a device so that you can become aware of something intangible, hidden, beyond.

But to love music is good, to love dance is good, to play music is good, to dance is good – but remember, that is not the end. You have to go far – away from music, away from dance – to understand the real beauty of any creative art. Every creative art brings you to your innermost being where there is just calmness, utter quietness, absolute silence.

Then you can say, "I have heard that which cannot be heard. And I have seen that which cannot be seen."

Beloved Bhagwan,
Until now I have not had many sexual experiences, but lately I have felt to become more sexually active. I seem to avoid heterosexual men, and desire those who are homosexual.
I am not clear if I am running away from sex out of fear, or towards people I really like and need. Would You please shed some light on this?

It is possible that avoiding sex for a long time and now getting interested in it you will have to go slowly towards it.

To be attracted to homosexuals is a step. Finally you will be attracted to the heterosexuals. The homosexual is half way. Nothing is wrong in it. It is good to go gradually, mature gradually.

And it is also possible that the homosexual person may be a person that you like, you love, that he deserves your love. His homosexuality may be a secondary thing. If it is a secondary thing, then perhaps you can stay with the homosexual person long enough, but if it is only a passing phase then moving from no sexuality or very little sexuality towards a heterosexual man, a direct jump, will be too much and can be dangerous. It may throw you back into your avoidance.

It is perfectly good that you are loving a homosexual. If he is a worthy person to be loved, that is even better; otherwise even his homosexuality is going to help you tremendously to reach to the heterosexual person.

These are the four stages: the auto-sexual person avoids sexuality. He wants to contain his sexuality within himself, he is a kind of miser, and such people suffer from constipation. It is now a well-established psychological fact. There is not a medical way to help them get rid of constipation, as their constipation has no cause in the body; their constipation has its cause in their mind.

You should be reminded that the sexual center is in the mind, not in the genitals. And strangely enough, by the way, the sexual center and the food center are very close – too close. So a person who stops his sexuality starts eating too much. The energy of the sexual center starts overflowing onto the next center, that is food. He becomes a food addict; he looks at food the way a lover looks at a beloved.

The second stage is homosexuality. It is a little better than being auto-sexual, confined to yourself – now at least you are connecting with your same sex. But there is a confinement still – although it is a bigger confinement – man to man, woman to woman.

The third stage is heterosexual, which is the maturity of sex – when you go beyond your femaleness or your maleness, where you transcend your class and move to the opposite. And because the tension between the opposite is great, love blossoms on a grander scale.

Between two homosexuals, love is – but there is no tension in it. It is not without any reason that homosexuals are called gay people, because there is no tension, there is no fight; they are always smiling, always looking happy. The happiness is shallow.

The heterosexuals are in a conflict, and in love. They laugh deeply, they weep deeply, they fight deeply, they feel for each other deeply; everything is deep because of the tension. They are known as intimate enemies. The intimacy is deep, the enmity is also deep.

The fourth stage is asexual, when you are fed up and you have seen all that sex can provide – its misery, its pleasure, its fights, its friendship – and slowly, slowly you see the routine, the same wheel moving. To change

that boredom of the same wheel moving you may change partners; that gives you a little energy for a few days more, but again the boredom comes back.

Once you are utterly bored with sex then the fourth stage is asexual. For the first time you are completely free. The first stage was very much confined to yourself; the second stage was confined to your class – man to man, woman to woman. The third was better, but still it was confined – man to woman, the same species.

The fourth stage is completely free from sex: you have known it, you have understood it. Its work is finished. It is no longer a burden on you, no longer a desire on you, no more a tension. You feel light, and for the first time you can enjoy being alone.

To me this is true celibacy, not a practiced celibacy. It is through the experience of all the stages that you come to true celibacy, and the true celibacy has to be understood: it is not anti-sexual, it is only asexual. It has no antagonism, no anti-attitudes. In the fourth stage you can have sex as fun, just a biological game.

So it is not that you have to drop sex; you can drop…you can either drop it or you can keep it. But it has lost all the old meaning and all the old implications, all the old bondage, all old fights, jealousies – all that is lost. If it drops, it drops; if it continues, then it is just casual friendship, with no strings attached to it, with no conditions attached to it.

Beloved Bhagwan,
There have been very few enlightened women in the world, and none that I know of in this century. Is there hope for us women?

It is not hard – but man has not allowed it. Man suffers from a deep inferiority complex, and to keep it repressed he keeps the woman in every possible way inferior to himself; otherwise if she is allowed freedom, allowed all her talents, her genius, the great fear of man is that she can prove superior in many dimensions. And she has many things which man is missing.

Naturally the only simple way was to cut all possible ways in which the woman could grow. So all women have been left retarded. Their roots have been cut: don't give education to them, don't let them have the freedom of movement in society, don't let them have friends from the other sex.

And for thousands of years it has been going on. Naturally if a woman cannot become a scientist, if a woman cannot become a poet, if a woman cannot become a great architect, a great sculptor, then the question of a woman becoming enlightened becomes very difficult. So many steps in between have been completely removed. My whole vision is to put those steps back.

And I am trying my best to put those steps back, so any woman of any quality has the full possibility, freedom and support to grow. Some of the women will grow to become enlightened, but no such possibility has ever existed before.

So it is true you have not heard of enlightened women, particularly in this century – although there have been a few women who, in spite of all this imprisonment of their being, became enlightened. But they are not the rule, they are the exceptions. They simply prove one thing: that just to be a woman does not mean that the doors of enlightenment are closed to you.

One woman was Rabiya al-Adabiya, in Arabia, one woman was Meera in India. One woman was in the very ancient times, in the days of the *Rig Veda* – that may be five thousand years old, or ninety thousand years old; it is undecided by the scholars…but these women can be counted on less than ten fingers.

But it is enough proof that to be a woman does not mean that enlightenment is not for you. As far as I am concerned, I feel that because you have been prevented from being enlightened, or even from moving in that direction, you have more possibility now than man, for the simple reason that just as land that has not been used for many years is more fertile, just it needs seeds… That means "Okay, Maneesha!"

The Most Blissful Moment — When You Cannot Find Yourself

Beloved Bhagwan,
When I sit in front of You and listen to You speak, I feel as if a process of osmosis is happening. I find I don't intellectually listen. Is this the right way or am I missing something?

This is the *right* way.

If you listen to me intellectually you miss, not something, but all. Intellectual listening is a kind of deafness. When I say something, you can listen to the word. You have a mind, a library in the mind of all your prejudices, philosophies, ideologies. The word has to go through all those preconceived patterns, and by the time it reaches to you it is no longer the same.

It has changed so many times, passing through the whole process of intellectual listening, that when it comes out it is absolutely something else. And yet it appears to be rationally the right thing; it fits with your mind. The process of listening has managed to cut it here and there, change it here and there; to color it here and there, to make it what you want it to be, not what it is. And you will agree with it; it is your own idea, it has nothing to do with *me*.

Listening intellectually is not listening at all. It is a way of avoiding. The right way is that you don't bring your mind in and you let me go into your innermost being without being hindered. Then there will be an understanding. Then there will be a communion, a *real* listening, because in the very process of listening, you have changed.

Now the agreement that arises in your being is not agreeing with your mind, it is agreeing with something new, which your mind knows nothing of. The mind is always old, and the truth is always new; they never meet, they never coexist.

You are fortunate that you can listen the right way – putting the mind aside, just allowing me to sink deeper and deeper within you. Then even though words have been used, silence has been conveyed. Even though words have been used, that which cannot be said has been said – at least has been heard.

And saying is not important, hearing is important.

Right listening means you will never ask how to do it. For example, if I am talking about silence and you are listening the right way, you will never ask how to be silent, because in the very listening you will have tasted it. In the very listening you will have experienced it – the window has opened.

The people who listen intellectually are bound to ask later on how to do it. Their question about how to do it signifies that they have missed what was conveyed to them.

It is not only words that I am saying to you – I am conveying my very heart. The words are only vehicles. Through the intellect the vehicles will reach, but I will be left behind. When you are listening without the mind, the vehicle becomes unimportant; its only use is that it helps me to reach to you. It is my outstretched hand, so that I can touch your heart.

Beloved Bhagwan,
I remember You talking about eyes and looking into people's eyes and hiding through not looking directly into someone's eyes. After this discourse I dropped my glasses, which I have had since I was one year old. Not wearing them, I found myself being more open in looking in someone's eyes, and I felt great power in my eyes. Would You please talk about the psychological need to wear glasses?

It is something truly significant to understand.

No animal needs glasses. It is very strange why man needs glasses. The reasons are two: the first is the physiological reason; and the second is the psychological.

The physiological reason is that our process of helping a mother to give birth to a child is basically wrong. For example, the child has been for nine months in deep darkness; his eyes are very delicate, fragile. And in any hospital where he is going to be born, he is going to face, immediately after the birth, glaring lights all around. That is the first shock to the whole delicate system of his eyes. And eyes are the most delicate part of your body – softer than a rose petal, very fragile and very important, because eighty percent of your life's experience depends on them. Only twenty percent is contributed by your other senses.

That is one of the reasons why a blind man suddenly creates a deep compassion in you. The deaf man does not create the same compassion. He is also missing something – he cannot hear. The dumb cannot speak…. In any other way the body may be crippled, but nothing can create more compassion in you than a blind man. Unknowingly, unconsciously, there is an understanding that the blind man is the poorest.

Eighty percent of his life experience is cut off; he is living only on twenty percent. His life has no color, his life has no experience of beauty, his life has no experience of proportion. His life has missed the beautiful sunsets and the starry night. His eyes have missed millions of other eyes which are loaded with experience; and to be in contact with them is to be in contact with different worlds.

But the way the hospitals have decided to give birth to a new child is dangerous. First they spoil the eyes. Second, they destroy the trust of the child. The child has lived for nine months in the mother's womb with immense trust – the question of doubt does not arise. Everything that he wants he gets; in fact before he wants, he gets it. No responsibility, no worry, no question of time. He does not think of tomorrow, and he has no memories of yesterdays. He lives moment to moment, utterly joyous. There is nothing to make him sad, nothing to make him miserable.

But the moment he is born, his whole life goes through a great, tragic change. The doctors are in a hurry; they cannot even wait for two minutes. They want to cut the cord that joins the child with the mother, immediately – and they cut it immediately, without bothering that the child has not yet breathed on his own, that his own system has not started functioning. They have cut the connection with the life source of the mother. This is one of the deep wounds that will be carried all along through his life.

And then to make the child breathe, they will hang it upside down and hit on his buttocks – a great reception! And because of the hit the child starts breathing. But this breathing is not natural and spontaneous. If they had just waited two or three minutes and left the child on his mother's belly…. He was inside nine months; with just three minutes outside on the belly – the same warmth, the same woman, the same energy – he would have started breathing on his own. And then to cut the cord would have been absolutely logical, rational, scientific.

And everything else that is being done takes no account of the implications. The child has been in the mother's womb in a certain warmth. He has been floating. The best way will be, once he starts breathing on his own, just to put him in a small bathtub of warm water consisting of the same chemicals as the mother's womb – it is exactly the same as ocean water. And that's what makes the evolutionists certain that man was born in the ocean.

You will be surprised to know, the first incarnation of God in Hinduism is a fish. It is very strange – just the idea…but to them God was life. And just a little translation is needed: instead of saying the reincarnation of God was as a fish, all that is needed is to say that life's beginning was as a fish.

Allow the child the same atmosphere so he does not feel, from the very first moment, in a strangers' world, afraid. But we make him afraid. We destroy his delicate eyes, we destroy his spontaneity, we even force his breathing. We don't give him a natural environment, one to which he is accustomed.

All these small things are going to affect his whole life. For example, whenever he is in anxiety, his breathing will become erratic. Whenever he is afraid, his breathing will be immediately affected. And sooner or later – because only man uses his eyes for reading, and his eyes are no longer as powerful as nature had made them – the child finds his eyes are weakening. He cannot see small letters, small figures, or he cannot see faraway things, and then the glasses become necessary. If glasses are avoided then his eyes will go on deteriorating. The glasses are simply to help him, just to compensate for the damage that has been done.

But glasses have their own psychology. With the glasses you are always behind a curtain, in some way hiding – not facing life as it is, trying to avoid this way or that, never being straight, sincere. Glasses are helping you to protect your eyes, but they bring their own problems with them. And these are the problems. They stand between you and the world, between you and the person you love, between you and the person you are communicating with.

Because of the glasses you never come in direct contact with the eyes of other people. And that is missing a great experience, because people are basically their eyes.

If you can see into a person's eyes, its depth will be that person's depth. A cunning person will not allow you to see directly into his eyes, because a cunning person's eyes reveal his cunningness.

The eyes are just an opening – the cunning person is afraid; he will always look sideways. He will be talking to you but looking at something else; his talking and his seeing will not be in the same direction. He will be listening to you but his eyes will not be concentrated on you. The man who wants to deceive you cannot confront you eye to eye. Only a simple, sincere person, a person with a loving heart and with no cunning desire will allow you to look into his eyes because he knows you will find his truth. He has nothing to hide.

So if you are using glasses, then use them only for particular purposes. If you need them for reading, use them for reading. If you use them continuously it is dangerous – not to your eyes, but to your whole being. If you need them to look far away, you can use them; but don't make it part of your being.

Your glasses should never become part of your being. Only when necessary use them. When you feel they are not necessary, put them away, so at least for long periods you are available to the world in your authenticity, and the world is available to you; there is no barrier.

You cannot do anything about the basic harm, but if you give birth to a child, it is better to give birth amongst your loving friends, with candlelight, with incense burn-ing, with flowers all around. Give the child at least a good welcome to the world.

And don't be technical – man is not a machine – be human. Let him first breathe; then cut the connection with the mother. There is no hurry. He should be given the chance to be spontaneous; otherwise he will suffer his whole life troubles and problems concerned with breathing.

And there is no need for glaring lights; otherwise you have started already destroying his eyes. Soon he will need glasses. If you have been using them since you were one year old, that shows what we have been doing with children. And nobody tells you to use glasses only when you need them; otherwise don't let them become an essential habit.

It is known about Mulla Nasruddin that one night he woke up and asked his wife, "Where are my glasses?"

She said, "What is the need in the middle of the night for glasses?"

He said, "I don't want to fight – I am not in a position right now – I will explain everything later on. First, my glasses!" With his glasses on he tried for a few minutes, then he said, "You destroyed it. If you had given them to me immediately, perhaps I may not have missed. I was having such a beautiful dream; just then I remembered, 'I cannot see without glasses.' Such a beautiful dream – I must be missing much. And you are so stupid that you started arguing with me.

"When I was asking for my glasses, you should have understood there must be some need, and later on you could have discussed it. But at that very time…and the gap became so big that I tried again and again with the glasses, but the dream was broken. And with it broken I could not manage to catch up with it again.

"And it was not only just a beautiful

dream, it had something to do with finances too. A man was promising to give me money, and we were haggling. He wanted to purchase something, and I had brought him up to ninety-nine rupees. But I was stubborn – I was trying to bring him to one hundred rupees; and it was only a question of one rupee. And the thing I was selling was not worth twenty rupees. I would have given it to him for ninety-nine, but I wanted to see the man accurately, and I wanted to count the money accurately. The glasses were needed.

"After I put on the glasses, I was saying to the man, 'Wherever you are, come back! Okay – ninety-nine I will accept, ninety-eight I will accept. I am willing to give it even for ninety.' But nobody responded. Just because of these glasses the whole profit was lost. And I don't know if I can ever meet this man again, because in the first place I cannot recognize him without my glasses. Even if I meet him tomorrow on the street, I will not be able to recognize him, because what I was seeing I don't know whether it was true or not true."

People are so accustomed to their glasses that they become almost their substitute eyes. Then it is dangerous. Your eyes need a little freedom: once in a while take the glasses off. And there are a few exercises available. Do those exercises which will make your eyes stronger, healthier, and perhaps you may not need the glasses at all.

Beloved Bhagwan,
My whole life I have been struggling with two huge desires: a desire to love and be loved, and the desire to understand and be understood. To see how misunderstood You are by the world and by Your friends astounds me, and Your not being affected by it astounds me even more. For the past ten years I have been consumed with desire to understand You every minute of every day. Today I feel I don't understand anything, and yet my desire to be understood has diminished. When You speak, the joy of being beyond these two dualities is heaven.

The desire to love and to be loved, the desire to understand and to be understood are very instinctive, very natural – but very binding, imprisoning. That's why, even if for a few moments listening to me – if you can forget these two desires, in that transcendence you will find the ultimate in joy.

I have been misunderstood perhaps more than anyone else ever, but it has not affected me, for the simple reason that there is no desire to be understood. It is *their* problem if they don't understand, it is not *my* problem. If they misunderstand, it is their problem and their misery. *I* am not going to waste my sleep because millions of people are misunderstanding me. If I was concerned about being understood they would have driven me mad. But they have not been able to even scratch a little bit.

All their misunderstanding is their problem. They are suffering from it, they are paying for it. Why should I be bothered by it? I have said what I felt is true. I have said it, not to be understood – I have said it because I wanted to share. If they are not willing, it is up to them; I cannot force them.

But both these desires – to understand and to be understood – are together. Unless *you* understand, you cannot drop the desire to be understood. Once you understand just the simple existence of your being, both disappear. There is nothing more to understand, and there is no question that anybody should understand you.

And the same is true about love.

The moment you understand what love is, you experience what love is, you *become* love. Then there is no need in you to be loved, and there is no need in you to love. Loving will be your simple, spontaneous existence, your very breathing. You cannot do anything else; you will be simply loving.

Now if in return, love does not come to you, you will not feel hurt, for the simple reason that only the person who has become love can love. You can give only that which you have. Asking people to love you – people who don't have love in their life, who have not come to the source of their being where love has its shrine – how can they love you? They can pretend. They can say, they can even believe, but sooner or later these things are going to…it is going to be known that it is only a pretension, that it is only acting, that it is hypocrisy.

There may not be an intention to deceive you, but what can the person do? You ask for love, and the other person also wants love. Both understand that you are expected to love, that only then can you get love – so you both try in every possible way to take the posture of love. But the posture is empty. And both are going to discover it, and both are going to complain about it against the other, that it is not right. From the very beginning it has been two beggars begging from each other, and both have only empty begging bowls.

Both are pretending that they can give, but their basic desire is to get. If you don't have it, you cannot give it.

And those who have it – this is to be understood very clearly – those who have found the source of love within themselves are no longer in need of being loved. And they *will* be loved.

They will love for no other reason but simply because they have too much of it – just as a rain cloud wants to rain, just as a flower wants to release its fragrance, with no desire to get *anything*. The reward of love is in loving, not in getting love.

And these are the mysteries of life, that if a person is rewarded just in loving people, many will love him. Because by being in contact with him, they will slowly start finding the source within themselves. Now they know one person at least who showers love and whose love is not out of any need. And the more he shares and showers his love, the more it grows.

The same is true about understanding. If you are close to a person of understanding you will see that he shares; sharing is his joy, it is not his business. He gives wholeheartedly, knowing perfectly well that he will find many doors closed in his face, but his understanding is deep enough to understand these people who misunderstand him.

They are miserable. They are afraid to let his understanding reach them, they are afraid of his light. They start closing their windows and their doors. They are afraid of his presence. They will condemn, they will create confusion, they will create rumors, they will create lies; they will do *everything* to prevent this man's light, his understanding, his insight from spreading. And the reason is that they are afraid.

This man's presence is a great fear to them. In his presence they become suddenly naked – with all their jealousies, with all their miseries, with all their pain, with all their wounds. In his presence they cannot hide. Before his eyes they are as if before x-rays which will penetrate to their deepest core and reveal all they have been somehow hiding from the society, and creating a certain good image. They are just the opposite within.

I have never been hurt by any misunderstanding. It was part of my understanding that it is going to be so, and once you are free of the desire to love and to be loved, you *will* love; but it will not be a desire, it will be an overflowing energy. And you *will* be loved, but it will not be an expectation, it will be a surprise.

Once you understand just yourself and you have gone beyond all kinds of misunderstandings, your light is so clear and bright, your certainty is so absolute, that the whole world can condemn you but it will not in any way hurt you. It will simply create more compassion and more effort to make these people somehow come out of their darkness and see the light.

And one thing is certain that you mention – that once both these desires are calmed down, one feels in heaven. One really *is* in heaven. One has always been; it was just that one was getting disturbed by small things and forgetting the immense beauty and joy the whole existence is ready to give to you – and without any price. It is just yours for the asking.

Beloved Bhagwan,
I have too many questions about You because in You I see a part of myself, and in that part I see everyone. Please nudge me if I am in the wrong lane.

You *are* in the wrong space.

You see a part of you in me. That is going to create many problems, because I don't have any part of you in me. And that is the beginning of a long journey; then in that part you see everybody else and all their problems. Then the small part you had seen in me becomes so big – because in that small part you are seeing everybody – that you are going to forget me completely. I will be covered all over with other people's parts – thick, not a thin layer, because *everybody*'s parts....

Just try the other way: see me just as a small corner in you. Give it to me, see me there, and in it see Chuang Tzu, see Gautam Buddha, see Socrates. See all the flowers that humanity has produced, and you will become a totally new person. Just seeing me, and in me bringing all those who can somehow be connected with me, you will be surrounded by the very salt of the earth, by all that is glorious. And you will disappear in it: you will not be able to find yourself, find where you have gone.

You will meet Socrates, you will meet Pythagoras, you will meet Heraclitus, you will meet strange but beautiful beings – Bodhidharma or Diogenes or Dionysius – but you will not find yourself. In fact, yourself does not exist. And the meeting of all these people within you will make you a paradise.

So please just give it a little turn: rather than seeing yourself in me – if you can do that, why can't you do this? it is the same – see me in you. And I am not asking for your whole being because I want you to leave it for other guests. Just give me a little corner, just a contact center from where buddhas can enter in you.

But we are so accustomed to misery that we can do anything to be miserable. And we have forgotten the language of blissfulness, so to make even a small effort seems to be very arduous. But I am asking you to do the same – just give it a little turn. It will be far easier, and the reward is going to be enormous. You will be lost, and you will never be found.

And that is the most blissful moment – when you cannot find yourself, and there is just utter silence.

Chapter 22
April 23, 1986, Morning

Freedom Doesn't Choose, It Discovers

Beloved Bhagwan,
What does it mean when You say, "Just be yourself"? How can I be myself when I don't know who I am? I know many of my preferences, likings, dislikings and tendencies, which seem to be the outcome of a programmed biocomputer called the mind. Does just being oneself mean that one totally lives out the whole content of the mind as watchfully as possible?

Yes, it exactly means that – to live as an awareness: awareness of all the programs the mind has been conditioned for, awareness of all the impulses, desires, memories, imaginations…all that the mind can do. One has to be not part of it, but separate – seeing it but not being it – watching it.

And this is one of the most essential things to remember, that you cannot watch your watchfulness. If you watch your watchfulness, then the watcher is you, not the watched. So you cannot go beyond watchfulness. The point that you cannot transcend is your being. The point that you cannot go beyond is you. You can watch very easily any thought, any emotion, any sentiment. Just one thing you cannot watch – and that is your watchfulness. And if you manage to watch it, that means you have shifted: the first watchfulness has become just a thought, now you are the second watcher.

You can go on shifting back, but you cannot get out of watchfulness because it is you: you cannot be otherwise.

So when I say, "Just be yourself," I am saying to you, "Just be unprogrammed, unconditioned awareness." That's how you had come into the world, and that's how the enlightened person leaves the world.

He lives in the world but remains totally separate.

One of the great mystics, Kabir, has a beautiful poem about it. All his poems are just perfect – nothing can be better. One of his poems says, "I will give back the soul that was given to me at the time of my birth as pure, as clean, as it was given to me. I will give it back that way when I die." He is talking about awareness, that it has remained unpolluted. The whole world was there to pollute it, but he has remained watchful.

All that you need is just to be watchful, and nothing will affect you. This unaffectedness will keep your purity, and this purity has certainly the freshness of life, the joy of existence – all the treasures that you have been endowed with.

But you become attached to the small things surrounding you and forget the one that you are. It is the greatest discovery in life and the most ecstatic pilgrimage to truth.

And you need not be an ascetic, you need not be anti-life; you need not renounce the world and go to the mountains. You can be where you are, you can continue to do what you are doing.

Just a new thing has to be evolved: whatever you do, you do with awareness – even the smallest act of the body or the mind – and with each act of awareness you will become aware of the beauty and the treasure and the glory and the eternity of your being.

Beloved Bhagwan,
You say freedom is the greatest value for You. You also say Your attitude to life is that of let-go. It seems to me that You have used Your freedom to choose to give up the freedom to decide anything, in favor of letting existence take care of You.

Is the ultimate in freedom actually total enslavement?

No, I have not chosen anything.
I have not chosen, out of my freedom, to allow the existence to take care of me. Freedom is choiceless. In freedom I have discovered, not chosen.

With the eyes free, with the consciousness free, I have discovered that let-go is the way existence functions. There was no question of choice – whether to be with existence or not. It was not either/or, but just the realization that this is the only way existence works. I relaxed with it.

The people who are not living a life of let-go are choosers, because they are going against nature, against existence; they have to choose. The ego is a chooser. When you are completely free of ego, of self, when you are simply freedom, you see it happening that the fight is disappearing and let-go is taking its place. You are nothing more than a watcher. If you choose it, then it is not let-go. How can it be let-go if you choose it?

It happened that one man came to Gautam Buddha, and he wanted to surrender himself unto Buddha's feet. Buddha looked at him and said, "You cannot surrender."

He said, "Why? Everybody else is allowed, and I am not allowed – what is my disqualification?"

Buddha laughed and he said, "There is no question of disqualification. Just the nature of surrender is such that you cannot do it – it happens. If you *do* it, it is your doing; it is not surrender. And if you do it, you can take it back. It is never total; you are outside of it. It was your action, so you can decide any moment: no more surrender! But if it *happens* then it takes all of you, the whole of you, leaving nothing behind which can ever do anything against it."

Simple things…but they become complicated because our mind is accustomed only to

FREEDOM DOESN'T CHOOSE, IT DISCOVERS

doing. And these are not mind things. Surrender, let-go – these are not mind things. For the mind it is impossible to think of them. It can agree to surrender, it can agree to let-go, but it has to be the master, doing it, and it has to be an act – and that's where everything goes wrong.

Surrender is once and forever; let-go is once and forever – just as death is once and forever, because nothing is left that can change the course of things. All has been taken in. *You* are no longer there to have a second thought.

Just the other day I was shown a statement of Rajen, one of our therapists, who is doing as much damaging work as possible. His statement was, "Up to now I was helping Bhagwan's work through surrender; now he has given me freedom. I will still continue to do his work but my work will be different. My work will be to help people to be free of Bhagwan."

Now, in the first place if he was really surrendered, then there is no going back: you cannot do anything about it anymore. It has happened, and you are dissolved in it.

Secondly, I cannot give you freedom, because if I give you freedom I can take it back. Freedom has to be your realization – and that would have come through surrender, on its own.

Surrender flowers into freedom, because in surrender the self is gone, and all the hell that the self creates is gone. Your whole energy is now available to blossom.

I cannot give freedom to anyone.

Freedom is not a commodity that I can hand over to you; it has to happen at the innermost core of your being. Surrender only removes the hindrances. You surrender only that which is blocking the way for freedom to come to you.

So on the second point also he is wrong.

And then on the third he goes really stupid, saying that now his work will be to help people to be free of Bhagwan.

The whole world is free of me – that is not helping them!

But what he means… He is now persuading sannyasins not to be sannyasins. And he thinks he is helping people to be in a state of freedom.

There are things which only happen.

Let-go is not an action on your part, but just an understanding of the fact that this is the only way the universe functions, and if you are not functioning in this way, you are going to remain in misery. You are not being punished, you are simply being foolish. The old religions have given the idea to people that if you do wrong, you will be punished; if you do right, you will be rewarded – because they were all dependent on doing, and that's their basic fallacy.

Religion begins when you cross the boundary of doing and enter into the world of happening. Then let-go happens, because you see that this is the only way things work. If you go against it, you are miserable.

Nobody is punishing you; you are simply being stupid. If you try to get out through the wall and hit your head, do you think it has been a punishment? And there is the door, always available for you to get out. Knowing about the door, you try to get out through the wall and smash your face. Old religions call it punishment. It is not punishment, it is simple foolishness. And the person who goes out of the door into the garden, in the sun, in the air, is not being rewarded; he is just being intelligent.

So if you ask me, I will say intelligence is the reward; unintelligence is the punishment. In its ultimate form: unintelligence is hell, intelligence is heaven.

Beloved Bhagwan,
Living decisively, knowing what one wants, seems easy. However, my reality is that I can never make up my mind about anything. I can always see both sides of an argument and can never decide which is right. So I am left hanging between the two. One part of me, listening to You, feels this is okay, but it makes me feel static, as if I am only partially alive. Please comment.

Mind is never decisive. It is not a question of your mind or somebody else's mind; mind *is* indecisiveness. The functioning of the mind is wavering between two polar opposites and trying to find which is the right way.

Mind is the wrong thing, and through the wrong thing you are trying to find the right way. It is as if by closing your eyes you are trying to find the door. Certainly you will feel yourself hanging between the two – to go this way or that; you will be always in a condition of either/or. That's the nature of mind.

One great Danish philosopher was Soren Kierkegaard. He wrote a book, *Either/Or*. It was his own life's experience – he could never decide about anything. Everything was always such that if he was deciding this way, then that way seemed to be right. If he was deciding that way, then this way seemed to be right. He remained indecisive.

He remained unmarried, although a woman was very much in love with him and had asked him. But he said, "I will have to think about it – marriage is a big thing, and I cannot say yes or no immediately." And he died with the question, without getting married. He lived long – perhaps seventy years – and he was continually arguing, discussing. But he found no answer which could be said to be the ultimate answer, which had not its equal opposite.

He never could become a professor. He had filled out the form, he had all the qualifications – the best qualifications possible – he had many books to his credit, of such immense importance that even after a century they are still contemporary, not old, not out of date. He filled out the form but could not sign it – because "either/or"…whether to join the service or not? The form was found when he died, in the small room where he used to live.

His father, seeing the situation – and he was his only son – seeing that even going somewhere he would stop at the crossroads to decide to go this way or to go that way, for hours…! The whole of Copenhagen became aware of this man's strangeness, and children nicknamed him "Either/Or," so urchins would be following him, shouting, "Either/Or!" wherever he would go.

Before he died his father liquidated all his businesses, collected all the money, deposited it into an account, and arranged that every month on the first day of the month, Kierkegaard should receive so much money, so for his whole life he at least could survive. And you will be surprised: the day he was coming home, on the first day of the month, after taking out the last installment of the money – the money was finished – he fell on the street and died. With the last installment! That was the right thing to do. What else to do? – because after this month, what will he do?

And because of the urchins and other people harassing him and calling him Either/Or he used to come out only once a month, just on the first day, to go to the post office. But now there was nothing left – next month he had nowhere to go.

He was writing books but was not decisive about whether to publish them or not; he left all his books unpublished. They are of tremendous value. Each book has a great penetration into things. On each subject he has written, he has gone to the very roots, to every minute detail…a genius, but a genius of the *mind*.

With the mind, that is the problem – it is not your problem – and the better mind you have, the more will be the problem. Lesser minds don't come across that problem so much. It is the genius mind that is opposed, with two polarities, and cannot choose. And then he feels in a limbo.

What I have been telling you is that it is the nature of the mind to be in a limbo. It is the nature of the mind to be in the middle of polar opposites. Unless you move away from the mind and become a witness to all the games of the mind, you will never be decisive. Even if you sometimes decide – in spite of the mind – you will repent, because the other half that you have not decided for is going to haunt you: perhaps that was right and what you have chosen is wrong. And now there is no way to know. Perhaps the choice that you had left aside was better.

But even if you had chosen it, the situation would not have been different; then this which would have been left aside would haunt you.

Mind is basically the beginning of madness.

And if you are too much in it, it will drive you mad.

I have told you that in my village I used to live opposite a goldsmith. I became aware at first, and then the whole town became slowly aware…and his life became hell. I used to sit just in front of his house, and I became aware that he had a curious habit: he would lock his shop, then pull the lock two, three times to see whether it was really locked or not.

One day I was coming from the river and he had just locked his shop and was going home. I said, "But you have not checked!"

He said, "What?"

I said, "You have not checked the lock!" He had checked it – I had seen him three times pulling it, but now I had created a suspicion, and mind is always ready…

So he said to me, "Perhaps I forgot – I must go back." He went back, and checked the lock again. That became my joy: wherever he would go…

In the market he would be purchasing vegetables and I would reach there saying, "What are you doing here? You have left the lock unchecked!"

He would drop the vegetables and he would say, "I will be coming back; first I have to go and check the lock."

Even from the railway station… He was purchasing a ticket to go somewhere, and I went and told him, "What are you doing? The lock!"

He said, "My God, have I not checked it?"

I said, "No!"

He said, "Now it is impossible to go to the marriage I was going to." He returned the ticket, went home, and checked the lock. But then it was too late to go back to the station – the train had already gone. And he trusted me because I was always sitting in front of his house. Slowly it became known to everybody, so wherever he would go, people would say, "Where are you going? Have you checked the lock?"

Finally he became angry with me. He said, "You must be spreading it, because wherever I go everybody is talking about the lock, and I have to come back home – sometimes so many times that I forget completely for what purpose I had gone in the first place to the market! The whole day I have been checking the lock!"

I said, "You don't listen to them. Let them…"

He said, "What do you mean, 'Don't listen to them'? If they are right then I am lost forever. I cannot take that chance. So knowing perfectly well that the man may be lying, I have to come back compulsively to check the lock. I know somewhere that I have checked it, but who knows for certain?"

Mind has no certainty about anything.

If you are between the two polarities of the mind, in a limbo – always to do or not to do, you will go crazy. You *are* crazy! Before it happens, jump out and have a look from the outside at the mind…and that's what I am telling you continuously.

Be aware of the mind – its bright side, its dark side, its right, its wrong. Whatever polarity it is, you just be aware of it. Two things will come out of that awareness: one, that you are not the mind, and second, that awareness has a decisiveness which mind never has.

Mind is basically indecisive, and awareness is basically decisive. So any act out of awareness is total, full, without repentance.

I have never in my life thought again about anything – whether something else would have been better. I have never repented. I have never thought that I have committed any mistake, because there is nobody else who has been left to say these things. I have been acting out of my awareness – that is my whole being. Now whatever happens is all that is possible.

The world may call it right or wrong – that is their business, but it is not my problem.

So awareness will take you out of the limbo. Rather than hanging between these two polarities of the mind, you will jump beyond both, and you will be able to see that those two polarities are two polarities only if you are in the mind. If you are outside it, you will be surprised that they are two sides of the same coin – there was no question of decision.

With awareness you have the clarity, totality, let-go – existence decides within you. You don't have to think about what is right and wrong; existence takes your hand in its hand, and you are moving relaxedly. That's the only way, the right way. And that is the only way you can be sane; otherwise you will remain muddled.

Now, Soren Kierkegaard is a great mind, but being a Christian he has no idea of awareness. He can think, and think very deeply, but he cannot just be silent and watch. That poor fellow had never heard about anything like watching, witnessing, awareness. Thinking was all that he had heard about, and he had put his whole genius into thinking. He had produced great books, but he could not produce a great life for himself. He lived in utter misery.

Beloved Bhagwan,
You spoke the other night about honest truth. Mystics have often spoken of the "ultimate truth." Can the truth be anything other than ultimate?

Truth cannot be anything other than the ultimate.
But the mystics had to speak about "ultimate truth" for a certain reason. The reason was that philosophers have been speaking of "relative truth," and they have been emphasizing the fact that every truth is relative. Albert Einstein in this century brought the conception of relativity to scientific truths; otherwise they used to be ultimate – they became relative. And he was right. Mahavira,

Gautam Buddha – they all have talked about relativity.

One thing that is missing is that nobody makes a distinction between truth and fact. Facts are relative, and truth is ultimate, but if you get mixed up and you start thinking of facts as truth, then they will be relative.

Two things first: Facts are relative, and you have to understand exactly what is meant by relative. It means that something can be true in a certain situation, and the same thing can be untrue in some other situation.

It was said that while Albert Einstein was alive there were only twelve people in the whole world who understood what he meant by relativity. It is a very delicate and subtle explanation about the universe. And Einstein was continually asked – wherever he would go, in a club, in a restaurant – wherever he would go people would ask, "Just say something about what this relativity is and say it so that a layman can understand it."

Finally he found a way: he said that if you are sitting on a hot stove, time will appear to you to be going very slowly; a single minute will look like hours because you are sitting on a hot stove. Your state is changing your conception of time.

But if you are sitting with your girlfriend, hours go by and it seems only seconds have passed.

He would say, "This is what I mean by relativity: time is relative to a particular situation. There is nothing like ultimate time so that whatever you do it is the same. It has always been known that when you are happy time passes fast, and when you are miserable, time passes very slowly."

He has established relativity so deeply that it has become almost interwoven with all scientific findings. But only one thing I want you to remember: he is talking about facts and calling them truth. And because of that the mystics had to use the word 'ultimate'. They want to tell you that there *is* an experience which is beyond relativity. That's all their meaning is: truth is ultimate.

For example, what I have experienced in these thirty-five years in different situations – it has remained the same, and I know even in my death it will not be different. This is truth: that which remains the same, whatever happens around it…the center of the cyclone.

But the whole world is full of facts. Facts are relative. Now, it has to be made very clear to the scientists that what Einstein was talking about was not truth but fact. But for science there is no truth other than what they discover. The mystic's truth they don't accept, because the mystic cannot put it in front of the scientist so that they can dissect it and find out what constitutes it – its measurement, weight, and things like that.

It is an experience, and totally subjective. It cannot be made objective.

So let us say it in this way, if they insist on calling it truth: objective truths are all relative, and subjective truth is always ultimate. But just not to get it mixed up, the mystics have been calling it the ultimate truth.

All truth is ultimate. But there are scientific truths which are really only facts. For example, if you are sitting on a hot stove the experience of time going very slowly is just a fact of your psychology; it has nothing to do with time. But nobody has pointed that out to Albert Einstein. When you are sitting with your girlfriend and time passes fast, it has nothing to do with time; it has something to do with your mind.

Time goes with its own speed. It does not change; otherwise there would be such a difficulty. Somebody is sitting on the hot stove, and somebody is sitting with his girlfriend –

what will poor time do? Go slow or go fast? Time remains the same; it is your mind, your concept of time which is relative.

All objective truths are relative. You cannot say that somebody is tall; that statement will not be correct, because the tallness of the person has to be relative. Tall in comparison to whom? You have to make it complete. Somebody is fat, but just that much is not right and not complete. You have to make it clear that he is fatter than Avirbhava, or thinner than Anando. Unless you make the comparison, you cannot use relative terms.

But we are using them. Because people are using relative words, the mystics have been compelled to say the "ultimate" truth; otherwise just saying "the truth" would be sufficient, because ultimateness is its intrinsic nature. But it has to be repeated; otherwise there are people who will get misguided, confused, because they have heard about relative truths and they will make your truth also into a relative truth. So a distinction has to be made. To draw that distinction, the word 'ultimate' is used – unwillingly.

I would not like to use it because it is a repetition, a tautology. "The ultimate" and "the truth" mean the same. You can use either, but to use both is an unnecessary repetition.

My father was very insistent that every Monday he had to receive a letter from me, while I was in the university. I told him, "If there is something wrong, if there is some problem, if I am sick, I will inform you. But unnecessarily writing the same thing again and again has no justification."

He said, "Justification or not, it is not a question of your arguments. I wait for seven days and I become worried about you. It is not your sickness that I am worried about; I am worried about what you are doing, what is happening to you. You may get into trouble any moment. So every Saturday you have to post a letter so that on Monday I receive it. If I don't receive it on Monday, then I will unnecessarily have to come two hundred miles to the university."

So what I had done…I had written one letter, "Everything is all right here. I am not in any trouble. You need not be worried." And on other letters I had just made the sign 'ditto.' He was very angry. When he saw me he said, "I feel like beating you! You write 'ditto' on the letters!"

I said, "That's exactly the situation, because I have to write the same thing again. And do you think I write every Saturday? I have just asked one typist to type the first letter, and a hundred letters with the 'ditto.' I have given them to one very particular man – because I may forget and unnecessarily you may have to come – and I have told him, 'You have to post one of these "ditto" letters every Saturday.' He is so particular in everything that once you ask him, he will do it." He was a student, living in the same hostel.

But my father was very angry, "Have you ever heard of anybody writing in the letter just 'ditto'? I wait for eight days and then I get a card on which the only message is 'ditto'! Not even your signature, because in 'ditto' everything is implied from the first letter: Refer to the last letter. You can read the first letter again when you get the ditto letter."

Life is not mathematics; it is not logic, it is not science. It is something more, and that something more is the most valuable.

The mystics have called that something more "the ultimate truth." They can be forgiven for calling it ultimate. But you have to understand that the reason they are calling it ultimate is because there are people who are calling *every* truth relative – not only scientists, not only people who are working with matter.

Mahavira says that truth itself is relative: he has no ultimate truth. Buddha has no ultimate truth. Again the difficulty is that Mahavira and Buddha can be misunderstood when they say that there is no ultimate truth but that every truth is relative: it can be one thing in one situation, it can be another thing in another situation, and because it is related to situations it cannot have any ultimacy. This goes against all the great mystics.

Only Mahavira and Buddha, two people… But I know both, and I understand both better than their own followers, because none of their followers have been able to make any sense out of it: either all the mystics are wrong, or Buddha and Mahavira are wrong!

I say nobody is wrong. What Mahavira says is that truth has seven aspects, and Buddha says that truth has four aspects. They are really referring to the expression of truth. Truth can be said in seven ways according to Mahavira. He is really a logician. But what he is saying is not about truth – there is a misunderstanding. What he is saying is about truth expressed, not experienced. When you experience it, it is always ultimate, but the moment you say it, it becomes relative. The moment you bring it into language it becomes relative, because in language nothing can be ultimate. The whole construction of language is relative. Buddha is not a great logician, so he stops at four, but the situation is the same.

They are not speaking of the truth which you experience in silence, beyond mind. Nothing can be said about it. The moment you say something about it, you drag it into the world of relativity, and then all the laws of relativity will be applicable to it.

Perhaps Ludwig Wittgenstein, one of the best logicians of this age, was right when he said, "That which cannot be said should not be said." This is a strange statement. It stands out in the whole history of thought, unique and original: "That which cannot be said should not be said" – because if you say it, you are contradicting yourself. First you say it cannot be said, and then you say it. You may make all kinds of conditions: "When I say it, it is no longer the same; when I say it, it even becomes untrue." But then, why say it?

Wittgenstein's statement will make it clear that Mahavira and Buddha both were talking about the truth *said:* then it is relative. And the mystics who are talking about "the ultimate truth" are talking about the truth experienced yet not brought into the world of language and objects. So I think it is better to allow them to use the word 'ultimate', although it is a repetition, because it keeps it separate.

Beloved Bhagwan,
Is it not true to say that because we can even formulate a question that we have an inkling somewhere of the answer – even though we are not aware of it?
It seems to me like a doctor looking at a patient: the fact that he asks the patient certain questions and not others indicates he has some idea of what the diagnosis – and hence the answer – is.

It is true. Whenever you ask a question, somewhere deep down you have some inkling of the answer, but it is in the darker parts of your consciousness. You yourself cannot pull it out and bring it to your consciousness.

The question is in the consciousness; the

answer is in the unconscious – vague, a shadow, with no certainty, but the inkling is certainly there.

The function of the master is exactly what Socrates has defined it as – the master is only a midwife. He helps to bring everything that is hidden in you to consciousness. When your question disappears, that means your answer from the unconscious has been brought to the conscious.

It has to be remembered that this is the distinction between a master and a teacher: a teacher will give you an answer, which will not bring your own answer from the unconscious. He will force an answer into your conscious, repressing your question. He will make the situation more complicated. First you had only a question, and if you had silently waited, meditated, perhaps the unconscious answer may have surfaced and the question would have disappeared. And once the question disappears, the answer has no relevance in being there; it disappears also, and a pure emptiness is left.

But the teacher forces an answer on your mind, and makes the situation more complicated. Now you have a question and you have an answer which has not been able to dissolve the question, which has only repressed it. And your unconscious answer is still lying down there, to be released so you can be unburdened. The teacher burdens you, complicates you.

The master never gives you any answer that is going to burden you.

His every answer is an unburdening. He brings your own unconscious answer to the surface, where first the question disappears, then the answer disappears – and not a trace of either remains behind.

This is real communion.

This is a clear-cut way, a criterion, to make the distinction between a teacher and a master.

In the West there seems to be no distinction. In the East the teacher is simply repeating inherited knowledge; he is not concerned with you, he is concerned with his own knowledge.

The master has nothing to impose upon you; he is empty and silent.

Your question does not give him a chance to impose something on you, but only gives him a chance to bring your unconscious answer to the surface. So if you go on simply listening to the master, slowly, slowly you will find your questions have disappeared…and strangely, you don't have any answer.

People ordinarily think that when the question disappears you will have the answer in its place. No, when the question really disappears the answer has no relevance. It also disappears. And left without questions and without answers, you have immense freedom…unburdened…open sky.

Chapter 23
April 23, 1986, Evening

Trees Grow Without Being Taught

Beloved Bhagwan,

Having heard You talk about competition and our childhood the other morning, it set me thinking of my own education. I realized that for twenty-one years solidly, every single event at school — from playing in the garden, through official sports, to Latin Grammar — was basically an exercise in how to beat the next person. It seems as if it was the single most damaging experience of my life. I can't think of a more perfect system to destroy children and make us completely inharmonious with the world around us.

How can we help children to grow to their full potential, without encouraging this competitive spirit?

The moment you start thinking how to help children to grow without any competitive spirit you are already on the wrong track, because whatever you are going to do is going to give the children a certain program. It may be different from the one that you received, but you are conditioning the children – with all the best intentions in the world.

The trees go on growing without anybody teaching them how to grow. The animals, the birds, the whole existence, needs no programming. The very idea of programming is basically creating slavery – and man has been creating slaves for thousands of years in different names. When people become fed up with one name, another name immediately replaces it. A few modified programs, a few changes here and there in the conditioning, but the fundamental thing remains the same – that the parents, the older generation, want their children to be in a certain way. That's why you are asking "How?".

According to me, the function of the parents is not how to help the children grow – they will grow without you. Your function is to support, to nourish, to help what is already growing. Don't give directions and don't give ideals. Don't tell them what is right and what is wrong: let them find it by their own experience.

Only one thing you can do, and that is share your own life. Tell them that you have been conditioned by your parents, that you have lived within certain limits, according to certain ideals, and because of these limits and ideals you have missed life completely, and you don't want to destroy your children's life. You want them to be totally free – free of *you,* because to them you represent the whole past.

It needs guts and it needs immense love in a father, in a mother, to tell the children, "You need to be free of us. Don't obey us – depend on your own intelligence. Even if you go astray it is far better than to remain a slave and always remain right. It is better to commit mistakes on your own and learn from them, rather than follow somebody else and not commit mistakes. Then you are never going to learn anything except following – and that is poison, pure poison."

It is very easy if you love. Don't ask "how," because "how" means you are asking for a method, a methodology, a technique – and love is not a technique.

Love your children, enjoy their freedom. Let them commit mistakes, help them to see where they have committed a mistake. Tell them, "To commit mistakes is not wrong – commit as many mistakes as possible, because that is the way you will be learning more. But don't commit the same mistake again and again, because that makes you stupid."

So it is not going to be a simple answer from me. You will have to figure it out living with your children moment to moment, allowing them every possible freedom in small things.

For example, in my childhood…and it has been the same for centuries, the children are being taught, "Go to bed early, and get up early in the morning. That makes you wise."

I told my father, "It seems to be strange: when I am not feeling sleepy, you force me to sleep early in the evening." And in Jaina houses early in the evening is *really* early, because supper is at five o'clock, at the most six. And then there is nothing else to do – the children should go to sleep.

I said to him, "When my energy is not ready to go to sleep, you force me to go to sleep. And when, in the morning, I am feeling sleepy, you drag me out of the bed. This seems to be a strange way of making me wise! And I don't see the connection – how am I going to become wise by being forced to sleep when I am not feeling sleepy? And for hours I lie down in the bed, in the darkness…time which would have in some way been used, would have been creative, and you force me to sleep. But sleep is not something in your hands. You cannot just close your eyes and go to sleep. Sleep comes when it comes; it does not follow your order or my order, so for hours I am wasting my time.

"And then in the morning when I am really feeling sleepy, you force me to wake up – five o'clock, early in the morning – and you drag me out for a morning walk towards the forest. I am feeling sleepy and you are dragging me. And I don't see how all this is going to make me wise. You please explain it to me!

"And how many people have become wise through this process? You just show me a few wise people – I don't see anybody around. And I have been talking to my grandfather, and he said that it is all nonsense. Of the whole household, that old man is the only sincere man. He does not care what others will say, but he has told me that it is all nonsense: 'Wisdom does not come by going early to bed.

I have been going early to bed my whole life – seventy years – and wisdom has not come yet, and I don't think it is going to come! Now it is time for death to come, not for wisdom. So don't be befooled by these proverbs.'"

I told my father, "You think it over, and please be authentic and true. Give me this much freedom – that I can go to sleep when I feel sleep is coming, and I can get up when I feel that it is time, and sleep is no longer there."

He thought for one day, and the next day he said, "Okay, perhaps you are right. You do it according to yourself. Listen to your body rather than listening to me."

This should be the principle: children should be helped to listen to their bodies, to listen to their own needs. The basic thing for parents is to guard the children from falling into a ditch. The function of their discipline is negative.

Remember the word "negative"…no positive programming but only a negative guarding – because children *are* children, and they can get into something which will harm them, cripple them. Then too don't order them not to go, but explain to them. Don't make it a point of obedience; still let them choose. You simply explain the whole situation.

Children are very receptive, and if you are respectful towards them they are ready to listen, ready to understand; then leave them with their understanding. And it is a question only of a few years in the beginning; soon they will be getting settled in their intelligence, and your guarding will not be needed at all. Soon they will be able to move on their own.

I can understand the fear of the parents that the children may go in a direction which they don't like – but that is *your* problem. Your children are not born for your likings and your dislikings. They have to live their life, and you should rejoice that they are living their life – whatever it is. They may become a poor musician….

I used to know a very rich man in the town who wanted his son, after matriculation, to become a doctor. But the son was interested only in music. He was already no longer an amateur; he was well known in the area, and wherever there was any function, he was playing the sitar and was becoming more and more famous.

He wanted to go to a university which is basically devoted to music. Perhaps it is the only university in the world which is devoted completely to music, and has all the different departments – dance, different instruments – but the whole world of the university is musical.

The father was absolutely against it. He called me – because I was very close to his son – and he said, "He will be a beggar all his life," because musicians in India cannot earn much. "At the most he can become a music teacher in a school. What will he be earning? That much we pay to many servants in our house. And he will be associating with the wrong people," because in India, music has remained very deeply connected with the prostitutes.

The Indian prostitute is different from any prostitute in the rest of the world. The word "prostitute" does not do justice to the Indian counterpart, because the Indian prostitute is really well versed in music, in dance – and India has so much variety. If you really want to learn the deeper layers of music, of singing, of dancing, you have to be with some famous prostitute.

There are famous families – they are called *gharanas*. *Gharana* means family. It is nothing to do with the ordinary family; it is the family of the master-disciple. So there are famous gharanas which have a certain way of their own. Presenting the same instrument, the same dance, different gharanas will produce it in different ways, with subtle nuances. So, if someone really wants to get into the world of music, he has to become part of some gharana – and that is not good company. According to a rich man it is certainly not a good company.

But the son was not interested in the company. Not following his father, he went to the music university. And his father disowned him – he was so angry. And because his father disowned him, and because he had no other ways – because the university was in a very remote mountainous area where you cannot find any job or anything – he came back and had to become exactly what his father was predicting, just a school teacher.

His father called me and told me, "Look, it is just as I have said. My other sons – somebody is an engineer, somebody is a professor, but this idiot did not listen to me. I have disowned him; he will not inherit a single cent from me. And now he will remain in just the poorest profession – a school master."

But my friend himself was immensely happy…not worried that he had been abandoned by his family, that he was going to live a poor man's life, that he would not be receiving any inheritance. These things did not bother him; he was happy, "It is good they have done all this – now I can become part of some gharana. I was worried about them, that they would feel humiliated. But now they have abandoned me, and I am no longer part of them, I can become part of some gharana."

Teaching in a school, he became part of a gharana, and is now one of the best musicians in India. It is not a question of his being one of the best musicians; what is important is that he became what he felt was his potential. And whenever you follow your potential, you always become the best. Whenever you go astray from the potential, you remain mediocre.

The whole society consists of mediocre people for the simple reason that nobody is what he was destined to be – he is something else. And whatever he will do, he cannot be the best, and he cannot feel a fulfillment; he cannot rejoice.

So the work of the parents is very delicate, and it is precious, because the whole life of the child depends on it. Don't give any positive program – help him in every possible way that *he* wants.

For example, I used to climb trees. Now, there are a few trees which are safe to climb; their branches are strong, their trunk is strong. You can go even to the very top, and still there is no need to be afraid that a branch will break. But there are a few trees which are very soft. Because I used to climb on the trees to get mangoes, *jamuns* – another beautiful fruit – my family was very much worried, and they would always send somebody to prevent me.

I told my father, "Rather than preventing me, please explain to me which trees are dangerous – so that I can avoid them – and which trees are not dangerous, so that I can climb them.

"But if you try to prevent me from climbing, there is a danger: I may climb a wrong tree, and the responsibility will be yours. Climbing I am not going to stop, I love it." It is really one of the most beautiful experiences to be on the top of the tree in the sun with the high wind, and the whole tree is dancing – a very nourishing experience.

I said, "I am not going to stop it. Your work is to tell me exactly which trees I should not climb – because I can fall from them, can have fractures, can damage my body. But don't give me a blank order: 'Stop climbing.' That I am not going to do." And he had to come with me and go around the town to show me which trees are dangerous. Then I asked him the second question, "Do you know any good climber in the city who can teach me even to climb the dangerous trees?"

He said, "You are too much! Now this is going too far. You had told me, I understood it…"

I said, "I will follow it, because I have myself proposed it. But the trees that you are saying are dangerous are irresistible, because *jamun*" – an Indian fruit – "grows on them. It is really delicious, and when it is ripe I may not be able to resist the temptation. You are my father, it is your duty…you must know somebody who can help me."

He said, "If I had known that to be a father was going to be so difficult, I would have never been a father – at least of you! Yes, I know one man" – and he introduced me to an old man who was a rare climber, the best.

He was a woodcutter, and he was so old that you could not believe that he could do woodcutting. He did only rare jobs, which nobody else was ready to do…big trees which were spreading on the houses – he would cut off the branches. He was just an expert, and he did it without damaging their roots or the houses. First he would tie the branches to other branches with ropes. Then he would cut these branches and then with the ropes pull the other branches away from the house and let them fall on the ground.

And he was so old! But whenever there was some situation like that, when no other woodcutter was ready, he was ready. So my father told him, "Teach him something, particularly about trees which are dangerous, which can break." Branches can break…and I had fallen already two, three times – I still carry the marks on my legs.

That old man looked at me and he said, "Nobody has ever come, particularly a father bringing a boy…! It is a dangerous thing, but if he loves it, I would love to teach him." And he was teaching me how to manage to climb trees which were dangerous. He showed me all kinds of strategies of how to protect yourself: If you want to go high up the tree and you don't want to fall onto the ground, then first tie yourself with a rope to a point where you feel the tree is strong enough, and then go up. If you fall, you will be hanging from the rope, but you will not fall to the ground. And that really helped me; since then I have not fallen!

The function of a father or a mother is great, because they are bringing a new guest into the world – who knows nothing, but who brings some potential in him. And unless his potential grows, he will remain unhappy.

No parents like to think of their children remaining unhappy; they want them to be happy. It is just that their thinking is wrong. They think if they become doctors, if they become professors, engineers, scientists, then they will be happy. They don't know! They can only be happy if they become what they have come to become. They can only become the seed that they are carrying within themselves.

So help in every possible way to give freedom, to give opportunities. Ordinarily, if a child asks a mother anything, without even listening to the child, to what he is asking, the mother simply says no. "No" is an authoritative word; "yes" is not. So neither father nor mother or anybody else who is in authority wants to say yes – to *any* ordinary thing.

The child wants to play outside the house: "No!" The child wants to go out while it is raining and wants to dance in the rain: "No! You will get a cold." A cold is not a cancer, but a child who has been prevented from dancing in the rain, and has never been able again to dance, has missed something great, something really beautiful. A cold would have been worthwhile – and it is not that he will necessarily have a cold. In fact the more you protect him, the more he becomes vulnerable. The more you allow him, the more he becomes immune.

Parents have to learn to say yes. In ninety-nine times when they ordinarily say no, it is for no other reason than simply to show authority. Everybody cannot become the president of the country, cannot have authority over millions of people. But everybody can become a husband, can have authority over his wife; every wife can become a mother, can have authority over the child; every child can have a teddy bear, and have authority over the teddy bear…kick him from this corner to the other corner, give him good slaps, slaps that he really wanted to give to the mother or to father. And the poor teddy bear has nobody below him.

This is an authoritarian society.

What I am saying is in creating children who have freedom, who have heard "yes" and have rarely heard "no," the authoritarian society will disappear. We will have a more human society.

So it is not only a question of the children. Those children are going to become tomorrow's society: the child is the father of man.

Beloved Bhagwan,
India, Your homeland, has treated You badly and without due respect. Yet sometimes when I hear You speak, do I not detect a subtle fondness in You for India and her people?
Bhagwan, what do You love about India?

India, to me, is not only a country, but a concept…not just a land, but a way of life, a tremendously significant philosophy.

So when I talk about India, it does not matter at all that they have treated me badly, that they would like me to be killed. They have made efforts – unfortunately they failed. These are small things, and I don't take them into consideration.

My consideration is for the India as a concept.

It is the only part of the world which has gone deep into the interiority of man, which has discovered for the first time the ultimate in consciousness, the universality of individual beings.

Science has discovered much, but no discovery of science can be compared to the discovery that India has made in the past. For ten thousand years continuously it has devoted its whole energy to finding out the meaning of life, the very essence of existence – and it has found it.

So when I talk about India, I do not talk about the India that you see on the map, I do not talk about the India that exists today. I am talking about a concept that has come out of centuries' work, of discovery. Nowhere has religion ever reached such heights. No community has ever given all her geniuses to the discovery of man's inner world. And that is the most precious thing in life.

You can have everything, all, but if you don't have yourself…you can know everything around you, but if you don't know what is within you, all your knowledge, all your wealth, all your power is futile – and sooner or later you will be drowned in your own wealth, in your own power. It will destroy you because it will go on increasing, becoming bigger and bigger, and you will be shrinking, becoming smaller and smaller.

The scientist is denying that he is, and asserting truths about things and objects. It is a very strange phenomenon. Then who is discovering all these things and objects? Every genuine scientific genius feels embarrassed – anybody like Albert Einstein – because he cannot say anything about himself…and he knows about the farthest star in the world, its whole history millions of years before it was created, and he knows how many more million years it will remain, and then it will dissolve. His knowledge is vast, but he knows nothing about the knower.

And what use is this knowledge? Not only is it useless, it is going to be harmful. And we know now that the whole of science is in the service of the war machine: that is, in the service of death. The objective experimentation, the enquiry into the outside world, has reached a stage which can only be called a global suicide; while in India the search was inner, and it culminated in the universal experience of life, of joy, of blissfulness, of nirvana.

I am not concerned with India as a geographical unit, but as a spiritual search. I can condemn the present-day situation. It is ugly; it is against all human values.

The country is becoming poorer every day, and the politicians cannot prevent it, for the simple reason that if they try to prevent it… And the only way to prevent it is to spread birth-control methods. That goes against the orthodox Indian mind, and to annoy the orthodox Indian mind means you lose your power; next election you will be gone. So you know that if you do something to prevent it, you are finished; if you want to keep yourself in power, then you know the country is going to die and starve.

Already India has nine-hundred million people. When I started speaking there were only four hundred million people. If they had listened to me, it would never have got into such a bad situation. But they threw stones at me.

Now countries are trying to prevent me even from landing at their airports; the question of entry into the country does not arise. Even countries about which I have never thought…

Just today Anando informed me that Venezuela – I have never thought about it! – has passed a resolution that I am banned, I cannot enter into the country. Even in Ireland, where we were for two weeks, the government is now denying it. They are not even courageous enough to say, "Yes, they were here and they are gone." They are denying, saying, "They have not been here. How could they enter into the country? – because they are banned." Just as we left they must have passed some resolution in the parliament to ban us.

The European parliament has a resolution now to ban me collectively, rather than separately, so all European countries who are members of the parliament automatically become closed.

The same situation was happening in India. At the stations my train would be delayed for two hours because there were people who did not want me to get down at their city, and were forcing the train to take me back.

I would be speaking in an Indian city, and the electricity would be cut off. And this was happening so often, again and again, that it could not be just accidental. The fifty thousand people would be sitting in darkness for half an hour, one hour, and the electricity wouldn't come on. And finally I would have to inform them, "Now it is pointless – you please go home. I will stay a little longer in the city so you will not miss any lecture of the series." And as the people were leaving, as I was leaving, the electricity would come on.

Just now the Indian government wanted me to stay in India, but with conditions. One: no foreign disciple should be allowed to come to see me. Two: no news media should be allowed to interview me. Three: I will not go out of the country. If I fulfilled these three conditions then I could stay in the country.

I said, "Why don't you simply shoot me? These conditions are just to kill me!" And I had to leave the country because…there are many sannyasins in high posts in the government who informed me that I should leave immediately because they were going to confiscate my passport so I could not get out of the country.

I had not enough time, they said, to get a visa, to go to another country. Moreover they had informed all the embassies in Delhi that nobody should give me a visa to their country. So the only country that was available was Nepal, because no visa is needed – that is a treaty between India and Nepal.

But then the American government was pressuring Nepal, the German government was pressuring Nepal, the Indian government was pressuring Nepal that I should not be allowed there. And when it became absolutely certain that they were going to take some steps – they could have arrested me there, they could have sent me back to India – as I was informed, I had immediately to leave.

Whenever I am saying something about India, I am not talking about this India – this India, which is absolutely corrupted, and politically in the worst shape.

Every day hundreds of people are being killed – and it goes on declaring that it is a democracy. But newspapers are not allowed to publish how many people are killed; it

seems to the outside world that everything is peaceful. But the reality is that India has never been one country; it was always many countries.

In Gautam Buddha's time there were two thousand kingdoms in India. Mohammedans tried to make it one whole; they could not succeed fully, but still they managed that half of India become one nation. Britain, with more brutality, managed to force the whole of India into one nation; otherwise "nation" and "nationality" are not Indian concepts. This unity of India was forced.

Winston Churchill, before he retired, said, "The day India becomes free, it will fall apart, into pieces." And he was right. Politically he had the insight, because he knew that they had somehow put all the pieces together, and it needs immense power to keep them together. If that power is removed, those pieces will start falling apart – and that's what is happening now.

First Pakistan and Bangladesh became separated from India, now Punjab wants to be separate from India. Assam has been fighting for forty years to be separate from India, Bengal wants to be separate from India, Tamil Nadu wants to separate from India.

There are thirty languages in India. For forty years they have been trying to make one language – Hindi – the national language, but they have not been able. If you cannot even make a national language, how can you manage to have a nation? And all these entities are not small. India is almost a continent. All these states – Punjab or Maharashtra or Tamil Nadu – are as big as France or England or Germany, and each has its own culture, its own language, its own dress, its own way of doing everything.

Now, to prevent separation they have made a law that nobody can speak in favor of dividing any part. Anybody who speaks of dividing any part from India will be immediately arrested, and there will be no legal way, no court trial for it. And this is democracy!

In Punjab they have killed thousands of Sikhs, Sikhs have killed thousands of Hindus; and it continues every day. And it is going to happen all over India. And it can be solved very easily.

India is facing today the question of separation. There is no need to kill people. India should remain one. My solution is simple – one just needs a little understanding. Freedom is everybody's birthright.

So I am not in favor of *this* India, which is absolutely corrupted. But to me, in my vision, there is a totally different, glorious India, which consists of men like Gautam Buddha, Nagarjuna, Vasubundhu, Shankara... a whole line of thousands of enlightened people.

That's *my* India.

Beloved Bhagwan,
How can I assert myself if I dissolve and accept whatsoever is happening?

The moment you start thinking about these things, problems arise. You just do it and see what happens.

You dissolve yourself into the whole, and if the situation needs assertion, *you* will not be asserting; the whole will be asserting. You will not be less, you will be more. You will not be alone, you will be supported by the whole.

Experience dissolves problems.

But we go on simply thinking, and if you think, then naturally the problem seems to be very relevant: "If I dissolve, then how am I going to assert myself?" Naturally it seems contradictory. Logically it is contradictory, but existentially it is not.

You dissolve, and see what happens.

If the situation needs assertion, there will be assertion...not yours, because now you are part of the whole. Now the whole will assert with you. You never lose anything. With the whole dissolving, you are always a gainer.

But before thinking about it, do it.

Only doing will solve the contradiction.

Beloved Bhagwan,
Before I see You each day, I am so excited at the thought of seeing You. But when I do I become blank, as if I have no face, no smile. I even find it difficult to namast'e You, as if I have become invisible in front of You.
Whatever my heart does looks childish, and it feels as if any act I did would be just dumping my rubbish on You.
Bhagwan, I have never expressed how much gratitude I feel, although my heart is full of it.

I know it. And what is happening is absolutely right, what you are feeling is perfectly in tune with my teaching.

You cannot express your gratitude. You can be full of it, but any act...it will look too small. And it can happen, it is very natural, that you are excited when I am coming, but when I come, you are almost absent. This is good, this is how it should be.

When I am here, you should not be here, because in this room only one can survive: either you or I.

So it is not a question... But you have expressed very accurately your feeling. You should be happy that it is happening to you.

Whenever the Ego Gains, You Are the Loser

Beloved Bhagwan,
For some time now You have been saying that You are our friend and we are friends. I'm having difficulty in truly getting it.
Bhagwan, to me You are my most beloved master. Please show me where I am missing.

The question is from Vivek.

I can understand her difficulty.

The same will be the difficulty of all those who have come close to me, loved me, received me in their hearts as a master.

I have been saying that I am your friend, and you are my friend for a very strange reason that may not be obvious to you. There was another question from Milarepa – why are a few sannyasins feeling very resentful towards you, angry with you?

This has been an historical thing, that amongst disciples there are always a few who are accidental. The wind was blowing this way and they arrived. They saw a tremendous energy in the disciples, and they became greedy. But it was not a search for truth, it was not a search for love; it was simple greed. They also wanted to be spiritually powerful.

They became sannyasins, they became disciples, but the distance between me and them remained the same. They could never become my intimate people. They could never become *my* people. Even though they were with me, deep down they were resentful, angry. I wanted them to drop their resentfulness, to drop their anger. It was not my problem, it was their problem, and I wanted to help them in every possible way.

It was for this simple reason that I had said, "I am your friend, you are my friend." Those who were not really with me were immensely happy that now their status and my status was the same. And amongst these were people that you would never have imagined...

Just the other day I had the message from a sannyasin that Teertha is saying to people that my state and his state are now the same – we are friends. For this he was hanging around for fifteen years. Rajen is saying to people, "Now I am no longer a disciple but a friend, and I have the same status."

These were the people that I wanted to get rid of as peacefully, as lovingly as possible. But those who had loved me felt hurt – because they have loved me as a disciple, and to be a disciple is something so valuable that who cares to be a friend?

There is a story in Gautam Buddha's life.... One of his closest disciples, Sariputta, was found to be not meditating enough. Even people who had come after Sariputta had gone deeper into meditation, people of lesser genius and lesser intelligence. Buddha called Sariputta one morning and said, "What is the matter?"

He said, "You know it. I never want to be enlightened while you are alive. I simply want to sit at your feet the way I have always been sitting. To be your disciple, to be showered with your love...who cares about enlightenment? This is my enlightenment!"

So I can understand Vivek's difficulty. She has been for sixteen years with me. When she came she was only twenty years old; now she is thirty-six, almost twice the age. And all these sixteen years, day in, day out, she has been taking care of me with as much love as possible, with a deep devotion. It is difficult for her to think of herself as being a friend. It would not be a gain to her, it would be a loss. Those who have understood the joy and the celebration of being a disciple, of being in love with a master, will all feel the same: that to be a friend is nothing compared to it; everything is lost. To be a friend becomes formal.

So those who were really with me have

been shaken, hurt, and those who were not really with me have been tremendously happy. Just by me calling you my friend, you do not achieve the state in which I am. If it was so easy I would have called the whole world my friend, and they all would have come to the same state.

Milarepa's question is concerned with it. After the American government destroyed the commune, illegally but systematically – it was a criminal act against human consciousness and its evolution – people had to leave the commune. Now, a few of these people are feeling resentful; that simply means they were around me for a certain reason. There was some greed – although I have been insistently destroying all greed, all ego, all jealousy, all competition, all ambition. But they are so deeply rooted that although intellectually you may feel they have left you, they are there.

These people are now feeling resentful because deep down they had the greed that if they die in the buddhafield they will become enlightened, and now the buddhafield has disappeared. They are angry, and they are angry at *me*, because in spite of me telling them continually that I do not believe in miracles, they continued to believe, so it was a shock to them that I was arrested. They would have loved it if I could have gone through the walls of the jail, and then a miracle... Those were their desires...the commune had been destroyed and I should have done something to prevent it from being destroyed. Naturally, they are angry.

But this is their misunderstanding. They can't see real miracles; they can't see how I lived for those twelve days in jail, how the people in the jail – the authorities and the inmates – almost became sannyasins. All these people in the jail were saying that it was absolutely unjust, unfair, against the constitution, and when I left their jail, there were tears in their eyes.

One of the jailers said, "This is the first time that I have tears in my eyes when I am releasing a prisoner; otherwise I am always happy to make somebody free. But if you ask me, I really want you to be here always! You have changed the whole atmosphere. How you have done it, I don't know; perhaps it was just your presence."

I was in the hospital section, and the head nurse told me, "This is the first time that the jailers, the assistant jailer, and other officers continually come to this department; otherwise nobody comes here. They come here, they sit with you, they talk with you. They are hurt that you have been harassed, and they are ashamed that they are all instrumental in the harassment."

They made every arrangement for me – they have never done that for anybody else. I call *this* a miracle, not coming out of the walls or breaking the chains; those are not miracles. But this impact on human consciousness... All the six nurses and the doctor – who was also a woman – were crying when I left. They said, "We know you have to go...we know that you have been only three days with us, and we have become so attached to you; what must be happening to your people, who have been living for years with you? You have to go, but our personal feelings do not listen to logic – we want you to be here. You have changed the whole atmosphere."

Even the inmates were not smoking so that I was not affected. They were trying in every possible way so that the government might think they are harassing me but I was not harassed. I was not taking showers – the prisoners' shower booth was so dirty that it felt cleaner not to have a shower – the nurses found out, and they made available to me

their own shower.

They made available to me their own place – the office of the nurses, the office of the doctor – so that wherever I wanted to sit, I could sit; wherever I wanted to lie down, I could lie down; I did not need to go to the cell. And whenever I wanted I had simply to knock and they would open the cell and bring me out. I said, "You need not be worried – I am perfectly good in my cell."

They said, "It is not a question of your being perfectly good in your cell; we love you to be in the office. We will remember forever that this is the place you used to sit."

The same happened in Crete: the chair I was sitting in for almost seven hours... By and by the chief superintendent relaxed, started talking to me, and finally he said, "I am feeling proud that you are sitting in my office. So many of your people come, and I have seen you only in the picture of their locket. Now I will be able to say to them, 'This is the chair your master has been sitting in for seven hours with me.'"

He phoned his wife, saying, "I will not come until Bhagwan is safely sent to Athens." He became so concerned that he allowed Devaraj to drive me to the airport. The police officers were sitting at the back, I was sitting in the front and Devaraj was driving! This would have never happened...

These people who feel resentment may have other causes also.

Just the other day Anando was showing me one book published against me in Australia by a couple who have been sannyasins for three years and have been in the commune. But just looking at their ideas, it seems they have never seen me. They are saying that they were working, working hard, and with their work I was purchasing Rolls Royces. You can see the absurdity: their work

WHENEVER THE EGO GAINS, YOU ARE THE LOSER

was not bringing any money. Their work was making their own houses to live in, the roads – which were needing money, not producing money. But in their mind – and for all those three years also – they must have been resentful.

Those Rolls Royces were *not* produced by the commune. They were presents from outside, from all over the world. And I was not their owner – I had given them to the commune. They were commune property, and I have not brought any of them with me; I have left them with the commune. Everything that I had has been left with the commune. I never owned anything. But there must have been the idea that they are earning money, and I am wasting money. That is their resentment.

What money were you earning? In fact you needed money to make houses, to make roads, to make a dam – a dam needed two and a half million dollars to make. You were contributing your labor, but we were not creating money out of it so that I could purchase Rolls Royces, so that I could purchase anything. I have not purchased anything from the money produced by the commune because the commune never produced any money. The commune was absorbing money. In fact all my royalties, all my books, all their profits were going to the commune. The situation is just the opposite – that I had given everything to the commune. Now, four hundred books in different languages were bringing millions of dollars in royalties, and those royalties were going to the commune.

If I had wanted to purchase Roll Royces, I could have purchased my own Rolls Royces, as many as I wanted, just out of my royalties.

But the resentment, the anger, is blind. In the commune we invested two hundred million dollars. Those sannyasins perhaps think they had brought two hundred million dollars there! Without me and the people who love me around the world, those two hundred million dollars would not have been possible. And now you can see: Sheela is trying hard but is not getting even enough money to pay the attorneys. No sannyasin is going to see her.

Shanti B and Puja have been given bail by the magistrate – ten million dollars each. But they cannot collect even ten dollars, what to say of ten million dollars! Who is going to put up ten million dollars for Puja, ten million dollars for Shanti B? These people played with two hundred million dollars, and they remained in the illusion that this money was coming to them! The money was given to me, but because I don't receive anything, I had given the whole money to the commune. And still they feel resentful towards me. They are angry at me.

Just to pacify these people, before I left I did everything: I dissolved the religion, because that gives hope to people – and they start believing that the responsibility is mine, that they should be raised in consciousness, awareness, and finally made enlightened.

I made them free – saying that you need not wear red clothes, you need not wear a mala, it is not compulsory anymore – simply to drop all the load of responsibility that they were unknowingly putting on me. They were hoping that just by wearing red clothes and putting the mala on, their work was finished, that now it is my responsibility to make them enlightened. I dropped that. They think that I was giving freedom to them; in fact I was simply making my own life as light as possible. I was simply dropping unnecessarily imposed responsibilities. And finally, not to let them feel that they were inferior to me in any way, I told them, "I am your friend and you are my friend."

And the people who wanted it, who had been waiting for it, rejoiced.

But the people who understood cried and wept.

Now in Rajen's groups even my name is not mentioned. What is the need of mentioning the name of a friend? You have many friends – you don't mention their names.

Teertha has made an academy. Devageet was there; he worked hard to find the place, to arrange it, hoping that it was going to be Bhagwan's meditation academy. But when he saw the board being put up it said simply "Meditation Academy."

He asked, "But no mention of Bhagwan?"

And Teertha and Vedana and others who were involved in it simply said, "We are all friends – why put Bhagwan's name there?"

They printed a brochure, and Devageet was saying to me, "I cried, and I had to fight almost physically because Your name was not even mentioned in the brochure. It was not even mentioned that the meditations they will be teaching have something to do with You. They have all their pictures in the brochure, but Your picture is not there." Because he fought so much, finally they agreed to put in a picture of me, a strange picture, an old picture that nobody would recognize – it must be a picture taken by someone in '74 – and that too a small picture, and without mentioning my name or saying anything about who the person is.

Devageet, simply out of disgust, left the place. And now these same people are trying to have a world festival – in which my name is not mentioned. There is no need, naturally, to mention the name of a man who is your friend; you have many friends! But they will be exploiting the sannyasins.

The strategy is very clear, because I have been seeing: when they advertise their groups in our newspapers, newsletters, magazines, then they are in orange clothes with the mala. None of them is using red clothes or mala, and in the group not even my name is mentioned. But in advertisements, to attract sannyasins to participate in the groups, all of them are publishing their pictures with malas, with orange dress – as if they are old sannyasins. Just to make these people feel at ease, I withdrew myself from their lives.

But, Vivek, you need not be worried about it. Those who love me, those who know me, know perfectly well that I am their master, and they have traveled a long way with me, in devotion and love. And of course, it is impossible for them at any moment – even if they become enlightened – to call me a friend. That will be simply ungratefulness.

Again, I remember Sariputta. One day finally he became enlightened, and Buddha said, "You have to go to preach. Now you are enlightened there is no need for you to sit here by my feet."

He said, "This was the trouble! I was ready to drop the idea of enlightenment. You forced me to go on deeper into meditation, and now I am in a fix. I knew that this was going to happen – once I become enlightened you will tell me to go to spread the word. I don't want to go anywhere. While you are alive, I want to be just your shadow."

But Buddha persuaded him. Finally he agreed, when Buddha was so insistent, but he said, "One freedom I want…" Just see the use of the word 'freedom', and you can see the freedom that your so-called resentful and angry sannyasins have: "One freedom I want, that wherever you are I should be allowed to bow down and touch your feet, from a faraway distance, in your direction."

But Buddha said, "You are already enlightened – you need not touch my feet!"

He said, "You have to give me that freedom."

Love asks for a freedom which logic cannot understand.

Sariputta was asked again and again in his journeys… Every morning he would get up, take his bath, and the first thing he would do was to bow down on the ground with folded hands towards the direction where he knew Buddha was dwelling.

They would say, "To whom are you praying this way?" – because there is no God in Buddhism.

And he would say, "I am not praying to any God, but Buddha is God to me; he is my master."

And they would say, "But you are enlightened!"

He said, "That does not matter. I am enlightened because of him. Without him I don't think it would have happened in many lives' time, I cannot conceive how it could have happened. So he may say he is not responsible for the happening, but I cannot accept the idea. This freedom I have asked from him, and this is a special privilege."

I am feeling very relieved – relieved of all those who were not my people but somehow were hanging around. Now I want only those who are really with me.

Yesterday while Vivek was reading the questions to me, when she read her own question she started crying. I said, "What is the matter? Whose question is this?"

She said, "It is my question."

And I know that is the situation of many hearts – but only those hearts who have learned to love a master.

All those egoist people were pretending to be disciples. I did not want to hurt them, so the best, the graceful way was that I declared: you are my friends, and I give you total freedom. And they accepted immediately, joyously, not knowing what they were accepting. They were free…they met me; now they are again free, in the same position. They have lost something, but they think their egos have gained something. Whenever the ego gains, you are the loser.

It is one of the reasons that I don't want to have another commune. I want only a mystery school, so those who really are interested can come, learn, go back. It has been a tremendously meaningful experience, but it was not new. At every turn of my life I have had to drop a few people. And I don't want to say to somebody, "I am dropping you." I can't be that unkind, ungraceful. I have managed things so that they drop themselves.

It has happened many times – this was not the first time. And it is natural that as you go along, you start gathering some junk, some unnecessary luggage, and there comes a point where it has to be dropped. But these are living people. Although they are junk, they are just luggage, useless, I am still respectful towards them. So I have to find a certain device so they can go happily, not feeling that they have been dropped, but on the contrary, that they have gained what they wanted.

It was simply hilarious when I read Teertha's letter. In the end he writes, "I am doing the same work as you are doing; the only difference is that you are doing it on a bigger scale and I am doing it on a personal scale, individual to individual. But the work is the same." And then came this second news that he told somebody on the phone, who informed me, "I am of the same state."

It is good that they are feeling good.

As far as reality is concerned, those who

were real disciples are still disciples – even if they become enlightened, they will not lose their disciplehood. In fact, they have attained to the ultimate of disciplehood. Their gratitude and their love towards the master is not less but more than ever.

Beloved Bhagwan,
Listening to You speak recently, I have had many moments when Your words go in and strike a deep chord. When this happens it seems like two opposite phenomena occur simultaneously: on the one hand it's like hearing something for the first time, and on the other, like remembering something just recently forgotten.
Could You say something about this?

They are not opposite phenomenon. My whole work is not to make something of you, but to help you to remember something. Your innermost reality, your truth, has not to be brought to you; it is already there. It just has to be remembered.

The word 'remember' is very beautiful. Ordinarily you don't think about words. 'Remember' means to "make it a member again." Its root meaning is that you have forgotten some member of your being. 'Remember' means you suddenly become aware that it is there.

And my talking to you is not the talking of a teacher, because I am not teaching any theology, any doctrine, any cult, any creed. I am speaking to you in a totally different context. I am speaking to you in such a way that it creates inside you a synchronicity, it hits a deep chord in you. And in that, simultaneously something is remembered… You feel that you have heard it for the first time and

you also feel that it is a truth that has always been with you, just you had forgotten it. Both are true. From the outside you have heard it for the first time. From the inside it is part of your being; you had forgotten it.

I know so many people in the world, and so intimately, but still I forget their names sometimes – but I never forget their faces, I never forget their eyes. Even in a crowd of millions of people I can find them. But as far as names are concerned…because deep down I know names are just given to you, they are not part of your reality. So I forget. Then I have a simple technique for how to remember… It is strange that there are a few names which I go on forgetting. I will remember and will forget again…there must be something in those names.

So what I do is I simply close my eyes and start repeating the alphabet – from A to Z, slowly – and it helps. I say to myself "A" and wait for a moment to see if something is remembered, if the "A" hits something…then "B," then "C." And it never fails.

For example, Geeta is sitting here. Now Geeta is one of the names that I should not forget; it is the bible of the Hindus – in India the most respected book, the holiest book. But perhaps that is the reason I go on forgetting it! So this poor Geeta suffers.

Yesterday I was answering her question, but I could not remember her name, and there was not time while answering to go through the alphabet. Later on, walking up the steps, I went through the alphabet and caught her immediately as "G" came; I immediately remembered – it is Geeta. And then I was surprised because this is such a common name; it is not uncommon. But perhaps it is the Hindus and their holy book – that seems to be the only reason. I have spoken on it…not in English, so you don't know; otherwise

WHENEVER THE EGO GAINS, YOU ARE THE LOSER

twelve big volumes I have spoken on it, twelve thousand pages, although it is a small book.

But I had to go always…it was not only once. Once I can understand – one can forget. Then the next day I saw her coming to clean my bathroom and I thought, "My God! I have to go through the alphabet again!" And I caught her at "G" immediately, that "G" hits some chord, and I remembered "Geeta." And there are many names like that, that I go on forgetting. But they are there, just waiting to be struck rightly, then they become alive.

Different people use different techniques for forgotten names; they make associations. For example, if I don't want to forget Geeta's name I can simply make it associated with Krishna. That name I never forget, and it is his message – Geeta. So I can simply connect these two, so that whenever I see Geeta I don't have to bother about her name; I have to think of Krishna, then immediately I will remember Geeta. That too I have tried just this morning. Coming in, I said, "Hey Krishna!" I remembered that she is Geeta and no one else.

So if it happens when I am speaking that something hits a deep chord in you, you feel it is something new that you have heard. But suddenly, in an even deeper and darker part of your being, something else is remembered. And suddenly you are in a puzzle: have you heard it new or you had just forgotten, and hearing this you have remembered?

Both are true – there is no need for any puzzle. It is new as far as you are concerned; it is as ancient as existence as far as your being is concerned. For your ego it is new, but for your being it is just a forgotten message.

Sometimes you feel you know something, you remember something. You are absolutely certain. In all the languages this kind of phrase is available, "It is almost on the tip of my tongue." It is, but still you cannot say it. And it feels very, very strange, a little awkward inside, with both the things together: you know, you are perfectly certain that it is on the tip of the tongue, but you cannot verbalize it, you cannot simply say it. The more you try, the more you become tense…tense because it is so close. And it *is* close, but something is hindering the path, something is coming in between – a very thin layer of something, some other word. But because you are becoming tense, it is not possible to remember it.

Then different people have different methods. you start smoking a cigarette – you forget all about it. Just smoking a cigarette you relax, and suddenly it is there. Or you go into the garden and start watering the plants – you forget all about it. You are no longer tense, you are no longer worried even about remembering it, and that is the moment you remember it. It seems relaxation plays a great part in letting it come to the surface.

Perhaps when I say something it relaxes you deep down, and that helps. Just sitting with me, listening to me, is not a tense affair. It is not the lecture of a professor, where you are taking notes.

In India I had continuously to tell people, "Please stop taking notes because you are destroying the whole atmosphere. I am not a professor and this is not a class, and when I am speaking and you are taking notes, you can't hear me. You are concentrated on taking notes; you will miss many significant things."

Listening to me, sitting relaxed, suddenly a deep relaxation happens inside, and something that you have forgotten….

Now I would like again to remind you of the meaning of the word 'sin.' The religions have destroyed the beauty of the word – so much so that it has become almost impossible to use it, because all the connotations that they have given to it are in everybody's mind.

But in reality the word 'sin' simply means 'forgotten.' In that sense I accept it.

Our only sin is that we have forgotten ourselves, and our only enlightenment will be that we remember again.

We Cannot Be Otherwise

Beloved Bhagwan,
Today is my eighth sannyas birthday.
Isn't eight years a very long time to miss the obvious?

The obvious has been missed for hundreds of lives, so no time is long enough to miss it. On the other hand, even a single minute is enough to recognize it.

In fact, it is a nontemporal phenomenon; time has no concern with it. If you think in terms of years, if you have missed it in the moment when it was possible to get it, you will go on missing. Time cannot help; on the contrary, the longer you have missed it the more is the possibility to miss it again when the moment comes to recognize it.

The question is from Devaraj. He should not be worried, because he has not missed it. And it is not the time of eight years that has helped him not to miss. It is his love – not the length of time but the depth of love that he did not miss it.

He has loved me immensely and in a very difficult situation. He is my personal physician, and anybody in that situation will be in a very difficult situation.

I am a difficult patient. I don't listen to him or to anybody; I simply tell *him* to do what he should tell *me* to do. And he has to manage somehow to do it – and to do it rightly, because he has to take care of medical science and he has to take care of a madman.

I won't listen, because I understand my body and its ways. Whatever he, or any doctor in the world has learned about bodies and ways... They have learned about corpses, not real bodies; they have been dissecting dead bodies.

Sooner or later medical science will have to accept the fact that their understanding is basically wrong, because a living body functions totally differently; the dead body does not function at all. You study the dead body and you apply your conclusions to the living body. That is one of the greatest flaws in modern medical science.

But with me the difficulty is even more; it is not only a question of a living body. Modern medical science has no understanding of a body in which enlightenment has happened, which changes its functioning absolutely, totally.

But Devaraj has been able to understand for the simple reason that he has been able to love. His science, his experience, and my body's different functioning may have created a great problem for him to understand – but love solves everything. He has followed *my* understanding of my body and its wisdom, still keeping in tune with his scientific medical knowledge. He has done something which has never been done before, and he has done it successfully.

He need not worry: eight years or eighty years make no difference. The first moment he saw me the obvious became a reality to him, and not for a single moment has he lost sight of it; otherwise you can live with an awakened person for your whole life and still not see what awakening is, what illumination is.

So remember, it is not the length of time but the depth of love that makes the obvious understood. And in that very understanding a tremendous transformation takes place.

Only such people know intimacy with a master.

Beloved Bhagwan,
What is the nature of this chatterbox mind of mine? It has been going on and on now for as long as I can remember. What are its origins? Is its source somewhere in the vast silence it dissolves into when I am in Your presence?

The mind is simply a biocomputer. When the child is born he has no mind; there is no chattering going on in him. It takes almost three to four years for his mechanism to start functioning. And you will see that girls start talking earlier than boys. They are bigger chatterboxes. They have a better quality biocomputer.

It needs information to be fed into it; that's why if you try to remember your life backwards, you will get stuck somewhere at the age of four if you are a man, or at the age of three if you are a woman. Beyond that is a blank. You were there; many things must have happened, many incidents must have occurred, but there seems to be no memory being recorded, so you cannot remember. But you can remember back to the age of four or three very clearly.

Mind collects its data from the parents, from the school, from other children, neighbors, relatives, society, churches…all around there are sources. And you must have seen little children, when for the first time they start speaking, they will repeat the same word many times. The joy! – a new mechanism has started functioning in them.

When they can make sentences they will make sentences so joyously, again and again. When they can start asking questions, then they will ask about each and everything. They are not interested in your answers, remember! Watch a child when he asks a question; he is not interested in your answer, so please don't give him a long answer from the *Encyclopaedia Britannica*. The child is not interested in your answer; the child is simply enjoying that he can question. A new faculty has come into being in him.

And this is how he goes on collecting; then he will start reading…and more words. And in this society, silence does not pay; words pay, and the more articulate you are, the more you will be paid.

What are your leaders? What are your politicians? What are your professors? What are your priests, theologians, philosophers, condensed to one thing? They are very articulate. They know how to use words meaningfully, significantly, consistently, so that they can impress people.

It is rarely taken note of that our whole society is dominated by verbally articulate people. They may not *know* anything; they may not be wise, they may not even be intelligent. But one thing is certain: they know how to play with words. It is a game, and they have learned it. And it pays in respectability, in money, in power – in every way. So everybody tries, and the mind becomes filled with many words, many thoughts.

And you can turn any computer on or off – but you cannot turn the mind off. The switch does not exist.

There is no reference about it, that when God made the world, when he made man, he made a switch for the mind so that you could turn it on or turn it off. There is no switch, so from birth to death it continues.

You will be surprised that the people who understand computers and who understand the human brain have a very strange idea. If we take out the brain from the skull of a human being and keep it alive mechanically, it goes on chattering in the same way. It does not matter to it that it is now no longer connected to the poor person who was suffering from it; it still dreams. Now that it is connected to machines, it still dreams, it still imagines, it still fears, it still projects, hopes, tries to be this or that. And it is completely unaware that now it can do nothing; the person it used to be attached to is no longer there.

You can keep this brain alive for thousands of years attached to mechanical devices, and it will go on chattering, round and round, the same things, because we have not yet been able to teach it new things. Once we can teach it new things, it will repeat new things.

There is an idea prevalent in scientific circles: It is a great wastage that a man like Albert Einstein dies and his brain also dies with him. If we could save the brain, implant the brain into somebody else's body, then the brain would go on functioning. It doesn't matter whether Albert Einstein is alive or not; that brain will continue to think about the theory of relativity, about stars and about theories. The idea is that just as people donate blood and people donate eyes before they die, people should start donating their brains too so that their brains can be kept. If we feel that they are special brains, very qualified – and it is sheer wastage to let them die – then we can transplant them.

Some idiot can be made an Albert Einstein, and the idiot will never know – because inside the skull of man there is no sensitivity; you can change anything and the person will never know. Just make the person unconscious and change anything you want to change in his brain – the whole brain you can change – and he will wake up with the new brain, with the new chattering, and he will not even suspect what has happened.

This chattering is our education, and it is basically wrong because it teaches you only half of the process – how to use the mind. It does not teach you how to stop it so that it can relax – because even when you are asleep it goes on continuing. It knows no sleep. Seventy years, eighty years, it has worked continuously.

If we can educate…and that's what I am trying to impress on you – that it *is* possible. We call it meditation.

It *is* possible to put a switch on the mind and turn it off when it is not needed. It is helpful in two ways: it will give you a peace, a silence, which you have never known before, and it will give you an acquaintance of yourself which, because of the chattering mind, is not possible. It has always kept you engaged.

Secondly, it will give the mind rest also. And if we can give the mind rest it will be more capable of doing things more efficiently, more intelligently.

So on both sides – on the side of mind and on the side of being – you will be benefited; you just have to learn how to stop the mind from functioning, how to say to it, "It is enough; now go to sleep. I am awake, don't be worried."

Use the mind when it is needed, and then it is fresh, young, full of energy and juice. Then whatever you say is not just dry bones; it is full of life, full of authority, full of truth, sincerity, and has tremendous meaning. You may be using the same words, but now the mind has collected so much power by resting, that each word it uses becomes afire, becomes power.

What is known in the world as charisma is nothing…it is simply a mind which knows how to relax and let energy collect, so when it speaks it is poetry, when it speaks it is gospel, when it speaks, it need not give any evidence or any logic – just its own energy is enough to influence people. And people have always

known that there is something…although they have never been able to exactly pinpoint what it is that they have called charisma.

Perhaps for the first time I am telling you what charisma is, because I know it by my own experience. A mind that is working day and night is bound to become weak, dull, unimpressive, somehow dragging. At the most it is utilitarian; you go to purchase vegetables – it is helpful. But more than that it has no power. So millions of people who could have been charismatic remain poor, unimpressive, without any authority and without any power.

If this is possible – and this *is* possible – to put the mind to silence and only use it when it is needed, then it comes with a rushing force. It has gathered so much energy that each word uttered goes directly to your heart. People think that these minds of charismatic personalities are hypnotic; they are not hypnotic. They are really so powerful, so fresh…it is always spring. This *is* for the mind.

For the being, the silence opens up a new universe of eternity, of deathlessness, of all that you can think of as blessing, as benediction; hence my insistence that meditation is the essential religion, the only religion. Nothing else is needed. Everything else is nonessential ritual.

Meditation is just the essence, the very essence. You cannot cut anything out of it.

And it gives you both worlds. It gives you the other world – the divine, the world of godliness – and it gives you this world too. Then you are not poor. You have a richness but not of money.

There are many kinds of richness, and the man who is rich because of money is the lowest as far as the categories of richness are concerned. Let me say it in this way: the man of wealth is the poorest rich man. Looked at from the side of the poor, he is the richest poor man. Looked at from the side of a creative artist, of a dancer, of a musician, of a scientist, he is the poorest rich man. And as far as the world of ultimate awakening is concerned he cannot even be called rich.

Meditation will make you ultimately rich by giving you the world of your innermost being and also relatively rich, because it will release your powers of mind into certain talents that you have. My own experience is that everybody is born with a certain talent, and unless he lives that talent to its fullest, something in him will remain missing. He will go on feeling that somehow something is not there that should be.

Give mind a rest – it needs it! And it is so simple: just become a witness to it. And it will give you both things.

Slowly, slowly mind starts learning to be silent. And once it knows that by being silent it becomes powerful, then its words are not just words; they have a validity and a richness and a quality that they never had before – so much so that they go directly, like arrows. They bypass the logical barriers and reach to the very heart.

Then mind is a good servant of immense power in the hands of silence.

Then the being is the master, and the master can use the mind whenever it is needed and can switch it off whenever it is not needed.

Beloved Bhagwan,
I remember You once explaining that tantra means expansion. My moments of greatest joy and my moments of greatest silence are invariably accompanied by an exquisite feeling of expanding. This feeling is also present in the urge to melt into someone or something – like a tree or a sunset – that I love.

Where does this desire come from? Is it an innate longing to be reunited with something of which we were once part?

Yes, it is not something coming from outside. It is your innate feeling to be one with something with which you were once one – and with which you are still one, but without being aware. So it is only a question of awareness, of remembrance.

You have never gone anywhere. You are still here; it is just your mind that goes on moving to faraway spaces. If the mind is silent, suddenly you discover this crystal clear moment, now and here, and the feeling of oneness with all.

We are one.

We cannot be otherwise.

There is no other way.

Life is one phenomenon, existence is undivided – but mind has the capacity to forget it.

The mind has the capacity to dream of faraway things. You sleep in the night in your bedroom and you can dream of being on the moon. Do you think if you are suddenly awakened you will ask, "How to get home? – because I am on the moon." If you are suddenly awakened you will not be on the moon, you will be in your bed. You have never been on the moon. Even when you were dreaming that you were on the moon, you were not on the moon. The moon was a dream, your being on it was a dream; you were on your bed, in your bedroom.

The mind has the capacity to go far away. So once in a while when it is not far away, when something very striking brings it back to herenow – a beautiful sunset, a beautiful painting, a great dance…anything can pull it back. If something so enchanting is happening *here,* it cannot wander out, here and there; it has to rush home. That's why, at the moment of seeing a sunset or listening to music, you feel a certain oneness. And it is so fulfilling, so satisfying that you would like it to persist every moment, forever.

And the joke is that it persists every moment, eternally. You just go on, here and there, again and again forgetting about it.

You have to be brought back.

Once you have understood the basic situation, then there is no need for anything. Just close your eyes and feel now and here, and suddenly existence opens its doors.

You have always been part of it.

You are part of it.

You cannot be otherwise.

Beloved Bhagwan,
All my life, including my years of being a sannyasin, I have never had a questioning attitude. This has not worried me up to date, but now since You have been inviting us to ask You questions, I wonder if it is okay that I am quite empty?

I t is absolutely okay.

Beloved Bhagwan,
My love for freedom makes me always give to my beloveds all the freedom I possibly can. So often, I put myself into an uncomfortable situation where I get hurt. Does this mean I don't love myself so much, and that's why I put myself second?

I t may be much more complicated than you think.

First, the very idea that *you* give freedom to your beloved is wrong. Who are you to give freedom to your beloved? You can love, and your love implies freedom. It is not something that has to be given. If it has to be given, then there will be the problems that you are facing.

So in the first place you are doing something wrong. You really don't want to give freedom; you would love that no such situation arises in which you have to give freedom. But you have heard me saying again and again that love gives freedom, so you force yourself unconsciously to give freedom, because otherwise your love is not love.

You are in a troubled situation: if you don't give freedom, you start suspecting your love; if you give freedom, which you cannot give...

The ego is very jealous. It will raise a thousand and one questions: "Are you not enough for your lover or beloved, that she needs freedom – freedom from you to be with someone else?" It hurts, and that's why you start feeling, "I am putting myself second."

Giving freedom to her you have put somebody else first, and you have put yourself second. That is against the ego, and it is not going to help in any way, because you will take revenge for the freedom that you have given. You would like the same freedom to be given to you – whether you need it or not, that is not the point – just to prove that you are not being cheated.

Secondly, because your beloved has been with someone else you will feel a little strange being with her. That will stand between you and her. She has chosen someone else and dropped you; she has insulted you. And you have been doing so much; you have been so generous that you gave her freedom. Because you are feeling hurt, you are going to hurt her in some way or other.

But the whole thing arises from a misunderstanding. I have not said that if you love, then you *have* to give freedom. No, I have said that love *is* freedom.

It is not a question of giving. If you have to give it, then it is better not to give it. Remain the way everybody is. Why create unnecessary complications? – ordinarily, there are enough.

If your love itself has come to that quality that freedom is part of it, that your beloved need not even ask your permission... In fact, if I was in your place and the beloved was asking my permission, I would be hurt. That means she does not trust my love. My love is freedom. I have loved her; that does not mean that I should close all doors and windows so she cannot laugh with somebody else, dance with somebody else, love somebody else – because who are we?

That is the basic question that everyone has to ask: Who are we? We are all strangers, and on what grounds do we become so authoritative that we can say, "I will give you freedom," or "I will not give you freedom," or "If you love me, then you cannot love anybody else"? These are stupid assumptions, but they have dominated humankind since its very beginnings.

And we are still barbarous; we still don't know what love is.

If I love someone, I am grateful that that person allowed me, my love, and did not reject me. This is enough. But I don't become an imprisonment to her: She loved me, and as a reward I am creating a prison around her; I loved her, and she, as a result, is creating a prison around me. Great rewards we are giving to each other!

If I love someone I am grateful and her freedom remains intact. It is not given by me. It is her birthright, and my love cannot take it away. How can love take somebody's freedom away, particularly the person you love? It is her birthright. You cannot even say, "I give freedom to her." Who are you in the first place? – just a stranger. You both have met on the road, by the way, accidentally, and she was gracious to accept your love. Just be thankful, and let her live the way she wants to live, and live the way you yourself want to live. Your life-style should not be interfered with.

This is what freedom is. Then love will help you to be less tense, less full of anxieties, less in anguish, and more in joy.

But what goes on happening in the world is just the opposite. Love creates so much misery, so much pain, that there are people who decide finally that it is better not to love anyone. They close the doors of their heart because it is simply hell and nothing else.

But closing the door to love is also closing the door to reality, to existence; hence I will not support it. I will say: Change the whole pattern of love! You have forced love into an ugly situation – change the situation.

Let love become a help for your spiritual growth. Let love become a nourishment to your heart and a courage so that you can open your heart, not only to one individual but to the whole universe.

Beloved Bhagwan,
Do we have to transcend sex before getting enlightened?

You don't have to transcend anything. You have to live everything that is natural to you, and live it fully, without any inhibition –

joyously, aesthetically. Just by living it deeply, a transcendence will come.

You are not to transcend anything. Remember my words. A transcendence will come by itself, and when it comes by itself it is such a release and such a freedom.

If you try to transcend, you are going to repress, and repression is the sole reason why people cannot transcend; so you are getting into a vicious circle. You want to transcend, so you repress, and because you repress you cannot transcend, so you repress more. As you repress more, you become more incapable of transcendence.

Live it out fully, without any condemnation, without any religion interfering with your life. Live it out naturally, intensely, totally – and a transcendence comes. It is not your doing, it is a happening. And when it comes by itself, there is no repression, there is no antagonism.

You are above all those things that you wanted to transcend – for example, sex. But a real transcendence does not mean that you cannot make love. Of course your love will have a totally different quality. It will not be sexual, it will not be a biological urge, it will not be animalistic; it will be simply a play between two human energies.

If transcendence comes by itself, then many things, more or less, disappear. But anything that disappears – you are not against it. You can still enjoy it. For example, in a state of transcendence you are not a food addict, but that does not mean that you cannot enjoy, once in a while, going to a Chinese restaurant.

Transcendence makes you free; it does not give you a new bondage: first you were so addicted that you had to go, now you are so addicted that you cannot go. Transcendence means that now all this addiction is gone – you can go, you may not go. You are neither against nor for.

You may be smoking. Transcendence does not mean that once in a while with friends you cannot smoke a cigarette. I don't think that a cigarette, once in a while, will destroy your spirituality. And if it destroys it, then that spirituality is not worthwhile.

I cannot smoke – not because of transcendence but because of my breathing trouble. I have no antagonism against poor cigarettes; it is just the smell of tobacco I cannot tolerate, the smoke I cannot inhale. But that is a problem with my body; it is my allergy. But when I see somebody smoking I don't feel that this man is condemned forever, is going to fall into hellfire.

No condemnation arises in me, because what he is doing is simply playing a game. Being alone, finding nothing else to do and being told continually by the parents and the society that it is better to do something rather than nothing…so the poor man is doing something rather than nothing. He is at least smoking.

Transcendence is a very childlike state.

My grandfather used to smoke cigars and cheroots, and he would send me to get his cigar and lighter. And rather than bringing both, I would take the cigar in my mouth and light it and bring it to him. He said, "This is not right. I had asked you to bring the cigar and the lighter."

I said, "When I can bring one, which does the work for both…I am not stupid."

He said, "That I know. But remember, don't learn this habit."

I said, "Don't be worried. Seeing you cough continually the whole night, it is enough. I don't have to go through the experience to learn it. I learn from others' experience too."

His doctors were saying to him, "Drop these cigars." But it was impossible for him...a whole life's addiction. He was ready to suffer – to cough and not to sleep well.

I said, "Seeing you is enough prevention for me, and just that one puff that I take when I light your cigar brings tears to my eyes. It is enough just to experience what kind of enjoyment you must be having."

The people you know as saints are not childlike. They are addicted as much as others; their addictions have just become reversed. Somebody is addicted to sex – they are addicted to no- sex. Somebody is addicted to smoking – they are addicted to no- smoking.

Transcendence is a state of no-addiction...just a childlike playfulness. There is no sin in sex. Just living it intensely, by and by you transcend, just the way you transcend playing tennis. One day you throw away the whole thing, "Enough is enough!" You transcend football, you transcend all kinds of things, and nobody calls you a saint.

To me transcendence comes out of your experience. You see the futility of something and the addiction drops. Then once in a while, just for a change, if you want to smoke I don't see any harm; if you want to make love I don't see any harm. The harm is in the addiction – the harm is not in the act. And transcendence is not concerned with the act; transcendence is concerned with the addiction.

And to be completely unaddicted gives an immense freedom.

Chapter 26
April 25, 1986, Morning

The Circle
Can Be Broken

Beloved Bhagwan,
I hear You often say that the politicians and the priests are exploiting and cheating people, as if they are a different race from outer space, forced upon us.
My understanding is, rather, that these politicians and priests just come out from amongst us, so we are totally responsible for their doings, and complaining about them seems like complaining about ourselves. Is not a politician and a priest hidden in every one of us? Would You please comment?

The politicians and the priests are certainly not coming from outer space; they are growing amongst us. We also have the same lust for power, the same ambition to be holier than others. They are the most successful people as far as these ambitions and desires are concerned.

Certainly we are responsible, but it is a vicious circle; we are not the only ones who are responsible. The successful politicians and priests go on conditioning the new generations for the same ambitions; they make the society, they cultivate its mind and conditioning. They are also responsible – and they are more responsible than the common people, because the common people are victims of all kinds of programs that are being imposed upon them.

The child comes into the world without any ambition, without any lust for power, without any idea that he is higher, holier, superior. Certainly he cannot be responsible. Those who bring him up – the parents, the society, the educational system, the politicians, the priests – the same gang goes on spoiling every child. Of course in his own turn, he will spoil…but it is a vicious circle. From where to break it?

I insist on condemning the priests and the politicians, because that is the place from where it can be broken. Condemning the small children coming into the world is not going to help. Condemning the common masses is also not going to help, because they have been already conditioned – they are being exploited. They are suffering, they are miserable. But nothing wakes them up – they are fast asleep. The only point where our condemnations should be concentrated is on those who have the power, because they have the power to contaminate the future generations. If they can be stopped we can have a new man.

I know that everybody is responsible. Whatever happens, in some way or other, everybody has his own part in it. But to me what is important is whom to hit, so that for the new generation of children the vicious circle can be avoided. Humanity has been revolving in it for centuries. That's why I don't condemn the common masses, I don't condemn you. I condemn those who are now in a position that if they just relax a little bit as far as their vested interests are concerned, and look at the miserable mass of humanity, a transformation is possible – the circle can be broken.

I purposely choose the politicians and the priests. There are many other things to be remembered. The priest knows perfectly well that there is no God. In this world the priest is the only person who knows there is no God, but his whole profession depends on this non-existential God. He cannot say the truth because all his vested interests will be lost – not only his, but for generations to come he will be spoiling the whole game. He knows the rituals are just hocus-pocus, that the mantras carry no power, that his theology is just a cover-up. Nobody else knows it better; he has studied the scriptures and he knows there is no evidence of God anywhere. He interprets the scriptures in such a way that they help his profession. He goes on making commentaries on the ancient scriptures, adding more and more things that are helpful for his profession.

As times change he has to make new additions. For example, Manu, a five thousand year old thinker, priest, the father of priesthood, in his *Manusmriti* – the memoirs of Manu which Hindus follow word by word – he created the caste system, one of the ugliest things in existence.

Because of it one fourth of Hindus have suffered a long slavery, exploitation and humiliation. They have been turned almost into subhuman beings – they are called *achoot,* untouchables. They have fallen so much that you cannot touch them; otherwise you have to take a bath immediately. Even their shadow touching you is enough to make you impure. Manu reduced one-fourth of the Hindus to eternal slavery it seems.

I know everybody is responsible, but not everybody is powerful enough to break the circle; hence I am hitting constantly on the priests and the politicians. And now they have become afraid of me – perhaps they have never been afraid of a single man before. All over the world they don't want me to enter into their countries. The priests are behind the politicians who are making rules and laws that I should be prohibited.

The commune in America was destroyed by the politicians, but behind the politicians were the fundamentalist Christians, the most orthodox group of Christian priests. Ronald Reagan himself is a fundamentalist Christian. And to be a fundamentalist Christian means to be absolutely orthodox. He believes that every single word in *The Bible* is holy, is from God's own mouth. They were in conspiracy together to destroy the commune.

Just the other day I received the news that

now they are making a memorial in The Dalles; bishops and politicians and all kinds of leading, prominent citizens are contributing money – a big memorial, a memorial that they have become victorious, that they have thrown away the evil forces who had created the commune. They have thrown me out, destroyed my work, and they are not satisfied with that; they want to create a memorial so that the future generations will know.

And both the priests and the politicians are very vulnerable; they have no ground beneath their feet. Just a good hit is needed and they will be finished. And once they are finished, society will have a taste of freedom.

We can bring up children in a more human way, unconditioned, intelligent, looking at the whole earth as one – not Christians, not Hindus, not Mohammedans, not Indians, not Chinese, not Americans. Nations and religions are creations of the priests and the politicians. Once they are finished, religions and nations are also finished.

And a world free of religions, free of nations, will be a human world – without wars, without unnecessarily fighting for things which nobody has seen....

It is so stupid that for thousands of years people have been killing each other in the name of God. None of them has seen, none of them has any proof, none of them has any evidence. And they don't even feel embarrassed, because nobody has, looking directly into their eyes, asked the question.... And they are going on crusades, *jihads,* religious wars, destroying all those who do not believe in their dogma, because their dogma is divine and every other dogma is the devil's creation.

They are trying to serve humanity by killing people. Their intention is to free those people from the clutches of the devil. But the strangest thing is that every religion thinks that the other religion is created by the devil. So the fight continues. Politicians are fighting war after war – for what? I don't see the point. The earth has no lines; then why make these maps and draw lines?

One of my teachers was a very intelligent man. One day he brought a few pieces of cardboard; he had cut the whole world map into small pieces, put them on the desk and asked, "Can anybody come and arrange them in the right order?" Many tried and failed. Just one boy, seeing that everybody was failing and they were not making the world map by putting the pieces together, he looked at one piece on the reverse side. Then he turned all the pieces over and he found the picture of a man. He arranged the picture of the man, which was very easy, and that was the key. On one side the man was arranged, and on the other side, the world map was arranged.

Perhaps the same is true about the real world...if we can arrange man, the world will be arranged. If we can make man silent, peaceful, loving, nations will disappear, wars will disappear, all dirty politics will disappear. And remember, all politics is dirty; there is no other kind.

But we have to hit on those who have the power. Hitting the poor common man will not help, because he has no power, he is a victim. Even if we can change him, it won't be a great change. But if we can abolish the conspiracy between religion and politics, priests and the politicians, it will be really a great change, a revolution – the only revolution that is needed and that has not happened yet.

Beloved Bhagwan,
When You spoke of greed, I was totally horrified. I have finally reached a point where I am willing to see how big a part it plays in my

life, and the misery it brings with it. Could You please shed more light on what this thing called greed is, where it comes from? — and perhaps offer some tools to help me?

Just to understand the nature of greed is enough. You need not do anything else to get rid of it; the very understanding will clarify the whole mess.

Man is full if he is in tune with the universe; if he is not in tune with the universe then he is empty, utterly empty. And out of that emptiness comes greed.

Greed is to fill it: by money, by houses, by furniture, by friends, by lovers – by anything, because one cannot live as emptiness. It is horrifying, it is a ghost life. If you are empty and there is nothing inside you, it is impossible to live.

To have the feeling that you have much inside you, there are only two ways: either you get in tune with the universe… Then you are filled with the whole, with all the flowers and with all the stars. They are within you just as they are without you. That is real fulfillment. But if you don't do that, and millions of people are not doing that, then the easiest way is to fill it with any junk.

I used to live with a man. He was a rich man and he had a beautiful house. And somehow he became interested in my ideas; he listened to a few of my lectures, and he invited me, saying, "Why live far away, out of the city? I have a beautiful house in the city and it is so big; you can have half of the house. And I am not going to charge you, I simply want your presence to be there in my house."

I was living outside, in the mountains, but it was difficult to come from there to the university. From his house the university was very close. His house had a beautiful garden and was in the best locality of the city, so I accepted his invitation.

But when I went into his house I could not believe it; he had so much junk collected that there was no place to live. The house was big, but his collection was bigger – and a collection which was absolutely stupid. Anything that he could find in the market he would purchase. I asked him, "What are you going to do with all these things?"

And he said, "One never knows, some day one may need it."

"But," I said, "where is one going to live in this house?" So much furniture of all ages… because the Europeans had left the country so they had to sell all their things. He could not have enough; he managed to purchase anything, things which he did not need. A car was standing in the porch which always remained standing because it was too old, broken. And I asked him, "Why don't you throw it away? At least to clean up the place…"

And he said, "It looks good in the porch."

All the tires were punctured – it was of no use. Whenever you had to move it from here and there, you had to push it, pull it back. And it was there, rotting. He said, "I got it at a very reasonable price. It belonged to an old woman who used to be a nurse here and who has gone back to England."

But I said, "If you were interested in purchasing a car then at least you should have purchased a car which moves."

He said, "I am not interested in movement. My bicycle is perfectly good." And his bicycle was also a marvel. You would know that he was coming from one mile away, the bicycle made so much noise; it had no mudguards, no chain cover – it must have been the oldest bicycle made. It had no horn.

He said, "There is no need for a horn. It

makes so much noise that at least for one mile ahead people are already giving way. And it is a good thing, because it cannot be stolen."

I said, "That is strange. Why can't it be stolen?"

He said, "Nobody else can ride on it. It has been stolen twice, and the thief was caught immediately – because it makes so much noise, and everybody knows that it is my bicycle, so people caught the thief and asked him, 'Where are you taking the bicycle?'

"I can leave it anywhere. I go to see a movie – I don't put it on a bicycle stand, because then you have to pay money. I put it anywhere, and it is always there – when I come back it is always there. Everybody knows that it is a trouble. And even if you can get it to your home you cannot ride on it in the city – you will be caught. So it is better not to bother with it."

He said, "It is a rare specimen."

I said, "The way you describe it, it looks like it."

And he had all kinds of things in his house…broken radios, because he could get them cheap. He was a Jaina and he had a broken statue of Jesus Christ on the cross.

I said, "What have you purchased it for?"

He said, "The woman gave it to me free when I purchased the car – she offered it to me as a present. I don't believe in Jesus Christ or anything, but I could not refuse a piece of art."

I said to him, "Half of the house from today you take to the other half – my part has to be empty."

And he was very happy to take everything. Already his house was so full you could not walk – you could not find your way. He took everything. He had so many kinds of furniture that he had piled up on the sofa; it was not used, because you cannot sit on a sofa that is touching the roof. And I asked, "Why?"

He said, "You don't understand – the price! And someday I may get married" – he was not married – "and I may have children and they may need all these things. You don't be worried, everything will be of some use sometime."

Even on the road, if he could find anything lying there which had been thrown by somebody, he would pick it up. One day he was walking with me from the garden to the house and he found a bicycle handle, and he picked it up. But I said, "What will you do with a bicycle handle?"

He said, "You don't understand. I will show you." I went with him. In his bathroom he had almost a bicycle – just a few things were missing. And he said, "All these things I have picked up from the road. And I go on joining them and putting them together. Now a few things are missing. The chain is not there, the seat is not there, but I will get them. Somebody is going to throw them away someday. Life is long, and what is the harm? It looks perfectly good in the bathroom."

Greed simply means you are feeling a deep emptiness and you want to fill it with anything possible – it doesn't matter what it is. And once you understand it, then you have nothing to do with greed. You have something to do with your coming into communion with the whole, so the inner emptiness disappears. And with it, all greed disappears. That does not mean that you start living naked; that simply means you do not live just to collect things. Whenever you need something you can have it.

But there are mad people all over the world, and they are collecting… Somebody is collecting money although he never uses it. That is strange. In the commune, we had made a sticker for cars: "Moses earns, Jesus saves, Bhagwan spends."

A thing has to be a utility; if it is not a utility then there is no need for it.

But this thing can take any direction: people are eating; they are not feeling hungry and still they go on swallowing. They know that this is going to create suffering, they will be sick, but they cannot prevent themselves. This eating is also a filling-up process.

So there can be many directions and many ways to fill emptiness, although it is never full – it remains empty, and you remain miserable because it is never enough. More is needed, and the more and the demand for more is unending.

I don't take greed as a desire – it is some existential sickness. You are not in tune with the whole, and only that tuning with the whole can make you healthy. That tuning with the whole can make you holy.

It is strange that the word *health,* and the word *holy* both come from 'wholeness'. When you are feeling one with wholeness all greed disappears. Otherwise…what have religions been doing? They have misunderstood greed as a desire, so they try to repress it: "Don't be greedy." Then one moves to the other extreme, to renounce. One kind of person collects – the greedy person; and the person who wants to get rid of greed starts renouncing. There too, there is no end.

Mahavira could never recognize Gautam Buddha as enlightened for the simple reason that he still carries three sets of clothes – just three sets of clothes, which are absolutely necessary. One you are using, one has to be washed, and one for emergency reasons… someday the clothes may not come from being washed or they are not dry, or it is raining the whole day. So three seems to be very essential – one emergency…

Mahavira is absolutely against greed. Now, that has taken to an extreme form – he is naked. Buddha carries a begging bowl. Mahavira cannot accept it because even a begging bowl is a possession, and an enlightened man, according to him, should not possess anything. A begging bowl…it is made of coconut. You cut the coconut in the middle…and there are special coconuts which are very big. You cut from the middle, you take all of the fruit out, and then two bowls are left, hard shells. That is the cheapest thing, because they are thrown away; you cannot eat them. To have a begging bowl and to call it being possessive is not right.

But when you take greed as a desire and you become stubborn, going against it, then everything is a possession. Mahavira lived naked, and instead of a begging bowl he used to make a bowl of his two hands. Now it was a very difficult thing: his two hands are full of the food and he has to eat just like the animals, because he cannot use his hands – so he has to use his mouth directly to take the food from the hands.

Everybody in the world eats sitting. But Mahavira's idea is that when you eat sitting, you eat more. Now this is going to the opposite extreme. So he was teaching to eat food standing – standing, with the food in your hands; it is such a strenuous thing. You can take food only one time, so whatever can fit in your two hands at one time is one meal. You have to eat it standing, and everything has to be taken together, sweet, salty, and they all get mixed. That is Mahavira's idea of making it tasteless, because to enjoy taste is to enjoy the body, is to enjoy matter.

To me, greed is not a desire at all. So you need not do anything about greed. You have to understand the emptiness that you are trying to fill, and ask the question, "Why am I empty? The whole existence is so full, why am I empty? Perhaps I have lost track – I am no longer moving in the same direction, I am no longer existential. That is the cause of my emptiness."

So be existential.

Let go, and move closer to existence in silence and peace, in meditation.

And one day you will see you are so full – overfull, overflowing – of joy, of blissfulness, of benediction. You have so much of it that you can give it to the whole world and yet it will not be exhausted.

That day, for the first time you will not feel any greed – for money, for food, for things, for anything. You will live naturally, and whatever is needed you will find it. And you will live, not with a constant greed that cannot be fulfilled, a wound that cannot be healed.

Beloved Bhagwan,
Many times I have heard You tell the Zen story that, "If you meet the master on the way, kill him."

Bhagwan, does it really have to be like that? If we meet on the path, can we not just laugh, and chat a little while, and then if we must part, do so gracefully, with a namast'e and a smile?

The story is not about any actual path, and not about any actual meeting with the master. The story is about when you are meditating and things are disappearing from the mind – it is becoming silent. The last to go will be the one you have loved most. That is, the last will be the master. It is in your meditation, when everything else is gone, that still you will be seeing the master. Now, chit-chatting will disturb your meditation, and preparing a cup of coffee will not help.

The saying looks hard, but it is true: Cut the head of the master! It is in your imagination that you are cutting. By chit-chatting or laughing or talking, you will not get rid of the master. You have to be very simple and straight; you need a sword, and cut the head of the master and pass on. Don't look back!

The master is saying this so that you can enter into *suneeta-shunyata,* into nothingness, into nirvana. The master is making you aware that even he should not be a hindrance to you.

And I will be a hindrance. You have loved me so much that you may be able to drop everything from the mind, but then I will be there – and you have to drop me too. It is not an actual thing, it is just about your imagination, about the last trick of your mind.

Your mind will bring in the master because the mind knows you cannot throw away the master. You have thrown away everything else, and that is the last resort of the mind to prevent you from going into meditation. And if you are afraid – if you feel this is being ungrateful, if you feel this is not the right thing to do – to cut the head of the master, then you are playing into the hands of the mind. It has nothing to do with the master, because there is no master – it is just your mind projecting.

And don't ask, "From where am I to get a sword?" It has been asked, down the centuries. Whenever masters have said to their disciples, "If you meet me on the way, cut my head," the disciples have asked, "But from where have I to get a sword?"

I will tell you a Sufi story. Mulla Nasruddin has applied for a job on a ship. He is being interviewed, and the captain and the high officials of the company are asking questions. The captain asks, "If the waters are in a turmoil, and the wind is blowing very strong and there is a danger of the ship being upturned or swayed into a direction it does not want to go, what are you going to do?"

He said, "Simple, I will throw out an anchor."

The captain said, "That's right. But suppose another storm comes up; what are you going to do?"

He said, "Nothing else; I will throw out another anchor."

The captain said, "It is right, but suppose a third storm comes up. What are you going to do?"

He said, "The same! I will throw out an anchor."

And the captain said, "But from where are you getting these anchors?"

And Mulla Nasruddin said, "From where are you getting these storms? From the same place!"

Just as the master is imagination, your sword is also an imagination. If the mind can provide you with one imagination, it is capable of providing you with the other thing – and perhaps happily, because you are going to kill the master. The mind is very happy when you are against the master – angry, resentful – and now he will be bursting with joy that you are going to kill the master. He will present you a beautiful sword immediately – just ask.

Both are imaginary, the master and the sword. And you have to go beyond imagination. So this must be the last barrier, and once there is nobody, nothingness opens up – you are connected with existence, you are connected with your reality.

**So Which Way
Are You Moving?**

Beloved Bhagwan,

Often joyously I hear You saying contradictory things, and emphasizing that everything just has its polar opposite to be complete.

But the other morning I got into trouble when You were talking about offering Your friendship to Your sannyasins.

I understood that some of them have taken this long-wanted opportunity for their self-aggrandizement, and haven't been aware of the fact that they were basically resentful and angry towards You at being mere disciples.

My understanding was totally different, when You were telling us in Kulu and Kathmandu that as far as You were concerned, You didn't have any disciples anymore, and now it was up to us to drop discipleship.

To me Your offer of friendship was just overwhelming, and I felt more reverence and love towards You than ever before, and very very grateful. I felt a very delicate, sensitive and precious kind of intimacy starting to grow between me and You, as my Master.

Now You say that all this was just a device to get rid of egoists, and that they enjoyed this offer of Yours. I don't understand anymore. Did I get it all wrong? Where am I hooked?

The question is from Premda.

His situation is different from those who were waiting for such an opportunity for their own ego-fulfillment. He is new. He has not known the phase of discipleship at all, so when friendship was offered it was not a nourishment to his ego; it went directly to his heart because he has no resentment, no anger at being a disciple.

This became a joyous intimacy and a loving growth for him. Now he is feeling more reverence, more love, more respect. This will bring in him the wonderful experience of discipleship. So the situation is so different that there is no question of contradiction.

The people who have been with me for ten years, twelve years, and were hankering deep down to become masters themselves were certainly feeling resentful towards me. And when I offered friendship, it was not a gratitude or reverence that grew in their heart but a deep and long-awaiting ego was fulfilled.

Now they could declare that they have the same status as I have, that their experience is the same as my experience. So my declaration of friendship was to them the end of their discipleship – and not the beginning of friendship either; it was simply the end of the road.

But to Premda the situation is different. He has not been around me for many years, and he has not for a single moment thought of being a master. His whole desire has been to be closer to me, to be intimate with me. So when I declared that I am your friend, this desire was fulfilled, and it has created a loving intimacy and reverence. And you can see it from the question. I call myself your friend, but he says he started feeling a reverence towards the master.

To those who have been calling me "Master," the declaration of friendship ended their discipleship, and to one who was simply longing for intimacy the same declaration made him a disciple. And the people who were longing to be masters were not many; they belonged only in the category of therapists – just a few therapists, not all. And those therapists got this longing because I was sending people to their therapies and they started thinking that they are some kind of master, and they are helping people to grow.

The reality was, I was sending these people to their therapies because these people were so full of rubbish that they needed some dry cleaning, and those therapists were nothing but dry cleaners. But thousands of people passing through their therapies…it is very human and very natural to get the idea that, "We can be masters on our own." They were just waiting for the opportunity.

It is not true about all sannyasins; it is only true about a special, small group of therapists. Their work destroyed them. They may have helped many people come closer to me, but they themselves went on going farther and farther away.

Premda has no desire to be a master, and nobody who has a desire to be a master can ever be a master. Only those who are desire-less happen to be masters. It is not something like a goal that you can achieve: it is something that happens by the way, unintentionally, without being sought for. You are doing something else, you are feeling more love, more intimacy, more reverence, and slowly, slowly, in this reverence and love and intimacy, your ego is disappearing. One day, when the ego is not there, you have become a master.

You were not seeking it – it is just a by-product. And those poor therapists missed – although they were with me for years – because they remained achievers, climbers. In their mind they were always thinking how to become a master.

It is good, Premda, that my offering of friendship created discipleship in you. That's how it should have been to everyone who is sincerely here for the search of truth, for the search of oneself.

You are blessed.

Beloved Bhagwan,

Hearing about the sannyasin therapists who are choosing to do their own thing, reminds me that once I also decided to do my own thing rather than be with You.

When I did come back, I judged myself, and felt judged by others – ironically, some of whom are among those of whom You have recently spoken.

Because I can alternately view my experience as a going astray or as a constructive learning, I am very cautious about judging others who would appear to have gone off track. Surely only an enlightened seer is in a position to indicate where we are.

My question is: What is it to miss? Is it something other than, through our sleepiness, choosing to take a longer, more devious route to that place which we must some day reach...that place which, in fact, You say we have never left?

Are we all missing every moment of every day until we are enlightened?

Yes, everybody is missing every moment until they are enlightened.

Whatever you are doing can either bring you close to the point of explosion, or can take you away from the point and make you more closed. These are the two possibilities within you: exploding into a lightning experience, or being closed in a dark night of the soul.

So which way are you moving?

If you are moving towards the dark night of the soul you are missing – and missing more every moment because you are going farther and farther away. And there is no end of going farther away. You can go away eternally; there is no time limit.

One can remain unenlightened forever – that's the danger. And one can become enlightened this very moment. The question is, towards what are you moving? If you are coming closer to your center of explosion, then every moment you are nearer and nearer to enlightenment. It depends on your speed. If your understanding is intense enough, it can happen this very moment; you have not to wait even for a single moment more.

So you see these are the two possibilities: either now or never. Both are possible, and man's prerogative is that he has the freedom to go either way.

There is no harm in doing your own thing – but you don't know who you are, how can you do your own thing? It is a dilemma. Those who know cannot do their own thing, because they know there is nobody inside as a self, as a separate entity from existence. Those who do not know themselves cannot do their own thing because they don't know even their own self.

So either you are accidental...one possibility; that's what you call "doing your own thing." You are accidental, or you are existential: that's what I call "doing the thing existence wants you to do." It is not your own thing. I am not doing my own thing – there is nobody to do such a thing. I am simply available to existence. So whatever and wherever it wants to lead me, I am available, because I am not.

Remember, these are the difficulties with language. I say I am available because I am not. Only when I am not, there is availability. If I am, then there is always choice, not availability. Then I will judge whether to go that way or not, whether to go this way or not, whether to do this or not. So whenever you are doing your own thing, one thing is certain: you are not in tune with existence. So what can it be? It can only be accidental.

I know people who had come accidentally to me. They had come to meet one of their friends who was a sannyasin; they had not come to meet me or to see me. They were not even remotely interested in me, but then listening to me they became interested, they became curious, they became involved. This is accidental. If I send them away to do something I can be certain some accident is going to happen.

I have tried – seeing some accidental people I have told them, "Go and open a center in your place," and they were very happy and they went there and fell in love with a woman, and forgot all about the center – got married and got into the whole mess of marriage.

You cannot depend on these people; they are not reliable. It is not their fault. They are just driftwood – any accident and they start doing things they have never thought about, doing things without ever thinking whether they really want to do them. Perhaps others are doing, so they start doing.

What you call "doing your own thing" is accidental, because you don't know yourself yet; you cannot do your own thing. And to be accidental is to remain in darkness – being thrown by winds here and there like a dead leaf…having no roots, having no integrity, having no individuality, having no sense of being connected with existence.

Doing your own thing, *you* were wrong – not that the things that you were doing were wrong, but that you were thinking that they were your own. They were only accidental. The people, the therapists, who criticized you were thinking they were doing *my* things, not their own. And that was creating deep resentment in them, that they have to do my thing. They really wanted to do their thing.

They criticized you just to strengthen in themselves that the very idea of "doing your own thing" is wrong. To repress their own idea they judged you wrong; they were really judging themselves. And once they got the opportunity…now they are all doing their own things, and thinking that this is freedom. They are telling people, "Bhagwan has given freedom to us." Now, this is such a foolish idea. Nobody can give you freedom, and if somebody can give you freedom, he can take it back any moment. Freedom cannot be a gift. You have to grow and be free; freedom has to be something that happens to you – it is not given.

Now they are saying, "Bhagwan has given freedom to us, and now we are doing our own thing." And they are doing the same thing they were doing here…perhaps less efficiently, more superficially, because the people they will be getting will not be meditators.

I used to choose people for their groups; seeing the need of the person, I used to choose which group he should go to. Now they will be doing things to people who don't need them; or these things may even harm them. There is every possibility that the people, through their therapies, will be harmed – because therapy is not anything spiritual. Therapy is only preparing the ground. And if you don't have the seeds, the ground that you have prepared will simply grow weeds, wild grass. It cannot grow roses.

Here I was using their therapy to clean the ground so that seeds of meditation can be sown, and people can blossom.

But soon they will understand. Seeing the results, people will start disappearing from their therapy groups. I know perfectly well that people *never* wanted to do therapy groups; I had to persuade them to go to do therapy groups. They had come to listen to me and to meditate.

Therapy groups are already out of fashion. Esalen – the original pioneer institution for therapy groups – is dying. Nobody comes anymore. Only on weekends a few old people turn up. And when they saw that thousands of people are coming to me and going through me to the therapies, they could not believe it, because they were the original people who had started the movement of therapies. It was unbelievable for them why people were not coming there.

The reason was that people had been there and had seen their therapies and found that they were only games you can play with. It feels good while you are playing them, but after two days all is gone; you are the same person, nothing has changed. And what is the point of going again and again, giving money and playing the same kind of games?

These therapists who had been working here in the world of the sannyasins will soon feel frustrated, tremendously frustrated. One thing, sannyasins will stop going to them, knowing that it is no longer part of a spiritual movement. Secondly, those who go will see that it is pointless. Just again and again clearing the ground and letting the weeds grow makes no sense.

I was using therapy simply as a preparation – it was not the end. And these therapists know nothing of meditation, because they felt that it was below them to go and meditate with the same people who are doing therapies with them; they are great therapists. So they never meditated; they missed meditation. They were so knowledgeable that they thought they knew everything. I don't think they have listened to me; otherwise the way they have betrayed me would not have been possible.

But they will have to come back; they cannot go on existing for long. Soon you will see those faces again, and this time they are not going to be therapists. This time I am going to work in a totally different way. Therapy will not be part of it; perhaps personal counseling may be there, but not therapy.

There is nothing wrong in doing your own thing – just remember that it is accidental. First know thyself, and then do anything that happens, that comes up out of your nothingness.

And out of nothingness always comes the lotus of nirvana.

Beloved Bhagwan,
In the Hindi incarnations of God there are a woman and a man together – like Vishnu and Laxmi, Shankar and Parvati, Krishna and Radha, Rama and Sita, etc. On the other hand, there are other religions like Jainism, Buddhism, Taoism, Mohammedanism, Christianity, et cetera, which have no place for women. Please comment.

Compared to Hinduism, all these religions – Taoism, Jainism, Buddhism, Christianity, Mohammedanism, Judaism – are very new. Hinduism is very old; hence it has some unique characteristics. Because it is the oldest religion in the world, a few things are in it which you will not find in other religions.

For example, you are asking that Hindu incarnations of God are always with a woman consort: Shiva is with Parvati, Krishna is with Radha. In India, Jainism and Buddhism flowered twenty-five centuries ago. They had to fight against Hinduism. Hinduism was the only religion.

You will be surprised: it was so alone that it had no name. A name is needed when there is more than one thing; if there is only one thing, what is the use of a name? Hinduism was the only religion, so it was simply called *dharma* – religion. There was no need to put an adjective to it. Jainism and Buddhism were born out of Hinduism, offshoots of the old religion, but then they had to make some specialities to stand aloof; otherwise the oceanic Hinduism would have drowned them.

Hinduism was very natural, that's why the reincarnations are not celibate. The idea of celibacy had not entered in the mind of the Hindus because it is unnatural, so even their incarnations of God have their wives. They are just as natural as you are.

Jainism and Buddhism both made it a point that man has to go above nature, beyond nature, only then he is religious – Hinduism is not religion.

What kind of a religion is it if just to be natural is to be religious? Then there is no difference between you and animals, because all animals are natural. They had a point there, and they created great logical systems against Hinduism. One of the basic points was that you have to go beyond nature – and that starts from celibacy, because that is the basic nature, sexuality.

So Buddha is alone, Mahavir is alone, and for these twenty-five centuries, all their monks and masters have been alone, celibate. You will be surprised to know that their celibacy was such a thing that the common masses became very impressed. Their ascetic attitude towards life...because Hindus were not ascetic – I mean Hindus before Buddha and Mahavir were not ascetic. Even their seers lived in comfort and luxury. They had their communes in the mountains, in the forests, which their followers went on donating to. The kings, their sons, their daughters – all had to go to be there in their monasteries to learn.

So they had immense power. One great Hindu wise man had many kings as his followers, and lived in luxury, comfort. His whole commune of disciples and teachers, they all lived beautifully. They were not other-worldly people.

Jainism and Buddhism are ascetic; they went on point by point against Hinduism, to make a distinct identity. Comfort is not even heard of; discomfort is the way. The more you can keep yourself in discomfort, the more spiritual you are – because the body is the enemy of your soul, so torture the body so you can find your soul. This world is the hindrance for the other world, so renounce it.

Jainism and Buddhism did so many strange things that even the Hindu masses became impressed; even Hindu wise men, brahmins, started thinking how to fight against the rebellious Jainas and Buddhists. The only way was that they also had to be ascetic – more than they were. So after Gautam Buddha you will not find any Hindu master with a woman. Shankaracharya, Ramanujacharya, Nimbarkha, Vallabha – great masters, but you will not find them with a woman. What happened?

They all had to be celibate. They *had* to be to fight with the Buddhists and the Jainas; otherwise they were ordinary people, they were not spiritual. And they were all ascetic, just like Jainas and Buddhists were; they were ascetic in their own way. They renounced the world, they renounced all comforts – just to counter-attack.

Hinduism got spoiled by Hindus themselves; otherwise it was a beautiful religion, very natural, very simple, very innocent. But it became more and more complicated. These three religions have been fighting for twenty-five centuries, arguing, writing treatises against each other. And those treatises have become more and more complicated – to such a point that even to understand them has become a difficult expertise.

And there are treatises which scholars

have been trying for years to translate into English but have not been able to. Because of the complexities of ideas, language, its nuances, it is difficult to be authentic to the original and to translate it; the translation looks very poor.

Judaism, Christianity, Mohammedanism, Sikhism, all are later additions to human consciousness – after Buddha. In fact Buddha should be the demarcation line, not Jesus. We say, "Before Jesus Christ, after Jesus Christ." Jesus has become the demarcation line dividing history, but that credit should go to Gautam Buddha, who came five centuries before Jesus and *really* divided human consciousness and its growth.

Jesus himself had traveled to India while he was young. *The Bible* has no account of him between the age of thirteen to thirty; *The Bible* has no account of where Jesus had been. This looks strange – a small life – he lived only thirty-three years – and in those thirty-three years *The Bible* has accounts of only three years, the last three years. About his earlier life are only two incidents – minor, meaningless. One was of his birth and the coming of the three wise men from the East to pay tribute; and second, his getting lost in the temple of Jerusalem, arguing with rabbis. These are the only two incidents. And then from the age of thirteen to thirty, seventeen years, nothing is mentioned – what happened to this man, where he was.

These seventeen years he traveled to Egypt, to India, to Ladakh, to Tibet, and all these places were Buddhist at that time. Buddha had died only five centuries before, and his impact was still very alive. Jesus visited Buddhist monasteries. I have been to a Ladakh monastery which Jesus had visited, and I looked in their records of visitors, which they have kept for two thousand years. And I

asked them if they had a record of all the visitors and their impressions about the monastery.

It is one of the most beautiful monasteries, and Jesus stayed there for almost six months, studying Buddhism from the monks. There are, in their official record, the impressions of Jesus, his signature, the date. He became immensely influenced by Buddhism, so his celibacy, his ascetic attitude, his praise for poverty, his condemnation for riches, were all borrowed ideas from Gautam Buddha.

Naturally these people followed a certain pattern that Buddha left behind him. They don't have a woman companion, which would be natural. Hinduism seems to be very natural – even its gods are very natural. There is no desire to be beyond nature; there is only one desire: to be totally natural. But in a way *all* other religions are reactions, rebellions against Hinduism.

It had no name. It was known as the eternal religion because it had always been there. Nobody can say when it was born, who was the founder of the Hindu religion. You can find founders of all other religions except Hinduism. Who was the original man? There seems to be no one. Hindus themselves used to call it *sanatan dharma:* the eternal religion. How did they become Hindus? Who started calling them Hindus? It was in a very strange way that they got the name, Hindus.

It was by the foreigners who were constantly invading India that the name was given, because every invader had to pass one of the greatest rivers of India, Sindhu. The first invaders, were the Hunas, who have disappeared from the world now – a wild tribe. In their alphabet they had no sound for 'sa', for 's'. The closest sound to 's' was 'h', – 'ha'. 'Sa – ha' – that was the closest. They could not pronounce the river *Sindhu;* they

241

pronounced it, the river *Hindu,* and because of their language, and because of their pronunciation, the people who lived beyond this river, they started calling *Hindus,* the people who live beyond the river Hindu.

It is beautiful sometimes to look at the history of how a word evolves, in what phases it moves, what turns it takes, what colors it takes.

Because of the word 'Hindu' the land of the Hindus became Hindustan, and the religion became Hindudharma, Hindu religion. And from the Hunas, invaders used to be continually coming. The country was so rich that another group of invaders, Mongols from Mongolia…who were the most terrible invaders, who produced Tamerlane, and Genghis Khan, the most terrible of men. In their language – now it had become established because of the Hunas – the name of the Sindhu became Hindu, the land became Hindustan, the people became Hindus. They did not have any sound in their alphabet for 'h', for 'ha' – the closest for 'h' was 'i'. They could not pronounce Hindu, they could only pronounce, Indu.

It looks close: Hindu-Indu. And because of the Mongols, the river became Indu and the country became India – from Indu – and the people became Indians. But it all happened because of that river which has a name, accidentally. But Hindus themselves don't have a name, neither do they have a name for their country. They have been always there, their religion has been always there. They don't know any beginning of their religion.

So it seems it has grown very naturally with the natural man. Buddhism was the first effort on man's own part to create a religion. That's why I say Buddha should be the demarcating line; because what was natural up to then became something man- made, manufac-tured. And now religion is manufactured, so many religions are manufactured.

Nature is one, but once you start manufacturing then you can manufacture, as you like, different religions, different creeds, different cults, different philosophies.

Buddha certainly stands just in the middle of this change.

If you understand me, my whole effort is to reverse the whole process. Man does not need man-made religions; man simply needs to be natural. Nature should be the only religion, and then there will not be divisions of Hindus and Mohammedans and Christians and Buddhists.

Nature does not make any divisions; it is undivided and it is one.

Beloved Bhagwan,
During the time with You in Oregon, I sometimes felt that leaving was an escape, a mistake – like removing the kettle from the fire just before the water boiled. Now look at us: we've all had to leave, and You are continents away. Yet this time seems even richer – a time when You are offering something vital, not to be missed…perhaps the chance to be "at home" everywhere. How to summon You, and how to slip quietly into our hearts as we drive cabs and bulldozers in the "outside world"?

Love knows no distances in time or in space. So wherever my people are, whatever they are doing, if their heart beats in tune with me, they are with me. Then all distances of time and space disappear.

The question is of the hearts beating in the same rhythm. That is the only closeness.

It was easy to miss in the commune

because I was so close to you. It was easy to forget me. I was too obvious. It was easy to take me for granted. But now that you are scattered all over the world, by the courtesy of the American government, we have made the whole world our commune.

There are great distances in space, but this will help you; it will not be a loss. This will make you remember me more. This will remind you of me more. In your silent moments, in your loving moments, just playing on your guitar, you will find me sitting by your side. Just in moments when you are silent, peaceful, you will start hearing my heartbeat too.

Everything that happens is good, is for the better, because existence goes on evolving. If we remember that existence is continuously in evolution, then whatever is happening…at the time it may seem disastrous, but finally you will find that it was not so; it has brought new flowers, it has created new experiences.

I know there are continents between me and you, but those continents cannot separate; they only join. They are not walls, they are bridges. And a bridge, however long, is a bridge; and a wall, however short, is a wall.

My own experience has always been that everything that has happened has always proved to be good. If we can trust, then even at the time of its happening we will not be sad, we will be celebrating. And our sannyasins did well, even though the most powerful government was destroying a small commune of five thousand people – which proves that they were afraid. Out of fear they were acting, but our people danced and sang and celebrated, knowing that out of this chaos some beautiful stars will be born.

The American government's fear has now become a world phobia. Now every government is afraid…not of a commune; the question of a commune does not arise. They are afraid even of me landing at their airport…not a question of entering in their country! Fear seems to be unlimited. What can I do if I just land at their airport?

England would not allow me to rest overnight in the airport, and in the parliament they had to discuss it, my being in the country. And that was a lie because I was only asking to stay overnight in the lounge of the airport – which it is meant for. I had my jet plane standing at the airport so that in the morning we could leave, thinking that they may say, "The lounge is only for first class passengers; now how can we decide about your jet, which class is it?" So we purchased tickets for first class traveling too, not giving them any chance. And that's actually what happened.

They said, "The jet is okay, that it is ready, but how can we be certain…? The lounge is only for first class passengers." So we produced our first class passenger tickets, saying that, "For your satisfaction we have tickets also."

Then they disappeared and came back about half an hour later and said, "There is some bylaw of the airport that we cannot allow you to stay the whole night – a few hours is okay."

I asked the man, "What do you mean by a few hours? And how do you decide that three hours is enough, or four hours is enough, or twelve hours is enough? And where is that bylaw of your airport?" The man disappeared and never came back.

Another man came back, and he said, "You have to understand it, that if you want to wait the whole night you have to wait in the jail. We cannot take the risk of leaving you free in the airport lounge." And I had to stay in the jail. And in the parliament, the prime minister answered the questions and said that my being there was dangerous for the country, for the country's safety.

An American establishment for nuclear weapons in England to bomb Libya is not dangerous; my just staying overnight in the airport lounge, from where I cannot go into the country by any way, is dangerous. You can see these politicians are made of straw. And the thing has gone around the world: now the whole European parliament, all the countries of Europe, are deciding together that I cannot land my jet at any airport; they will not refuel it. And then small countries are bound to follow.

Now the Bahamas have decided that I cannot enter; other countries – Panama and two or three other countries near Panama – afraid that I may come there, have decided. Strange, that they are afraid of a single man so much. Soon I think they will be deciding in the U.N. that this man should not be allowed to stand on earth anywhere.

But I take it as a good sign. It means they have recognized one fact: that what I am saying they cannot refute, that what I am saying is dangerous to their very roots. And if their roots are so weak, do you think they are going to survive? Even without me they will die; even without me they have to die.

Their *fear* shows death.

And all these governments are lying without any evidence of anything! Now they are spreading the rumor around the world that they have nothing against me, but the people who are with me, three of them, are criminals. They don't give the names, of the three people who are criminals and what crime they have committed. Some evidence should be proved. And even if they are criminals, I cannot be punished for their crimes. But just because they have traveled with me, I cannot be allowed to remain in a country.

In Spain, the government took one month to decide: the parliament discussed, the cabinet meetings went on for seven days, and finally they decided – the president and the prime minister, all were involved in it – that I should be allowed in. And then came a letter from the German government that three criminals are traveling with me. They called my secretary, Hasya, and told her, "We don't have anything against Bhagwan, but from the German government there is tremendous pressure that three criminals are with you."

She asked, "Who are the three criminals, and what crimes have they committed?" By insistently asking, we have come to know only that one is German, one is Canadian, one is American. Strangely enough, there is no German in the group, so one third of the information is absolutely wrong. There are a few Americans, but none of them are criminals, and none of them remembers that he has committed any crime! One is a Canadian: he is shocked by hearing it – that he is a criminal. There are no charges against him.

Just today I have received a letter from the U.S. Supreme Court in Oregon. They could not prove the case for which they were harassing me for twelve days in jail; they failed to prove the case in North Carolina. The U.S. attorney has had to accept in the court that, "We have not been able to prove anything; still, we want everybody else to be released on bail but Bhagwan should not be released on bail."

This must be something unprecedented! They have not proved anything against me. Why should I not be granted bail? The reasoning was that I was capable of jumping the bail, whatever the bail would be – ten million dollars or twenty million dollars. Does it mean nobody in America who has money will ever be allowed bail?

Strange! The people who don't have money cannot be allowed bail because from where will they get money for bail? And the people who have money cannot be allowed bail because they can jump. So bail is simply out of the question in America.

Simple logic can show the stupidities. Then finally they had to drop the case, but they had taken three persons on bail – Jayesh, Devaraj, Vivek – at twenty-five thousand dollars each. But you can see the cunningness! If governments are so cunning then I don't think criminals are doing anything bad. Governments are criminals.

The letter that I have received today says that because these three people have refused to appear as witnesses, we are dropping the case. These three people have never received any summons to appear. Now, this is simply strange! We were waiting that these people should be sent for any day; our attorneys were waiting there. They said, "You give us the time and the date, and we can call our people and they will be here." But because they had dropped the case, now they were afraid that they would have to return the seventy-five thousand dollars.

To keep that money, this letter has been sent: Because these three people have not appeared, their bail money is to be taken up by the U.S. government.

And they have confiscated my things, which they had said would be released when I am released – they were not given back. Then they told my attorneys, "After three days we will be releasing them." They were not released; then seven days…months have passed and they go on postponing.

Now the case is dropped. Even the bail money has been transferred to the government account. What about my personal things? My attorneys are continually going to

them, saying, "Decide something about his personal things." They want to divide them half and half – half will taken by the government, and half will be given to me. Strange! For what should the government get half? And we were ready even for that.

I told the attorneys, "Let them have half. Half you take, and then we will fight for the other half." But they simply *say* – they don't do anything. Perhaps some other day I may receive a letter in which all those things are confiscated and taken by the government – for some reason they can find or invent, because my people did not appear in the court on the hearing day.

And there has never been a hearing, there has never been a hearing day; the case was dropped a few weeks ago. We have been informed by the attorneys that the case has been dropped, knowing that they have nothing to prove in it.

It seems on the surface, with all these things, that they are destroying my work, destroying my message. But they are wrong. This is the way, not of destroying any truth – this is the way the truth enters into people's minds, gets their sympathy, their heart.

So wherever you are, it does not matter. Just your heart has to beat with me. If it stops beating with me, then there is distance.

Now look at Chetana, sitting there in the corner: now she is almost sitting on the moon. The reason is that she had asked a question. She herself had asked, "If I am wrong, please nudge me a little." I nudged her a little and said, "You are wrong," and that has hurt her so much that since that day she has become a miserable person. I have never seen her in any misery before. She has always been light, joyful. But since that day, because I said, "You are in a wrong space…" And she herself had asked, "Nudge me a little." And I really nudged her a little…just a little, and she has gone so far away; she is sitting on the moon.

Remember one thing, when you ask a question be ready for any answer. Don't expect a certain answer that you would like; otherwise there is not going to be any learning, there is not going to be any growth. If I say you are not right at a certain point, try to look at it. I will not be saying it just to hurt you. If I am saying it, I mean it.

And if you start feeling hurt by small things, then it will become impossible for me to work. Then I have to see what you would like. Then I will not be a help, then I will not be a master to you.

So you can be here, but if your heart is not beating with me, you are far away. And vice versa.

Going Just With His Flute and A Bottle of Wine

Beloved Bhagwan,
I have carried this sutra You spoke on in Poona with me for many years. It reads:

The Buddha said,

*It is better to feed one good man
than to feed one hundred bad men.*

*It is better to feed one who observes
the five precepts of Buddha
than to feed one thousand good men.*

*It is better to feed one srotapanna
than to feed ten thousand of those
who observe the five precepts of Buddha.*

*It is better to feed one skridagamin
than to feed one million of srotapannas.*

*It is better to feed one anagamin
than to feed ten millions of skridagamins.*

*It is better to feed one arhat
than to feed one hundred millions
of anagamins.*

*It is better to feed one pratyak buddha
than to feed one billion of arhats.*

*It is better to feed one of the buddhas
either of the present or of the past
or of the future
than to feed ten billions of pratyak buddhas.*

*It is better to feed one who is above
knowledge, one-sidedness, discipline, and
enlightenment than to feed one hundred
billions of buddhas of past, present, or future.*

It says so much about Your height and our darkness, and has produced two feelings in me: the blessing and joy of being in Your magnificence, and the arduousness of how far we have to travel just to have a taste of Your consciousness.
Would You please speak on this again?

One of the most fundamental things to be understood is that the distances are only dream phenomenon, they do not exist in reality. One may be asleep very lightly, one may be asleep very deeply, one may be almost in a coma.

There are distances... If you want to wake them up, then the first, who is in a very light sleep, half awake, half asleep, can be awakened soon; but every one of them can be awakened. It is only a question of the intensity of the effort needed to awaken from the outside, and the intensity needed to be awake from the inside.

You all must have felt moments of nightmare when you want to wake up but you cannot move. And then, in a minute, you wake up. It looks so strange that just a moment before it looked impossible even to open your eyes or move your hands, and after just one minute you are fully awake.

The distance between me and you is only a dream distance, so there is no need to feel any sadness, no need to feel that it is going to be a very arduous and long journey. It is a very simple and very natural phenomenon. If you can relax – and nothing can be easier than relaxation – things will start happening on their own.

About the sutra of Gautam Buddha...it is symbolic. Feeding somebody means nursing somebody, respecting somebody, loving somebody, doing something for somebody – out of compassion, kindness, or love, or respect. So food has not to be taken literally.

The sutra says: *It is better to feed one good man than to feed one hundred bad men.* Who is the good man? The good man is one who spontaneously acts in the right way. Remember the word 'spontaneously'. The good man is not one who makes efforts to act in a certain way that is accepted by the society in which he is born as good...it may not be good. There are hundreds of societies in the world, hundreds of civilizations have existed, and there is not a single thing that has not been either praised as good by someone or condemned as bad by somebody else.

Now, to be naked the Jainas will say is a good act – it shows that the man has renounced the world completely. But to be naked according to any other society will be considered bad, even sick. According to Sigmund Freud, the naked man simply wants to show his naked body to others; it is a very perverted, precarious, satisfying sexuality – it is perversion. And he has given a certain name to this sickness: exhibitionism.

So it is not a question to be decided by the outside morality. The decision has to be according to your spontaneity. Whatever you do out of your heart – so it is not a reaction but a response – that act is good.

Buddha says, *It is better to feed one good man* – because it is very difficult even to find a good man, a man of spontaneity, a man whose actions arise out of his heart – *than to feed one hundred bad men*. As far as the bad man is concerned, everybody who is acting in sleep, unconsciously, is bad. The bad and good are not concerned with the act; they are concerned with the consciousness through which they have been done. Spontaneous consciousness, a little alertness, or unconsciousness...the act may be perhaps the same, but its quality changes by the touch of the man who is doing it.

Buddha is saying that taking care of one hundred sleepy men, unconscious, not knowing who they are, not knowing why they are, not knowing where they are going, for what they are going, they are just part of the crowd, they are not yet men, they are sheep...Buddha says it is better to be respectful to the spontaneous, alert man.

I have to emphasize the word 'respect', because ordinarily it simply means honor. But the root meaning of the word 'respect' is 're-spect' – a man whom you would like to see again and again; a man who somehow touches your heart, has a magnetic impact on you, so that you want to look at him again and again.

It is better to feed one who observes the five precepts of Buddha than to feed one thousand good men. Buddha is simply giving you the vast expanse of consciousness, its responses, and how you have to behave – because your behavior is going to be a transformation to you. The five precepts of Buddha are in a way very simple, if they are done exactly according to Buddha's teaching; otherwise they become self- torture. And he says, *It is better to respect one who observes the five precepts of Buddha than to feed one thousand good men.*

The good man acts spontaneously, but the man with five precepts has a certain responsibility with his spontaneity, has a certain goal with his spontaneity, has a certain very clear-cut vision with his spontaneity. He knows what he is doing, why he is doing it and he knows what is going to be the result of it. He is acting very consciously. The five precepts are simple, but awareness has to be the base of it...and it has to be, because Buddha is saying, *It is better to feed one who observes the five precepts of Buddha than to feed one thousand good men.* One thousand good men, with all their spontaneity, he is comparing with one man.

The five precepts: The first is nonviolence; whatever the situation, he should not act in a violent way. His response should always be nonviolent, because we are part of one exis-tence. Whomsoever you are hurting, you are hurting yourself in the long run. Today you may not realize it, but one day when you will become more aware, then you will say, "My God! This wound was inflicted by me – upon myself." You had hurt somebody else thinking that people are different. Nobody is different.

This whole existence is one cosmic unity.

Out of this understanding comes nonvio-lence.

The second is non-possessiveness. If the whole existence is one, and if the existence goes on taking care of trees, of animals, of mountains, of oceans – from the smallest blade of grass to the biggest star – then it will take care of you too. Why be possessive? Possessiveness shows simply one thing: that you can't trust existence; you have to arrange separate security for yourself, safety for your-self. You cannot trust existence.

Non-possessiveness is basically trust in existence.

There is no need to possess, because the whole is already ours.

The third is non-stealing. If it is one cosmos, to steal is simply as foolish as... I have heard that one pick-pocket sometimes used to have difficulty in finding people, to pick their pockets. But he was so habituated, and it was so difficult for him to accept the fact that he had not been able to do anything today, that he would pick his own pocket! People can deceive themselves that way.

I have heard about one man who went in the evening to the fisherman's shop and said, "I want that fish. You throw it, and I will catch it."

The man said, "What is the need of throwing it? I can give it to you."

He said, "No, you have to throw it and I will catch it – because I never want to lie. And when I go home my wife is going to ask, 'Where have you been?' I have been catching fish, but I could not catch any. And this one I will have certainly caught. I have not purchased it; you have thrown it and I have caught it. So I can say with a straight face, 'This is my catch – a beautiful fish.' But I cannot lie. That's why you have to throw it, and I have to catch it."

In fact that is what we are doing. It is all ours and we are in subtle ways stealing. It does not mean that you have to steal money or you have to steal things; you can steal thoughts, you can steal words. And all your knowledge is stolen. It is not something that you have discovered, it is something you have picked up – from here, from there. And then, without thinking twice, with a straight face, you say to the world, "This is my opinion." It is *not* your opinion! You are not even aware of yourself – what opinion can you have? So all this is part of stealing.

The fourth is no-taste. It became a torture, but it was not meant so. A man of the sensibilities of Gautam Buddha cannot make it a self-torture. His idea of no-taste was simply not to hanker after taste. Food is for nourishment of the body; taste is secondary – don't make it primary. And secondly, his disciples were all monks; they had to beg. And he was a very careful man. He never wanted his people to become a burden on the society. If they start asking, "We want this, we want that…please prepare this dish for tomorrow when I come to beg," then they will be heavy and burdensome.

He made it a rule: don't ask from just one house. Your one meal – and the Buddhist monk was to eat only one meal – your one meal has to come from five houses. He was simply trying to spread the burden, otherwise…he was moving with ten thousand *bhikkus,* his disciples, wherever he was going, and it would have been really troublesome if ten thousand bhikkus had come into a small town

– which may not have had the population of ten thousand – and they started asking for their preferences. The poor people of the town would be in a difficulty.

Buddha's whole effort about no-taste was that you should never be unwelcome wherever you go. People should know that out of compassion you go to five houses – just for a single meal. He denied more than one meal. It looks to us that it is ascetism, that it is self-torture. Even in the poorest countries, people need at least two meals. In richer countries like America people are eating five times, or as many times as they go and visit the fridge…the whole day. It is not a question of times.

There are thirty million people in America today who are dying because of over-eating. They know that this over-eating is killing them, but they cannot stop it. It is just like being an alcoholic; they have become so addicted, that they need something. If they have nothing then at least they chew gum, so their mouth goes on and on. In a way it is good; otherwise they would talk – yakety yak, yakety yak – because somehow they have to go on using their mouth. Their talking is just a substitute. Chewing gum keeps them silent at least!

Buddha's insight is really deep, because modern experiments, particularly by the psychologist Delgado, have proved it beyond doubt that with one meal per day man's life can be doubled. The more you eat the less you will live; the less you eat the longer you will live. He was trying one experiment…for thousands of times he tried, then he gave his conclusion.

He had two rows of white rats. One row was given as much food as they wanted – American way. The food was always available; they could eat as much as they want. And the second row, the way of the bhikku, had just one meal – nourishing, complete for the body. And thousands of times the experiment was tried and always the American style rats died half way. The Buddhist bhikkus lived double the time of the Americans.

So there Buddha had a deep insight: eat one time and don't hanker for taste; otherwise you would like to eat many times.

It is known about Nero that he used to eat so many times that he had to keep four doctors with him; so when he eats they will help him vomit everything, so he can eat again. Just madness…but he was simply hankering for taste. And that was the only way; otherwise you cannot go on eating the whole day. He was eating from the morning till night when he went to bed – he was either eating or vomiting. And the doctors' only purpose was to help him vomit easily so he could eat again.

Buddha's insight is right. It is not self-torture. It is simply a profound insight into health, longevity – and perhaps sooner or later science will like everybody to eat only once. Of course the food should be sufficient, should have all that is needed by the body, but only once. It looks to us a little difficult, but it is only a question of habit. In Africa there are many tribes who have never eaten – for thousands of years – more than once a day. They were simply surprised when Christian missionaries reached Africa. They could not believe it: they start with tea in bed, then breakfast, then lunch, then coffee break, then supper, then dinner…and snacks here and there. They could not believe it, "What are these people doing? Are they living or simply eating?" – because they had eaten only once, and they were far more healthy and they lived longer.

They are still eating once. Their bodies are more proportionate, they live longer, they run faster – just like animals, like deer they can run. And their bodies have just the proportion that people are trying to get in thousands of gymnasiums around the world. They have it without any effort, just by a single meal.

Non-violence, non-possessiveness, non-stealing, no-taste…and the fifth precept is compassion.

We live in passion – our lives are passionate. Passion is always a turmoil: ups and downs, one day good, another day bad, day follows night… In the same way the life of passion is continuously going into pleasure, into pain – and they are balancing each other.

Compassion is not to live passionately, but to live calmly, quietly, silently. Compassion can be without ups and downs – a deep serenity. Whatever happens on the outside does not matter, but the center of your being remains still, undisturbed.

So Buddha says, *It is better to feed one who observes the five precepts of Buddha than to feed one thousand good men.*

It is better to feed one srotapanna than to feed ten thousand of those who observe the five precepts of Buddha.

Srotapanna is a very beautiful word. It means "who has stepped into the stream." Literally, *srot* means "the source"; *srotapanna* means "who has stepped into the stream which leads to the source." He is no longer standing on the bank. The man who follows the five precepts may be still standing on the bank.

Before a srotapanna, Buddha says, *ten thousand of those who follow the five precepts of Buddha…* One srotapanna is weightier, more valuable. He has risked the journey. He has moved from the bank into the river; he is ready to go to the source. He has taken the most courageous step a man has to take, ever in his life.

The bank seems to be so safe, and you can make it so cozy. And stepping into an unknown stream – no one knows where it is going; it is certainly going into the unknown, and perhaps ultimately into the unknowable... The man who has the courage to step in, that srotapanna is better to feed – just one srotapanna – than to feed ten thousand of those who observe the five precepts of Buddha.

It is better to feed one skridagamin than to feed one million of srotapannas. One million of srotapannas are nothing in comparison with one *skridagamin:* one who has reached the source. One million srotapannas may have stepped – but they may remain stuck there. Their first step may be their last step, because the journey is going to become more and more mysterious, more and more unknowable, more and more beyond their minds and beyond their control.

So many will step, but only a few will go to the very end. One who reaches to the end, the skridagamin, he is equal to one million of srotapannas.

It is better to feed one anagamin than to feed ten millions of skridagamins. Those who have reached the source are not necessarily going to stay there. They may come back. *Anagamin* means "who is not going to look back" – coming back is out of question.

The skridagamin may have gone for strange reasons – maybe his ego: he is a strong person; when the weaker ones are stepping down or stopping, he will go to the very end, but he has all the desires in him – which can be fulfilled, or at least you can hope for them to be fulfilled, only on the bank. He will come back. He cannot remain there at the source.

Only one who remains at the source and does not come back, anagamin... These words are from the same root. *Gamin* means

"going." The English word *go* comes from the same root as the Pali word *gamin.* Anagamin means "one who is not going back." *It is better to feed one anagamin than to feed ten millions of skridagamins.*

It is better to feed one arhat than to feed one hundred millions of anagamins. Now things are a little more subtle. *Arhat* means "the victorious." Now there is nothing for him to achieve; he has come home. The anagamin has come to the source. He is not going back, but there are weaknesses in him which do not allow him to be totally victorious. He has reached the place from where victory is possible. He is not going back – but he is not going ahead either.

An arhat is one who goes ahead of the anagamin. The anagamin becomes so happy with the source that he has reached that he feels that this is all there is; he has arrived – and that's an illusion. There is much more. The arhat is not satisfied – although it is very pleasant, nice. But he has not come on this journey, on this pilgrimage to reach a pleasant state. He wants truth, and he is ready to lose all pleasures – even this spiritual pleasure of being at the source. His search is for truth, not for pleasure. *It is better to feed one arhat than to feed one hundred millions of anagamins.*

It is better to feed one pratyak buddha than to feed one billion of arhats.

Pratyak buddha means "a man who has attained enlightenment." The arhat is victorious but he is not illuminated. There is still darkness at the very center of his being. A pratyak buddha is one whose whole darkness has disappeared; he is simply light. The arhat has discovered the truth; the pratyak buddha has become it.

You have to understand the difference. One has discovered it, but it is still there and he is separate from it. The pratyak buddha has become it. There is no question of victory, because there are not two; hence the difference. You can see: *It is better to feed one pratyak buddha than to feed one billion of arhatas.* The distance goes on becoming bigger and bigger and bigger. *It is better to feed one of the buddhas, either of the present or of the past or of the future than to feed ten billions of pratyak buddhas.*

What is the difference between pratyak buddhas and buddhas? The pratyak buddha is one who has become enlightened, but he never becomes a master. He has experienced it, but he cannot explain it. Neither is he interested in anybody else, or in sharing his experience with anybody else. He has the same status as a buddha, but the difference is that the buddha wants to share it, and the pratyak buddha simply keeps it within himself. He has become the truth, but his great achievement is confined only to himself. A buddha works hard, against all kinds of oppositions, difficulties, to reach people, to reach those who are on the path but are in darkness.

The story about Gautam Buddha is that when he reached the gates of nirvana he stood there, his back towards the gates. The gates were opened, and the guards wanted him to enter. They were ready to welcome him – because centuries pass and then once in a while those gates open. And they were immensely happy that someone has again become a buddha.

But Buddha refused. The story is symbolic. He says, "Unless every living being passes by me into nirvana, I am going to stay here. I will be the last. I cannot go alone, I have to take everybody with me. They are struggling in pain and misery, and do you think I should enjoy nirvana and its tremendous blissfulness? It is not possible. I will wait. You can wait; but waiting here I will try to help those struggling souls, stumbling in darkness, groping in darkness. Unless I am satisfied that everybody has passed in, I will not come in and close the doors."

Buddha is certainly one of the most insightful men. He does not stop at himself. Anybody would have stopped there – it is a natural tendency to put oneself at the highest point and then stop.

He says, *It is better to feed one who is above knowledge, one-sidedness, discipline, and enlightenment than to feed one hundred billions of buddhas, of past, present or future.*

The last category is tremendously significant, because it will be the category which will be misunderstood the most. One who is above knowledge – he will not be consistent, he will be self-contradictory. One who is above one-sidedness, who cannot favor one side of the truth, one aspect of the truth – at the risk of being contradictory he will support all the aspects of truth. He will support the opposites, and naturally he will look illogical, he will look absurd. One who is above discipline – who has no discipline, who lives moment to moment, who has no certain order to follow – he does not follow anything. Each moment decides what he is going to do.

You cannot categorize such a man. You cannot call him good, you cannot call him bad; you cannot call him religious, you cannot call him irreligious, because he follows no discipline. And not only discipline, but he transcends enlightenment.

Enlightenment is the ultimate experience, but still it is an experience…the highest, but still part and parcel of all other experiences: they may be lower, this may be the highest. Finally one transcends it too. One simply forgets about it. It becomes one's nature.

In the beginning, when you reach from

your ignorance into enlightenment, it is such a difference that you are immensely gratified. But now ignorance is gone. Enlightenment slowly, slowly loses the excitement it had in the beginning. It is no longer ecstasy, it is simply your nature. And nobody remembers one's nature.

This is the ultimate category Buddha manages to talk about: beyond knowledge, beyond discipline, beyond enlightenment. This kind of man will be opposed by all, this kind of man will be condemned by all. This kind of man is bound to stand alone against the whole world, for the simple reason that all that they value, he has transcended.

In Japan there is a beautiful series of pictures depicting the whole range of the pilgrimage to the truth. In the beginning – the name of the Zen painter who made it is not known – it had ten pictures. But even the Zen masters suppressed the tenth picture, and for centuries it was known only as having nine pictures. It was only later on that it was discovered in some old scripts that the original had ten pictures, and the description of the tenth is the description Buddha is giving of the last.

It is a series of pictures: A man loses his bull. In one picture, he looks all around and he cannot see it. There are mountains, there are trees, there is a lake and the man is standing there looking all around – and the bull is not anywhere to be seen. In the second picture he finds the footmarks of the bull. He cannot see the bull yet, but footmarks are there and he follows the footmarks.

In the third he sees just the back of the bull, who is standing under a tree. In the fourth he finds the bull. In the fifth he tries hard to catch hold of it; it is a bull – it is difficult, he is really powerful. But in the seventh he manages. In the eighth he rides on the bull. The bull won't allow it, and tries this

way and that to throw him off. In the ninth he reaches home with the bull.

The tenth was repressed even by the people who can be said to be the most meditative, to be the most alert in the whole world. Perhaps they were afraid that the tenth picture may confuse people or may help them to go astray, because in the tenth – he has got the bull, and the bull is in the shed, tied up – in the tenth he takes a bottle of wine and a flute and goes back near the lake. He is going just with his flute and a bottle of wine. Now this picture was repressed, destroyed; it has been recovered now. But this is the picture of the last state. Now there is no discipline: he can drink wine, he can play the flute.

The bull is the self, your inner reality. Finding it represents nirvana. At the ninth, logically it should stop. But existence is not logical, and who will know better then Gautam Buddha that it is not logical? The tenth goes beyond all logic, all comprehension. Even enlightenment is dropped. The man becomes absolutely ordinary, without any discipline – a hobo with a bottle of wine to enjoy under a tree, and playing the flute – utterly ordinary.

But his ordinariness is not the ordinariness we are aware of; his ordinariness is something most extraordinary. But he is going to be misunderstood, he is going to be condemned. Now, who is going to accept him as a master? Who going to accept him as a buddha?

But Gautam Buddha has put him above himself. He says, *It is better to feed one who is above knowledge, one-sidedness, discipline, and enlightenment, than to feed one hundred billions of buddhas of past, present, or future.*

This sutra shows the beauty of the man, his grandeur, his greatness.

Chapter 29
April 26, 1986, Evening

Come
A Little Closer

Beloved Bhagwan,
In a speech prepared for his followers after his car accident, Gurdjieff said, "Again I repeat that the institute is closed. I died. The reason is that I was disenchanted with people after all that I have done for them; I have seen how well they have paid me for it. Now inside me everything is empty."

Recently, when Krishnamurti died, I felt that somehow he too died disenchanted.

Bhagwan, over the years with You, we have built great castles in the sand and have seen them destroyed; yet when I see You these precious mornings and evenings, You seem so genuinely happy to see us. Do You ever get disenchanted with us?

It is not only for George Gurdjieff or J. Krishnamurti, it is true for hundreds of masters down the ages, and there are reasons. They all died disenchanted, disappointed, disillusioned.

Let us go deeper, first into George Gurdjieff's last statement. The last statement of anybody is the most significant statement of his whole life; in a certain way his whole life is condensed in his last statement.

He was disenchanted because the disciples failed him, betrayed him, went against him, did everything to harm him – and these were the people for whom he had devoted his whole life, each single moment of it. But still in his place I would not be disenchanted. He thought that he was doing a very serious work. That's where the seed of his disenchantment was.

I am not doing any serious work. I am not doing work at all; it is my joy to share with you. Now what you do with it is your problem, not mine.

You cannot disappoint me.

You can betray me; there are people who have done that. You can do any kind of harm imaginable – and people have done that. You can go against me, you can tell lies about me; still I will not be disenchanted, because in the first place I have never expected anything from you.

The disappointment comes from expectation.

The disenchantment comes from a deep hope that "these people are going to fulfill my work". I don't have any expectation, any hope – I am just so blissful that I cannot contain it; I want to share it unconditionally. It is the conditions which create disappointment.

Gurdjieff had worked hard with great expectations. And even people like P.D. Ouspensky, who had learned everything from the master, denied him. Ouspensky himself became a master; he even stopped using Gurdjieff's full name. When he had to mention him at certain points, he would use only G. He would not allow his own disciples to go to Gurdjieff, even to see him, and Gurdjieff had worked on this man for years, for decades.

And whatever Ouspensky said after separating himself from Gurdjieff – each single word, each single insight – was borrowed, it was not his own. Certainly he had a great talent; he was one of the best writers I have come across. Gurdjieff was not a writer. Ouspensky was a great logician, a world famous mathematician, a great writer. Gurdjieff was none of these things, he was purely a mystic.

Gathering everything from the system of Gurdjieff, Ouspensky was in a position to write beautiful treatises, as if they were his own experience. Gurdjieff could not compete with him in writing, nor in speaking. Ouspensky was a very talented genius, well educated. Gurdjieff was uneducated, coming from a very undeveloped tribe in the Caucasus, in Soviet Russia. But he had the whole mine of diamonds – it is just that they were all uncut, unpolished. Only a man who had the eyes of a jeweler would be able to recognize them; otherwise they were just stones.

Ouspensky had the eyes of a jeweler; he recognized that this man had a treasure, but had not the talent to spread it…a great chance for exploitation. He learned everything from Gurdjieff, and the day he felt that now it was enough – he could make a system out of it all – he betrayed him. And he had to prevent his disciples from going to Gurdjieff, because personality-wise Ouspensky was just a schoolteacher – he looked like a schoolteacher. Even while teaching mysticism there was a blackboard – he was a mathematician. He would be teaching mysticism and writing on the blackboard; it was like a class, a university class. His students were taking notes.…

Gurdjieff had a tremendously charismatic personality. Anybody who had seen him once could not forget the man; in a crowd of millions he would still stand out. If you had looked into his eyes once, those eyes would follow you your whole life. He was not a man of words, but a man of a tremendously powerful being.

And that was the fear of Ouspensky – that if his disciples went to Gurdjieff, then whatever he had been saying against Gurdjieff would be exposed. And if they listened to that man…although he was not articulate, in a way he *was* the most articulate master ever. To say a simple thing he would take hundreds of pages. You have to find out where it is – what he really wants to say. He will make up his own words, big long words spreading out over the whole line, a single word that you have never heard before – it is his invention. He knew nothing about how to write; one paragraph will go running on for pages. No publisher was ready to publish his books; he had to publish them himself.

When his first book was published it was one thousand pages. It is one of the strangest books in the world, *All and Everything*. He kept nine hundred pages uncut, and only one hundred pages – that is the preface – were cut, with a note to every customer who purchases it: "You read the preface and if you feel that it is worth reading on, then you can cut the remaining nine hundred pages. But if you feel it is not worth it you can take your money back – return the book – but don't cut the uncut pages. Those one hundred pages are enough example."

Even to understand those one hundred pages is a strange experience, particularly for those who don't know anything about mystics and their strange ways. Now he was not in any way able to compete with his own disciple Ouspensky. His books are so lucid, so beautifully written, so poetic, that I have not seen any other man who comes close to him, even close to him. Kahlil Gibran writes well, Mikhail Naimy writes well, but they don't even come close to Ouspensky.

Gurdjieff had much hope that Ouspensky would carry on his work. Rather than carrying on, he simply opened his own school against Gurdjieff – teaching everything, because it is impossible to add to it; the system is complete and perfect. You cannot take anything out, you cannot put anything in. He was a great teacher, Ouspensky, but he was not a master. He influenced many people around the world; millions of people came to know of Gurdjieff only through Ouspensky. What a strange fate! And he was consistently trying to oppose him.

It was very difficult, because his whole teaching was borrowed from the man, but it was a logical necessity. He had to oppose

Gurdjieff so nobody would think that he had borrowed all this teaching from Gurdjieff. It is an existential necessity that any disciple who betrays and wants to use the master's teaching to become himself a master, is bound to oppose the master, to create lies about the master. And naturally it was hurting Gurdjieff – and it was not only Ouspensky, there were many others who were doing the same. For years Gurdjieff would work on them, and then one day they turned into his enemies. And to justify why they have left Gurdjieff they had to invent lies, they had to create a false image of Gurdjieff.

Ouspensky had a strategy. He said, "While I was with Gurdjieff he was right, and when I saw that he was going astray, I left him" – Gurdjieff had gone astray, that's why the disciple had left. Up to that point Gurdjieff was right, and he could use his teachings without any difficulty. But beyond that point, for him Gurdjieff did not exist at all.

This was being done by many disciples, and if Gurdjieff was working with great expectations, naturally he was getting wounded, hurt. He could not believe that these were the people for whom he had lived and he had died; his whole life he had sacrificed, and these were the people.... That's why he said, "The institution is closed, is dead."

He was afraid that after his death his institution will also be used in the same way. "The institution is dead because I am dead." And these were all the wounds of his life saying it together. This statement is the statement of his whole life: "Man is cunning, cowardly, deceptive, hypocritical – you cannot trust anybody."

This was his whole life's experience: You cannot trust anybody. He trusted many and he gave everything that he had, and still what had they returned? – not even gratitude. And he was not asking for anything else. But his people had given him no reverence, no gratitude, no respect – on the contrary, great antagonism, opposition, all kinds of fictions condemning him... Naturally he was disappointed.

But my approach is totally different. I trust you, not because of your trustworthiness; otherwise the same will be my experience. I do not have to wait for my death to come; already I have worked with people for years and they have repaid me very well. I trust you because I cannot distrust; so there is no burden on you – you can betray me, but you cannot hurt me. I have trusted you, not because of you, but because of me. And I am still there, the same.

See the difference. To trust a person is possible in two ways: either because of his trustworthiness – then there is danger, there is risk – or because you enjoy trusting. The trustworthiness or unworthiness have no relevance.

Secondly Gurdjieff and all these people took their work very seriously – the transformation of man, the transformation of human society...they took it too seriously. And when people did not live up to their seriousness they felt that something is basically wrong with man, that nothing can be done about him. Then a great hopelessness arose in them.

It cannot happen to me, because I am not serious at all. I do not think that existence has given me a certain responsibility, to transform man or human society. Who am I to bother about all this? One day I was not here – the society was there, man was there, existence was there.... One day I will not be here, so just for a few days in between.... And existence has not given me any job that has to be done. Why should I be serious?

I am simply playful.

If everybody betrays me I will have the last laugh; I will enjoy that moment too. I will say to myself, "Great! I love to play; I played well. And these people were good; as long as they could continue to be with me, they managed and continued – in difficulties, in troubles. When they found it was too much, they went on their own."

Even if I am left alone I will not be disappointed. I will simply enjoy the moment, that this has been a great life – so many seasons, so many changes, so many people, so much love, so much trust. And I am going out of life without leaving any footprints behind. I will not feel that I have wasted my life. I don't think that there could have been any better way to live, and to love, and to laugh.

J. Krishnamurti was very serious – I don't think he ever smiled. A long life: ninety years. His fame started very early, at thirteen years old; so really he had a very long life of work and disappointments. Even the closest ones betrayed him. His whole life seems to be just a series of betrayals, and those who remained never managed to understand what he was saying. They listened to him for half a century, but still he could not cross their thick minds and reach to their being. And every day...if you look at his life, in the beginning he was very hopeful, very excited that man can be changed, that a new man can arrive. But slowly, slowly that hope disappeared, that excitement was no more there. And as he grew older, he became sadder.

For twenty years, just because of his seriousness, he suffered from migraine continuously. No medicine could help, no physician...and every physician told him, "You are straining your whole brain system too much. You are too serious, you should relax; you have taken too much of a burden on yourself."

Sometimes his migraine was so much that he would like to have hit his head against the wall.

While speaking he was almost screaming, shouting, hitting his own head, because he could not understand that you are unable to understand such a simple thing. For example, he was explaining the same thing his whole life: that meditation cannot be done, it is a happening. And he would talk for one hour about the difference between doing and happening, and then somebody who was just sitting in front of him listening attentively, would stand up and ask, "How can we do meditation?"

I would have laughed at the whole thing, but he would hit his head…too serious. And as death was coming closer he was becoming more and more serious, knowing now that his life had been a failure. He worked hard, immensely hard. His approach was very clean and very clear. His way of working was very logical, very intellectual, absolutely contemporary: an impeccable life of worth – he was a perfectionist.

But in the end the hands are empty. As far as results are concerned, nothing has happened, as if he had not been here. The world goes on…the old routine, the old rut. Do you see anything that has changed because J. Krishnamurti was born, and lived for ninety years? Has it made even a scratch? Naturally he died in the same state.

And this has been the case with thousands of masters; humanity remains unevolving because they are so serious in wanting man to evolve. And naturally they fail.

But I cannot fail, because I am not concerned at all whether humanity evolves or not, whether the new man is born or not. I enjoy these ideas and I enjoy communicating them to people, and there I am perfectly

victorious. I don't need to wait to be victorious until you have changed; that will be your victory. My victory is that I have been able to communicate what I wanted to communicate. Now what you do with it is your freedom.

I will not call it betrayal, and I will not call it opposition, and I will not call your things lies. If you are enjoying doing these things it is perfectly good – enjoyment is good. If somebody is creating lies about me and is feeling perfectly happy about it, why should he be stopped? He has all my blessings.

In India it happened, one man wrote a book against me and he sent me the proof copy. I looked into it – it was all rubbish, lies, fictitious stories with no evidence. Still, I sent him my blessings and told him to print it on the first page of the book. He could not believe it; he was so disturbed: what kind of man is this?

He lived in Baroda, a thousand miles away from me, but he came to see me – he had never seen me. He was just collecting third-rate yellow newspapers and cuttings and gossips, rumors…and he managed to make a book. And he asked me, "Have you seen inside or have you simply sent blessings?"

I said, "I have gone through it word for word; it is all bullshit, but you have done so much work collecting bullshit, you need blessings."

He said, "But this looks strange – with your blessings. I know this book: even while I was collecting and writing…. My purpose is to earn money – this book is going to become a bestseller – but now seeing you and your response, I feel perhaps I should not have done this."

I said, "No, you continue. Let this book go into the market. Collect more, because while I am alive more and more lies will be there, more and more gossips, rumors – you can always earn money; this is a good way. It is not doing any harm to me. And the picture you have chosen for the cover is really beautiful."

He said, "My God! I was thinking you would be angry, ferocious."

I said, "Why should I be angry, why should I be ferocious? Life is too short to be angry, to be ferocious. Even if we can manage to be blissful, that's enough; if we can manage to bless, that's enough. What you do is your business, but you have done it well. Your writing is good; what you have written is nonsense, but the way you have put it and presented it is really good. And you devoted almost one year to my service. I cannot pay you, but I can give you my blessing."

And the book was published with my blessings and *every* criticism that appeared in newspapers about the book mentioned it: "It is strange that Bhagwan blesses it." And just that simple blessing cancels the whole book.

My whole approach is different, so totally different that it has never been used before. I am enjoying everything that has happened, is happening – perhaps tomorrow I will be arrested, deported, but I have been enjoying it. Then Hasya has to find a new place, so I can be deported again! We are not going to leave a single country unblessed.

In fact I cannot conceive a situation that will be a disappointment to me. You have to forgive me – I am simply so fulfilled and so happy, so centered that nothing can affect me. Any new kind of situation is really a great excitement. And to live without any conditions, to live with people who have total freedom to be the way they want to be, is already a transformation. All old approaches have failed. Now let us see what happens to my approach. As far as I am concerned I cannot fail, because I am squeezing the juice of life every moment; I don't leave it for another moment.

What has to be seen is how many people can become as successful, as victorious as I am. I am giving them all the cues, now it is their problem. If they fail they should be disappointed; why should I be disappointed? If they succeed, they should rejoice. I can participate in their rejoicing, but there is no way to disappoint me.

Just include me out of the category of Gurdjieff, Krishnamurti and others.

Beloved Bhagwan,
I have tried for so long to write a question to You about money. The question is so complex, I can't even get it on paper. It involves friendships, self-image, integrity, trust, intelligence, identification, letting-go, holding-on, guilt, relationships, and most importantly, my discipleship.
Please help me with the question and the answer.

Money is a strange thing.

If you do not have it, it is a simple matter – you don't have it. There is no complexity. But if you have it, then it certainly creates complexities.

One of the greatest problems that money creates is that you never know whether you are loved or your money is loved, whether you are desirable or your money is desirable. And it is so difficult to figure out, that one would have preferred not to have had money; at least life would have been simple.

Just a few days before, Hasya was telling me about Aristotle Onassis' daughter. I remember seeing her picture when Onassis was alive, perhaps ten years ago. She was a beautiful, well-proportioned, charming young girl. But Onassis died and left her with a lot of money, and that created hell for her. Since then she has married three times, and each marriage fails because she thinks the person loves her money, not her.

And this starts from the very beginning; the day of marriage is really the day of divorce. On the day of marriage she takes a guarantee from the person – a legal document before the court – that he will not take her money. In case divorce happens, he will not ask for money. Now can you conceive a marriage to be worthwhile, when on the first day the woman is asking you to give in writing before the court that you are interested in her, and not in her money; and that in case a divorce happens you will not ask for money? The divorce has already happened.

In the fourth marriage she got into more troubled waters. Before I describe the fourth marriage, something else has to be said which was happening on the side. She was becoming fatter, uglier, as if deep down in her psychology she wanted to prove, "You love me whether I am beautiful or ugly, shapely or fat – you don't love my money."

And she has become so ugly now that she avoids photographers, news media: she hides and does not want her pictures to be taken. Perhaps it is because she was uncertain whether she is loved, or her money. And most probably the people who have been with her *were* for the money, not for her. She did not receive love. The proof is that she started eating too much. If you are loved, you are so full of love, so filled with love that you don't eat too much.

I have been traveling in India, staying with different families, and I have come across at least three women who told me the same thing, that while I am staying in their homes they cannot eat.

When I was told this for the first time I said, "This is strange. Why can't you eat?"

They said, "We don't know, but we don't feel hungry either. We feel perfectly good, with more well-being than we have ever felt. You stay three days and we can't eat. And we wait the whole year again when you will be back in the city for three days; those three days become a beautiful memory."

When I was told by another woman, and then by another woman…I had to look into the fact – what is the matter? They felt so loved, and they loved me so much that there was no need for any food, as if love was enough nourishment. And after three days they did not look hungry, they did not look starved. One of these three was a Jaina woman, and she said, "Now I know what a real fast should be." She had been fasting for almost ten years, long fasts of ten days.

In the Jaina tradition, those Jainas who are very orthodox, fast for ten days every year in the rainy season. This woman has been fasting for ten days for almost ten years, and she said to me, "Now I know that was not fasting, that was simply starving because I was continuously thinking of food, food and food. I could not sleep in the night because of hunger; even if I fell asleep for a few moments or a few hours I was dreaming of food. I was thinking of food, I was dreaming of food; except food there was nothing in me. For these three days while you stay in my house I know what fasting is. I never think about food at all. It just comes naturally that I don't feel any hunger; I feel so fulfilled."

Onassis' immense riches have created a hell for the poor girl, a feeling that she is not loved. And not coming in contact with a man like me who could have told her…. The question is not that you should be loved, the question is that *you* should love. Why bother about why the other loves you? Have you ever thought about why *you* love the other? For what? And then you will understand the situation. Perhaps it is because of his hair? Then you don't love the man. Perhaps because of his eyes? Then you don't love the man. Perhaps because of his nose? Then you don't love the man. If you have any reason to love, then you don't love the man. So why are you making so much fuss about money?

You should love and you should be loved, and you should be loved *more* because of your money. There is nothing wrong in it; you have something *more* than any other woman has. Otherwise, each thing will start creating problems: you have a beautiful face, that's why this man loves – he does not love *you*. If you had a face with pockmarks this man would not love you. Because you have eyes, this man loves you; if you were blind, this man would not love you. Then you are creating unnecessary problems for yourself. This man certainly loves you, in your totality, and your money is part of you. Why make it separate? You are rich, just as somebody is beautiful; you are rich just as somebody is a dancer. But the dancer will not ask the question, "Do you love me or my dance?" If she asks the question she will be in trouble.

In the fourth marriage Onassis' daughter found a rich man, just to be certain that "He is himself so rich that he will love me, he will not love my riches – he himself is a big industrialist." And because of this she did not repeat the ritual of going to the court after marriage, and taking a certificate from the man, that in case of divorce he will not ask for money. Seeing that the man is so rich, it looked absurd to ask. But this man proved really cunning, and because there was no certificate he divorced her and took almost half of her fortune.

Now, something like money, that could

have been a great pleasure, has turned out to be immense anguish. But it is not money, it is your mind. Money is useful. There is no sin in having money, there is no need to feel guilt; otherwise everybody should feel guilty. I should start feeling guilty – "Why am I enlightened, when there are so many millions of people who are not enlightened? I must commit suicide, because the world is full of unenlightened people, and I must be immensely selfish to be enlightened."

I don't ask you, "Why do you love me? Do you love me or do you love my enlightenment? If you love my enlightenment then – finished! Then you don't love me." But why make these divisions? This is how mind creates misery. You have money, enjoy it! And if somebody loves you, do not pose this question because you are putting the person in a really bad situation. If he says he loves you, you are not going to believe it, and if he says he loves your money you *are* going to believe it. But if he loves your money, then the whole affair is finished. Deep down you will go on suspecting that he loves your money, not you. But there is nothing wrong: the money is yours, just as the nose is yours, and the eyes are yours, and the hair is yours, and this man loves you in your totality. The money is also part of you – don't separate it, then there is no problem.

Try to live a life with as little complexities and as few problems as possible. And it is in your hands; we go on creating unnecessary problems. At least being with me, you should learn that all problems are created; there is no real problem.

This question is from Avirbhava. She has suffered from this question her whole life, and absolutely unnecessarily. Your money should make your life richer, more lovable, and it is making it difficult.

Whenever anybody starts loving you, you are constantly thinking about the money – "this man is interested in the money, not in me." Even if he is interested in the money…who is not interested in money? He is simply being human. He is not a Buddhist monk, he is interested in money. But this does not mean that he is not interested in you. He is interested in you more because you are not only a woman, but a rich woman. Enjoy the idea, and drop this problem forever.

Beloved Bhagwan,
How to catch the light from your candle?

J ust come a little closer. People are afraid of coming closer, particularly to a person like me.

The fear is that coming closer to me they may be dissolved.

Coming closer to me they may disappear.

So they keep a certain distance, they come only so far, so they can remain themselves; if the time comes and their mind decides to move away, they can.

But if you come really close, that means you have taken a total jump, a quantum leap; now there is no going away, now there is no possibility of going away. Now you are melting and dissolving into the unknown. People come close but only so far, so they can escape if they want to, they can turn their back if they want.

Do you know the meaning of the word "hippie"? It simply means showing your hips – turning your back. The hippie is one who is turning his back towards the world, its problems, its challenges; he is running, escaping.

Coming close to me…don't stop as long as

you *are,* only then your candle will be lighted. And this is the beauty of candles: you can light one candle in this room, or one thousand candles in this room. The candles may be one thousand, but the light will be one. So when a disciple comes too close to the master, the candles remain two, but the light becomes one. The flames remain two. That's why I have to make a seemingly contradictory statement: that when you dissolve into the master, for the first time you are not, and for the first time you are. You are not your old self, but now you have a new individuality. What you have lost was never yours; what you have gained was always yours, but was covered with the false.

Two lighted candles will create only one light in the room. There can be two thousand, there can be two million – it will not make any difference, the light will be one. So in a certain way they will all be individuals, and in a certain way they will all be part of an oceanic existence.

New Bottles for the Old Wine

Beloved Bhagwan,
The other night You spoke of the mystery school. At that moment I thought of Pythagoras. Since You started speaking again, I've wanted to ask questions about him – his name comes to me often. The main part of his teachings I love are the three P's: Preparation, Purification, Perfection.
Would You speak on them again?

Pythagoras is a link between East and West, between a civilization that disappeared in the Atlantic and a civilization that we are living in; hence he has a significance of his own.

He traveled almost all his life in search of fragments of truth. Most of his time he was in Egypt, in Alexandria. In those days Alexandria had the biggest library in the whole world, particularly scriptures containing all the discoveries of consciousness made in the lost civilization of Atlantis – a whole civilization drowned with the whole continent in the Atlantic ocean. The name Atlantic comes from the continent Atlantis, that went down into it. The only fragmentary knowledge available about it was in Alexandria – and perhaps Pythagoras was the first and the last man of such integrity, intelligence, ingenuity, to look into those scriptures.

That library exists no more, so whatever we know about Atlantis we know through Pythagoras. That library was destroyed by Mohammedans. The man who destroyed it, Mahmud Gaznavi, destroyed many beautiful things in India, in Afghanistan, in Egypt. But the most precious was the vast library that contained everything about that whole civilization, which had reached to the peaks of consciousness. The day this man destroyed the library, he took Koran Sharif in one of his hands and a burning torch in another, entered the library and asked the learned librarian, "Listen carefully – the existence of your library depends on your answers. My first question is: Is there anything in your whole library which goes against the holy *Koran*? And my second question is: If there is nothing which goes against the holy *Koran,* then the holy *Koran* is enough; why bother about this big library?"

The librarian must have been in a dilemma – whatever he says will be dangerous. If he says there are many things in the library which are not in the *Koran,* Mahmud is going to burn the library, because that which is not in the *Koran* is untrue – the *Koran* contains all and ultimate truth. And if he says that everything that is in the library is substantially and essentially contained in the *Koran,* then too he is going to burn the library, saying, "Then it is useless; the *Koran* has it all." And the library was so huge and so immense that you can only conceive… He burned it, and the fire continued for six months. For six months continuously books were burning; perhaps the greatest treasure of humanity was destroyed.

Pythagoras studied in that library for many years. He was a Greek, but he found in Greece itself only sophistry. Sophistry is something ugly. It comes from a very beautiful word 'sophia', which means wisdom, but sophistry is only a pretension of wisdom. And the whole of Greece was so interested in sophistry. There were sophist teachers moving all over the country teaching people, and the basic teaching of sophistry was: There is no truth. It is all a question of better argument. Truth as such does not exist, it is a fallacy. When two persons argue, whoever is better in argument seems to have the truth, but it is really the better argument and nothing else.

Their teaching was to give you all possible ways of arguing and to make you a great arguer, and then you can argue from any side – it doesn't matter. When truth does not exist, what side you take and argue for does not matter. It is a question of convenience: which side is going to declare you victorious? Which side do you have more arguments for?

I have been interested in sophistry, although the name sophistry has disappeared. Socrates was the cause of destroying it. He emphasized that truth *is,* and arguments do not prove it, they only discover it. They do not disprove it either; they can only prevent its discovery. One single man, Socrates, destroyed the whole tradition, hundreds of years old, of sophistry. But it has remained running underground. I see it in theologians, in religious philosophies, in political ideologies…no concern for truth, the only concern is to present a very solid argument.

There is a story: one very famous sophist teacher, Zeno…and he was not just a sophist, he was a genius. It is unfortunate that his genius became associated with sophistry because that was prevalent. You pay him money and he can prove anything – anything in the world. You just say it, he has a price for it. He proved strange things which logicians have not been able to disprove even now, after two thousand years, and whatever he has proved goes against all common sense. But logic listens to the argument, and his arguments are so fine, so refined.

For example, he says that when you kill a bird with an arrow, the arrow does not move at all. This is absurd, because if the arrow does not move at all, then how does it reach the bird? From your bow to the bird there is a distance. The arrow reaches there, the bird is killed – there is proof. This question was asked by one king, thinking that Zeno would not be able to prove this – and he was ready to give any amount of money if Zeno should prove that the arrow does not move.

Zeno proved that the arrow does not move, and even up to now there is no way to disprove him. His argument is that for movement, the arrow has to go from point 1 to point 2 to point 3 to point 4; obviously it has to move from one place to another place, then only will it reach the bird.

Moving from A to B or from 1 to 2, it has to pass a passage between A and B; it cannot simply reach from A to B, so you have to make another point between the two. So where there were two points, now there are three points – and you have got into difficulty. Now he has to reach not only three points but five, because these two gaps are there, and this goes on growing. If you fill these two gaps, then there are five points and there are gaps. And you go on filling ad infinitum…the arrow will never reach the bird.

The argument is very solid. What he is saying makes sense – but it is absolute nonsense: the arrow goes and kills the bird.

Zeno is not interested in the arrow or the bird. He says, "My argument proves that nothing moves, nothing can move; there is no movement in the world."

These kinds of people were all over Greece. They dominated the mind; they were constantly debating. Pythagoras was not interested at all in this kind of stupid game. It sharpens your intellect, but it does not lead you to any truth, to any discovery, to any realization. And even the greatest sophists were getting into trouble, because Zeno himself – who had many arguments which go against reality but could not be disproved – was defeated by his own student.

This was the routine: he was so confident, and he had the genius to be confident, that he used to take half the fees in the beginning, and half when the student won his first argument. This student was strange: he gave half the fee but he told him that he would never give him the other half. Zeno said, "How?" He said, "I am never going to argue! I will accept defeat without arguing. I may lose everything that I have but I am not going to give you the other half of your fee."

Zeno waited, but the man would not even talk about the weather, because some argument may start and there may be trouble. And he was determined not to pay the fees so as to teach Zeno: "You may be a great logician, but there is a possibility of going higher than you."

But Zeno was not going to sit silently. He put a case in the court against the student: "He has not paid me half the fee." His idea was that if he wins the case, then he will tell the court, "Force that student to pay the fee." If he loses the case, no harm – outside the court he will catch the student and will say, "You have won your first argument – my fee!" So whether he wins or whether he loses, he is going to get half the fee.

But he forgot that it was his own student who knew all his techniques and arguments. From the opposite side the student was thinking, "That's good: if I win in the court, I will appeal to the court that this man should not bother me outside the court, because that will be a contempt of court. And if I lose the case, then there is no problem. Outside I will catch hold of Zeno and say, 'Master, I have lost my first argument – you cannot get the fee.'"

The whole genius of Greece was involved in that, in that atmosphere. Pythagoras is very unique. He got out of Greece – it was not the right place. People were simply arguing and arguing, but nobody was concerned in evolving consciousness.

He was coming to India. On the way he remained a few years in the library of

Alexandria, where he picked up knowledge about the lost continent of Atlantis.

We have only that proof; no other proof exists – although recently scientists have started looking into the matter. What they have been finding in the Atlantic ocean suggests that there must have been a great civilization; whole cities are drowned there. The whole continent simply went down into the ocean.

Such changes happen on the earth: new islands come up, new mountains come up.

The Himalayas are a new mountain range – the newest. It was not there when *Rig Veda* was written, because it is impossible that *Rig Veda* should not mention such beautiful mountains – the highest and the most glorious. But there is no mention about them. And the people who wrote *Rig Veda* had come from Mongolia. Certainly there was no mountain on the way; otherwise to cross the Himalayas and to come to India would have been impossible. Even today, there are only two places from where you can cross the Himalayas; otherwise it is uncrossable. Changes go on happening on the earth.

Pythagoras reached India, but he got caught again – in the Buddhist atmosphere. It was so real; although Buddha was dead, the whole country was throbbing. His impression, his impact, had been very deep. When Pythagoras reached India, whatever he learned was learned in Buddhist universities. You will be surprised to know that Buddhist universities are the oldest universities in the world. Oxford is only one thousand years old. Nalanda, a Buddhist university, and Takshila, a Buddhist university, existed twenty-three hundred years ago. They were destroyed by Hindus and Mohammedans both.

But they were rare universities – they fulfilled the real meaning of the word. Not everybody was allowed to be in the university. Outside the university campus there were places where people could live for preparation. At the gate the gatekeepers were no ordinary people but very qualified Buddhist bikkhus, and they had to give people an examination at the gate. When you had passed those examinations, you could enter into the university campus; otherwise it was not even possible to enter it. Even just to see it was not possible; it was so sacred. Wisdom was thought so sacred – it was not everybody's thing, only those who could put their whole life into the search.

These three P's – Purification, Preparation, Perfection – come from the Buddhist sources of wisdom. Of course, Pythagoras made them more logical – he had a Greek mind – made them more systematic. But those words are really significant.

Preparation does not mean preparing for a verbal examination or a written examination. Preparation means preparing for an existential examination; it means going deeper into meditation. Unless you were meditative you could not enter those universities. And they had big campuses: Takshila had ten thousand scholars in it, Nalanda had twelve thousand scholars in it. Even today the greatest universities don't have more than that number, but their quality is very ordinary; students have simply passed the school examinations and they are ready to enter. No existential preparation is needed.

Preparation means that you drop all your conditionings, you drop your prejudices, you drop what you think you know and you do not know: you get as innocent as possible. Your innocence will be the preparation – that will allow you to enter into the university campus.

Then purification... In preparation you drop the conditionings which were given by

NEW BOTTLES FOR THE OLD WINE

the society, prejudices which were given to you or caught by you from the surroundings; it was borrowed knowledge in some way or other. You go like a child – but even the child is not pure. That is something very significant to understand, because people take it for granted that the child is pure.

He is certainly innocent, but his innocence is equivalent to ignorance, and behind his innocence are all his feelings: anger, hatred, greed, jealousy. You can see, children are very jealous. If one child has a doll, the other becomes so jealous that they will start fighting. If some child has something, then the other child also wants to have it. They are very competitive. Even in the family children have a hierarchy, and they are constantly fighting to be higher than others. Whatever is needed to be done…if obedience makes them the most loved in the family, they will follow obedience. But they are not following obedience; they are really trying a power strategy.

So preparation simply takes away the layers that society has put on your mind. But you have brought with nature, with your birth, so many ugly instincts, that a purification is needed.

You have to understand that competition is meaningless. You have to meditate deeply and recognize that you are not like anybody else. And competition can be only among similar people – and everybody is dissimilar, unique.

Once the competitive mind disappears, many things change in you; then you are not jealous. If somebody has a beautiful face and somebody has more money, and somebody has a more powerful body, you simply accept the fact that a few trees are tall and a few trees are small. But existence accepts them all.

The disappearance of competitiveness will also help you to get rid of greed. People go on accumulating – they want to be in a better position than you, with more money than you, with everything better than you. And their whole life is wasted in that.

Purification is almost going through a fire of understanding in which all that is instinctive and ugly burns down. And it is a great experience that only the ugly burns. That which is beautiful blossoms. In purification you lose all trace of hate, and instead, suddenly a spring of love bursts forth – as if the rock of hate was preventing the spring.

Once the cruelty…and children are very cruel. The idea that they are angels is just stupid. They are very cruel; they will beat dogs, they will beat cats. A small insect passing by – and a child will simply kill it for no reason, he just enjoys destruction. There is a destructiveness in him. Once that is gone, creativity arises.

So purification is a deeper meditation than preparation. Preparation was very simple, but purification is going deeper into meditation – the deepest possible – so everything that is not worthy of human beings is transformed. Everything has energy in it – hate, jealousy, greed – and when these things change, their energy becomes available to you in its purified form. And they *can* turn: greed can turn into compassion, sharing; hate can turn into love. Everything will turn into something which makes your heart a garden.

And when the purification is complete, utterly complete, not a corner of your being remains in the dark, everything is light and fragrant, fresh…

What we have called the awakened man, the enlightened man, Pythagoras calls perfection. It is simply a different name: the perfect man.

The first two you have to do; the third is the ultimate outcome of it. In these three simple words he has condensed the whole alchemy of human transformation.

Pythagoras is one of the most important people that Greece has given to the world. But strangely enough, nothing much is talked about all the best geniuses that Greece has given to the world. Pythagoras, Socrates, Heraclitus, Epicurus – these are the ones who should be talked about. But instead of them, in the universities Plato is studied, Aristotle is studied.

Plato is simply a record-keeper – he has not a single idea of his own! He is a devoted lover of Socrates, and whatever Socrates says, he goes on recording it, writing it. Socrates has not written anything – just as no great master has ever written anything. And Plato is certainly a great writer; perhaps Socrates may not have been able to write so beautifully. Plato has made Socrates' teachings as beautiful as possible, but he himself is no one. Now the same work can be done by a tape recorder. And Aristotle is merely an intellectual, with no understanding of being, or even a desire to search for it. These people are taught in the universities.

I was constantly in a fight with my professors. When they started teaching Plato, I said, "This is absolute nonsense, because Plato has nothing to say of his own. It is better to teach about Socrates." Plato can be referred to – he has compiled it all. But Socrates' name has become almost a fiction, and Plato has become the reality – just the way I was saying to you last night that Ouspensky has become the master, because he has written the books, beautiful books. One day Gurdjieff will be forgotten – he is already forgotten – and Ouspensky will be remembered for centuries. And sooner or later what he has written will be thought to be his own ideas. None of it is his own ideas.

Pythagoras is not at all bothered about any university in the world, for the simple reason that he is not a routine scholar; he is an original seeker, and he is ready to go anywhere. He traveled all his life to find people who may have had a little glimpse and may be able to impart something to him. He was collecting pieces, and he managed beautifully.

But Greeks don't talk about him because he is not talking about Greek philosophy; he is bringing foreign ideas, strange ideas from Alexandria, from Nalanda, from Takshila – he is almost not a Greek. They are not interested in what he is bringing, although what he is bringing has nothing to do with Greeks or Indians or Egyptians. But he is ignored – one of the most significant men, utterly ignored.

The same has happened to Diogenes. He is ignored because he looks embarrassing to the Greeks. And he is very original – not only in thoughts but in life. In everything that he does he is original and very sincere – a man of tremendous courage, who could say to Alexander the Great, "You are behaving like a fool. The very idea of conquering the world is nonsense. For what do you want to conquer the world? What will you do after it?"

He said, "After it? I am going to relax and enjoy." And Diogenes looked at his dog – they were friends, they used to live together – and he told the dog, "Did you hear? He is planning to relax and enjoy after conquering the world, and we are enjoying right now, without conquering anything! Why take so much trouble?" A naked man who can say to Alexander, "You are behaving like a fool," must have guts – and Alexander had to recognize it. And he was a man of tremendous power himself, of great intelligence. He had to recognize it – that he has never met a man of the quality of Diogenes.

But Greeks go on avoiding, the same way they have done with Epicurus. It is very strange, but perhaps this is the way of humanity to behave with its own greatest sons – to ignore them, not to take any note of them.

But amongst all these, Pythagoras has created a complete system to create a Buddha. He himself became an enlightened man – it was not only theoretical. When he came back to Greece, he was not the same Pythagoras who had left; he was a new man. And that was one of the greatest difficulties – his own country could not recognize him. In fact they had no category of enlightenment, awakening, buddhahood, so where to put Pythagoras? The category just does not exist in their mind, so he remains uncategorized, and for two thousand years nobody has commented upon him.

I am the first man to have commented on the great genius and realization of this unique individual. He has a more perfect way of presentation than you will find in Indian scriptures, because Indian scriptures are more poetic, and he is, after all, a Greek! He is very logical and very scientific.

Beloved Bhagwan,
You are famous for Your contradictions. But it seems that one of the most powerful confirmations that You are who You are – for the world in general and posterity – is that, in all those millions and millions of words, spoken spontaneously over several decades, You really never ever contradicted Yourself at all.

That's true!
I have never contradicted myself. I cannot do it. In the first place I don't remember anything that I have said before – how to contradict it?

Secondly, it is not my thinking, it is my experience. Contradictions happen in thinking, but not in experience. I have said things which may appear to people contradictory, but they are really evolutionary. My experience I have expressed in different ways; that may create the idea that I am contradictory. I was expressing it in different ways so if you have missed one way, perhaps the other way you may get it.

I have tried to describe it from all aspects possible, just to help people, because sometimes it happens that one aspect does not reach you but the other aspect is more in tune with you. I have used all possible, multidimensional expressions, but there is no way for me to contradict. It is my experience. I am not taking about others' experience. Even if I am talking about others, it is always according to my experience. They may agree with it, they may not agree with it – but I cannot go against my experience.

During the years, talking to you, I have been sharpening my arrows, my words, so that they can penetrate directly to your heart. But contradiction is not there at all. And you are right: the day all of my words will be understood, there will be found an undercurrent running through all of them and joining them. They are like flowers of a garland – a thin thread, invisible, is running through all the flowers – and that is my consistency, that is my experience.

It is true, I don't think anybody else has spoken so much. Much of it is lost because it was not recorded; almost half of it is lost, but whatever remains is still more than anyone else has ever tried to convey.

The reason is simple: I enjoy it, I love it. When I see a word settling in your heart, my joy knows no bounds. When I see a glimpse in your eyes that you have caught the meaning, I am immensely happy.

And I had to speak so much because nobody before me has addressed the whole world. They were addressing small fragments of humanity. Jesus remained confined to Judea, Buddha remained confined to Bihar, Socrates remained confined to Athens. Fortunately they don't let me remain in one place, so I have to be all over the world. And I have to speak again and again through different angles about the same experience, because in that also my life has been unique: people have been coming to me and leaving me – new people coming, old people going. It has been beautiful. It has not been like a dead pond where the water only evaporates, and soon there is left nothing but muddy mess.

It is almost as if I have been speaking by the side of a river, which is running so fast that each time I look at it there are new faces to whom I have to speak again. In thirty years so many people have changed. It was not true about Socrates or Buddha or Lao Tzu, they worked with a group their whole life. I have been working with so many new people, and I have always to find out a new mode, a new phase, new expressions, new bottles for the old wine...but the wine is old, and it is the same wine that I have been offering to all.

Chapter 31
April 27, 1986, Evening

The Courage to Be Ignorant

Beloved Bhagwan,
What are the qualities of the seeker of truth?

Every child is born with an innate search for truth. It is not something learned or adopted later on in life. Truth simply means, "I am, but I do not know who I am." And the question is natural – "I must know the reality of my being." It is not a curiosity.

These are the three differences, or three categories the world can be divided into: there are things which are, but they do not know that they are; hence there is no opening for any enquiry. They are closed, their existence is windowless. Then there are animals who know that they are, but they don't have the intelligence to enquire what it is that they are. Their windows are open, but their intelligence is not enough to look out and see the stars and the sky and the birds and the trees. Their windows – whether opened or closed – don't make much difference.

Perhaps once in a while a rare animal uses the window. In Shri Raman Maharshi's ashram…and he was one of the most significant people of this century. He was not a master; that's why people don't know him as they know George Gurdjieff or J. Krishnamurti. They don't know him even as they know Sri Aurobindo or P.D. Ouspensky who were only teachers – profound teachers, but not mystics.

Raman Maharshi was a silent pool of energy. Every morning he used to sit for a silent *satsang,* communion. He never talked much, unless asked something. Then too his answer was very short – having profundity, but you had to look for it. There was no explanation in it. His literature is confined to two, three small booklets.

His teaching was mostly to be in silent communion with the disciples. Naturally, very few people were benefited by him. But every morning he was sitting, people were sitting, and a cow would come and stand outside, putting her neck through the window, and she would remain standing there while the satsang lasted. It must have continued for years. People came and went, new people came, but the cow remained constant...and at the exact time, never late. And as the satsang would disperse she would move away.

One day she did not appear, and Shri Raman said, "Today satsang cannot be held, because my real audience is absent. I am afraid either the cow is very sick or she has died, and I have to go and look for her." He lived on a mountain in the south of India, Arunachal. The cow belonged to a poor woodcutter who lived near the ashram. Raman left the temple where they used to meet, went to the woodcutter and asked, "What happened? The cow has not come today for satsang."

The woodcutter said, "She is very sick and I am afraid she is dying, but she goes on looking out of the door, as if she is waiting for someone. Perhaps she is waiting for you, to see you for the last time. Perhaps that is why she is hanging around a little longer."

Raman went in and there were tears in the eyes of the cow. And she died happily, putting her head in the lap of Raman Maharshi. This happened just in this century, and Raman declared her enlightened, and told his people that a beautiful memorial should be made for her.

It is very rare for human beings to be enlightened; it is almost impossibly rare for animals to become enlightened, but the cow attained. She will not be born again. From the body of a cow she has bypassed the whole world of humanity, and she has jumped ahead and joined with the buddhas. So once in a while – there are a few instances only – it has happened. But that cannot be called the rule; it is just the exception.

Things are, but they do not know that they are. Animals are, they know that they are, but they don't have the intelligence to ask who they are. And it is not something to be wondered about. Millions of human beings never ask the question – that is the third category.

Man is, is aware that he is, and is capable by birth to enquire who he is. So it is not a question of learning, cultivation, education; you bring the quest with yourself. You *are* the quest.

Your society destroys you. It has very sophisticated ways and means to destroy your quest, to remove the question from your being, or at least cover it up. And the method it uses is this: before the child has even asked who he is, the answer is given. And any answer that has been given before the question has been asked is futile; it is going to be just a burden.

He is told that he is a soul, that he is a spirit, that he is not a body, that he is not material. Or, in communist countries he is told that he is a body, just material, and that only in the old days, out of fear and ignorance, did people believe that they have souls – that that is just a superstition. But in both cases, the child is being given an answer for which he has not asked. And his mind is delicate, pure...and he trusts his mother, his father – there is no reason for him not to trust.

He starts a journey of belief, and belief kills the quest. He becomes more and more knowledgeable. Then education is there, religious education is there, and there is no end to collecting knowledge. But all this knowledge is futile – not only futile, but poisonous, because the first step has gone wrong. The question was not asked, and the answer has been implanted in his mind, and since then he has been collecting more and more answers. He has completely forgotten that any answer that is not the finding of a question is meaningless.

So the only quality of a seeker of truth is that he does not believe, that he is not a believer, that he is ready to be ignorant rather than to be knowledgeable, because ignorance is at least natural, simple, innocent. And out of ignorance there is a possibility, almost a certainty, that the question will arise, that the journey will begin. But through knowledge you are lost in a jungle of words, theories, doctrines, dogmas. And there are so many, and they are so contradictory to each other, that soon you will find yourself more and more confused...more and more knowledgeable and more and more confused.

As far as I am concerned the basic quality of a seeker of truth is to cut himself away from all belief systems, from all borrowed knowledge – in other words, to have the courage to be ignorant rather than to have borrowed knowledge. Ignorance has a beauty; it is at least yours, authentic, sincere. It has come with you. It is your blood, it is your bones, it is your marrow.

Knowledgeability is ugly, absolute rubbish. It has been poured upon you by others, and you are carrying the load of it. And the load is such that it will not give you any opportunity to enquire on your own what truth is. Your collection of knowledge will answer immediately that this *is* truth. If you are filled with *The Holy Bible,* then the question will be answered by *The Holy Bible*. If you are filled with the *Vedas,* then the question will come out of the *Vedas*. But it will come from some source outside yourself; it will not be *your* discovery. And that which is not your discovery is not yours.

Truth brings freedom because it is your discovery. It makes you fully into man; otherwise you remain on the level of the animals: you are but you don't know who you are.

The search for truth is really the search for the reality of your being.

Once you have entered your being, you have entered into the being of the whole, because we are different on the periphery but at the center we meet – we are one. You can draw many lines from the periphery of a circle towards the center; those lines on the periphery have a certain distance from each other. But as they come closer to the center the distance goes on becoming less. And when they reach to the center the distance disappears.

At the center we are one.

At the periphery of existence we appear to be separate.

And to know the truth of your being is to know the truth of the whole.

There is just one quality, one courage: not to be afraid of being ignorant. On that point there can be no compromise, no cheap borrowed knowledge to decorate yourself with as a wise man. That's enough! Just be pure and natural, and out of that purity, naturalness, ignorance, innocence, the quest is bound to be born.

Every human being would be a seeker of truth if the society were not interfering with children.

The class of children is the most harmed, oppressed, exploited, distorted class of all classes – and the most helpless. And you are taking advantage of the helplessness of small children. But you are also not responsible. The same has been done to you. It is difficult to find out who was responsible in the beginning. But as long as we can look back, this has been the situation: every generation corrupts the new generation, and anybody who wants to prevent this corruption is condemned as corrupting the youth.

Socrates was condemned for corrupting the youth, and all that he was doing was the simple process of removing borrowed knowledge and helping his disciples to be themselves and then "to know thyself." If anybody has served truth the most sincerely it was Socrates. But he was condemned by the court, by the law, by the people who were in power, for corruption, for corrupting young minds.

Strangely, in the land of Socrates I was also condemned as corrupting people's minds. It seems the technology of corrupting the youth has evolved immensely in two thousand years, because it took Socrates his whole life to corrupt, and I was only there for two weeks! And the archbishop was already threatening to burn my house, to stone me to death.

Why are they afraid? They know perfectly well that they have no foundations. So if anybody shows the young people that their knowledge is unfounded, that all their answers are bogus because they don't even have questions, that they are only repeating things parrot-like but they don't have any understanding of what they are saying…then anybody who has a little intelligence will be able to understand it immediately.

Is this corruption of the youth?

To bring people to the quest of the truth – is this corruption?

It seems it is the greatest crime in the world in which – unfortunately – we are living.

Beloved Bhagwan,
Probably no enlightened master has spoken so many millions of words about the truth as You have. Lao Tzu says, "The truth that can be spoken is not the truth."
Beloved Master, what do You say?

Lao Tzu is right. The truth that can be spoken is no longer true, because the mechanism of language distorts the experience – which happens beyond mind, beyond words. To pull it down to the darker valleys of language is certainly distorting it.

On the one hand it is true that the truth cannot be spoken; on the other hand, because the truth cannot be spoken it has to be spoken in thousands of ways. The problem is not that the truth will reach to you through thousands of ways, but you may become infected with the search. If a man speaks about the truth he may not be able to say it…but you can get a glimpse from his eyes, you can get something from his gestures – something not from the words but the way the words are spoken, the emphasis, the gaps. The presence of such a man speaking may be just an excuse to allow you to be showered by his presence.

Lao Tzu cannot speak truth, but to be with Lao Tzu you may get the right direction. His presence may prove to you that there exists something that you know nothing about, and that it is so precious that all that you know and all that you have is worth sacrificing…that what you see in the presence of the master, of a realized man, is so precious that it has to be discovered; it has to become your experience too.

I have spoken millions of words just in order to give you a taste, a feel. Truth I cannot give to you – nobody can give it to you – but I can open my heart to you, which has known the truth, lived the truth. And that opening may help you in a very indirect way to go on your own pilgrimage. It may give you confidence that all this talk about truth is not just talk, that it changes people, that it changes their very presence, that it gives them a certain fragrance, a certain power, a certain authority. They don't speak like anybody else. They are not orators, they are not speakers; they simply open their heart. Perhaps the rhythm of their heart will change the rhythm of your heart.

Listening to them you may not get the truth, but you may be transported into another world: a world of silence, a world of immense peace, a world of benediction. And all those are immensely helpful for the search.

So Lao Tzu is both right *and* wrong: right because what he is saying is exactly so – the spoken truth is no longer true. But that is not all. If the truth is spoken by someone, and if it is out of experience – and it can only be out of experience – then that very person, his every act radiates something. It is contagious. Hence, whether truth is conveyed to you or not is not important. What is important is that if you become convinced that there is something like truth, there is a certain transformation that brings the full flowering of the being, then the word, the language, has done more than can be expected!

So I say again, Lao Tzu is right and not right. And my emphasis on *not* right is more than on his being right; otherwise I would not have spoken millions of words, I would have remained silent.

But I saw that it is not only a question of speaking; much more is involved. It shows why no mystic in the whole history of man has ever written anything. The reason is that the written word will miss all that the spoken word has. It will be the same word – spoken or written makes no difference. It will be the same statement written or spoken, but why has no mystic agreed to write? The reason is that they were all aware that the spoken word has a living quality, because experience is behind it, a heart is beating behind it, a consciousness is making arduous effort to reach to you.

The written word is dead, just a corpse. You can worship it but it cannot give you anything. All scriptures are dead. Perhaps when they were spoken it was a different phenomenon. If the man who had spoken them was speaking out of his own realization, then something – the very vibe – is carried away by the word.

Truth may not be expressed, but truth becomes a reality. Seeing the master, seeing one who is a realized one, you become certain: if you are groping in the dark, don't be worried, and don't feel hopeless. Go on groping! Every night has a morning to it, and sooner or later you will find the door, you will reach to the point. If one man has reached, the whole humanity can reach. He is enough proof.

So the question is not whether truth can be spoken or not, the question is whether a presence can create a conviction that there is something that you are missing – and unless you find it your life will not be complete, will not be perfect.

Beloved Bhagwan,
For me You seem to be pointing the way so strongly these days and I've almost become unattached to the finger...but then there is the arm, and the twinkling eyes, the sound of Your voice, and the beautiful graceful atmosphere that surrounds You. With You it is so easy to say ma nana to the moon. What to do?

There is nothing to do.
Say ma nana to the moon!
Just live the moment with intensity and totality. Live it with as much joy as possible, with as much love as possible, with no fear, no guilt. This existence is yours and this moment is a gift – don't let it go to waste. And don't be worried about enlightenment, the moon.

This moment, living totally, is enlightenment.

Just the other day I was telling you the Buddhist sutra…. Gautam Buddha is really a miracle, because he even puts himself down. He creates a category beyond himself: a man who has gone beyond knowledge, beyond discipline, beyond enlightenment. Then billions of buddhas are not equal to him. That last part of the sutra is so valuable, particularly for you, because here is a man in front of you who has no knowledge, who has no discipline…

Just when we came here I was sleeping twenty hours a day. Nobody has done it before, and no religious person will forgive me – twenty hours a day! I was getting up in the morning for two hours to take a bath and take my food and go to sleep again, and two hours in the evening to take my bath, eat my food and go to bed again. And I loved it.

I don't have a discipline; that's why I don't impose any discipline on you. When it has to be transcended, why bother in the first place to impose it? I am not telling you to read this holy book or that because finally it has to be transcended – transcend it right now!

Even enlightenment has to be transcended.

I have never said it to anybody, but I have left enlightenment far behind. I have not said it because you will not understand it. It is difficult to understand enlightenment, and if I start saying that there is something even beyond it, you may lose all hope. You will say,

"This is too much! First enlightenment was too much, and we were trying hard and nothing was happening. And now, beyond enlightenment…it is better to be ordinary and not bother about these things."

That's why I have not said it. But yesterday, the sutra, suddenly…I had no desire, but I could not deny the truth of what Buddha is saying. Experience, even the highest experience of enlightenment is still a duality: the experiencer and the experienced. And that duality has also to be dropped. But the moment you drop the experience, the experiencer also disappears – they can exist only together.

And that is the state of nirvana.

All has disappeared, the whole drama – the actors, the audience, everything has disappeared. Just an absolute silence prevails.

So don't be worried. Just try to live this moment as sincerely, as totally as possible, without being disturbed by the past or by the future. Undistracted, go deep into it, and that's enough. It *is* enlightenment.

One day it will explode. You need not wait for it; even your waiting will be a distraction. You forget all about it. That's why in my presence you feel so good – because there is no yesterday, no tomorrow. Just here…this is our whole world for the moment. One day that atomic explosion within you happens. And finally, one day you go even beyond it – then everything disappears.

That's why I say again and again that what has happened in the East as far as spiritual growth is concerned is incomparable. All other religions are far behind. Now, no religion can say that knowledge disappears, discipline disappears, enlightenment disappears – only then you are at home.

Buddha is saying billions of buddhas are not worth it: it is so valuable, the ultimate value. And it is available to all, every moment of your life. It is so mysterious how you go on missing it; it is the one thing that should not be missed. But a centuries old wrong upbringing is destroying your small precious moment.

It is up to you to throw away all that upbringing and let this small moment be all – and you have attained everything. Then you need not worry. Existence takes care. Existence is very compassionate.

Beloved Bhagwan,
Where is my question disappearing to? It is there one minute, and when I want to write it down it is gone, blank. Is it going into hiding in my subconscious? and why?

It is not going into your unconscious. It is coming from your unconscious, but when you start writing it, it becomes conscious. And this is a simple process: anything unconscious becoming conscious starts disappearing; it loses meaning.

On this simple principle the whole of psychoanalysis stands. Your dreams are unconscious. Tell them to the psychoanalyst – by telling them you will be making them conscious. And once they are conscious, they disappear.

Unconsciousness is a kind of basement where you go on throwing things, repressing things. Things that you don't want to see, things that you don't want to hear, things that you don't want to accept, you go on throwing into the unconscious. It is your rejected parts – allow them to surface. And that is what is happening while you are asking the question, and why I am insisting that you go on asking.

My answer may help you or not, but your asking is going to help you certainly. If it is something unconscious that wants to come into light, and you start writing it, you find it is losing meaning. Its whole meaning is in repression. Unrepressed it bursts like a soap bubble.

So it is tremendously good. Go on doing it. Only intellectual questions will not disappear; intellectual questions will remain. But if a question is coming from the unconscious and is significant... Intellectual questions are rubbish; they don't have anything to do with your being and your change. Let your unconscious reveal, and you will start seeing changes – not that the questions are disappearing, but your attitudes, your approaches, your behavior, even your dreams are changing.

It is a beautiful exercise to write down whatever you feel is somewhere lurking in the darkness of your mind. It is not very clear; there it is dark – bring it into the light. And if you can bring all the contents of the unconscious into the conscious mind, your unconscious mind and your conscious mind will become one; they will be both conscious.

And it is such a gift – because right now one-tenth of the mind is conscious, and nine-tenths is unconscious – naturally it is nine times more powerful. So you decide something by the conscious mind, but the unconscious mind can cancel it – it will cancel it! You decide that tomorrow morning you are going to get up at five o'clock – the morning is so beautiful, so healthy, so fresh. Exactly at five the alarm wakes you, and something happens. You don't want to get up. You say, "We will see tomorrow. It is so beautiful right now under the blankets, so cozy." And you take a turn and go to sleep.

When you do wake up, you will condemn yourself, you will feel guilty. But you don't understand what has been happening. Your conscious mind had decided to wake up at five. The unconscious was never in agreement with it. You had never asked for the agreement – there is no way to ask for agreement.

If you are hypnotized and your unconscious mind is told, "Wake up at five," then there will be no change; you will wake up at five, alarm or no alarm. But right now you take the decision with the conscious mind, and when you are asleep the conscious mind is no longer functioning.

It is the unconscious mind which is in power and functioning in your deep sleep. So when at five o'clock the alarm goes off, you pick up the alarm clock and throw it away – because the unconscious mind has no idea what the conscious mind has decided, and it looks so foolish to the unconscious mind, an unnecessary disturbance. You simply go back to sleep. But when you wake up, the unconscious mind has gone back; the conscious mind has come into function. It remembers, "I had decided to wake up at five o'clock, and I cheated myself." It feels guilty, but it has not done anything; it is not responsible for it.

You decide not to be angry, you decide not to be tense, you decide a thousand things and the unconscious mind goes on cancelling them. It goes on doing the way it has always been doing. But if all the contents of the unconscious mind evaporate, then you have only one mind, *conscious* mind, day in, day out. Every decision will be followed, no decision will ever be cancelled. Your life will have integrity.

That's what I mean when I use the word 'integrity.' You will have a kind of oneness. You can promise, and you can rely on your promise, because there is nobody in you who can cancel it. It is a decision of your total mind. And a decision of a total mind is immensely powerful.

It is good – go on doing it. If questions are not enough, then you can make a notebook. Just write anything unconscious, and don't be worried that anybody will see it, because there will be many things which you don't want anybody to see – that's why you are keeping them in the dark. Don't be worried, just bring them into the open. Nothing is wrong.

Keeping it in the dark is wrong. Bringing it into the light changes the whole quality…it disappears.

Beloved Bhagwan,
The silence that happened the other day – was that a taste of where You are pointing Your finger?

R ight!

Life Consists of Small Things

Beloved Bhagwan,
Why is it that I feel I need to have approval and be recognized, in my work especially? It puts me in a trap — I cannot do without it. I know I am in this trap but I am caught in it and I cannot seem to get out of it.
Can You help me be able to find the door?

The question is from Kendra.

It has to be remembered that the need to have approval and be recognized is everybody's question. Our whole life's structure is such that we are taught that unless there is a recognition we are nobody, we are worthless. The work is not important, but the recognition. And this is putting things upside down. The work should be important – a joy in itself. You should work, not to be recognized but because you enjoy being creative; you love the work for its own sake.

There have been very few people who have been able to escape from the trap the society puts you in – like Vincent Van Gogh. He went on painting – hungry, without house, without clothes, without medicine, sick – but he went on painting. Not a single painting was being sold, there was no recognition from anywhere, but the strange thing was that in these conditions he was still happy – happy because what he wanted to paint he has been able to paint. Recognition or no recognition, his work is valuable intrinsically.

By the age of thirty-three he had committed suicide – not because of any misery, anguish, no, but simply because he had painted his last painting, on which he had been working for almost one year, a sunset. He tried dozens of times, but it was not up to his standard and he destroyed it. Finally he managed to paint the sunset the way he had longed to.

He committed suicide, writing a letter to

his brother, "I am not committing suicide out of despair. I am committing suicide because now there is no point in living – my work is done. Moreover, it has been difficult to find ways of livelihood. But it was okay because I had some work to do, some potential in me needed to become actual. It has blossomed, so now it is pointless to live like a beggar.

"Up to now I had not even thought about it, I had not even looked at it. But now that is the only thing. I have blossomed to my utmost; I am fulfilled, and now to drag on, finding ways of livelihood, seems to be just stupid. For what? So it is not a suicide according to me, but just that I have come to a fulfillment, a full stop, and joyously I am leaving the world. Joyously I lived, joyously I am leaving the world."

Now, almost a century afterwards, each of his paintings is worth millions of dollars. There are only two hundred paintings available. He must have painted thousands, but they have been destroyed; nobody took any note of them.

Now to have a Van Gogh painting means you have an aesthetic sense. His painting gives you a recognition. The world never gave any recognition to his work, but he never cared. And this should be the way to look at things.

You work if you love it. Don't ask for recognition. If it comes, take it easily; if it does not come, do not think about it. Your fulfillment should be in the work itself. And if everybody learns this simple art of loving his work, whatever it is, enjoying it without asking for any recognition, we will have a more beautiful and celebrating world.

As it is, the world has trapped you in a miserable pattern:

What you are doing is not good because you love it, because you do it perfectly, but because the world recognizes it, rewards it, gives you gold medals, Nobel prizes.

They have taken away the whole intrinsic value of creativity and destroyed millions of people – because you cannot give millions of people Nobel prizes. And you have created the desire for recognition in everybody, so nobody can work peacefully, silently, enjoying whatever he is doing.

And life consists of small things. For those small things there are no rewards, no titles given by the governments, no honorary degrees given by the universities.

One of the great poets of this century, Rabindranath Tagore, lived in Bengal, India. He had published his poetry, his novels, in Bengali – but no recognition came to him. Then he translated a small book, *Gitanjali*, Offering of Songs, into English. And he was aware that the original has a beauty which the translation does not have and cannot have – because these two languages, Bengali and English, have different structures, different ways of expression.

Bengali is very sweet. Even if you fight, it seems you are engaged in a nice conversation. It is very musical; each word is musical. That quality is not in English, and cannot be brought to it; it has different qualities. But somehow he managed to translate it, and the translation – which is a poor thing compared to the original – received the Nobel prize. Then suddenly the whole of India became aware... The book had been available in Bengali, in other Indian languages, for years and nobody had taken any note of it. Every university wanted to give him a D.Litt.

Calcutta, where he lived, was the first university, obviously, to offer him an honorary degree. He refused. He said, "You are not giving a degree to me; you are not giving a recognition to my work, you are giving recognition to the Nobel prize, because the book has been here in a far more beautiful way, and nobody has bothered even to write an appraisal."

He refused to take any D.Litt.s. He said, "It is insulting to me."

Jean-Paul Sartre, one of the great novelists, and a man of tremendous insight into human psychology, refused the Nobel prize. He said, "I have received enough reward while I was creating my work. A Nobel prize cannot add anything to it – on the contrary, it pulls me down. It is good for amateurs who are in search of recognition; I am old enough, and I have enjoyed enough. I have loved whatever I have done. It was its own reward, and I don't want any other reward, because nothing can be better than that which I have already received." And he was right. But the right people are so few in the world, and the world is full of wrong people living in traps.

Why should you bother about recognition? Bothering about recognition has meaning only if you don't love your work; then it is meaningful, then it seems to substitute. You hate the work, you don't like it, but you are doing it because there will be recognition; you will be appreciated, accepted. Rather than thinking about recognition, reconsider your work. Do you love it? – then that is the end. If you do not love it – then change it!

The parents, the teachers are always reinforcing that you should be recognized, you should be accepted. This is a very cunning strategy to keep people under control.

I was told again and again in my university, "You should stop doing these things…you go on asking questions which you know perfectly well cannot be answered, and which put the professor in an embarrassing situation. You have to stop it; otherwise these people will take revenge. They have power – they can fail you."

I said, "I don't bother about it. I am enjoying right now asking questions and making them feel ignorant. They are not courageous enough simply to say, 'I do not know.' Then there would be no embarrassment. But they want to pretend that they know everything. I am enjoying it; my intelligence is being sharpened. Who cares about examinations? They can fail me only when I appear in the examinations – who is going to appear? If they have that idea that they can fail me, I will not enter the examinations, and I will remain in the same class. They will have to pass me just out of fear that again for one year they will have to face me!"

And they all passed me, and helped me to pass, because they wanted to get rid of me. In their eyes I was also destroying other students, because other students started questioning things which have been accepted for centuries without any question.

While I was teaching in the university, the same thing came about from a different angle. Now I was asking the students questions to bring to their attention that all the knowledge that they have gathered is borrowed, and they know nothing. I told them that I don't care about their degrees, I care about their authentic experience – and they don't have any. They are simply repeating books which are out of date; long ago they have been proved wrong. Now the authorities of the university were threatening me, "If you continue in this way, harassing students, you will be thrown out of the university."

I said, "This is strange – I was a student and I could not ask questions to the professors; now I am a professor and I cannot ask questions to the students! So what function is this university fulfilling? It should be a place where questions are asked, quests begin. Answers have to be found not in the books but in life and in existence."

I said, "You can throw me out of the university, but remember, these same students, because of whom you are throwing me out of the university, will burn down the whole university." I told the vice-chancellor, "You should come and see my class."

He could not believe it – in my class there were at least two hundred students…and there were no spaces, so they were sitting anywhere they could find – on the windows, on the floor. He said, "What is happening, because you have only ten students?"

I said, "These people come to listen. They dropped their classes; they love to be here. This class is a dialogue. I am not superior to them, and I cannot refuse anybody who comes to my class. Whether he is my student or not, it does not matter; if he comes to listen to me, he *is* my student. In fact you should allow me to have the auditorium. These classrooms are too small for me."

He said, "Auditorium? You mean the whole university to gather in the auditorium? Then what will the other professors be doing?"

I said, "That is for them to think out. They can go and hang themselves! They should have done it long before. Seeing that their students are not going to listen to them was enough indication."

The professors were angry, the authorities were angry. Finally they had to give me the auditorium – but very reluctantly, because the students were forcing them. But they said, "This is strange, students who have nothing to do with philosophy, religion or psychology, why should they go there?"

Many students told the vice-chancellor, "We love it. We never knew that philosophy,

religion, psychology can be so interesting, so intriguing; otherwise we would have joined them. We thought that these are dry subjects; only very bookish kind of people join these subjects. We have never seen any juicy people joining the subjects. But this man has made the subjects so significant that it seems that even if we fail in our own subjects, it does not matter. What we are doing is so right in itself, and we are so clear about it, that there is no question of changing it."

Against recognition, against acceptance, against degrees…but finally I had to leave the university, not because of their threats but because I recognized that if thousands of students can be helped by me, it is a wastage. I can help millions of people outside in the world. Why should I go on remaining attached to a small university? The whole world can be my university.

And you can see: I have been condemned.

That is the only recognition I have received.

I have been in every way misrepresented. Everything that can be said against a man has been said against me; everything that can be done against a man has been done against me. Do you think this is recognition? But I love my work. I love it so much that I don't call it work even; I simply call it my joy.

And everybody who was in some way elder to me, well-recognized, has told me, "What you are doing is not going to give you any respectability in the world."

But I said, "I have never asked for it, and I don't see what I will do with respectability. I cannot eat it, I cannot drink it."

Learn one basic thing: Do whatever you want to do, love to do, and never ask for recognition. That is begging. Why should one ask for recognition? Why should one hanker for acceptance?

LIFE CONSISTS OF SMALL THINGS

Deep down in yourself, look. Perhaps you don't like what you are doing, perhaps you are afraid that you are on the wrong track; acceptance will help you feel that you are right. Recognition will make you feel that you are going towards the right goal.

The question is of your own inner feelings; it has nothing to do with the outside world. And why depend on others? All these things depend on others – you yourself are becoming dependent.

I will not accept any Nobel prize. All this condemnation from all the nations around the world, from all the religions, is more valuable to me. Accepting the Nobel prize means I am becoming dependent – now I will not be proud of myself but proud of the Nobel prize. Right now I can only be proud of myself; there is nothing else I can be proud of.

This way you become an individual. And to be an individual living in total freedom, on your own feet, drinking from your own sources, is what makes a man really centered, rooted. That is the beginning of his ultimate flowering.

These so-called recognized people, honored people, are full of rubbish and nothing else. But they are full of the rubbish which the society wants them to be filled with – and the society compensates them by giving them rewards.

Any man who has any sense of his own individuality lives by his own love, by his own work, without caring at all what others think of it. The more valuable your work is, the less is the possibility of getting any respectability for it. And if your work is the work of a genius then you are not going to see any respect in your life. You will be condemned in your life…then, after two or three centuries, statues of you will be made, your books will be respected – because it takes almost two or three centuries for humanity to pick up as much intelligence as a genius has today. The gap is vast.

Being respected by idiots you have to behave according to their manners, their expectations. To be respected by this sick humanity you have to be more sick than they are. Then they will respect you. But what will you gain? You will lose your soul and you will gain nothing.

Beloved Bhagwan,
Would You talk to us about the difference between love and trust? It seems to me that trust is of greater significance in our relationship to You than love. When I say, "Bhagwan, I love You," I'm speaking of a feeling that is colored and defined by other love relationships, a feeling that is limited by my state of unenlightenment. I speak as if I have some comprehension of what my love towards You implies.
When I say, "Bhagwan, I trust You," I am saying, "Do with me whatever needs to be done. Lead me into unimagined and unimaginable places: I am Yours."
Trust seems to embrace the understanding that it is available even to things beyond its comprehension. Love, unenlightened love, also seems outgoing, somewhat aggressive; the "I" very conscious of itself as an entity. While trust – even in its unenlightened form – seems to have a quality of utter let-go in it. The "I" is only attached to it for linguistics, because the trusting person acknowledges that he himself may disappear.

It is Maneesha's question.
It is not a question at all. She has answered it herself, and beautifully. She has said exactly what I would have said. And that's what I

would like for each of you, by and by: to come to an understanding that when you ask a question, you can answer it exactly the way I will be answering it.

Trust is certainly a higher value than love. In trust, love is implied; but in love, trust is not implied. When you say, "I trust in you, Bhagwan" it is understood that you love. But when you say you love, trust has nothing to do with it. In fact your love is very suspicious, very untrusting, very much afraid, always on guard, watching the person you love.

Lovers become almost detectives. They are spying on each other. Love is beautiful if it comes as a part of trust. And it always comes as a part of trust, because trust cannot be without love. But love cannot be without trust, and a love without trust is ugly; deep down it has all kinds of jealousies, suspicions, distrust.

It is also true that when you say, "I love you," it is not a surrender, it is not a readiness to be dissolved. It is not a readiness to be taken to unknown and unknowable spaces. When you say, "I love you," you stand equal, and there is a certain aggressive quality in it. That's why from the very beginnings of humanity everywhere, and in every time, the woman has not taken the initiative to say "I love you." She has waited for the man to say, "I love you" – because the heart of the woman feels that aggressiveness. But man has a harder heart; he does not feel that aggressiveness – in fact he enjoys it.

But when you say, "I trust you," it is a deep surrender, an openness, a receptivity, a declaration to yourself and to the universe that, "Now if this man takes me even to the hell, it is okay with me: I trust him. If it looks like hell to me, it must be a fault of my vision. He cannot take me to hell."

In trust you will always find faults with yourself; in love you will always find faults with the one you are in love with.

In trust you are always, without saying it, in a state of apology: "I am ignorant. I am sleepy, unconscious. There is a possibility of saying something wrong, doing something wrong, so be merciful towards me, have compassion on me." Trust implies so much. It is such a treasure.

When you say, "I love you," there is a subtle current of possessiveness. Without being said, it is understood, "Now you are my possession, nobody else should love you."

In trust there is no question of possessing the person you trust. On the contrary, you are saying, "Please possess me. Destroy me as an ego. Help me to disappear and melt in you, so there is no resistance in going with you."

Love is a constant struggle, a fight; it demands. "I love you," means, "You have to love me too. In fact, I love you only because I want you to love me." It is a simple bargain; hence the fear: "You should not love anybody else. Nobody should love you, because I don't want anybody to be partners in my love, to be sharers in my love."

The unconscious mind of man goes on thinking as if love is a quantity, that there is a certain quantity of love. If I love you, then you should possess the whole quantity. If I love a few other people, then the quantity will be distributed, you will not get the whole of it; hence the jealousy, the spying, the fighting, the nagging. And all that is ugly goes on behind a beautiful word, love.

In trust there is no question of any fighting. It is really a surrender. When you say, "Bhagwan, I trust in you," it means, "From this moment my fight with you stops. Now I am yours; you can do whatever you want. You can kill me, but I will not resist because I am no longer there – I have given myself to you.

LIFE CONSISTS OF SMALL THINGS

Now it is up to you: whatsoever you feel right, do it."

And trust is not competitive; hence there is no jealousy. You can trust me, millions of people can trust me. In fact, the more people will trust me, the more you will be happy. You will be rejoicing that so many people are trusting…not so with love.

But in trust, all that is beautiful in love is implied.

The moment you say, "I trust in you, Bhagwan," you have also said, "I love you." But now, because of the trust, the "I" is no longer existent, only love. And love without the ego creates no problems: "Many people can love you, and the more people love you, the more I will be happy." But this is because of trust.

Trust is perhaps the most beautiful word in the human language.

And trust is so close to truth that if it is total, then this very moment your trust becomes a revelation, a revolution.

Beloved Bhagwan,
This weekend there is a big sannyasin festival in Florence with dance and meditation and music. Is Your heart with all these thousands of sannyasins?

In the first place, there are not going to be thousands of sannyasins there, for the simple reason that the people who are organizing it are no longer with me. They are trying to cheat the sannyasins. Only three hundred sannyasins have booked for it, and the organizers are declaring it to be the first world festival since the last one in the commune in Oregon, America.

But my name is not mentioned in it. It is not my festival. It is those few people, those few therapists, who want to exploit the sannyasins. But they are in trouble, because three hundred sannyasins coming will only cover the expenses – they were hoping thousands would come. And also, the three hundred are coming because they are not aware that these people have started working against me.

My heart will be with my people wherever they are. I will be with my sannyasins – and I have to be, particularly to show to them that this is not my festival, that they have been deceived, that the people on the stage have ugly ideas. They are all pretending to be masters, that they have become enlightened.

But the festival is going to be a fiasco, because on the stage there is not going to be my presence but my utter absence. I will be present in the audience…. These three hundred people who are coming are going to ask, "By what right have you called the sannyasins for a world festival when yourself are no longer a sannyasin? On whose authority?" But it is a good chance for sannyasins to see who are the people in the role of Judas, selling their own master for thirty pieces of silver.

As far as sannyasins are concerned, I am always with them. In this so-called world festival I will be more strongly there in the audience, to make them feel that the stage is empty, that the stage is dark and there is no light. The people who are pretending are going to be exposed, and they will never try anything like this again.

So inform all your friends: Go there and ask the people on the stage, "On what authority have you called the sannyasins? *You* are not a sannyasin. *You* are not a master, you are not enlightened, and you had no guts ever to say this in the commune. But now, because Bhagwan is not present, you are trying to play the role of an enlightened master."

In fact, I would have loved to go there and suddenly walk onto the stage and see what happens to those therapists, but I cannot enter Italy. The government is stubborn, although sixty-five very eminent people from different professions, known worldwide, have protested that there is no reason why I should be prevented.

But the government is simply silent, because the pope is heavy and the politicians are beggars. They are not afraid of intellectuals, painters, musicians, sculptors, architects, writers – they are not afraid of these people. They are afraid of the pope, because he holds the votes.

But more protests are going to be presented to the government, and really eminent people are showing a tremendous interest in why a single individual who has done no harm to the country, who has never been in the country, should be prevented.

So I will not be able to go there. But my presence will be with my sannyasins, wherever they are. And you have to write to all your friends in Italy: "Make it clear to these people that you cannot exploit sannyasins. If you are no longer sannyasins, then simply get out from here. This is a festival of sannyasins – we will manage it. Leave the stage! The empty stage is far better than a stage full of those who have betrayed."

Beloved Bhagwan,
The most painful experience in the world is to be angry with You. This is not a question – only an expression of sheer joy at feeling free again to love You.

That's right! It must be from Chetana! It is one of the most difficult things, to be angry with me.

You can ask Vivek, because she suffers many times for my sake, for my safety. And I can understand that if she becomes angry it is not against me. But then she suffers so much because of anger.

You love me so much – you cannot conceive of being angry with me. But once in a while, just a taste is good. That will prevent you for the future from going into such spaces.

Of course for Vivek it is difficult. Now she has been continuously sad and worried because I have been continuously mistreated by the police, jail authorities, governments, deported from one place to another. And she knows that she cannot do anything to prevent it. This whole sadness sometimes turns into anger. Now she cannot even be angry with those governments; she can only be angry with me. But then to be angry with me is really difficult. It is almost an impossible task! And those who have to pass through it know its hell.

But one thing is good about it – there is always something good, even in the worst situation – that nothing remains forever. You come out of it, and then you feel a tremendous freedom and joy and understanding.

Chapter 33
April 28, 1986, Evening

Prayer — Your Psychological Armor

Beloved Bhagwan,
The other day when You were speaking about coming closer to You, I was aware that I still feel a thin armor around me that keeps me from coming closer. This armor is incongruous with my openness to You. I don't know where it is coming from.
Please help me to melt it away.

Everybody has that kind of armor. There are reasons for it. First, the child is born so utterly helpless into a world he knows nothing of. Naturally he is afraid of the unknown that faces him. He has not yet forgotten those nine months of absolute security, safety, when there was no problem, no responsibility, no worry for tomorrow.

To us, those are nine months, but to the child it is eternity. He knows nothing of the calendar, he knows nothing of minutes, hours, days, months. He has lived an eternity in absolute safety and security, without any responsibility, and then suddenly he is thrown into a world unknown, where he is dependent for everything on others. It is natural that he will feel afraid. Everybody is bigger and more powerful, and he cannot live without the help of others. He knows he is dependent; he has lost his independence, his freedom. And small incidents may give him some taste of the reality he is going to face in the future.

Napoleon Bonaparte was defeated by Nelson, but in fact the credit should not go to Nelson. Napoleon Bonaparte was defeated by a small incident in his childhood. Now history does not look at things in this way, but to me it is absolutely clear.

When he was just six months old, a wild cat jumped on him. The maidservant who was looking after him had gone for something in the house; he was in the garden in the early morning sun and the fresh air, lying down, and the wild cat jumped on him. It didn't harm him – perhaps it was just being playful – but to the child's mind it was almost death. Since then, he was not afraid of tigers or lions; he could have fought a lion without any arms, with no fear. But a cat? – that was a different affair. He was absolutely helpless. Seeing a cat he was almost frozen; he became again a six-month-old small child, with no defense, with no capacities to fight. In those small child's eyes that cat must have looked very big – it was a wild cat. The cat may have looked into the eyes of the child.

Something in his psyche became so much impressed by the incident that Nelson exploited it. Nelson was no comparison to Napoleon, and Napoleon was never defeated in his life; this was his first and last defeat. And he would not have been defeated, but Nelson had brought seventy cats at the front of the army.

The moment Napoleon saw those seventy wild cats his mind stopped functioning. His generals could not understand what had happened. He was no longer the same great warrior; he was almost frozen with fear, trembling. He had never allowed any of his generals to arrange the army, but today he said, with tears in his eyes, "I am incapable of thinking – you arrange the army. I will be here, but I am incapable of fighting. Something has gone wrong for me."

He was removed, but without Napoleon his army was not capable of fighting Nelson, and seeing the situation of Napoleon, everybody in his army became a little afraid: something very strange was happening.

A child is weak, vulnerable, insecure. Autonomously he starts creating an armor, a protection, in different ways. For example, he has to sleep alone. It is dark and he is afraid, but he has his teddy bear, and he believes that he is not alone – his friend is with him. You will see children dragging their teddy bears at airports, at railway stations. Do you think it is just a toy? To you it is, but to the child it is a friend. And a friend when nobody else is helpful – in the darkness of the night, alone in the bed, still he is with him.

He will create psychological teddy bears. And it is to be reminded to you that although a grown-up man may think that he has no teddy bears, he is wrong. What is his God? Just a teddy bear. Out of his childhood fear, man has created a father figure who knows all, who is all-powerful, who is everywhere present; if you have enough faith in him he will protect you. But the very idea of protection, the very idea that a protector is needed, is childish. Then you learn prayer – these are just parts of your psychological armor. Prayer is to remind God that you are here, alone in the night.

In my childhood I was always wondering… I loved the river, which was just close by, just two minutes walk from my house. Hundreds of people used to take a bath there and I was always wondering… In summer when they take a dip in the river they don't repeat the name of God – "Hare Krishna, Hare Rama" – no. But in cold winter they repeat, "Hare Krishna, Hare Rama." They take a quick dip, repeating, "Hare Krishna, Hare Rama."

I was wondering, does the season make a difference? I used to ask my parents, "If these are devotees of 'Hare Krishna, Hare Rama,' then summer is as good as winter."

But I don't think that it is God or prayer or religion; it is simply the cold! They are creating an armor with "Hare Krishna, Hare Rama." They are diverting their minds. It is too cold, and a diversion is needed – and it helps.

In summer there is no need; they simply

forget all about what they have been doing the whole winter.

Our prayers, our chantings, our mantras, our scriptures, our gods, our priests, are all part of our psychological armor. It is very subtle. A Christian believes that he will be saved – nobody else. Now that is his defense arrangement. Everybody is going to fall into hell except him, because he is a Christian. But every religion believes in the same way that only they will be saved.

It is not a question of religion. It is a question of fear and being saved from fear, so it is natural in a way. But at a certain point of your maturity, intelligence demands that it should be dropped. It was good when you were a child, but one day you have to leave your teddy bear, just the same as one day you have to leave your God, just the same as one day you have to leave your Christianity, your Hinduism. Finally, the day you drop all your armor means you have dropped living out of fear. And what kind of living can be out of fear? Once the armor is dropped you can live out of love, you can live in a mature way.

The fully matured man has no fear, no defense; he is psychologically completely open and vulnerable.

At one point the armor may be a necessity – perhaps it is. But as you grow, if you are not only growing old but also growing up, growing in maturity, then you will start seeing what you are carrying with you. Why do you believe in God? One day you have to see for yourself that you have not seen God, you haven't had any contact with God, and to believe in God is to live a lie: you are not being sincere.

What kind of religion can there be when there is no sincerity, no authenticity? You cannot even give reasons for your beliefs, and still you go on clinging to them.

Look closely and you will find fear behind.

A mature person should disconnect himself from anything that is connected with fear. That's how maturity comes.

Just watch all your acts, all your beliefs, and find out whether they are based in reality, in experience, or based in fear. And anything based in fear has to be dropped immediately, without a second thought. It is your armor. I cannot melt it. I can simply show you how you can drop it.

It is not a simple thing; there are many things around it…. In India there are so many temples. Many people don't have houses, but there are so many gods – thirty-three million gods – and they all need their temples. In some places, like Varanasi, you will find two houses then one temple, three houses then another temple…the whole city is a city of temples. In Khajuraho, which is a ruined city, still there are one hundred temples, and hundreds of other temples are in ruins. Once it must have been a big city, but looking at the temples, I could not figure out where men were living, because the whole city seems to be composed of temples and temples. There seems to be no space.

I used to go for a morning walk in Jabalpur, in a silent street, and one man used to follow me – because we were the only two who used to go for a walk in the morning. His habit was to pay respect to every god on the road, so this temple will come and he will pay respect, and that temple will come and he will pay his respect.

I told him, "Just listen, if you have to come with me then you cannot continue this stupidity; otherwise you are free – you can do it, but I cannot wait at every temple. It looks embarrassing: you are doing this idiotic act and I am standing by your side!"

But he loved me. He said, "I also think that it is useless. Nobody else does it, but my father used to do it, and because of him it has become almost a heritage: I am doing it, my children are doing it. And now there is great fear…my father has left it with me, perhaps his father had left it with him. The fear is that if you pass the temple of any god without paying respect, he may be angry at you. And gods are very revengeful; they are not going to leave you alone. You will suffer. So the fear is, why unnecessarily make enemies, powerful enemies against whom there is no other defense? It is better to pay respect – it costs nothing."

I said, "Then you can do it, but you cannot come with me."

And he loved to come with me, so he said, "Tomorrow I will try – just give me one chance, because I can see that you don't pay any respect, and nobody takes any revenge. Nobody else is paying respect – thousands of people are passing and only I am… It seems all the gods are waiting for *me* to pay respect, otherwise I will suffer revenge. They are not concerned with anybody else."

I said, "That's what I am saying – they are not there. There is nobody in the temple; all temples are empty. There are no gods and there is no need to be afraid. You come with me, but tomorrow this habit has to be stopped; otherwise our friendship for this morning walk is at an end."

He said, "Just one day…" He tried hard, and I could see how psychological chains exist. He had promised me, and I was with him so he could not deceive me. On one side was the god…and he was caught between the two sides. I could see his feet stopping; I could see his hands getting ready to pay respect, but seeing me he would drop his hands.

It took almost double time that day, because he was stopping…almost an automatic break. And I had to stop and look

at him severely, so he would say, "Okay, I will not do it. But are you certain there is no god?"

I said, "You just forget all about gods. We have come for a morning walk, and this continuous stopping… And there are so many temples; I am fed up!"

But you will be surprised. In the evening he came to see me. He was looking very happy. He said, "Do you know what? I had to go another time. When I left you I went again to pay respect because I was so disturbed that so many gods would be angry. And I am a poor man, how I am going…? But now I am feeling at ease." So he said, "That's perfectly good: with you I will come and will not pay respect, but I can go twice – the second time just to pay respect to the gods."

I said, "It seems you are incurable. You see me every day with you – nobody is being angry, nobody is taking any revenge. You see thousands of people passing by."

He said, "I see everything, but what am I to do with my own mind?"

I said, "Then it is better you go one time and pay respect, and I will stop going on that street. I will go on another street, because I will not force you to go twice, wasting your time."

When people are psychologically in such a bondage they always find reasons. One day he came to me and told me, "Now I go walking alone, without you, the whole joy of the morning walk is gone. And I know you will not come with me unless I leave these gods; I have to choose. So today I tried it – perhaps you are right! So I tried it on my own: I didn't pay any respect. And when I came home my mother was dead. Now it is absolutely certain that I angered so many gods."

But I said, "Everybody's mother is going to die. Do you think it is because the gods are angry that mothers die? and that only your mother is special? Everybody's father is going to die, everybody is going to fall sick, everybody is going to have accidents!"

But he said, "I cannot think of anything…when I had gone for the walk she was perfectly okay and when I came back she was dead. The doctors say she had a heart attack, but I know that really I have killed her by not paying respects."

I said, "If you had not paid respect, *you* should have died from a heart attack, not your mother. Can't you see a simple thing – that your mother has nothing to do with it."

But the psychological conditioning makes you almost blind. He said to me, "This is a warning to me, 'Look, this time we are taking your mother, next time *you* are gone!' They have given me an opportunity, a chance – a chance because I have always been respectful. They are being kind towards me, but now I am not going to listen to you."

Your psychological armor cannot be taken away from you. You will fight for it. Only you can do something to drop it, and that is to look at each and every part of it. If it is based in fear, then drop it. If it is based in reason, in experience, in understanding, then it is not something to be dropped, but something to be made part of your being.

But you will not find a single thing in your armor which is based on experience. It is all fear, from A to Z.

We go on living out of fear – that's why we go on poisoning every other experience.

We love somebody, but out of fear: it spoils, it poisons.

We seek truth, but if the search is out of fear then you are not going to find it.

Whatever you do, remember one thing:

Out of fear you are not going to grow. You will only shrink and die.

Fear is in the service of death.

Mahavira is right: he makes fearlessness a fundamental of a fearless person. And I can understand what he means by fearlessness. He means dropping all armor.

A fearless person has everything that life wants to give to you as a gift. Now there is no barrier. You will be showered with gifts, and whatever you do you will have a strength, a power, a certainty, a tremendous feeling of authority.

A man living out of fear is always trembling inside. He is continuously on the point of going insane, because life is big, and if you are continuously in fear… And there is every kind of fear.

You can make a big list, and you will be surprised how many fears are there – and still you are alive! There are infections all around, diseases, dangers, kidnaping, terrorists…and such a small life. And finally there is death, which you cannot avoid. Your whole life will become dark.

Drop the fear! The fear was taken up by you in your childhood unconsciously; now consciously drop it and be mature. And then life can be a light which goes on deepening as you go on growing.

Beloved Bhagwan,
In discourse when You say things like, "Live totally in the moment," I always think, "Of course!…that's it! From now on I am always going to do that." And of course, a moment later, I have forgotten already. In every discourse I decide the time has come to be more meditative, more religious, more loving, more aware – and I immediately forget.

Is it possible that just by sitting with You, one of these days I will really get it in spite of myself?

It is possible you may get it in spite of yourself. But your question is very significant. If you look at it, you can see what is going wrong. You listen to me talking about living totally, intensively... moment to moment, living now, living here and you say to yourself, "Of course, that is it! I am going to do it." It is not that later on you forget it; you have already forgotten it. By saying, "Of course! this is it," by deciding that you are going to do it, you have already postponed it for tomorrow; by deciding that you are going to live this way, you have already missed the point.

You have missed the point *now*.

You think that later on you find you have forgotten it just a moment afterwards. You are not forgetting it just a moment afterwards; you have not listened to it at all! Otherwise you would not say, "Of course! This is it!" You would simply understand it non-verbally. You would not verbalize it, because in verbalizing it you are missing the moment...the moment is a very small thing.

Your mind is really deceiving you. Your mind is saying, "I have understood it, don't be worried. Of course, this is it! We are going to live this way." But when? The question was now, and your mind has already postponed it. The question was here, and the mind has already brought the future in. It is not that you forget later on; later on you only recognize that you have forgotten. But the truth is that you have not even understood, because if you understand it there is no possibility of forgetting it.

A truth has a quality: understood, it is impossible to forget it. That's why if you are a man of truth you need not remember it, but if you are accustomed to lying then you need a very good memory, because then you have to remember continually what lie you had told this man yesterday, and you have to repeat the same lie – because meanwhile you may have been lying to other people, about other things. A liar has to be very very alert, and if he is caught, then he has to be very logical, almost a sophist, so he can manage.

One Sufi story is that Mulla Nasruddin was chosen by the Shah of Iran to go to the king of India as his messenger, to make a friendship between two great countries. All the other important people in the court of the Shah of Iran were very jealous. They were trying in every way to spoil Nasruddin's journey, to create in the mind of the king antagonism against Nasruddin, and they were spying on Nasruddin to find out what he was doing.

What Nasruddin did was this: he went to the emperor of India, and before the whole court of the emperor he said, "Seeing you is a great privilege for me. My king, the Shah of Iran is just a young moon – just two days old. You are a full moon."

The emperor was certainly very much impressed – that the ambassador of Iran is comparing him not with a two-day old moon, which is barely visible for a few minutes, but with the full moon! He gave him many presents to give to his king and said, "Let him know that I am very much pleased with his messenger."

But the spies of the Shah's court, the conspirators against Nasruddin, had reached the Shah's court before him. They told everyone that Nasruddin had insulted the Shah of Iran, calling him just a young moon, two days old, and had compared him with the emperor of India by saying that the emperor of India is a full moon, perfect in its glory!

Naturally the Shah of Iran was very much offended. He said, "Let that Nasruddin come! I used to think that he is a wise man, but he seems to be very cunning." Nasruddin came with big, valuable presents, but the Shah was angry. He said, "I don't want any presents. First you have to give the explanation to me: is it right that you compared me with the emperor, saying that I am just a two-day old moon, and he is as the perfect full moon?"

Nasruddin said, "Yes, and the emperor is a fool! He did not understand my meaning."

The Shah said, "What is your meaning?"

He said, "My meaning is that the full moon is on its deathbed, from tomorrow it will start declining. The two-day old moon is on the increase: tomorrow it will be bigger, the day after tomorrow it will be even bigger! So my Shah of Iran is expanding, becoming bigger and bigger. The emperor does not have any future – my Shah has a future; he has only past, and his future is death."

The Shah of Iran was very impressed. He gave all the presents that were given by the emperor of India for him to Nasruddin, and he gave many more presents to Nasruddin, and told him, "You are really a wise man." And the whole court was silent, seeing that the whole thing had changed completely: "This Nasruddin is really a strange fellow; we had never thought that he would interpret it in such a way."

That night they went to see him, because now he had become the most important man in the court, second only to the Shah, and they all praised him. He said, "Don't be bothered – I am just an incurable liar! Whatever the situation is, I manage somehow to interpret it in such a way that it appeals to the party concerned: both the India emperor and the Shah of Iran are idiots! And I am just an incurable liar. I don't mean anything!"

Truth has a quality, it has a validity which is intrinsic. You need not prove it; its experience is its proof. No other logic is needed.

So just look into your acts, into your thoughts, into your feelings: you will find the armor everywhere. Wherever you see fear, you have created it. It was needed at one time – now it is no longer needed. A simple understanding that it is no longer needed…now it is a barrier, a hindrance, a burden. If you find something truthful, it will have its own validity. But in the armor you will not find anything that has any connection with truth. The whole armor is made of fear – layers and layers of fear.

The woodcutters and the scientists who work with wood count the age of the tree from the layers of the bark. When you cut a tree you will see layers of the bark on the trunk. Each year the tree gathers one layer – that's how they manage to know how old the tree is. There are trees which are four thousand years old; they have four thousand layers.

Your armor has also as many layers as you have lived. Not one every year; perhaps one, two, three – it depends on conditions: what kind of upbringing, what kind of education, what kind of people you have lived with. But each year you are collecting layers, and the armor goes on becoming thicker and does not allow you to touch life. There is such a gap between you and life.

You are carrying an imprisonment around yourself. But because you yourself have created it, you are capable of dropping it any moment…this very moment. But don't postpone, don't say, "I will do it tomorrow." Tomorrow never comes. And when I am saying, "Do it…," in fact doing it is not needed; just seeing is enough. If you have seen it, don't verbalize it: "This is it," because in verbalizing it you will miss – the moment is gone. Without verbalization, just see it and it will evaporate. It has no substantiality. It is not something real. It is something unreal that you have created, and this goes on happening every day.

I tell you to live intensely herenow, but the barrier which is there immediately shifts it into the future. You *feel* that you have understood it; right now it will shift it towards the future and give you the feeling of understanding. But next moment you will have forgotten it, because in the first place you had not understood it at all. Understood, it is never forgotten.

My professors in the university were very angry with me because I would never take any notes, and every other student was taking notes. They would see me just sitting, and they would ask me, "Don't you want to take notes?"

I said, "There is no need. I am trying to understand, and if I understand it, there is no need of any notes; the understanding will remain with me. Understanding becomes part of your blood, part of your bones, part of your marrow. These people who are taking notes are the ones who are not understanding. They are thinking that by taking notes they will be able to remember – but what will they remember? They have not understood in the first place. These notes will be dead. Perhaps they will be able to repeat these notes in the examination papers.

"You are responsible – because these people will take these notes into the examination, and then they will be caught. In fact you are responsible; you should have stopped them from taking notes. It is a simple logic: they are not understanding and they are trying to take notes. They can't do two things together. In the end, only the notes are in their hands and no understanding, and in the examination, what will they do? They will try to bring in the notes in a thousand different ways."

People will write small notes on their hand, people will write on their clothes…and in India you wear a *kurta,* a very long robe, on the underside you can write big notes. Nobody can see it; only when you want to see it you can just turn it up and look at the note, and you are not carrying any notes or anything. And the people who are a dangerous type, and are known to be dangerous, will bring their copies with them, with a knife. They will put the knife on the table with the copy, and they will be copying from the copy before the teacher who is standing there. He knows that the man is dangerous and that the knife is symbolic, "If you prevent me or do anything wrong to me, I can do anything – I can kill you." But who is responsible?

"And you," I used to tell them, "you are angry at me, who is trying to understand?"

In my own class, when I became a professor in my own turn, I prevented it completely…nobody could take notes. I said, "The mind can do only one thing at a time, so try to understand so that you need not sneak notes into the examination."

First my students were very much puzzled. They said, "Every professor says, 'Take notes, so you don't forget.'"

I said, "The question of forgetting arises only when you have not understood. I am saying, 'Understand, and don't worry about forgetting.' Anything understood is never forgotten, and anything not understood is bound to be forgotten."

So that's what is happening…. I say, "Live now." You say, "This is it! Enough is enough, now I am going to live moment to moment." But why the decision?

Just start! Whatever you are doing here…you are listening here, just listen. There is no need to verbalize it. The mind is a commentator – it goes on commenting – but if you try intensely to hear, the commentating mind will stop because it is a question of energy. You have a certain energy. If you stake the whole energy in listening, then this continuous commentary in the mind automatically stops. It has no more energy; you are not nourishing it.

And yes, it is true: it is going to happen in spite of you. How long are you going to not listen to me? Just tired, one day you will say, "Let us listen!"

Beloved Bhagwan,
George Gurdjieff said, "Bravo, America!" After seeing how inhumanely the United States treated You, I say, "To hell with America!"
Beloved Master, what do You say?

I cannot say anything against Gurdjieff. I will still say, "Bravo, America!" for the simple reason that America has not mistreated me. The small group of bureaucrats who mistreated me are not America; they are mistreating America too. Don't say, "To hell with America!" say, "To hell with the American government!" Make it a clear distinction.

America has not much knowledge about me. It was the American government's behavior, mistreatment, that made me known to every American. And wherever I went in those twelve days – I passed almost all over America – I was greeted with love and respect by strangers. Everybody could see that the American government was behaving like a fascist government; everybody could see that this was religious persecution, that this was not democracy. Even amongst the bureaucrats who came in contact with me – the jailers, the doctors, the nurses, the other attendants in the jail, the inmates – there was not even a single exception. I was surprised, because those inmates had no way of knowing me. They had just known what was happening with me from the television – small bits and pieces.

But they were certain that I was being persecuted by the Christian fanatics and by the bureaucracy; that the government was afraid for some reasons and the church was afraid for some reasons. They simply wanted some excuse so I could not enter America, because they knew that if I was out of America my people, naturally, would disperse.

But from the American people I experienced great love. The first jail I was in, so many telegrams and so many telephone calls…in the thousands. I asked the jailer, "You must be getting tired?"

He said, "No, we have had to appoint three, four more people to receive phone calls, open telegrams."

The first day somebody from Germany phoned and asked the jailer, "Perhaps Bhagwan must be the first in your jail who is a man of international standing?"

And the jailer said, "No, we have had cabinet ministers, leaders of political parties, and many celebrities."

I had no idea what had happened, but as the second day came and flowers started coming… There were so many that in that jail, a big jail – they had six hundred inmates or more – they had no place to keep them. They had only one room empty, a big room, bigger than this room, and it was full of flowers.

The jailer came to me, saying, "What to do with the flowers?"

I said, "Send them to schools, colleges, universities, hospitals, sick people in the city – wherever you feel, just send them, from me."

He said, "One thing more, I am sorry and I want to apologize. I don't know the number of the man who called from Germany…you had come recently and I had no awareness of what kind of man you are. Now, in two days, I have seen that the whole world is interested in you. There is not a single country in the world from where we are not receiving calls and telegrams, and flowers. And from America everywhere people simply want to know why you have been arrested.

"So I cannot phone that man and apologize to him, but I can say to you what I want to say to him: please forgive me. Those cabinet ministers and political leaders – you don't belong to their category. Perhaps we will never have another man like you in this jail. These two days have been my life's most precious days."

The jailer used to take me to the court everyday, and returning he would say, "It is sheer injustice. I have never seen such injustice. They can't prove a thing against you, and still they are not ready to give bail. This is unprecedented," he said, "in my whole life – and I have been here for twenty years."

On the street people were standing on both sides whenever I was coming to the court, going back from the court – perhaps for hours, because they did not have any idea at what time I would be taken out – shouting, showing two fingers for victory, throwing flowers on the police cars.

No, America has not mistreated me. The government – and that is a totally different thing….

The politicians and the church conspired; both were in danger. And now they are trying to create the fear in all the other countries where they can have some pressure. Because they help the poor countries with money, the poor countries are under obligation, so whatever America says to them they have to follow. Their whole effort is not to let me settle again and create a commune, because that commune will be an answer that proves that all their accusations, allegations, are absolutely wrong.

But as far as the people of that land are concerned, they are beautiful. And Gurdjieff was right.

This government is not going to last long. They have already started doing suicidal acts. With the attack on Libya they have shown their real face. A small country like Libya, and a nuclear power like America – there is no comparison… The only reason for attacking Libya is that the man who leads Libya, Kaddafi, is really a brave man, outspoken, and he says whatever is the truth. He is not a politician.

And he said that Ronald Reagan is Adolf Hitler Number Two. This statement was the root cause for attacking Libya; all other things were not of any consideration. But he does not know that before attacking Libya he should attack me – fortunately I don't have any land – because I have immediately corrected Kaddafi: "You are wrong. Ronald Reagan is not Adolf Hitler Number Two; he is Adolf Hitler Number One."

The poor Adolf Hitler of the second world war cannot be number one. He is now second, for the simple reason that Ronald Reagan has a million times more power than Adolf Hitler had. Now he is calling Kaddafi "the mad dog of the Middle East," calling him "the bad smell."

Ronald Reagan and his government started dying the day they arrested me. It takes a little time. Let them do a few more stupid things and let the American people understand what kind of a government they have got. It is not a democracy: it is not for the people, it is not of the people, it is not by the people.

It is a fascist gang that is ruling America, and it will be good that the American people get rid of it; otherwise.... People naturally think the government and the so-called political leaders are the leaders of the people. That is not so.

Just recently I have received news from Crete about a few incidents that happened after they arrested me. Eleven old people – fifty to sixty years old – just as I left the house with the police, reached the house and said, "This should not have happened without us. Why did you not inform us? We have our hunting guns, we would have come and shown those police people what it means to misbehave."

One journalist had asked me, "Any message for the people who live here?"

I said, "Just tell them to reach the airport in the night to show that they are with me – not with the church and not with the government." There were three thousand people at the airport. They had waited for hours to support me, and to say that what the police had done and what the government had done was not right. Fifty people met one sannyasin; they were immensely angry about what had happened and were asking, "What can we do?" Just poor people, simple people.... Another group of forty people met another sannyasin, and they were asking, "Show us... we want to do something. This thing should not be allowed to happen. And everything that Bhagwan was saying was right, about the church; there was nothing wrong in it."

These simple villagers understood that what I was saying about the church is true; nothing was wrong in it. And even when I had left Greece, people from Crete sent a delegation to the president saying, "This behavior of the police and the government has disgraced us."

So always remember to make a differentiation between the government and the people. The government is not necessarily the representative of the people. In most cases it has cheated people, exploited people. It is not *for* them.

I know...the question is from Milarepa. I can understand your anger. Every sannyasin would like to say, "To hell with America!" But just say, "To hell with the American government!"

America is far bigger, far more important, and I still hope that the new man will be born in America.

These governments come and go; the people remain. The people are the very soul. A country is not made of land, it is made of the people. In those twelve days in jail, moving from one jail to another, I came in contact with the common people and with the lowest of the low – the criminals – and I have seen so much love in their hearts. Whenever I entered into a new jail I was received...I did not feel that it was a jail because the reception was so warm.

Of course those people were behind bars, but they were shouting, "Bhagwan, we know you, and you are right!" in the face of the jailer, the doctor and the other officials. They would line up, and whenever I reached my cell, soon inmates would start coming with fruits...somebody with milk, somebody with soap, somebody with a toothbrush, somebody with toothpaste. They would say, "These people will not give you anything. They want to torture you. But as we had heard just the day before that you will be brought here, we have been saving; all these things are fresh."

These people are criminals, and Ronald Reagan is not a criminal?

And he killed unnecessarily Kaddafi's daughter, bombed his three houses which are

in the civilian area. He himself is a mad dog –
and he is calling Kaddafi a mad dog!

I can understand your anger, but
remember always to be careful to draw fine
lines so that only the criminal is hit, not the
simple, poor, innocent people.

Chapter 34
April 29, 1986, Morning

Rocks, the Earth...They are All Alive

Beloved Bhagwan,

I heard You say that if a person can remember his birth and being in the womb, then the memory of his last death may come. I have tried to remember, but only imagination is there. I also heard You say that it is not possible to remember beyond three to four years old because the baby has no mind.

Is there a remembrance that is not of the mind?

There is no remembrance that is not of the mind, but you don't know the whole mind. When you are trying to remember, you are using only the conscious mind, and the conscious mind can go only up to the age of four. But below the conscious is the unconscious mind.

Sometimes in your dreams you go deeper than the conscious mind can ever lead you. Many of your dreams are memories of your past lives, but you have no way to recognize that they are of a past life. So there is a special method which is something like hypnosis. It can be done by somebody else to you – which is simpler because you can relax completely, and he can lead you deeper into the past life.

In hypnosis or in Buddhist or Jaina terminology – because they discovered the method first – it is called *jati-smaran:* remembering the past lives. In hypnosis you don't hear anybody else except the person who has hypnotized you. He can talk to you, you can answer him, yet you will remain fast asleep, you will not come to the conscious mind. So only in hypnosis can your unconscious be communicated with, asked questions.

This can be repeated again and again, and if the same fact comes up without exception, the same memory comes up, the same story comes up, then certainly it is not imagination.

Another thing... Through hypnosis the

other person can reach you, but not through your conscious mind – because in whatever the conscious mind does there is an effort and tension, and that prevents the unconscious mind from surfacing. The conscious mind has to be completely relaxed so the unconscious can surface. In hypnosis it is better to begin with someone else. And it is such a simple method that anyone can do it – it does not need any expertise. I will tell you about the method, how you can help each other.

When you have become a good medium, so that you can slip very easily into the unconscious, then finally the unconscious can be told that you are able to reach your past lives. It can be given a certain symbol to avoid the conscious mind completely. For example, it can be told that if you repeat, "Om, om, om," three times, you will fall into hypnosis. Before using this mantra – anything can be used, "One, two, three," it doesn't matter, the words are not significant – before doing it, you have to tell your conscious mind, "Wake me up after ten minutes." The other person can also do the same, but it is easier for you because you are not doing anything. But once you have been able to go into deeper layers of your past life or past lives, the other person can tell the unconscious, "This is your mantra: one, two, three. And whenever I say it, you will fall into an unconscious state." But remember to tell the conscious to wake you; otherwise, who will wake you out of unconsciousness? It can become a coma.

The unconscious mind is nine times bigger than the conscious; it has tremendous treasures, all the memories of your past. And below the unconscious there is the collective unconscious. One can descend into the collective unconscious also – at first with somebody's help. That used to be the work of a mystery school – that the master will take you slowly towards the unconscious and the collective unconscious. In your collective unconscious you have memories of your past lives as animals, as birds.

Below the collective unconscious is the cosmic unconscious. Slowly, slowly one can go deeper and deeper, and the cosmic unconscious has memories of your being trees, rosebushes, stones.

So mind is not only that which you know; there is much to be discovered in your own mind. It is yours, it is there – but not easily available. There are reasons why it is not easily available. Nature makes barriers, because it would confuse you if there were no barriers between the conscious, the unconscious, the collective unconscious, and the cosmic unconscious. Even this small mind – the conscious mind – is so confusing, so disturbing. If you knew all that you have lived for millennia, from the very beginning, naturally you would get in such a mess, in such a madness.

For example, you love a woman. She may have been your mother in a past life, and if you remember it then you will be in trouble. But she may have been, in your collective unconscious, your murderer; then things become even more complicated. And those realities are as authentic as the realities of your life. You will get mixed up: how are you going to behave with this woman who is your wife, who was your mother, who was your murderer? Whatever you do with this woman will create guilt in you. You will not be at ease. That's the reason why nature goes on putting barriers between your past existences and allows you only this life's memories.

The science of hypnosis has been condemned by all religions, and the reason is that if hypnotism becomes accepted as a scientific enquiry – and once it is explored it has to be accepted, because it fulfills all the criteria of being a science – then there will be trouble: Christians cannot say there is only one life, Mohammedans can't say there is only one life, Darwin can't say that man has evolved from the apes. It will depend on the research done through thousands of peoples' total minds, and what they say.

Hindus believe that man's consciousness has evolved from the consciousness of cows – that's why they call them "mother." And I think a cow being a mother looks more relevant than a monkey being a father. The Hindus are saying this through a certain research into the mind, which has been available for centuries in the East: how to go into past lives. And there has not been a single exception – whenever you cross the border of the collective unconscious mind, you pass from the body of a cow, not from the body of a monkey.

It is not a question of hypotheses. With Darwin it is only hypothetical, just a conjecture, and now he is being refuted, even by scientists. Now there are not many Darwinians; they are out of date.

The latest research into evolution does not help Darwin and his theory. They say that for thousands of years we have not seen any monkey evolving into a man, and neither have we seen the reverse – that a man reverses into a monkey. And Darwin could not provide the missing link – which he was asked for again and again his whole life; it was a nightmare for him! It cannot be just a jump from a monkey to a man: this moment you are a monkey and next moment you decide to be a man, and you become a man. There must be a missing link…not only a link, perhaps many links, many steps slowly, slowly, but they should be available.

Darwin could not even find dead bodies

that would have been a proof of a link. We have been searching for dead bodies and we have found one ninety thousand years old – a human body in China. But it is still human; it is not a monkey. It was preserved by the snow. It is still human, as human as you are.

But Hindus have a totally different approach. It is to be remembered that this is the only point on which all the three religions that were born in India agree: about everything else they have their own philosophy, but about reincarnation they all agree. And that is not just an accident, because all three religions were working on the same lines – looking into the unconscious of man – and they all found the same results. To call the cow mother…the whole world laughs at it, but I don't think anybody understands why Hindus call the cow mother. If they are right – the cow has the qualities of a mother, and it is far better to be connected with the cows than with the monkeys.

So don't try to remember. It is not a question of remembering. You cannot cross the barrier with the conscious mind; you can only imagine, and you will know that it is only imagination because it changes every time, so you know perfectly well that you are imagining. Go through a hypnotic process. And the hypnotic process is very simple – the simplest.

The mind, the conscious mind, has to be focused on something just for a few seconds – for example, an electric light bulb. Don't have anything in the room so that the mind can wander here and there; just have a bare room with only one thing: an electric light which is on in the darkness. Lie down, be relaxed, and take the help of a person whom you trust. That is the most important thing, because the conscious mind will not relax unless there is trust. It will keep itself alert, because the man may do something, take you someplace, and you will not be aware of it. That's why I said hypnosis was part of a mystery school where there were masters whom people trusted, or there was one great master who helped you. You trusted him, and he said to you, "This man is going to take you into hypnosis. Your trust in me should be your trust in him too; I am choosing him." Or if it was possible for the master himself, if the school was small, then he would do it once in a while, just to show others what happens.

The process is very simple. You have to lie down relaxed, the whole body relaxed. Looking inside the body starting from the toe, see if there is any tension. If there is any tension near the knee or near the stomach or anywhere, then relax it there. Bring that relaxation up to your head – and keep your eyes focused on the light.

And it is easy to recognize when you have come to the point where you are on the border of conscious and unconscious: your face changes; it starts looking sleepy, it loses the quality of awakening, and at that moment the master says, "Sleep is coming…deep sleep is coming…you are falling into a sleep which you have never fallen into before." And a moment comes when even if you try to keep your eyes open… You have been told that until your eyes close by themselves, in spite of yourself, go on keeping them open. That keeps the conscious mind engaged.

Soon – it takes two minutes, three minutes, at the most five minutes – your eyes start drooping. That means you are just crossing the border. The master says, "You are falling, and I will count up to seven. With each number you will be going deeper." And he starts counting, "One…" and goes on repeating, "the sleep is becoming deeper. Two…the sleep is becoming deeper. Three…" And at seven he stops it. At seven he says, "You have

fallen into deep unconsciousness. Now you will be available only to me; you will not hear anything else, anybody else. Now the only communication with the world is through me; you will be able to hear me, you will be able to answer me…"

And the beauty of the unconscious is that it never lies, because it has never been part of civilization. It has never been educated, it has never been turned into a hypocrite; it is very simple, very innocent. It simply says whatsoever is the case. Then for a few seconds the master leaves you, so that you can settle into that state. And then he starts asking you where you are. Perhaps you are in the womb of your mother, perhaps you have been conceived, perhaps you are dying in a past life somewhere. And you will answer where you are. He asks, "Describe it in detail," and you will describe it in detail. This can be taped, recorded, so that when you come back you can listen to it.

The process has to be repeated many times, because this is the proof: if it is imagination or dream it will go on changing every time you do it, but if it is a reality then nothing can be done about it. Each time you come to that place you will describe exactly what it is. And all that you say can be recorded, so that it can be compared later on when you are conscious. If you are saying the same thing again and again it is not a dream, it is not imagination; you are coming across a real memory. You are reliving it; it is not only remembered, but relived.

Once you have succeeded in getting one life back, then with the same process you can go on deeper, into other lives. There will come a barrier where human lives stop and animal lives start: that means you have come to the collective unconscious.

Now the master needs to put you in an

even deeper unconsciousness, and that can be done in your unconscious state. The first thing was done when you were conscious; it brought you to the unconscious. The second step has to be done in the same way: "I will repeat seven times that you are falling deeper into the collective unconscious, and you will start falling." Giving a little rest, he can again ask where you are, and you may say, "I am a rosebush," or anything else that you have been. You relive it; you can make every detailed description. Again the barrier will come when you pass from animals, from plants, to what you call matter — because matter is also consciousness, fast asleep.

And that's the end of the journey in the lower depths of your mind. If this is completed, your consciousness will go on changing. With each new revelation your consciousness will become richer. And then a point comes – when you have traveled all the way down backwards, downwards – that you can move upwards from consciousness to superconsciousness until you reach to the cosmic consciousness. We are exactly in the middle. On both sides of the conscious there are three stages: below it is unconscious, collective unconscious and cosmic unconscious; above it is superconscious, super-superconscious, and cosmic conscious.

Our mind has seven worlds. To know the past, to know our background, is to know the whole history of consciousness and its evolution until this moment. But that makes it clear that this is not the last stage – it cannot be. If there is so much behind you, there must be something ahead of you. So what Western psychology goes on doing is only working with one thing: unconsciousness, the first lower rung of the ladder. Eastern psychology has worked on all the seven.

As you move from the conscious mind,

hypnosis is the method. And hypnosis is not yet recognized by the scientists because they have not even tried it. It is very strange. Perhaps the reason is that science is a development of the West, and because the West has a Christian conditioning it simply denies that there is anything other than this life, so from the very beginning one is prejudiced – why bother about hypnosis?

A few people have dared and tried, but they were all condemned by the society – badly. Mesmer tried it, but was condemned, and there was a tradition of women who Christianity condemned as witches. They were trying hypnosis, and they were closer to the truth than Christianity has ever been. But thousands and thousands of witches were burned alive; their whole tradition was completely erased, all their literature was burned. Only one copy of each book has been preserved in the Vatican.

It is the duty of the U.N. to take over the library of the Vatican. It is underground; it has tremendous treasures that Christianity has destroyed. They are still afraid to bring those books out in the light because then the condemnation for Christianity will be immense, even from Christians, "What you were saying was not true, and those who said the truth were killed, burned."

But they are keeping at least one copy in their vast library. Nobody is allowed to enter into that vast library; only when you become a cardinal are you allowed in the library, but by that time you are so much conditioned. Those books are written in a different way, particularly to avoid the attention of Christians. They have used parables, diagrams, and other things, as if they are not about religion, as if they are about something else.

It is the duty of all the intelligentsia of the world to insist to the Vatican: "That library does not belong to you. You have done enough harm; now at least give that library to the U.N. and let scholars find out what beautiful literature you have destroyed. And it should be published, and made available to anybody who wants it."

One of the things that got destroyed in this way was hypnosis – the method, the science and the results. It is now simply a condemnatory word. If you love me, if you trust me, anybody can say you are just hypnotized. He does not know even the meaning of the word; he does not know its implications, but he is using it to condemn you. But really, to be hypnotized and to go into the darker realms of your being is the first step in going into the lighter realms of your being.

You contain the whole evolution – past, present, future. You have such an enormous being, and only a small window of the conscious mind is allowed…this is you.

Your vastness is denied.

Your universality is denied.

So if you really want to remember, not only to remember but to relive, then you will have to use the method of hypnosis. I am going, as we settle somewhere, to start a section which will be totally devoted to hypnosis and its implications, and I want every sannyasin to go through it.

I am reminded of two incidents… One is in Gautam Buddha's life, and one is in Vardhaman Mahavira's life. A man takes sannyas, becomes part of the community of Buddha, but finds it hard, difficult, arduous. He is sad, depressed, and thinks many times to leave it. One day Buddha called him and told him to sit in front of him and go into the method of *jati-smaran* – that is, hypnosis.

He had not yet tried it, so somebody gave him the instructions to go into past lives. And it was an amazing revelation: for almost five lives in the past he had taken sannyas and dropped it. That had become a routine of his consciousness. So Buddha said, "Now you are doing it again. It is up to you, but you have done it five times before. It is simply repetitive; you are wasting time. Either stop taking sannyas and do whatsoever you want, or be courageous; if you have taken it, then go into it this time. This should not be repeated. Five lives have been a waste."

Looking at his own five lives…the same pattern, almost mechanical, the same wheel moving: first getting attracted to a great master, getting initiated with great enthusiasm, and then seeing the arduousness, the difficulties of transforming himself and escaping, renouncing sannyas itself. And he comes back to it again and again.

Buddha said, "You can do it as long as you want. In your next life you will do it again. And for five lives nobody reminded you, because the masters you were working with were not masters of jati-smaran."

The man remained. It changed his whole attitude: "This is stupid. If it is hard then it has to be faced. If it is a challenge then it has to be taken." And he became one of the enlightened disciples of Buddha.

There is a similar story in Mahavira's life. A prince becomes enchanted with Mahavira's individuality, but he does not know that Mahavira's life is really arduous. Nobody has lived the way Mahavira has lived – naked in the winter, in the hot sun, hungry for months, fasting, eating once in a while, barefooted, walking on the burning earth in the hot sun.

He did not use shoes because shoes were made only of leather in those days, and to use shoes meant you were indirectly supporting the industry of violence, because the best leather comes when you kill young calves. If you want really perfect leather, then you have to take the leather from the calf while it is alive; you don't kill him first. First you take the leather, and in taking the leather of course he dies. That leather is the most soft and the best. Mahavira was absolutely against in any way supporting anything which is based on violence.

This prince became – and naturally, you can understand it – the prince became impressed by the man, his integrity, his authority, his teaching. He was not aware that life with him is going to be tremendously hard – and he had lived very luxuriously. But in a moment of enthusiasm he took sannyas and entered into Mahavira's commune.

Now, ten thousand sannyasins used to move with Mahavira, and they were staying in a big caravanserai, and it was the routine that the elder ones – that means those who had been longer in sannyas – should have better places, and the others accordingly. This prince was just a one-day-old sannyasin, so in the night he got a place just near the door, the main door, where people left their shoes, umbrellas and other things. He was the son of a king, and by that door sleeping was impossible; people were continuously coming and going. When there are ten thousand sannyasins... He had never slept in such a situation, and he immediately thought, "This is not the life I would like. Next morning I will give my apology, and I will say, 'This is not the life for me.'"

But before he reached Mahavir, Mahavir reached him, and asked him to let himself be taken into jati-smaran – and it was the same process. For three lives he had been doing the same thing: getting impressed by magnetic people, charismatic people, and then finding it difficult over small matters and leaving them. In all those three lives he could have become enlightened, because those three people were capable of triggering the process of enlightenment.

Mahavira said, "You have missed three lives, and you are missing the fourth. You can decide. But you are a warrior, not only a prince. Don't emphasize that you are a prince and you have lived only in luxury; remember that you are a warrior and you have been fighting in wars. And there is nobody in this area who is a better swordsman, a better archer. Don't insult yourself, don't humiliate yourself. This is escape."

And the man remained. But the factor that helped these two men to remain was their reliving their past experiences. It is of tremendous use, but in the West it is so much condemned that the condemnation has reached to the East too – because now the East is just a parrot. Now the East is not the East it used to be; it is just a shadow of the West. All the Eastern scholars are produced by the West. They learn in Western seats of education – in Paris, in London, in Oxford, in Cambridge, in Harvard.

I have been continuously fighting, in many universities in India, that these scholars should not be called Eastern scholars because whatsoever they have learned is Western; even though it is about Indian philosophy, they have learned it in Oxford.

This is ridiculous – that to understand Indian philosophy you have to go to Oxford. These scholars are not Eastern in any way; their whole approach is Western. So there is no more East really, now it is all West. The East has become so interested in Western success, in materialism, in technology, that it has forgotten that it has also become successful in a different world – the world of the inner – and has reached the highest peaks of illumination.

So don't try to remember, but take the help of someone whom you trust, who can hypnotize you. Soon, as existence allows me to settle somewhere, I will create people who can help everybody to go into the past, and experience and relive those moments.

They will change your every attitude. They will make you aware that you are moving in a circle, and it is time to get out of it, because this is nonsense: each life you are doing the same thing, moving in the same circle. And you can go on doing it eternally – nobody is going to prevent you – unless you decide to jump out of this viciousness.

Beloved Bhagwan,
While traveling in Greece with a group of sannyasins we visited Delphi, the place of the ancient oracle, and where it is said Pythagoras once lived. We all felt a peaceful happiness while walking around the ruins, and in the end we all gathered on the top of the stadium and sat silently with each other. What happened to us?
Why does one have such different feelings about different places?

People like Pythagoras, Socrates, Plotinus, Gautam Buddha, Lao Tzu, Chuang Tzu…the people of such state are continuously radiating – not with any effort, but effortlessly and spontaneously. Their experience, just like a candle, radiates light; their consciousness has become a light. Their being has attained to a fragrance, to a flowering, and everything around them is going to catch it. For centuries it will continue to vibrate.

I have not been to Delphi. I was thinking to go, but before being at Delphi I was arrested and thrown out of Greece. But Delphi was one of the places I would have liked to visit.

In India I have visited a few places… The place where Gautam Buddha became enlightened is called Bodh Gaya. It is a small temple – some follower made the temple as a memorial, by the side of the tree under which Buddha became enlightened. That tree still remembers something, and I came to know later on that the bodhi tree has a certain substance which no other tree has, and that is the substance which makes a man a genius. Only geniuses have that substance in their mind, and in the world of trees only the bodhi tree has that substance. Perhaps it is more perceptive, more receptive; it has a certain genius.

Buddha remained under that tree for many years. The whole area is still fragrant, and just by the side of the tree is the place where he used to walk. When he used to get tired of sitting and meditating then he would walk and meditate, so that place is marked by marble stones. But sitting under the tree or walking on those marble stones, you can feel you are not in this world, that this place has something which no other place has. Perhaps the moment Buddha became enlightened something exploded in him and was caught by everything that could catch it. We used to think before…but it is not the case. Now it is well proved that trees are very sensitive, more sensitive than man – their sensitivity just has a different level.

One scientist was working on trees. He had put on the tree a certain mechanism, just like a cardiogram, that takes the graph of the feelings of the tree, and he was surprised that when the gardener came… He had told the gardener, "You go and cut one of the branches of the tree. I want to see the effect." But there was no need to cut the branch. As the gardener came with his axe, the graph was already going mad!

The scientist said, "Don't do that – the tree has already caught the idea that you are going to cut and hurt her." Later on he became more amazed, because when you cut one tree, all the other trees in the surrounding area, their graphs go mad. When the same gardener comes to water the tree, the graph remains perfectly balanced – it becomes even more harmonious. It seems the tree is able to catch your thoughts, your ideas.

Perhaps the same may be found about rocks, the earth, because they are all alive. Their life may be on a different level, but they are all alive – and certainly they are more simple and more innocent. People have been keeping… In Tibet they have been keeping the bodies of enlightened people, because if the trees and the stones and the earth are impressed by the great experience, then certainly the body of the man, his bones, must be impressed – they are closer.

Perhaps Tibetans were the first to understand it: they have covered ninety-nine great masters' bodies with gold. That used to be the most sacred place in Tibet. It is just… If you have seen the picture of Potala, the palace of the Dalai Lama, it is just underneath it. Potala is high in the mountains, and underneath there are many caves. One cave is devoted only to those ninety-nine bodies.

Why did they stop at ninety-nine? A strange figure! A hundred would have been more appropriate. They had to stop because the lineage of Dalai Lamas dropped from the height it used to be, and the country could not produce anybody worthy of taking the hundredth seat in the sacred, secret temple. It was opened once a year for the people, and just to pass through it was to pass through another world.

Now it is completely closed so that the communists cannot find it – because they will not be interested in the bodies; they will be interested in the gold. They will destroy those bodies and take the gold – and it is a great quantity of gold. So before the Dalai Lama left Lhasa because of the communist invasion of the country, he sealed it in every possible way so that they cannot discover it. And they have not been able yet to discover it.

Slowly, slowly in all the countries where spirituality has flowered, people became aware that something happens… So people have preserved things that were used by these people, or just have made memorials of their bodies. In India bodies are burned, but you will be surprised to know that the remains left after burning a body are called "flowers." Ordinary people's ashes are thrown into holy rivers, but enlightened people's "flowers" are preserved in *samadhis* – in beautiful marble memorials. Just to go and sit there is in itself a meditation. But the trouble is that the world is ruled by those who know nothing of this.

For example, Delphi should not be open for everybody, because they will destroy its subtle vibration. But the government is interested in tourism!

Delphi should be open only to a few people who are chosen – chosen by a mystery school that should exist there. Delphi was a mystery school. In the days of Pythagoras and Socrates, Delphi was the temple – the most famous temple – of wisdom. And the priestess used to go into a trance. While praying and dancing and singing in the temple, she would go into a trace, and in her trance she would say things which always proved to be true. She herself could not remember anything when she came back from the trance; perhaps the trance was taking her higher into the mind, perhaps to the cosmic mind.

In such a trance she declared that Socrates was the wisest man in the world. And a few people visiting her from Athens were very happy, because Socrates was an Athenian. They reached Socrates – he was old – before his death, before his murder, and said, "You should be happy; the oracle of Delphi has declared you the wisest man in the world."

Socrates said, "It is too late. When I was very young I used to think that I was very knowledgeable, very wise. The more I came to know, the more I became ignorant – aware that what I know is nothing, and what I do not know is so much. Now, in my old age, I can say without any hesitation that I do not know anything. The oracle, for the first time it seems, has missed."

The people were very much surprised, because Socrates should have been happy hearing it. They went back and the priestess again danced, fell into a trance. They asked her in the trance, "You said Socrates is the wisest man in the world, but he denies it. He says, 'I do not know anything…'"

And the priestess in her trance said, "That's why he is the wisest man in the world. Only idiots say that they know. Those who are wise cannot say that."

Places like these, or Bodh Gaya, should not be available to tourists – which is an ugly race with all their cameras, binoculars, and stupid things. And they are not interested in the place at all; they are taking photographs and rushing from here to there. Later on, sitting at home, they will look at the photographs and say, "Great! Our tour has been great. We visited beautiful places – you can see." But they were never there; they were with their cameras. They should sit there, should allow themselves to absorb the subtle vibe of the place… Something of Gautam Buddha must be there; it has to be there!

Falling Above the Mind

**Beloved Bhagwan,
What is madness?**

There are two possibilities:
Madness literally means going out of the mind; hence the two possibilities. You can go out of the mind either below the mind or above the mind.

Ordinarily, people go below the mind because it needs no effort, you don't have to do anything. Any shock can shatter the stability of your mind: somebody you loved died, your business has gone bankrupt – the shock is so much that you cannot keep your normality. You fall below the mind, your behavior becomes irrational.

But you go beyond the misery – if you had remained in the normal mind the shock would have created immense misery. It is a natural way to avoid the shock. It simply pulls you down; now you don't know what has happened. Your business has gone bankrupt, your wife has died or your child has died – it doesn't matter, in fact you don't even remember. You have entered into a new phase, you have become a new person. But it is going to be irrational, abnormal, unpredictable. This is ordinarily called madness, insanity, all over the world.

Only in the East have we found that there is another kind of madness, too, that comes from deep meditation: going beyond the mind. Both are outside the mind; hence there is some similarity. So sometimes you will find that the madman once in a while behaves almost as a wise man. He has insights – he has no control over them, they are just flashes, but sometimes he can see things which you cannot see.

In the East, where mind has been the sole center of all research down the centuries, we have discovered that you can go above the mind. Sufism accepts that state and calls it the state of a *masta* – a divine madman. He is mad, but he is superhumanly mad. His behavior is irrational as far as our logic is concerned. But perhaps there is a higher logic, according to which his behavior is not irrational.

In India such a man is called *paramhansa*. Ramakrishna, in the last century, was one of the men who was called paramhansa. The behavior of a paramhansa is utterly mad, but intensely beautiful, and has a depth which even the greatest genius of the mind does not have.

It happened that in Ramakrishna's time… He lived just outside Calcutta, on the bank of the Ganges in a small temple. Now many temples have arisen, and in Calcutta… At that time Calcutta was the capital of India, not New Delhi, so the cream of intellectuals, creative people, was in Calcutta. And anyway, Bengalis are the most intelligent people in India, mostly intellectual.

Keshav Chandra Sen was a great genius as far as intellect is concerned, and he was a co-founder of a religion, *Brahmasamaj* – the society of the divine. He was known all over India. Ramakrishna was not known, except to a few people in Calcutta on the riverbank where he lived. He was uneducated, and people thought he was mad – the people of the mind – because his behavior was not explainable by mental concepts.

But slowly, slowly his influence was increasing, particularly in Calcutta – which was very close; people could come to see him.

And Keshav Chandra Sen was worried that a villager, uneducated… And even professors of the universities were becoming devotees; they would touch his feet. And whatever he was saying was so ordinary. The man had nothing exceptional. One day finally he decided to go and argue with this man and finish this whole thing.

He went. Hundreds of people who knew Keshav Chandra and a few who knew Ramakrishna, they all gathered to see what would transpire. Ramakrishna's followers were very much afraid, knowing that Keshav Chandra could defeat anybody if it was a question of rationality. He had proved his mettle hundreds of times, all over India. He had defeated great scholars without much effort. Now, how was poor Ramakrishna going to stand up before him?

Everybody among the followers was nervous, but Ramakrishna was not. He was again and again asking, "Keshava has not come yet?" He would not use even his whole name: Keshav Chandra Sen. He would say simply, "Keshava has not come yet?"

Finally Keshav Chandra arrived with his great following. Ramakrishna hugged him. Keshav Chandra was not prepared for that. He had come to fight, and he made it clear to Ramakrishna, "These things won't help. I have come to discuss each and every point of your philosophy. Don't try to create a friendship. I have come as an enemy: either you defeat me and I will be your follower, or be ready to become my follower."

Ramakrishna said, "That we will be doing soon – hugging has nothing to do with it! I have always loved you. Whenever I have heard about you and your ideas, that you say there is no God…and I know there is God, but still I enjoy and love you. In fact your great intelligence is proof that existence is intelligent; otherwise from where does intelligence come? You are a proof to me that God is – but that we will discuss later on. What is the hurry? And there is no need for any enmity. The discussion can be in deep friendship.

"And you know, I am a poor man. I don't

know any logic. I have never discussed with anybody. It is going to be a very easy job for you, so you need not be so tense! I have prepared some sweet for you; first take the sweet. I have prepared it with much love. And then you can start your so-called discussion."

Keshav Chandra was finding it a little difficult. The man was strange; he offered him a sweet, he hugged him. He had already destroyed the animosity, the aggressiveness – in a very subtle way, without saying a word. And strangest of all, he says that my presence – that is, Keshav Chandra's presence – is enough proof of God, there is no need of other proof. Without God how is such intelligence possible? The world would be dead. The world is intelligent, and God is nothing but the intelligence of existence.

After taking his sweet, Ramakrishna said, "Now you start your game!" And Keshav Chandra was arguing against whatever he had found in Ramakrishna's small books – his followers collected his sayings and stories, anecdotes from his life. And Ramakrishna would enjoy it, and would say to his followers, "Look how beautifully he has criticized it!" And many times he would stand up and hug him and say, "You are a genius! Your criticism is perfect."

Keshav Chandra said, "I have not come here to get your approval; I have come to argue." Ramakrishna said, "I don't see there is any question of argument. You are the proof. I don't need to give any other proof; I can take you to the whole world as a proof that God exists – Keshav Chandra is the proof!"

Keshav Chandra had never come across such a man, and what he was saying had immense significance; it was penetrating Keshav Chandra's heart. And the presence of the man, and the way he behaved, his lovingness... Something happened to Keshav Chandra that his followers could not believe.

By the end of the discussion, Ramakrishna said, "You tell me who is defeated and who is victorious, and I will follow it. If you are victorious, I will become your follower. But I don't know the ways of discussion and I don't know the judgment. You judge; you are efficient enough to make the judgment. You can say to me, 'You are defeated,' and I am defeated."

And Keshav Chandra's followers were shocked to see that Keshav Chandra fell at the feet of Ramakrishna. They could not believe their eyes! When they had gone, everybody was asking, "Keshav Chandra, what happened to you?"

He said, "I don't know. One thing is certain, that that man has experienced something about which I have been only talking. I can talk efficiently, but he *has* it; he radiates it. I have that much intelligence at least to see the aura of the man, to feel the radiance of his love, to see his simplicity, sincerity; to see his trust, that he says to me that, 'You decide, and if I am defeated...' And he has not argued at all. How can you defeat a person who has not argued at all? On the contrary, he was appreciating my criticism and he was telling his disciples, 'Listen, this is the way a thing should be criticized.'

"And as I was sitting by his side, slowly, slowly something melted in me – the antagonism, the aggressiveness. And this is the first time this has happened with anybody. People think he is mad, but if he is mad, then I would like also to be mad. He is far superior to our so-called sanity."

It was very difficult to take Ramakrishna from one place to another place, because anywhere on the road, in the middle of the road... And Calcutta is a very overpopulated city, with more than ten million people in one city. And the traffic is the worst in the world. It is bound to be because thousands of people are walking; there are all kinds of vehicles – cars, trams, buses. He would start dancing in the middle of the road because something reminded him of God.

And anything could remind him of God…a beautiful child, and he would start dancing and singing. His followers would feel very embarrassed – they had to protect him from all sides – that in this traffic… And the police were bound to come, and that man was creating a traffic jam.

But outside India he would have been in a mad asylum because in the West madness is madness; there are no two categories. In India he became almost a divine being, a god, because people realized, slowly, slowly, that he looks irrational but there is something divine in his irrationality.

He had been doing things from his very childhood. His family was worried – what is going to happen to this child? People suggested – as it is customary in India and in other countries too – that it will be good to marry him so he will forget all about God and all about meditation and will become engaged in worldly affairs. But they thought that he would refuse – and that would have been the ordinary expectation. But he was a madman; he does not follow your expectations.

When his father asked, fearing that he is going to say no, Ramakrishna said with great joy, "Yes! But where is the girl?"

They said, "This boy is mad! This is not the right way. He is so ready… immediately! And he is asking, 'Where is the girl? To whom am I going to be married? Do it soon!'"

Just in a nearby village, another village, he was taken on a particular day to see the girl. And in India this is the way: the girl will come with some sweets to put on your plate, and that's the only moment you can see her – just for a moment – and decide.

When he was going to see his future wife, his mother had given him three rupees, just in case he needs them. When the girl came with the sweets, he looked at the girl, took out his three rupees and put them at her feet, touched her feet and said, "Mother, you are the right girl. I am going to marry you."

His father said, "You idiot, you don't understand that nobody calls his wife mother."

But everybody knew that he was a little eccentric – first putting those three rupees at the feet of the girl…everybody was shocked. And then touching her feet and telling the girl then and there, "Mother, you are really beautiful. I am going to marry you – it is settled."

But just by a very strange coincidence, the whole family of the girl wanted to deny this marriage because they said, "This boy is mad, and if he is starting this way what will happen in their married life nobody knows." But the girl insisted that if she will marry anybody, she will marry this man.

He was a beautiful man. So the family had to decide for the marriage. The marriage happened; they lived together their whole life. Ramakrishna continued to call her mother. There was never any husband-wife relationship between them. On the contrary… In Bengal they worship the mother goddess, Kali. So in those days when they worship the mother goddess all over Bengal – and in other places also, wherever Bengalis are in India…they are the only people in India left who still conceive of God as a mother.

In those days, every year he would put Sharda, his wife, naked on a throne and worship her – just as naked as the statue of the mother goddess is in the temples. He would not go to the temple; he would say, "When I have a living mother with me, why should I go and worship a stone statue?"

Anybody will say this is madness, sheer madness. But in so many ways his madness cannot be categorized with that of other mad people. His madness is beyond mind, not below mind. Each of his statements is of tremendous importance, simple but full of meaning. Just like a villager, he tells small stories. But those stories are so beautiful that you can get out of them much more meaning than out of a whole scripture. And his life…if you watch carefully, you will find that he is not an ordinary man; he is superhuman.

One day Ramakrishna and his followers are passing the Ganges in a boat and suddenly in the middle he starts crying, "Don't beat me! I have not done anything wrong. Why are you beating me?" And tears started flowing.

And his people said, "Nobody is beating you – what are you doing?" Even his own followers once in a while suspected that he was insane, because they were only followers. Nobody was beating him, and he was crying. And they could see from his face that he was being whipped very badly.

And he said, "You don't believe me? Just look at my back." They removed his clothes and they could not believe it: there were so many lines, blood oozing; he had been whipped badly. They could not believe… what to make of it? This man is mad and he is making his followers mad.

But when they reached the other shore, they found a man who had been beaten, and there was a crowd. And they looked at his back and they were surprised: the marks of the beating were exactly the same on both Ramakrishna's and this man's back.

Such oneness of feeling, that when somebody else is being beaten – innocently, he has not done anything – Ramakrishna becomes part of that person, they become one. This is not madness, this is a tremendous experience, a man of Himalayan heights… And although he was not a preacher, not a scholar, in everything that he says you can find the insight of the greatest men who have walked on the earth.

Of course his way is that of a villager….

One man came to Ramakrishna and said, "I am going to Varanasi to take a dip in the Ganges to get rid of my sins" – that's Hindus' belief.

Ramakrishna said, "Very good idea, you can go. But do you know that on the bank of the Ganges there are big, huge trees?"

The man said, "Yes, I know."

He said, "When you take a dip in the Ganges your sins will leave you, but they will sit on the trees. And how long can you remain under the water? You will have to come out, you will have to come home. And when you are dressed and ready to go home, those sins jump back on you. So it is futile, but it is up to you."

He will not say that this is stupid – that the Ganges cannot take your sins away. But he says it in his own way, without hurting the man's feelings. And he has said it in a beautiful way: "You can go. The Ganges will do its work, it will purify you – but how long you will remain in the Ganges? Sooner or later you will have to come out. And what do you think? Those trees are standing there, they are the resting places for the sins.

"And sometimes it happens that even other people's sins jump upon you. Seeing a better man, they change. So I will not suggest it. Find some other way. This is dangerous – so many people are taking a bath in the Ganges, and all their sins are on the trees; they get mixed up. And then it is up to them to choose.

"It is better to have your own sins. At least you are acquainted with them. You may come back with some new sins, more dangerous. "But I will not prevent you; I never prevent anybody. You can go and try, but I have told you the whole story. Nobody talks about the trees because the priests who are sitting on the banks of the Ganges, their whole business will flop if people come to know about the trees and the real secret. And sins, nobody can see, they are invisible; so they sit on the trees and wait."

This man, in India, became paramhansa. *Paramhansa* means literally "the greatest swan"...because in Indian mythology it is thought that the swan eats only pearls; that is his food. And the swan is the only bird in existence that if you put before him milk mixed with water he will drink the milk and leave the water behind. He has the capacity to discriminate between water and milk.

Paramhansa means "the greatest swan" who has become capable of discriminating between darkness and light, between right and wrong. It is not an effort on his part; it has become simply his nature. But his behavior may look mad.

This is my feeling, that there are many madmen in India who are really mad, who have not gone beyond mind – I have seen a few – but they are worshipped as paramhansas. Their irrational acts are interpreted by great scholars in such a way that they start having meaning. I have watched these people and they are really mad, they are not paramhansas.

Perhaps the case may be similar in the West; there may be a few paramhansas who are living in mad asylums, because you don't have any other category. Once a man starts behaving in a bizarre, berserk manner, he is mad. So on both sides there is confusion. But I think, still, the Eastern confusion is better. There is no harm in worshipping a madman;

you are not doing any harm. But to put a paramhansa into a madhouse and force him through medicines and injections and treatment to come back into the mind is real harm.

Western psychology has still no category for the second one, which it needs. But that category will arise only when it accepts supermind. Before Sigmund Freud it had not even accepted the unconscious mind – only the conscious mind. For thousands of years in the West there was no idea of the unconscious mind.

With Sigmund Freud, the unconscious mind became established. With Jung, the collective unconscious mind became established. Now somebody is needed to establish the cosmic unconscious mind. A tremendous field is available for any genius to establish it. Because in the Eastern psychology all these three are accepted, have been accepted for thousands of years.

And this is below the conscious mind. Above the conscious mind are also three: the superconscious, the collective superconscious, and the cosmic superconscious. On those, no work has been even started. The second category of madmen that I am talking about is somewhere in these three categories; certainly in the superconscious but perhaps if it grows deeper, it may become collective superconscious. And in a man like Ramakrishna it is cosmic superconscious.

When he was dying he had a cancer of the throat, and it became impossible for him to eat anything or drink anything. And his followers were telling him again and again, "You just close your eyes and tell the existence – it will listen to you." He would close his eyes, but would forget all about it. After a while, when he would open his eyes...the disciples were waiting; they would say, "What happened?"

He said, "Nothing, because when I close

my eyes everything becomes silent. What are you expecting to happen?"

They said, "We had asked you to ask existence...." Finally they forced his wife, Sharda: "Perhaps only you can persuade him."

Unwillingly, reluctantly, she asked him. With tears in her eyes she said, "I don't want to tell you to do *anything* because that is interfering, and my whole life I have never said a single word to interfere. You are far above; my hands cannot reach. But because these people are so deeply in anguish, I have agreed to say to you, just once: Close your eyes and ask existence, 'What are you doing to me? Remove this cancer from my throat.'"

He said, "Because you have never asked anything – every wife is asking everything, any day, every day; for your whole life you have never asked anything – and this is maybe my last day, or last days, I will fulfill it."

He closed his eyes, opened his eyes and said, "Sharda, I asked. And I heard a voice saying to me, 'Ramakrishna, can't you drink with other people's throats? Can't you eat with other people's throats? Do you necessarily need your own? Are you still attached to your own body?'

"And I said, 'No' – I had to say the truth. So the voice said, 'From now onwards, you eat with everybody's throat, drink with everybody's throat.'"

This is the stage of cosmic consciousness. This man may look mad, may behave in some ways which do not fit with our mind...and psychology has to find a place for this man, separate from the madman we know.

So there is a possibility of becoming mad below the mind, and with that too you can be on three levels. You can be mad, just unconscious; you can be mad collectively unconscious. And each step down you will become more and more mad. You can be mad at the level of the cosmic unconscious mind; that is the worst that can happen to a man. He will live just like a stone, a rock. He has lost all touch...he is so far away, miles away from consciousness.

Psychology has tried to pull these people back to the mind – not very successfully, but still, if the person has only fallen one step, it can pull him back. From the second step it becomes more difficult; and from the third step I don't think psychology has yet been able to find any way to pull the person back.

It is very difficult to pull the person down from superconsciousness, but it is possible. And psychology *is* doing it – at least in the West – with a few people who may not be mad in the ordinary sense.

For example, Vincent Van Gogh was kept for one year in a madhouse; and I don't think he was mad, he was painting things the way we don't know things are. During that one year in the madhouse he had painted his best paintings. And that is proof that he was perhaps in a higher state than the ordinary mind.

Perhaps he had reached the superconscious. In that one year he painted one painting in which the stars are spirals. And everybody laughed, "This is absolutely mad! Who has seen stars as spirals?" And just recently, a few days ago, physics has come to the same conclusion, that stars are spirals. It is because of the distance that we cannot see it. A hundred years after Van Gogh...

Perhaps that man, when we thought that he was mad, was on a higher level of consciousness and was capable of seeing one century ahead of science, with no instruments, with nothing; just with his pure consciousness – a visualization that stars are spirals.

There are other paintings in which he has painted strange things. Perhaps by and by we may come to know that they are not strange, they are exactly as he has painted them. In his whole life… After this one year he didn't live long, but he painted one painting in which trees are going higher than the stars. The stars are just on the way, and trees have passed them and are going higher. Even the painter's friends laughed, that "You are now making a fool of yourself! Trees going above the stars?"

Van Gogh said, "I don't know, but whenever I sit by the side of a tree I feel the ambition of the tree: it is the ambition of the earth to go beyond the stars. I don't know whether those trees are lying to me or I am deceived, but this happens every time I sit by the side of a tree. And I suddenly feel the tree is saying to me, 'I am the aspiration of the earth to go beyond the stars.'"

Perhaps man going to the moon, man going to Mars, man going to the stars, is also part of the same ambition, that the earth wants to go as far as possible, to enquire, to investigate.

Now, Van Gogh looks mad, but what he is saying is not absolutely senseless; it has a certain credibility about it. If in man there is a desire to reach to the stars, then in the trees also there must be a desire to reach beyond the stars, because we are all part of one life. Trees are a different expression, we are a different expression, but the life is the same.

You ask me, "What is madness?" Madness can be defined as either falling below the mind or falling above the mind. Falling below the mind is sickness; falling above the mind is health, wholeness.

Beloved Bhagwan,
For the past seven years I have heard You speaking about truth. But this is still an empty word for me. Often You say that one knows truth when one is silent inside. I know this delicious feeling that takes me over when I close my eyes and become quiet inside, but what is truth to do with that?

That *is* the truth.

Truth is not an object that you will find somewhere when you are silent. Truth is your subjectivity.

Just try to understand. *You* are there, and the whole world is there. Whatever you see is an object, but *who* is seeing it is the subject.

In silence all objects disappear – and the word 'object' has to be remembered; it is the same word as 'objection.' 'Object' means that which prevents you.

So all preventions, all objects, all objections, disappear; you have the whole infinity, and just silence. It is full of consciousness, it is full of presence, of your being. But you will not find anything as the truth – that will become an object. And truth is never an object.

Truth is subjectivity.

To discover your subjectivity – unhindered, unobjected to by anything, in its total infinity and eternalness – is the truth.

"The truth" is only a way of speaking; there is not something labeled "Truth," that one day you will find and open the box and see the contents and say, "Great! I have found the truth." There is no such box.

Your existence is the truth, and when you are silent you are in truth. And if the silence is absolute then you are the ultimate truth. But don't think of the truth as an object – it is not an object.

It is not there, it is here.

Beloved Bhagwan,

Since being with You so much growth and maturity has happened in me — I have changed in every aspect. At the same time, when I look into myself, I feel the same as I did when I was a little child.

Is this my witness, or something else?

It is your witness.

Just remember one thing, that the feeling of being a child can be experienced in two ways. You can be a witness and the experience of childhood can be an object. Then one more step is needed: you have to become the purity, the innocence of the child...not separate — you *are* it.

It will come. This is how it comes: first it comes as an object; you are still separate and watching it. This is beautiful and a great experience – that all rubbish is thrown out and you are feeling a very pure, innocent state – but you are still separate from it. Just go on witnessing it, and soon even the childhood will disappear, and there will be only the witness, the subjectivity. There will be only the mirror without mirroring anything. Then you have arrived home.

You can mirror beautiful things, and it is good, but when the mirror is absolutely empty...

One of the Buddhist scriptures has the name "The Empty Mirror." That exactly describes the ultimate state of consciousness, when you simply are and there is nothing – not even childhood, not even silence, not even peace, not even blissfulness...nothing that you can observe it.

This ocean of nothingness surrounding you is nirvana.

There is nothing more to explore.

There is nothing more to find.

But as it is going it is good: you *are* changing, and even to feel one's childhood is a great experience. But greater experiences are ahead. Don't stop, just continue till only you are left, alone, without a second.

Chapter 36
April 30, 1986, Morning

Wake Up
and You are It

Beloved Bhagwan,

When You speak about the many states on the way to enlightenment I am not even able to see where I am on the way. I always think I must be thousands of lifetimes away from the highest state. On the other hand, You are saying that it can happen now and here, for all of us. I cannot imagine that a quick change can be possible — from a state of unawareness like my own, to a state of total consciousness. In my reality I often see myself as an idiot, very stupid. I do have a taste of understanding, especially through Your so-called contradictions, but this understanding creates in me even more absurdities. For example: "The highest freedom is in the highest slavery."

I am totally confused — and at the same time, I am not. Even when I say that I don't believe in the unexpected happening here and now, I don't believe in my believing, because it might be just the tricky mind which has carried the memory of Your saying that enlightenment is the only thing that cannot be desired.

So I am here, just enjoying, grateful for Your being and Your words. To be one of so many people in the world to be allowed to sit by the feet of the most beautiful man in the world gives the insight that existence takes so much care of me that I cannot really be an idiot; at least I must be a blessed fool.

Please help me to know a little bit who I am.

A man asleep, can dream himself anywhere in the universe. From that point, to be awake will look thousands of lives away. But it is a dream; as far as the real sleep is concerned, awakening is just close by.

Any moment you can wake up.

Any situation can make you awake.

And the master's work is to create devices in which you can become awake. Sometimes very small things – just throwing cold water in your eyes will make you awake. Asleep you were so far away, but when you wake up then you will see that it was a dream that created the distance. Dreaming is the distance. Of course, for dreaming, sleep is necessary, but the moment you are awake sleep disappears, and with it the whole world of dreams too.

The truth is that awakening is the nearest reality to you, just by the side of you. It is not far away; hence it cannot be made a goal. All goals are dreaming, all achievements are dreaming. Awakening cannot be a goal because the man who is asleep cannot even think of what awakening can be. He cannot make, in his sleep, a goal of enlightenment – it is impossible. Or whatever he makes will be totally different from the reality of enlightenment.

Enlightenment is part of your waking consciousness.

In the East we have four layers of consciousness. First is the one we know as so-called wakefulness. It is not really wakeful, because just underneath it dreams are floating. Close your eyes and you will have a daydream. Close your eyes and you will immediately see – imagination takes over, and you start going away from this moment, from here. In reality you are going nowhere, but in your mind you can go anywhere.

So the first state is the so-called waking state; the second state is called sleep. We are aware of these.

The third is called the dreaming state, because sleep can be without dreaming; then it has a different quality. It is very peaceful, very silent, dark and deep…very rejuvenating.

So sleep is the second stage, below the so-called waking stage, and then comes the third stage, dreaming. Most of the time in your sleep you are dreaming. If you sleep eight hours, then six hours you are dreaming. Just here and there, like small islands, you are asleep; otherwise it is continuous dreaming.

You don't remember it, that's why people think this seems too much – six hours of dreaming and only two hours of sleep. You remember only the last dreams when you are waking up, because only with your waking up your memory starts functioning; so it catches only the tail end of your dream world. You don't remember all the dreams, but only the dreams that happen just before you are waking up – the morning dreams.

It was always understood in the East that these six hours of dreaming are as essential as those two hours of silent sleep. But in the West, within the last ten years for the first time new researches have proved the Eastern insight totally right. In fact, the new findings say that dreaming is even more essential than sleep, because in dreaming you are throwing out the rubbish of your mind.

The whole day the mind is collecting all kinds of words, all kinds of desires, ambitions – too much dust! It has to be thrown out. In the day you don't have any time to throw it out; you are gathering more and more. So in the night when you are asleep the mind has a chance to clean itself up. Dreaming is a kind of spring cleaning. But it is an everyday business: again you will collect, again you will dream, again you will collect…

These are the states known to us. The fourth is not named in the East but is simply called the fourth, *turiya*. It is a number, it is not a word. No name is given to it so that you cannot interpret it, so that your mind cannot play with it and deceive you. What can the mind do, just listening to the number four? The mind simply feels paralyzed. Give any name with meaning, then the mind has a way –

meaning is its way. But the number four has no meaning.

The fourth state is the real awakening. The fourth state has to be understood in reference to the other three states. It has something similar to the first, the so-called waking state. The so-called waking state is very thin, almost negligible, but it has some quality… The fourth consists only of that quality; it is *pure* awakening. You are fully awake.

It also has some similarity to the second stage – the sleep. Sleep has silence, depth, peacefulness, relaxation, but in a very small measure – just as much as is needed for day-to-day affairs. But the fourth has its totality: total relaxation, total silence, abysmal depth.

It has also some quality of the dream. The dream takes you far away from yourself. You may go to the moon in the dream, you may go to some star in the dream, although you remain here, in your bed. In reality you don't go anywhere, but in imagination – as long as you are dreaming – it looks absolutely real. You cannot think in a dream that it is a dream. If you can think in a dream that it is a dream, the dream will be broken – you are awake, and you cannot catch hold of the dream again.

One Sufi story about Mulla Nasruddin is that one night he dreams that an angel is giving him some money, "Because you are so virtuous, so wise, God has sent some reward for you." But as the mind is, he gives him ten rupees, and Mulla says, "This is not a reward – don't insult me." And slowly slowly he brings the angel up to ninety-nine rupees. But Mulla is stubborn; he says, "I will take a hundred or I will not take anything. What a miserly approach it is – and from God! You represent God and you cannot make it a hundred?"

He shouted so loudly, "Either a hundred or nothing!" that it woke him up. He looked all around – there was nobody, just he was sleeping in his bed. He said, "My God, I lost ninety-nine rupees unnecessarily, just being stubborn for one rupee more." He closed his eyes, tried hard, "Please come back, wherever you are. Ninety-nine is okay; even ninety-eight will do…ninety-seven is also all right – anything will do. You just come back! Where are you?"

He came back to one rupee, "I will take only one rupee…anything from God is great. I was foolish to call God a miser; in fact, I was greedy. Forgive me, and give me just one rupee." But the angel was not there.

You cannot catch hold of the same dream again; once you are awakened there is no way to catch hold of the same dream.

A dream takes you away from yourself; that's its basic quality. Perhaps that's why it cleanses you and helps you to have a certain relaxation: you forget your worries. For a few moments at least you can be in paradise, you can be in a situation you always wanted to be in.

The fourth stage also has something similar, but just similar. It also takes you away from yourself – but forever. You cannot come back to yourself. In the dream you cannot come back to the same dream; in the fourth stage you cannot come back to the same self. It takes you really so far away that you can be the whole universe. That's what the Eastern mystics have said: *Aham brahmasmi* – I have become the whole.

But you have to lose the self.

You cannot come back to it.

This fourth stage has been given different names. This is the most mathematical name, the fourth. It was given by Patanjali, who was a very scientific and mathematical mystic. His treatise has remained for thousands of years the only source of yoga. Nothing has been added, because nothing is needed. It is very rare that one person creates a complete system, so complete and so perfect that it is impossible to change anything in it.

In the West it used to be thought that Aristotle was such a person – he created logic, the whole system of logic alone, and for two thousand years it has remained the same. But in this century things have changed, because new discoveries in physics have made it absolutely necessary to find something better than Aristotle. The new findings in physics have created a problem, because if you follow Aristotle's logic then you cannot accept those findings. Those findings are against Aristotle's logic, but you cannot deny reality. Reality is reality! You can change the logic – which is man-made – but you cannot change the behavior of electrons. It is not in your power, it is existential. So a non-Aristotelean logic has grown up.

The second case was geometry. Euclid has reigned for hundreds of years as a perfect master as far as geometry is concerned, but in this century that too has got into trouble. Non-Euclidean geometries have evolved. They had to be evolved because of the new discoveries of physics. For example, you have heard that the closest distance between two points makes a straight line, but the discovery of the physicists is that there is no straight line at all. A straight line is impossible, for the simple reason that you are sitting on a global earth. You can draw a straight line here on the floor, but it is not a straight line because it is part of a circle. If you go on drawing it from both ends, one day they will meet somewhere and you will see that it has become a circle. So the small piece that you were thinking was a straight line was not a straight line; just it was just such a small part of a circle that you could not see the curve. The curve was invisible – it was so small, but it was there.

Where are you going to draw a straight line? – because all stars, all planets, everything is global, is round. So wherever you draw a line, howsoever small it is, it looks absolutely straight – even with scientific instruments you can see that it is straight – but go on making it bigger and bigger, and it will become a part of a circle. So it was an arc, not a straight line. In the same way everything from Euclid has been cancelled.

Patanjali remains the only person yet, and perhaps may remain the only person, who has created a whole science alone, and has remained for five thousand years without any challenge from any corner. He calls it the turiya, the fourth. He is so scientific a man that one simply feels amazed.

Five thousand years ago, he had the courage, the insight, the awareness, to say that God is only a hypothesis. It can help you to become awakened but it is not a reality, it is only a device. There is no God to be achieved; it is only a hypothesis.

A few people can be helped by hypotheses – they can use it – but remember, it is not a reality. And once you have become awakened, it disappears, the same way as when you wake up your dreams disappear. They were so real that sometimes it happens that even after you have awakened there is some effect left of the reality of the dream: your heart is beating faster, you are perspiring, trembling, still afraid. Now you know perfectly it was a dream, but you are still crying, your tears are there. The dream was non-existential, but it has affected you because for that period you had taken it to be real.

So it is possible. You can see the devotees crying before their god, emotionally very much affected, dancing, singing, worshipping, and feeling the truth of it, but is is just a hypothesis. There is nothing, no God, but these people are taking the hypothesis as a reality. One day when they will be awake, they will laugh at themselves, that it was only a hypothesis.

But there are other masters who have given different names according to their own philosophical background. A few have called it enlightenment: becoming full of light – all darkness disappears, all unconsciousness disappears – becoming fully conscious.

There are others who have called it liberation, freedom – freedom from yourself, remember. All other freedoms are political, social. They are freedom from somebody, from some government, from some country, from some political party; but it is always freedom *from*...

Religious freedom is freedom not from somebody else, but from yourself.

You are no more.

Because you are no more, a few masters in the East have called it *anatta* – no-selfness. Buddha called it nirvana – which is very close to anatta, no-selfness, or selflessness – just a zero, a profound nothingness surrounding you. But it is not emptiness, it is fullness: fullness of being, of ultimate joy, fullness of being blessed, fullness of gracefulness. All that you have known before is no more there; hence is it empty of all that. But something new, absolutely new you had not even dreamt about, is discovered.

Some have called it universal existence, but what name you give does not matter. I think the fourth still remains the best, because it does not lead you into mind trips; otherwise you are going to think about it, "What is emptiness? What is nothingness?" And nothingness can create a fear, emptiness can create a fear, anatta, no-selfness, can create a fear. The fourth is absolutely right.

Three stages you know; the fourth is just a little deeper. It is not far away.

The idea of being lifetimes away from it is a dream.

In reality it is just by the side...wake up and you are it.

Beloved Bhagwan,
I heard You saying that enlightenment is the transcendence of mind – conscious, unconscious, sub-conscious – and that one dissolves into the ocean of life, into the universe, into nothingness. I also hear You talking about the individuality of human beings. How can the individuality of an enlightened person manifest itself if he is dissolved in the whole?

The ordinary, unconscious human being has no individuality; he has only a personality. Personality is that which is given by others to you – by the parents, by the teachers, by the priest, by the society – whatever they have said about you. And you have been desiring to be respectable, to be respected, so you have been doing things which are appreciated, and the society goes on rewarding you, respecting you more and more. This is their method of creating a personality.

But personality is very thin, skin-deep. It is not your nature. The child is born without a personality, but he is born with a potential individuality. The potential individuality simply means his uniqueness from anybody else – he is different.

So first, remember that individuality is not personality. When you drop personality, you discover your individuality – and only the individual can become enlightened. The false cannot become the ultimate realization of truth. Only the true can meet with the true, only the same can meet the same. Your individuality is existential; hence when your individuality blossoms you become one with the whole.

Here is the question: if you become one with the whole, then how can you remain individual?

The problem is simply a non-understanding. The experience of becoming the whole is of consciousness, and the expression of it is through the body, through the mind. The experience is beyond the body/mind structure. When one becomes absolutely silent, goes into *samadhi,* reaches the fourth stage, he is not body, he is not mind. They are all silent – he is far above them. He is pure consciousness.

This pure consciousness is universal, just as this light in all these bulbs is one, but it can be expressed differently. The bulb can be blue, the bulb can be green, the bulb can be red; the shape of the bulb can be different. The body/mind are still there, and if the man of experience wants to express his experience, then he has to use the body/mind; there is no other way. And his body/mind are unique – only he has *that* structure, nobody else has that structure.

So he has experienced the universal, he has become the universal, but to the world, to the others, he is a unique individual. His expression is going to be different from other realized people. It is not that he wants to be different; he has a different mechanism, and he can only come through that mechanism to you.

There have been enlightened painters. They have never spoken because word was not their art, but they have painted. And their paintings are totally different from ordinary paintings, even of the great masters. Even the greatest master painters are unconscious people; what they paint reflects their unconsciousness.

But if a realized man paints, then his painting has a totally different beauty. It is not only a painting, it is a message too. It has a meaning to be discovered. The meaning has been given in code, because the man was capable only of painting, so his painting is a code. You have to discover the code, and then the painting will reveal immense meanings. The deeper you go into those meanings, the more and more you will find. The other paintings are just flat; they may be made by masters, but they are flat. The paintings made by a realized man are multidimensional, they are not flat. They want to say something to you. If the man is a poet, like Kabir, then he sings, and his poetry is his expression.

If the man is articulate in speaking the unspeakable, then he speaks; but his words will have a totally different impact. The same words are used by everybody, but they don't have that impact because they don't carry the same energy, they don't come from the same source. A man of experience brings his words full of his experience – they are not dry, they are not the words of an orator or a speaker. He may not know the art of speaking but no orator can do what he can do with words. He can transform people just by their hearing him. Just by being in the presence of him, just by letting his words rain over you, you will feel a transformation happening: a new being is born in you, you are reborn.

So when I say that even enlightened people have individuality, I mean that they remain unique – for the simple reason that they have a unique body/mind structure, and anything that comes to you has to come through that structure.

Buddha speaks in one way, Mahavira

speaks in another way. Chuang Tzu speaks in absurd stories – he is a great story-teller – but his stories, side by side, go on playing with your heart. The stories are so absurd that your mind cannot do anything.

That's the reason why he has chosen the stories to be absurd, so that your mind cannot come in between. With his absurd stories he stops your mind, and then his presence is available to you and to your heart; you can drink the wine he has brought for you. And he has put your mind away by telling you an absurd story. The mind is puzzled and is not functioning.

Many people have wondered why Chuang Tzu writes such absurd stories, but nobody has been able to explain the fact for the simple reason that the people who have been thinking about why he is writing the stories have no idea that it is a device to make the mind stop functioning – then you are available, fully available from your heart. He can contact you in that way.

But Buddha cannot tell an absurd story. He uses parables, but they are very meaningful. He does not want to avoid the mind… these are the uniquenesses of the people. He wants the mind to be convinced and then, through that conviction of the mind, he wants to go to your heart. If the mind is convinced it gives way. And Buddha's parables, his discourses, are all logical; the mind has to give way sooner or later.

Different masters… For example, Jalaluddin Rumi did nothing but whirling. He became enlightened after thirty six hours of continuous whirling, without any stop – non-stop whirling.

In fact every child likes to whirl. Parents stop him; they say, "You will fall. You may have a fit or you may get hit by something – don't do such a thing." But all children all over the world love whirling, because somehow while the child is whirling he finds his center.

Without finding the center you cannot whirl. The body goes on whirling, but the whirling has to happen on a center; so slowly, slowly he becomes aware of the center.

After thirty-six hours of continuous whirling, Rumi became absolutely clear about his center. That was his experience of the ultimate, the fourth. Then his whole life he was not doing anything but teaching whirling to people. It will look absurd to a Buddhist, it will look absurd to any other religion – because, what you can get out of whirling? It is a simple method, the simplest method, but it may suit you or it may not.

For example, for me it does not suit. I cannot sit on a swing; that is enough to create nausea in me. And what to say about sitting myself on a swing? I cannot see somebody else swinging! That is enough to give me a feeling of nausea. Now, Rumi is not for me. And there may be many people to whom whirling will give nausea, vomiting. That means it is not for them.

We *are* individually different. And there is no contradiction. One can experience the universal, and yet when the question of expression arises, he has to be individual.

Beloved Bhagwan,
The other morning I heard you saying that the so-called self is just an idea of the mind, because it seems hard for the mind to accept that our being is just pure nothingness, surprisingly containing the whole. Then who and what is the witness You talk about so much? Is it a masterly device which has to be dropped at some point?

WAKE UP AND YOU ARE IT

t is. Everything is a device, because the truth cannot be said. So only devices can be given. You have to be convinced about the devices, but they will have to be dropped at the last moment – but that does not mean that you have to drop them now! Dropping them now will not help; now you have to use them to their utmost possibility. And then that moment will come by itself...when the device has reached to the peak, it disappears – and you are in the experience of the fourth.

The whole problem arises because the truth cannot be said, so something has to be devised which will bring you to truth. And the device has to be such that it will not become an obstruction in itself. So the great master is one who gives you a device which is made in such a way that it is going to disappear automatically, autonomously, the moment you come close to truth.

There are many devices which are good but dangerous, because they can become obstacles. For example, I told you that Patanjali says God is a device. Nobody before him or after him has ever said that. There have been people who have said God is a truth, and there have been people who have said there is no God, but Patanjali's attitude is totally different from both. He is not a theist, he is not an atheist, he is simply a scientific mind. He says God is a hypothesis. The fight about its existence or non-existence is baseless – you don't fight about any other hypothesis.

But it is a dangerous hypothesis. Even in the life of a man like Ramakrishna it became an obstacle.

So the device is not going to leave you automatically at the right moment. It is dangerous – it will cling, it will obstruct your vision. It will take you to the final step, but it won't allow you to take it. A great attachment with the device itself will become the barrier.

Ramakrishna was a devotee of the mother goddess Kali, and not an ordinary devotee, not formal; he really loved her. Sometimes from the morning till the evening he would go on dancing and singing in the temple. And sometimes he would lock the temple for days together and not even go into it. It was reported...because the temple belonged to a very rich woman, Rani Rasmani; Ramakrishna was a paid servant, he was the priest. People said that it is not right that for a few days the temple does not even open. Other devotees come and have to go back because Ramakrishna is not in the mood to open the doors. And sometimes Ramakrishna is so much in the mood that the devotees get tired...

When you go into a temple you wait for *prasad* – the food that is offered to God has to be distributed to all the worshippers who are there. It is thought – *prasad* means grace – that it is God's grace and his gift. So people wait for it; but how long can they wait? This man goes on dancing, singing, from morning till evening... worshippers have come and gone, because the prasad can be distributed only when the priest has stopped worshipping.

And all priests are paid, so they are always in a hurry. In fact one priest will go to many temples, so he can get salaries from all those temples; so he is in such a hurry that he does as short a worship as is possible or acceptable, and immediately distributes the prasad and runs to another temple. There are so many temples in India that a priest can manage five, six temples, very easily. But Ramakrishna was not such a priest; he was really a lover. To him the goddess was not just a statue, and the worship was not just a ritual; it was a reality, not a dream.

The owner of the temple, Rasmani, called him and asked him, "What is the matter? I have been hearing different kinds of complaints about you. One is that sometimes you worship the whole day. In what scripture is this written?"

Ramakrishna said, "I don't know any scripture, and I had made it clear even before you employed me that I am uneducated. I don't know any scripture, I know only devotional songs – so I sing. And to me it is not a question of worshipping for a certain time. Time disappears – I don't have any idea. Once I am in it, I don't know when the morning has become evening. So if you don't want me, I can leave. But I am going to be this way."

Rasmani said, "This is not the only complaint – because this can be allowed. The whole day worshipping…there is no harm. But sometimes you don't open the doors of the temple."

He said, "That's true. Sometimes I get angry at the goddess. I love her, but she does not listen to me, and once in a while – after all, I am a human being – I get cross, so I say, 'Okay, remain closed for two, three days. That will bring you to your senses.' No food, no worship! But if you have any trouble with this, I can leave."

Rasmani could not tell him to leave – the man was so beautiful and so authentic, and what he was saying had a beauty of its own. Even not opening the doors was part of a love affair, just the quarrel of lovers. She said, "Even that can be allowed, because I want you to be here. But one thing is very bad: I hear that before offering the food to the goddess you taste every sweet yourself."

He said, "That's true, because my mother used to make these sweets" – and Bengalis make the best sweets in India – "she would make them and then she would taste them. If they were really good then she would will give some to me, give some to my father; otherwise not – she would make them again. My wife prepares the sweets. She prevents me, 'This is not right. First they have to be offered to the goddess and then they can be distributed.' But I cannot offer anything which is tasteless or is not made well; I have to taste them first. If you don't want it, I am ready to go, but I will continue in the same way."

The man was very simple, and what he was saying was a beautiful thing: he cannot offer to the goddess something that may not be the best. Only the best should be offered, but how to find out? – one has to taste it.

He worshipped in Dakshineswar, near Calcutta, his whole life. Towards the end of his life, just a few years before he died, he told the goddess one morning, "Now the doctors are saying that I have cancer of the throat. It is not growing but it can start growing any moment, and before I die I want to experience the truth. I am ready and I will do everything: I will dance today before you, sing before you." In every temple of mother Kali there always hangs a big sword, because in the past that sword was used – and it is still used in the main temple of Calcutta – to cut off the heads of animals as sacrifice.

Ramakrishna was not doing that, but the sword had become part of the temple. He said, "If by the evening I don't have the experience, I will take the sword and kill myself – the responsibility will be yours."

A few worshippers were there. They rushed out and told everybody, "That madman is going to do something… Now this is too much. All that he was doing before was okay, but now he is going to kill himself!"

A great crowd assembled in the temple, and Ramakrishna danced madly, sang madly, the whole day. And as the sun was setting he pulled out the sword and said to the goddess, "So I am going to cut off my head as a sacrifice to you. Either the experience – or my head will be at your feet." And as he was going to cut himself with the sword, the sword fell from his hands and he fell down on the floor. He remained there for six hours; to the outside world he was unconscious, but in his own experience he was in *samadhi,* in a beautiful state, utterly silent and blissful. And after six hours when he was woken up, he awoke with tears and he said, "Why have you woken me up? You should have left me in the same state."

Just a few days afterwards there was a master passing by who heard about Rama-krishna, that he had a six-hour samadhi. The master came. Ramakrishna was a very humble man; he touched the feet of the master and said, "Help me, because I attained that experience but it was only for six hours – then I was back to my old state."

The master said, "You don't understand, it was not a real experience. You forced that experience upon yourself by your stubborness because you were going to kill yourself. After dancing the whole day and singing, your mind simply stopped, seeing the situation – 'The man is going to kill himself!' It had nothing to do with Kali or anybody; it was simply the stopping of the mind. And that experience was only an experience of when mind is not chattering, and you feel immense silence and beauty and joy. If you really want the ultimate experience, the fourth, then you will have to do one thing which is very hard, and that is to cut all attachment with the mother goddess.

"That is your problem. You have passed all other barriers, but now this last barrier is the most difficult because you have staked everything on her. So do as I say: you sit in meditation, close your eyes, and when you see the mother Kali arising near your third eye – which is going to happen…"

He said, "Yes, it happens. Whenever I close my eyes she *is* there."

So he said, "That's good. That is the moment…this time you are not to cut *your* head; take the sword and cut the mother goddess in two pieces."

Ramakrishna said, "My God, that is very difficult! I cannot hurt her – and you are telling me to kill her!"

But the man said, "Unless you do it, you will never attain. You try it and see."

He would close his eyes, tears would flow from his eyes, and there was great joy on his face, and radiance. He would open his eyes, and the master would ask, and he would say, "Yes, I saw her, but I forgot all about killing her – she is so beautiful, and the attachment is so long…as long as I can remember." He was very small when he became the priest.

Two or three times he tried.

The master said, "This is the last time. If you cannot do it, then I will do it. I have brought this piece of glass. When I see that tears have started flowing from your eyes I will know that you are seeing the mother goddess. I will cut your forehead with the sharp piece of glass to remind you that this is the time: you do the same, cut her in two pieces. It is just your idea – there is nobody else. It is just a hypothesis."

The master had to cut his forehead, and the mark remained for his whole life. Blood started flowing over his face, but deep inside he managed to gather courage and cut the mother goddess in two pieces.

And as she fell in two pieces, it was as if a door had opened and the whole universe was his.

It took six days for him to come back. The first words that he uttered when he came back are immensely important. He said, "The last barrier has fallen."

Any device can become a barrier too. It may help you to get rid of other things, but finally you have to get rid of it – and that may be a difficult thing. It was so difficult for Ramakrishna. And that was the last day... never again did he go into the temple. Afterwards he lived three, four years; he simply forgot all about Kali.

But there are devices which will not create such a trouble, and there are devices which will fall automatically. The moment when you are reaching to the climax of your being they will simply fall down.

I call a master a great master, the perfect master, who creates devices which are going to fall on their own accord when the moment has come for the person to experience the ultimate. Other devices are created by smaller people. Perhaps they don't know that these devices can become attachments themselves.

So everything I say is a device. My speaking to you is a device so that you can just be here – your mind is engaged, listening to me, and something invisible can go on transpiring between me and your hearts. That's the real thing.

The words will help the mind to remain engaged. They are like just toys. When you don't want children to disturb you – you are studying – you give them toys and they start playing with the toys, so you can do your work or study or do anything you want to do, and the children won't come to you to bother you and ask you questions and this and that.

The mind is just like a child.

The words are just toys for the mind – not truths, but simply toys. But while the mind is engaged something can happen from my depth to your depth. You may not understand it, but it will start bringing changes in you, transformations in your being.

Sometimes simply sitting silently with me

...but then there is always the problem that your mind will disturb you. I have tried sitting in silence with you, and I have seen that the problem is, I can reach your heart less; your mind is disturbing you too much. Speaking seems to be a better device: your mind remains engaged, and once in a while if I give a gap between two words, the mind does not disturb. The mind simply looks and waits: "What is going to happen? What is going to be said?"

And meanwhile the real work is happening. The real work is from my heart to your heart.

Chapter 37
April 30, 1986, Evening

Beloved Bhagwan,

It feels very dangerous to me, the way Your therapists are working at the moment: claiming to be on the same level as You are, and doing the same work. What they say they have to offer — flying schools and "freedom" — sounds very appealing to the ego, but doesn't seem to have any connection with Your work.

I'm concerned that innocent people, wanting to be closer to You and wanting spiritual guidance, will put their trust in these people who have authority as Your chosen therapists.

We saw with Sheela what happens with the misuse of worldly power. The misuse of spiritual power seems a far greater menace as it works with people's very beings.

You have always said that this is what happens when a master leaves his body. Is there any advice You can give now so that history will not repeat itself this time?

Each Moment Is Insecure

The unconscious human mind is the cause of the whole trouble.

There have been people around me who were doing all kinds of things – there were doctors, there were dentists, there were plumbers, there were carpenters – but none of them got such an ego as the people who were working as therapists.

Therapy basically has nothing to do with spirituality. I was using it just to clean the rubbish that the mind has gathered down the ages. The work of the therapist with me was exactly that of cleaners, nothing superior to them in any way. But in the West therapy has connotations of spirituality because there is nothing in the name of spirituality. There is a vacuum, and therapists seem to fill it.

It is only apparently so. They don't fill the gap, they cannot; they themselves have no spiritual experience. All that they know are certain techniques through which your mind can be cleaned. But even that cleaning of the mind makes you feel fresh only for a few days, because it does not change the base, the foundation of your being; it simply cleans the surface. You remain the same person. You will again collect the same garbage, so therapy will be needed again and again and again.

The same is true about every other kind of psychotherapy, psychoanalysis, analytical psychology – they are just different names. There is not a single person in the whole world that psychologists can claim is purified – now there is no need for him to go through analysis, therapy, or any kind of processing.

Even the psychotherapists, psychoanalysts have to go through therapy, analysis, be under some psychotherapist once in a while, because they are also collecting garbage. In fact they are collecting more because so many people are unloading themselves in their therapy sessions, and it is bound to affect the therapist. People will become a little lighter, but the therapist will become a little heavier – he will need therapy himself. This is a vicious circle.

My effort was to bring the West closer to the East. The East has developed spiritual techniques, but when those techniques were developed, man was not so loaded with knowledge, degrees, and all kinds of meaningless garbage. Those techniques were developed for innocent people.

Now the situation is different: if you give those techniques directly to the people, the people are so loaded that in their garbage your techniques will be lost.

My understanding was, and still is, that therapy can be a good beginning, but it is not the end, it is not the answer. It can clean the mind only for a short period, but in that short period a spiritual technique can be introduced to you before the mind gets loaded again.

If the spiritual technique is introduced to you, then that garbage is not going to disturb you; it cannot create confusion, and you do not need any therapy anymore. You are on the way – now this ordinary garbage cannot prevent you.

But if you are loaded already, then to introduce you to a spiritual technique is futile; it is throwing seed onto stones. The seed is not going to live, to become a plant, to become a tree, to blossom.

So I was using these therapies just for the moment to clean the ground and let me put in the seed. Then we are not worried about the garbage that you will be collecting. The seed has enough force; once it has found its soil, there is no problem. It will bring its branches and foliage, its fruits and its flowers, in spite of all the garbage around – that doesn't matter.

But I was aware of the danger – that these therapists themselves have no spirituality, and they will start feeling as if they are guides, spiritual guides; as if they are helping so many people on the path. It is so easy to blow your ego up bigger and bigger.

These therapists came from the West to me because in the West therapy was going out of fashion. People were tired, because what is the point? – for a few days you feel great and then come the dumps. You feel worse than before. Then to go again to the therapist becomes a kind of addiction.

And there is no end to it. People go on moving from one therapy to another therapy their whole life, always feeling, "This is going to work." And it seems to work for a while, but it does not change anything basic, just superficial touches, so you are again back to zero.

All these therapists had failed in the West; nobody was coming to them. When they came to me they had no need to search for clients: thousands of sannyasins were coming, and I wanted a certain synthesis between Western methods of therapy and spiritual growth, so I allotted them the work.

But these therapists forgot completely that the people had not come for their therapies. In fact people were very unwilling to do their therapies; I had to persuade them. But slowly people started understanding the fact that just a little cleaning helps to take a long jump into meditation. So the people who passed through therapies went deeper into meditation than the therapists. The therapists were going deeper into their egos.

The therapists were not meditating. They were not asking questions, because to ask a question means that you are ignorant, you do not know the answer to it; they were not even humble enough to ask a question. And they were happy, tremendously happy that now there was no burden on them of finding people. People were coming by themselves, and I was sending them to their therapies.

I made them great therapists. I tried to refine their methods to make them the best possible therapists. I used to meet every therapy group and ask the people who had participated how they were feeling, what had happened. And indirectly – and the therapist was present – I was suggesting what more could be done, what should have been done. I was also asking the therapist what difficulties he was finding, what problems were arising with people – in an indirect way, because I don't want to hurt anybody, even by giving advice.

Through the years I had worked on these therapists and their therapies, and they started feeling that they had become kinds of gurus, masters. And deep down there was great competition amongst them: Somendra left because of his competition with Teertha about who was a better therapist – just fights of egos.

Deep down, unconsciously, they must be thinking that sooner or later I will have to die. Teertha had taken it for granted, without anybody saying it to him, that he was going to be my successor. Perhaps he was spreading the idea that he was going to be my successor.

The day I announced in the commune that nobody is going to be my successor, only two persons were unhappy – and I looked at both the persons: one was Sheela and the other was Teertha. Everybody was happy, rejoicing, but these two people were sad. That was their aim – perhaps not consciously, but unconsciously. That was the beginning of Sheela trying to destroy the commune in different ways.

And when the American government… Now all the governments of the world are together in a conspiracy against a single man; they have made me so important, so powerful. They are just behaving so idiotically. They have all the powers; I have no power, and they are all conspiring against me. Their whole effort is to stop me, my work, not to let me settle anywhere, not to allow another commune to come into existence.

Our therapists are immensely happy, seeing the opportunity that now I don't have a commune, and every government is against me; perhaps I will not find a place anywhere in the world. This is a great chance for them.

And all the sannyasins are in a state of vacuum, so these therapists are trying to exploit that vacuum. Now they are telling people that they will teach them freedom, they will teach them spirituality, they will teach them this and that; their whole effort is not to miss this opportunity.

The people are in a need because suddenly…they were working, growing, and the work has stopped. I am being prevented from every direction, so that I cannot work. And the therapists are immensely happy: they have suddenly become spiritual masters. They know nothing about spirituality, not even the ABC.

But there is nothing to be worried about. They can only talk about freedom, and that too will be just a repetition of what they have heard me say to you. They don't have anything original to say, anything coming out of their own experience, so they can only talk. Let them talk – the talk is not going to change people. And soon people will feel that these therapists are just exploiting the situation.

Meanwhile, somewhere we are going to create the mystery school. Existence cannot be so uncompassionate towards a man who has been working simply for truth, simply for existence.

My trust is absolute.

These governments and churches don't matter at all. They may try their best, but the mystery school will be established, although it may take a little time, a little trouble. And this time things will be done in a totally different way so nobody gets this idea of gurudom.

History will not be repeated, because I am still here. I know all those therapists, and I know their problems. I know they are in the same boat as their clients; they are not in any way of superior consciousness. They can give consultations, they can help people to some clarity, but that is from their *knowledge*. In the same situation they don't have that clarity.

To everybody else they can show the way of clarity: it is very easy when you are not in trouble. You can simply advise anybody, "It is simple. Do it this way." The real thing is, when you are in the same trouble, whether you have the clarity, whether you are capable of following your own advice – and those therapists are not capable of that. So there is no harm. Let them enjoy a few days of glory.

They are not even mentioning my name.

That is enough proof that they know that whatever they are saying and doing is related to me, and if they mention my name they will become immediately secondary. And for the first time they have got the chance to be on the top. With me, it was impossible.

So I don't see that there is any problem. It is good – let them enjoy for a few days. Their enjoyment is not going to last long. Soon they will lose the people.

Once the mystery school starts functioning nobody is going to bother about them. Even they themselves will have to come to the mystery school, and this time not as therapists but simply as disciples. There is not going to be any therapy. Now the school will function in a totally different way.

**Beloved Bhagwan,
What are the qualities of a mature person?**

The qualities of a mature person are very strange.

First, he is not a person. He is no more a self. He has a presence, but he is not a person.

Second, he is more like a child – simple and innocent.

That's why I said the qualities of a mature person are very strange, because maturity gives a sense as if he has experienced, as if he is aged, old. Physically he may be old, but spiritually he is an innocent child. His maturity is not just experience gained through life. Then he will not be a child, and then he will not be a presence; he will be an experienced person – knowledgeable but not mature.

Maturity has nothing to do with your life experiences. It has something to do with your inward journey, experiences of the inner.

The more he goes deeper into himself, the more mature he is. When he has reached the very center of his being, he is perfectly mature. But at that moment the person disappears, only presence remains…

The self disappears, only silence remains.

Knowledge disappears, only innocence remains.

To me, maturity is another name for realization: you have come to the fulfillment of your potential, it has become actual. The seed has come on a long journey, and has blossomed.

Maturity has a fragrance. It gives a tremendous beauty to the individual. It gives intelligence, the sharpest possible intelligence. It makes him nothing but love. His action is love, his inaction is love; his life is love, his death is love. He is just a flower of love.

The West has definitions of maturity which are very childish. The West means by maturity that you are no longer innocent, that you have ripened through life experiences, that you cannot be cheated easily, that you cannot be exploited, that you have within you something like a solid rock – a protection, a security.

This definition is very ordinary, very worldly. Yes, in the world you will find mature people of this type. But the way I see maturity is totally different, diametrically opposite to this definition. The maturity will not make you a rock; it will make you so vulnerable, so soft, so simple.

I remember… A thief entered a master's hut. It was a full-moon night, and by mistake he had entered; otherwise, what can you find in a master's house? The thief was looking, and was amazed that there was nothing. And then suddenly he saw a man who was coming with a candle in his hand.

The man said, "What are you looking for in the dark? Why did you not wake me up? I was just sleeping near the front door, and I could have showed you the whole house." And the man looked so simple and so innocent, as if he could not conceive that anybody could be a thief.

Before his simplicity and innocence, the thief said, "Perhaps you do not know that I am a thief."

The master said, "That doesn't matter, one has to be someone. The point is that I have been in the house for thirty years and I have not found anything, so let us search together! And if we can find something, we can be partners. I have not found anything in this house – it is just empty."

The thief was a little afraid – the man seems to be strange. Either he is mad or…who knows what kind of man he is? He wanted to escape, because he had brought things from two other houses that he had left outside the house.

The master had only one blanket – that was all that he had – and it was a cold night, so he told that thief, "Don't go this way, don't insult me this way; otherwise I will never be able to forgive myself, that a poor man came to my house in the middle of the night and had to go empty-handed. Just take this blanket. And it will be good – outside it is so cold. I am inside the house; it is warmer here."

He covered the thief with his blanket. The thief was just losing his mind! He said, "What are you doing? I am a thief!"

The master said, "That does not matter. In this world everybody has to be somebody, has to do something. You may be stealing; that doesn't matter, a profession is a profession. Just do it well, with all my blessings. Do it perfectly, don't be caught; otherwise you will be in trouble."

The thief said, "You are strange. You are naked and you don't have anything!"

The master said, "Don't be worried, because I am coming with you! Only the blanket was keeping me in this house; otherwise in this house there is nothing – and the blanket I have given to you. I am coming with you – we will live together. And you seem to have many things; it is a good partnership. I have given my all to you. You can give me a little bit – that will be right."

The thief could not believe it. He just wanted to escape from that place and from that man. He said, "No, I cannot take you with me. I have my wife, I have my children, and my neighbors, what will they say? – 'You have brought a naked man!'"

He said, "That's right. I will not put you in any embarrassing situation. So you can go, I will remain in this house." And as the thief was going, the master shouted, "Hey! Come back!"

The thief had never heard such a strong voice; it went just like a knife. He had to come back.

The master said, "Learn some ways of courtesy. I have given you the blanket and you have not even thanked me. So first, thank me – it will help you a long way. Secondly, going out – you opened the door when you came in – close the door! Can't you see the night is so cold, and can't you see that I have given you the blanket and I am naked? Your being a thief is okay, but as far as manners are concerned, I am a difficult man. I cannot tolerate this kind of behavior. Say thank you!"

The thief had to say, "Thank you, sir," and he closed the door and escaped. He could not believe what had happened! He could not sleep the whole night. Again and again he remembered…he had never heard such a strong voice, such power. And the man had nothing!

He enquired the next day and he found out that this was a great master. He had not done well – it was absolutely ugly to go to that poor man; he had nothing. But he was a great master.

The thief said, "That I can understand myself – that he is a very strange kind of man. In my whole life I have been coming in contact with different kinds of people, from the poorest to the richest, but never…even remembering him, a shivering goes through my body.

"When he called me back I could not run away. I was absolutely free, I could have taken the things and run away, but I could not. There was something in his voice that pulled me back."

After a few months the thief was caught, and in the court the magistrate asked him, "Can you name a person who knows you in this vicinity?"

He said, "Yes, one person knows me" – and he named the master.

The magistrate said, "That's enough – call the master. His testimony is worth that of ten thousand people. What he says about you will be enough to give judgment."

The magistrate asked the master, "Do you know this man?"

He said, "Know him? We are partners. He is my friend. He even visited me one night in the middle of the night. It was so cold that I gave him my blanket. He is using it, you can see. That blanket is famous all over the country; everybody knows it is mine."

The magistrate said, "He is your *friend*? And does he steal?"

The master said, "Never! He can never steal. He is such a gentleman that when I gave him the blanket he said to me, 'Thank you, sir.' When he went out of the house, he silently closed the doors. He is a very polite, nice fellow."

The magistrate said, "If you say so, then all the testimonies of the witnesses who have said that he is a thief are cancelled. He is freed." The master went out and the thief followed him.

The master said, "What are you doing? Why are you coming with me?"

He said, "Now I can never leave you. You have called me your friend, you have called me your partner. Nobody has ever given me any respect. You are the first person who has said that I am a gentleman, a nice person. I am going to sit at your feet and learn how to be like you. From where have you got this maturity, this power, this strength, this seeing of things in a totally different way?"

The master said, "Do you know that night how bad I felt? You had gone; it was so cold. Without a blanket sleep was not possible. I was just sitting by the window seeing the full moon, and I wrote a poem: 'If I was rich enough I would have given this perfect moon to that poor fellow, who had come in the dark to search for something in a poor man's house. I would have given the moon if I had been rich enough, but I am poor myself.' I will show you the poem, come with me.

"I wept that night, that thieves should learn a few things. At least they should inform a day or two ahead when they come to a man like me, so we can arrange something, so they don't have to go empty-handed.

"And it is good that you remembered me in the court; otherwise those fellows are dangerous, they may have mistreated you. I offered that very night to come with you and be partners with you, but you refused. Now you want... There is no problem, you can come. Whatever I have I will share with you. But it is not material: it is something invisible."

The thief said, "That I can feel – it is something invisible. But you have saved my life, and now it is yours. Make whatever you want to make of it. I have been simply wasting it. Seeing you, looking in your eyes, one thing is certain – that you can transform me. I have fallen in love from that very night."

Maturity to me is a spiritual phenomenon.

Beloved Bhagwan,
Often I hear You saying that we can wake up any moment. Your words, and how You say them, thrill me so much that I often start shaking. What is really preventing me from waking up? Is the unconscious really so mighty? Do I need more and more dry cleaning?

The unconscious is certainly very powerful and immense. It is your whole past, from the very beginning. All that has happened in existence is part of your unconscious. It is as long and infinite as your past – but so is your superconscious. It is as long and as infinite as your future. You are just in the middle – you are always in the middle.

The past is very powerful because it has already happened, so it has left its marks on you. The future is not so powerful because it has not happened yet; it is only a possibility. The past is a reality; it is a history. Your unconscious is your history, and tremendously vast; your superconscious, which means awakening, is only a probability. You can go on postponing it.

And that's what your past manages to do. It goes on telling you the idea is good – one *has* to wake up, you have to try it – but all these are the ways of postponing. The past goes on questioning how to wake up. The idea is appealing, but *how* to wake up? That "how" is also a way of postponing. So when I say, "Wake up!" something in your superconscious gets stirred and a thrill goes through you.

The unconscious is a very thick wall, but it cannot prevent you from waking; it can only postpone it – and that too depends how deeply you are listening to me, whether you are only hearing or listening. And remember the distinction between these two words.

Hearing is simple, everybody who has ears can hear, but listening is something more than hearing. Listening means hearing without your mind coming in between, interpreting, meddling, giving colors of its own to what you have listened to, bringing connotations, associations from your past – that is, from your unconscious.

When I say, "Wake up!" I have one meaning. If you *hear* it you may have a different meaning, but if you *listen* to it then you will have the same meaning as I have. Listening means putting the mind aside, so what is being transferred to you goes directly to your very heart, to your very being.

Then perhaps you can wake up any moment. Any small thing may trigger it. It is unpredictable; one cannot say when, one cannot say what will help. I can only go on explaining in different ways so the meaning of waking gathers around you. Then *anything*...

People have become enlightened, awakened, in strange situations – there is no causal relationship. Lao Tzu became enlightened when he was sitting under a tree and a dry leaf started falling from the tree. There was no strong wind so the leaf was falling very slowly, like a feather, and he simply watched it falling. And as it rested on the ground, something happened in him which had nothing to do with the leaf.

He simply saw the way of the leaf, its let-go – no effort to cling a little longer with the tree. It had been with the tree its whole life, but not even a look back, no hurry to reach anywhere, just a tremendous let-go, that wherever the wind takes it... A great trust. All these things, with the dropping of the dry leaf, happened in Lao Tzu. From that day he was a different man.

The master can only do one thing: he can go on spinning around you meanings of a thousand kinds. Perhaps one of them may trigger the process, but nothing can be said about what was the trigger; it depends on so many things that it is unpredictable. But howsoever big the unconscious may be, its value is nothing.

Waking up, even for a single moment, has tremendous value, and remaining awakened you have become an emperor in existence.

To live unconsciously is to be just a beggar.

Beloved Bhagwan,
There is an old saying that, "You are what you eat." But in California it's, "You are what you drive," in Italy it's, "You are what you wear," and in France, "You are what you drink."
The other day someone said, "You are what you are," and then I thought, "You aren't who you think you are." Bhagwan, I'm getting confused – who are I?

Y ou simply are not!
Don't get confused, because there is nobody. All these definitions are a futile exercise because it is defining something which does not exist. You are not, so no definition can define you. Your nothingness is your inde-

finability. It makes you infinite, it makes you eternal, it makes you part of the unknowable mystery of existence.

Anything that can be defined is worthless.

Beloved Bhagwan,
Those of us who have the good fortune to be with You on Your visits to various countries over the past few months have had with us constantly the reminder of how precious our time with You is. It has been impossible to slip into complacency and imagine that You will be with us indefinitely.

Living in such insecurity could send us into a panic – a self-defeating reaction because it renders us unavailable to those moments we *do* have with You. The alternative is to ride on the uncertainty we live with to sharpen our awareness and soften our hearts, and thus be more open to You than we have ever been.

I see You – who represent everything of value to be contributed to the world, who are the most magnificent expression of existence's fulfillment – accept with grace and dignity and humor whatever that same existence ordains.

Then how can *I* be anything but gracious, and grateful for what has been, for what is right now, and for what might be in the future, even if it is not of our choosing?

It is a great opportunity for you all.

I have been saying my whole life that we are all living in insecurity. You have listened to it, you thought you had understood it, but it was not the case.

Now it is the reality. I need not even say to you that each moment is insecure.

In fact that's how it is always. All these stupid governments have just made it more clear to you that each moment is uncertain, insecure; you cannot take me for granted.

But this has not to make you afraid, to panic, to be sad, to be worried, because all those things will not change the insecurity. All those things will simply make you forget the insecurity, and they will help you to miss the present moment – which you have got already, which is secure. The next moment may be insecure.

So I would like to say to you: use the moment that is secure to the fullest, and don't be bothered with the next moment; it is always insecure. In our situation it has become more apparent. And it is good that it has become more apparent. That will throw you into the present moment; otherwise one can be sleepy. One knows tomorrow is there.

But in the situation in which we are, tomorrow is not certain; anything can happen tomorrow. But don't panic, because that is not going to change the situation. That is simply missing the opportunity.

And I can understand, it is difficult to live in such insecurity. But this is the reality, it is not a special case. The whole world is living in the same insecurity, only they are not in such a situation where the insecurity is so clear that there is no need to say anything about it. It is there; it is everywhere. There is no distinction at all, no differentiation, only you are fortunate because you cannot miss this moment. You know tomorrow I may be taken away from you. You cannot afford to miss this moment; this is all you have got, so you have to drink of me.

Coming here and going from here I pass a room in which there is a beautiful carving of The Last Supper. Jesus and his followers must be in a deep insecurity – tomorrow anything is possible. But you are even more in insecurity, because they knew what was going to happen tomorrow. It was well known that Jesus would be crucified; hence this was the last supper with the master. They would not be eating with him again. So in a way it was not so insecure; it was certain – tomorrow he is going to be crucified. There was a certainty.

Even that certainty is not here. Anything can happen tomorrow – to me, to you. As far as I am concerned, I know that this is something that was bound to happen. Sooner or later the whole world was going to be against me, because I was fighting against the whole rotten world.

It is a wonder that they tolerated so much. They can destroy me very easily, they can shoot me, but they are afraid: if they kill me, then they will make the biggest religion in the world ever. Jesus had only a dozen followers but his crucifixion gained so many sympathizers – if they kill me it will go against them, so they cannot kill me.

All they want is to cripple me, to create such a situation that I cannot enter any country, that people cannot come to meet me, that I am isolated from the news media, that the people who are working for me get tired, harassed so much so that they start thinking, "This is too much," so the whole work stops…because I cannot do the whole work. The work can stop, and I can be isolated, because if they close the doors of all the countries wherever I go, if they start closing the doors there…

Now they are doing it here. And I am amazed: I had never thought that even departments of justice are nothing but cunning politicians. They arrested me in North Carolina without any arrest warrant. They would not tell me even the reason why they were arresting me – which is absolutely illegal. They would not allow me to inform my attorney – which is unheard of in a democracy. And finally they could not prove the case; they could not prove anything against me. They released the people who were with me – three were simply dismissed because they were in a different plane, and the three who were with me were released on bail for seventy-five thousand dollars.

Just yesterday we received a letter from the attorney general's office, with the seal of the department of justice, and it is such a cunning letter – one cannot imagine! Seeing that they are going to fail completely, they have nothing to prove, they want to drop the case. They harassed me for twelve days; they took the personal things of all the people who were on the plane and they have not released those things. And seeing that they cannot prove anything – they don't have anything – they want to drop the case. But dropping the case meant that they would have to return the seventy-five thousand dollars deposited for bail for three persons – because if there is not going to be any trial and you are dropping the case, then that money should be returned. Why should that money be kept?

But you can see the greed and cunningness… They did not want to return the money and they wanted to drop the case. So with the magistrate's seal, what they did was they claimed that they had called these three witnesses and they did not appear in the court; hence their deposits of seventy-five thousand dollars are confiscated by the government, and the case is dropped.

They never informed us that there was any hearing, and they don't have any proof that we have refused. Our people were ready to go and we were asking, our attorneys were asking continually, "When is the date?" They never told our attorneys, never informed us. Even courts – federal courts – are lying that they informed us, and because we did not appear in the court we have lost the money.

And they don't even mention the personal effects – which are worth nearabout three million dollars. They have not returned them either.

They have sent the letter here. About me, they say that they don't have any charges against me, but for the future they cannot say anything. If I assassinate any U.S. official, then there will be charges against me. And they say because one of my sannyasins has attempted murder or assassination, then there is a possibility.... They don't name the person. It is Sheela.

I exposed her. I invited the government, I told the government all the crimes that she had committed, and now they are associating her with me – as if one Christian murders and that means the pope is responsible. Out of five thousand sannyasins in a commune, if one sannyasin commits some crime, that does not mean that I become a possible candidate for doing the same thing.

And strangely enough, it simply says, "U.S. official." If I kill some U.S. citizen, then what? According to that letter I am free to kill U.S. citizens – that will not be a charge against me – only it should not be a U.S. official!

It seems so stupid – either you should state a whole list of all possible crimes that a man can commit, or you should not state even a single crime. You don't have any charges against me right now. You could have simply said, "We don't have any pending charges against him." That's enough. Who is saying that this means that in future if I murder your president you will not have charges against me?

But now that you have said that if I assassinate some U.S. official then there will be charges, that means I can assassinate anybody else – just he should not be a U.S. official. Including this one class makes me free to commit any crime, and you cannot put any charges against me; otherwise, why did you not include it in the letter?

But just to create a fear, a paranoia... Before the letter reached us, it went to the president, and he has become shaky, afraid.

And these people belong to the same race – the politicians. They think in the same way. Their parties may be different, their countries may be different, but their basic reasoning is the same. If they see that America is afraid, being such a big power, then a small country like this should not take the risk.

Germany is insisting to this government, to every government, that I am a dangerous man. It is not wrong, but the meaning they give to "dangerous man"...perhaps I will kill their president or create a terrorist movement or start throwing bombs on people and hijacking their airplanes. What do they mean by "dangerous man"?

One man in Spain, a famous novelist, was very much interested in me because he has read a few of my books which have been translated into Spanish. He was working for one month continuously for me to go to Spain, and he is well-known in the whole Spanish speaking world, well respected, even by the politicians. He was talking to the president, to the prime minister, to the royal family, and they were all willing for me to come there. Then these letters from America, from Germany, from Greece, from Italy, started pouring in.

Just yesterday he informed me, "Now it has become difficult. Even the president has told me, 'You don't get involved in it. That man is very dangerous. Even your association with that man may bring difficulties to you; you just keep out, don't mention his name!'"

But he asked, "What danger is there?"

He said, "You don't ask! It is a very dangerous situation."

So many countries… The European parliament is passing a bill that I should not be allowed in any airport in Europe. Countries like the Bahamas, and other countries – Panama, and a few other islands near Panama, I have not even heard their names – and their parliaments have started discussing and deciding that I should not be allowed in their country.

Every man's life is in insecurity, but you are not so aware of it. You go on, sleepily. Yes, people die, people are murdered, everything happens, cancer and AIDS and everything, but still you go on thinking that it is not going to happen to you. But with me it is not a question that it is not going to happen: it is already happening.

So each moment *is* insecure.

And you have to be courageous, alert, and capable of using the opportunity that may be cut any moment. Make it a point that it is good that reality, which to others is hidden, to us is no longer hidden; it is clear and open. Face it! And the only way to face it is to live moment to moment as totally and intensively as possible.

You cannot afford to be sleepy and unconscious, just dragging on. You have to become alert. You have to become a flame so that whatsoever happens the next moment does not matter: you have lived my presence, my love, as totally as possible.

Chapter 38
May 1, 1986, Morning

A World
Beyond Time

Beloved Bhagwan,
Your vision is so beautiful, and most of all, so simple. But when I think about what man has to cleanse himself of, it seems to get complicated. I think the thing hardest for man to drop, for Your vision ever to be, is his so-called power — worldly and spiritual. To me, such people would rather see their world blow up than to give up their precious power. Is this so?

It is so. People are so unconscious that they can do anything to keep their power, their respectability – even if it means blowing up the whole world. They can risk anything to save their ego. And these are the people who naturally reach to the positions of power, because they are the only seekers of power.

No creative, intelligent person seeks power. No intelligent person is interested in dominating others. His first interest is to know himself. So the people with the highest quality of intelligence go towards mysticism, and the most mediocre go after power. That power can be worldly, political; it can be of money, it can be of holding spiritual domination over millions of people, but the basic urge is to dominate more and more people.

This urge arises because you don't know yourself, and you don't *want* to know that you don't know yourself. You are so afraid of becoming aware of the ignorance that prevails in the very center of your being. You escape from this darkness through these methods – lust for money, lust for power, lust for respectability, honor. And a man who has darkness within himself can do anything destructive.

Creativity is impossible from such a person, because creativity comes from your being conscious, a little alert…light, love. Creativity is not at all interested in dominating anyone – for what? The other is the other;

neither you want to dominate anyone, nor you want to be dominated by anyone. Freedom is the very taste of being just a little alert.

But these people are completely asleep. In their sleep they are making atomic bombs, nuclear weapons, not knowing what they are doing. Only one thing keeps them moving, and that is: more power, more power. And whoever comes in their way has to be destroyed. They don't know anything else. They are barbarians who have not evolved into human beings. Yes, they can destroy the whole world; they are already prepared to do so. They are all against me because I am exposing them.

And I am surprised: in this big world nobody else is there to join hands with me, because people are afraid of the powerful ones – they can destroy them. One is fearless only when he knows that he is indestructible; you can kill him but you cannot destroy his being. But such people have slowly disappeared from the earth. We have not nourished them. We kill them and then worship them.

This also has to be understood, why all the people that we have killed – for example, Jesus, Socrates, Al-Hillaj Mansoor, Sarmad – are immensely respectable *after* they have been killed. When they were alive they were condemned by everybody, not only by those who were in power but even by those who were not in power. Those who were not in power condemned them to show to the powerful, "We are with you." And the powerful condemned them because these people were bringing a vision. If it succeeds, then there will be no domination in the world; then there will be human beings – everybody unique, flowering in his own way.

But all these people are worshipped when they are dead. That comes out of guilt. First people kill them… It is the powerful who kill

them, and it is the powerless, the dominated, who support them – unwillingly, but very fanatically, because they want to show to everybody, "We are more against them than you are, and we are more in favor of the powerful than you are."

But once the man is killed, crucified, poisoned, these are the people who start feeling guilty, because from the very beginning they were not ready to kill the man. They had no problem with the man; he was not destroying any of their vested interests. They simply supported the powerful because they were afraid that if they didn't support, if they remained silent, they would be suspected of supporting the person who has been killed.

A disciple of Jesus was in the crowd when Jesus was crucified, and he was asked – because he looked different from others, was not from the same place, was a foreigner, and nobody recognized him – he was being asked again and again, "Who are you? Do you know this man who is being crucified?" And he said, "No, I have never heard about him. Just seeing that so many people are going this way, just to see what is happening, I have come." Even he cannot admit that he is a follower of Jesus, because he knows the result will be another cross.

So finally, when these people are crucified, the people who had supported it unwillingly start feeling very guilty, "What have we done against an innocent man, who has done no harm to anybody? And whatever he was saying, he was right." They can understand that these people in power are exploiting everybody.

It is a strange world. You know people now as kings and queens, and if you follow their ancestors, in the beginning, they were robbers. From where did they get their kingdom? They are great robbers who have killed many people, accumulated money, land, declared themselves as lords of the land, and now they have royal blood. They are in the lineage of criminals – and not ordinary criminals, big criminals. But they have power, they have money – naturally their blood is special.

The ordinary people have known all along that they are being crushed, murdered slowly. They labor hard and they cannot manage even one meal a day. They produce – but all that goes to those people who are in power. So when they support these people, it is unwillingly. That unwillingness, when the man is dead, turns into guilt; they start feeling that they have been participants in a criminal act. They have not done anything, but they were participants in a way; they were showing that they are in support of the powerful people.

To remove that guilt, worship arises. Worship is simply the removal of the guilt, to wash away the guilt. That's how such big religions like Christianity…otherwise Jesus had not that genius to produce such a big religion. There were hundreds of rabbis far more intelligent, far more scholarly than him, he was just an uneducated young man, but the crucifixion changed the whole situation. Once they crucified him, they made him a god – god to all those people, who are millions, who had supported the crucifixion. They started feeling guilty.

And you can see it, if you look deeply. Jesus was killed by the order of the Roman emperor, by his viceroy, Pontius Pilate in Judea, with the agreement of the high priest of the temple of the Jews. Today Rome has been the citadel of Christianity for twenty centuries, but the order to kill that man had come from Rome. There was a day when the whole Roman civilization turned into a Christian civilization. Today the pope has only a small piece of land – eight square miles – but it

is an independent country. It has been shrinking slowly; once he had the whole of Italy. He was higher than the state.

People were killed in Rome for being Christians. Christ was the first one, then whosoever turned Christian was killed in the same way; hundreds of people were crucified. And this whole crucifixion created so much guilt in people that a great religion came out of it. But such a religion can only be a psychological cover-up; it cannot be a true religion. It is simply covering up your guilt. The more fanatic a religious person is…you can measure by his fanaticism how guilty he is feeling, what he is hiding behind it.

But Christianity became the world's biggest religion for the simple reason that not only Christ but many other people, who had turned Christian, were crucified without any trial. And the masses were supporting the powerful people but deep down feeling hurt – what is happening is simply inhuman, should not happen. But they are poor, they have no power; they cannot do anything except worship.

A real religion is always of meditation.

A false religion is always of worship.

Worship is a psychological method of washing from your hands the blood that you can see on your hands. Even Pontius Pilate…the first thing he did after ordering the crucifixion of Jesus was to wash his hands, because he was not willing to kill this innocent man. He had talked to him, he had listened in disguise where he was talking to his disciples, and he had started loving something in that man. He is innocent. He says some crazy things but the way he says them is beautiful. He is uneducated but he speaks poetry. He does not know much, but whatever he knows he presents it with tremendous authority. And he is not doing any harm to anybody: if you don't want to listen to him, don't listen; if you don't want to follow him, don't follow. He is not preaching any dangerous ideas to people.

Pontius Pilate wanted him to be freed. He tried to persuade the priests that he should be freed because he seems to be innocent. But Jews were not ready to free him – and they committed a great mistake. They are responsible for creating Christianity. So all the bloodshed that Christianity has done, deep down, Jews are responsible for, and Christianity has taken revenge, tortured Jews, killed Jews, made them homeless. For centuries it has been going on.

Who are the people who became Christians? A few Jews who felt the innocence of the person but were afraid of the priesthood, the religious hierarchy in power. But many more people were crucified in Rome – and many more Romans became Christians.

It was a convention that every year the Jews were allowed to ask Pontius Pilate to save one life, because it was just before their religious holiday; it was a religious mercy and compassion.

Pontius Pilate was hoping that they would ask – because there were three people who were going to be crucified – that they would ask Jesus to be released, because the other two were great criminals. But the priests and the hierarchy of the rabbis shouted, "We want Barabbas!" – one criminal who had committed seven murders. Even Barabbas could not believe that he was being released, and this poor guy, Jesus – he knew him – they were not asking for him to be released. And he had not done anything!

Barabbas was saved. Christians don't talk much about Barabbas but he is a tremendously powerful character, and very important, because the miracle happened to *him,* not to Jesus. It was expected that God would save Jesus. God missed his target. Barabbas could not believe it. When they released him he looked back again and again – there must be some mistake. He was such a criminal; there was not any crime that he had not done – rape, murder... And he was always drunk, he was a drunkard.

But the face of Jesus remained in his mind and tortured him. He also started feeling guilty, "I should not have been released. It was perfectly right for me to be on the cross. That poor man... I have taken his place and he has taken my place." He felt a soft corner for Jesus. And within six months he committed a rape, he committed a murder, and he was caught again.

But this was the rule, that once the Roman emperor releases somebody from crucifixion, he cannot be crucified again. So they had to find an alternative for such people, because those people are bound to do something if they are such diehard criminals. In Rome they had a dangerous coal mine; they used to send those people to that coal mine to dig coal. It has reached to such places that once in a while it used to collapse, and thousands of the people who were working under it would be killed. That was their way of avoiding crucifixion.

Barabbas was sent to the coal mines in Rome. Within three months the coal mine collapsed. There were at least three thousand people; only Barabbas remained alive, everybody else was dead. That was the second miracle! He could not believe what was happening! He had been hanged on the cross and then brought down. He could not believe it that day; he was completely ready to be crucified, and he knew that he had done so many criminal things that it was perfectly right; there was no question of his being released.

Now what had happened? Three thousand

people had died and only he was saved. Even the emperor of Rome, the empress of Rome, became aware that this man seems to be a man of God – twice he has returned from death. So he was called to Rome. He had become so famous that people started touching him. He had become almost divine; just to touch him was a great experience. Even the empress wanted to touch Barabbas.

But the emperor said, "One test more; these two things may have been just accidental." And the last test was... Every year they had games in which criminals were thrown without any weapons before hungry lions, to fight with them. Barabbas was thrown before a hungry lion, and he managed a third time: he killed the hungry lion. Then even the emperor thought, "Now it cannot be an accident." He had never seen before... All criminals were eaten by the lions! This was the first time that a man had killed the lion; unscratched, he was victorious.

He was freed, he was given citizenship. He was no longer a slave – because in those days there were two categories of people, slaves and citizens. He was given citizenship. That was a great honor, and especially for a criminal...but he had proved three times that he can come back from death.

Christians have so much difficulty in proving that Jesus is a man of miracles. Barabbas is a man of miracles. They prove hard that Jesus is the only begotten son of God. It seems there is some mistake – Barabbas seems to be the only begotten son of God!

But all these years he was carrying the innocent Jesus' face, and feeling guilty that he was saved: "There has been some mistake. And I have been saved thrice!" He started meeting Christians in underground caves, where they used to meet so that nobody would

know. He listened for the first time to what Jesus used to say – and he became a Christian. The day he became a Christian he was caught and crucified, and then no miracle happened! It is a very strange story.

But the Roman people, who are now Italians, started feeling: Thousands of people are being crucified just because they are getting involved with Jesus and his teachings. The Roman empire disappeared, and the whole land of the Romans became Christian. And from there Christianity started moving all over the world.

A guilt feeling is very basic for being a Christian, for being a false religious person. Real religiousness arises not out of guilt but out of silence, out of love, out of meditativeness.

These people who are in power are almost on the brink of destroying the world, rather than lose their power. I can understand their logic – they may not be aware of it. Their logic is: We are going to die anyway, so what if the whole world dies? Our death is certain, so why should we bother about whether the world lives after us or not? We should live in power as long as we are here, and there is no need to be bothered about what will happen if the world explodes into a third world war.

The inner logic is: the day one is dead, the whole world is dead for him. You were not here one day; whether the world was here or not would not have made any difference to you. You will not be here one day; whether the world is there or has been blown up by nuclear weapons will not make any difference to you. What makes the difference to them is that they are in power, and they want to prove to the whole world that they are the most powerful people.

Now the competition has reached to a suicidal point, and America is in a hurry for the third world war to happen. Russia wants to delay it a little, because America has evolved certain microwave patterns around the whole country – billions of dollars have been put into it. You cannot see it, it does not obstruct anything; it only obstructs nuclear weapons. If a nuclear weapon is fired at America, if a missile comes to America, it will be returned; it cannot enter the country. So America is feeling safe. That's why this Libya episode happened.

The Soviet Union has not yet been able…they are working hard to create a protective armor around the country. Their country is big, vast; their finances are not as great as American finances, but still they are preparing – there is no other way.

Those two nuclear powers are preparing their protection. Then America can send missiles to the Soviet Union, and they will also be returned. Now, where they will fall, nobody knows – they will fall somewhere. But those two countries are protected, and the whole world is unprotected. So the whole world is in danger. Right now the Soviet Union is not ready with its protection; Libya was just a way to check whether Russia is ready or not. If they had been ready, the third world war would have been on.

The Soviet Union is ready to support Libya but is afraid to, for the simple reason that it does not yet have any protection for its own country; it needs some time. That's why the Soviet leaders are talking about cutting the production of nuclear weapons in such a way, step by step, that by the end of this century all production completely stops – and the whole world is impressed by it.

America cannot accept it because it has put billions of dollars into the protective armor that will be useless…billions of dollars into nuclear weapons, and no chance to use them. America is in a hurry; it wants any excuse. And the gap is not big; perhaps within one year the Soviet Union will be ready. So if the war has to happen, America wants it quickly.

Kaddafi's daughter died because America bombed his houses – even his tent in the desert they did not leave – and Kaddafi was silent, taking no action. On the contrary, he said that if America bombs anywhere else, their whole strategy will be to bomb the place and blame Libya for it. Libya is a small country, but Libya is just an excuse to provoke the Soviet Union. And Kaddafi said, "Next time Libya is bombed then be certain, that will be the beginning of the third world war." But why next time? The Soviet Union needs a little time.

If the world has some intelligent people in it, they should protest together to the U.N.: "Now it is intolerable. Patience has a limit, and all nuclear weapons should be banned, should be thrown in the oceans, or some way should be found that they are made useless or turned into some creative force."

Perhaps we are not far away now, not even ten, fifteen years… America is in such a hurry, and the hurry has a reason…before the Soviet Union completes its project of protection, because after that protection those two countries will be safe. Then everybody else will be killed who is not fighting, who has nothing to do with the fight, who is out of the war but they don't have any protection. The returning nuclear missiles will fall all over the world.

The intelligentsia of the world has to create an atmosphere in the world that now it is a question not of the Soviet Union and America; it is a question of the whole world. Because the whole world is going to suffer, the whole world should unite against both these nations and force both these nations to stop this mad race of nuclear weapons and power.

But there seems to be no protest, there seems to be no worry. The world goes on in a routine rut. It seems people don't have any alertness, don't have any clarity about the problem.

I can see clearly that there is more possibility of the world blowing up than being saved, because nothing is being done to save it and everything is being done to blow it up. And because I speak against it, America is against me, the Soviet Union is against me. This is a rare phenomenon; otherwise it happens that if America is against me, the Soviet Union will be favorable to me. And vice versa too is true. But both are against me, because I am not really against America or the Soviet Union; I am against this game of power, which is simply idiotic.

Beloved Bhagwan,
We have experimented with communes in both the East and the West that did not last. Buddha and other enlightened masters created communes that did last.
What is the difference?

Gautam Buddha and other masters never created communes the way we have created them. Buddha had followers, but not staying in one place…moving continuously. Mahavira had followers, but not staying in one place…moving continuously. So nobody has created the way we created communes. Five thousand people living together is a totally different experience than five thousand Buddhist monks moving from one place to another place, only staying three days at one place. And even in that, man's cunningness comes in.

Jaina monks have to move continuously, except during the rainy seasons. In India, before atomic experiments started, the seasons used to be very fixed. Even dates and days were fixed – on what day the rains will begin and on what day the rains will stop – and there were three clearcut seasons, four months each. So for four months in the rainy season they had to stop. But that also does not mean that thousands of sannyasins will be stopping in one place, but wherever they are.

But the cunningness of man's mind is such that I have seen Jaina monks who have lived their whole life in Bombay – somebody is there for fifty years… I enquired, "How is it being managed? – because it is against their basic rule and discipline. After three days they have to move."

And I was told that in Mahavira's time there were not such big cities as Bombay. Now the Jaina monk moves from one part of Bombay to another part of Bombay, and in this way he goes on moving around Bombay, inside Bombay, from one place to another place. But he remains in Bombay; he never leaves Bombay. Clever idea! From one suburb he will move to another suburb; that is another place. And in Mahavira's time there were not such big cities; these suburbs would have been different cities, different towns. So "We are moving!" and they go on circling.

Bombay has a population of… the daily population is nearabout ten million people. Forty million people come every day to work, from nearby towns, and they return in the evening. Fifty million people are there in the town. They are logically right, that there was no city in Mahavira's time of such population. But the whole point is missed. The point was simply that you don't become attached to a certain place, that you don't start having friendships, likes, dislikes. In three days you cannot do much. One day you come, just one day you really stay, and the third day you have to move. It is not enough time to get into any politics, or any local problems. To avoid power politics, to avoid local problems, attachments, the device was created that you move after three days.

But after three days they go on moving in the same city – for fifty years, sixty years. They have immense contact with people. They are almost residents of Bombay! The people who like them come to listen to them wherever they are.

Nobody had any commune the way we tried, and both the experiments have given great insights into human nature, so nothing has been a failure. We have learned much. So now I am not going to create a commune. I am going to create a totally different thing: a mystery school…forty, fifty people will be there to take care of the school, and two hundred, three hundred, five hundred people can come for a one month course, or a two month course, or a three month course, and move on. And slowly, slowly we can train people so that they can open mystery schools around the world. A school is a different thing. You come for three months to learn something, to go through some experiences, and then you are back in the world, to your work, to your job.

The commune experiment has made it clear that if five thousand people are living in a commune, they will have to do many things – make roads, make houses, make other facilities for five thousand people, and for the guests who will be coming for festivals. These people will not have any time left for the real search they had come for in the first place. They will not have time for meditation. They will not have time to go within themselves, to find techniques and work upon them, because the work is such that you cannot just work five

hours a day, five days a week; it will never be completed. You have to work ten, twelve hours a day seven days a week. You are tired – and moreover, what you are doing is only the necessary facilities for yourself. Soon you will have to start production; otherwise from where are you going to get your food, your clothes? So this is a vicious circle.

And when five thousand people are there, then there is bound to be power politics. Then you have to find group leaders, coordinators. It is not possible to give freedom to five thousand people: "Do whatsoever you like" – because they will all go swimming and trekking and playing their guitars, but then who will make the roads and the houses and do the farming? And how are your food and your clothes to be arranged? How long can we depend on donations? Sooner or later you will have to make factories and you will have to create something. Then this commune becomes just an ordinary world – so why make so much unnecessary trouble? Our basic reason was to give you an insight into yourself. That is completely forgotten in unnecessary trivia.

So my new phase of work is a mystery school. You work in the world, where roads are already there, houses are already there, you need not make them. Factories are already there…in thousands of years the world has created all that. So you can manage – five hours, work five days a week is enough. On the weekend you can meditate, you can go into silence or you can go to some isolated spot and just relax. And in a year you will be able to earn so much money, save so much money, that you can come here for one month, two months, three months…as much as you can manage.

Then being with me has no connotations of work. Then being with me is simply joy, celebration, meditation, singing, dancing. Those three months are simply holiday. You forget the world for those three months. They are pure search for the truth. And after three months, whatever you have learned, continue it at home; there you have time. Five hours you work – you have enough time; you can get at least two hours for yourself.

Not only this…when you start living with me there is a possibility that you may start taking me for granted, that I am always here. Nine months being away will bring you closer to me, because distance creates longing, creates love, creates understanding. So each year you will be coming, then going. Whatever you can manage…you can come twice. You will not be a burden on anybody, and there is no need for anybody to dominate you; there is no need for any strict discipline – work needs that. There is no need for coordinators, so we can avoid the power trip.

But both our communes have helped to bring us to this point where we can start a mystery school. Without those two communes it would have been impossible. This is my way of looking at things. Even failures bring you closer to success, because each failure gives you insight into what went wrong, how it went wrong. So both the experiments have been immensely significant.

Now we are in a position to create a totally different kind of place, which is simply a festival all the year round. People will be coming and going. They will take whatever they learn and they will practice it in the world, and they will come again to renew, to refresh, to go further, deeper. Only a skeleton crew will be here to take care of you.

Beloved Bhagwan,
I've been here with You now for two weeks, and find myself not thinking or talking about the place and the people I was with before. It feels as if I have been here for three months or more, so many things have happened. How come that time loses all its meaning when we are with You?

Time is a relative phenomenon. It is nothing absolute, so in different contexts it will have different meanings. You are in pain – time will look longer. Your tooth is hurting – seconds will look like minutes, minutes will look like hours. It depends how much the tooth is hurting! In pain you want to finish it, finish this pain, somehow to get rid of it. You don't want to prolong it, so time seems to be long.

Christians have never been able to explain why their hell is eternal, and they cannot explain it because the grounds on which they have made it eternal are foolish. If it is punishment, then it is absolutely impossible to prove that somebody has committed so many sins that his punishment is going to be eternal.

Bertrand Russell, one of the genius minds of our times, wrote a book, *Why I Am Not A Christian,* and this is one of the points that he makes clear, "I am absolutely against the idea of eternal hell, because as far as I know, if all my sins in my long life" – and he lived long, almost a century – "can be accumulated, and even those sins which I have not committed but only contemplated, those sins which I have dreamed of but I have not really committed… Combine all of them and the hardest judge cannot give me more than four to five years in jail. Now, eternal hell? It is so absurd and illogical – that puts me off." And he recounts other points. The Christians have not been able to answer, for the simple reason that they have based their argument on wrong things.

My answer would have been that because hell is the idea of suffering, immense suffering...it may be only for a single moment but it will appear as eternal, unending. It is a relative concept. And Bertrand Russell would have immediately understood it, because he wrote a book, *The ABC of Relativity*. He understands the idea of relativity: when you are joyous and happy with a friend, with a lover, time becomes short; it seems to go faster. Hours pass, and suddenly you see that so many hours have passed but it seems only a few minutes have passed. In pain time becomes long – it is very elastic. In pleasure it becomes very short.

But to be with me is something more than pleasure; it is peace, it is silence. It is something that is beyond the words. But my presence can make you feel it: time can disappear completely. It can be felt as if time has stopped. This is a beautiful experience.

Time stopping means you are entering into a world beyond time.

And that's what I am trying to do.

To be avilable to you, to call you here to be with me, simply means that I want to give you some taste of that which is higher than pleasure. And in that moment, times comes to standstill.

Chapter 39
May 1, 1986, Evening

Your Mind Is Not Yours

Beloved Bhagwan,

Why is it that Western society reacts so strongly to any individual deviating from the norm, particularly as far as his mental state is concerned? It looks on those who have fallen below the mind in such a way as to cast a stigma on them, and regards the possibility of going beyond the mind — enlightenment — with skepticism. It does allow a slight margin of deviation in its creative people and geniuses; hence such people are excused for their "eccentricities."

It is as if the mind is the touchstone of one's adjustment to society, and any aberration that might threaten the status quo is regarded with fear. What is that fear? — both of the sick mind and the enlightened no-mind?

The mind is within you, but it is really a projection of the society inside you. It is not yours.

No child is born with a mind. He is born with a brain. The brain is the mechanism; the mind is the ideology. The brain is fed by the society, and every society creates a mind according to its own conditionings. That's why there are so many minds in the world. The Hindu mind is certainly separate from the Christian mind, and the communist mind is certainly separate from the Buddhist mind.

But a fallacy is created in the individual that the mind is yours, so the individual starts acting according to the society, following the society, but feeling as if he is functioning on his own. This is a very cunning device.

George Gurdjieff used to tell a story... A magician deep in the mountains had many sheep, and to avoid servants and to avoid looking after the sheep and going in search of them every day when they were lost in the forest, he hypnotized all the sheep, and told each sheep different stories.

He gave different minds to each sheep. To one he told, "You are not a sheep, you are a man, so you need not be afraid that one day you will be killed, sacrificed, like other sheep – they are only sheep. So you need not be worried as far as returning home is concerned." To some he said, "You are a lion, not a sheep," and to some, "You are a tiger." And since that day the magician was at ease: the sheep started behaving according to the mind that was given to them.

He could kill a sheep – every day he used to kill sheep for his own food, his family's food – and the sheep who believed that they were lions or men or tigers would simply look and giggle, "This is what happens to sheep." But they were not afraid, not like in the old days.

When he killed a sheep before, all the sheep were trembling, afraid, "Tomorrow is going to be my day. How long can I live?" And that's why they used to escape in the forest – to avoid the magician. But now nobody was escaping. There were tigers, there were lions…all kinds of minds had been implanted in them.

Your mind is not your mind – this is something basic to be remembered. Your mind is an implantation of the society in which you have accidentally been born. If you were born in a Christian home, but immediately transferred to a Mohammedan family and brought up by the Mohammedans, you would not have the same mind; you would have a totally different mind that you cannot conceive of.

Bertrand Russell, one of the geniuses of our times, tried hard to get rid of the Christian mind, not because it was Christian, but simply because it was given to him by others. He wanted his own fresh outlook about things. He did not want to see things from somebody else's glasses; he wanted to come in contact with reality immediately, and directly.

He wanted his own mind.

So it was not a question of being against the Christian mind; if he had been a Hindu he would have done the same, if he had been a Mohammedan he would have done the same, if he had been a communist he would have done the same.

The question is whether the mind is your own or implanted by others – because the others implant a mind in you which does not serve *you*, but serves their purposes. Now in the whole Soviet Union, each child is being brought up with a communist mind.

One of my friends, Rahul Sankritayana, was visiting the Soviet Union. He went to see a school and he asked a small boy, "Do you believe in God?" The small boy looked at him in shock and he said, "At your age, in this century, you ask such a question! In the past when people were ignorant they used to believe in God. There is no God." Now this child will believe for his whole life that this is his voice. It is not so. It is the voice of the society, and it serves the purposes of the vested interests of the society.

You are prepared by the parents, by the teachers, by the priests, by your educational system to have a certain kind of mind, and your whole life you go on living through that certain kind of mind. That is a borrowed life. And that is why there is so much misery in the world: because nobody is living authentically, nobody is living his own self; he is simply following orders implanted in him.

Bertrand Russell tried hard and wrote a book, *Why I Am Not A Christian*. But in a letter to a friend he wrote, "Although I have written the book, although I do not believe that I am a Christian, I have dropped that mind, still, deep down… One day I asked myself, 'Who is the greatest man in history?' Rationally I know it is Gautam Buddha, but I could not put Gautam Buddha above Jesus Christ.

"That day I felt that all my efforts have been futile. I am still a Christian. I know rationally that Jesus Christ stands no comparison with Gautam Buddha – but it is only rational. Emotionally, sentimentally I cannot put Gautam Buddha above Jesus Christ. Jesus Christ remains in my unconscious, still affecting my attitudes, my approaches, my behavior. The world thinks I am no longer a Christian, but I know… It seems difficult to get rid of this mind! They have cultivated it with such acumen, with such craftsmanship."

And it is a long process. You never think about it. A man lives at the most seventy-five years, and for twenty-five years he has to be in the schools, colleges, university; one third of life is devoted to cultivating a certain mind. Bertrand Russell failed because he had no knowledge of how to get rid of it. He was fighting, but groping in the dark.

There are absolutely certain methods of meditation which can take you away from the mind, and then it is very easy if you want to drop it. But without first becoming separate from the mind it is impossible to drop it – who is going to drop whom?

Bertrand Russell is fighting with one half of his mind against the other half, and both are Christian – it is impossible. And now it has been proved scientifically. One of the most important scientific contributions is from Delgado. He has found seven hundred centers in the brain. Each center is capable of containing an immense quantity of knowledge; it is just like a recording. And his experiments are very shocking: he touches a certain center in the brain with an electrode, and the man starts speaking. He takes away the electrode and the man stops. He puts the electrode back on the same center, and the man starts speaking again – from the very beginning.

Delgado himself has not been able yet to figure out how the tape gets reversed – because the man always starts from the beginning. Wherever you leave him makes no difference. It is not that he starts where you left him. Some automatic process in the mind will be discovered…

Some electrode can be implanted in the mind, permanently, and it can be controlled from far away by remote control. Delgado exhibited it in Spain, in a bullfight. He planted an electrode in the mind of the toughest bull, and he stood in the field showing a red flag. The bull rushed towards him ferociously, and the people almost stopped breathing: "The bull is going to kill one of our best geniuses!" But they did not know that he had a remote control switch in his pocket – just a small box with a switch.

Just when the bull was about to attack, from one foot away, he pushed the button and the bull stopped, just frozen. And he did it many times. Again and again the bull came with the same ferocity, and again and again he stopped whenever Delgado pushed the button.

Delgado says, "Sooner or later, this discovery will either become a blessing to humanity, or it will become a curse."

Every child's mind can be easily implanted with an electrode. You will have very obedient people; you will not have any rebels, you will not have any revolutionaries, but the whole charm of life will be gone. People will be simply vegetables, enslaved scientifically. And they will not know, because the remote control unit may be in the capital, in the hands of the government.

It can be useful – criminals can be

prevented, murderers can be prevented, thieves can be changed, rapists can be transformed – but it is dangerous also. Anybody who is in power can make the whole country just a crowd of slaves. And you cannot do anything, because you don't know. Remember one thing, inside the skull, where the brain is, you don't have any sensitivity. Even if a stone is put inside your skull, you will never know; you just don't have sensitive nerves there which can inform you.

This came to be known in the second world war. A man was shot with a bullet, and somehow the doctors thought that the bullet was not inside him, but had missed, just touching his head. So they treated the wound, it healed and the bullet remained inside his head for ten years – and he was never aware of it. It was for some other reasons that he was being x-rayed, and they were surprised to find that there was a bullet inside him. Then the wound was opened and the bullet was found. That made it clear that anything can be planted in the mind.

Delgado's mechanism is scientific, but society has been doing the same by planting ideas… It is an old bullock cart method. It takes so long, twenty-five years, and it is not foolproof, because a few revolutionaries escape, a few rebels are still born. And it is good that there are people who escape from the enslaving structure of the society, because these are the people who have advanced knowledge, who have given all scientific progress, who have changed all superstitions.

But the society wants you simply to be a carbon copy, never an original.

The strategy to create a mind in you is to go on repeating certain things continuously. And even if a lie is repeated continuously it starts becoming a truth; you forget that it was a lie in the beginning.

Adolf Hitler started lying to the German people that all the misery of their country is because of the Jews. Now this is such an absurd thing – like somebody saying that all the misery of the country is because of bicycles, so if we destroy all the bicycles all the misery will disappear.

In fact the Jews were the very backbone of Germany, they had created all the wealth of Germany. And they had no other nation, so any nation – wherever they were – was their nation. They had no other alternative in their minds; they could not betray, and they had been doing all the things that any other German was doing for the welfare of the country.

But Adolf Hitler in his autobiography writes, "It doesn't matter what you say, because there is no such thing as truth. Truth is a lie that has been repeated so often that you have forgotten that it is a lie."

So the only difference, according to him, between truth and a lie is that the lie is fresh and truth is old; otherwise there is no difference. And there seems to be some insight in it.

For example, Christianity, Hinduism, Mohammedanism – these three religions repeat to their children, "There is a God." Jainism, Buddhism, Taoism, three other religions, say "There is no God." The first group of three religions have a certain mind. Their whole life is filled with the idea of God, hell, heaven, prayer. The second group of three religions has no prayer because there is nobody to pray to, there is no God. And the very question does not arise.

r332   Now, half of the world is communist. They don't believe even in the soul of man, and every child is continuously told that man is matter, that when man dies he simply dies, nothing remains; that there is no soul –

consciousness is a by-product. Now half of the humanity repeats it – as the truth.

Adolf Hitler cannot be accused of being absolutely absurd. It seems to be the case that if you repeat anything to people, they will slowly, slowly start believing it. And if it has been repeated for centuries, it has become a heritage.

Your mind is not yours. And your mind is not young; it is centuries old – three thousand years old, five thousand years old. That's why every society is afraid of anybody creating a doubt about the mind.

That's my crime: that I create a doubt in you about your mind. And I want you to understand that it is not *your* mind, and your search should be to find your own mind. To be under somebody else's impact is to remain psychologically a slave. And life is not for slavery. It is to taste freedom.

There *is* something like truth, but with this mind you can never know it, because this mind is full of lies, repeated for century after century. You can find the truth when you put this mind completely aside and look at existence with fresh eyes, like a newborn child; then whatever you experience is truth. And if you remain constantly alert not to allow others to interfere with your inner growth, there comes a moment when you become so attuned with existence, so one with existence... Only this experience is religious experience. It is not Jewish, it is not Christian, it is not Hindu. How can any experience be Jewish, Hindu or Mohammedan? You never see its ridiculousness. You eat something and you say it is delicious, but is it Christian, or Hindu, or Buddhist? You taste something and you say it is sweet, but is it communist? – is it materialist or spiritualist?

These questions are nonsense. It is simply sweet, it is simply delicious.

When you feel existence immediately, without any mediator, with no mind given by anybody else to you, you taste something which transforms you, which makes you enlightened, awakened, which brings you to the highest peak of consciousness.

A greater fulfillment there is not. A higher contentment there is not. A deeper relaxation there is not.

You have come home.

Life becomes a joy, a song, a dance, a celebration.

And I call this life religious.

I want everybody to be religious, but I don't want anybody to be Christian, Hindu, Mohammedan, because those are the barriers which will never allow you to become religious. And you can see it clearly: Gautam Buddha is not a Buddhist, he never heard the word Buddhist; Jesus Christ is not a Christian, he never heard the word Christian and certainly he is not a Jew; otherwise Jews would not have crucified him.

If Jews decided to crucify Jesus, that simply means he has dropped the mind that they have given him to carry his whole life, that he is saying things that are not part of their given mind. And Jesus continuously reminds them of it. He says, "It has been said by the old prophets" – and who were those old prophets? all Jews – "it has been said, 'An eye for an eye is the law.' But I say unto you that if somebody slaps you on one cheek, give him the other cheek too."

This was not part of the Jewish mind. The Jewish God declares, "I am not a nice person! I am a very angry God, I am very jealous. Remember that I am not your uncle." These are actually the words: "I am not your uncle, I am not nice, I am jealous, I am angry." And Jesus says, "God is love."

I am trying to show you that he has

dropped the Jewish mind, and that's the reward he got – the crucifixion. The crucifixion was the reward for dropping the Jewish mind. He was dangerous in the sense that he would create doubt in other people's minds: "Our God says he is angry, jealous – he will destroy those who are against him, and Jesus is saying that God is love. He is going against our vested interest."

He was killed – he was not a Jew; he was not Christian because the word 'Christian' does not exist in the Hebrew language, the word 'Christ' does not exist in the Hebrew language. He was called the messiah – that is equivalent to 'Christ.' 'Christ' is a Greek word. It was three hundred years later that Jesus' sayings were translated into Greek; then messiah became Christ, and the followers became Christians.

What I am trying to say to you is that Gautam Buddha was not a Hindu. He was born in a Hindu family, but he has renounced it; he renounced it the very day he started his search for truth. See the simple point: the Hindu need not search for the truth; the Hindu has already got it ready-made. It has been given by the tradition, by the religion, by the scriptures; he need not go in search.

The day Gautam Buddha went in search for truth, he dropped the Hindu mind. And of course he was not a Buddhist; that was a name his followers were given later on by Hindus, to keep a distinction. But he had his own mind.

To have one's own mind in the world is the richest thing possible. But no society allows it; every society keeps you poor. On your account every society, particularly those who are in power – either through money or through politics or through religion or through knowledge, or for any reason – those who are in power don't want people to have their own minds. It is dangerous to their interests. They want not men but sheep, not individuals but crowds, who are always in need of being led, who are always in need of being told what to do, what not to do; who don't have their own minds, their own insights, their own consciousness. They are always dependent.

The fear of anybody being different, being a stranger, being an outsider, is always the same for the simple reason that no society will have the courage to accept you – because that society has not made your mind, and that society cannot trust that you will always be obedient to it, that you will never object about anything, or create doubt about anything, or be skeptical about anything.

For example, in India the cow is worshipped as the mother. Anybody who has not been brought up as a Hindu is simply going to be skeptical, "This is nonsense!" And this is not all. Hindus do things that nobody can even conceive of: they drink the urine of the cow because it is holy, they eat cowdung because it is holy.

And it is not only the villagers or the uneducated, or the uncultured. In Mahatma Gandhi's ashram there was a man, a professor, who lived for six months only on the urine of cows and cowdung – not eating anything else, not drinking anything else. And Mahatma Gandhi praised him, saying that he is a saint.

Now, Hindus are angry at me because I cannot accept this kind of stupidity – that it can make somebody a saint. It simply proves that man was an idiot! But Mahatma Gandhi is a politician; he is also not a saint. If he was a saint he would also have said, "This is nonsense. You cannot become holy by eating cowdung." But he is a politician *par excellence,* in the garb of a religious saint. Saying that this man is a saint, he has satisfied the whole Hindu community; now he is the sole leader of all the Hindus. Anybody who has not been brought up by the Hindus will not be able to accept it.

So any deviation from the norm in any society... There are many people who you call mad, but they are not mad. They are simply not agreeing with *your* madness; they have a private madness of their own. You have a collective madness.

Now, for example, if all four hundred million Hindus accept without any question the idea that drinking the urine of cows makes you holy, and somebody starts drinking the urine of a horse, they say he is mad. I simply say that he is *privately* mad, you are collectively mad. But you both are mad!

I would like that man more than this collective madness; at least he has the courage to do something private, individual. It will look foolish to all the Hindus, but they will not look foolish to themselves, to their own mind.

No society wants strangers, outsiders. Why is the whole world afraid of me? I am not a terrorist; I am not making bombs and killing people. I am a nonviolent person. But they can accept terrorists.

In Germany it actually happened at the same time... They prevented me from entering Germany, passed a resolution that I am a dangerous man and I should not be allowed any entry into Germany, and at the same time they allowed all the terrorist groups of Europe to have a world conference.

I was simply amazed! All the terrorist groups that have been murdering people, that have hijacked airplanes, that have bombed embassies, that have kidnapped people – their international conference is allowed, but I cannot be allowed four weeks of being a tourist in the country.

Those terrorists are not of a different mind.

It is a very strange phenomenon. When Pontius Pilate had asked... Three people were being crucified the same day as Jesus, and it was the convention that one can be forgiven – and it was the people's decision. And Pontius Pilate was absolutely certain that they would ask, "Release Jesus." He was innocent; he had done no harm to anybody. But the Jews shouted, the high priests shouted, "We want Barabbas" – and Barabbas was a confirmed criminal. He had committed seven murders, rapes...any kind of crime you name and he had done it.

But you should not be surprised, because Barabbas belongs to the Jews. He may be a murderer, but his mind is still of a Jew. This Jesus may be innocent, but his mind is no longer that of the Jews; he is an outsider, he is dangerous. Barabbas is not dangerous. What can he do? A few more murders at the most. But this Jesus can destroy the whole structure of the society, because it is standing only on superstitions.

Even Barabbas could not believe it. He thought something must have gone wrong: "There is not another criminal in the whole country who can compete with me, and this poor Jesus, who has never done anything except talking to few people here and there... And nobody is asking for him." Not a single voice shouted for Jesus to be released, and thousands of people shouted, "Barabbas! We want Barabbas!"

If you go into the psychology of it, it is very simple. All those terrorists having a conference in Germany are acceptable: they have the same mind, the same politics. They belong to the same rotten society.

But I cannot be allowed. Against me they have the idea that I will corrupt people. The same was their condemnation of Socrates – that he corrupts people – and all that Socrates was doing was teaching people to have their own mind.

All the great masters in the world have been saying only one thing down the centuries, "Have your own mind and have your own individuality. Don't be a part of the crowd; don't be a wheel in the whole mechanism of a vast society. Be individual, on your own. Live life with your own eyes; listen to music with your own ears."

But we are not doing anything with our own ears, with our own eyes, with our own minds; everything is being taught, and we are following it.

Deviation is dangerous to the rotten societies. And particularly in the West – where no idea of enlightenment has ever existed – it is more so, because enlightenment simply means going beyond the mind. And going beyond the mind you will be yourself.

The West has never nourished the idea of enlightenment. It is against the society, against the religion; they have never bothered about it.

Think about truth – that is allowed! That's why in the West philosophy has grown to great heights and depths. But it is always thinking *about* truth. It is like madmen thinking about sanity, blind men thinking about light. However the blind man tries to think about light…he may create a big system of thought about what light is, but it is not going to be anything like light. For light, you need eyes.

You cannot think about truth, because thinking will be done by your mind – which is full of lies, nothing but lies. How are you going to think about truth? Truth can be found only when you have put the mind aside.

In the East we say truth is the experience that happens in the state of no-mind or in the state of beyond mind. But in the West the very idea has not existed. And that will make one thing clear to you: philosophy is a Western thing. In the East there is nothing like philosophy.

It is very strange: the East is far older, at least ten thousand years old, but there is nothing like philosophy in the East. What is called Eastern philosophy is a wrong name. In the East it is called darshan – darshan means "to see." It has nothing to do with thinking. The very word darshan means "to see."

I had to coin my own word for it: I call it *philosia,* as against philosophy, because philosophy means "to think," and philosia means "the love of seeing." Philosophy means "the love of thinking" – but what can you think? Just to avoid the danger of people going beyond mind, and becoming dangerous to the society, a substitute, a toy has been created. That is philosophy.

No philosopher comes to experience anything. No philosopher becomes enlightened or awakened; he remains on the same ground as you are, as unconscious as you are.

Darshan – philosia – is a totally different approach. It's approach is by witnessing your mind, not by thinking but just becoming a watcher of your mind and creating a distance between you and your thoughts. Just seeing them, as if you are on a hill and the whole mind and its traffic is going on down in the valley, a moment comes when thoughts start disappearing, because their life is in the identity. Their life is the life of a parasite; they suck your blood.

If you are far away and you are not giving any juice to your thoughts, they start shrinking and dying. And when there are no thoughts around you but immense silence, tremendous nothingness, just a watcher and nothing to watch…this is the moment you are freed from the fetters of the mind. And this is the moment of the beginning of a new life.

But you may look mad to people, because from this moment your behavior will be different. From this moment you will have an originality; you cannot be part of the crowd. People will think you have gone wrong somewhere. It is strange – the people are wrong! But in a way it is not strange. If you go into a society of blind people with eyes, nobody is going to believe that you have eyes. You must be having some mad illusion – eyes don't exist. Nobody has eyes, how can you have?

The enlightened person in the West will be condemned as mad.

The people who are mad in the West are mad because you have created so much tension and anxiety and anguish, and you have given them such a rotten mind, that it cannot manage. A point comes when it breaks down. When the mind breaks down, the person falls below the mind; hence psychoanalysis is a Western phenomenon. In the East there is nothing parallel to psychoanalysis.

In the East we have tried for a break-*through,* not for a breakdown. The breakthrough takes you above the mind, and the breakdown simply pulls you to a subhuman level. But for that too society is responsible. It gives you too much ambition, which it cannot fulfill. It gives you too much desire – for money, for power – which it cannot fulfill. It only teaches you how to go on climbing the ladder of success, higher and higher, and tells you to be quick, because you have only a small life, and so much has to be done! There is no time for living, no time for loving, no time for rejoicing.

People go on postponing everything that is meaningful. Tomorrow they will laugh; today, money has to be gathered…more money, more power, more things, more gadgets.

Tomorrow they will love – today there is no time. But tomorrow never comes, and one day they find themselves burdened with all kinds of gadgets, burdened with money. They have come to the top of the ladder – and there is nowhere to go except to jump in a lake.

But they cannot even say to other people, "Don't bother to come here – there is nothing," because that will make them look stupid. You have become the president of the country and you are saying, "Here is nothing – don't bother. This is simply a ladder which leads nowhere" – you will feel stupid.

So they go on pretending that they have achieved, that they have found; and deep down they are empty, meaningless, and they have wasted their whole life. If they break down under such pressure, the society is responsible. The society is driving people mad.

In the East you will not find so many mad people, so many people committing suicide – and the East is poor, so poor that people can't manage to have one meal a day. Logically there should be more people committing suicide, more people going mad. But no, they are not going mad, they are not committing suicide. they seem to be in a certain contentment, because ambition is not being part of the mind given by the society; their society also gives them ambition, but for the other world, not for this world. This world is condemned.

You try to understand… Their society also gives them ambition – ambition to reach to paradise, to realize God – but that ambition is against the ambitions of this world. "Renounce this world! Here there is nothing but shadows; it is illusory." For thousands of years they have thought it is illusory, it is worthless to bother about it – why not look for the real thing? So they don't go mad. In utter poverty, in sickness, in death…but you will not find them tense, anxious, and they don't need any psychotherapy.

Psychotherapy is absolutely Western; it is the need of the Western mind. First the Western mind creates all kinds of desires and ambitions, which are going to create a breakdown sooner or later; then psychotherapy comes in. It is now the most highly-paid profession, but the strangest thing is that psychotherapists commit suicide more than people from any other profession, twice as much as any other profession, and psychotherapists go mad twice as much as any other profession. And these are the people who are helping other people to be sane! It is really a mess.

It can be cleaned up. It is simply a question of understanding that the mind that we have is not capable of encountering reality, because reality is contemporary, and the mind is two thousand years old. The gap is big, and the mind fails to encounter reality. The mind has to go *with* reality, step by step; it has not to lag behind.

And that is possible only if each individual has his own mind, his own individuality.

I am basically an individualist, because only the individual has a soul. No group can claim a soul – they are all dead arrangements. Only the individual is a living phenomenon. We have to help the living phenomenon to be contemporary, and to remain contemporary, because what is contemporary today will not be contemporary tomorrow, so you have to learn the methods of flowing like a river with existence, each moment. Die each moment to the past, and be born each moment to the new.

Unless that becomes your religion, you are going to be in trouble, and your society is going to be in trouble.

Beloved Bhagwan,
Why is it that in spite of the vast range of subjects that You cover in Your talks – perhaps a wider range than any man who has ever lived – whenever I discuss You with press and any other interested parties, they seem preoccupied with only one subject: sex?

I am reminded of Doctor Johnson. He had made one of the best dictionaries of his times. It was a very big, voluminous book – more than one thousand pages. Three old ladies came to him, very angry; they must have been seventy, seventy-five, eighty, they all had glasses. And they said, "Are you not ashamed of your book? There are three words in it which are obscene!"

Doctor Johnson said, "My God, in a book of one thousand pages, in which there are thousands of words, how could you manage at your age, with such thick glasses, to find three obscene words? You are great researchers. You must have been looking for them. Nobody else has objected to me; nobody has even mentioned them."

I have almost four hundred books in my name. I have not written anything, but these are a collection of my talks. Out of four hundred books there is only one book on sex, and that too is not really on sex; it is basically on how to transcend sex, how to bring the energy of sex to a sublimated state, because it is our basic energy.

It can produce life… That is only one thing that we know about it, but that even animals manage. And scientists say even trees have their own kind of sexuality, so the whole of existence manages some kind of sexual energy. It is only man who has the privilege to change the character and the quality of sexual energy.

The name of the book is *From Sex to Superconsciousness* – but nobody talks about superconsciousness. The book is about superconsciousness; sex is only to be the beginning, where everybody is. There are methods that can start the energy moving upwards, and in the East, for at least ten thousand years, there has developed a special science, Tantra. There is no parallel in the West of such a science.

For ten thousand years people have experimented with how sexual energy can become your spirituality, how your sexuality can become your spirituality. It is proved beyond doubt – thousands of people have gone through the transformation. Tantra seems to be the science that is, sooner or later, going to be accepted in the whole world, because people are suffering from all kinds of perversions. That's why they go on talking about sex as if that is my work, as if twenty-four hours a day I am talking about sex. Their repressed sexuality is the problem.

A great poet, Heinrich Heine, once got lost in the forest. For three days he could not find the way out. Hungry, tired, worried about wild animals the whole night, sitting in the trees, and the whole day stumbling, trying to find some human being... But for three days he could not meet anyone to show him the way. The third night was a full-moon night. He was sitting in a tree, utterly exhausted. He looked at the moon, and suddenly he laughed.

He laughed because he had written so many poems about the moon and he has read so many poems about the moon. The moon is such a romantic phenomenon that no poet of any standing can leave it out, no painter can leave it out. Its impact is deep, its beauty is great. So why did he laugh? He laughed because when he looked at the moon, he didn't see all those romantic things that he was talking of in his poems; he saw a round loaf of bread, floating in the sky.

He said, "My God! What has happened to me?" After three days of hunger and tiredness, it is natural, but perhaps his experience was unique: nobody else has ever seen a floating round loaf of bread floating in the sky! He laughed at himself, and for the first time he understood that what he had been saying about the moon had nothing to do with the moon; it had something to do with himself.

So the people who talk about sex and condemn me don't understand that it is their repression. I have been speaking on thousands of subjects, but they are not concerned with them because that is not their repression. Sex has been repressed traditionally all over the world. Naturally it is bound to come up in some way or other. You cannot avoid it.

Even *The Holy Bible* has five hundred pages of pure pornography. And it is not an exception – all other religious scriptures... Hindu scriptures are the worst. They go into such details that you will be worried, "Are these people talking about spirituality, or what?" They have even made temples like Khajuraho, Konarak, Puri. Each temple has thousands of naked women, naked men, in different sexual postures...temples! If you suppress something in man it is going to come up somewhere or other, in some way or other.

This repression of sex by all the religions has helped the pornographic literature of the world – magazines like *Playboy* – to be read more than anything else. Now *Playboy* is published in almost all languages, and there are many magazines of the same kind.

When I was in jail in America, in the first jail I was surprised: every inmate had a *Bible,* and one inmate, who was just next to me, every day ritually in the morning, in the evening, would put his head on *The Bible,* kneel down on the floor – *The Bible* on the bed, his head on *The Bible* – and pray. He looked really pious.

But I asked him, "This is very beautiful, you are doing good, but why do you have all over the room these pictures of naked women that you have cut from magazines? and not a single picture of Jesus Christ? Jesus Christ among all these nudes would have looked very beautiful."

He was shocked he said, "I never thought about it. I am a very devoted Christian, a fundamentalist."

I said, "You must be a fundamentalist; otherwise how to explain all these pictures? For these pictures to exist, a fundamentalist Christian is absolutely necessary. Don't be worried! They are not contradictory, they are complementary. It is a conspiracy between the churches and the people who are exploiting your mind."

My whole effort has been how to make your sex a natural, accepted phenomenon, so there is no repression – and then you don't need any pornography; so that there is no repression – and then you don't dream of sex. Then the energy can be transformed. There are valid methods available through which the same energy that brings life to the world can bring a new life to you. That was the whole theme of the book. But nobody bothered about the theme, nobody bothered about why I have spoken on it. Just the word 'sex' was in the title, and that was enough.

That word has created so many rumors that I am really amused! People are thinking that we are having sexual orgies the whole day. People really have imagination! Just because out of four hundred books, on one book the word 'sex' has appeared in the title,

their imagination has moved so far away. But it reflects their mind; it has nothing to do with me.

In Khajuraho, the Indian temple, the most famous temple in the world…there are thirty temples – perhaps it would have taken thousands of years to make those temples. As sculptures they are just the best; you cannot create better. But the sexual postures are so absurd that you cannot even imagine…

Absolutely all kinds of postures that man – sane and insane, whoever! – has imagined are there: men are making love to animals, a man and a woman are standing on their heads and making love. Have you ever imagined…? But why has this happened? – and these people must have worked hard! Repress anything and it will take pervert proportions.

Now there is homosexuality, lesbianism, sodomy, and all kinds of other perversions, and nobody ever thinks about who is responsible. Animals in the wild are never homosexual, but in a zoo, if females are not available, then animals turn homosexual. That gives a clue. It seems we have made our society a zoo, not a natural phenomenon. We have repressed sex so much that now it goes on taking strange shapes.

For example, homosexuality must have been born in monasteries, so I call it a religious thing. In monasteries men are kept separate – no woman is available. In nunneries women are separate – no men are available. In Athos, in Europe, there is one monastery, one thousand years old, which you can enter – but you cannot get out alive. You renounce the world forever: Enter the monastery and the world is finished. In this monastery, not even a six-month-old baby girl is allowed. I sometimes wonder: are monks living inside, or monsters? A six-month-old baby girl is not allowed; no woman of any age

YOUR MIND IS NOT YOURS

has ever entered there, dead or alive.

Now, you are forcing people... These people will become homosexuals, the nuns will become lesbians, and you go on preaching celibacy! You still go on preaching that monks should be celibate, nuns should be celibate, and they are all reading pornographic literature...of course, hiding it in *The Bible*!

We are living in a very sick society, which could have been very healthy, and *can* be healthy immediately...just a question of understanding.

Chapter 40
May 2, 1986, Morning

The Body Does Not Have Beliefs

Beloved Bhagwan,
Hearing You talk about hypnosis the other morning, I reached into a very quiet, relaxed state. I felt totally safe and wrapped in a wonderful softness.
When I did a three-month dehypnotherapy with Santosh at the ranch, however, I often found myself in total horror and fear, regressing into my early childhood. What did I experience with You?

Hypnosis is such a simple, innocent experience, that even hearing about it can give you a taste of it. And that's what happened. Even when I am not talking about hypnosis, the same is happening to those who are really listening to me. A softness, a calmness, a silence starts surrounding them. That is a signal that whatever is being said is being heard too, that I am not talking to the walls.

About your experience with Santosh and his dehypnotherapy, I can only say one thing: Santosh knows nothing about dehypnotherapy. He himself is so tense, so continuously worried, has so many problems...but he had studied hypnosis as a student for years in Germany so he knows the technique; but he has never been in those spaces himself.

It is just like...you can read the map of the whole world and you have never been to those places, ever. Knowing where Constantinople is does not mean that you have been there. Knowing about it is one thing; being there is a totally different phenomenon. And in the schools only the technique, the know-how, is being taught.

So when Santosh came to me he had the know-how of hypnosis. I engaged him in hypnotherapy, and I tried my best to make him understand that we have first to create a state of de-hypnotherapy – because every child is being hypnotized, from the very childhood. That's how conditioning happens; that's how you get your mind. Your parents may not know, your teachers may not know, your priests may not know what they are doing: they are practicing hypnotic techniques. By the time you leave the university, you know all the techniques for conditioning others. So whoever comes to me is already conditioned.

I was trying to make Santosh understand, "First dehypnotize these people, let them get rid of what society has forced upon them, and only then will hypnosis be clean, young, fresh, just born."

He was only a student, so he changed the name of his therapy to dehypnotherapy on my suggestion. But what he has been doing is still the same techniques that he had learned in Germany. And those techniques can create horror, because first you are filled with social conditionings, and on top of it you are hypnotized.

In hypnosis you reach to your unconscious mind, where all conditionings exist. You are in a volcanic state. There are going to be horrors because you may remember your childhood, and all that has happened to you since your childhood, which you have repressed. Remember, nobody represses any pleasant experience – why should one repress a pleasant experience? In fact one tries to exaggerate it, to himself and to others, as much as he can. One represses only things which are unpleasant.

So your unconscious is full of serpents and scorpions and dragons that you have repressed because you did not want to know about them and you did not want others to know about them. Without unconditioning you, if you are lead into hypnosis directly you will reach a hell of your own creation: whatever is repressed will show its true face to you

– and it is natural that you will become terrified.

The problem of these therapists like Santosh is that they have never gone through the process themselves; they have simply studied from a teacher. They have never been part of a mystery school, which would have cleaned them. And in a mystery school the technique is given to you only when you are able to use it, and not get into dark spots, horror spaces, terrible states. They are all imaginary, but when you are in them they are real.

So with Santosh, what happened with you was a nightmare that was repressed, and he opened the bottle and the *djinn* came out. These kind of people are dangerous. I told him again and again, to the point that he was angry with me…because he used to think that he was a hypnotist, and he had studied for twelve years in Germany – what more could anybody teach him? I said, "It is not a question of teaching. You have not gone through these spaces into which you are leading other people, and you don't know what will happen to them."

Now all these therapists are befooling themselves. Because the commune has been destroyed by the American government, it has been a tremendous blessing to the therapists.

We had a property of the commune in Laguna Beach in America, and our sannyasins were running it; we had made a board of directors. It was a three million dollar property. What Santosh did was, he took three hundred sannyasins from the ranch to Laguna Beach, and all the sannyasins became members of the Laguna Beach commune – and of course they changed the whole board of directors. Santosh brought his own directors, his own board, and he opened a dehypnotherapy institute in Laguna Beach. My name is not mentioned. He has appropriated the property without thinking of its legal implications. And we had been fighting for years, four years, to win the case....

It was a strange case. There used to be a Christian Church, but of a very independent character. The man who was leading the church, the priest, did not belong to any organization; it was independent, it had four hundred members. But the priest became interested in me. He and his wife came to Poona and became sannyasins, and then he went back. Instead of *The Bible* he started teaching through my books. His congregation could not believe what had happened.

But many of his congregation were thrilled – they were tired of listening to *The Bible,* bored. Many of his congregation came to Poona and became sannyasins, almost thirty persons became sannyasins. And then there was a conflict. The conflict was...the non-sannyasins left the congregation because it was no longer Christian, and they had joined it because it was Christian. So they left the congregation; it became purely a sannyasin commune.

Then the old priest retired.... He used to come to festivals in the commune with his wife – he was still alive and still had love for me – but he wanted to retire, he was old. So he retired, appointing sannyasins as the priests of the congregation. When he retired, the people who had left the congregation went to the court, saying that the buildings and the grounds – and it is a beautiful place, Laguna Beach – belong to them, and these people are not the owners of it. We had to fight the case for four years continually.

The case was decided in our favor for the simple reason that these people had left the congregation; they were no longer members

of it, and they had no right.... They should have remained part of the congregation and appealed to the court, then the situation would have been different. They were the majority, but they had left, and now seeing that sannyasins had captured the whole property and the church, they wanted it back. The court dismissed the case because they had no right any longer. The moment you leave the congregation, you have no right....

So we were keeping that property, fourteen sannyasins were there, and we wanted to sell it; for the new mystery school you will need money!

Santosh has done a great service to us. Now he is the head priest. He knows nothing as far as experience is concerned, and he will destroy many people. So I have informed our people that something has to be done and Santosh has to be removed from there; or he has to pay three million dollars, and then he can do whatever he wants to do in the property. And our sannyasins have to be informed that his hypnotherapy is not going to help them.

I have told you about a world festival that Teertha, Rajen, Poonam and others were arranging in Italy. Just yesterday the news came that very few people reached there; they have made a great loss of fifteen thousand dollars, and the whole thing was absolutely dead and flat. All these great therapists were on stage, but there was no celebration, there was no feeling that you are in the presence of someone who is enlightened. People left disappointed, disgusted with the whole thing.

I told you just a few days before that they will soon be in trouble. People will desert them, because people were not coming for them – these therapists had got a wrong idea. But for fifteen years...one can get easily into a wrong idea, that people are coming for them.

Soon they will be lost in the crowd. And it is good that they should be lost; otherwise they will play with people's psychology, no knowing what they are doing and what is going to happen.

Hypnosis is really a very soft method …very mellow music. It can happen just sitting by my side in silence. It can happen just by listening so intently that all your worries, tensions disappear, and you start moving deeper into your being. But those worries, tensions, anguishes, anxieties should disappear first.

And 'hypnotherapy' is an old word. 'dehypnotherapy' is my construction. I told Santosh to make it dehypnotherapy, and he never asked, "What will be the difference between dehypnotherapy and hypnotherapy?" He simply made it dehypnotherapy. Now he has become the director of a dehypnotherapy institute, and he does not know what the difference is between dehypnotherapy and hypnotherapy.

The process is going to be totally opposite. Hypnotherapy can take you into a deliberate sleep; dehypnotherapy can take you into a deliberate awakening. But I was puzzled: he did not even ask what the difference between the two will be.

It is unfortunate, but I will have to make my people aware of the dangers of these therapists, because they will exaggerate their claims, saying that they have been with me for fifteen years. But they have not been with me for fifteen seconds. They were playing their own small role of being a guru to a small group of people. They had come for themselves, but they forgot completely. This is what happens to accidental people: they come for one thing and buy something else.

I have heard about a real estate agent who was thought to be the top man in that profession, in a big city. He was part of a big company. The boss was very angry that day and was waiting for the man. And when the man came the boss burst out in anger and said, "This is too much. The man to whom you have sold land at double price has just gone. That we can understand; you are clever and intelligent and you managed that, and that's why we pay you so much. But the man had come to say, 'It has rained, and now the land you have sold me is under eight feet of water. What kind of company is this? This is really cheating!'"

The salesman said, "Don't be worried boss, I will take care of him. I am going." And after an hour he came back, smiling, and he said, "You have to give me some reward today."

He said, "First you tell me what happened to that man and his land?"

He said, "Nothing happened. We have had two rotten boats for many days; I have sold them to that man. I told him, 'You are a fool. Such beautiful land, which becomes a lake in the rainy season…have two boats. Make a house high enough so you will have both things together. When it is the rainy season you enjoy the lake – and the boats I have brought with me.' And those boats are so rotten that they will drown the man the first time he sits in them. You don't be worried. They had been lying with the company for no one knows how many years. And we got a good price for them."

The boss said, "This is too much! You have still cheated that man – and now you have put him in a dangerous situation. Those boats will kill him."

The man said, "This world goes on this way. You don't have to think about what happens to others; you have to just think about your own pockets."

And that seems to be the state of these therapists: they are thinking about their own pockets. They are not worried about what happens to the people. What they are suggesting, they themselves have not lived; it is not their experience. And it is dishonest to tell somebody something that is not your experience, and put him into a state which can drive him crazy.

Hypnosis can be dangerous too. In wrong hands anything can be dangerous; otherwise hypnosis is a simple form of relaxation. But it can be dangerous, because the man, if he is bent upon cheating you, in those states when you are under hypnosis can suggest to you things that you don't want to do. But you will have to do them when you wake up.

I used to work with one of my students. I lived in his house for six months. His brother was my friend, and I was alone and there was no point in getting a house – and who was going to take care of it? So he said, "You'd better stay with me." And I discovered really a beautiful medium in his younger brother.

I started hypnotizing him. Just to give an example to you: one day I told him, "Tomorrow, exactly at twelve o'clock, you will kiss your pillow madly." The second day, nearabout quarter to twelve, he started looking a little strange, afraid, watching everybody, everywhere, and just in front of him I took his pillow and locked it in my suitcase. I could see tears coming into his eyes. I said, "What is the matter? Why are you crying?"

He said, "I don't know, but something like this has never happened to me. It is so strange…I cannot describe." And exactly at twelve he came to me and he said, "Please return my pillow."

I said, "What will you do at twelve? In the evening I will return it."

He said, "You have to return it to me right now."

I gave him the pillow and before six other people he started kissing the pillow madly, and looking at people thinking that he must look mad…and he himself thinking that he *is* mad – what is he doing?

I said, "Don't be worried, that's what everybody is doing. When a man is kissing a woman, a woman is kissing a man, that is a natural hypnosis, a biological hypnosis; the biology has hypnotized your chromosomes. It is not that you are doing it…and feeling so awkward, you don't want to do it before others, you want some lonely place of your own. Don't be worried! It makes no difference whether it is a pillow or a woman. What you are doing, *you* are not doing – it is your unconscious which is forcing you to do it."

He said, "That is the trouble. That's what I feel. Something in me says, 'Kiss,' and I know that this is stupid. This is only a pillow. Why should I kiss it?"

You can, under hypnosis, manage anything if you are a person who is just trying to cheat people. You can even tell the person to murder someone and he will murder – and he will be punished. He may be sentenced to death, and he will not have any explanation to give. And nobody can touch you who hypnotized him, because nobody will ever know what you did in hypnosis, while he was asleep.

Hypnosis can be misused. Everything great can be misused. Perhaps that is one of the reasons why most of the countries and cultures have tried to avoid any entanglement with hypnosis. And the word 'hypnotism' has become a condemnatory word. But that is not right; it can do immense good too. Somebody who has some difficulty in any subject can be simply hypnotized and told, "You don't have that difficulty. That subject is simple, and you have enough intelligence to understand it." And the man will start behaving differently from the next day – his unconscious got it. There is no need to fear.

People can be helped with diseases, because almost seventy percent of diseases are mental. They may be expressed through the body, but their origin is in the mind. And if you can put in the mind the idea that the disease has disappeared, that you need not worry about it, it does not exist any more, the disease will disappear.

I have tried very strange experiments with it. My work was concerned with something else. For example in Ceylon, Buddhist monks every year on the birthday of Gautam Buddha, dance on red-hot burning coal – and they don't burn. One professor from Cambridge University, a professor of psychology, had gone especially to see it, because he could not believe that it is possible. But when he saw twenty monks just dancing in the flames, and that they were not burned, he thought, "If these people can do it, why cannot I do it?" So he tried…just coming a little closer it was so hot that he ran away. He would have died if he had jumped into the pit where the fire was burning and the monks were dancing. Now, it needs a tremendous effort of hypnosis.

I tried it on the same boy, because he was a good medium. Thirty-three percent of the whole population are good mediums, and you should remember this thirty-three percent. Thirty-three percent of the people are the most intelligent too, and this thirty-three percent is the more creative, most innovative people too. These are the same people who can go into deep hypnosis; it needs immense intelligence. People with greater intelligence – if they are ready to go into it – can go to very

deep layers. And the deeper the layers are, then things can be done which look almost miraculous.

With this boy – his name was Manoj – I tried putting a hot burning piece of coal on his hand and telling him that it is a beautiful roseflower. He saw it and he said, "So beautiful, and so fragrant," and it did not burn. I tried otherwise also: putting a roseflower on his hand and telling him it is a burning hot piece of coal. He threw it immediately, but it burned his whole hand.

Mind has tremendous power over your body. The mind directs everything in your body. Seventy percent of your diseases can be changed by changing the mind, because they start from there; only thirty percent of diseases start from the body. You fall down, and you have a fracture – now, that fracture cannot be helped by hypnosis saying that you don't have any fracture. You will still have the fracture. The fracture has started from the body and the body cannot be hypnotized. The body has its own way of functioning. But if the process starts from the mind and extends to some point in the body, then it can be easily changed.

Religions have exploited it. There are many religions in India – Mohammedans do it, Tibetans do it, Burmese do it…dancing in the fire without being burned. But these are not ordinary people, they are monks. For years they have been hypnotized, and this thing has settled in their unconscious – that fire cannot burn them. But remember, only seventy percent… And that reminds me of a strange phenomenon that physiologists, medical people, and others who are concerned with man's body, are very much disturbed about and have no answer…

Allopathy succeeds only in seventy percent of cases; homeopathy succeeds only in seventy percent of cases; ayurvedic medicine succeeds only in seventy percent of cases; Greek medicine succeeds only in seventy percent of cases; Tibetan medicine succeeds only in seventy percent of cases; Chinese acupuncture succeeds only in seventy percent of cases – all the methods for curing the body succeed only in seventy percent of cases. This is a very strange coincidence.

Looked at from the outside it is a mystery. Homeopathy has nothing in it – just small sugar pills – but it succeeds, and succeeds to the same percentage. The only factor is: it succeeds if the person believes in homeopathy. The only difference in allopathy is that you need not believe in it and still it succeeds. Naturopathy, homeopathy, ayurveda – their basic need is that you should believe.

I had one ayurvedic physician, a man of rare intelligence, a nice man. He used to take care of me, and he was very famous in that area. But he became a victim of tuberculosis. When I heard it, I went to his house and there I found out he was in the hospital. I said, "This is strange. He is such a great ayurvedic physician, why should he go to allopathy?"

I went to the hospital; I asked the physician, "This is strange behavior. You have helped so many people through your medicines, can you not help yourself with your tuberculosis?"

He laughed and he said, "No I cannot, because the basic thing in ayurvedic medicine is that you have to have faith in it. I don't have faith in it. I know all about it – it is nonsense. But if people are healed, I keep my mouth shut. I don't say anything to anybody, but one thing is certain, it won't help me. I will die if I take those medicines – which cured innumerable people, even of tuberculosis! So don't be surprised, and don't tell anybody anything,

because if I survive I will have to continue my practice. If I die then you can tell the truth."

But the truth is, you need faith. It is the faith that changes the mind and affects the body – but not vice versa. The body is not superstitious, nor is it faithful; it is simply natural. It doesn't care about anything else.

There used to be a sect in America…I think it still survives in a few places, but in the beginning of this century it was very prominent. It was a Christian group, they used to call themselves Christian Scientists. They believed that everything can be cured, you just have to believe in Jesus Christ, and that your diseases are nothing but your beliefs – you believe that you have tuberculosis, so you *have* tuberculosis.

One young man met on the road with one old woman and she asked, "I don't see your father in the meetings…" They used to have meetings every Sunday.

He said, "He's sick, very badly sick."

The old woman said, "Nonsense, because we are Christian Scientists. He is a Christian Scientist; he only *believes* that he is sick."

The young man said, "If you say so, perhaps he only believes that he is sick."

After two, three days, he came across the same woman again and she asked, "What happened?"

The young man said, "Now he believes he is dead, so we had to take him to the graveyard. We tried to shake him and shouted, 'Don't believe such a thing. You are a Christian Scientist. Believe that you are alive!' But nothing happened and the whole neighborhood laughed. Now the poor man is in a grave, still believing that he is dead."

The body does not have beliefs or disbeliefs, but the mind has. And mind has immense control over the body.

One of the greatest sincerities in working

with people is to take care that what you are saying or what you are doing is not going to destroy them. And I am afraid all those therapists... While they were working in the commune in my presence there was no danger. I could have put anybody back into his right position. But now they are working without any understanding, they can prove to be very dangerous.

All the sannyasins all over the world have to be informed: beware of the therapists. In my presence I allowed them to do anything because there was no problem; if something had gone wrong I would have taken care. But now if something goes wrong – and it is bound to go wrong because they themselves are wrong – then who is going to take care?

The master's work is not easy. He has to change you, he has to transform you. But he has not to cripple you, he has not to destroy you. It is almost like walking on a razor's edge, because anything that can be helpful can also be used in such a way that it can be disastrous.

Beloved Bhagwan,
Traveling with You over the past few months and seeing the hardness of the world, instead of being hardened in response I find myself only becoming softer and softer. Would You please comment?

The ordinary response will be to become even more hard, but you are not in an ordinary situation. Even a small touch of meditativeness, of silence, of love, of compassion, a small touch of the master's presence, will mean you have totally different responses.

Seeing the hardness of the world, you will feel more compassionate towards them, you will feel softer. You will not react violently because that will be joining them in their same stupidity. Being with me, whether you know it or not you are learning thousands of things. One of them is that you cannot react.

The world may be hard – that hurts. It makes one sad that unfortunately man is still barbarous, but it does not give you the idea to curse them. On the contrary, it gives you the idea to help them, to be compassionate to them, so they can come out of their hard shells. Perhaps they are also suffering in their hardness, and there is nobody to tell them how to get out of this hardness. They are also miserable. It is out of their misery that they misbehave, because they have been mistreated. They know only that violence is power.

Seeing the world you will see that violence is not the real power. The real power is love, and that love will make you softer, forgiving, without any anger; in fact laughing at the whole hilarious situation that this world believes that it is civilized, that Charles Darwin thought that we have evolved from animals. But our behavior shows that we are still animalistic. There has been no evolution at all. Perhaps we have lost the tail, but that is not evolution; perhaps we can stand on two feet, but that is not evolution. We are still behaving so crudely, so cruelly. And nobody is there to say it, because whoever is going to say it will be crushed, will be killed.

And you have chosen to be with a man who *is* saying it, and who is going to say it to the very last breath.

But as far as you are concerned, this whole experience of world travel, and finding the politicians the same everywhere, finding the nations, governments, the police behaving in the same manner...it seems that we are living in a nightmare. Only someone who is out of it can say, "This is a nightmare!" But when somebody in a nightmare is shouting and screaming, you don't feel hard towards him; you feel soft, you want to help him.

It has been a good experience. Later on when you will recapitulate, you will see it has given you a maturity which takes lives to gain.

Beloved Bhagwan,
It seems that masters have always been betrayed by their chief disciple. The same has happened to You, with those to whom You have given so much love and attention, and on whom you have worked so hard. Bhagwan, is it that people who have more potential go higher and then can fall even lower than the ordinary human being? You have been harassed by the police and the bureaucracy. I feel they are not doing right, but they can't do otherwise; but when I hear about old sannyasins' behavior, my heart cries and it hurts me deeply.

The sannyasins I have worked harder on are not the ones who have the best potential – they were the worst; hence they needed hard work. Those who are the best I have not worked on at all. Just my presence has been enough for them, just my love has been enough for them.

So it is not that I worked hard on them because they had more potential to go high, and then to fall even below the ordinary. I worked on them because they had no possibility to go high. Even with hard work, at the most I could bring them to the normal. And they are behaving normally – I am not disappointed in them.

Whenever a person of higher potential has come to me, he has received my love, but there has been no need to work on him. He needs just a slight push, and he will be flying in the sky. None of those people have fallen, or will fall down, because one who has known the freedom of the sky cannot go back to the state where he was not even aware of his wings, and he cannot be disgraceful towards the master who helped him. It is impossible, simply impossible.

His gratitude will grow more and more because the master has not only made him aware of his wings but has pushed him into the sky and has given him total freedom. How can you be ungrateful to a person who has given you total freedom to be yourself, who has not tried in any way to impose any image, any ideal on you? Most of the sannyasins are feeling more loving than ever, more grateful than ever – and it is really a time of difficulties, when your mettle is tested.

Those who have fallen from grace were expected to. They never reached to the point where they could open their wings. If they are not grateful towards me, the simple reason is that they have not experienced anything that would make them grateful towards me. They have remained closed in their own darkness, in their own ego.

Vivek goes on asking me again and again, "Why don't you work on me?" And it is difficult to explain that there is no need of any work on her. She has to work for me, and in that work, in that care, she is growing, she is maturing.

It is a very complicated situation. I have to choose to work on the worst; they need the attention. Even if they can grow a little bit it will be good. I don't hope that they will become enlightened. Even with hard work they will not become enlightened, because the work on the worst people has a difficulty: they fight with you. While working on them, they

THE BODY DOES NOT HAVE BELIEFS

are continually fighting you! On each single step they don't want to grow; you are doing something against them. With the best quality people it is different. They want to grow.

You need not do any hard work. Just looking in their eyes is enough, just being with them is enough; it is nourishment. It is nourishment to open their wings – and they will be grateful.

The people on whom one has to work hard are not going to be grateful; they will be revengeful, because you were working against them. They never wanted to fly.

I remember an old story of a man who loved freedom immensely, who had made his country free from foreign rule, but was so much in love with freedom that he would not take the reins of the government in his own hands. Once the country became free, he left the country towards the mountains. He said, "My work is done."

The last stop was a *caravanserai*. It had a beautiful parrot, and the owner of the *serai* was also in love with the idea of freedom. If he had really been a lover of freedom he would have made the parrot free, but the parrot was in a golden cage. His idea of freedom was just a mental luxury. Because he loved freedom so much – just the idea – he had taught the parrot to repeat the word, "Freedom, freedom, freedom." The whole day, the parrot would suddenly burst into shouting, "Freedom, freedom!" He knew only one word. And this man who had fought for the freedom of his country, had been in jails, had been in dangers, he was staying there.

He thought, "This poor parrot wants freedom. He is not happy in this golden cage, nobody listens to him. The whole day he is shouting 'Freedom!'" He decided that in the night he would open the cage and let him be free, so in the middle of the night he came to the cage, opened the door of the cage, and tried to pull out the parrot. But the parrot was hitting the man with his beak, and with one of his legs he was holding onto the cage.

The man could not understand: the door was open, and he was still shouting, "Freedom!" But the man was also a strong fighter for freedom; he somehow pulled the parrot out of the cage and threw it into the sky. He had damaged both of his hands; there was blood on both of his hands where the parrot had scratched. But he was happy that the poor parrot who longed so much for freedom was at last free.

He went to his room, went to sleep, but in the morning he woke up with the sound of the parrot who was shouting, "Freedom!" He said, "Strange! Where is the parrot?" He opened the window: the parrot was sitting in the cage and the door was open, and he was repeating his routine: "Freedom…freedom!" It was just a word.

The owner came out; he knew this famous man. He looked at his hands, he looked at the open cage. He said, "You don't understand, he is only a parrot. I have taught him the word 'freedom' because I like the idea of freedom. He is a parrot; he does not even know the meaning of freedom. You should not have unnecessarily tried and got harmed. A few other people have tried it before, but he always comes back. Who wants to leave the golden cage?

"As far as I am concerned, it is only an idea; otherwise I would have thrown him out of the cage and removed the cage. But I love to hear the word 'freedom'. It is my idea; I don't want to do anything about it, it is simply philosophical – neither does the parrot want to do anything about it. For him it is not even philosophical, for him it is simply a recording, memory…not even mind. You are a man who has sacrificed his whole life for freedom. You are in a different category. You should not have bothered about this parrot – he is an idiot. It is just that he has learned the word."

The sannyasins who think they have betrayed me.... They have not betrayed me: they have betrayed themselves. How can they betray me? I had no involvement of any kind. I was not in any way expecting anything from them. I worked because I enjoyed, loved it.

They cannot betray me, they can only betray themselves. It does not affect me, it will only affect *their* lives. They will get again into their cages and start shouting, "Freedom, freedom!" and the door will remain open.

Chapter 41
May 2, 1986, Evening

Times of Crisis are Just Golden

Beloved Bhagwan,
As society's hold on people's minds begins to disintegrate, in times of social crisis such as now there seems to be a tendency for an increasing number of people to fall below the mind into madness. Also, is it true that this is paralleled by a tendency for people to look at the possibility of going beyond the mind into enlightenment?

Times of crisis are both dangerous and immensely important – dangerous for those who have no courage to explore new dimensions of life. They are bound to disintegrate into different kinds of madness, because their mind was made by the society. Now the society is disintegrating, the mind cannot remain; its roots are in the society. It is constantly nourished by the society – now that nourishment is disappearing.

Because the society is disintegrating, a great suspicion, a doubt that was never there before, is bound to arise in the individuals. And if they were just obedient people who have never gone beyond any limit that society has decided, who have always been respected, honorable citizens – in other words, just mediocre – they will immediately go mad.

They will start committing suicide, they will start jumping from high buildings...or even if they live, now they don't have a mind which can help them to figure out the situation for their life. They will become retarded, stupid, idiotic, may become schizophrenic, split into two persons – or perhaps a crowd.

In times of crisis, the danger is for those who have enjoyed the times when the society was settled, when there was no problem, everything was at ease, they were honored, respected. These were the people who had enjoyed the obedience of the mind, and these are going to be the sufferers. It is a simple arithmetic. They will go psychotic, they will go neurotic – and these words don't make much difference.

I have heard a definition. One psychoanalyst was asked, "What is the difference between psychosis and neurosis?"

And the psychoanalyst said, "The psychotic person believes that two and two are five. And the neurotic person knows that two and two are four, but is not at ease with the fact that two and two *are* four." So the difference is very fine. Both are in trouble.

But times of crisis are of tremendous significance for those daring souls who have never bothered about society's respectability, its honors; who have never bothered about what others think about them, but have done only that which they felt right to do; who have in a certain way been always rebellious, individualistic. For these people the times of crisis are just golden, because the society is disintegrating. Now it cannot condemn anybody – it is itself condemned, cursed. It cannot say to others that they are wrong. It is itself proving wrong; its whole wisdom is proving just foolish, superstitious.

The daring individual can use this opportunity to go beyond mind, because now the society cannot prevent him, cannot hinder him. Now he is free.

It is almost like a situation in a jail…when the doors are open, the guards have disappeared and the jailer is nowhere to be found. The people who have some sense, some intelligence, will use it for freedom. But those who have become so enslaved that they cannot think of freedom – imprisonment has become their home – they will simply panic, "What is going to happen today? No guards? No jailer? The doors are open! Who will take care of us? Who will provide food for us?"

There will be people whose slavery has penetrated to their very soul; these people will go berserk. But the people who always were in search of a moment when they can escape from the prison will be immensely happy. This was the time they have been waiting and praying for. They will escape out of the prison into the open sky. Going beyond the mind is going into the open sky, full of stars, the moon, the sun – the immensity of it… It becomes yours; the whole existence becomes yours.

The mind is a small cage.

So moments of crisis are both…and that is what is happening all around the world. There has never been so intense a search for spiritual growth, for meditation. But there has never been so much madness either. Both are happening because the status quo is no longer powerful; it has lost control.

When Galileo found that the earth moves around the sun, not vice versa as *The Bible* says, the pope asked him to be present in his court. Many things happened that day. One was very important. Galileo asked, "What does it matter if one statement in *The Bible* is proved wrong? It does not prove the whole *Bible* wrong. I am a devout Christian, a practicing Christian, and I don't see the point that if one statement is wrong it makes a difference."

But the pope said, "You don't understand" – and the pope was right. He said, "When one statement is proved wrong then thousands of problems will arise. One – that God can be wrong. And if he is wrong about one statement, what is the certainty about other statements?" Just one brick taken out of the palace, and the whole palace may collapse.

"I cannot allow," the pope said, "any statement in *The Bible* to be wrong."

His argument is significant. Today not

only one thing about the old mind, the old society, is wrong, but so many things are wrong that it needs an absolute idiot to still believe in it. Just a little intelligence and it is impossible to be part of the old mind. It has lost credibility – and not in one place, but all over the world. There are different kinds of old traditions, but they all have come to a point where so many things are scientifically proved wrong.

You will be surprised to know… One Jaina monk had come to see me; he had collected millions of rupees to make a lab to prove that man has not reached the moon. He wanted my support, that I should be the director of his lab. He would give any finance that was needed, but it had to be proved that no man has stepped on the moon.

I said, "Why are you so much worried about it?"

He said, "You don't understand. In Jainism, the moon is a god, not a planet. You cannot walk on a god. And they have not only walked on a god, they have brought stones and other things from the moon to be studied on the earth. It has to be proved that they are deceiving the whole world, that all these things they had taken from the earth, and they have brought them back… Nobody has been to the moon; nobody can have been, otherwise the whole system of Jainism will collapse." I said, "Just for a single thing, that the moon proves to be a planet not a god…?"

He said, "If one thing is wrong, then everything becomes suspicious. We cannot afford anything to be wrong."

I said, "You are too late! Many things have already been proved wrong. You are not very knowledgeable. You have been simply reading the newspapers, and because it is a recent event, man landing on the moon… otherwise in three hundred years science has destroyed much that all the religions have believed in for centuries."

That man was really in tremendous anguish. And I said, "For you, being a monk, it does not matter whether anything is wrong or right – your search is for the truth, for peace and silence. And you are getting so much upset. Your very anguish shows that your own mind is shattered. It is not a question of Jaina scriptures, or the Jaina tradition, it is a question of *your* mind.

"You are collecting all this money, not for Jaina scriptures but to save your sanity; otherwise you would go insane. You have sacrificed your whole life, and now you find that the gods you have been worshipping are not gods but just planets, as ordinary as the earth, and very poor – no water, no plants, no life. It is your mind that is going to be shattered. How will you account for your whole life…?"

This is the situation of many people of intelligence. Either they are going insane …you can see it – psychotherapy and other schools of therapies are growing fast. They are the most highly paid people, people are going through psychoanalysis for years at a time. In fact people have started boasting… In women's clubs you can go and hear it, that one woman will be saying, "How many years have you been in psychoanalysis? – just seven years? I have been in psychoanalysis for fifteen years." It has become something of pride. But to be in psychoanalysis simply means you are insane; otherwise why are you taking the treatment? And it is spreading.

But the most intelligent people are rushing towards the East to find some way, some method, some meditation – Yoga, Zen, Sufism, Hassidism. Somewhere somebody must know how to get over this critical stage, how to go beyond the traditional mind and still remain centered, sane, and intelligent.

Thousands of people are moving towards the East.

It is very hilarious because thousands of people are coming from the East to the West to study science, medicine, engineering, electronics, and the people who know all these are going to the East, just to learn how to sit silently and do nothing.

But it is a beautiful time. The grip of society is lost. Yes, the mediocre will suffer, but anyway they were not enjoying, they were not really living; they were simply being hypocrites. By being insane at least they will be real, authentic. They won't lose anything – of course they won't gain much....

But the people who will go beyond mind will create the new man, the new mind. And the most special thing to be remembered about the new mind is that it will never become a tradition, that it will be constantly renewed. If it becomes a tradition it will be the same thing.

The new mind has to become continuously new, every day new, ready to accept any unexpected experience, any unexpected truth... just available, vulnerable. It will be a tremendous excitement, a great ecstasy, a great challenge.

So I don't think this crisis is bad; it is good. A few people will lose their masks, and will be actually what they are – neurotic, psychotic – but at least they will be true and they will be honest. You may think they are mad; they are not mad, they are simply in a state of very great surprise. They have believed too much in the old mind, and it betrayed them.

But the best of the intelligence will reach to heights unknown before. And if even in a traditional world, a man like Gautam Buddha or Chuang Tzu or Pythagoras is possible, we can conceive that in the atmosphere that the new mind will create, a thousandfold more awakened people, enlightened people will become easily possible.

If the new mind can prevail, then life can become an enlightening process. And enlightenment will not be something rare, that it happens once in a while to somebody very special; it will become a very ordinary human experience, that only once in a while some really idiotic person misses.

Beloved Bhagwan,
I have hesitated for long to ask this question because it seems to reach deep down into my unconscious, and there is a lot of fear connected with it.
For the past fifteen years I have experienced tension of varying degrees in my heart area, for which there has been no physical explanation. It can vary from sharp, breath-taking pain, which can last for hours, to a slight feeling of pressure. It disappears when I love, melt, let-go, and when I am in harmony with my body. Does it have something to do with the name You gave me? Do I hold back?
I would be grateful if You could throw some light on this.

The question is from Premda, and his name has certainly to do something with the problem.

It is not physical; it is certainly concerned with relaxation, total melting, forgetting oneself completely. In those moments it disappears, so certainly it is not physical. You have to learn to give more love. This is not only your problem; in varying degrees it is the problem of everybody.

Everybody wants to be loved; that is a wrong beginning.

It starts because the child, the small child, cannot love, cannot say anything, cannot do anything, cannot give anything; he can only get. A small child's experience of love is of getting: getting from the mother, getting from the father, getting from brothers, sisters, getting from guests, strangers – but always getting. So the first experience that settles deep in his unconscious is that he has to get love. But the trouble arises because everybody has been a child, and everybody has the same urge to get love; nobody is born in any other way. So all are asking, "Give us love," and there is nobody to give because the other person was also brought up in the same way.

One has to be alert and aware that just an incident of birth should not remain a constant prevailing state of your mind. Rather than asking, "Give me love," start giving love. Forget about getting, simply give – and I guarantee you, you will get much. But you are not to think about getting. You are not even indirectly, by the side, to watch whether you are getting it or not. That much will be enough disturbance. You simply give, because to give love is so beautiful that getting love is not so great. This is one of the secrets.

Giving love is the really beautiful experience, because then you are an emperor. Getting love is very small experience, and it is the experience of a beggar. Don't be a beggar. At least as far as love is concerned, be an emperor, because it is an inexhaustible quality in you. You can go on giving as much as you like. Don't be worried that it will be exhausted, that one day you will suddenly find, "My God! I don't have any love to give anymore."

Love is not a quantity; it is a quality, and a quality of a certain category that grows by giving and dies if you hold it. If you are miserly about it, it dies. So be really spendthrift. Don't bother to whom – that is really the idea of a miserly mind: I will give love to certain persons with certain qualities.

You don't understand that you have so much…you are a raincloud. The raincloud does not bother where it rains – on the rocks, in the gardens, in the ocean – it doesn't matter. It wants to unburden itself. And that unburdening is a tremendous relief.

So the first secret is: Don't ask for it, and don't wait, thinking that you will give if somebody asks you. Give it!

The founder of the theosophical movement, Madame Blavatsky had a strange habit her whole life – and she lived long, and traveled all over the world and created a world movement… In fact no other woman has been so powerful in the whole history of man, has had influence worldwide. She used to carry many bags with her, full of seeds of flowers. Her whole luggage was nothing but seeds of flowers. Sitting in the train by the side of the window she would go on throwing seeds outside the window, and people would ask, "What are you doing? You carry so much unnecessary luggage, and then you go on throwing those seeds out of the window for thousands of miles."

She said, "These are seeds of flowers, beautiful flowers. When the summer goes and the rains come, these seeds will become plants. Soon there will be millions of flowers. I will not be coming back on the route and I will never see them, but thousands of people will see them, thousands of people will enjoy their fragrance."

She actually made almost all the railroads in India full of flowers, and people said, "When you will not them again, what is *your* joy?"

She said, "My joy is that so many people will be joyful. I am not a miser. Whatever I can do to make people joyful, happy, I will do;

it is part of my love." She really loved humanity, and did everything that she felt was right.

Just give your love to anybody – a stranger. It is not a question that you have to give something very valuable, just a helping hand and that will be enough. In twenty-four hours, whatever you do should be done with love, and the pain in your heart will disappear.

And because you will be loving so much, people will love you. It is a natural law. You get what you give. In fact you get more than you give.

Learn giving, and you will find so many people being loving towards you who had never looked at you, who had never bothered about you.

Your problem is that you have a heart full of love but you have been a miser; that love has become a burden on the heart. Rather than making the heart blossom you have been hoarding it, so once in a while when you are in a moment of love you feel it disappearing. But why one moment? Why not every moment? It is not even a question of a living being. You can touch this chair with a loving hand. The thing depends on you, not on the object.

Then you will find a great relaxation and a great disappearance of your self – which is a burden – and a melting into the whole.

This is certainly a disease, in the literal meaning of the word: it is a dis-ease. It is not sickness, so no physician can help you. It is simply a tense state of your heart which simply wants to give more and more. Perhaps you have more love than other people, perhaps you are more fortunate, and you are making out of your fortune a great misery for yourself. Share it, without bothering to whom you are giving. Just give it, and you will find

tremendous peace and silence. This will become your meditation.

One can come to meditation through many directions; perhaps this is going to be your direction.

Beloved Bhagwan,
What I find really amazing about Your childhood is that, unlike most of us as children, You seem to have an intrinsic and undeniable understanding that Your parents' interpretation of reality and Your experience of reality were often two different things. You insist that You are no different from us, yet this facet of Your childhood alone is more than enough evidence that You house the most unique sort of intelligence.
I would be grateful for Your comment.

Every child understands that he sees the world in a different way than his parents. As far as seeing is concerned, it is absolutely certain. His values are different. He may collect sea shells on the beach and the parents will say, "Throw them away. Why are you wasting your time?" And for him they were so beautiful. He can see the difference; he can see that their values are different. The parents are running after money – he wants to collect butterflies. He can't see why you are so interested in money; what you are going to do with it? His parents cannot see what he is going to do with these butterflies, or these flowers.

Every child comes to know this, that there are differences. The only question is: he is afraid to assert that he is right. As far as he is concerned, he should be left alone. It is a question of just a little courage, which is also not missing in children. But the whole society is managed in such a way that even a beautiful quality like courage in a child will be condemned.

I was not willing to bow down in the temple to a stone statue. And I said to them, "If you want, you can force me. You have more physical force than me. I am small; you can force me, but remember you are doing an ugly act. It will not be my prayer, and it will destroy even your prayer, because you are doing violence to a little child who cannot resist physically."

One day while they were inside praying in the temple, I climbed on the top of the temple, which was dangerous. Only once a year a painter used to climb it, but I had seen the painter and how he had managed. He had put nails at the backside as steps. I followed him and I was sitting on the top of the temple. When they came out they saw me sitting there and they said, "What are you doing there? In the first place, do you want to commit suicide?"

I said, "No, I simply want to make you alert that if you force me, I can do anything that is within my power. This is the answer, for you to remember that you cannot force me to do anything."

They begged me, "Be quiet. We will arrange for somebody to bring you down."

I said, "Don't be worried. If I can come up, I can come down." They had no idea about those nails. I had been particularly watching the painter, how he manages, because everybody wondered – that this painter was really great. He was painting all the temples.

I came down. They said, "We will never force you about anything, but don't do such a thing! You could have killed yourself."

I said, "The responsibility would have been on you."

It is not a question that intelligence is not in the children. It is that they just don't use their assertiveness because it is condemned by everybody. Now, everybody condemned my family because I had gone up on top of the temple – that means beyond their god. That was insulting to their god. And I said, "If a painter can go… And do you know the painter is a Mohammedan? I am at least not a Mohammedan yet."

My father said, "What do you mean, that you are not a Mohammedan yet?"

I said, "Exactly what I have said. If you torture me too much I can become a Mohammedan."

I had even asked the *malvi* of the mosque nearby, "Are you willing to initiate me into Mohammedanism?"

He said, "You want to be initiated? Your parents… There will be trouble in the town."

I said, "Don't be worried, because you are not forcing me. I am accepting Mohammedanism. I will stand in front of the mosque and tell my parents and to the whole town that I have not been forced."

He said, "This is dangerous. It may create a riot in the city and a few people may be killed."

I said, "Don't be worried, I am not going to be a Mohammedan. You just remember, if my father asks you, you say to him, 'Yes, he has come, and if he wants to become a Mohammedan we cannot refuse.' I am not going to come, but this much you have to tell him."

And my father asked him, "Has he come to you?"

He said, "He has come, and he is very insistent."

My father said, "It is better to leave him alone!"

They had a meeting of the whole family,

"Leave him alone; he is really dangerous. If he becomes a Mohammedan we will be condemned by the whole city. And he really has gone, and he is insisting, 'If anything happens again to force me, then I am going to change my religion.'"

That was the last…! They remained silent; they never told me to come to the temple. I never went to the temple. Slowly they learned one thing, that I am not dangerous, just they should not force me into a corner.

Each child has to be assertive, that's the only thing. And what is there to lose? But children are so dependent, and I don't see that they have to be so dependent. They told me many times, "We will stop giving you food."

I said, "You do it. I can start begging – in this very city. I have to survive, I have to do something. You can stop giving me food, but you cannot stop me from begging. Begging is everybody's birthright."

There is not any difference of intelligence, but I see differences of assertiveness because children who are obedient are honored.

In my family, my other brothers would be called when some guests would be there; my uncles would be called, "He has come first class. He has come this, he has done this…"

And I would introduce myself, "I have done nothing, and all these people are just at a loss what to do with me. They never wanted me to be introduced to you, so I thought I should introduce myself!"

This happened… One member of parliament was visiting the house – he was a friend of my father. They were introducing everybody, and I was not called; I was simply ignored. When I came in and I introduced myself to him he said, "But this is strange. Nobody called you."

I said, "Nothing is strange. These are all obedient people. I am disobedient – and you will have some taste of it soon."

And my father said, "Leave him alone. Why should he have a taste?"

I said, "He is going to speak in my school" – I was in the ninth class – "he is going to address my high school, and I am going to create trouble. I am just informing him beforehand that I am going to ask questions, and he should not think that because he is a great orator and a parliamentarian that I will be impressed by these things. Nothing impresses me."

My father told him, "You be aware of him. He will ask something, something that you cannot answer, because he is continuously harassing us. He will never ask anything that you can answer, and he has a capacity for finding…how he finds, we don't know. He asks questions that you cannot answer, and in a public meeting where you are addressing hundreds of people he can make you look a fool."

That man became really afraid. He asked me, "It will be good if you come with me, in the car" – just to persuade me not to create any trouble.

I said, "Nothing will help. I can come in your car that will simply shock my headmaster, my masters, and the whole school. But there is no way of giving me any bribe."

He said, "You look to be so strong…at this age?"

I said, "I am not strong, I simply ask simple questions and I want their answers. When you come to address the school, I have every right to ask you a few things. You are continually asking in the parliament: I see your name in the newspapers everyday – questions to the prime minister, to this minister, to that minister – you should not be so much afraid of a small child. What can I ask?"

But he said, "Your father is so afraid, and we have been colleagues, we have studied together; I trust in his judgment. And you also look dangerous."

We went to the school. He started speaking; I stood up and asked him, "Be honest and tell everybody, why have you brought me in your car? Just be sincere!"

And he said, "Your father was right. You ask questions which cannot be answered."

I said, "This is a simple question. If you cannot answer it I can answer. You know the answer, I know the answer, I want everybody else also to know the answer."

My principal tried to settle the matter saying, "You sit down. He is our guest, and much depends on him for grants and this…"

I said, "That is not my business. I am not the principal of this school, I am simply a student. And I am not asking a very complicated question or any question which is dangerous to the security of the country or anything. I am just asking him why he has brought me in his car. If he accepts it sincerely I will not ask another question."

He said, "I am sorry, but it is true. What he is saying is right – it was a bribe. I thought that sitting in my car he would feel good and he would not harass me." But he looked so embarrassed saying such small things. When I came back home, my father said, "Did you create any trouble?"

I said, "I did not create any trouble, he himself created it. He asked me to sit in his car. I was going myself, walking to the school. He created the trouble."

Each child, if supported by the parents to be courageous, has the intelligence to make clear that his values are different, his perceptions are different. But nobody supports, everybody tries to repress the child. The only difference you can make is in that… To me

anything that was repressive was a challenge. Then I was provoked to do something – and they had to learn the lesson.

So the next time I was the *first* to be called to be introduced, because they knew that I would come by myself and then it would become more difficult. It was better to introduce me. But they had nothing to say about me – what to say about me?

So I told them, "You can say exactly the truth: 'He is disobedient; he is a problem. He is continuously creating trouble for the family, for the neighborhood, for the whole town – teachers, students. And the whole day we are tired of listening to complaints coming…' You can simply introduce me the way I am. Why are you so afraid, when I am not afraid? These are true things."

A situation was created that instead of my being afraid, my whole family was afraid of me. And each child can do that…just a little courage. One day my father said, "You have to be back in the house before nine o'clock in the night."

I said, "If I don't come – then?"

He said, "Then the doors will not be open."

I said, "Then keep your doors closed. I will not even knock on the doors, and I am not going to come before nine. I will sit outside, and tell everybody! Whoever will be passing, they will ask, 'Why are you sitting in darkness in this cold night?' And I will tell them, 'This is the situation…'"

He said, "That means you will create trouble for me."

I said, "I am not creating it. You are giving this order. I have never thought about it, but when you say, 'Nine is the deadline,' then I cannot come before nine. It simply is against my intelligence. And I am not doing anything; I will be simply sitting outside. And if somebody asks, 'Why are you sitting...?' And anybody is going to ask. If you are sitting in the road, everybody who will be passing is going to ask, 'Why are you sitting here in the cold?' Then I will have to explain, 'This is the situation...'"

He said, "Forget about that limit. You come whenever you want."

And I said, "I am not going to knock. The doors have to remain open. Why should the doors be closed – just to harass me? There is no reason to close the doors." In my part of India the town is awake up to twelve, because it is so hot that only after twelve it starts cooling down. So people remain awake, work continues. The day is so hot that they may rest in the day and work in the night. I said, "There is no reason to close the doors when you are sitting inside and working. Leave the doors open. Why should I knock?"

He said, "Okay, the doors will remain open. It was my fault to say to you, 'Come before nine,' because everybody comes before nine.'"

I said, "I am not everybody. If it is suitable for them to come before nine they can come. If it is suitable for me, I will come. But don't cut my freedom, don't destroy my individuality. Just let me be myself."

It is a simple question of asserting yourself against those who have power. But you have subtle powers that you can use against them. For example, if I said, "I will simply sit in the road," I am also using power. If I am sitting on top of the temple, I am also using power. If they can threaten me, I can also threaten them. But children simply fall in line just to be respectable, just to be obedient, just to be on the right path. And the right path means whatsoever their parents are showing them.

You are right, I was a little different. But I don't think it is any superiority, just a little bit of difference. And once I learned the art, then I refined it. Once I knew how to fight with people who have power – and you don't have – then I refined it, and managed perfectly well. I always found out some way. And they were always surprised because they thought, "Now he cannot do anything against this" – because they were always thinking rationally.

I have no devotion to reason.

My devotion is basically towards freedom.

By what means it is achieved does not matter. Every means becomes good if it brings freedom to you, individuality to you, and you are not enslaved. The children just don't have the idea. They think that their parents are doing everything good for them.

I always made it clear to them, "I don't suspect your intentions, and I hope you don't suspect my intentions either. But there are things on which we disagree. Do you want me to agree on everything with you? – whether you are right or wrong? Are you absolutely certain, that you are right? If you are not so absolutely certain, then give me the freedom to decide for myself. At least I will have the pleasure of going wrong on my own decision, and I will not make you feel guilty and responsible."

One just has to be alert about one thing: whatsoever your parents say, they cannot do. They cannot harm you, they cannot kill you, they can only threaten you. Once you know they can only threaten you, their threats don't make any difference; you can also threaten them. And you can threaten them in such a way that they will have to accept your right to choose what you want to do.

I made it absolutely clear to them, "If you can convince me that what you are saying is right, I will do it. But if you cannot convince me then please don't dictate. Then you are teaching me to be a fascist; you are not helping

TIMES OF CRISIS ARE JUST GOLDEN

me to be a liberated man, but somebody imprisoned."

So there are differences, but nothing that is special or superior. And children can be taught; they all can do the same, because I have tried that too, even in my childhood. Students were puzzled: I harassed the teachers, I harassed the principal, and still they could not do anything against me. And *they* would do something wrong and immediately they were in trouble. They started asking me, "What is the secret?"

I said, "There is no secret. You have to be very clear that you are right and that you have a reason to support it. Then whoever is against you will see. Whether he is a teacher or the principal does not matter."

One of my teachers went in great anger into the office of the principal and fined me ten rupees for my misbehavior. I just went behind him, and while he was fining me I was standing by his side. As he moved away, with the same pen I fined him twenty rupees for *his* misbehavior.

He said, "What are you doing? That register is for teachers to fine the students."

I asked, "Where is it written? In this register, nowhere is it written that only teachers can fine the students. I think this register is to fine anybody who misbehaves. If there is anywhere else where it is written, I would like to see it."

Meanwhile the principal came in. He said, "What is the matter?"

And the teacher said, "He has spoiled the register. He has fined *me* twenty rupees for misbehavior."

The principal said, "That is not right."

I said, "Do you have any written document that says that no student can fine a teacher, even if the teacher is misbehaving?"

The principal said, "This is a difficult matter. We don't have any document, it is just a convention that teachers punish."

I said, "It has to be changed. Punishment is perfectly right, but it should not be one sided. I will pay those ten rupees only if this man pays twenty rupees." Because the principal could not ask him for twenty rupees, he could not ask me for those ten rupees, and the fine is still there! When after a few years I visited the school, he showed me, "Your fine is still there."

I said, "Leave it there for other students to know."

One just has to find ways…!

So there must be some difference, but it is not of superiority. It is just a question of using your courage, your intelligence, and risking. What is the danger? What could those people have destroyed? At the most they could have failed me in their class – of which they were afraid, because that meant I would be again in their class the next year! – so it was really favorable to me. They wanted to get rid of me as quickly as possible. That was the only power in the teacher's hands, to fail a student.

I had made it clear to every teacher, "You can fail me, it doesn't matter. Whether I pass a class in two years or three years does not matter. This whole life is so useless – somewhere I have to pass my life. I can pass my whole life in this school, but I will make your life hell, because once the fear of failing disappears then I can do anything." So even the teachers who were against me were giving me more marks than needed just to help me move into another class, so I was no longer a burden to them.

If parents really love children, they will help them to be courageous – courageous even against themselves. They will help them to be courageous against teachers, against society, against anybody who is going to destroy their individuality.

And that's what I mean: the new mind will have these different qualities. The children born under the new mind and the new man will not be treated the way they have been treated down the centuries. They will be encouraged to be themselves, to be assertive, to be self-respectful. And that will change the whole quality of life. It will become more shiny, alive, and more juicy.

Chapter 42
May 3, 1986, Morning

Everybody
is Enough

Beloved Bhagwan,
The gift of being here with You is over-shadowed by a sense of unworthiness. It troubles me because I don't feel as available to You as I could be.
Can You help me to dissolve this?

It is something very essential to understand, that people who are really worthy always feel unworthiness, and the people who are really unworthy never feel it. Not feeling it is part of unworthiness; feeling it is part of worthiness.

The question is from Kirtan.

It is good that one feels it, because there are no limits to unworthiness – you can go as high as you desire; it is just like the sky. And to feel it means the ego is dissolving. The ego never feels unworthy; it wants to prove that everybody else is unworthy and only it is worthy. It is humbleness that feels unworthiness and pain which can give birth to a new life.

So don't take it as a problem. Accept it as a blessing. Let the ego completely dissolve. It cannot stand the feeling of unworthiness. There are a few things in life which function in a strange way. A real lover never feels that he is loving as much as he should. He is always feeling something more can be done, something better can be done. These feelings are part of real love. And a hypocritical lover always feels that he is the biggest lover in the world. He is fake, he has no love; hence the feeling that more can be done does not arise in him. On the contrary he will try to prove that the other is not loving enough.

Life in one sense is very simple, and in another sense, very complex. Don't take it at its face value. It is perfectly good to feel unworthy on the way. It will create humble-ness, egolessness, gratitude, selflessness. And once you have understood that this feeling of unworthiness is one of the most beautiful gifts of life, once you start enjoying it, then it goes on opening doors of more mysteries. A point comes when you disappear, and with your disappearance unworthiness also disappears, because it cannot hang on without you.

So go on keeping it as a religious phenomenon, as part of your meditation, and it will lead you to the right place, where the last trace of your self disappears. With it, unworthiness also disappears. That does not mean you start feeling worthy; it simply means that worthiness and or unworthiness become irrelevant. You are beyond both.

So what is happening to you is perfectly right. Go deeply into it, and go on rejoicing – not with a sadness, "I am unworthy." That sadness will prevent... Not taking it as a problem that has to be solved, no. It has not to be solved, it has to be dissolved, but the dissolution is not in your hands. When it reaches to its ripeness, is dissolves itself. And when one does not think in terms of worth, one becomes part of the vast *isness* that surrounds you.

There are millions of flowers. No flower feels unworthy – it may be just a grass flower – but neither does the lotus feel worthy. Those qualities don't exist in nature because the ego does not exist there. All our problems are somehow or other related with the ego.

If you were feeling worthy then it would be dangerous: that will feed the ego, nourish the ego. But you are feeling unworthy. That is perfectly the right thing to go deeply into.

Beloved Bhagwan,
In discourse the other morning I had a realization that was so obvious I cannot believe I just got it: I've been dehypnotized.

The process started the moment I heard Your voice ten years ago. Today I felt so close to something. You could have said, "Count to three and you will be awake."
I can't believe how deeply programmed we are against hypnosis, and however so gently You have been pointing that out to us – so much so that we even think it is an insult when people say, "Bhagwan has hypnotized you," when in fact it's the greatest gift on the earth.
Your patience, brilliance, compassion, mastery and wisdom has me in constant awe.

I was really going to say, "Kaveesha, one...two...three!" But then I thought, "Dehypnotizing Kaveesha before everybody else is not good manners!" so I remained silent. But she heard it anyway.

What she is saying is exactly true. My talking to you has not the ordinary purpose that talking serves: indoctrination – that is not the purpose of my talks. I don't have any doctrine; my talking is really a process of dehypnotization. Just listening to me, slowly, slowly you will be free of all the programs that the society has forced you to believe in. Just by listening with an open heart, with a receiving gratefulness, it is bound to happen.

There have been hypnotists but nobody has ever tried speaking itself as a method of dehypnotizing. It can become a music in you; it can relax you, can make you silent, can give a new rhythm to your heart...a new feeling of my presence, a new perception of reality.

And I may be talking about anything. It is not the question that I am talking about *these* things; these are by-products. I may be talking about A or B or C – which are absolutely unrelated to dehypnosis. The question is your way of listening. If it is right, then whatever I am saying will relax your being totally, and slowly, slowly your conditionings will start falling apart.

And I want to do it this way. I don't want to hypnotize you – that means to make you first unconscious. This way there is no need to make you unconscious. You become more conscious, more alert. You are becoming conscious and alert in order to listen to me. But my purpose is not to teach you something, but to use teaching as an excuse to make you conscious, alert, so you can start touching the superconsciousness in you.

And from superconsciousness a higher quality of hypnosis arises.

The ordinary methods of hypnosis can be dangerous; you can be in the hands of a person who can use you against yourself, because you *are* unconscious. You are not in a better state than your normal consciousness.

Nobody before has used speaking to help you to become superconscious, so I need not say to you, "Drop this, drop that" – I do not have to give you post-hypnotic suggestions. Everything will be happening here-now, and it will be happening in your fully-alert state, so you cannot be used, cannot be misused; you cannot be exploited.

Hypnotism became condemned because people started exploiting it. Anybody who is as unconscious as you are can use the technique of hypnotism. That's why it became condemned; otherwise such a beautiful phenomenon which can help you towards meditation would not have been condemned.

My way cannot be misused. And when people say to you that you are hypnotized, don't feel hurt. Tell them, "Yes, we have been hypnotized to wake up. We have been hypnotized to enter into superconsciousness. We have not been hypnotized to go into lower realms of the mind, but to the higher super-conscious or collective superconscious" – and

finally if you simply go on listening to me, doing nothing, the cosmic consciousness is going to be your experience.

But I have never said it before, and people have always wondered: if I don't have a religion, don't have a doctrine, don't have a teaching, then why do I go on talking to people? I could not tell them; they would not understand. Only those who will experience the relaxation of superconsciousness will be able to see the point. And then certainly, as Kaveesha says, they will understand how long I have been waiting, and how long I have been patient, and how I have been condemned for things which have nothing to do with me. But I have remained silent – because it does not bother *me;* the only thing that I am interested in is that my people should attain to the state from where they cannot fall before I leave the body.

I cannot give you anything more precious.

Beloved Bhagwan,
How might we sannyasins best relate with one another?
We are such an amazing assortment of unique individuals – all determined to be ourselves and avoid society's impositions. Yet we are all joined by a common thread: love – our love for You – and we all long for the moment when we can melt into You, when we can finally come home.

It is not difficult.
Only individuals can relate; personalities cannot. Personalities are like shadows. They cannot meet, they cannot merge, because they don't exist. Personalities are fake. That's why in the whole world people are talking of love, but there is no love. They are talking of

friendship, but there is no friendship – even talking of trust. But for that a tremendously powerful individuality is needed. Personalities cannot trust; they are always afraid – afraid that their reality may be exposed, may be known.

As far as my people are concerned, there is no problem; it is not a question of fighting for individuality. I declare you individuals, so your individuality is not a problem – that you have to protect it. You can mix and merge, you can be friends, you can be lovers. You can work together; you can work under each other without any fear because you have dropped the personality, which was always afraid. Now you have individuality, a solid rock which is fearless.

I have told you the story of Diogenes, that he was caught by four thieves. They wanted to sell him in a slave market. They were very happy to find such a beautiful, healthy individual. First they were afraid and they were hiding behind the trees near where Diogenes was sitting, thinking, "He alone is enough to finish all four of us!" He was a strong man.

Diogenes was listening to their whispers, "What to do? We are four, but he alone is enough…" Diogenes finally said, "Don't bother – just come and take me where you want."

They were very much afraid: what kind of man is this? They said, "We are thieves and we want to take you to the slave market, because for you we can get the highest price anybody has ever got. We cannot normally find slaves of your individuality, beauty, proportion, strength."

Diogenes said, "Don't be worried." They started trying to tie him up; he said, "Stop, there is no need to bind me. You come behind me, I know the way."

They could not believe it – that man is mad or what? And he started moving towards the slave market. And everybody who saw them on the way thought that he was the master and they were the slaves. Those four poor thieves were so afraid: "This man can do anything. We got unnecessarily involved with this man!"

And this is what he did: he stood on the pulpit where the slaves have to stand so every buyer can see them, go around and look at them, and he shouted, "Listen, all you slaves who are here! For the first time a master is for sale. If any one of you has guts, you can purchase me. And these poor fellows, four fellows you see – they need money. And it does not matter to me where I am. My individuality cannot be destroyed."

There was great silence. The whole marketplace became utterly silent, because he had said, "A master is for sale." One king who had come to look for a few slaves became interested, and he was ready to pay any price. Diogenes asked the thieves, "How much do you want? Don't be shy – just ask it. Get the money and get lost!"

They got the money. Diogenes sat on the chariot with the king, and the king said, "This is strange. You should not have done that."

Diogenes said, "Those poor fellows were in need, and as far as I am concerned, wherever I am I will remain myself." Even the king became afraid, because only those two were in the chariot, and the man was so strong: grabbing the neck of the king, he could have simply finished him.

Diogenes said, "But don't be worried. I could finish you right now, but I will not. You have helped those four poor men. I will come with you, and I will serve as a slave, because even in slavery my freedom is intact. I am choosing it; nobody is imposing it upon me."

Do you see the difference? Only a slavery imposed is slavery; a slavery accepted, chosen, is the highest expression of freedom. You are so certain of your being, of your individuality, that you are not worried, even of becoming a slave. The king was happy. He said, "No, I will not make you a slave, but a friend. As far as I understand you must be Diogenes. I have heard about the man, and I feel that there cannot be many Diogeneses. You *must* be Diogenes."

Diogenes said, "I am," and he lived with the king in the palace, naked, as he used to live in his own way. The king told him, "In the palace it looks odd, embarrassing. You should use clothes."

Diogenes said, "Then it is better you don't make me a friend; you make me a slave. If friendship cannot allow freedom, what kind of friendship is this? You make me a slave, then whatever you say I will do." But the king had started loving the man. His sincerity, his authority, his power was magnetic. He freed him. He said, "I cannot make you a slave and I know I cannot make you a friend. In the palace, living naked, where other kings come and stay, it will be always a problem."

Diogenes said, "This is your decision. I am simply your slave. If you make me free, that's perfectly okay. I am happy that those four poor people have been helped. And I have found a beautiful way to help poor people: if sometimes somebody is poor I can tell him, 'Take me to the slave market and sell me.'"

Here with me your individuality is accepted, declared, so you need not be worried that it will be taken away, that it can be crushed by others, that somebody may enslave you, force you to do things.

Don't be worried – nobody can force you. You have always the choice. Ultimately, you are to decide, and it is good to decide in a way so the people who are with me don't feel any antagonism between them. They love me –

that is a joining thread. There is no organization. Each sannyasin is connected to me individually, but because he is *my* sannyasin… Other sannyasins who are joined with me have to be respectful of each other, because each of my sannyasins somehow represents me. Your love for me must be shared with my people too.

Beloved Bhagwan,
I understand You to have said that in hypnosis one's problems can be worked out on an unconscious level, and that this method has the advantage over psychotherapy in that it can cover a lot more ground in a far shorter time.
Is it necessary merely for the contents of the unconscious to surface during hypnosis, or does the conscious mind need to be made aware of those contents for the clearing to be complete?

The conscious mind has to be made aware; otherwise there will be no change. The contents of the unconscious mind are repressed by the conscious mind. To reverse the process, they have to be brought back to the conscious mind, and the conscious mind has to express them instead of repressing them.

Because of repression they had gone into the unconscious; unless the reverse process of expression is there, they will remain. They can be available to the hypnotists, but the conscious mind does not know about it. For the conscious mind they are still repressed, and it is only through the conscious mind that they have a way to go out of your being.

From the unconscious mind directly, there is no door. A contact can be made, but there is no way for any content to go out of the unconscious mind directly; first it has to come to the conscious mind. It is just like your main gate. You have entered at the main gate. If you want to go out you will have to go to the main gate; otherwise you will remain confined.

The deeper you go into the unconscious mind, the thicker the walls become. The collective unconscious mind has even thicker walls, and the cosmic unconscious mind is almost unapproachable. It is very difficult even for the hypnotist to find out what is hidden there. For the first time the unconscious mind's contents are released through the conscious mind, bringing them to the notice of the conscious mind – not only to the notice, but the recognition, acceptance and expression. That's why I said it should be recorded as a proof; otherwise the conscious mind will deny it.

If you say to somebody, "You want to marry your mother," the conscious mind will simply deny it, "It is all nonsense – what are you saying? I have never thought about it." And he is right, he has never thought about it. But his mother was the first woman in his life, and he loved her and he got her love, and he has been jealous of his father since then. That's why every society has made it a discipline to respect your father. That is just to prevent the natural tendency of being jealous and disrespectful.

And every society has made it a point that you cannot even be allowed to think that you would like to love your mother; even to think of it, you will feel that you are just being mad. But there was a day in your childhood when you had longed for it. Slowly, slowly you repressed it; it was not allowable.

If the hypnotist just tells you that this thing is in your unconsciousness, you are not going to accept it. So it should be recorded, and not one time but many times so that you can be made clearly alert that this content is there. Then you can relax and let that content come directly to your conscious mind – not through the information from the hypnotist.

You follow me? He is telling you, but that will not help. His telling can only do one thing: if he can convince you that such a content exists in your unconscious mind, and you allow it in your silence to surface to the conscious mind, from there it can be released. You know that it is absurd; it has no meaning.

Perhaps in your childhood you had the desire, but now you can understand it is meaningless and you can release it; rather than repressing it inside, you can throw it out. And as the unconscious becomes empty, then the collective unconscious starts speaking – only then. As the collective unconscious becomes empty then there is a possibility for the cosmic unconscious to speak. And once the whole lower part of your mind, the depth of your mind, is cleaned away, it is such a freshening experience, as if twenty-four hours a day you are taking showers. And once this lower part is unburdened, then you are ready to move upwards very easily.

But the conscious mind is the only door for the higher, for the lower. So anything that is going to happen has to happen through the conscious mind.

Sigmund Freud and his school have not been very successful for the simple reason… You will be surprised to know that first he had been an apprentice of a hypnotist, a very famous hypnotist in France. It is only there that he developed the idea of psychoanalysis, that what comes up in deep hypnosis, can be brought up through dreams. But he forgot one thing, and that's what is missing in psychotherapy.

First, you cannot remember all your

dreams. For six hours you are dreaming; you can remember perhaps one dream – the last, when you were just waking up. Secondly, you cannot be convinced that a dream is a reality. Thirdly, the dream is not going to repeat itself; and for any scientific work, repeated experimentation is absolutely necessary, so that you can come to a conclusion without exception. A dream may come once and may not come again, because there are so many dreams. So the person's conscious mind is never convinced that this dream content has any reality.

Fourthly, the dream is a different language. It is not the language of the conscious mind, it is pictorial, it is not alphabetical. That is one of the greatest troubles, and because of it, psychoanalysis has to disappear; it cannot continue. So the whole thing depends on the psychoanalyst interpreting. You can tell him the dream, but the dream says nothing unless he interprets it.

Now that interpretation may be just his personal prejudice. That's how, if you go to Freud, everything comes to sex. Whatever you dream, you cannot dream anything which he will not conclude is sexual repression. You take the same dream to Jung and it will be from the collective unconscious – a myth, a mythology from your past lives. Take the same dream to Adler and it is nothing but ambition, will to power. So if there are thousands of interpreters, there will be thousands of meanings to the dream.

In hypnosis it is not a pictorial language that the unconscious uses. It uses the same language as the conscious mind uses, because it is talking to a person's conscious mind – the hypnotist's. So it is very simple and very clear.

Sigmund Freud thought that he had developed a better method, for the simple reason that it discarded hypnotism – because it was condemned, condemned by the society. But psychoanalysis has not helped.

What I am doing here…if you are just listening to me and your conscious mind becomes silent, the unconscious mind itself starts releasing its vapor. No language is needed, neither of dream nor ordinary language; it is just a repressed energy that starts coming up to the conscious and is released through the conscious. Once we have cleaned the lower mind, then we can easily move to the upper realm. But for that too, one has to go through the conscious mind.

And the upper wing does not have anything; nothing is repressed there. So there is no question of psychoanalysis ever discovering it, or any other school of psychology ever discovering it, because it has no dreams, it has no repressions. It is utter purity.

Clean the lower mind and just a simple method of meditation will give you the wings to move upwards. There is no barrier. You get more and more into light, deeper and deeper into bliss, and finally you come to a point where even you are no more…nirvana.

Beloved Bhagwan,
Why is it that we are never quite satisfied with who we are, and what existence has given us? We are always looking for something better to do, looking for someone else to be, always wanting what the other one has more than what we have been given. Like the saying goes, "The grass is always greener on the other side of the fence."
Why is this?

It is because you have been distracted. You have been directed where nature has not meant you to be. You are not moving towards your own potential. What others wanted you to be, you are trying to be, but it cannot be satisfying. When it is not satisfying, the logic says, "Perhaps it is not enough – have more of it." Then you go after more; then you start looking around. And everybody is coming out with a mask which is smiling, happy looking, so everybody is deceiving everybody else. You also come with a mask, so others think you are happier. You think others are happier.

The grass looks greener on the other side of the fence – but from both sides. The people who are living on the other side of the fence, they see your grass and it looks greener. It really looks greener, thicker, better. That is the illusion that distance creates. When you come close, then you start seeing that it is not so. But people keep each other at a distance. Even friends, even lovers keep each other at a distance; too much closeness will be dangerous, they may see your reality.

And you have been misguided from the very beginning, so whatever you do you will remain miserable. Nature has no idea of money, otherwise dollars would have been growing on the trees. Nature has no idea of money; money is a pure invention of man – useful, but dangerous too. You see somebody with much money, and you think perhaps money brings joy: look at that person, how joyous he seems to be, so run after money. Somebody is healthier – run after health. Somebody is doing something else and looks very contented – follow him.

But it is always the others, and the society has managed so that you will never think about your own potential. And the whole misery is that you are not being yourself. Just be yourself, and then there is no misery and no competition and no botheration that others have more, that you don't have more.

And if you like the grass to be greener there is no need to look at the other side of the fence; you can make the grass greener on your side of the fence. It is such a simple thing to make the grass greener. But you are just looking everywhere else, and all the lawns are looking so beautiful – except yours.

Man has to be rooted in his own potential, whatever it is, and nobody should give him directions, guidance. They should help him, wherever he is going, whatever he is becoming. And the world will be so contented that you cannot believe it.

I have never felt any discontent, even from my childhood, for the simple reason that I never allowed anybody to distract me from what I was doing or what I was trying to be. That helped me immensely. It *was* difficult, and the difficulties went on growing, and now the whole world is against me. But it does not disturb me. I am perfectly happy, perfectly content. I can't think that I could have been otherwise. In any other position I would have been miserable.

I don't have a home, I don't have a place to live, I don't have any money. Still, I have something that gives me absolute contentment. I have lived according to my potential, and even if death comes it will not upset me. I have lived my way. The whole world may be against me – it does not upset me. People get upset even if one person is against them. They get so upset; I cannot even understand it.

Hasya was saying, "Bhagwan, soon we will be running out of countries."

I said, "That does not matter. First we will run out of countries, then we will find something else. We can have a big boat and live on the boat." Because I said in Crete, "If you don't allow me any land anywhere, I will have a jet plane and I will be living on that," they immediately started a movement that I cannot

EVERYBODY IS ENOUGH

land at any airport in Europe. I am really enjoying that a single person who has no power can make these pygmy politicians just go out of their minds! I had just mentioned it, and immediately the European parliament tabled a resolution, which they will be discussing soon and passing, that I cannot land at any airport in Europe.

But we will find some way... In Europe there are communist countries – Yugoslavia, Czechoslovakia – we can land at their airports. They cannot prevent me just landing. But we can have a big ship with thousands of sannyasins on it, and just live on the ship. And let them do what they can do – bomb the ship or do whatsoever they want to do – but one thing is certain, they cannot upset me.

They tried in the American jails to upset me in such ways that anybody would have been upset. They would wake me up at four o'clock; sleep was impossible, so it was not a problem to me because I was just lying down with closed eyes. They would wake me at four o'clock, saying, "You get ready. At five o'clock the U.S. marshal is coming and he will be taking you to the airport." So I would get ready and wait. From five o'clock in the morning till five o'clock in the evening I was just sitting, waiting, and the man would appear at five o'clock in the evening.

And I said to him, "You must have got into some trouble – twelve hours late, and you just live three blocks away..." As we became friendly, after three days he said, "These are the tactics used to harass people. You forgive me. I was going to come at five in the evening but I said that I would come at five in the morning, so the whole day you would be sitting and waiting."

But I said, "What is upsetting in it? Anyway I would have been sitting and...there is nothing else to do."

The world is against individuality.

It is against your being just your natural self.

It wants you just to be a robot, and because you have agreed to be a robot you are in trouble. You are not a robot. That was not the intention of nature, to make a robot of you. So because you are not what you were meant to be, what you were destined to be, you are constantly looking: "What is missing? Perhaps better furniture, better curtains, a better house, a better husband, a better wife, a better job..." Your whole life you are trying and rushing from one place to another. But the society has distracted you from the very beginning.

My effort is to bring you back to yourself, and you will suddenly find all that discontent has disappeared. There is no need to be more – you are enough. Everybody is enough.

Chapter 43
May 3, 1986, Evening

Beloved Bhagwan,
You told a story about ten years ago that I have not been able to understand:
A seeker is lost in the mountains; he is tired and thirsty. It is night and he sees a silver bowl with crystal clear water which he drinks and then sleeps. In the morning light he sees that the bowl was in fact a dirty old skull.
He laughed and became enlightened.
What did he see, Bhagwan?

The story is simple, but with immense meaning. The seeker saw in the skull the whole reality, and our illusions about it. He saw what we think is, and what really is – and the difference is tremendous.

He would not have taken that water, drunk that water, if he had known that it was in a dirty old skull. He thought it was a beautiful bowl with crystal clear water.

Our life is lived in illusions of crystal clear water, but reality is totally different. Seeing the difference he laughed at himself. And to be able to laugh at oneself can become a breakthrough – one can become enlightened.

People laugh at others, and people feel hurt if somebody laughs at them, but to come to an understanding where you see your own stupidity… And your whole life is full of it. We live in dreams, illusions, hallucinations. They do not correspond to reality at all. The reality is the dirty old skull. He laughed at himself, and in this very laughter he became a different man. Now he will live with reality, whatever it is. Now no illusions will be needed, no hallucinations will be needed to cover it, to hide it.

He has seen the point.

The story is simple but it is the story of the whole pilgrimage from darkness to light, from illusions to reality.

Logic Should Serve Love

Just watch your mind, how it creates illusions about everything and then gets disillusioned and disturbed. You love a man, you love a woman – you create a certain illusion about the man or the woman. It is not the truth. Deep down you know it too. You are imposing an image. Soon it will be shattered, because against reality no illusion can last long. Soon you will find a dirty old skull.

Then ordinarily you will be disappointed, miserable, and you will miss the point. If you could have laughed you would not have missed it.

Even when you understand that things are not the way you had imagined them to be, you dump the whole responsibility on the other person. A woman who was beautiful turns out to be a bitch. A man you had thought to be a hero turns out to be just a henpecked husband. You are not going to laugh at yourselves. You will throw the whole responsibility on the other person: that he deceived you, that he pretended to be something that he was not, that she was not so beautiful as she was pretending – with all the make-up she deceived him. But no make-up is needed. Your illusions, your hallucinations, your lust is enough – the greatest make-up in the world.

So whatever you want, whatever you desire, you project, and when that projection proves wrong, there are two possibilities. One is to dump the whole responsibility on the other person, who is simply innocent of what you were seeing in her.

In fact, when you say to a woman, "You are beautiful…" and this and that, she wonders, because she also looks in the mirror and she does not find anything that you are talking about. But why disturb yourself unnecessarily? Why not enjoy? It fulfills her ego. Even the ugliest woman will not object, say that you are wrong. She will smile and accept all your compliments. And standing before a mirror she may think that perhaps she is wrong. How can that man be wrong? Why should he be wrong?

In each love affair both the persons are innocent, as far as they are concerned. But both are responsible for projecting upon the other something which the other is not.

A Sufi story tells that Mulla Nasruddin had a beautiful house in the hills and once in a while he used to go there. And sometimes he would say it would take three weeks for him to rest or two weeks, or four weeks, but he never managed to keep the date that he had given for his return; he would always come sooner. If he had gone for three weeks, within two weeks he would be back.

His friends started asking, "You plan for three weeks, then you come back in two weeks, sometimes even in one week. What is the matter?"

He said, "You don't know. I have an old woman servant."

They said, "What has that to do with your remaining in the hills and relaxing?"

He said, "First listen to the whole thing. She is so ugly. That's why I have chosen her – she is my criterion. When she starts looking beautiful to me, then I escape, then I know: 'Now, Mulla, this is not a safe place, and you have lost your mind. So I go for three weeks, but what can I do? In three days she starts looking beautiful. And if I stay one day more I may propose. And she is really ugly. It is difficult to tolerate her, but I have kept her specially for this purpose, so that when I start losing my mind I will know it is the exact time to leave and come back home into the world."

You project; the projection fails. If you could laugh at yourself… That is the message of this story.

The man was thirsty in the night. It was a

projection. Even in the full moon night a skull is a skull and the dirty water is dirty water. But he was thirsty; it was his thirst that projected clean, crystal clear water in a beautiful bowl. And he drank with joy. In the morning he was not thirsty and there was sunlight. He looked at the bowl; it was a dirty old skull – and he had drunk from it! If he had known that it was a skull filled with dirty water, he would have rather suffered thirst than drink from it. But his thirst projected an illusion.

We are doing it every moment of our lives, projecting illusions – about people, about things – and getting frustrated continuously, disgusted.

The story is saying to you: these are the moments; if you can understand that it was your projection… This is the time to laugh at yourself, at your own stupidity, at your own foolishness. That will be an act of tremendous intelligence. And it will be freeing you from that constant projection, frustration – that whole vicious circle.

An old monk with his young disciple was passing through the forest, going to another town. But the young man was very much puzzled, because the old man had never walked like that – he was almost running and clutching his bag. And once in a while he would feel something inside the bag. The young man could not imagine what he had in the bag. And the old monk was again and again asking, "Will we be able to reach the town before sunset?"

The young man said, "Even if we don't reach, we have nothing to fear. We can stay in the forest. We have stayed here many times, so it is not new. But today you seem to be strange."

The old man said, "We will discuss it later on. First, be fast. I don't want to stay in the forest tonight."

By the side of the road was a well, and the sun was just setting. Before the sun set they washed themselves. They were really tired. They drank, and while the old man was washing his face he gave his bag to the young man and told him, "Be careful."

The young man said to himself, "He has never been this way before." And out of curiosity he looked into the bag. In the bag he was carrying two bricks of gold. Now everything was clear: why the monk cannot stay in the forest, why for the first time he is so afraid.

While the old monk was washing his face and doing his evening prayer, the young man threw those two bricks into the forest, found two stones weighing almost the same as the bricks, and put them in the bag. The old man finished his prayer in half the time – he was in such a hurry! He immediately took the bag from the young man and the weight showed him that everything was okay. They rushed on. After a mile, it was getting dark. The old man said, "It seems to be difficult to reach to the town, and this place is dangerous."

But the young man said, "Don't be afraid. As far as the danger is concerned, I have thrown it by the side of the well."

He said, "What do you mean, you have thrown the danger by the side of the well?"

He said, "Look into your bag and you will know."

He looked into the bag and he said, "My God!" The old man laughed, threw the bag, and sat under a tree; he could not stop laughing.

The young man said, "Why are you laughing so much?"

He said, "I am laughing because you have done the right thing, and for almost one mile I have still been befooling myself with those stones, thinking they were gold. Now we can sleep under this tree. It is good. There is no fear and there is no hurry." He could have been angry at the young man and missed the point. But he laughed, laughed madly, because he could see the point: "It was so stupid of me. The young man has proved far more intelligent than me. My own disciple had to teach me the lesson."

They slept the whole night, and in the morning the old man touched the feet of the young man and thanked him, "Although I am your master, you helped free me from an illusion. And I slept so deeply the whole night. I had not slept for a few nights because of that bag; those golden bricks would not let me sleep. Even in the night I was groping in the bed and trying to find out whether they were there or not. Those bricks had become so important that I lost my joy, I abridged my prayers, I abridged my meditation."

As far as existence is concerned, gold and rock are not different – it is human illusion, we have projected it. If man is no longer in this world, gold will not be gold; although it will still be itself, there will be no difference in valuation between it and a rock. The valuation and the difference is our projection – and then we suffer.

So the insight in that small anecdote is great. If you can laugh at yourself when any of your illusions fall away, soon you will be able to live without illusions, to live without hallucinations, to live without projections. And to live without all these things means to live in peace, and to live in silence, and to celebrate the small things of life.

Beloved Bhagwan,
I remember once hearing You tell us that Buddha's definition of truth was: that which works.

It struck me as almost audacious, and yet totally pragmatic, and for both reasons I loved it.
My understanding is that Your definition of truth is probably the same, that you will do and say anything at all, in the name of truth, that might prod us in the right direction.
I would love to hear You speak to us on this.

It is true. I can say anything if it directs you towards truth. Of course truth cannot be said, it can only be pointed at. I can use anything that points towards it. Perhaps for different people different pointers are needed. To me it does not matter what I say. What matters is whether it leads you in the right direction – towards your illumination.

Yes, my definition is exactly the same: truth is that which works. It is pragmatic, and Gautam Buddha was a very pragmatic man, very scientific. This definition can be called scientific also.

All definitions of science are nothing but proof for this definition. We don't know what electricity is, we only know how it works. We don't know anything about atomic energy, what it is, but we know how it works. And that knowledge of how it works is the whole science of it.

The ultimate truth is not different. And the master's function is to lead you, to direct you, to push you in a direction where you will find the truth. He cannot give it to you, but he can create devices which will lead you to it. In a very subtle way what the master says is not meant to be understood; it is meant to be drunk so that it reaches to your blood, to your bones, to your marrow, and you start moving in a certain direction – not knowing where you are going, but the master knows where you are going.

If you are going on the right track, you will find his blessings and his love showering on you. That will be the only indication that you are on the right path. One day you will find the truth and then you will laugh, because what was said had nothing to do with it. But it certainly turned your attention towards it.

I have always told this story: A house is on fire and small children are in the house playing. They are so involved in their play that the whole neighborhood is shouting, "Come out! The house is on fire!" But they are enjoying that too. The flames are all around and the children are in the middle of the house – they have never seen such fireworks.

And they are not listening to the crowd. Then comes the father who had gone to the market, and people say, "Now do something. All your children will be dead. The house is almost going to collapse."

The father went close and shouted, "I have brought your toys – all the toys that you have asked for. Come out." Just the back door of the house was not burning yet.

They all rushed out and asked the father, "Where are the toys?"

And the father said, "You will have to forgive me. I have not brought them today, but tomorrow I will bring them certainly."

They said, "Why did you unnecessarily disturb our game?"

He said, "I have not disturbed your game. You do not understand. The house is on fire; you would have been dead. I simply lied to you about the toys, because I knew that it was the only thing that could bring you out."

Now, toys and fire seem to have no connection, but in that particular situation the father functioned as a master. He gave the children an indication that saved their lives. Although now they are aware he lied, they will not complain about it. He lied out of compassion. He lied because he loved them; he lied because he wanted to save their lives.

Truth cannot be said, so whatever *can* be said is going to be a beautiful lie – beautiful because it can lead towards truth. So I make a demarcation between lies: beautiful lies and ugly lies. Ugly lies are those which take you away from truth, and beautiful lies are those which take you closer towards truth. But as far as their quality is concerned, both are lies. But those beautiful lies work; hence in some way they hold the flavor of truth.

Beloved Bhagwan,
A question I have had since I was a kid and started seeing the ways of the world is: Why do people treat each other like they do? Where is the love, the compassion and the respect for each other? I think that everybody is longing to live in love and harmony with himself and all the human beings around. And I don't think there is any longing for hate, violence, and power over other people – but this is what I see happening.
What is it that makes people live this unnatural and miserable life? Is it all conditioning, or is there something in man that makes him willing to go astray?

It is both.
First, there is something in man that leads him astray. And secondly, there are people whose interest it is to lead human beings astray. Both together create a false, fake human being. His heart longs for love, but his conditioned mind prevents him from love.

You will be surprised to know that Adolf Hitler never allowed his girlfriends to sleep in his room for one simple reason: how can you trust? The woman may shoot you in the night,

LOGIC SHOULD SERVE LOVE

mix poison in your water. What is the guarantee? She may be just pretending that she loves you. It may be just a conspiracy. There is no way to find out whether it is a conspiracy or true love for him. To be on the safe side he never allowed any woman with whom he had been in contact to sleep in his room.

He never allowed anyone to be friendly with him – Goebbels, or any of his other close associates. He always kept them at a distance. It was said that there was not a single person who could put his hand on his shoulder, like a friend. Too much closeness is dangerous – that was his conditioning. The other may do harm to you. He may come to know something about you which he may use against you. It is better to keep him at a distance. And everybody is ambitious, everybody wants to be in his place, so although they are looking very friendly, deep down they are all enemies, competitors; they can kill him. He had no friends. And what kind of love is this, that he cannot trust the woman in his room.

One of his women remained for many years in love with him, and there was no reason to suspect her. But suspicion needs no reason. One day she wanted to go and see her mother who was ill, in the same town. And Adolf Hitler said no. Yes was very difficult for him to pronounce, for anything.

There is a deep psychological meaning in it. No gives you power. Yes does not give you power. Whenever you say no, you can feel power; whenever you say yes, you can feel love, you can feel compassion, but not power. Words have their own qualities. Those qualities you cannot find in the dictionaries. But in actual life if you go into the psychology of words, each word has its unique individuality. No is not simply a denial; it is an assertion of power.

There was no need to say no. She was going just to see her sick mother, and she would be back before he returned from the office. But yes was not his word. He only knew how to order, how to reject anybody else's idea. Even such a small thing, that had nothing to do with power...

He went to the office; the woman thought that she could manage: she could go and see her mother and return – he would not be back yet. She went, came back, and certainly she managed. But the first thing he enquired from the guard of the house was, "Has she been out? – how long?"

And Hitler loaded his gun and just went in and shot her – he did not even ask, he did not even give her an opportunity to say anything. That was enough. And it had to be a proof for everybody else, that not to follow his order meant death.

Hitler longed for love, but his mind longed for power – and you cannot ask for both.

This is the problem. The child is born with a heart which longs for love, but he is also born with a brain which can be conditioned. And the society has to condition it against the heart, because the heart will be always rebellious against the society, it will always follow its own way. It cannot be made into a soldier. It can become a poet, it can become a singer, it can become a dancer, but it cannot become a soldier.

It can suffer for its individuality, it can die for its individuality and freedom, but it cannot be enslaved. That is the state of the heart.

But the mind... The child comes with an empty brain, just a mechanism, which you can arrange the way you want. It will learn the language you teach, it will learn the religion you teach, it will learn the morality you teach. It is simply a computer; you just feed it with information.

And every society takes care to make the

mind stronger and stronger so that if there is any conflict between heart and mind, the mind is going to win. But every victory of the mind over the heart is a misery. It is a victory over your nature, over your being – over *you* – by others. And they have cultivated your mind to serve *their* purposes.

For example, the British government ruled in India for three hundred years, and it created a certain kind of education that only produces clerks, postmasters, stationmasters.... The whole program is such that it does not produce great intellectuals, geniuses, scientists – no. So if a person studies for one third of his life, he comes out of the factory of the university just a clerk. But the British government needed clerks.

By the way, because the capital of India at the beginning of the British empire was Calcutta, Bengalis were the first to be indoctrinated by the British education system. They were the first to become mediators between the land and its people, and the rulers. The rulers did not know the language of the people; the people did not know the language of the rulers. These mediators knew both.

They were respected by the masses because they were so close to the rulers – second only to the rulers. But the rulers hated them. It was just a necessity to create an army of mediators; otherwise they could not rule such a huge country – there would be no understanding, no communication.

But they hated these people, and just as an example I will tell you... They called these Bengalis *babus* and the word *babu* became respectful all over India. Because the rulers were calling the Bengalis *babus,* the word *babu* became very important – so significant that even the first president of India was called Babu Rajendra Prasad. And nobody ever thought about what this word means.

I told Rajendra Prasad, "You should drop this and you should make it known to the country that nobody should use this word, because it is condemnatory." It means a man with a bad smell. Bengalis eat fish – fish and rice, that is their only food – and they smell of fish. Just eating fish continually...

Bengal is a beautiful place, and you will find there one beautiful thing: next to every house you will find a small lake. The richer people have big lakes with their palaces. And those lakes are there simply to produce fish. Those lakes are not for any other purpose but to get fresh fish – the kind of fish the people like. Every house, even a poor man's house has a small pond – it looks very beautiful, because a small pond with palm trees...it may be a small hut.

But the smell is too much. Only once have I traveled in Bengal, and then I said, "I cannot go further than Calcutta." It stinks – everybody stinks of fish, every house stinks of fish. That is their main diet.

Babu is a Persian word. *Bu* means smell and *ba* means with. The British got India from the Mohammedans, whose languages were Persian, Arabic and Urdu, and it was from them that they got this idea of *babu*. It was a condemnation, but to the masses it became the most respectful word.

India must have more universities than any other country – one hundred universities and thousands of colleges – and the whole purpose is just to serve the Empire. The whole education is to be obedient, not to be rebellious. It is absolutely against any idea of revolution.

India would have remained a slave country for centuries, but Britain committed just one mistake: it allowed a few rich people's sons and daughters to be educated in England, and that was the trouble. These were the people who brought the idea of freedom to India. No Indian educated in India had any idea of freedom, but a few rich people sent their sons, their daughters, to be educated in England – because if they were educated in England then they would be given the highest posts in India. A holder of the same degree from an Indian university would never reach that post, but from England he comes qualified for the highest post.

Britain created its own enemies unknowingly. These were the people who found in Britain a different kind of education, who learned about democracy, who learned about freedom, who learned about individual rights, who learned about freedom of expression. And they came back to their country full of utopian ideas about how India could become independent.

So all the fighters against the British regime were basically educated in England. And I don't think the British have even realized the fact, because nobody has noted it anywhere.

One man who was very influential in India, Subash Chandra, was educated in Britain. And anybody who was educated in Britain was immediately absorbed in the highest government service, the Indian Civil Service – I.C.S. Every student coming back from England had to give an interview to the governor of his state. And Subash had come with the full desire to fight the British Empire, not to serve it.

But still he went to give his interview. And Bengalis have a certain habit: they always carry their umbrellas. Nobody knows why. I have asked many people because it is not raining, it is not hot… But traditionally it is part of them. Without an umbrella, a Bengali is not a full Bengali; his umbrella is absolutely necessary.

And they give reasons, because they are intellectual people. They say, "Rains can come at any time, it is unpredictable. One should always be prepared for anything. Right now it is cloudy, but the sun can come out and it will be hot. And moreover, there are so many dogs, and for this and that you can use your umbrella. Even if you have to fight with someone, the umbrella is handy."

So Subash went with his umbrella and his hat into the governor's office, and the governor was very much annoyed that an Indian should behave in this way. He should remove his hat, to be respectful – and he has come to give an interview. So the governor said, "First you remove your hat. You don't know even how to be respectful."

And Subash took his umbrella out, and on the other side of the table was the governor. He hooked his neck with his umbrella and said, "If you want respect, then you should be respectful too. You should have stood. If you cannot stand you should not expect any respect from me. And I am not interested in your I.C.S. I have just come to see how you behave with people. But don't think that you can misbehave with me. People like you used to polish my shoes in England" – naturally in England a white man will polish the shoes – "so just because you are white does not mean anything. Keep your service to yourself."

These were the people who created the whole freedom movement. The British government forgot completely: if you have created a certain educational system in India to produce only clerks, servants, slaves, then you should not allow Indians to be educated in England, because these people will be dangerous to the Empire. And they proved dangerous – they destroyed the Empire – but the whole credit goes to the British universities.

So mind is empty, it is brain; you can put anything in it. And with twenty-five years of education you can make it so strong that you forget your heart; you will always remain miserable. The misery is that your heart can only give you joy, can only give you happiness, can only make you dance. The mind can do arithmetic, but it cannot sing a song. Those are just not the capacities of the mind. So you are torn apart between your nature, which is your heart, and the society that is in your head. And certainly you are born – everybody is born – with these two centers. That is the difficulty.

And one center is empty. In a better society it will be used in accordance with the heart, to serve the heart. And then it will be a great life, full of rejoicings. But up to now we have lived in an ugly society, with rotten ideas. They have used the mind. And that vulnerability is there – mind can be used.

Now communists are using it in one way; fascists used it in Germany in one way; all the other religions are using it in different ways. But that vulnerability is with every individual: that you have a mind which you bring empty. In fact it is a blessing of existence – but misused, exploited. It is given to you empty so that you can make it perfectly subservient to your heart, to your longings, to your potential. Nothing is wrong in it. But the vested interests all over the world have found it a beautiful opportunity for them – to use the mind against the heart. So you remain miserable and they can exploit you in whatever ways they want.

That's why the whole world is miserable. Everybody wants to be loved, everybody wants to love; but the mind is such a barrier that neither does it allow you to love, nor does it allow you to be loved. In both cases the mind comes in the way and starts distorting everything. And even if by chance you meet a person you feel love for and the person feels love for you, your minds are not going to settle. They have been trained by different systems, different religions, different societies.

One of my friends married an American girl. He was a professor of physics, and while studying in America he fell in love with a girl, a beautiful girl, and he married her against his parents wishes. So they became enemies. His parents did not receive them in their home when they came back to India.

I had to give a party, a reception for their marriage. But in a month I saw that it could not last. One of my friends was staying with me and he is a very beautiful person – jack of all trades, master of none…but he knows everything. So he is very interesting and very influential.

Superficially he will impress you on any subject, on anything. You will find out later on that it is just superficial, but by that time he has done his work.

All that he does is borrow money. He has a Ph.D. He could have been a professor, but he says, "I don't want to bother with all this. I enjoy borrowing."

I said, "You should think about how long this can last."

He said, "You don't see. I never borrow from the same person again. And the world is so big and life is so short. I will manage."

So he started flirting with the American girl. She was very much impressed – he is a very impressive person – and the professor who had married her was feeling so jealous. He had just an Indian mind. The Indian mind cannot conceive that his wife can go with somebody else to the swimming pool. In the first place no Indian woman will go to the swimming pool and even if she goes, she will go with her husband. But she was going with some stranger.

She was going out with him on bicycles; they were playing cards. The husband was in the university, but he was continually worried about his wife and that fellow – because he was completely free; he did nothing.

Soon the marriage broke up. They were fighting continuously. I told them, "You love each other, but you don't understand the situation. Your minds are cultivated very differently. She can't see that there is anything wrong if she goes to the swimming pool with some friend. She has been doing that from her childhood. You cannot conceive the idea. Your idea is what you have seen in your family, in your society – that the wife should not even open her cover." The sari that is used by the Indian women is pulled down to make a cover over the face. She should not take the cover off before strangers. "You have been brought up with such people; you cannot understand your wife holding hands with some stranger. They are enjoying and playing tennis and going for a walk, and you are just sitting and boiling up unnecessarily. You should have thought. Your parents were right – that this kind of marriage is not going to succeed."

And I have not seen any marriage between Indians and foreigners succeeding. They always fail, for the simple reason that the two minds are brought up with different ideas, filled with different programs.

It is everybody's birthright to be happy, but unfortunately the society, the people with whom we have been living, who have brought us into the world, have not thought anything about it. They have just been reproducing human beings like animals – even worse because at least animals are not conditioned. This conditioning process should be completely changed. The mind should be trained to be a servant of the heart. Logic should serve love. And then life can become a festival of lights.

Watchfulness is the Greatest Magic

Beloved Bhagwan,
When I go to sleep at night, I am swept away by such incredibly surreal dreams that I wake up in the morning surprised I am in my same bed.
Bhagwan, is there a way to channel this phenomenal energy that goes into dreaming at night, into watchfulness?

The phenomenon of dreaming and watchfulness are totally different things. Just try one thing: every night, going to sleep, while you are just half awake, half asleep, slowly going deeper into sleep, repeat to yourself, "I will be able to remember that it is a dream."

Go on repeating it till you fall asleep. It will take a few days, but one day you will be surprised: once this idea sinks deep into the unconscious, you can watch the dream as a dream. Then it has no grip over you. Then slowly, as your watchfulness becomes more sharp, dreams will disappear. They are very shy; they don't want to be watched.

They exist only in the darkness of the unconscious. As watchfulness brings light in, they start disappearing. So go on doing the same exercise, and you can get rid of dreams. And you will be surprised. Getting rid of dreams has many implications. If the dreams disappear then in the daytime your mind chattering will not be so much as it used to be. Secondly, you will be more in the moment – not in the future, not in the past. Thirdly, your intensity, your totality of action will increase.

Dream is a disease.

It is needed because man is sick. But if dreams can be completely dropped you will attain a new kind of health, a new vision, and part of your unconscious mind will become conscious. So you will have a stronger individuality. Whatever you do, you will never repent, because you will have done it with such consciousness that repentance has no relevance.

Watchfulness is the greatest magic that one can learn, because it can begin the transformation of your whole being. It is only through watchfulness that resurrection happens…you are reborn.

Beloved Bhagwan,
Why is it difficult for some people to be hypnotized? Is it because we do not trust the person who is doing it to us, or are we not as receptive as those who can be?

There are many reasons possible. The most important is, if the person's intelligence quotient is very low he will not be able to understand what hypnosis is, and what he is supposed to do. Idiots cannot be hypnotized. It is something to be remembered, that animals can be hypnotized, but idiots cannot be hypnotized. Animals may not have our kind of intelligence, but they are not idiots.

The idiot is one whose mind has not grown at all, who is zero. He cannot understand what is being said, where it is going to lead him, and why he should do it. Intelligent conversation is impossible. The idiot looks like man, but inside he is far behind even the animals.

First, the idiot cannot be hypnotized. Second, the man who is always suspicious of everything, who has an ingrained suspicion, cannot be hypnotized. His suspicion will not allow him to go with the hypnotist. Thirdly, the people who think they are intellectuals, who are full of borrowed knowledge, but don't have any intelligence of their own, cannot be hypnotized, because they have an idea that intellectuals cannot be hypnotized – and they are intellectuals. Finally and basically, a man who cannot trust.

It needs total trust, because you are going into darkness, the unknown, and you don't know what the intentions of the man are, and you don't know what he can make you do while you are under hypnosis.

Once I was in Bombay, staying with a very rich family, and they insisted to me, "You are always working, involved with people, meetings, committees; this evening you keep free. We are going to invite a great hypnotist and he is going to show us a few tricks of hypnotism – you will enjoy it."

Not for entertainment, but just to see what kind of person this great hypnotist was, I remained. They had in the house itself a small auditorium. They had invited their rich friends, so there were at least two hundred people. And the hypnotist called for five people – "Anybody can come."

Five people went up. He hypnotized them and then told them, "Just in front of you cows are standing. Now start milking them." And they immediately sat in the Indian way and started milking the cows. There were no cows, and people were laughing and enjoying, but the hypnotized person could not hear anybody. Things like this he did.

After the show he was introduced to me. I told him, "You stop this nonsense. Hypnotism is condemned because of people like you. Now the people who have seen how you befooled the ones who had come to be hypnotized will never be able to be hypnotized. They have lost trust. You will make a laughingstock of them. You are not doing any service to the science of hypnosis, you are an enemy. Find some other job. You don't see the simple point that two hundred people are seeing you befooling five people. Now these people will carry this idea in their minds."

All the intellectuals all over the world have this idea that intellectuals cannot be hypnotized. But the real reason is because they cannot trust. Trust needs a man of heart, of feelings, not of thoughts. And all these people who are using hypnotism as an entertainment should be stopped by law – it is a crime. They are spoiling a tremendously valuable science.

Only a master should be allowed – and then too, he should hypnotize only his own disciples. And not to make a mockery of it, but to increase the consciousness of the disciples, to increase the intelligence of the disciples, to change their wrong habits, to make them more integrated, more consolidated, to give them more courage and stamina.

And when other students, other disciples see that hypnotism can be a blessing – the same man who was so much afraid has lost all fear, even the fear of death; the same man who was always miserable has lost his misery and is always in a state of joy – more trust will be created, more and more people will be ready to be hypnotized. That readiness, that trust, that receptivity is missing because for centuries hypnotism has been misused.

People like magicians, showmen, entertainers – the wrong kind of people – have made hypnosis condemned.

It can become such a great benediction to humanity. You need trust, you need receptivity, you need intelligence to go into it. And all these things will be strengthened when you attain new dimensions, new talents, new genius. And then you will be more able to go back into it.

And soon everybody who has been hypnotized by a loving, compassionate master who cannot harm you, who cannot imagine hurting you…after a few sessions of your being hypnotized, he will start a new phase: self-hypnosis.

In deep hypnotic states he will tell you, "Now you are able to hypnotize yourself – you don't need me, you don't need anyone else." So he is not going to use hypnosis to create a spiritual slavery. He will use it to give you more spiritual freedom than you ever had before. And the day you can hypnotize yourself is a great day; something valuable has been achieved.

Then you can do miracles with it, upon yourself. You can change things that you have always been trying to change; but the more you try to change them, the more difficult it becomes.

I used to stay in Calcutta with an old man, Sonalal. He was famous all over India as the greatest gambler. He never paid a single cent to the government in taxation because he never kept any books. I was surprised at how he maintained all his businesses – gambling winnings of millions – how he kept the accounts. And when I stayed in his house, I asked him. He took me to his bathroom – all over his bathroom were his books, on the walls.

So no income tax officer can conceive that on his walls in the bathroom he keeps all the accounts from different countries, of different people – where, in which bank, what number, telephone numbers…everything. He said, "This is my accounts office."

And even in his bathroom he had six telephones. He was continuously on the phone…two phones always in his hands. You could not talk with him easily; it was so difficult.

He told me that he belonged to a certain religion which values celibacy as the greatest spiritual thing. He had taken the vow of celibacy three times. A man was with me and he was very impressed. When Sonalal had gone for some work inside the house he said, "This is a great man – three times!"

I said, "You are an idiot. When he is saying three times he took a vow for celibacy, that simply means that the fourth time he never took it. He understood that it is impossible."

He said, "But…I never thought about it. I simply thought, 'Three times!'"

Sonalal came back and I asked him, "What happened the fourth time?"

He said, "I could not gather the courage, because three times I failed, and each time I became more guilty, ashamed of myself. And I am old." He was at that time seventy years old. "In the first place, to stand up in the congregation and take the vow for celibacy, people laugh – they see this seventy year old…and that too for the fourth time."

I said, "There is no need. Your religion and your religious leaders don't know. Celibacy *is* possible without repression, and at such a stage I will not call it a crime, but it has to be done through self-hypnosis. There is no need for any vow to be taken."

He was immensely excited. He said, "Do whatever…but I want to be celibate before I die, because this is the only thing in which I have failed in my life. I have never failed in anything." He gave millions of dollars to the freedom movement. So all the leaders who became prime ministers, and presidents and cabinet ministers looked to him as a father figure.

Pandit Jawaharlal Nehru, who was the prime minister, told him, "It was okay not to give taxes to the British government, but now it is your own government."

He said, "Remember, it does not matter to me which government it is. I can donate twice the amount that you think I should pay in taxation, but taxation? – that I cannot do. And you cannot catch hold of me, because I don't have any books. Except for me, nobody knows how much money I have, how much money is invested, where it is invested, how it is invested. I don't even have a secretary. So never ask for any tax.

"You can always ask for a donation. If your government needs a donation, I am ready. Just as I was giving to you when you were fighting for freedom, I can give to you now, when your government needs it." And he never gave any tax, even to the independent Indian government.

He said, "I have my own principles. I am nobody's servant. But about this celibacy there is a wound in me. Three times I have failed. And I don't want to die a failure in anything." And he was a man of rare courage. I have seen people of different kinds, but I have never found any man of that courage.

When he had met me first in Jaipur – that was his home town – listening to me, he came, touched my feet and gave me ten thousand rupees. But I said, "I don't need rupees, because I am simply traveling alone and my friends can take care of my expenses, traveling, food, accommodation. There is no need."

Tears came to his eyes, and he said, "Don't refuse. Don't hurt me, because I am a poor man. I don't have anything I can give to you – I have only money. You can't find a more poor man than me – just money and nothing else. So when somebody refuses money, he is refusing me, because I don't have anything else. Don't refuse. If you want to throw it you can throw it; once I have given it to you, it is none of my concern."

I gave that money to the institution that was organizing my lectures in Jaipur, and from that day – he was very old – he became very friendly to me, and he said, "I have houses in all the big cities of India. So wherever you go, you can stay in my house. And just inform me so I will be there."

He had beautiful mansions everywhere – Bombay, Hyderabad, Madras, Simla, Calcutta. He said, "I have earned enough, just this celibacy is heavy on me."

I said, "That's a very simple matter. At this age it is perfectly right." I hypnotized him two, three times while I was with him. And then I gave him a posthypnotic suggestion: now you will be able to hypnotize yourself.

And once that posthypnotic suggestion is given, the person becomes able to hypnotize himself. Any strategy can be used: Count from one to seven, or one to ten, and tell yourself, "I will be back in ten minutes" – never forget that, because otherwise there is nobody to wake you up. You will not die, but you may spend almost the same period under hypnosis as in sleep – six to eight hours. If you have time then there is no need to say that, because the hypnotic sleep has a totally different beauty: it is so soft, so silent; it is as if you are no more. And suddenly you come back.

I said, "Before going into hypnosis, repeat three times, 'I want to remain celibate,' and that's enough."

After six months I met him again in Madras, and I asked him, "What about celibacy?"

He said, "This is a wonder. Without any vow, without going to a spiritual head, confessing, it has simply disappeared. I simply wonder why sex so dominated me. I don't even remember it."

You will be surprised to know that in hypnosis even operations can be done; without any anesthesia, big operations, dangerous operations can be done.

It is an unexplored science, unnecessarily condemned by a few idiots who have been making an entertainment of it.

Trust is the foundation to begin with. You can even start by yourself, but the problem is, you don't trust yourself; otherwise there is no problem, there is no need for anybody else to hypnotize you. You can hypnotize yourself.

But that is the difficulty: nobody trusts himself.

You know yourself, you know how deceptive you are, you know how cunning you are, you know you say one thing and you don't mean it. You know that you decide that tomorrow morning you will get up early, and when you are deciding it, even at that time you know that it is not going to happen.

So you cannot trust yourself – that is the problem. That's why somebody else is needed, somebody you can trust, somebody in whose hands you can leave yourself without any fear. And the person who hypnotizes you, if he really loves you, would like you to get into self-hypnosis as soon as possible, because then you are totally free. Then you can do whatsoever you want to do with it.

If you want to stop smoking you can do it so easily. If you want to change anything in you which you think is impossible, you can give it a try – nothing is impossible. You have decided many times to change this, to change that, but you have always failed, because the decision remains in the conscious and the action comes from the unconscious – they don't meet.

The unconscious never hears anything that the conscious is deciding, and the conscious cannot control the unconscious – the unconscious is so vast.

The secret of hypnosis is that it takes you to the unconscious, and then you can put the seed of anything in the unconscious, and it will grow, blossom. The blossoming will happen in the conscious, but the roots will remain in the unconscious.

As far as I am concerned, hypnosis is going to be one of the most significant parts of the mystery school. Such a simple method, which only demands a little trust, a little innocence, can bring miraculous changes in your life – and not in ordinary things only. Slowly it can become the path of your meditation.

You meditate, but you don't succeed. You don't succeed in watching; you get mixed up with thoughts, you forget watching. You remember later on, "I was going to watch, but I am thinking." Hypnosis can help you; it can make the watcher and the thoughts separate.

For spiritual growth I don't think there is anything more important than hypnosis.

Beloved Bhagwan,
As You have announced each new phase of Your work, I have been immensely excited and said to myself, "Great! Now we are really going to begin the work." And each phase in its turn has been more amazing than the one before it.

Now You speak of a mystery school. My mind shouts out, "Hey, that sounds esoteric, and Bhagwan always insists that truth is not esoteric, but absolutely pragmatic, an open secret." That's what my mind says.

If things are otherwise though, then count me in. I am coming with You all the way.

Also, the mystery school has begun already, has it not?

It has begun. And truth is both: it is pragmatic and it is esoteric.

I was emphasizing that it was pragmatic, because in those phases I did not want my people to be involved in any esoteric work. The pragmatic work is the right foundation.

Without that foundation, esoteric work is just dreaming. So I was continuously against esoteric work.

I am a very mathematical person, in the sense that when the foundation is being laid, you should not talk about the temple that is going to be built upon it, and how it is going to be, what kind of architecture – because all that will disturb the work on the foundation. I wanted you to be totally concerned only with the foundation, so that later on we can forget the foundation and we can start building the temple.

Truth is a mystery, and it can be discovered only in a mystery school. And this phase is going to be the most valuable. All that we have done before was a preparation. The mystery school will create the purification, and the outcome will be perfection.

That's why people who look at me only intellectually will find contradictions. But those who have a more comprehensive view of life will not find any contradiction. I have denied esoteric work, knowing perfectly well that one day I will have to introduce you to the esoteric work. But everything in its time, not before; otherwise it can simply create confusion. And if esoteric work is introduced to you without any foundation, you are not going to work for the foundation, because that is not interesting. The esoteric work is really very interesting, but I don't want you to make a temple without a foundation. It has happened many times; then the temple falls and destroys those who were building it.

The word 'esoteric' simply means: you cannot put it objectively, scientifically. It is something inner, something subjective, something so mysterious, so miraculous that you can experience it but you cannot explain it. You can have it, but still you cannot explain it. It remains beyond explanation. And it is good that there is something in life which you cannot bring down to language, which you cannot bring down to the objective world…something which remains always beyond. You can become one with it – and that is going to be the work of the school.

I have been spontaneous in my work, but these are the mysteries of life, that existence itself has taken care. I have left it to existence, "Whatever you want me to do, I will do." I am not the doer; I am just a passage for existence to reach people. So I have never planned, but existence functions in a very planned way. So all the phases that have passed were necessary, and now we are ready to enter into the last phase – the ultimate ecstasy.

Ecstasy cannot be pragmatic.
Love cannot be pragmatic.
Trust cannot be pragmatic.
All that is valuable is esoteric.

Beloved Bhagwan,
In last night's discourse, listening to You, I went into a state where Your words became sounds, Your voice became music, and in the gaps between Your words, it felt as if I found myself rising up into the sky. At first I thought I was going to fall asleep, but it turned out not to be like this.
Would You please help me in understanding this?

I have told you the story of the Sufi mystic who was thought to be a little eccentric. Even his disciples were afraid that he could create a situation which would be very embarrassing to them.

Once it happened… He was going to the mosque to deliver a religious discourse and he sat on his donkey in such a way that the whole city laughed. And the disciples were just feeling ashamed, because he was not facing the way the donkey was going; he was sitting with his back towards the mosque where the donkey was going and he was facing his students who were following him.

Naturally people came out of the shops, out of their houses and laughed and they said, "This man is really mad. It is strange that a few people think he is a master. Now look at what nonsense he is doing. Is this the way to sit on a donkey?"

And all the students were feeling very badly: to go with the master anywhere is a trouble. When they had reached the mosque the students asked, "Before we enter we want some explanation: Why did you do this?"

He said, "I thought over it very much, meditated over it. If I sit the way people sit on their animals then my back will be towards you, and that is insulting; that is not being respectful towards you."

One student said, "Then you should have told us. We could have been ahead of you."

He said, "Then it would have been insulting towards me. Your back towards me? – that would be even worse. So finally I figured out that the best way is that I sit facing you, and you follow me. And there is no religious scripture in which it is written that you should always sit on the donkey in such a way. It is not irreligious. There is no book of etiquette in which it is written how to sit on a donkey.

"It is our donkey and nobody has the right to be bothered about it. And I have found absolutely the right way: I am facing you, you are facing me; nobody is being disrespectful towards anybody else. What is wrong in it?"

This master was staying with a devotee, and they were worried that he may do something… "He is bound to do something to

WATCHFULNESS IS THE GREATEST MAGIC

create a scene, and the neighbors will gather. It is good that he has come in the night. We should put him in the basement and lock it so no problem arises – at least in the night – so we can sleep silently and the neighbors can sleep silently."

But in the middle of the night they heard roaring laughter coming from the roof. They said, "My God, how has he managed to reach the roof?"

They rushed up, and he was laughing and rolling around, and he said, "It is such a great experience. You did well to put me in the basement, otherwise I would have missed."

They said, "Please tell us, what has happened?"

He said, "I started falling upwards. The whole credit goes to the roof. Somehow I clung to the roof, otherwise you would not have found me. I was falling upwards so fast. I have heard that things only fall downwards – this is a new experience of falling upwards."

The whole neighborhood was there and everybody was coming with lamps, and they started asking, "What has happened?" And the people of the house could not even say what had happened.

The master said, "Don't be worried, I will explain; these people cannot. I started falling upwards."

They all laughed and they said, "We have been telling these people, 'Don't get involved with that madman. He can create any situation and make you all look foolish.'"

But it is a famous Sufi statement, that one can fall upwards. The state you are asking about, when you found that my words became sound, that my voice became music, that in the gaps between, you felt you were rising upwards…this is what the Sufis mean by falling upwards.

The story is just symbolic – nobody can fall from the basement to the roof – but it says much.

Just look at what you felt: my words became sound. Sound is the source. Sound is meaningless; when a sound is given meaning then it becomes a word. Words are secondary; sound is the source.

That is why I have criticized the Biblical story that there was word in the beginning. That is impossible, because word cannot be in the beginning. Word means it has to be meaningful. But who will give it meaning? There was nobody else.

In the East they are far more profound. Each ancient Hindu scripture begins with *om*. That is a sound; it is not a word. *Om* does not mean anything. It would have been better to say, "In the beginning there was sound."

You say, "Then your voice became music." That means you are listening totally, so totally that you are not even thinking about what is being said. Naturally meaning will disappear, words will become sound. And if meaning disappears, then the voice will become music. And in the gaps between the sound and the music, the silent gaps, you felt you were rising upwards.

In the East we have, and science has to accept it sooner or later, the opposite idea to gravitation. It is called levitation: just as things fall downwards, things can rise upwards. Gravitation is a way downwards; levitation is a way upwards. In utter silence you are no longer confined to your body. Your body is under the impact of gravitation; it cannot fall upwards.

But you are not the body, you are pure consciousness. In fact it is a miracle that you are in the body. Because of the gravitation that affects the body, you remain attached to the earth. But in absolute silence, suddenly all your attachment to the body disappears, your attachment to the mind disappears – because now words have become sound. The mind cannot conceive it. The voice has become music. For the mind to figure it out is not possible, and because the mind is in a state where it cannot control, your connections with the body become loose.

Mind is your connection, and in that looseness you can feel as if you are floating upwards. Your body is still sitting on the ground, so if you open your eyes you will be puzzled. But what you have experienced is not imagination; it is as true as gravitation, it is just invisible. You can feel it, but you cannot see it. Don't be afraid of it. Let it happen more and more. Suddenly one day you will find you are close to the stars and not to the earth.

The same thing can be possible through hypnosis. If a person is deeply hypnotized – that means he has been hypnotized many times and has become more and more trusting… And there are ways to check whether he has come to the point where you can experiment. You can simply say to him, "Come out of the body. You will be able to remember whatever you see."

Your consciousness, your soul, or whatever name you give to it, will float above you like a balloon, still attached to your navel with a very shiny cord, looking like silver. And you can see your body lying on the bed.

In a mystery school we will need places where nobody disturbs. If such an experiment is being done, any disturbance can be dangerous. The cord can be broken – then the soul cannot enter the body again; then the person is dead. No harm to the soul, but to the world you have killed a person. There should be no disturbance of any kind.

The soul can see everything from above, and then you can say, "Now slowly come back to the body." And you can feel that you are settling back into the body, slowly spreading into different parts of the body. Because you are told that you will remember everything, you will be able to tell about it when you wake up and you are asked – you will tell the whole thing, what has happened.

And this has been experimented with for at least ten thousand years, and it has been always the same. That's why I say it is the science of the interior, of your inner being, because there has been no exception. All the reports from people who have gone out of the body are exactly the same. For example, they all feel that they are connected by a silver cord to the navel.

Out of this experience scientists may think that life is centered in the heart, that if the heart stops you are dead. It is not true. There have been experiments proving certainly that the heart can be stopped and the person does not die. After ten minutes he comes back, and the heart starts again. According to the spiritual science, life is just two inches below the navel. The child was joined by the navel to the mother. And the navel was nursing the source inside, two inches below… It has been cut from the mother's life, but it is still joined with the universe from the same place. It is not in the heart, it is just two inches below the navel.

And because of this, in Japan a certain thing developed: *harakiri. Harakiri* is a special kind of suicide. *Hara* is the name of the center below the navel, where life is. And only in Japan has it been possible to locate it exactly. A certain development in Japanese tradition led to this point: if you want to kill yourself, the best, the quickest, and the most comfortable way is just to put a knife in the center of the *hara,* so the cord is cut. That happens within seconds, and the person is dead, but he does not suffer any agony.

And the science of health, medicine, has to take note of it, because if it is the real center of life, then it should be nourished when a person is dying or sick. Rather than working on other places which are only offshoots, work at the center. Perhaps a totally new science of medicine and health can come out of it.

The *hara* has not been recognized anywhere except Japan. But Japan has proved it, that *there* is the center of life, because within a second the person is finished – and with no agony, no anguish. His face is as it was when he was alive – not even any tension.

Harakiri developed for a strange reason. It is part of the *samurai* training in Japan. The *samurai* is a special kind of warrior. He is a meditative warrior. Life and death are equal to him, but honor, respectability, dignity, is higher than anything else. So if anything happens that he feels is humiliating, then it is not worth living, and he commits *harakiri*. It is not good to translate it as suicide, but there is no other way.

Thousands of *samurai* have committed *harakiri*. You cannot hurt the integrity of any *samurai*. It is dangerous – he will not kill you, he will kill himself. Life has lost meaning; if people cannot respect him, there is no reason why he should live. And he lives with dignity. The *samurai* is a special development of human individuality, and utterly devoted to freedom. Anything hurting him, or anything destroying his freedom or his honor…

In the second world war it was a danger, that you can destroy Japan but you cannot win. It was the atomic bombs which changed the situation; otherwise the ordinary war…

Just a few years ago, thirteen years after the second world war, a man was found hiding in a forest, still fighting. Whenever he could find an opportunity, he would kill an American and then go back to the forest. He was caught thirteen years after the second world war, and when he was told that Japan had been defeated, he could not believe it.

He said, "That is impossible. Japan can be destroyed, but cannot be defeated. It is a land of *samurais*. We live with dignity, we die with dignity." He could not believe it – thirteen years had passed, and he was still fighting for Japan, alone.

Meditation and swordsmanship, or archery, or other ways of the warrior, have been joined together. To us it seems too much, that a person should destroy himself, but to those thousands who have committed *harakiri* it is not the case. They are not destroying themselves, they are simply leaving this life – this life is not worth living, something has gone wrong. It is against their honor to be here.

Through hypnosis we can make a person aware of how this rising upwards happens, and how he can enter the body again. And once you have done it, a posthypnotic suggestion can be given, that you can do it on your own, any time you want. And it is a tremendously beautiful experience, for the simple reason that for the first time you find that the prison is not you. Your body is one thing; *you* are totally different: you are eternal, immortal.

Bodies have come and gone; you have been here since eternity, and you will be here until eternity.

Some Biographical Facts and Events from the Life of Bhagwan Shree Rajneesh

The Childhood Years

1931

Bhagwan Shree Rajneesh was born in Kuchwada, Madhya Pradesh, India, on December 11, 1931, the eldest son of a modest cloth merchant who belonged to the Jain religion. He spent his first seven years with his grandparents who allowed him absolute freedom to do exactly as he liked, and who fully supported his early and intense investigations into the truth about life.

1938

After the death of his grandfather, he went to live with his parents at Gadawara, a town of 20,000. His grandmother moved to the same town and remained his most generous friend until she died in 1970, declaring herself to be a disciple of her grandson.

1946

Bhagwan experienced his first satori at 14 years of age. Over the years, his experiments with meditation deepened. The intensity of his spiritual search took its toll on his physical condition. His parents and friends feared he might not live long.

The University Years

1953

At the age of 21, on March 21, 1953, Bhagwan attained enlightenment, the highest peak of human consciousness. Here, he said, his outer biography ended, and he has since lived in an egoless state of at-oneness with the inner laws of life. Outwardly, he continued to pursue his studies at the University of Saugar, from which he graduated with First Class Honors in Philosophy in 1956. He was All-

India Debating Champion and won the Gold Medal in his graduating class.

1957

Bhagwan taught at the Sanskrit College, Raipur. A year later he became philosophy professor at the University of Jabalpur. He gave up this post in 1966 in order to dedicate himself entirely to the task of teaching modern man the art of meditation. Throughout the sixties, he traveled the length and breadth of India as the "Acharya (teacher) Rajneesh," arousing the wrath of the Establishment wherever he went.

He exposed the hypocrisy of the vested interests and their attempts to obstruct man's access to his greatest human right – the right to be himself. He addressed audiences of tens of thousands of people, touching the hearts of millions.

The Bombay Years

1968

He settled in Bombay, living and teaching there. Regularly, he held "meditation camps," mostly in hill stations, where he introduced his revolutionary Dynamic Meditation, a technique that helps to stop the mind by first allowing it to cathart. From 1970 he started initiating people into Neo-Sannyas, a path of commitment to self-exploration and meditation, helped by his love and personal guidance. He began to be called "Bhagwan" – "The Blessed One."

1970

The first seekers from the West arrived, among them many professional people. Bhagwan's fame began to spread throughout Europe, America, Australia and Japan. The monthly Meditation Camps continued and in 1974 a new place was found in Poona, where the teaching could be intensified.

The Poona Years

1974

On the 21st anniversary of Bhagwan's enlightenment, the ashram in Poona opened. The radius of Bhagwan's influence became worldwide. At the same time, Bhagwan retreated more and more into the privacy of his room, emerging only twice daily: lecturing in the morning and initiating and advising seekers in the evenings.

Therapy groups combining Eastern insight into meditation with Western psychotherapy were created.

Within two years, the ashram earned a reputation as "the world's finest growth and therapy center." Bhagwan's lectures encompassed all the great religious traditions of the world. At the same time, his vast erudition in Western science and thought, his clarity of speech and depth of argument made the time-honored gap between East and West disappear for his listeners.

His lectures, taped and transcribed into books, fill hundreds of volumes and have been absorbed by hundreds of thousands of readers. By the late seventies, Bhagwan's ashram in Poona had become a mecca to modern seekers of truth. Indian Prime Minister Morarji Desai, devout traditional Hindu, thwarted all attempts of Bhagwan's disciples to move their ashram to a remote corner of India where they would be able to experiment with applying Bhagwan's teachings to create a self-sufficient community living in meditation, love, creativity and laughter.

1980

An attempt was made to murder Bhagwan at one of his lectures by a member of a traditional Hindu sect. Although the official religions and churches opposed him in the East and in the West, Bhagwan by then had over a quarter of a million disciples worldwide.

A New Phase – Rajneeshpuram, USA

1981

On May 1st Bhagwan stopped speaking and entered a phase of "silent heart-to-heart communion" while his body, now seriously ill from a back condition, was resting. He was taken to the USA by his doctors and caretakers in view of possible emergency surgery. His American disciples purchased a 64,000 acre ranch in the Central Oregon desert. They invited Bhagwan there – where he recovered rapidly. A model agricultural commune evolved around him with breath-taking speed and impressive results, re-claiming overgrazed and depleted land from the desert and turning it into a green oasis feeding a city of 5,000.

At yearly summer festivals held for Bhagwan's friends from all over the world, up to 15,000 visitors were housed and fed at this new city of Rajneeshpuram.

Parallel to the rapid growth of the commune in Oregon, large communes sprang up in all major Western countries, and Japan, supported by their own independent businesses. Bhagwan had by then applied for permanent residence in the U.S. as a religious leader, but was refused by the American government; one of the reasons given was his vow of public silence. At the same time the new city was under increasing legal attack from the Oregon government and the Christian majority in the state. Oregon's land use laws, meant to protect the environment, became a major weapon in the fight against a city that had put enormous effort into reclaiming barren land and enhancing the environment – in fact a city which had become an ecological model for the world.

In October 1984, Bhagwan started speaking to small groups in his residence, and in July 1985 he started giving public discourses every morning to thousands of seekers in Rajneesh Mandir.

1985

On September 14, Bhagwan's personal secretary and several members of the commune's management suddenly left, and a whole pattern of illegal acts committed by them came to light. Bhagwan invited the American authorities to the city to fully investigate the matter. The authorities used this opportunity to accelerate their fight against the commune.

On October 29, Bhagwan was arrested without a warrant in Charlotte, NC. At the bail hearings he was put in chains. The trip back to Oregon where he was to appear in court – normally a five hour flight – took eight days. For two of those days there was no trace of Bhagwan. Later he revealed that in the Oklahoma State Penitentiary he was signed in under the name of "David Washington" and put into an isolation cell with a prisoner suffering from infectious herpes, a disease that could have proven fatal for Bhagwan. Just an hour before being finally released, after a 12-day ordeal in prisons and chains, a bomb was discovered at the Portland, Oregon jail in which Bhagwan was kept. Everybody was evacuated except Bhagwan, who was kept inside for an hour.

In mid-November his lawyers urged him to

plead guilty to two of thirty-four minor "immigration violations" with which he had been charged, so as to avoid further risks to his life in the hands of the American judicial system. Bhagwan acquiesced and entered an "Alford plea," a plea peculiar to the U.S. judicial system, whereby he could accept the contention of guilt while at the same time maintain his innocence. He was fined four hundred thousand dollars and ordered to leave the USA, not to return for five years. He left by private jet the same day and flew to India, where he rested in the Himalayas.

A week later, the Oregon commune decided to disperse.

In a press conference, U.S. Attorney Charles Turner made three telling points in answering the question: Why weren't the charges brought against his secretary also brought against Bhagwan? Turner said that the government's first priority was to destroy the commune and that the authorities knew that the removal of Bhagwan would precipitate this. Second, they did not want to make Bhagwan a martyr. Third, there was no evidence whatsoever implicating him in any of the crimes.

The World Tour – A Study In Human Rights

December 1985

Bhagwan's new secretary, his companion, his doctor and other western disciples accompanying him were ordered out of India, their visas cancelled. No reason was given by the Indian government for this unprecedented action except, "You are not wanted here." Bhagwan left to join them in Kathmandu, Nepal, where he resumed his daily discourses.

February 1986

Bhagwan went to *Greece* on a 30-day tourist visa, where he lived in the villa of a Greek film producer and started to speak twice daily. Disciples flocked to hear him. The Greek Orthodox clergy threatened the Greek government that blood would flow unless Bhagwan was thrown out of the country.

March 5, 1986

Police broke into the villa and arrested Bhagwan without warrant, shunting him off to Athens where only a twenty-five thousand dollar bribe could move the authorities not to put him on the boat to India.

March 6, 1986

He left in a private jet for *Switzerland* where his 7-day visa was cancelled by armed policemen upon arrival. He was declared 'persona non grata' because of "immigration offenses in the United States" and asked to leave.

He flew on to *Sweden* where he was met the same way – surrounded by rifled policemen. He was told he was "a danger to national security," and ordered to leave immediately.

He flew on to *England*. His pilots were now legally bound to rest for eight hours. Bhagwan wanted to wait in the First Class Transit Lounge, but he was not allowed; nor was he allowed to stay in a hotel overnight. Instead, he and his companions were locked up in a small, dirty cell crowded with refugees.

March 7, 1986

Bhagwan and his group flew to *Ireland*, where they were given tourist visas. They went to a hotel near Limerick. The next morning police arrived and ordered them to leave immediately.

However, this was not possible because *Canada* had by then refused Bhagwan's plane permission to land at Gander for refuelling on the intended flight to *Antigua* in the Caribbean.

This extraordinary denial of the right to refuel was made in spite of a bond from Lloyds of London guaranteeing that Bhagwan would not step outside the plane.
On the condition that there was no publicity that might embarrass the authorities, he was allowed to remain in Ireland until other arrangements could be made.
During the wait, Antigua withdrew permission for Bhagwan to go there. *Holland*, when asked, also refused Bhagwan.
Germany had already passed a 'preventive decree' not to allow Bhagwan to enter their country. In *Italy*, his tourist visa application remained stalled – and in fact has still not been granted 15 months later.

March 19, 1986

At the last moment, *Uruguay* turned up with an invitation, and so, on March 19th, Bhagwan, his devotees and fellow travelers flew to Montevideo via Dakar, Senegal. Uruguay even opened up the possibility of permanent residence. However, in Uruguay it was discovered why he was being denied access to every country he tried to enter – telexes with "diplomatic secret information" (all from NATO government sources) mentioning INTERPOL rumors of "smuggling charges, drug dealing and prostitution" concerning Bhagwan's circle had invariably preceded them to their prospective host countries.
The source of these stories was found to be the USA. Uruguay soon came under the same pressure.

May 14, 1986

The government decided to announce at a press conference that Bhagwan had been granted permanent residence in Uruguay.

That night Sanguinetti, the President of Uruguay, received a call from Washington, DC, saying that if Bhagwan stayed in Uruguay, current U.S. loans of six billion dollars would be called in, and no future loans given. Bhagwan was requested to leave Uruguay by June 18th. On the day after he left, Sanguinetti and Reagan announced from Washington a new U.S. loan to Uruguay of one hundred and fifty million dollars.

June 19, 1986

Jamaica granted Bhagwan a 10-day visa. Moments after he landed there, a U.S. navy jet landed next to Bhagwan's private jet, and two civilians descended. The next morning, the visas of Bhagwan and his group were cancelled, "for reasons of national security."

Bhagwan flew on to Lisbon via Madrid, and remained "undiscovered" for some time. A few weeks later policemen were placed around the villa where he was resting. Bhagwan decided to return back to India the next day, July 28.

In all, twenty-one countries had either deported him or denied him entry.

July 29, 1986

Bhagwan arrived in Bombay, India, where he settled for six months as a personal guest of an Indian friend. In the privacy of his host's home, he resumed his daily discourses.

January 4, 1987

Bhagwan moved into the house at the ashram

in Poona where he had lived for the major part of the seventies. Immediately upon Bhagwan's arrival, the police chief of Poona ordered him to leave on the grounds that he was a "controversial person" who may "disturb the tranquility of the city." The order was revoked the same day by the Bombay High Court.

The same Hindu fanatic who, in May 1980, tried to murder Bhagwan by throwing a knife at him during a public lecture began making aggressive threats about forcing his way into the ashram with 200 commandoes trained in martial arts – unless Bhagwan was expelled from Poona.

At the same time Indian Embassies around the world, and immigration officers at Bombay airport, began refusing entry to Westerners "known to be followers of Acharya Rajneesh."

November 6, 1987

After a 7-week illness in which a simple infection failed to respond to any treatment, Bhagwan's physicians diagnosed a general deterioration of his physical condition due to poisoning; a further analysis concluded thallium poisoning. During public discourse, Bhagwan stated that he believed the government of the USA had slow-poisoned him during the 12 days he was in their custody in September 1985.

April 1988

At the time of writing, despite the attempts of the governments of the "free world" to isolate Bhagwan in virtual internal exile, thousands of disciples have managed to travel to Poona to be with their Master once again.

WORLDWIDE DISTRIBUTION CENTERS
FOR THE WORKS OF BHAGWAN SHREE RAJNEESH

Books by Bhagwan Shree Rajneesh are available **AT COST PRICE** in many languages throughout the world. Bhagwan's discourses have been recorded live on audiotape and videotape. There are many recordings of Rajneesh meditation music and celebration music played in His presence, as well as beautiful photographs of Bhagwan. For further information contact one of the distribution centers below:

EUROPE

Denmark
Anwar Distribution
Carl Johansgade 8, 5
2100 Copenhagen
Tel. 01/420218

Italy
Rajneesh Services Corporation
Via XX Settembre 12
28041 Arona (NO)
Tel. 02/8392 194 (Milan office)

Netherlands
Rajneesh Distributie Centrum
Cornelis Troostplein 23
1072 JJ Amsterdam
Tel. 020/5732 130

Norway
Devananda
Rajneesh Meditation Center
P.O. Box 177 Vinderen
0386 Oslo 3
Tel. 02/123373

Sweden
Madhur Rajneesh Meditation Center
Hag Tornsv. 30
12235 Enskede (Stockholm)
Tel. 08/394946

Switzerland
Mingus AG
Asylstrasse 11
8032 Zurich
Tel. 01/2522 012

United Kingdom
Purnima Rajneesh Publications
95A Northview Road
London N8 7LRa
Tel. 01/341 4317

West Germany
The Rebel Publishing House GmbH
Venloer Strasse 5-7
5000 Cologne 1
Tel. 0221/57407 42

Rajneesh Verlags GmbH
Venloer Strasse 5-7
5000 Cologne 1
Tel. 0221/57407 43

Also available from nationwide
bookshop distributor VVA Vereinigte
Verlagsauslieferung GmbH
An der Autobahn - Postf. 7777
4830 Guetersloh

ASIA

India
Rajneeshdham
17 Koregaon Park
Poona 411001 M.S.
Tel. 0212/60963

Japan
Eer Rajneesh
Neo-Sannyas Commune
Mimura Building 6-21-34
Kikuna, Kohoku-ku
Yokohama, 222
Tel. 045/434 1981

AUSTRALIA

Rajneesh Meditation &
Healing Center
P.O. Box 1097
160 High Street
Fremantle, WA 6160
Tel. 09/430 4047

AMERICA

United States
Chidvilas
P.O. Box 17550
Boulder, CO 80308
Tel. 303/665 6611
Order Dept. 800/777 7743

Also available in bookstores
nationwide at
Walden Books and B. Dalton

BOOKS BY BHAGWAN SHREE RAJNEESH
ENGLISH LANGUAGE EDITIONS

RAJNEESH PUBLISHERS

Early Discourses and Writings

A Cup of Tea *Letters to Disciples*
From Sex to Superconsciousness
I Am the Gate
The Long and the Short and the All
The Silent Explosion

Meditation

And Now, and Here (Volumes 1&2)
The Book of the Secrets (Volumes 1-5)
    Vigyana Bhairava Tantra
Dimensions Beyond the Known
In Search of the Miraculous (Volume 1)
Meditation: the Art of Ecstasy
The Orange Book
    The Meditation Techniques of
    Bhagwan Shree Rajneesh
The Perfect Way
The Psychology of the Esoteric

Buddha and Buddhist Masters

The Book of the Books (Volumes 1-4) *The Dhammapada*
The Diamond Sutra *The Vajrachchedika Prajnaparamita Sutra*
The Discipline of Transcendence (Volumes 1-4)
    On the Sutra of 42 Chapters
The Heart Sutra *The Prajnaparamita Hridayam Sutra*
The Book of Wisdom (Volumes 1&2)
    Atisha's Seven Points of Mind Training

Indian Mystics:

The Bauls

The Beloved (Volumes 1&2)

Kabir

The Divine Melody
Ecstasy – The Forgotten Language
The Fish in the Sea is Not Thirsty
The Guest
The Path of Love
The Revolution

Krishna

Krishna: The Man and His Philosophy

Jesus and Christian Mystics

Come Follow Me (Volumes 1-4) *The Sayings of Jesus*
I Say Unto You (Volumes 1&2) *The Sayings of Jesus*
The Mustard Seed *The Gospel of Thomas*
Theologia Mystica *The Treatise of St. Dionysius*

Jewish Mystics

The Art of Dying
The True Sage

Sufism

Just Like That
The Perfect Master (Volumes 1&2)
The Secret
Sufis: The People of the Path (Volumes 1&2)
Unio Mystica (Volumes 1&2) *The Hadiqa of Hakim Sanai*
Until You Die
The Wisdom of the Sands (Volumes 1&2)

Tantra

Tantra, Spirituality and Sex
    Excerpts from The Book of the Secrets
Tantra: The Supreme Understanding
    Tilopa's Song of Mahamudra
The Tantra Vision (Volumes 1&2)
    The Royal Song of Saraha

Tao

The Empty Boat *The Stories of Chuang Tzu*
The Secret of Secrets (Volumes 1&2)
    The Secret of the Golden Flower
Tao: The Golden Gate (Volumes 1&2)
Tao: The Pathless Path (Volumes 1&2)
    The Stories of Lieh Tzu
Tao: The Three Treasures (Volumes 1-4)
    The Tao Te Ching of Lao Tzu
When the Shoe Fits *The Stories of Chuang Tzu*

The Upanishads

I Am That *Isa Upanishad*
Philosophia Ultima *Mandukya Upanishad*
The Supreme Doctrine *Kenopanishad*
That Art Thou *Sarvasar Upanishad,*
   Kaivalya Upanishad, Adhyatma Upanishad
The Ultimate Alchemy (Volumes 1&2) *Atma Pooja Upanishad*
Vedanta: Seven Steps to Samadhi *Akshya Upanishad*

Western Mystics

Guida Spirituale *On the Desiderata*
The Hidden Harmony *The Fragments of Heraclitus*
The Messiah (Volumes 1&2)
   Commentaries on Kahlil Gibran's The Prophet
The New Alchemy: To Turn You On
   Mabel Collins' Light on the Path
Philosophia Perennis (Volumes 1&2)
   The Golden Verses of Pythagoras
Zarathustra: A God That Can Dance
Zarathustra: The Laughing Prophet

Yoga

Yoga: The Alpha and the Omega (Volumes 1-10)
   The Yoga Sutras of Patanjali
Yoga: The Science of the Soul (Volumes 1-3)
   Originally titled Yoga: The Alpha and the Omega
   (Volumes 1-3)

Zen and Zen Masters

Ah, This!
Ancient Music in the Pines
And the Flowers Showered
Bodhidharma The Greatest Zen Master
   Commentaries on the Teachings of the
   Messenger of Zen from India to China
Dang Dang Doko Dang
The First Principle
The Grass Grows By Itself
The Great Zen Master Ta Hui
   Reflections on the Transformation of
   an Intellectual to Enlightenment
Hsin Hsin Ming: The Book of Nothing
   Discourses on the Faith-Mind of Sosan
Nirvana: The Last Nightmare
No Water, No Moon
Returning to the Source

Roots and Wings
The Search *The Ten Bulls of Zen*
A Sudden Clash of Thunder
The Sun Rises in the Evening
Take it Easy (Volumes 1&2) *Poems of Ikkyu*
This Very Body the Buddha
   Hakuin's Song of Meditation
Walking in Zen, Sitting in Zen
The White Lotus *The Sayings of Bodhidharma*
Zen: The Path of Paradox (Volumes 1-3)
Zen: The Special Transmission

Responses to Questions:

Poona 1974-1981

Be Still and Know
The Goose is Out!
My Way: The Way of the White Clouds
Walk Without Feet, Fly Without Wings
   and Think Without Mind
The Wild Geese and the Water
Zen: Zest, Zip, Zap and Zing

Rajneeshpuram

From Darkness to Light
From the False to the Truth
The Rajneesh Bible (Volumes 1-4)

The World Tour

Beyond Psychology *Talks in Uruguay*
Light on the Path *Talks in the Himalayas*
The Path of the Mystic *Talks in Uruguay*
Socrates Poisoned Again After 25 Centuries
   Talks in Greece
The Transmission of the Lamp *Talks in Uruguay*

The Mystery School 1986 - present

Beyond Enlightenment
The Golden Future
The Great Pilgrimage: From Here to Here
The Hidden Splendor
The Rajneesh Upanishad
The Razor's Edge
The Rebellious Spirit
Satyam-Shivam-Sundram *Truth-Godliness-Beauty*
Sermons in Stones

Personal Glimpses

Books I Have Loved
Glimpses of a Golden Childhood
Notes of a Madman

Interviews with the World Press

The Last Testament (Volume 1)

Intimate Talks between Master and Disciple – Darshan Diaries

Hammer on the Rock
(December 10, 1975 - January 15, 1976)
Above All Don't Wobble
(January 16 - February 12, 1976)
Nothing to Lose But Your Head
(February 13 - March 12, 1976)
Be Realistic: Plan For a Miracle
(March 13 - April 6, 1976)
Get Out of Your Own Way *(April 7 - May 2, 1976)*
Beloved of My Heart *(May 3 - 28, 1976)*
The Cypress in the Courtyard *(May 29 - June 27, 1976)*
A Rose is a Rose is a Rose *(June 28 - July 27, 1976)*
Dance Your Way to God *(July 28 - August 20, 1976)*
The Passion for the Impossible
(August 21 - September 18, 1976)
The Great Nothing *(September 19 - October 11, 1976)*
God is Not for Sale *(October 12 - November 7, 1976)*
The Shadow of the Whip *(November 8 - December 3, 1976)*
Blessed are the Ignorant *(December 4 - 31, 1976)*
The Buddha Disease *(January 1977)*
What Is, Is, What Ain't, Ain't *(February 1977)*
The Zero Experience *(March 1977)*
For Madmen Only (Price of Admission: Your Mind)
(April 1977)
This is It *(May 1977)*
The Further Shore *(June 1977)*
Far Beyond the Stars *(July 1977)*
The No Book (No Buddha, No Teaching, No Discipline)
(August 1977)
Don't Just Do Something, Sit There *(September 1977)*
Only Losers Can Win in This Game *(October 1977)*
The Open Secret *(November 1977)*
The Open Door *(December 1977)*
The Sun Behind the Sun Behind the Sun *(January 1978)*
Believing the Impossible Before Breakfast
(February 1978)
Don't Bite My Finger, Look Where I'm Pointing *(March 1978)*

Let Go! *(April 1978)*
The 99 Names of Nothingness *(May 1978)*
The Madman's Guide to Enlightenment *(June 1978)*
Don't Look Before You Leap *(July 1978)*
Hallelujah! *(August 1978)*
God's Got a Thing About You *(September 1978)*
The Tongue-Tip Taste of Tao *(October 1978)*
The Sacred Yes *(November 1978)*
Turn On, Tune In, and Drop the Lot *(December 1978)*
Zorba the Buddha *(January 1979)*
Won't You Join the Dance? *February 1979)*
You Ain't Seen Nothin' Yet *(March 1979)*
The Shadow of the Bamboo *(April 1979)*
Just Around the Corner *(May 1979)*
Snap Your Fingers, Slap Your Face & Wake Up! *(June 1979)*
The Rainbow Bridge *(July 1979)*
Don't Let Yourself Be Upset by the Sutra,
Rather Upset the Sutra Yourself *(August/September 1979)*
The Sound of One Hand Clapping *(March 1981)*

Compilations

Beyond the Frontiers of the Mind
Bhagwan Shree Rajneesh On Basic Human Rights
The Book *An Introduction to the Teachings of
Bhagwan Shree Rajneesh*
Series I from A - H
Series II from I - Q
Series III from R - Z
Death: The Greatest Fiction
Gold Nuggets
I Teach Religiousness Not Religion
Life, Love, Laughter
Meditation: The First and Last Freedom
The New Child
The New Man: The Only Hope for the Future
A New Vision of Women's Liberation
Priests and Politicians: The Mafia of the Soul
The Rebel: The Very Salt of the Earth
Rebelliousness, Religion and Revolution
Sex: Quotations from Bhagwan Shree Rajneesh

Photobiographies

The Sound of Running Water
Bhagwan Shree Rajneesh and His Work 1974-1978
This Very Place The Lotus Paradise
Bhagwan Shree Rajneesh and His Work 1978-1984

Books about Bhagwan Shree Rajneesh

Bhagwan Shree Rajneesh: Crucifixion and Resurrection
  *Was Bhagwan Shree Rajneesh poisoned by the United
  States of America under Ronald Reagan's fascist,
  fanatic regime? (by Sue Appleton, LL.B., M.A.B.A.)*
Bhagwan Shree Rajneesh:
  The Most Dangerous Man Since Jesus Christ
  (by Sue Appleton, LL.B., M.A.B.A.)
Bhagwan: The Buddha For The Future
  (by Juliet Forman, S.R.N., S.C.M., R.M.N.)
Bhagwan: The Most Godless Yet The Most Godly Man
  (by Dr. George Meredith M.D. M.B.,B.S. M.R.C.P.)
Bhagwan: Twelve Days that Shook the World
  (by Juliet Forman, S.R.N., S.C.M., R.M.N.)

OTHER PUBLISHERS

UNITED KINGDOM

The Art of Dying *(Sheldon Press)*
The Book of the Secrets *(Volume 1, Thames & Hudson)*
No Water, No Moon *(Sheldon Press)*
Roots and Wings *(Routledge & Kegan Paul)*
Straight to Freedom *(Sheldon Press)*
The Supreme Doctrine *(Routledge & Kegan Paul)*
Tao: The Three Treasures *(Volume 1, Wildwood House)*

Books about Bhagwan Shree Rajneesh

The Way of the Heart: the Rajneesh Movement
  *by Judith Thompson and Paul Heelas, Department
  of Religious Studies, University of Lancaster
  (Aquarian Press)*

UNITED STATES OF AMERICA

The Book of the Secrets *(Volumes 1-3, Harper & Row)*
Dimensions Beyond the Known *(Wisdom Garden Books)*
The Great Challenge *(Grove Press)*
Hammer on the Rock *(Grove Press)*
I Am the Gate *(Harper & Row)*
Journey Toward the Heart
  (Original title: Until You Die, Harper & Row)
Meditation: The Art of Ecstasy
  *(Original title: Dynamics of Meditation,
  Harper & Row)*
The Mustard Seed *(Harper & Row)*
My Way: The Way of the White Clouds *(Grove Press)*
The Psychology of the Esoteric *(Harper & Row)*
Roots and Wings *(Routledge & Kegan Paul)*
The Supreme Doctrine *(Routledge & Kegan Paul)*
Words Like Fire *(Original title: Come Follow Me,
  Volume 1, Harper & Row)*

Books about Bhagwan Shree Rajneesh

The Awakened One: The Life and Work of
  Bhagwan Shree Rajneesh *by Vasant Joshi
  (Harper & Row)*
Dying for Enlightenment *by Bernard Gunther
  (Harper & Row)*
Rajneeshpuram and the Abuse of Power
  by Ted Shay, Ph.D. (Scout Creek Press)
Rajneeshpuram, the Unwelcome Society
  by Kirk Braun (Scout Creek Press)
The Rajneesh Story: The Bhagwan's Garden
  by Dell Murphy (Linwood Press, Oregon)

FOREIGN LANGUAGE EDITIONS

Chinese
I am the Gate (Woolin)

Danish
Bhagwan Shree Rajneesh Om Grundlaeggende
    Menneskerettigheder (Premo)
    Bhagwan Shree Rajneesh On Basic Human Rights
Hu-Meditation Og Kosmik Orgasme (Borgens)
    Hu-Meditation and Cosmic Orgasm
Hemmelighedernes Bog (Borgens)
    The Book of the Secrets (Volume 1)

Dutch
Bhagwan Shree Rajneesh Over de Rechten van de Mens
    (Rajneesh Publikaties Nederland)
    Bhagwan Shree Rajneesh On Basic Human Rights
Volg Mij (Ankh-Hermes) *Come Follow Me (Volume 1)*
Gezaaid in Goede Aarde (Ankh-Hermes)
    Come Follow Me (Volume 2)
Drink Mij (Ankh-Hermes) *Come Follow Me (Volume 3)*
Ik Ben de Zee Die Je Zoekt (Ankh-Hermes)
    Come Follow Me (Volume 4)
Ik Ben de Poort (Ankh-Hermes) *I am the Gate*
Heel Eenvoudig (Mirananda) *Just Like That*
Meditatie: De Kunst van Innerlijke Extase (Mirananda)
    Meditation: The Art of Inner Ecstasy
Mijn Weg, De Weg van de Witte Wolk (Arcanum)
    My Way: The Way of the White Clouds
Geen Water, Geen Maan (Mirananda)
    No Water, No Moon (Volumes 1&2)
Tantra, Spiritualiteit en Seks (Ankh-Hermes)
    Tantra, Spirituality & Sex
Tantra: Het Allerhoogste Inzicht (Ankh-Hermes)
    Tantra: The Supreme Understanding
Tau (Ankh-Hermes) *Tao: The Three Treasures (Volume 1)*
Het Boek der Geheimen (Mirananda)
    The Book of Secrets (Volumes 1-5)
De Verborgen Harmonie (Mirananda)
    The Hidden Harmony
Het Mosterdzaad (Mirananda)
    The Mustard Seed (Volumes 1&2)
De Nieuwe Mens (Volume 1) (Zorn) *Compilation on
    The New Man, Relationships, Education, Health,
    Dutch edition only*

De Nieuwe Mens (Volume 2) (Altamira) *Excerpts from
    The Last Testament (Volume 1), Dutch edition only*
Het Oranje Meditatieboek (Ankh-Hermes)
    The Orange Book
Psychologie en Evolutie (Ankh-Hermes)
    The Psychology of the Esoteric
De Tantra Visie (Arcanum)
    The Tantra Vision (Volumes 1&2)
Zoeken naar de Stier (Ankh-Hermes) *10 Zen Stories*
Totdat Je Sterft (Ankh-Hermes) *Until You Die*
Priesters & Politici: De Maffia van de Ziel
    (Rajneesh Publikaties Nederland)
    Priests & Politicians: The Mafia of the Soul

Books about Bhagwan Shree Rajneesh
Een Tuin der Lusten? Het rebelse tantrisme van
    Bhagwan en het nieuwe tijdperk *by Sietse Visser*
    (Mirananda) *A Garden of Earthly Delights?*
Oorspronkelijk Gezicht *by Dr. J. Foudraine* (Ambo)
    Original Face
Bhagwan, Notities van een Discipel *by Dr. J. Foudraine*
    (Ankh-Hermes) *Bhagwan, Notes of a Disciple*
Bhagwan, een Introductie *by Dr. J. Foudraine*
    (Ankh-Hermes) *Bhagwan, an Introduction*

French
Je Suis la Porte (EPI) *I am the Gate*
La Meditation Dynamique (Dangles)
    Meditation: The Art of Inner Ecstasy
L'Eveil a la Conscience Cosmique (Dangles)
    The Psychology of the Esoteric
Le Livre des Secrets (Soleil Orange)
    The Book of Secrets (Volume 1)

German
Und vor Allem: Nicht Wackeln (Fachbuchhandlung fuer
    Psychologie) *Above All Don't Wobble*
Der Freund (Sannyas Verlag) *A Cup of Tea*
Vorsicht Sozialismus (Rajneesh Verlag)
    Beware of Socialism
Bhagwan Shree Rajneesh: Ueber die Grundrechte des
    Menschen (Rajneesh Verlag)
    Bhagwan Shree Rajneesh On Basic Human Rights

Italian

Bhagwan Shree Rajneesh parla Sui Diritti dell'Uomo
(Rajneesh Services Corporation)
Bhagwan Shree Rajneesh On Basic Human Rights
Dimensioni Oltre il Conosciuto (Mediterranee)
Dimensions Beyond the Known
Estasi: Il Linguaggio Dimenticato (Riza Libri)
Ecstasy: The Forgotten Language
Dal Sesso all'Eros Cosmico (Basaia)
From Sex to Superconsciousness
Guida Spirituale (Mondadori) *Guida Spirituale*
Io Sono La Soglia (Mediterranee) *I am the Gate*
Meditazione Dinamica: L'Arte dell'Estasi Interiore
(Mediterranee) *Meditation: The Art of Inner Ecstasy*
La Mia Via: La Via delle Nuvole Bianche
(Mediterranee) *My Way: The Way of the White Clouds*
Nirvana: L'Ultimo Incubo (Basaia) *Nirvana: The Last Nightmare*
Dieci Storie Zen di Bhagwan Shree Rajneesh:
Ne Acqua, Ne Luna (Mediterranee) *No Water, No Moon*
Philosofia Perennis (ECIG) *Philosophia Perennis (Volumes 1&2)*
Semi di Saggezza (Sugarco) *Seeds of Revolution*
Tantra, Spiritualita e Sesso (Rajneesh Foundation Italy)
Tantra, Spirituality & Sex
Tantra: La Comprensione Suprema (Bompiani)
Tantra: The Supreme Understanding
Tao: I Tre Tesori (Re Nudo)
Tao: The Three Treasures (Volumes 1-3)
Tecniche di Liberazione (La Salamandra)
Techniques of Liberation
Il Libro dei Segreti (Bompiani)
The Book of The Secrets (Volume 1)
L'Armonia Nascosta (ECIG)
The Hidden Harmony (Volumes 1&2)
Il Seme della Ribellione (Rajneesh Foundation Italy)
The Mustard Seed (Volume 1)
La Nuova Alchimia (Psiche)
The New Alchemy To Turn You On (Volumes 1&2)
Il Libro Arancione (Mediterranee) *The Orange Book*
La Rivoluzione Interiore (Mediterranee)
The Psychology of the Esoteric
La Bibbia di Rajneesh (Bompiani)
The Rajneesh Bible (Volume 1)
La Ricerca (La Salamandra) *The Search*
La Dottrina Suprema (Rizzoli) *The Supreme Doctrine*
La Visione Tantrica (Riza) *The Tantra Vision*

Japanese

Shin Jinkensengen (Meisosha Ltd.)
Bhagwan Shree Rajneesh On Basic Human Rights

Seimeino Kanki – Darshan Nisshi (Rajneesh Publications)
Dance Your Way to God
Sex kara Choishiki e (Rajneesh Publications)
From Sex to Superconsciousness
Meiso – Shukusai no Art (Merkmal)
Meditation: The Art of Inner Ecstasy
My Way – Nagareyuku Shirakumo no Michi
(Rajneesh Publications)
My Way: The Way of the White Clouds
Ikkyu Doka (Merkmal) *Take it Easy (Volume 1)*
Sonzai no Uta (Merkmal)
Tantra: The Supreme Understanding
Tao – Eien no Taiga (Merkmal)
Tao: The Three Treasures (Volumes 1-4)
Baul no Ai no Uta (Merkmal) *The Beloved (Volumes 1&2)*
Diamond Sutra – Bhagwan Shree Rajneesh
Kongohannyakyo o Kataru (Meisosha Ltd./LAF Mitsuya)
The Diamond Sutra
Koku no Fune (Rajneesh Publications)
The Empty Boat (Volumes 1&2)
Kusa wa hitorideni haeru (Fumikura)
The Grass Grows by Itself
Hannya Shinkyo (Merkmal) *The Heart Sutra*
Ai no Renkinjutsu (Merkmal)
The Mustard Seed (Volumes 1&2)
Orange Book (Wholistic Therapy Institute)
The Orange Book
Kyukyoku no Tabi – Bhagwan Shree Rajneesh
Zen no Jugyuzu o Kataru (Merkmal)
The Search
Anataga Shinumadewa (Fumikura) *Until You Die*

Korean

Giromnun Gil II (Chung Ha)
Giromnun Gil Ih (Chung Ha)
Tao: The Pathless Path (Volume 1)
Haeng Bongron II
Haeng Bongron Ih
Tao: The Pathless Path (Volume 2)
Joogumui Yesool (Chung Ha) *The Art of Dying*
The Divine Melody (Chung Ha)
The Divine Melody (Sung Jung)
Salmuigil Hingurumui Gil (Chung Ha) *The Empty Boat*
Seon (Chung Ha) *The Grass Grows by Itself*
Upanishad (Chung Ha) *Vedanta: Seven Steps to Samadhi*
Sesoggwa Chowol (Chung Ha) *Roots and Wings*
Sinbijuijaui Norae (Chung Ha) *The Revolution*

Mahamudraui Norae (Il Ghi Sa) *The Supreme Understanding*
Sarahaui Norae (Il Ghi Sa) *The Tantra Vision*
Meongsang Bibob (Il Ghi Sa) *The Book of the Secrets*
Banya Simgeong (Il Ghi Sa) *The Heart Sutra*
Kabir Meongsangsi (Il Ghi Sa) *The Path of Love*
Salmui Choom Chimmoogui Choom, Il (Kha Chee)
   Tao: The Three Treasures (Volume 1)
Salmui Choom Chimmoogui Choom, Ih (Kha Chee)
   Tao: The Three Treasures (Volume 2)
Salmui Choom Chimmoogui Choom, Sam (Kha Chee)
   Tao: The Three Treasures (Volume 3)
Sarangui Yeongum Sool (Kim Young Sa) *The Mustard Seed*
Yeogieh Sala (Kim Young Sa) *I am the Gate*
The Psychology of the Esoteric (Han Bat)
Soomun Johwa (Hong Sung Sa) *The Hidden Harmony*
I Say Unto You (Hong Sung Sa)
Sunggwa Meongsang (Sim Sul Dnag)
   From Sex to Superconsciousness
From Sex to Superconsciousness (Ul Ghi)
The White Lotus (Jin Young)
Beshakaui Achim (Je Il)
   My Way: The Way of the White Clouds
Iroke Nanun Durotda (Je Il) *The Diamond Sutra*
Meong Sang (Han Ma Um Sa)
   Meditation: The Art of Ecstasy
The Orange Book (Gum Moon Dang)
Jameso Khaeonara (Bum Woo Sa)
The Search – The Ten Bulls of Zen
The Teaching of the Soul (compilation) (Jeong-Um)
Alpha Grigo Omega (Jeong-Um)
   Yoga: The Alpha and the Omega (Volume 1)
Come Follow Me (Chung-Ha)
Philosophia Perennis (Chung-Ha)
Sinsim Meong (Hong-Bub)
   Hsin Hsin Ming: The Book of Nothing
Maumuro Ganungil (Moon Hak Sa Sang Sa)
   Journey towards the Heart
Saeroun Inganui Heong Meong *Neo Tantra*
Hayan Yeonkhot *The White Lotus*

Books about Bhagwan Shree Rajneesh
Jigum Yeogiyeso (Je Il) *The Awakened One*

Portuguese
Sobre Os Direitos Humanos Basicos (Editora Naim)
   Bhagwan Shree Rajneesh on Basic Human Rights
Palavras De Fogo (Global/Ground)
   Come Follow Me (Volume 1)

Dimensoes Alem do Conhecido (Cultrix)
   Dimensions Beyond the Known
Extase: A Linguagem Esquecida (Global)
   Ecstasy: The Forgotten Language
Do Sexo A Superconsciencia (Cultrix)
   From Sex to Superconsciousness
Eu Sou A Porta (Pensamento) *I am the Gate*
Meditacao: A Arte Do Extase (Cultrix)
   Meditation: The Art of Inner Ecstasy
Meu Caminho: O Caminho Das Nuvens Brancas (Tao)
   My Way: The Way of the White Clouds
Nem Agua, Nem Lua (Pensamento) *No Water, No Moon*
Notas De Um Homem Louco (NAIM) *Notes of a Madman*
Raizes E Asas (Cultrix) *Roots and Wings*
Sufis: O Povo do Caminho (Maha Lakshmi Editora)
   Sufis: The People of the Path
Tantra: Sexo E Espiritualidade (Agora)
   Tantra, Spirituality & Sex
Tantra: A Suprema Compreensao (Cultrix)
   Tantra: The Supreme Understanding
Arte de Morrer (Global) *The Art of Dying*
O Livro Dos Segredos (Maha Lakshmi)
   The Book of the Secrets (Volumes 1&2)
Cipreste No Jardim (Cultrix)
   The Cypress in the Courtyard
A Divina Melodia (Cultrix) *The Divine Melody*
A Harmonia Oculta (Pensamento) *The Hidden Harmony*
A Semente De Mostarda (Tao)
   The Mustard Seed (Volumes 1&2)
A Nova Alquimia (Cultrix)
   The New Alchemy To Turn You On
O Livro Orange (Pensamento) *The Orange Book*
A Psicologia Do Esoterico (Tao)
   The Psychology of the Esoteric
Unio Mystica (Maha Lakshmi) *Unio Mystica*

Russian
Bhagwan Shree Rajneesh On Basic Human Rights
   (Neo-Sannyas International)

Serbo-Croat
Bhagwan Shree Rajneesh (Swami Mahavira)
   (Compilation of various quotations)
Bhagwan Shree Rajneesh O Osnovnim Pravima Covjeka
   Bhagwan Shree Rajneesh on Basic Human Rights
The Ultimate Pilgrimage
Vrovno Hodocasce *A Rajneesh Reader*

Spanish

Sobre Los Derechos Humanos Basicos (Futonia, Spain)
Bhagwan Shree Rajneesh on Basic Human Rights
Ven, Sigueme (Sagaro, Chile) *Come Follow Me (Volume 1)*
Yo Soy La Puerta (Diana, Mexico) *I am The Gate*
Meditacion: El Arte del Extasis (Rosello Impresiones)
Meditation: The Art of Inner Ecstasy
El Camino de las Nubes Blancas (Cuatro Vientos)
My Way: The Way of the White Clouds
Solo Un Cielo (Collection Tantra) *Only One Sky*
Introduccion al Mundo del Tantra (Rosello Impresiones)
Tantra: The Supreme Understanding (Volumes 1&2)
Tao: Los Tres Tesoros (Sirio, Espana)
Tao: The Three Treasures

El Sutra del Corazon (Sarvogeet, Espana) *The Heart Sutra*
El Libro Naranja (Bhagwatam, Puerto Rico)
The Orange Book
Psicologia de lo Esoterico: La Nueva Evolucion del Hombre
(Cuatro Vientos, Chile) *The Psychology of the Esoteric*
¿Que Es Meditacion? (Koan/Rosello Pastanaga)
What Is Meditation?

Swedish

Den Vaeldiga Utmaningen (Livskraft)
The Great Challenge

RAJNEESH MEDITATION CENTERS
ASHRAMS AND COMMUNES

There are many Rajneesh Meditation Centers throughout the world which can be contacted for information about the teachings of Bhagwan Shree Rajneesh and which have His books available as well as audio and video tapes of His discourses. Centers exist in practically every country.

For further information about Bhagwan Shree Rajneesh please contact:

Rajneeshdham Neo-Sannyas Commune
17 Koregaon Park
Poona 411 001, MS
India